CONSENSUS AND DISUNITY

The Lloyd George
Coalition Government
1918–1922

CONSENSUS AND DISUNITY

The Lloyd George Coalition Government 1918–1922

KENNETH O. MORGAN

Fellow of The Queen's College, Oxford

CLARENDON PRESS · OXFORD
1979

Oxford University Press, Walton Street, Oxford OX2 6DP

OXFORD   LONDON   GLASGOW
NEW YORK   TORONTO   MELBOURNE   WELLINGTON
KUALA LUMPUR   SINGAPORE   JAKARTA   HONG KONG   TOKYO
DELHI   BOMBAY   CALCUTTA   MADRAS   KARACHI
NAIROBI   DAR ES SALAAM   CAPE TOWN

Published in the United States by
Oxford University Press, New York

British Library Cataloguing in Publication Data

Morgan, Kenneth Owen
   Consensus and disunity.
   1. Great Britain – Politics and government –
   1910–1936
   I. TITLE
   320.9′41′083   JN231   79–40263
   ISBN 0–19–822497–4

*Set, printed and bound in Great Britain by
Fakenham Press Limited, Fakenham, Norfolk*

For David and Katherine

Preface

England, in Disraeli's famous phrase, does not love coalitions. That led by David Lloyd George between the end of the First World War in November 1918 and the resumption of party politics in October 1922 is perhaps the most unloved of all. It has been popularly used as a scapegoat for the manifold ills, domestic and external, from which Britain suffered in the inter-war period, and for the nation's alleged 'loss of nerve' and sense of decline over the past sixty years.

Amongst historians, however, the Coalition government of 1918–22 has not so much been condemned as ignored. It forms a dark age in modern British historiography. It has been treated either as an appendage to the wartime years or else as a precursor to the 'normalcy' of 1922–39. The exciting events of post-war Britain have been too often compressed into a search for the personal and party origins of the downfall of Lloyd George himself. The history of the government as a whole has been lost sight of. Only one recent book has treated the period of post-war political change in Britain with the seriousness that it deserves. This is Maurice Cowling's quite brilliant *Impact of Labour* which surveys the period 1920–4, self-consciously and in deliberate isolation, from the standpoint of 'high politics', of rhetoric and manœuvre by an élite group of politicians anxious to retain power for themselves and deny it to the emergent labour movement. This approach is a valuable aid to understanding, to which I am myself much indebted. My own concern has been to try to build on Mr. Cowling's work, to study policies as well as politics, and to relate them to patterns of social and economic change and to shifts in the national psychology. For it seems to me that what is most crucial about the period of Coalition government in Britain after 1918 is the light it sheds on a society trying to adapt itself to fundamental structural changes within itself and in its international role, changes which underlay the arguments over the ebb and flow of coalition in 1918–22. I have tried, therefore, to write the history both of a government, in depth and in the round, and also of a changing social order, with what success others must judge.

This is an historical study of a particular experiment in coalitionism. I have deliberately rejected any attempt to construct a social science model of coalition or bi-partisan government, and its significance in the general evolution of British politics. Indeed, whether any useful generalizations can be made about the immensely diverse coalitions that Britain has known between 1783 and 1945 must be doubtful. Still less is this book a cautionary tale or an argument in favour of coalitions in general or of 'governments of national unity' in Britain in the 1970s or later. My own view is that such a coalition now would be impracticable and, indeed, undesirable. It would be a barrier against needed change. In 1918–22, circumstances were different, the pressures for political and social unity, temporarily at least, more compelling. On the other hand, my close concern with British politics in the 1960s and 1970s has, to some degree, influenced my historical research. Recent events have shown with brutal clarity, for instance, how inexorable economic difficulties can make the rhetoric of parties and the ideals of would-be reformers almost redundant, how the cosmetic exercises of public relations have become inseparable from the political process, how the manic-depressive mood in which modern governments operate can alternate, almost daily, from serene confidence to inhibiting despair. The world of Mr. Callaghan, Mrs. Thatcher, and Mr. Steel is not very distant from that of 1918–22.

I am much indebted to the Provost and Fellows of The Queen's College, for help towards the cost of my research, and to Pat Lloyd for once again typing my manuscript with such expertise. I have benefited from conversations with Lord Blake, Maurice Cowling, Colin Matthew, Ross McKibbin, Philip Waller, Andy Cooper, Michael Hart, and Michael Freeden. I am much indebted to John Stubbs for transcripts from the Garvin and Astor Papers, to Philip Williamson for transcripts from the Baird diary, to Philip Waller for access to the manuscript of his study of the history of Liverpool, and to the late Sir Colin Coote for fascinating reminiscences. I have also greatly benefited from the intellectual companionship of my colleague, Alastair Parker. I received enormous assistance from the Bodleian and other libraries where the courtesy and helpfulness of the staff were always beyond praise. I am also grateful to the History Society of Peterhouse College, Cambridge, to the History Society of the University College of Swansea, and to the summer School of the Open University at Keele, where helpful comments and criticisms were made on some of my conclusions. Finally, to my wife, Jane, for her constant encouragement and for allowing me to draw on her own unpublished research on the period, I can offer no more than mute gratitude.

KENNETH O. MORGAN

Oxford
September 1978

Acknowledgements

The following people and institutions have very kindly granted me permission to quote from documents of which they hold the copyright:

Mr. A. J. P. Taylor and the Beaverbrook Foundation (Lloyd George and Bonar Law correspondence and Frances Stevenson diary); Mr. John Grigg (Sir Edward Grigg correspondence); University of Birmingham (Austen Chamberlain correspondence); Viscount Bridgeman (Bridgeman diary); The Dowager Lady Addison (Lord Addison correspondence); Principal Mary Bennett (H. A. L. Fisher diary); the Master and Fellows of Trinity College, Cambridge (Edwin Montagu correspondence); Mrs. K. Idwal Jones (Sir Herbert Lewis diary); University of Texas and Lazard Brothers & Co., Ltd. (Astor correspondence); the late Sir Colin Coote (letter to the author); Mr. J. B. Priestley and Messrs. Heinemann (extract from *Postscripts*).

Contents

1

The Invention of National Unity

'Fear of Lloyd George and his influence'. This, according to a Conservative ex-Cabinet minister writing to Thomas Jones, was the dominant motive behind the formation of the 'National' government in August 1931.[1] No doubt, as a judgement on that momentous crisis, this verdict is crude and over-simplified. Yet it contains a profound insight into how the making of coalition in 1931 was deeply permeated by recollections of the unmaking of that of 1918–22. Indeed, the political and social history of Britain in the inter-war period can be explained in considerable measure by the memories and legends generated by the post-war administration presided over by Lloyd George, the only plausible inter-party government of national unity that modern Britain has known, other than during times of war. In *Guilty Men* in 1940, 'Cato' depicted Baldwin and MacDonald, respectively Prime Minister and leader of the Labour opposition at the time, conversing on Crewe station at the height of the general election of 1929. 'Well, whatever happens,' MacDonald is reported as saying, 'we shall keep out the Welshman.'[2] This anecdote, questionable in detail, is true in essence. Baldwin and MacDonald both rose to political leadership essentially as alternatives to Lloyd George and his post-war Coalition. Baldwin symbolized the decencies of orthodox independent Conservatism, cleansed from the impurities of its unsavoury association with 'the goat'. His denunciation of Lloyd George, in his famous speech at the Carlton Club on 19 October 1922, as a 'dynamic force' which was 'a very terrible thing', and which might split the Conservative Party as it had already riven the Liberals into fragments, struck the right note of apprehension and of nostalgia for Britain in the twenties. It evoked the 'normalcy' of pre-war. MacDonald, forced into uneasy liaison with Lloyd George in 1930–1 through the exigencies of minority government and the agency of such go-betweens as Christopher Addison, still represented something of

the spirit of internationalism and idealism, in stark contrast to the
'system of Versailles', and the sordid adventures of 'arms to Poland',
Genoa, and Chanak.

Baldwin and MacDonald illustrate, by their very rise to party
leadership so dramatically in 1922–3, and their dominance over the
British political scene for almost a decade and a half thereafter, the
intensity of the revulsion against the Coalition system that they helped
overthrow. Not only was the Lloyd George government of the post-
war years denounced for sabre-rattling in industrial relations, for
presiding over mass unemployment on a scale unknown in British
history, for the 'reprisals' in Ireland and unsuccessful adventures in
foreign affairs. It was credibly represented as debasing the tone and
the currency of British public life. It was impregnated with the whiff
of corruption, through the glittering millions of the Lloyd George
fund, largely raised through the sale of honours, as its visible legacy.
This reputation survived years after Baldwin and MacDonald had
themselves passed from the scene and become discredited in their
turn. In the early 1960s for instance, during the Profumo and other
scandals that rocked the Macmillan government, the test of corruption and moral decay was taken to lie in its resemblance to the Lloyd
George era of 1918–22. This had become established as the touchstone of public degeneracy. Its manic-depressive atmosphere has been
imperishably captured by Arnold Bennett's *Lord Raingo* (really set in
the war years) where Sam Clyth, Celtic Prime Minister, master of
'chicane', burdened with an all-powerful secretary or mistress, Rosie
Packer, was all too easily identifiable. Stained with corruption and the
traffic in honours, the Coalition of the post-war years has found few
friends. Perhaps, to misappropriate a famous phrase of Mr. A. J. P.
Taylor's, it did not deserve any.[3] Contemporaries were hard-pressed
to understand, later in the twenties, how such honourable figures as
Austen Chamberlain and H. A. L. Fisher, for example, took such
pride in their post-war association with the new Ishmael of public life.
When Fisher used to expand in the New College common room in the
late 1920s on the good old days under Lloyd George, younger dons
like Lionel Robbins averted their gaze or stopped their ears, until the
urbanity and sanity of their Warden duly returned. It reminded
Robbins of 'a good man who had unwittingly entered a brothel—*and
rather enjoyed it*'.[4]

This universal disapproval of the post-war Coalition was shot

through every major segment of political opinion in the 1920s and
1930s. It survived to colour the preconceptions of the new post-war
governors after 1945. Such few defenders that Lloyd George managed
to retain only confirmed the general revulsion or distrust. Lord
Beaverbrook's enthusiasm for much of Lloyd George's premiership,
and his lament at the cathartic, momentous impact of his downfall in
October 1922 merely underlined the prevailing impression of the
Welshman as a maverick and an outsider. He sought the 'driver's seat'
but appeared not to care in which direction the vehicle was travelling.
Many of those most closely associated with him were consigned to
oblivion. Coalition Liberals such as Macnamara, McCurdy, Munro,
Kellaway, Shortt, and Fisher were by the late 1920s utterly irrelevant
politically, one with Nineveh and Tyre. Only if they managed to find a
new political anchorage did any future present itself for them. For
instance, there was Addison who began in 1923 a new and distinguished career in the Labour Party and served in high office under
MacDonald and Attlee. Much more typically, there were Mond,
Greenwood, Guest, Grigg, Hilton Young, and, above all, Churchill,
who moved rightwards and found in the Conservative Party the true
custodian of the values of order associated with the Coalition of
1918–22. To the extent that they obliterated their Coalitionist past,
their careers prospered—Addison is a leading example here. To the
extent that their Coalitionist background was recalled and reflected in
their manœuvres in the inter-war period, it was still held against
them—witness the case of Churchill until September 1939. Otherwise, it had, long before 1931, become the established orthodoxy to
decry the Coalition and all its works. In so far as the Liberal Party,
through Lloyd George's still being a leading member of it, retained
the closest links with the Coalition, it was inevitably to suffer the most
acutely, as 'Cato's' anecdote on the 1929 general election suggests.

   Of those who led the outcry against the Coalition, it was perhaps the
anti-Coalition Liberals who were most vocal and most bitter. The
'coupon' had fatally split the Liberal Party; the Coalition had dis-
orientated the Liberal mind. It is not surprising that it was Asquith and
his followers, the main injured parties, who led the tirade of criticism
against the post-war government after its fall. From Simon and Runciman on the right to Masterman and Wedgwood Benn on the left, the
ex-Wee Frees throughout the 1920s regarded the Coalition with total
contempt. Asquith himself took the lead after being elected for Paisley

in early 1920. The tone of the House of Commons of that time he found deplorable—'the worst in which he had ever sat' with an absentee and cynical Prime Minister and a coterie of kept coalitionist retainers.[5] Similar language was to be used by others. Josiah Wedgwood, Liberal turned Labour, thought the parliament of 1918–22 'the wickedest I have known', dominated by men who were not so much 'hard-faced' as 'empty-headed'. J. M. Kenworthy wrote that it embodied 'hatred and hostility in the mass'.[6] Through the powerful pens of the Writers' Group of the Reform Club, through the *Nation* and other periodicals still largely dominated by Liberal men of letters, through Liberal intellectuals such as Murray and Keynes, the sniping against the era of Coalition was incessant. To such men, the vigorous presence of Lloyd George at Liberal summer schools in Oxford and Cambridge from 1924 onwards was a constant embarrassment. After all, his post-war administration had seemed to ride roughshod over every principle that Liberals most valued—free trade undermined; Ireland coerced with martial law; the rule of law and established political institutions treated with contempt. To such Liberal ancestral voices, Lloyd George's claim to Scott of the *Manchester Guardian*, to have led in reality a Liberal-minded government, with domestic reform, peace, and disarmament as its main programme, was either an impertinence or a bad joke.[7] Not only did Asquithian Liberalism triumph in the constituencies, the clubs, and common rooms. It was victorious in the history books as well. Through such authors as J. A. Spender and A. G. Gardiner, biographies of recent or more distant Liberal heroes proliferated; popularizers like Ramsay Muir handed on the tablets of Liberal historiography to a new generation. By contrast, until the publication of Lloyd George's own Memoirs from 1933 onwards, with their multiplicity of targets and *ad hominem* tone, the Coalitionist Liberal voice was silent, perhaps dead. A pro-Coalition publication like the *Lloyd George Liberal Magazine* (October 1920–November 1923) has virtually disappeared from bookshops and libraries.

Conservative revulsion against the late Coalition was hardly less emphatic. After all, it had been the nationwide revolt of the Unionist rank and file between January and October 1922, first at the grass-roots level in the constituencies, then via the under-secretaries and other junior ministers, finally in the parliamentary party in defiance of the directives of most Unionist Cabinet ministers, that had brought the government down. Bonar Law's voice may have been influential in the Carlton Club, but the issue was probably settled before he uttered a single word. Sir George Younger and his 'cabin boys' had indeed taken over the ship. Not surprisingly, then, Conservative ideology in the 1920s was concerned to construct a series of positions that would erase the traces of coalitionism in its ranks. Baldwin's final reunion of the ex-Coalitionists headed by Austen Chamberlain and Balfour with the party majority in 1924 was decisive here. The higher the Tory, the more vocal his contempt for Lloyd George. It was the most aristocratic layers of the party who led the outcry now against the 'little Welsh attorney'. Curzon, of course, had his own list of complaints about the conduct of foreign policy. To Lord Salisbury and his 'connection', the Coalition had been a time of radical adventures, of extravagance in social expenditure epitomized by the hapless figure of Addison, and of erratic lurches in foreign policy such as the attempt formally to recognize Bolshevik Russia and to write off the claims of British bond-holders.[8] These Tory onslaughts could lead in contradictory directions. The Coalition could be denounced for being too ready to give way to Labour as in the 1919 rail strike. Alternatively it could be criticized for seeking a confrontation with the unions as on Black Friday. It could be attacked for constitutional innovation as over the cabinet or for inertia as over the House of Lords. It could be criticized for seeking peace with the enemy, as at Genoa, and for being too tender to Junkers and Bolsheviks, or for making war at Chanak. These aristocratic assaults, then, tended to some confusion. In any event, Lloyd George could plausibly claim that the bulk of the older landed families in the Tory ranks had stuck to him in 1922.[9] The true-blue Oxford Carlton Club, with young officers such as Ralph Assheton and David Maxwell-Fyfe, backed up Austen Chamberlain at the time of the fall of the government.[10] Evidently not all Conservatives were repelled by Lloyd George's vulgarity or his style of dialectic.

It was, more fundamentally, the ethical quality of the late government that rallied Conservatives against the late Coalition. It was here that Baldwin emerged as an interpreter of genius of the Conservative psyche. His quiet passion, directed against the immoderate greatness of the Coalition and the lack of principled consistency of its leader, conveyed the right note for a party and a people desperate for tranquillity and for 'no adventures' at home or abroad. When Baldwin

attacked Lloyd George in 1929 for 'plastering together the true and
the false and therefrom manufacturing the plausible', he touched an
important chord[11]—even if it was Labour who largely reaped the
immediate electoral benefit. It was here that the Lloyd George fund,
so misguidedly flourished by its owner as late as 1929, served as a kind
of talisman of the rottenness of Britain in those earlier years, a reminder of the discordances of the one-man band. Conservatism had
become again the hallmark of honesty and integrity, of familiar
institutions and traditional standards of morality. Four decades later,
in the writings of Conservative historians, this interpretation had lost
little of its bloom.

Finally, Labour also had its own, vehement causes for revulsion
against the Coalition. After all, whatever its broad-based antecedents
at the end of the war, the Coalition had been fuelled during much of its
course by anti-Labour propaganda, from Downing Street and elsewhere. 'Fusion' of the parties in 1920 had been in essence an anti-
Labour and anti-socialist programme. It was hostility towards the
claims of the 'so-called Labour Party' that was Austen Chamberlain's
ultimate justification for the Coalition during the critical months of
1921.[12] Labour men everywhere viewed the Lloyd George era as a
time of class war and class rhetoric. There was strong-arm strike-
breaking to crush the railwaymen in October 1919 and the miners in
April 1921. There was bland deception such as the casual disavowal of
nationalization of the coal mines after the verdict of a majority of the
Sankey commission. There was the artifice used on Black Friday in
isolating Frank Hodges and using J. H. Thomas to break up the
Triple Alliance. In overseas policy, there was intervention in Russia
on behalf of the reactionary 'Whites' and the attempt to ship arms to
Poland, from which, so legend had it, only 'direct action' by the
Councils of Action had delivered the nation. On a broader front,
Labour's own committee of inquiry had exposed and condemned the
reprisals policy in Ireland, while imperialist adventures in Egypt,
Persia, Mesopotamia, and India were Labour's contribution to the
stockpile of Anti-Waste propaganda. In Labour's case, also, it was the
atmosphere of the government that finally mattered. It was an
administration in which Lloyd George had condemned the railway
strike as 'an anarchist conspiracy' (headed by Jimmy Thomas, of all
people). It was a government in which Churchill had repeatedly
denounced Labour as 'unfit to govern' and had poured contempt on

the 'baboonery of Bolshevism', by which Clynes and Henderson
were apparently bracketed with Lenin and Trotsky along the socialist
continuum. It was a period when the patriotic euphoria of 1918 was
turned into an inward-looking xenophobic jingoism, when the
Labour movement, so honoured during the war years, suddenly
found itself branded as sectional and disloyal. After all, the Coalition
alone was a major argument for the success of the Labour Party.
Whatever his friendly relations with individuals such as Philip Snowden or George Lansbury, Lloyd George could never claim again to
have any kind of special relationship with Labour, or to act as the
spearhead of the British left.

   Liberals, Conservatives, and Labour, then, were united after 1922
in seeing the post-war Coalition as an ignoble aberration, a deviation
from a healthier norm. The very concept of coalition was besmirched
for years to come; it could not be considered as an abstract proposition. The Lloyd George Coalition could be viewed as an abnormal
sequel to the political vacuum of wartime, in which the promises and
pledges to create 'a land fit for heroes' were systematically betrayed.
J. B. Priestley used this interpretation to bolster the nation's morale at
the time of Dunkirk twenty years later:

I will tell you what we did for young men and their young wives at the end of
the last war. We did nothing—except let them take their chance in a world in
which every gangster and trickster and stupid insensitive fool or rogue was let
loose to do his damnedest. After the cheering and the flag-waving were over,
and all the medals given out, somehow the young heroes disappeared, but
after a year or two there were a lot of shabby young-oldish men about who
didn't seem to have been lucky in the scramble for easy jobs and quick profits,
and so tried to sell us second-hand cars or office supplies we didn't want, or
even trailed round the suburbs asking to be allowed to demonstrate the latest
vacuum cleaner. (Broadcast of 28 July 1940.)[13]

Alternatively, it was a precursor and alternative to the familiar, reassuring world over which Baldwin and MacDonald presided after
1922—a world of party contention within constitutional,
parliamentary guidelines that almost all the nation accepted and
understood. Either way, as a sequel to the war or as a launching-pad
for the peace, the Coalition had become a scapegoat for all the ills that
Britain endured after 1918, a scapegoat indeed for national decline.

   Just as his government has irretrievably lost the battle in the newspapers and the history books, so Lloyd George's own reputation has

suffered almost beyond repair from the peacetime Coalition. Until
1922, the prevailing treatment of him by biographers and other commentators, Welsh and non-Welsh alike, had usually been one of
enthusiasm, even of hagiography. The war years added to the saga of
the 'cottage-bred boy' the legend of 'the man who won the war'.
Authorized biographies even in the Coalition years, by Harold Spender in 1920 and 'E. T. Raymond' in early 1922, still retained the old
glow of greatness. The great divide in Lloyd George historiography
was the fall of the Coalition in October 1922. Thereafter, Lloyd
George's reputation was totally transformed. Critical biographies now
multiplied—and, significantly, focused their attention mainly on the
period 1918–22. Charles Mallet's book in 1930, written by a former
Asquithian candidate, devoted three-quarters of its space to the years
of the peacetime Coalition, which it regarded as a period of extravagance and dangerous experiment.[14] Conversely, friendly authors felt it
necessary to concentrate on the happy years of social reform and
progressive radicalism before the outbreak of war in 1914, with
perhaps a coda on the pre-coupon phases of the wartime leadership.
The years after that were an embarrassment to be passed by as
speedily as possible. Watkin Davies's account, published in 1939,
stopped short at the outbreak of the 1914 war. He hinted that he
regarded the death of old Uncle Lloyd in early 1917 as marking a great
divide in Lloyd George's career. Henceforth, 'the foundations of the
old life at Criccieth were sapped'. His populist hero was 'left to his
own devices and seconded by charlatans whose grip of political principles was even weaker than his own'.[15] Only thus in Davies's view
(and he wrote as one who was variously offered Wee Free, Labour,
and Coalition Liberal candidatures in Wales in 1921–3)[16] could the
disastrous aberrations of 1918–22, so profoundly at variance with
Lloyd George's radical, nonconformist youth, be explained. The later
torrent of denigration on Lloyd George in the years after 1945, a phase
that lasted at least until the opening up of his private papers at the
Beaverbrook Library in 1967, again concentrated largely on the mistakes or crimes of that disastrous post-war interlude. The further
revelations of his private liaisons with Frances Stevenson and perhaps
others, while usually much exaggerated, enabled a variety of authors
in a Gibbonian sense to link the personal immorality of the Prime
Minister with the lack of probity of his administration. The private
and the public were held to be one and indivisible.

We have, then, a problem in recent historiography which at first appears to present no problem at all—a rare unanimity amongst journalists, commentators, and academics about the inadequacies of the government of Britain, and its leadership, between 1918 and 1922. Even after the opening of the Lloyd George archives, there has not been hitherto any significant shift in interpretation of this crucial phase of Britain's political and social evolution. The Coalition government of 1918–22 serves as a cautionary tale of the corruption of noble radical ideals, and the debasement of a spurious mood of 'national unity'. It has served as a moral to divide the British people into parties, sections, and interest-groups ever since. Far more than in 1918, we are all 'faddists' now. This may well be a legitimate conclusion. Historical truth on 1918–22 may well lie with the big battalions. What still remains necessary, however, is to try to peel away the accretions of legend, to see the evolution of the Coalition not as a cautionary tale but as an historical phenomenon, above all to try to see it in terms of the perceptions and attitudes of men and women at the time. What still remains is the treatment of the post-war phase of social and political change in Britain not as pre-history but as history. Until some effort is made to achieve this, an understanding of twentieth-century Britain will still remain partisan and incomplete.

The idea of a supreme government of national unity had scant appeal in Britain prior to the First World War. After the watershed of the Boer War, which encouraged observers as diverse as Lord Rosebery and Keir Hardie to believe that a totally new alignment of parties was under way and that the 'slate' would be universally wiped clean,[17] Britain rapidly returned to its familiar path of partisan conflict. Traditional issues such as free trade, licensing, and church schools again dominated the public mind. Ideas of a new supreme command to promote 'national efficiency' remained the chimera of intellectuals such as the Webbs or outsiders such as Milner.[18] The years which led to the landslide Liberal victory of January 1906, and even more the period of partisan conflict thereafter down to the First World War, were a time when, in the view of many observers, Britain was almost being reduced to 'anarchy' by political and social turmoil. The People's Budget, National Insurance, Irish home rule, votes for women, the upsurge of labour all heightened the temper of partisan debate. Liberal England seemed almost ungovernable.

There was only one exception to the partisan strife of these years—Lloyd George's famous draft memorandum proposing a Liberal–Conservative Coalition, somewhat on the lines of Theodore Roosevelt's New Nationalism in the United States a year or two later.[19] This was made during the height of the conflict over the House of Lords and the Parliament Bill in the summer of 1910, though it reflected a yearning for a supreme all-party national synthesis that dated back many years in Lloyd George's relatively short career. He argued that the needs of a new century made the old party battles irrelevant and damaging. The House of Lords controversy showed vividly how sectional conflict over time-worn issues could consume the national energies, and deflect attention away from the supreme needs of the time. Irish home rule, Lords reform, the Welsh church, even free trade could be disposed of on a non-partisan basis as 'non-controversial issues' and left to scientific examination by commissions of experts. Instead, a combined Liberal–Unionist government (significantly, Labour was already left out) could devote itself to the supreme causes of social reform—national insurance, unemployment, housing, education, and temperance—and perhaps military preparedness as well. There was even a hint of military conscription, though defence and foreign policy issues loomed much less large in Lloyd George's proposals in 1910 than he was to suggest in his *War Memoirs* over twenty years later.[20] But the coalition idea was a false dawn at this time, and made scant long-term impact. It aroused some interest from those of a similar cross-bench persuasion—Churchill on the Liberal side, F. E. Smith on the Unionist, later two of the four-man inner Cabinet of 1921–2—as well as separate groups such as the social imperialists of the Round Table group, Philip Kerr, Edward Grigg, and the like. But in the party atmosphere of 1910, it was a distraction and an irrelevance. Neither the Liberal nor the Unionist party leaders felt any enthusiasm for Lloyd George's schemes. There would have been less still at the grass roots. To Asquith and to Austen Chamberlain, Lloyd George's 'non-controversial' issues were the very stuff of party politics. The result was an even more acrimonious phase of party conflict, symbolized in the famous occasion in the House in 1911 when the Unionist 'Hughligans' howled down Asquith in a violent scene. The Marconi affair made Lloyd George still more controversial personally; Leo Amery now derided him as 'St. Sebastian of Limehouse'. By August 1914, with the Unionists under their belligerent new leader Bonar Law, going to near-treasonable lengths in their support of Ulster and with the menace of civil war if Irish home rule were carried through under the provisions of the Parliament Act, the prospect of national consensus, or of any agreed priorities on either domestic or external questions, appeared more remote than ever.

Of course, the outbreak of war in August 1914 had a profound effect on political alignments and social attitudes. Yet for a long period it seemed to bring no nearer any viable form of consensus, let alone coalition. Until the formation of the first wartime Coalition under Asquith in May 1915, party government and adversary politics went on, despite the uneasy truce which followed Britain's declaration of war on Germany. There was, it was true, a cessation of party hostilities at by-elections, which was enshrined in a truce signed by the three party whips and renewed at intervals until after Lloyd George became Prime Minister.[21] There were striking gestures towards a supra-party form of government symbolized in the towering figure of Kitchener being brought in as Secretary of State for war, with almost omnipotent powers over strategy and war materials. There were important developments in industrial relations, most notably the concluding of the 'Treasury agreement' by Lloyd George in March 1915, under which the trade unions undertook to refrain from strikes for the duration of the war in return for government pledges to sustain collective bargaining and to restrict wartime profiteering. Despite the total failure to observe this last requirement, the Treasury agreement survived as a monument to the new-found community of outlook of its main authors, Lloyd George and Arthur Henderson. But the electoral truce was wearing thin by the spring of 1915. Bodies such as the Unionist Business Committee, under the chairmanship of W. A. S. Hewins, were providing a focus for back-bench protests about tariff and trade policies. There were wider protests about the organization of military supplies, particularly the so-called 'shell shortage' on the western front. When the crisis exploded in May 1915, Asquith's remodelled administration, 'the first coalition' with Unionist and Labour ministers, was essentially the product of efforts by the leaders of the two major parties, Asquith and Bonar Law, to preserve their credibility and to perpetuate their leadership in more durable form.[22]

The Asquith Coalition staggered on somehow in the face of a series of disastrous reversals and setbacks on the western front, on the eastern Mediterranean, and in inter-Allied diplomacy, until 6 December 1916. But it was hardly a precursor for the kind of 'national unity' which was later to emerge. It was a poor advertisement for consensus, despite the unifying pressures of total war. In reality, party considerations dictated much of its composition and its programme. After all, the government had been formed through a successful attempt by Asquith, temporarily backed by Lloyd George, to preserve Liberal ascendancy in the government. McKenna, Grey, Simon, all Liberals, retained key portfolios. Lloyd George took over the vital new department of the Ministry of Munitions. Bonar Law, the Unionist leader, had to be content with the Colonial Office. As a result, the critical issues that agitated the government had strictly party implications. Unionists such as Long and Lansdowne were much involved in blocking Lloyd George's schemes in June–July 1916 to try to provide a final settlement of the Irish home rule issue, based on the temporary exclusion of Ulster. Far more seriously, the long-drawn-out battles over conscription in the winter and spring of 1915–16 had desperate effects on Liberal Party morale, even though a Liberal, Lloyd George, was now the most fervent advocate of conscription. The eventual adoption of universal conscription for all males up to the age of forty-five, unless excluded by professional or trade qualifications, had a shattering effect on Liberal attitudes towards the Coalition government. It led to a deep schism that foreshadowed that of December 1916. It seemed to be deliberately undermining traditional Liberal principles in relation to freedom of conscience and civil liberties. Labour was scarcely less hostile, since it was widely believed that industrial conscription would be the next stage of wartime collectivism.

The government, therefore, limped along in the face of military disasters and party onslaughts from every wing, expressed in the newspapers rather than in parliament. It was, indeed, a party attack, though from a different quarter, a challenge by Unionist backbenchers to Bonar Law's leadership over the sale of German assets in Nigeria in November 1916, which was the occasion of the final crisis which brought Asquith's Liberal-dominated Coalition tumbling down. The government had done little more than paper over the party sectionalisms of pre-war years. Nor had it made any concerted effort

towards wrenching the economy in a collectivist direction. The autonomy of private business and industry survived remarkably intact.
The coal mines, transport, and shipping remained under the in-
efficient control of their private capitalist owners. The one conspicuous exception was the 'war socialism' introduced by Lloyd George and
his assistant Addison at the Ministry Munitions. By a vigorous programme of controls over production and over the distribution of raw
materials, of wide-ranging intervention in collective and plant bargaining, of a radical extension of social welfare in the government's
armaments factories, and of other novelties ranging from 'diluted'
labour in the form of women munitions workers to Britain's first
nationalized public houses at Carlisle, the new ministry became the
pioneer of state interventionism on a dramatically new scale. The
multi-volume *History of the Ministry of Munitions*, an official publication written after the war, graphically showed how state control fed
upon itself, and expanded not through ideology but in the light of
specific wartime needs. It was not surprising that it was in Munitions,
and through the links it built up with men like Milner and his Round
Table supporters, that demands were heard for the reconstruction of
the government and the removal of the Prime Minister.[23] In other
areas of government also, in food production, in the control of
imported raw material, in the development of new technology and
scientific enterprise, a series of disparate and uncoordinated initiatives
were impelling the government towards new forms of collective control. It is difficult in this period to detect any precise boundary
between Liberal defenders of *laissez-faire* and collectivist advocates of
'national efficiency'.[24] Still, it was basically a free-enterprise world
over which Asquith still shakily presided in November 1916. It was
business as usual, run by the familiar or notorious procedures of the
capitalist system. The euphoria of 'national unity' that enveloped the
conduct of the war on the front and on the high seas, and which the
government had mass-produced through propaganda on behalf of
recruitment or to denounce the 'frightfulness' of 'the evil Hun'[25] had
yet to be translated in any meaningful way to the running of the
political and economic system at home.

By most tests, it is the advent of Lloyd George as Prime Minister in
December 1916 that provides the essential divide between the world

of party and of sectionalism that survived largely unscathed until the
fall of Asquith, and the new consensus that endured well into the years
of peace. Of course, Lloyd George came to power in a fashion that in
no sense was conducive to a mood of supra-party unity. The discussions between himself, Bonar Law, and Carson, delicately orchestrated by Max Aitken, between 20 November and 1 December, may
not have been the conspiracy or intrigue that was once claimed. It is
also true that Asquith finally accepted, late on 3 December, the
revised form of War Committee that was proposed. It was he who
provoked the ultimate split by throwing it over on the morning of 4
December. This was supposedly after reading a leading article in *The
Times*, a mysterious enough *casus belli*. Until then, Asquith had
unquestionably been intended by the leading participants in the
negotiations to remain in 10 Downing Street, whatever his defects in
energy or decisiveness. Nevertheless, the new government arose from
the ashes of Asquith's regime tainted from the start with an aura of
party chicanery. In the crucial manœuvres of 4–6 December, the
impact on the Liberal Party was disastrous. A fundamental schism in
the party emerged between followers of Asquith and of Lloyd George
(a matter of temperament rather than ideology); it has not recovered
from this schism down to the present day. Lloyd George had been
suddenly propelled to the leadership of a kind of emergency government or Committee of National Safety. Its duration was widely pre-
dicted as a matter of weeks rather than months.

For all that, it was a more genuinely integrated all-party coalition
that he could claim to lead, although one dominated at first largely by
the Unionists. Even if the War Cabinet contained only one Liberal,
the Prime Minister, as against three Unionists (Law, Curzon, and
Milner) and Henderson, representing Labour, even if the government
faced party opposition in a manner quite unknown to Churchill in
1940, still the government was broad-based enough. Lloyd George
had been assured by Addison that he could command the certain
support of 49 Liberal members and probably of 126 others, two-thirds
the parliamentary party.[26] More crucial still, by a majority of one, the
Labour Party's national executive decided to back the new government, and Henderson served in the War Cabinet, with Clynes,
Hodge, and Roberts in the lower ranks. Soon, as the Prime
Minister's authority was confirmed, the new government broadened
still further. In July 1917, there were brought into the government

two powerful Liberal ex-ministers, Winston Churchill, who went to
the Munitions ministry, and Edwin Montagu who went to the India
Office. Henceforth, it could be plausibly claimed that the government
was truly coping with the wartime emergencies in a non-party spirit.
For the first time, the mood of wartime national unity was being
reflected in the administration and its policies. The great debate over
the running of the war, above all the conflict between the politicians
and the generals over the strategy on the western front—a conflict
which reached a climax after the débâcle of the Flanders offensive in
1917—was in no sense one which kindled partisan passions as the
conscription arguments had done earlier. In the struggles with Haig
and Robertson in the winter of 1917–18, Lloyd George, Bonar Law,
and Milner saw basically eye to eye. Their alliance became more firmly
based, their personal relations more intimate. The government now
bore a truly coalitionist appearance. Nor did the parliamentary opposition in fact adopt an unduly aggressive or partisan posture. Asquith
himself was diffident in leading attacks on the government. Even in
the crisis of the Maurice debate on 9 May 1918, when he moved in
effect a vote of no confidence in the government for withholding
reinforcements from the army in France, Asquith remained half-
hearted.[27] In practice, by maintaining an unspoken alliance between
government and opposition, Asquith was acting as a patriotic prop for
the Coalition himself.

Labour was more of a threat. After Arthur Henderson left the
government in August 1917, following a celebrated row with Lloyd
George over his attending an international socialist conference at
Stockholm, Labour built up its party machinery so as to challenge the
government at the next election. Trade union disaffection, over 'trade
cards' and other issues, was also mounting, as the regional
Committees on Industrial Unrest anxiously warned. On the other
hand, Labour's challenge, too, was a muted one. It showed scant
sympathy with the anti-war militancy of the shop stewards in
Clydeside or the unofficial rank-and-file movements among the South
Wales miners. Labour was still represented in the government,
George Barnes taking Henderson's place in the War Cabinet. The
Treasury agreement still held firm. In addition, Lloyd George could
plausibly claim that 'patriotic labour' in the TUC still supported the
government, despite the anti-war enthusiasm kindled by the revolution in Russia. Whatever its dubious origins, whatever the aura of

press and clubland intrigue that clung to the government through its association with newspaper barons such as Northcliffe and Beaverbrook, it could still claim to be national in emphasis and aspiration. The party factionalism of the past had been set aside. With the fortunes of war at last turning decisively in favour of the Allies in August 1918, Lloyd George's emergency wartime regime was poised to emerge as one of Britain's few truly successful and creative coalitions, and to extend its existence into the post-war era.

It is, then, in the period that followed the triumph of Lloyd George in December 1916 that the new mood of 'national unity' can best be detected. This was far more than a matter of party by-election truces, of muted opposition in the Commons and suspended party activity in the constituencies. It went far beyond narrow political considerations. There are many pointers to a profound change in political and economic practice and ideology that marked the later period of the war. As men's eyes increasingly focused on the possibility of peace, the passion for a new kind of government, transcending the sectionalisms of the past, became almost overwhelming.

One pointer to the new mood of the time, of course, lies in the fabric of government itself. The very centre of decision-making had been transformed, with a supreme War Cabinet detached from departmental burdens. In other branches of government, the introduction of uncommitted businessmen was the portent of a new style of administration—Sir Albert Stanley, pitchforked from running the London underground railway to the Board of Trade; Lord Devonport removed from the London port authority to run food supplies; Lord Rhondda brought from his Cambrian collieries to administer food rationing; Sir Joseph Maclay, who never confronted parliament at all, brought in to run shipping. Most spectacular of all, there was the charismatic figure of Sir Eric Geddes, the head of the North Eastern Railway who moved to the Admiralty and then Transport, the very prototype of a new type of businessman politician, and the only wartime appointee to survive for most of the peacetime Coalition.[28] Men like these, like Lord Cowdray or Sir Andrew Weir, were truly liberated from ideology, impatient with party politics, dedicated only to business efficiency and collective control within an increasingly corporate state.

Underpinning them was a mighty leviathan of government, symbolized by the new Cabinet secretariat, run by Sir Maurice Hankey

and his Welsh assistant, that 'fluid person', Thomas Jones.[29] This was
a kind of Prime Minister's department to reinforce his control of the
supreme command, with wide powers of intervention into government departments. More striking at the time was the so-called 'Garden Suburb' or Prime Minister's secretariat, a dramatic illustration in
itself of the difference in style between the new government and the
party-based administration of pre-December 1916. The Garden
Suburb's leading figures all were detached from the party scene—Professor W. G. S. Adams, an Oxford don; Joseph Davies, a commercial
statistician; Waldorf Astor, proprietor of the *Observer* and a rare
Unionist MP who had backed Lloyd George's National Insurance
Bill; David Davies, a millionaire industrialist and philanthropist;
above all, the eccentric imperialist visionary, Philip Kerr, one of
Milner's protégés. The influence of the Garden Suburb over policy,
especially foreign policy, has often been exaggerated.[30] Still, its very
existence was a portent of the new style of bureaucratic, centralized
government. In the five-man War Cabinet, the presence of Milner
reinforced this approach. He was a man almost arrogant in his
detachment from the party scene, a 'social imperialist' of Bismarckian
inclinations.[31] His dominant position in the government, notably in
the so-called 'X Committee' of the War Cabinet from March 1918
onwards, showed how far Lloyd George's method of government had
moved from the pre-war party system, how it was aspiring to a new
level of efficient and patriotic synthesis.

   A further pointer to the new mood lay in the extensions of collectivist controls over a wider and wider area of social and economic life. No
longer was the Ministry of Munitions a lonely pioneer in war socialism
or autarchy. The mines, the railways, and shipping were in effect
placed under public ownership for the duration of the war. A vast
range of economic controls were imposed, on production, supplies,
prices, and rents, in commandeering stocks, centralizing purchases,
and licensing exports. Direct industrial controls were imposed by the
War Office on textiles, leather, and medical supplies, by the munitions ministry on iron and steel, engineering, aircraft production, and
chemicals and explosives, and by the Admiralty on shipbuilding.
Unprecedented powers were taken over agriculture. R. E. Prothero,
at the Board of Agriculture, presided over an astonishing revolution in
food production, as a result of which four million acres were added to
the tillage area of the United Kingdom.[32] The 1917 Corn Production

Act provided guaranteed prices for wheat and oats, and minimum wages for agricultural labourers, a group largely ignored by all previous legislation on agriculture. New restrictions were imposed upon labour—and were extended to the unfamiliar area of female labour as well. Over municipal housing, over the liquor trade, over scientific research through such bodies as the Department of Scientific and Industrial Research, over designated 'key' industries such as optical and chemical instruments, tungsten, and dye-stuffs, controls were relentlessly extended. Everywhere, it seemed, *laissez-faire* lay in the dust. How efficient these controls really were must be debatable. R. H. Tawney's panegyric for controls written in 1943 was a product of the passion for planning during the Second World War, and the reaction against the ethos of the 1930s.[33] Even he admitted that decontrol after the war was a response to widespread popular demand. The official historians of the Ministry of Munitions admitted that wartime controls were unscientific in application, and that private industry was 'subject to many inconvenient and irksome restrictions', of which export licences were particularly disliked.[34] Many forms of control were unpopular with the trade unions as well as with private manufacturing and industry. One eminent economic historian has judged them to be in general 'wasteful and provocative'.[35] The permanence of these controls was uncertain at the time. The Balfour committee which considered Britain's industrial and commercial policy after the war linked a searching diagnosis of the structural weaknesses of the British economy, which the war concealed, with the need to suspend controls and free the export trade from 'unnecessary restrictions' as soon as the war came to an end.[36] Even so, it is difficult to discover a serious examination of British economic and social policy in the 1917–18 period which does not take as its starting-point the decisive and permanent change wrought in the running of industry, agriculture, and commerce by the new collectivism.

Elsewhere, too, this new mood spread and gained remarkably wide acceptance. Another straw in the wind in the later wartime era is the apparent change in the attitudes of businessmen, and their new willingness to accept centralized restrictions upon business and industry. Naturally, socialism was unthinkable. The corporatist forms of control in the mines, shipping, and transport were imposed on industries which retained in full their capitalist system of management and of stock-holding. Nevertheless, the mood of business, implacably suspicious of state intervention and of a dialogue with the trade unions in the past, does show significant change at this time. The annual reports of the newly-formed Federation of British Industries were a hymn of praise to the new partnership between the state and private industry, with emphasis on how new efficiency had been brought to flagging industries such as textiles and shipping, with a vast boom in production and profits in consequence. Businessmen were not oblivious to the benefits of a more tranquil and equal relationship with organized labour. Taking their cue from Sir Eric Geddes, the 'czar of transport', they welcomed the settlement of industrial disputes on a more peaceful basis. For instance, the placating of the engineers in the summer of 1917 after the withdrawal of the 'trade card' scheme (which, in effect, enabled the unions to determine recruitment to engineering plants), was widely welcomed, even if it did Addison's reputation some temporary harm. Nor did businessmen react in immoderate fashion to the growing tide of labour unrest in the mines and engineering factories in 1917. The Commission on Industrial Unrest's reports encouraged an emphasis on positive measures to conciliate labour.[37] It recognized the social pressures on working people, notably the rapid rise in wartime prices, dismal housing, and community conditions, and the erosion of differentials amongst grades of workmen on the railways, in engineering workshops, and elsewhere. Businessmen now urged that the moral of the war was to build on the mood of conciliation, especially on the Industrial Councils formed within individual industries, and which Bridgeman, the Under-Secretary at the Ministry of Labour, considered the one really significant achievement of the war on the labour front.[38] The Whitley Councils, with joint representation for employers and employees in individual trades, seemed to many industrialists at the time just the kind of initiative to be adopted to build on the wartime mood of unity without falling into the perils of socialism or worse.

The new mood of reason amongst employers was to some fair degree mirrored amongst trade unions also. At the rank-and-file level, as has been seen, protests were increasingly numerous throughout 1917 and 1918. Movements such as the classes of the Central Labour College in the Welsh mining valleys preached a total rejection of capitalism or corporatism. The shop stewards' movement, amongst engineering and shipyard workers, was a sign of how the changes in industrial relations during the war, with the emphasis on negotiation at the level of the individual pit, plant, or factory, had placed new power in local, and perhaps more militant, leadership.[39] How far the writ of union executives, let alone that of the TUC Parliamentary Committee, ran was increasingly debatable. Nevertheless, at the summit, the mood of unity and conciliation remained dominant amongst the unions also. The euphoria of the Russian revolution, the dismissal of Arthur Henderson from the government, general war weariness, the new political challenge embodied in the constitution and machinery of the Labour Party in 1918—all these did not destroy it. After all, trade unions had experienced during the war the greatest period of growth in their history, building on the upsurge of 1911–14. They had been direct beneficiaries of the wartime collectivism. At the cost of some 'dilution' of skilled trades, trade union membership had soared to over six million. Wages had risen sharply, too, with wartime bonuses enjoyed by railwaymen, miners, and others. Indeed, wage increases had substantially outstripped the rise in prices since 1913. The eight-hour day was widely extended. Lloyd George, like Franklin Roosevelt, had exploited his reputation as a 'patron' of organized labour.[40] As promised, he had taken the mines and transport into public control. As promised, he had protected the processes of collective bargaining. More predictably, social welfare provisions had been dramatically extended. Adult and infant mortality was diminished; public health improved. Agricultural workers benefited from the new guaranteed minimum wage. Industrial workers profited from subsidized housing and pegged rents. Food rationing and price controls, however laxly administered, were also popular with the unions. They became, therefore, major clients of the new political and social order. The Labour Party's commitment to 'socialism' in the 1918 party constitution was simply another version of the unions' vision of wartime collectivism. As the TUC reflected on the industrial condition in 1918 and such pronouncements as Lloyd George's Westminster Hall declaration on war aims, it viewed with satisfaction its new wealth and status. The socialist R. H. Tawney applauded the unions' new partnership with the state. They had become 'the industrial organs of England at war'.[41]

Tawney's observation suggests that political and economic ideas were also changing in the light of the new imperatives of Lloyd George's corporate regime. The anti-socialist phobias of Property Defence Leagues and the like in pre-war days, their hysteria in the face of syndicalism, 'direct action' and other threats, now seemed ludicrously out of date. The prophets of collectivism now made all the running. Tory collectivists took pride in the effective centralism implied in conscription and the undermining of pure pre-war free trade. In the pressures of the war years, Joseph Chamberlain had truly come into his own, imperial preference and all. Even such a traditional figure as Lord Salisbury headed a committee which pressed for a dramatic new initiative in subsidized public housing and environmental planning.[42] Amongst Liberals, *laissez-faire* zealots such as Runciman were swamped by 'New Liberals' of the schools of Hobhouse or Seebohm Rowntree, who found in the social programmes of the war years a logical continuation of their own welfare proposals of pre-war years. J. A. Hobson, now in a kind of limbo between radical Liberalism and the Independent Labour Party, by way of the Union of Democratic Control, viewed with satisfaction the new controls over industrial production and public spending. He took it for granted that public control of the mines and transport would lead to a permanent nationalization of the iron and steel and other industries when peace returned. 'The war will have advanced State Socialism by half a century.' The important issue was to ensure that wartime idealism was not exploited by bogus patriotism and the 'impropriety' that arose from militarism and wartime profiteering.[43] That was why Hobson attached such importance to a new foreign policy as advocated by the UDC, as the key to a permanent revolution in the national psychology. That was also why he took the time in 1918 to produce a lengthy biography of that highly anti-collectivist radical, Richard Cobden.

The war above all gave new respectability to socialists of all shades, just as it fortified the consensus approach of a non-socialist collectivist like William Beveridge.[44] It impelled G. D. H. Cole away from his earlier anti-centralist, anti-bureaucratic guild socialism towards a frank acceptance of the new statist controls. It impelled Tawney towards a worship of the fiscal controls of wartime. Years later, his critique in an academic journal of the 'decontrol policy' of 1919–21 was to serve as the *locus classicus* for a certain kind of left-wing attack on the Lloyd George Coalition. At the same time, Tawney's main emphasis was on a moral concept of citizenship: he still feared the crude power of the overmighty servile state. The socialist theorist whose ideology most reflected the new mood was Sidney Webb.[45]

Suddenly, his years of preaching the new gospel of collectivism and efficiency reaped their reward and gave him a receptive national audience. Writing to Shaw, he advocated 'universal submission to the National Need.'[46] In a sense, this was the Fabians' war, with its general acceptance of planning and collectivism. The imposition of conscription in 1916 made it all the more crucial to deflect this collective spirit in a socialist direction. Much of the Webbs' writings and propaganda necessarily appeared under the auspices of the Labour Party. Its War Emergency Committee became the forum for new diagnoses of the administrative and economic structures of a socialist commonwealth. Webb went on to advocate more radical measures such as the 'conscription of wealth' through more drastic direct taxation and a levy on capital. The theoretical aspects of the 1918 Labour constitution, Clause Four and all, bore the stamp of Webb's ideas. Nevertheless, his brand of socialism had in some ways become a new orthodoxy. Men such as the 'microbe', Thomas Jones, diffused it throughout the entire nexus of central government. Lloyd George, on coming to office, sought and received a distinctly Fabian memorandum, prepared in part by Jones and Tawney, which called for 'a new spirit in government and the conduct of the war'. Montagu even suggested Webb as a possible President of the Local Government Board.[47] The message was for a drastic new extension of state control, with the conscription of all working or employable men up to the age of sixty. None embraced this gospel more wholeheartedly than 'Czar' Geddes, with his programme of centralization for national power supplies and transport services. With the Bismarckian Milner in the War Cabinet, many of his disciples in the civil service and the Garden Suburb, and Webb capturing the public mind, 'social imperialism' with all its Fabian implications was the dominant creed of the time.

    These diverse and disparate movements in policy and ideas operated at different levels throughout the period of Lloyd George's wartime premiership. None could by itself serve as the political or ideological base of a more permanent drive towards national unity. A striking portent, however, of the change in emphasis in political debate at this period is the attempt seriously made in 1917–18 to reduce these different forces and pressures to some kind of comprehensible form. This was the idea of 'reconstruction' which loomed so large in governmental policy-making in early 1918, at the height of desperate Allied attempts to ward off German assaults near Amiens, and equally desperate efforts by Lloyd George and Clemenceau to bring American military strength to bear on the western front before the war was irretrievably lost. The Ministry of Reconstruction was its main institutional focus. This is a largely forgotten episode in administrative experiment. It has tended to be treated summarily by those few who have discussed it. It has tended to be regarded as a classic example of a ministry set up with a confused and over-ambitious brief, ill-equipped, with inadequate powers over industry and finance.[48] Addison's massive memorandums on post-war recon-struction have usually been dismissed as a grand irrelevance, with little practical impact. It had its critics at the time. Bridgeman thought that Addison 'was given powers, which no one but a Prime Minister should wield, of interference with other departments—and having no experience of the Civil Service, and not enough capacity to realize his ignorance, embarked on all sorts of works which were already being done by one dept. or another'.[49] Significantly, Addison's salary dropped from £5,000 at Munitions to £2,000 at Reconstruction.[50] The Ministry of Reconstruction has been the popular scapegoat for the failure of the government after 1919 to deliver as promised that brave new land 'fit for heroes'.

That is not the way it appeared to contemporaries. There is little doubt that the Ministry of Reconstruction was taken very seriously both as a new departure in the coordination and stimulation of new social policies, and as an imaginative new gesture that would form the basis of a new political platform. It was close to the strategy for perpetuating the wartime feeling of unity to which Lloyd George was now applying his mind. The idea of a new governmental agency to supervise and co-ordinate post-war planning in the social and economic spheres was not new. Asquith had set up a Cabinet committee to consider reconstruction. Lloyd George, on the advice of Montagu amongst others, had himself chaired a more ambitious committee in March 1917, with Beatrice Webb amongst its members. But it was with the new ministry set up in July 1917 under Addison that reconstruction became a practical political theme, and a major priority for the government. Nothing more conclusively illustrates the foolishness of claiming that Addison was pushed out of Munitions because of his alleged mishandling of the engineers' strike than the fact that he was given charge of such a potentially significant new department.[51] It began work on a variety of tasks in the autumn of

1917. A radical report proposed in effect the abolition of the old Poor
Law. It embodied 'all the conclusions of the Minority Report of the
Poor Law Commission' in Mrs. Webb's opinion. Equally impressive
was a scheme for a new programme to build 300,000 houses which
Addison himself inspired. The earlier moves, in fact, led to very little.
The Poor Law report gathered dust and was forgotten. The housing
scheme met with the implacable opposition of Hayes Fisher and the
Local Government Board. However, in the spring and summer of
1918, the ministry's labours gained far more momentum. Persistent
stone-walling by the Local Government Board was partly overcome.
After all, Addison's work chimed in with Lloyd George's new overtures to the unions and the Labour Party which were heralded by his
speech on 'war aims' to the trade unions in January 1918 and which
lasted until his attempt to 'get at' the Webbs in June. By the end of the
summer, Addison's ministry had sketched out a totally new social
agenda, a socialism for consumers if not yet for producers.[52] A new
programme for public housing and slum clearance would be based on
subsidies to the local authorities. A new scheme for the demobilization
of soldiers after the war was linked to a programme of land settlement.
A new Ministry of Health would co-ordinate the nation's insurance
and medical services. Technical and secondary education would be
extended, much on the lines of H. A. L. Fisher's Education Bill of
1918. The Poor Law would be scrapped and replaced by a new
structure of public assistance committees. Unemployment insurance
would be made comprehensive and universal. Finally, devolution in
industry would be encouraged through the spread of 'Whitleyism' in
the form of Joint Industrial Councils, a cause particularly dear to
Addison and to Seebohm Rowntree. Much of this remained paper
proposals only. The devising of an appropriate machinery of government had still to be worked out. Universal unemployment insurance
was shamefully neglected, to the dismay of Beveridge, its leading
advocate. Nevertheless, reconstruction and the political energy that
went into it, may be taken as the supreme indication of the new
constructive mood of wartime.

   It is not surprising that reconstruction has not received much later
attention. The ministry was dismantled soon after the armistice, and
its proposals had varying fortunes—though, as will be seen, many
were implemented with success. The ministry operated at the level of
civil service expertise. It made little impact on the national public.

There was no dramatic, much-publicized document such as the 1942 Beveridge report to direct the public's gaze to new social horizons. The fact remained that this interlude, over which the uncharismatic Addison presided, managed to bring together all the different threads that the war years had released. If there was a realistic supra-party basis for a post-war coalition government, reconstruction would form the core of it. It was a cause particularly close to the Prime Minister's heart—and he would clearly be the transcendent figure when hostilities ended. It chimed in with his coalition scheme of 1910. It spelled out his instinctive belief that the war had totally transformed the political and social priorities, and had reduced the party issues of pre-war (always excluding Ireland) to minor significance. Here indeed was the opportunity to relegate free trade, Lords' reform, home rule, temperance, the Welsh church, and other albatrosses of pre-1914 to their appropriate niche as 'non-controversial issues'—and, by implication, non-partisan. Reconstruction, allied to the successful outcome to the war, suggested to Lloyd George in the late summer of 1918 the strategy for perpetuating his new style of government, and turning it into a new and progressive orthodoxy, challenging in tone while retaining the best of the fabric of the old order. At Criccieth on 21–2 August, Addison, Kerr, Milner, Hankey, Amery, Henry Norman, Bertrand Dawson, Dudley Ward, and other intimates fleshed out the skeleton of this new radical programme, especially the politics of public health. They assembled there in such numbers that Kerr feared that the food suppliers of rural Caernarvonshire might prove inadequate for the task of nourishing these zealous planners.[53] The relaxed atmosphere was encouraged by a paddling expedition in the River Dwyfor in which the Prime Minister 'paddled up to his middle in his shirt and pink pants, Milner doing the whole business in his trousers.' As the war rapidly approached its end in September and October, Lloyd George pondered the way towards formulating a new kind of consensus. The war had provided the mood and the momentum. Reconstruction had provided much of the agenda. The task of far-sighted statesmanship now was to invent the democratic mechanism to generate a more durable form of coalition, and give the unity of wartime political reality in the years to come.

2

Coupon and Coalition

The transition from wartime to peacetime government was one of immense complexity. One transcendent problem, of course, was gauging precisely when the war period was likely to come to an end. The best informed guesses in the spring of 1918 maintained that hostilities were likely to continue for at least another year, perhaps until the spring of 1920. Only then would the military and industrial power of the United States make its full impact, and the pressure of the Allied naval blockade starve the German population into submission. The withdrawal of Austria–Hungary as a belligerent power, locked in seemingly static conflict in the Italian mountains, was widely expected, and a major objective for Lloyd Georgian diplomacy in the late winter of 1917–18. Turkey, it was surmised, would not too long survive Allenby's new drive through Palestine and Syria, backed up by the uprising of the Arab chieftains under Feisal. But there seemed no obvious grounds for supposing in mid-1918 that German resistance was not as tenacious and implacable as at any stage in the war. The negotiations for the forthcoming general election in Britain, in fact, took place on the assumption that they would apply to a wartime not a peacetime election. In any case, the millions of new voters, including women for the first time, newly enfranchised under the 1918 Representation of the People Act, could not be expected to wait indefinitely.

It was, in any event, peculiarly difficult for Lloyd George and his advisers to outline any future political strategy. The exact import of what had taken place in December 1916 was still obscure. The tacit assumption seemed to be that, as soon as peace returned, the party truce would end, Lloyd George and Asquith would reassemble their respective forces under the banner of Liberalism and under Asquith's leadership, and party warfare would resume, with the significant presence of Labour as a much-strengthened third force. Lloyd George himself well knew that the Liberal Party machine, and the control of Liberal local associations in the constituencies everywhere save in Wales, were in the hands of the Asquithians operating from Abingdon Street. Lloyd George himself had no obvious nationwide strength to bring to bear. Truly, he was a premier without a party, a fortuitous product of the political vacuum of wartime, powerful only at the level of executive decision-making. If he were to suggest precipitately any kind of peacetime renewal of the Coalition he now led, it would be likely to cause a massive crisis amongst pro-government Liberals everywhere. They still dreamed of a peaceful reunion with their Asquithian comrades, with whom they generally remained on good terms. For example, Addison, Lloyd George's ardent lieutenant in 1916, retained his close friendship with his fellow-London member, Wedgwood Benn.

Now and again, in intervals from direction of the Allied war and diplomatic strategy, Lloyd George and a few friends turned to contemplate the shape of politics and government to come. To a man, they took as axiomatic the new priorities and principles mapped out by the wartime collectivism. But the political implications were most uncertain. In December 1917, Lloyd George met with an oddly assorted quartet of advisers, Milner, Addison, Waldorf Astor, the 'sentimental Socialist' proprietor of the *Observer*, and Victor Fisher of the firmly anti-Bolshevik British Workers' League. There was general agreement that the Prime Minister's basic weakness was the absence of any political machine or accepted slate of candidates to promote his cause. 'The country is ready for a bold move forward under State inspiration.'[1] George Riddell, the proprietor of the *News of the World*, Sir William Sutherland, the Prime Minister's Rabelaisian patronage secretary, and Freddie Guest, the government Liberal chief whip, gave advice in much the same sense. Lloyd George told Riddell in January 1918 that he believed the old Liberal Party to be a thing of the past. All parties, including Labour, would be split and reconstituted. 'He thinks it may come to a fight between him and Henderson.'[2] Apart from such generalized intuitions, however, Lloyd George had nothing immediately to offer. In any case, his main concern was winning the war—or, at least, not losing it. The uncongenial topic of electoral organization, a relatively unfamiliar area for him ever since he entered Welsh politics in the late 1880s, was hardly foremost in his mind. Throughout the spring of 1918, as the German army launched a massive new offensive around Amiens, the prospective pattern of post-war politics remained totally obscure. Pinpricks such as right-wing nationalist votes in by-elections, on the model of Pemberton Billing at Hertford, and the much more serious growth of Sinn Fein in Ireland were the sole diversions from the bipartisan unity of wartime which suffocated genuine political argument.

The situation was transformed by the Maurice debate of 9 May 1918. This followed serious allegations in the newspapers by General Frederick Maurice, lately Director of British Military Intelligence, that Lloyd George and Bonar Law had lied to the House of Commons about the state of British reserves under arms in January 1918, and that they had held back reinforcements to Haig in France since the abortive Flanders offensive the preceding September. Asquith, in a half-hearted but potentially dangerous speech, called for a full-scale committee of inquiry. Lloyd George warded off this threat with a triumph of passionate oratory rather than of factual argument. Indeed, the evidence seems to suggest that Maurice's allegations were correct, though whether Lloyd George knew this is less certain.[3] In the vote, 98 Liberals voted against the government. Certainly, most of them were merely confirming once again a persistent anti-government voting record over the preceding fifteen months. What is more significant is that the Maurice debate gave Lloyd George an irresistible argument for marshalling his Liberal followers in more permanent form. On 17 May a group of Liberal advisers, headed by Churchill, Addison, Illingworth, Hewart, Montagu, and Shakespeare, met to form the nucleus of a Coalitionist Liberal group. Guest was confirmed as their chief whip. The germ of a new party and, therefore, of a vital political bargaining weapon was in being. Guest reported that it was still inopportune to create organizations in the constituencies to challenge the traditional Liberal Associations, but that the activity of the Coalition Liberal whips should be stepped up and a Liberal programme prepared for projection throughout the country when the time came.[4] From this moment on, inspired by the political centre, as was typical of Coalition Liberalism throughout its shadowy history, the pressure mounted up for building a specifically Lloyd George brand of Liberalism, a creed that would merge almost imperceptibly with the coalitionist spirit of wartime. Sympathetic editors such as Sir William Robertson Nicoll, the veteran editor of the influential Free Church newspaper, the *British Weekly*, were harnessed to the cause. A *putsch* in September 1918 secured the purchase of the *Daily Chronicle* as a pro-Lloyd George daily.[5] Sir Henry Dalziel, a Liberal MP, arranged for most of the capital, much of it from the munitions organizer, Andrew Weir, later Lord Inverforth. The former editor, Robert Donald, a biting critic of the government who had had the temerity to employ General Maurice as his military correspondent, was dispatched into oblivion. After a fighting speech at Manchester from the Prime Minister in September, newly refreshed by the light-hearted confabulations at Criccieth, a National Election Committee was set up, with Sir Henry Norman, the old organizer of the Budget League in the happier days of 1909, in charge of its propaganda.[6]

The organization, then, was in being. What of the programme of the putative Lloyd George party? The crucial figure was the self-effacing Dr. Addison, Minister of Reconstruction, key member of the organizational committee set up in May, all-purpose contact man and trouble-shooter for his master. Addison chaired the 'Policy for Government Committee' which met in 12 Downing Street on 19 July with Dalziel, Hamar Greenwood, Shakespeare, Beck, Lord St. David's, Guest, Dudley Ward, and others among its members—not a particularly radical membership, it may be noted.[7] Its proposals, if often ill-defined, drew irresistibly from the collectivist experience of the recent past. There would be a joint development of imperial resources and the determined prosecution of the war to a successful conclusion. Essential industries would be given 'national assistance', with nationalization certainly not ruled out. On the social side, the effects of unemployment would be 'mitigated' by reform of the insurance scheme, there would be a Ministry of Health, a new housing and transportation programme, and a comprehensive policy of 'industrial conciliation' along the lines of the Whitley Councils. Conservative in some crucial details (notably in the insistence that 'freedom' be restored to industry and trade after the war), in general the main lines of this programme could have come out of the very maw of the Ministry of Reconstruction. Truly, 'that ogre, tradition', lay in the dust. The programme's silence on the traditional Liberal areas of free trade, the status of nonconformism, temperance, and the power of the landlord class was highly significant. The Old Liberalism was a casualty of total war.

Armed with this organization and programme, Lloyd George

encouraged Guest to approach the Unionists formally about an electoral agreement designed to perpetuate the Coalition.[8] In the course of
July, the irrevocable decision was taken to bind the Lloyd George
Liberals with their Unionist allies, and—who knew?—with perhaps
their Labour ones as well. The corollary that this meant a decisive split
in the Liberal Party was accepted without question. By the end of the
month, Guest and the Unionist whips had arrived at the electoral
agreement they sought, the notorious 'coupon' which was to dictate
the immediate shape of the politics of post-war.[9] Their attitude
towards the Prime Minister, so long distrusted as a Welsh radical
adventurer, had undergone a profound metamorphosis since
December 1916. Bonar Law and Balfour had both established
positions of intimacy and trust with the Prime Minister; they had
come to accept his directives on the running of the war without
question. Over the great crises of wartime politics, such as the sacking
of General Robertson, the CIGS, in February 1918, or the Maurice
allegations in May, they backed him up to the hilt. They indulged his
zeal for domestic reconstruction; they applauded his determination to
fight the war to a finish; they admired his enthusiasm for binding the
imperial dominions more closely with the mother country through the
Cabinet and through preferential trade arrangements. They trusted
his judgement. Even more surprisingly, they now trusted his integrity. They would have echoed the judgement of the American Ambassador, Walter Hines Page, another caustic critic of Lloyd George won
over by his war leadership, who saw him as 'the one public man here
who has an undoubted touch of genius', a man of 'vision and imagination, even if his imagination at times runs away with him'.[10] Willie
Bridgeman, a Shropshire squire and a warm defender of the Welsh
church, not obviously attributes to endear the Prime Minister to him,
was quite clear in his mind about his leader by February 1918. 'I
believe he is single-hearted about this war, and does not really think of
his future position afterwards, though his reception of Winston
Churchill into the Govt. looked as if he were afraid of losing hold of all
his Liberal colleagues & being absorbed by us.'[11] By the early autumn,
there was less certainty about who was to absorb whom, about who
played the whale and who, Jonah, as the dramatic turn in Allied
fortunes at the front enormously increased the Prime Minister's
authority.

Bonar Law even looked forward with equanimity to Lloyd George's being impelled towards as close a relationship to the Unionist Party as that once enjoyed by that other provincial radical, Joseph Chamberlain—and perhaps even becoming the Unionist leader. 'That would, however, I am inclined to think not be a bad thing for our Party and a good thing for the Nation. I am perfectly certain, indeed, I do not think anyone can doubt this, that our Party on the old lines will never have any future again in this country.' Such awkward items as tariffs, Ireland, and the Welsh church were all capable of happy adjustment. With its leadership in such an accommodating mood, it is not surprising that the Unionist Party was no less eager for a more durable alliance with Lloyd George and the greater post-war security that this 'combination of parties' would bring with it. It was generally accepted that the Prime Minister had even decided the date of the forthcoming general election, though he coyly refused to divulge to Unionist colleagues when it might be.[12]

Set against this background, the 'coupon' arrangements in the summer and autumn of 1918 seem more intelligible, even defensible. The 'coupon' has been much attacked subsequently for its damaging effects upon the Liberal Party and for associating Lloyd George disastrously in a subservient relationship with the Unionists. Keynes, in a famous passage, went on to link these political manœuvres with the outcome of the Treaty of Versailles with its punitive and vindictive terms imposed on Germany, as he saw them.[13] Lord Reading at the time felt that 'Ll.G. was too headstrong and too impressionistic, and needed to be held back if he was to be saved for Liberalism.' His present associates were 'thoroughly bad for him'.[14] Many later writers, far less charitably, have adopted this line of interpretation. In the wisdom of hindsight gained by a knowledge of party politics after 1922, there can be little doubt that the 'coupon' was a disaster for Lloyd George, one which forever damaged his credibility as a consistent leader of the British left. But the events of post-1922 were quite unforeseeable in the heady wartime atmosphere of 1918. The logic of events then, as almost all observers in all parties agreed, was to force politics into the new mould of consensus which the success of the Coalition had created. Those who had rejected that consensus must inevitably be rejected by the post-war Coalition. It could not seriously be argued that men like Simon, Runciman, or McKenna, with a persistent record of opposition to Lloyd George's government over the past two years, should now magnanimously be taken back into the

fold as ardent loyalists all along. That was political nonsense. The
'coupon' was the realistic outcome of the politics of war. Party on the
traditional lines was the world of pre-war and therefore repugnant to
the majority of political leaders. In the assumptions generally held in
mid-1918, something like the 'coupon' to determine supporters and
opponents of the Coalition at the next election was inescapable, as was
the agreed Coalition manifesto that followed.

As it worked out, the electoral arrangement concluded between
Freddie Guest and the Unionist whips in July 1918, and subsequently
filled out in detail constituency by constituency, caused relatively
little acrimony.[15] In general, it confirmed the known alignments of the
House of Commons voting lists over the past eighteen months. While
there were certainly some unfortunate casualties who found their
loyalty to the government unrewarded, and others who found an
unwanted 'coupon' forced upon them, these were a small minority.
Trevor Wilson's contention that the 'coupon' arrangements generally
were haphazard in impact and cynical in tone is hard to support by a
close examination of what was agreed.[16] The first draft accepted in
July specified 98 Liberals (including 25 ministers) who would receive
Unionist support at the next election, together with sixteen 'other
candidates', the Labour ministers, and the seventeen followers of
Victor Fisher's British Workers' League. In each case, the acid test
was the member's voting record and political outlook over the previous eighteen months. By the end of October, when the early end of the
war was clearly imminent, Guest's terms had hardened. Bonar Law
and the Unionists had finally agreed to give their support to 150 Lloyd
George Liberal candidates, '100 of whom are our Old Guard'.[17]
Younger noted ruefully that it was the Prime Minister himself who
insisted on 150,[18] a round number governed by the available candidates and finance, and that even more could have been squeezed out of
the pact with the Unionists. Reinforced by military victory and the
mood of domestic consensus, it was Lloyd George who was calling all
the tunes.

Of course, the party organizers and election agents did not care for
these arrangements. It was a quite unfamiliar exercise in self-
effacement that they had to undergo, just like trade unions who agree
to forsake free collective bargaining in the interests of an incomes
policy. There was much tension on all sides. The Liberals had
difficulty in reconciling many local associations to a passive accep-

tance of the electoral pact. Adoption of Lloyd George's list of 'men of proved loyalty' meant the proscription of 'pacifist' or 'Asquith' Liberals, plus a claim for seats where a Liberal was retiring and where Liberal constituencies were being split into two or more seats under the new redistribution of constituencies.[19] There was much tense negotiation with the Unionists about getting Liberals accepted in formerly Unionist-held seats. Guest wondered anxiously whether Younger and Sanders would 'deliver the goods'. He was angered that the Liberals seemed to be granted less than their fair share of seats in such old Liberal territory as Scotland. He even raised the wholly unreal threat of the Coalition Liberals fighting the election on their own.[20] The Unionists, who would clearly provide the majority of the new Coalition and whose organizers therefore felt that they were making the major concessions, were even more uneasy. Independent right-wingers such as Lord Salisbury felt that the arrangements were 'not satisfactory' with Guest claiming one of the Wandsworth seats and 'Eddy' Hartington being unceremoniously bundled out of the nomination in Chesterfield.[21] In Liverpool (a stronghold of Coalitionist sympathy where the Liberal Party, dominated by the Holt shipping family, was notoriously weak) Salvidge and Petrie objected to a Liberal—and a Jew—claiming the Fairfield constituency over the head of a sitting Unionist, and others putting in a bid for Wavertree and Exchange as well.[22] In the event, Salvidge was to use his influence to crush the 'couponed' Liberal, Joseph, at Fairfield. There was further difficulty over at least six Scottish seats. Forfarshire was a particular problem with a Coalitionist Liberal and a Coalition Unionist in confrontation.[23] In Wales, the Unionists in Swansea West refused to yield the seat. A local newspaper editor stood against a Liberal minister, Sir Alfred Mond, an abrasive capitalist and, more serious, 'a pure bred German who has not one drop of British blood in his veins'.[24] At Central Office, in the minds of party managers such as Younger and Malcolm Fraser, the entire procedure caused much alarm. Younger complained of how 'the P.M. seems always to be barging in, but I should fancy without much knowledge. His people have no idea of fulfilling their agreements.' The Prime Minister, for instance, was putting on pressure to secure more women candidates, like Christabel Pankhurst, who was found a seat in Smethwick.[25] This kind of difficulty was inescapable. In putting their electoral machinery in suspense in almost one hundred and fifty constituencies and

giving muted support to the old Liberal enemy, the Unionist organizers were being forced to act contrary to all their traditions and
instincts. It is a tribute to the logic of the 'coupon' arrangements that
both on the Liberal and Unionist side, constituency problems were
ironed out in all save a very small minority of cases, and that the
sentiment of 'unity' triumphed almost everywhere.

Agreement on a Coalition manifesto caused hardly more difficulty.
Lloyd George approached Bonar Law with confidence on this point.
He and Addison had sketched out a list of agreed priorities in July
—trade and industry, finance, land and housing, health, the Poor
Law, education, women, drink, and local government.[26] The schemes
of the Ministry of Reconstruction provided substance for these
skeletal outlines. Lloyd George agreed with George Barnes on the
need to combat 'Labour extremists' in Glasgow and elsewhere in
Scotland. But the answer to them lay not in reaction but in a bold and
challenging social programme, which would emphasize housing and
other issues and would make clear the government's determination to
deal equitably with all classes and stamp out wartime profiteering.[27]
With much of this, Bonar Law and the Unionist leaders instinctively
agreed. There were three sticking-points for them, none decisive. The
most important for the Cecils, yet undoubtedly the most trivial, was
the future position of the Welsh church, or more specifically its
endowments. Salisbury was particularly anxious on this and felt that
the prospect of a federal solution to the Irish question would make the
lot of churchmen in Wales more precarious.[28] Lord Robert Cecil was
shortly to resign from the government on the question of Welsh
disendowment. Beaverbrook mischievously raised the Welsh church
in the *Daily Express* as an issue likely to embarrass Lloyd George's
discussions with the Unionists.[29] But this was a question that the
passage of time had already eroded, one of scant interest outside Wales
and of declining interest even there. The disestablished church in
Wales already had a constitution drafted, while the Bishop of St.
Asaph was quietly lobbying Bonar Law over a compromise settlement
on the tithe question.[30] The Welsh church was no problem. Few
outside Hatfield House thought it ever would be.

Neither, more surprisingly in view of British political history since
1903, was free trade. The government had already swallowed a fair
number of concessions to the tariff reformers. Liberal ministers such
as Churchill and Addison were prepared to accept a good deal of

imperial preference as well. As the Prime Minister delighted to point out, it was the previous Asquith regime which had begun the erosion of pure and undefiled free trade, with McKenna's duties to protect key industries such as optical and chemical instruments in 1915, and Runciman's acceptance of the protectionist Paris resolutions in 1916. There was little difficulty in spelling out what the war years had indicated as generally acceptable to all parties—retaining the fabric of free trade and returning to free exchange and currency convertibility as soon as war ended, but using special powers to protect 'key' industries, to assist producers and manufacturers in the Empire, and to restrict the dumping of cheap foreign goods protected by 'collapsed' foreign exchanges such as the German mark.

Ireland was the major difficulty. Throughout 1918, the Irish tangle had become worse. Lloyd George's attempt to link conscription in Ireland with home rule after the war had proved disastrous. The constitutional convention had broken down and with it disappeared any hope of a middle way between Unionism and nationalism. Moderates like Sir Horace Plunkett were henceforth sad irrelevances. The rise of the Sinn Fein party headed by such hard men as de Valera, a survivor from the Easter rising in Dublin, and the introduction of hard-line government by the Irish administration showed vividly how Ireland, at least, was one part of the United Kingdom totally unaffected by the consensus of the war years.[31] Its political and sectarian divisions were as deep-rooted as ever. In the circumstances, none of the pre-war party solutions for Ireland was immediately practicable. The party leaders were able to arrive at an agreement without too much heart-searching in which home rule for Ireland, perhaps on a federal basis, was still held to be the ultimate objective, but Ulster's special position was reserved. 'Coercion' of her Protestant majority was specifically ruled out. In the meantime, British politicians could agree on a vigorous effort to stamp out lawlessness as manifested by the Irish republicans, as the essential preliminary to a post-war resolution of the Irish problem on constitutional lines. Apart from this, all the difficulties between the two wings of the Coalition were dealt with speedily and with much ease. One possible source of contention, a reform of the House of Lords to modify the defeat suffered in 1911, a cause dear to the hearts of Unionist peers, was safely shelved and given a suitably low place in the Coalition's manifesto. Otherwise, with a strong social emphasis and a ringing patriotic tone, the manifesto drafted in October 1918 supplied an agreed agenda of priorities towards which almost all wartime Liberals and Unionists, 'couponed' and 'uncouponed' alike, could subscribe. The historian, Herbert Fisher, gave it some literary style.

The Unionist members accepted all these points without demur and gave Bonar Law a unanimous vote of confidence on 12 November, the day after the armistice. In two important meetings on 6 and 12 November, the Liberal ministers and back-benchers did so as well. One or two Liberal ministers had misgivings on particular items, Fisher about Ireland, Montagu about India, Addison about wartime pledges, Churchill about anti-dumping and, more important, his own standing in any future Coalition government. On this last point, Lloyd George had to give him a famous dressing-down and to urge him to keep his ambition within bounds. 'National interests are completely overshadowed by towering personal concern.' The 'master and servant' relationship was never more apparent between them.[32] The finale came at a mass meeting on 12 November of over a hundred Liberal members of parliament, together with assorted Liberal peers and such activists as Dr. Shakespeare and Sir William Robertson Nicoll. A resolution was moved by that austere symbol of academic rectitude, H. A. L. Fisher, the education minister, seconded by Lord Leverhulme, which endorsed the Coalition manifesto and a continuing alliance with the Unionists. Lloyd George delivered a powerful radical address—'It is reaction that I am afraid of!' The motion was carried with acclamation.[33] The Coalition as the political embodiment of the new consensus was assured of a thriving future.

However, national unity, as the polls approached, was inevitably incomplete. There was Mr. Asquith. More seriously, there was Labour. As far as the Asquithian supporters were concerned, there were clear problems of identification and an abiding sense of grievance on the part of some candidates who felt that they had been unjustly victimized under the 'coupon' arrangements. Asquith himself was in a special category. It was a part of the 'coupon' conditions that after agreement had been reached with the Unionists, Lloyd George should make a public offer to Asquith inviting him to join the government. Scott of the *Manchester Guardian* had impressed on Asquith the need for a positive response, with perhaps the Lord Chancellorship as the reward.[34] It seems most improbable, though, that Asquith would have accepted office under the 'conspirators' of 1916. However diffidently, he had acted as a kind of implicit leader of the opposition throughout 1918, as the Maurice debate clearly showed. Fortunately, the offer that Asquith did not choose to accept was not unambiguously extended to him. When he saw Lloyd George in his room in the Commons a few days after the armistice, no clear offer was made by the Prime Minister; in return, Asquith offered no gesture of concilia- tion. It is futile to judge which of the two Liberal leaders was respon- sible for the breach: E. D. Simon of Manchester met both of them during this period and found the logic of each for his proposed course of action almost irrefutable.[35] This logic was founded on the new consensus built up by the 'Decembrists' of 1916. It was a consensus from which Asquith was, by definition, politically excluded, and he could have no complaint. His relative feebleness when he returned to the House in early 1920 does not suggest that the government was either weaker or less national in complexion for his absence.

The withdrawal of Labour was a much more serious matter, and a far more significant argument against the Coalition's being truly non-partisan. The claims of the Lloyd George–Bonar Law partner- ship to represent Labour were largely spurious. The two dozen of the Victor Fisher National Democratic Party were a small and unimpor- tant rump, with no figure of any political or industrial weight.[36] 'Patriotic Labour' was always something of an illusion, and Milner's rapid demotion in status in the government in 1919 was a decisive blow to its influence. The presence of George Barnes, a distinctly passé figure now who had ceased to be an important member of his party since 1911, lent little weight to the War Cabinet. What mattered was the mainstream Labour Party, with its mass trade union backing, and its defection from the government was predictable. The with- drawal of Henderson from the government in August 1917 did not eliminate Labour representation in ministerial ranks—apart from Barnes, J. R. Clynes, John Hodge, and G. H. Roberts also served under Lloyd George down to the armistice. Labour faithfully observed the party truce, and the bulk of the parliamentary Labour Party generally supported the government in the lobbies and applauded its social reform. But the parliamentary Labour Party was now, more than ever, a façade for more profound pressures. The immense growth of trade unionism, its dominance over the structure and machinery of the Labour Party, as indicated in the 1918 party

constitution, its new impatience for change fuelled by the revolution
in Russia and by grass-roots militancy amongst miners, engineers,
and railwaymen, made a break with the Coalition inevitable. Led by
Henderson the national executive voted on 14 November to leave the
government. A party conference, whipped up to unexpected fervour
by Bernard Shaw, endorsed the decision overwhelmingly; ministers
like Barnes and Roberts who refused to obey it were expelled from the
party.

In party terms, then, Labour contracted out from 'national unity' as
Lloyd George and Bonar Law defined it. In Shaw's words, it simply
said 'nothing doing'. In a wider ideological sense, however, this
exclusion is not so clear. Labour well knew how many of its demands
had become the conventional wisdom during the war, how the higher
wages and shorter working hours, backed by the new freedom of
access of trade union leaders to Downing Street, were an essential part
of the new social agenda flowing from the Ministry of Reconstruction.
The war had brought public control to major segments of industry.
There seemed no reason why this should not be confirmed after the
election, or even extended, for instance to the new electricity power-
stations that were promised by Geddes. A government backed
by allegedly 'hard-faced' businessmen such as Geddes was not
automatically alarming to Labour, particularly when it preached
'Whitleyism' and national control of industry. Over a peace settlement, the government's apparent attitudes were largely shared by the
trade unions, who did not favour the utopianism of the largely
middle-class UDC and its passion for 'open diplomacy' openly arrived
at. (Indeed, the latter body was essentially the creation of Liberals
such as Ponsonby, Trevelyan, Morel, and Angell, and its overtures to
the unions in 1916–17 had been tentative and unsuccessful.[37]) Most
Labour leaders took their cue from the Prime Minister that a balance
must be struck between creating a new network of democratic states
based on liberal principles of national self-government, and exacting
some kind of justified recompense from the German aggressors and
retribution from its leaders. Some kind of economic reparation from
Germany and a public trial for the Kaiser were the common coin
amongst Labour leaders of the Thomas/Hartshorn/Clynes type in
November 1918. In foreign policy as well as on domestic issues,
Labour felt far from alarmed by, or excluded from, the kind of unity
embodied in the Coalition. Labour, truculent, assertive, and

powerful, was on the outside during the 'coupon election'. But, in a way never true of the Independent Liberals, it was on the outside looking in, and at a world it could reasonably hope to enter and to influence.

The consecration of the new political order came at the polls that December. The tone of the campaign of the 'coupon election' has for ever been influenced by Keynes's bitter attack on it in *The Economic Consequences of the Peace*. Here he described how the mood of jingoism and of the lust for vengeance built up, with ministers such as Barnes demanding the hanging of the Kaiser and Sir Eric Geddes prophesying, for the benefit of Cambridge electors, the squeaking of German pips. Keynes admits that Lloyd George began the campaign in quiet, restrained vein, but argues that he was forced to change his tone in response to pressure from the press and an inflamed public. By the end, he was demanding indemnities from Germany which would pay the uttermost cost of the war. The punitive clauses of the Versailles settlement were the inevitable and tragic outcome.[38] Now it is not necessary to go to the extreme of producing a blanket justification of Lloyd George's tactics during this election. His political position was sufficiently unassailable for him to take the lead in educating the public in the economic facts of life with regard to a settlement with Germany. He failed to do so. He did make individual statements during the campaign which, even if scattered and incidental in nature, added their colouring to the election, just as Churchill's unguarded phrase in the 1945 election about the Labour Party instituting a 'Gestapo' fatally influenced the course of that campaign.

Nevertheless, it must be made plain that Keynes's account is highly inflated. Lloyd George made only six formal public speeches during the entire campaign. Otherwise, as Philip Kerr suggested, he preserved a detached presidential style, and kept aloof from the 'party ding-dong'.[39] Of these six speeches, the first three (at Wolverhampton on 23 November, at Newcastle-upon-Tyne on the 29th, and at Leeds on 7 December) all dealt solely with questions of domestic reconstruction, and emphasized strongly the progressive record of the Coalition since 1916. He went on at inordinate length in these urban centres to expound on his favourite theme of agricultural reform, the scientific cultivation of the land, the rural settlement of ex-servicemen, the guarantee of corn prices, and so forth. The fourth speech, an address to women electors at the Queen's Hall on 9 December, discussed in very general terms a 'sternly just peace' before turning to praise women's work during the war and the need for widespread reforms in relation to health, housing, and temperance. It was noticeable that Lloyd George evaded direct appeals by questioners to declare in favour of the immediate expulsion of 'enemy aliens'. The fifth, at the Colston Hall, Bristol, on 11 December did deal with the war. It contained the notorious declaration about Germany's 'paying to the limit of her capacity' to which Keynes drew attention. Even here, though, Lloyd George did try to emphasize that there were genuine limits to this capacity and that the payment of reparations could well take the unwelcome form of dumped German goods, manufactured by sweated German labour. The final speech, at Camberwell on 13 December, was purely a party knockabout, a fierce attack on Labour as a class, sectional party and on the sniping of the Asquithians. To these six speeches, there should be added some other pronouncements. While at Newcastle on 29 November, he received the freedom of the city and took the opportunity there to emphasize that Germany 'must pay the costs of the war up to the limit of her capacity to do so'. He also issued a statement to the press on 5 December which itemized several priorities, the first three of which were the prosecution of the Kaiser, the expulsion of enemy aliens, and provision for exservicemen, before listing various aspects of domestic reform and reconstruction.

Taken as a whole, however, Lloyd George's speeches surely bear out his claims in his book, *The Truth about Reparations and War Debts* (1932). They hardly add up to a saga of sustained and unqualified jingoism. He made reasonable efforts, given the fact that he was fighting an election campaign, not conducting a university seminar in moral philosophy, to ensure that the main emphasis was on issues of domestic progress. His observations on reparations and a peace settlement largely echoed the general themes of the time, with more restraint, indeed, than did other speakers, including some Asquithians and Labour men such as Clynes and J. H. Thomas. It was not electorally necessary for Lloyd George to concentrate on a punitive post-war settlement. He did not do so, nor could the Northcliffe press have forced him to. Much the least forgivable speech during the campaign was not the Bristol speech on Germany's capacity to pay, which was relatively unexceptional even if delivered with characteristic panache, but the Camberwell speech at the end, with its biting attacks on political opponents and its comparisons between Independent Liberals at the polls and German snipers leaping out of the trenches and crying 'Kamerad!'[40] This kind of demagogic style, seldom heard from Lloyd George since the days of the Budget League, was not merely a lapse in tone but a serious political error which made the creation of post-war political unity that much more difficult. Otherwise, it was clear that Lloyd George would have won the election whatever line he took on indemnities. In the event, he adopted a stance that was politically acceptable while leaving his hands open at the peace conference as the advocate of moderation he sought above all to be.

The 'coupon election' was not a story of jingo emotion at all. On the whole, it was remarkably quiet—'slow' and 'passionless' Lloyd George called it at Camberwell. One observant Unionist, Sir Alfred Hopkinson, commented on how election audiences were small and undemonstrative. They were bemused by the absence of traditional party labels and the disappearance of well-loved party cries of pre-war days.[41] The presence of so many new voters on the register, women in particular with their political inexperience, was thought to add to the air of quiet puzzlement.[42] The Times thought it 'the most orderly campaign of our time'—certainly much more so than that of December 1910.[43] Many political voters, of course, were abroad in the armed forces. In fact, the total poll was only 57 per cent,[44] far lower than in the past. Lloyd George and Bonar Law, as has been seen, in the main adopted an air of studied detachment from the hustings, and added to the mood of tranquillity. Lloyd George's statements on post-war treatment of Germany did not seem shocking or repugnant to most observers. What he had to say about punishing those specifically responsible for wartime atrocities was the common coin of the time. In any case, concentrating on the probably unattainable objective of trying the Kaiser could deflect popular emotion from the wider issues of 'making Germany pay'. The general tone of most Asquithian Liberal and Labour candidates was no less patriotic and anti-German than that of the Prime Minister or almost all his colleagues. Some Labour men, like Brace and Hartshorn in Wales, claimed that they were loyal to the government's programme which they saw as basically one of imaginative reform. Hartshorn was especially anxious to declare his support for the Prime Minister.[45] They were rewarded in many cases by being protected from a contest

with a 'couponed' government candidate. Certainly, some candidates
in individual constituencies did suffer cruelly from the pressures of
the electorate. MacDonald in Leicester, Trevelyan in Elland, Ponsonby in Dunfermline, Snowden in Blackburn, the Revd. T. E.
Nicholas in Aberdare (where Keir Hardie's anti-war stand was still
resented) were all vindictively attacked for their record in opposing
the war.[46] The ILP suffered desperately everywhere through being
identified with Bolshevism and pacifism. In fact, the immediate reaction of these candidates seems to have been to blame the local right-
wing press and 'the Bottomleys and Billings'. Lloyd George himself
escaped largely without censure. After all, only a few months earlier,
Arthur Ponsonby had concluded that Lloyd George's basic view on
international questions in Europe and the Middle East was still the
product of Liberal idealism. He was 'a responsible, sympathetic
human being who had still an appreciation of the larger moral
issues'.[47] Nor did the House of Commons that Lloyd George was to
dominate arouse the kind of instinctive reaction that Keynes was later
to impress on willing, quasi-pacifist minds in the 1920s and the 1930s.
The 'hard-faced' profiteers of 1919 are yet another element in post-
war mythology. The Coalition was returned with a vast and unreal
majority. It had 526 supporters in the new House, including 473
possessors of the 'coupon'—127 Liberals, 13 Labour and NDP, and
333 Unionists. A high number of its Unionist and Liberal members
were politically inexperienced businessmen,[48] although contrary to
the judgement of many contemporaries including Lloyd George himself, businessmen MPs did not form a majority of the House. The
predominance of members of this type was not necessarily sinister, or
the symbol of a mandate for right-wing reaction. The results, considered one journal, showed that the country was 'left centre to the
core'.[49] The emphasis during the campaign on new issues such as
housing was noted.[50] The literature of a Unionist minister such as
Laming Worthington-Evans in Colchester which stressed pensions
and other social themes was not untypical.[51] Generally, the 'coupon
election', so much maligned, was a verdict, soberly arrived at, on the
new politics of wartime, that 'centralized politics' for which Lloyd
George had called during the campaign.[52] If it embodied anything, it
was a mandate for peace, reconstruction, and reform.

The new politics that emerged after the polls was truly extraordinary. Against the serried masses of five hundred-odd Coalitionists

were a meagre 57 Labour men, largely distinctly pro-war trade unionists like Clynes, Sexton, Thomas, and Hodge under an obscure Scottish miner, William Adamson. The 'uncouponed' Liberals were
annihilated, with only Maclean, Acland, Wedgwood Benn, Lambert,
and Wedgwood (soon to join Labour) to provide any kind of
front-bench challenge to the government. Donald MacLean, an obscure Scottish border member previously, was given the newly-
invented post of leader of the parliamentary Liberal Party, an
arrangement designed to preserve the status of national party leader
for Asquith who had been defeated at East Fife. As it happened,
George Lambert, a supposed Wee Free, was soon to emerge as chairman of the Coalition Liberal group of MPs. Hilton Young also
defected to the government benches and the non-Coalitionist Liberals
added up to barely two dozen.

But the misadventures of Labour and the Independent Liberals
were not really what the election had been about. It had been called to
confirm the wartime consensus and to direct the wartime collectivism
to new social ends. Here, the new government gave much cause for
hope. There had been the inevitable jockeying for position, the more
pronounced as the prospective balance of power in the Cabinet was
totally unclear in the post-war confusion. Lloyd George wanted to
retain the small five-man War Cabinet of pre-election days. Very
reluctantly indeed did he concede that the new Chancellor of the
Exchequer, the Unionist Austen Chamberlain, would be admitted to
membership of it.[53] In his government overall, his ministers reflected
a fair coalition of attitudes, with eleven Unionists holding portfolios of
Cabinet rank (if we include such a non-party figure as Sir Albert
Stanley, the President of the Board of Trade), eight Liberals, and one
Labour. Lord French, Viceroy of Ireland, and Lord Inverforth,
Minister of Munitions, were additional members of the Cabinet on a
non-party basis. By no stretch of the imagination could the new
administration be termed 'die-hard'. The most widely-heard criticism
of it concerned the number of Jews which 'gave rise to comment'.[54] Its
Liberal members included such a dynamic figure as Winston
Churchill, on whom Lloyd George insisted in the face of Tory doubts
dating from the Dardanelles: Churchill, however, went to the War
Office, not the Admiralty as he had wished. Sir Eric Geddes, not
Churchill, was made the principal demobilizer of the armed forces.
This left Churchill 'sulky and hostile',[55] though not for long. On the

Unionist side, middle of the road figures such as Austen Chamberlain
and Robert Horne were reinforced by the experience of Arthur
Balfour, the Foreign Secretary, Lord Curzon, Lord President (and
Balfour's probable successor), and Walter Long, First Lord of the
Admiralty and another notable instance of how an undynamic party
patriarch of pre-war days had been stimulated and liberalized by the
war. Another Unionist of crucial importance was F. E. Smith, unexpectedly raised from the Attorney-Generalship to the Woolsack as
Lord Birkenhead, a vigorous enthusiast for social reconstruction, in
part a result of his knowledge of social conditions in Liverpool.[56]
Within twelve months, Birkenhead, Chamberlain, and Churchill
were to emerge as the main sources of power and energy in the
Cabinet, beneath the tranquil partnership of Lloyd George and Bonar
Law. All these were anxious to retain the class collaboration of wartime. A businessman minister such as Geddes, far from being a
symbol of 'hard-faced' reaction, was an index of the government's
commitment to retain the planning structure that had carried the
nation through after 1916.

On balance, the new government began under favourable auspices.
It commanded as wide an acceptance as could be expected in a
democratic country after the fluid politics which had marked the late
election. Outside Ireland, where the 73 Sinn Fein members stayed
away from Westminster and formed their own Dail, the government's
leading critics were the socialist left of the ILP, a party going through
hard times at this period, though shortly to surge back with new
strength. More immediately significant, the Coalition's anticipated
radicalism raised alarm amongst orthodox financiers on the right. To
them the polls had brought back to office the big spenders of the war
coalition. They had endorsed the 'wanton recklessness of national
finance' which had sacrificed the gold standard, vastly increased the
public debt, and fuelled price inflation to astronomic heights.[57] For
the rest, the new government confronted the post-war world with
genuine, if not extravagant, optimism. The reappointment of the
Home Affairs Committee, with the Liberal, Fisher, as chairman, was
a portent of its anxiety to promote radical legislative change.[58] It was
presided over by a premier eager to remind his colleagues of their
election pledges on behalf of social reform, and to sustain the improved working conditions that the war had brought.[59] And, as
Montagu sycophantically proclaimed, 'there has never been an elec-

tion like this in its one-man nature'.[60] The passions of the election campaign soon receded. An anxious, sombre mood gripped the nation. The new Coalition faced a unique opportunity to replace the political vacuum with an imaginative, questing programme that the vast majority of the nation appeared to endorse.

3

Priorities and Policies: Labour

'The uprising of Labour' was foremost amongst the challenges to the
Coalition and its claim to be custodian of the consensus, as soon as the
elections were over.[1] This was not a discovery which dawned upon the
government suddenly or unforeseen. The threat which Labour posed,
both through Austen Chamberlain's 'so-called Labour Party' and
through immensely more powerful and militant trade unions, had
been apparent to ministers during the last year of the war. Much of
Lloyd George's political finessing in the early months of 1918, from
his address to the trade unions at Westminster Hall in January
onwards, had been inspired essentially by the awareness of the gains
labour had made during the war and the need for its continued
appeasement. Labour, then, formed the primary preoccupation of
government and civil service as soon as the war ended.

In political terms, of course, it was the new vitality of the Labour
Party which alarmed the government. Lloyd George was not deceived
by the modest tally of 57 seats which Labour captured. Much more
significant were the 2.5 m votes Labour attracted, with its evident
appeal to newer voters, male and female. The election also confirmed
that Labour was a nationally-organized party for the first time, with
massive financial resources; the pre-1918 days of the loosely-
structured confederation that made up Keir Hardie's 'Labour
alliance' were emphatically over. The electoral threat posed by
Labour emerged even before the victory in the three-cornered by-
election at Spen Valley in December 1919 to which Dr. Cowling has
rightly drawn attention.[2] For several months in a series of by-elections
in 1919, Labour showed its ability to attract support in a wide diversity of constituencies throughout the land. In virtually every contest,
Labour candidates significantly improved their share of the poll.
There were two early Labour by-election gains—the Bothwell
division of Lanarkshire in July (at the expense of a Coalition Liberal)

and at Widnes in Lancashire where Arthur Henderson comfortably defeated a Unionist. Swansea East in July almost brought another victory. Attention was drawn in the press to the fact that in Widnes, Henderson gained the overt support of Independent Liberals;[3] but their failure to contest the election indicated that Labour was capable of mounting a far more effective challenge to the Coalition in industrial seats. In each contest, also, the poll was spectacularly high. Labour's new vitality was confirmed in another by-election in the Rusholme division of Manchester on 7 October. An ILP candidate came in second, far ahead of the Independent Liberal, the unfortunate Pringle, and produced a swing of over 17 per cent against the government. In the municipal elections in November, there were sweeping Labour gains, especially in London where Labour now claimed control of twelve metropolitan boroughs, and raised its total of London borough seats from 48 to 573, including several dozen women councillors. Spen Valley, therefore, where a relatively obscure miner headed the poll at the expense of Sir John Simon, for the Wee Frees, and a Coalition Liberal, Fairfax, only underlined the well-established pattern of the past twelve months. Labour, fully organized and geared for independent action at a time when other parties were confused by the continued impact of the wartime electoral truce and the effect of the 'coupon', had totally transformed the electoral geography as understood for the previous half-century.

It was, however, the industrial aspects of the upsurge of Labour that most preoccupied the mind of the governors. The success of the Labour Party had propagandist implications. The 'unrest' of the trade union movement seemed to penetrate to every recess of the social and economic fabric. Within a month of the 'coupon election', there were industrial disputes in many sectors of industry. In each case, trade unionists were striving to maintain the gains of the war years, the bonuses on wages, the reduced hours of work, the newly-defined trade differentials which had been the price exacted for involvement in the building up of war collectivism. Fundamental issues relating to wage regulation by government were now being raised. On the other hand, the measures adopted during the social compact of the war to increase productive efficiency—'dilution', leaving certificates, and the like—were a clear abandonment of their privileges by trade unions. They could not be expected passively to confirm this surrender now that peace had returned. By the end of January, there were troubles in the engineering and shipbuilding trades, a threatened strike in the London underground railway, a 30 per cent wage demand by the miners, pressure by railwaymen for an extended definition of the eight-hour day, a dispute with the railway clerks over union recognition, even a possibility of a national stoppage by the police. Most frightening of all, there were violent scenes in George Square, Glasgow, with a strike for a forty-hour week which the Secretary for Scotland, Munro, described as 'a Bolshevist rising'.[4] Maclean, Gallacher, Kirkwood, Shinwell, and other strike leaders ended up in prison; armoured cars and cavalry patrolled the streets of the city of Glasgow. The Cabinet responded with a mixture of bewilderment and truculence. Winston Churchill urged that 'there should be a conflict to clear the air'. He added, though, that 'they should be careful to have plenty of provocation before taking strong measures. By going gently at first, we should get the support we wanted from the nation, and the troops could be used more effectively.' The Cabinet should wait until 'some glaring excess were committed', and then act.[5] This determined attitude found many echoes in the Cabinet at this period. By contrast, the moderate tones of George Barnes, the Labour representative, made slight impact. There was much talk of arresting the leaders of the strike, of using the restrictive clauses of the Trade Union Act of 1875, and of denying insurance benefits to strikers. Measures were considered, for instance, by Bonar Law, for curbing the use of the strike funds of the unions themselves.[6] An air of fatalism seemed to grip the government at an early stage. During discussion of the railway clerks' dispute, it was suggested that 'a big general strike was probably coming sooner or later, and if and when it came the strike would be on ground chosen by the government'.[7] The early settlement of some of these disputes did not calm the government's nerves. In fact, the London Tube strike passed by quickly, the engineers' strike did not materialize, and the Railway Clerks Association won their major objective of being recognized as the representatives of supervisory grades (such as station-masters), as well as of the men supervised. Bonar Law specifically admitted the need to extend white-collar unionism in this field lest press and public opinion turn against the government.[8]

Throughout that spring, however, the labour situation continued to look increasingly ominous. It caused Lloyd George grave concern during his prolonged absence in Paris for the peace conference, even if the impact of domestic labour troubles on the conduct of peace negotiations was more remote and tangential than Professor Mayer has suggested.[9] Throughout January and February, indeed, the government seemed almost paralysed in dealing with the unions, in the absence of their dominant figure, one thought to have a unique flair in labour negotiations. Bonar Law as commander-in-chief on the home front failed to carry conviction. A stream of alarmist messages was sent off to the Prime Minister in Paris, conveying the mood of crisis gripping the government after barely two months in office. As a result, Lloyd George's responses became increasingly strident in tone. He agreed on the need to win over public opinion. But, particularly in relation to a possible miners' strike, he claimed that more direct methods were required, both to preserve law and order, and to ensure that the miners were deprived of food and other supplies should a national strike take place. 'Once the strike begins, it is imperative that the state should win. Failure to do so would inevitably lead to a Soviet Republic.' He and his Foreign Secretary, Balfour, believed that a national strike by the miners would be quite different in character from any previous labour dispute. It would menace the very foundation of democratic government. It should, therefore, be fought with all the physical and moral weapons at the administration's command. Transport should be seized so as to starve the mining communities into submission. They deserved no less, since they had 'challenged society to a duel'.[10] This kind of vision in part underlay the Fontainebleau Memorandum drawn up by Lloyd George and some close advisers during this very week in March. It emphasized the social dangers of Bolshevism in central Europe, should Germany be treated too harshly over frontiers and reparations. It was enveloped throughout by the rhetoric of class war.

This kind of response by Lloyd George and his government has usually been taken as revealing the basic attitude that dictated labour and industrial policy in this period—a stern determination from the Prime Minister downwards to fight off the challenge of a powerful and aggressive trade union movement with coercive force. Harold Laski saw the Prime Minister as 'ignorant of economics, ignorant of the working class temper, and so full of a kind of neo-Napoleonism as to be useless'.[11] Ample evidence could be cited from Cabinet and other records to show that alarmist talk filled the air until the late autumn of 1919. Every major labour dispute brought approaches from the

government to the army and naval chiefs of staff to ensure that the
maximum fighting power could be brought to bear to suppress a
revolutionary working class. There was talk of citizens' guards and
local militia. Sir Auckland Geddes talked of battalions of university
dons, clerks, stockbrokers, and other patriotic members of the community being formed in university towns and similar centres of loyal-
ism.[12] But the actual outcome of these serious confrontations, so
different in tone from the 'unity' of wartime, suggested that the
government's response to pressure from organized labour was more
flexible and sophisticated than might appear to the unwary. Even in
handling the upsurge of labour, the vision of the national consensus of
wartime retained its mystique even amongst the crudest sabre-rattlers
in governmental circles. An assessment of the Coalition's handling of
labour and industrial policy, therefore, must take into account the
different styles of response that coexisted in Whitehall, and the complicated and often subtle fashion in which they were translated into
action.

One thing must be conceded at once about the government's reaction to the labour troubles of 1919–21. The ministers and civil servants responsible for handling them were often peculiarly ill-
equipped for treating such a sensitive and vital area of policy. The
departments most directly concerned were the Board of Trade and the
Ministry of Labour. The first of these was in the hands of manifestly
inadequate ministers throughout the entire first year of the government. Sir Albert Stanley, who retained the Board of Trade in January
1919, was a rare survivor of Lloyd George's regime of businessmen
appointed in the purge of December 1916. He had been director of the
London underground railways and had no political background or
experience of any kind. When he succeeded Max Aitken at Ashton-
under-Lyne in December 1916, in an unopposed and unpublicized
by-election, there was some surmise that he might have been a Liberal. Guest's negotiation for the 'coupon' in July 1918, however,
placed Stanley firmly in the ranks of the Coalition Unionists, and it
was under this heading that he was 'couponed' in the general election.[13] Stanley's handling of labour unrest was a sad mixture of the
timid and the inept. His skills lay in his being a paternalist employer,
not a labour negotiator. It was an unhappy accident that his own
London underground was amongst the earliest challenges that he had
to face. Lloyd George immediately denounced his own minister.

'[Stanley] has all the glibness of Runciman and that is apt to take in innocent persons like you and me . . . Stanley, to put it quite bluntly, is a funk, and there is no room for funks in the modern world.'[14] At the same time, Stanley had little sense of when to concede, let alone of the wider changes that had transformed the trade union world during the war. Alone of the Cabinet, he resisted recognition of the moderate and quiescent railway clerks, when even such cautious figures as Austen Chamberlain and Walter Long agreed that their claim for official recognition must be upheld.[15] With Stanley as its spokesman, the government's dialogue with the unions was muffled and incoherent.

Astonishingly, when Stanley was removed from office in May 1919, he was succeeded by a minister even less well equipped. Sir Auckland Geddes, along with his brother, Eric, was another of Lloyd George's selections from the ranks of 'non-partisans' during the war. Auckland Geddes, who had begun public life as a professor of anatomy, was thought to be an expert on the stimulation of exports. No doubt he went to the Board of Trade (after a brief period as Minister of Reconstruction) with manufacturing and commerce in mind. In labour questions, he was hopelessly adrift, slow-witted, rigid, personally unsympathetic. Bridgeman found him inadequate as a department head. 'Geddes used to make up his mind, very often with undue haste, and never took me or the office properly into his confidence . . . utterly untrained for parliamentary or official work and consequently very hard to work with.'[16] Another problem contemporaries noted was Geddes's willingness to be used by Lloyd George in a multiplicity of roles, with the result that the work of the Board of Trade suffered as a first priority. In dealing with the trade unions, Geddes was quite out of his depth. Experienced labour advisers such as David Shackleton had little influence on him. Without doubt, Geddes played his part in hastening the national strike of the National Union of Railwaymen in September 1919, when he succeeded in alienating even so profoundly moderate a union leader as J. H. Thomas. Geddes's handling of the decisive negotiations with the NUR that summer was disastrous, culminating in his describing the government's latest proposals as a 'definitive offer' (the word 'definite' was later substituted by Lloyd George). At the start of 1920, it became clear that Geddes was going to be Ambassador to Washington in succession to Lord Grey. In fact, he limped on as caretaker President

of the Board of Trade until mid-March, having presided over a
disastrous period of mutual incomprehension between unions and
government.

The Ministry of Labour was, from January 1919, under a very
different kind of leadership, that of Sir Robert Horne who followed
two Labour men in that department, Hodge and Roberts. Horne
emerged from total political obscurity to become the great political
discovery of the government.[17] When Bonar Law retired through
ill-health in March 1921, there were speculations that Horne might
even replace him as Unionist leader. A year later, Lloyd George could
regard him as the second-ranking member of the government. Horne
was an amiable, party-going bachelor, a splendid mimic and racon-
teur. 'Swift in pursuit' was Beaverbook's description of his approach
both to tennis and to the opposite sex. Ladies declared his style on the
dance floor to be 'poetry in motion'.[18] Contemporaries testified to his
charm and good humour as a ministerial colleague. He was to succeed
Auckland Geddes at the Board of Trade in March 1920, thus gaining
command of a great well-established department for the first time. At
the Ministry of Labour, he was much less well-endowed with staff or
authority.[19] The department lost its two main civil servants,
Beveridge and Askwith, in 1919 and was unable to recruit young men
of ability thereafter. Its two main departmental heads, Horace Wilson
and F. W. Bowers, were both treasury-minded economists. They
were in no mood to resist the encroaching control of the
Treasury—symbolized by the recognition of Warren Fisher, the head
of the Treasury, as head of the entire civil service in 1919. The
ministry's general approach to labour questions was timid and negative. It compared unfavourably with the pre-war Board of Trade in the
Lloyd George–Churchill era. The Geddes committee in 1921 thought
that the Ministry of Labour might well be one that could conveniently
be abolished on grounds of economy, and its functions transferred to
the Board of Trade, the Home Office and elsewhere. The ministry
could in no sense serve as a kind of voice for trade union demands
within the administration, despite the presence of Sir David Shackleton, once a Labour MP, now its Permanent Secretary. Its main tasks
now lay in intelligence and conciliation.

In the first category, from the summer of 1919 onwards, special
intelligence reports were prepared under the Home Office Directorate
of Intelligence, largely by Basil Thompson, head of the Special

Branch. They provided an exciting weekly diet of reports of revolutionary activities in various parts of the British Isles. Woolwich was 'a happy hunting-ground for agitation', South Wales was a 'prey to Marxist extremists', ex-servicemen were 'drifting into the hands of extremists' in their tens of thousands. All these were grist to Thompson's ever active mill: he urged that the workers be encouraged to play football 'as an antidote to extremist teaching'. These reports were taken less seriously by the leading members of the government than they were by literal-minded historians of the 1960s. The reports on the conspiratorial features of the Workers Educational Association were widely ridiculed.[20] Much more representative of the Ministry of Labour mind were the weekly reports the department produced, presumably written by Horne himself. These took a much more positive view of labour demands. Horne recognized here the ambiguous situation in which he found himself, with the government both serving as a conciliator and also being a leading party in industrial disputes as an employer. He recognized also the importance of genuine social hardship in stimulating working-class demands, and in particular the importance of curbing high prices and rents. In dealing with labour, the government, he repeatedly insisted, should take care to enlist public opinion—which was largely labour opinion. It should rely ultimately not on brute force but on 'the moral supremacy of the community'.[21] He decided to drop a scheme to train working-class speakers and organize press communiqués as part of an anti-Bolshevik crusade when it was put to him that this would offend the Labour Party 'who at present trust him'.[22] The whole scheme was transferred to the Coalition whips' office which allowed it to gather dust over subsequent years.

These and other sensible sentiments made Horne a successful and popular Minister of Labour, especially as he had constructive legislation on unemployment insurance to show for his efforts. Bridgeman sang his praises—'a splendid person to work with' who concentrated on his departmental work and took his officials fully into his confidence. Horne also had a breezy self-confidence that stood him in good stead in exchanges in the Commons and in handling the press.[23] He seems to have enjoyed reasonably good relations with the miners' president, Bob Smillie, and to have struck up almost a friendship with Jimmy Thomas of the NUR whose outgoing, convivial temperament Horne warmly responded to. Horne's misfortune was that he went to the Board of Trade in March 1920 when the economy was at a turning-point, with a collapse in demand, falling prices, mounting unemployment, and a huge trade depression over the next twelve to eighteen months. The result was that Horne now interpreted his role largely in financial terms and seemed to have an excessively narrow view of his brief. 'His foot instinctively sought the brake rather than the accelerator,' one of his civil servants later commented.[24] In dealing with the economics of the coal industry in 1920–1, Horne took it as axiomatic that wage negotiations over the basic rate per shift should be governed by the over-all necessity for abolishing state assistance, that is for decontrol of the mines. 'I do not remember a single occasion when the statement of the miners' case ever appeared to touch a chord of sympathy in his being,' Bob Smillie wrote of him. The result was that, for all his bonhomie and human warmth, he took a series of decisions—or, rather, was encouraged to take them by an admiring Prime Minister who now saw in Horne a self-made Scots Presbyterian well within the Liberal mould—which made a confrontation with the miners the more inevitable. By 1921, he was *privately* not unwishful for a fight'.[25] From the increase in domestic coal prices in May 1920 to the ending of the government subsidy and the termination of contracts leading to a national strike in April 1921, Horne's attitude was both financially logical and industrially disastrous. With all his ability and amiability he was ironically to take the country even nearer to an industrial battle with the unions than were his less skilled predecessors in the department.

Measured, then, by those who were the government's spokesmen in collective-bargaining sessions with the major unions, the Coalition's reputation as guardian of the consensus seems improbable, if not absurd. By the first summer, Herbert Morrison could declare that the government was 'making war against the trade union movement'.[26] And yet, the strategy dictating labour policy was far from incompatible with the claims and the mood of the general election of 1918. Certainly, the Cabinet accepted the need for determination if a head-on conflict with the Triple Alliance or individual unions came about. In January 1920, Cabinet ministers were to discuss a confrontation with a national strike by the unions, 'revolutionary in character and with a commissariat organized through the co-operative societies'.[27] When such a clash came in April 1921, with the Miners Federation, none could doubt the grim resolve of Lloyd George and his Cabinet to fight it out. The equivalent of 56 infantry battalions and of 6 cavalry regiments were used on strike duty.[28] The union's surrender on Black Friday owed everything to the mediation of individual back-bench MPs and the lack of common purpose between the unions comprising the Triple Alliance. They owed nothing to conciliatory moves on the part of the government, in which even a left-winger like Addison was convinced that Frank Hodges and his MFGB colleagues were irrational extremists. At this time, Lloyd George cited Britain's need for military force in Britain as a justification to Briand and the French government for her inability to assist in the occupation of German towns in the Rhineland after Germany's default on the reparations payments schedule.[29]

Black Friday was, however, a case when head-on conflict did indeed arise. The government's basic strategy was to ensure that it did not. It was framed in the light of two premisses: firstly the changed relation of government and industry as a result of wartime collectivism, secondly the inevitability and permanence of arranging for wage bargaining exclusively through the mediation of the unions and ensuring that they retained their easy access to Downing Street. The authority of the unions and the need to protect it was accepted by government and civil servants. The unions' essential weakness was that their influence locally over shop-floor and pit-head was so limited, declared Churchill. 'Trade Union organization was the only thing between us and anarchy' exclaimed Walter Long.[30] The government's responses to the breakdown of negotiations with individual unions were framed in this spirit. The need not to be inflammatory or provocative was shot through each discussion.

It was also reflected in the organizational base set up to try to maintain essential services during labour disputes. The first was the Cabinet Committee on Industrial Unrest, set up on 4 February 1919 during the London tube and bus strikes.[31] Its head was Edward Shortt, a mild-mannered and somewhat colourless Liberal Home Secretary. He was popular with the metropolitan police which stood him in good stead when handling the 1919 police strike.[32] His committee appointed subcommittees to deal with public utilities, transport, communications, electricity supplies, and its work was co-ordinated with the Coal and Food Controllers as well. Its most active phase of activity was in July–August 1919 when there were fears that a strike of South Yorkshire miners might lead to a national stoppage, and there were also fears of a bread famine. The proudest achievement of this committee was the organization of milk distribution and supply, directed from Hyde Park, in August. The following month, it was replaced by Sir Eric Geddes's Supply and Transport Committee, formed during the national railway strike and at first simply called 'the strike committee'.[33] However, it would not be correct to view this Industrial Unrest Committee and its sequels as wanton government attempts at strike-breaking. The more inflammatory alternatives, military intervention, citizens' guards, and the like, were carefully ruled out. Shortt argued in favour of doing no more than recruit special constables, and that cautiously. He stressed that their role should be strictly non-military, purely local, and severely under the control of the police.[34] The military chiefs of staff also argued against the use of troops to quell labour troubles on the Tonypandy pattern. Further, the Industrial Unrest Committee kept what is now termed a strictly low profile. It held only 29 meetings in eight months, many of them quite perfunctory. Its administrative structure consisted wholly of civil servants. The emphasis would throughout be on the government as the defensive organiser of essential supplies and services, not the aggressive party seeking a war with the unions.

The same philosophy governed Sir Eric Geddes's committee which lingered on for a year after the rail stoppage in September–October. The Cabinet's Finance Committee acknowledged, in the aftermath of the rail strike, that the total of troops left in Britain and Ireland was particularly low in the light of the industrial troubles. 'The maintenance of order was primarily a matter for Police Forces or a Civic Guard.'[35] Geddes's committee was an even greyer body than its predecessor. Geddes himself proposed in the Cabinet several times over the next twelve months that it be abolished. It took its lead from departmental officials in the Board of Trade, the Home Office, and the Ministries of Transport, Food, Shipping and Labour. It set up sub-committees of civil servants, under the guidance of the formidable 'honest John' Anderson, to prepare for the co-ordination of national and local services in the areas of finance, communications, coal, road transport, protection of order, petrol supplies, electricity services, sea transport, and publicity.[36] This eventually gave way to the more formal guise of the Emergency Powers Act of October 1920, a legislative sanction for the kind of civil service contingency planning that

had been going on since March 1919. It was intended to keep collective bargaining and negotiations with the unions in being, not to crush
them with coercive force. It is noteworthy that the identical structure
was preserved by the Labour government of Attlee in March 1946, 'to
maintain essential services in time of widespread disturbances'; Bevin
and other trade unionists in the Cabinet agreed that this did not
amount to strike-breaking. It was also agreed in 1946 that to consult
the trade unions in advance about the running of such an organization
of supplies would nullify its purpose and effectiveness.[37] It was the
safest way of preserving civil order without confrontation.

In addition to this pacific approach to industrial stoppages, something also survived of the wartime efforts at conciliation and joint
industrial planning by both sides of industry, to which the FBI and
the TUC both paid tribute. The Joint Industrial Councils and Whitley
Councils of wartime seemed to offer a model for the future pattern of
industrial relations. Immediately after the armistice, on 13 November
1918, Lloyd George had proposed a national conference of the representatives of employers and employed to consider norms for wages
and working conditions.[38] After the election, the idea was taken up in
the press and also by the FBI and by J. R. Clynes of the Labour Party.
On 27 February, a conference of eight hundred delegates duly met at
Central Hall, Westminster. Lloyd George and Horne both made
remarkably conciliatory speeches, and a joint committee was set up to
consider hours, wages and working conditions generally; the problem
of unemployment; and the best methods of promoting co-operation
between capital and labour. Allen Smith and Arthur Henderson
represented each side of industry on this committee. On 4 April the
conference met a second time, and on this occasion passed with
remarkably little dissent the main proposals of the joint committee.
They included a legal maximum forty-eight hour week; a minimum
time wage; various proposals for dealing with unemployment including organized short time, limits on overtime, a new housing programme, and the state development of new industries; and more
adequate insurance provision. Finally, a permanent National Industrial Council of four hundred representatives of both sides of industry
was to meet twice a year. The conference also had before it a far more
radical memorandum largely devised by G. D. H. Cole, which
demanded sweeping powers of public ownership over major industries and services, more stringent taxation such as a capital levy, and

the establishment of a new concept of the public service in view of 'the breakdown of the existing capitalist system of industrial reorganization'. This, however, occasioned no debate, and did not mar the good humour of the occasion. Despite the background of recurring labour troubles that spring, there seemed a real prospect of the wartime consensus on industrial policy being given a new lease of life. Another pointer to this approach was the government's decision to leave the gold standard on 31 March, following the unpegging of the sterling–dollar exchange rate on the 20th. This decision, taken in the face of Treasury pressure that the pound be protected, was based on the need to placate labour with a 'cheap money' policy that would keep down unemployment and mollify unrest. One result was that the pound floated down to a very low level against the dollar: the rate fell steadily from $4.70 in March 1919 to a nadir of only $3.30 a year later. Complaints by the Treasury and the Bank of England that this made an early return to gold impossible were for the moment set aside. External monetary considerations were for the present subordinate to domestic peace.

The National Industrial Conference soon petered out. It aroused expectations that could not be met. Disagreement soon loomed over the implementation of a minimum wage. The government dragged its feet, while the new bitterness kindled by the Sankey commission and the tension in the mining industry made the conference and its joint committee seem redundant. It never met again. Still it would be wrong to regard it as solely a tactical manœuvre by the government to suppress union pressure, though that element certainly played its part. As Dr. Lowe has shown, there was a lack of support for consensus policies on both sides of industry whatever the government attempted. The conference could flourish only if employers and unions were prepared to collaborate in such a way. In a democratic society, corporatism could not be imposed on them by central government. It represented a genuine, if short-lived, attempt by the administration to sustain the unions in their new role, and to try to obtain a series of working agreements over social legislation. It yielded some valuable fruits. Trade boards were greatly extended, with a £20,000 grant from the Treasury. A forty-eight hour week bill was introduced, over the opposition of some employers, that autumn, while the radical re-drafting of the unemployment insurance scheme was also a by-product of the NIC. Above all, the conference retained enough impetus to encourage the spread of wage agreements on an industry-wide basis, in most major industries. 'Home rule for industry' reinforced collective bargaining on wage rates and minima. It also sponsored a trend towards industrial devolution with joint councils set up in place of control by government departments. The NIC represented an effort by the government to govern side by side with the trade unions even if it could not govern over them.

The real efforts made by the government to retain the atmosphere of wartime conciliation, and the profound difficulties that this encountered, is best illustrated by the two major unions that produced crises for labour in 1919—the railwaymen's and the miners'. The relative success of the government in placating the one, and its total failure in handling the other, showed both the possibilities of working in partnership with major unions, and the distance that remained to be travelled.

A conflict between the government and the National Union of Railwaymen, whose President and Secretary respectively were Charlie Cramp and J. H. Thomas, loomed large once the general election was over. The railways had flourished during the war, and its workers had flourished with them. There had been public control of rail services. Many ministers, Churchill among them, repeatedly declared their support for nationalization, thus going beyond the aspirations of unions, who would have been satisfied with state control without ownership. The Coalition's manifesto prior to the election had, at one time, included a declaration in favour of public ownership of the railways. Eric Geddes's Ways and Communications Bill, presented to the Cabinet in February 1919, seemed to go most of the way towards this objective.[39] In addition to a national amalgamation of the private railway companies, it included powers by order-in-council for the state to purchase any form of transport, rail or road, in the public interest. As far as railway workers were concerned, they had received a 'war bonus' of a flat advance of 33s. for all grades. Furthermore, the government had reached an agreement for continuing the wartime wage structure with ASLEF, the engine-drivers' and firemen's union, with which the NUR were in sharp rivalry. It was hard to resist 'a demand for more human conditions for the working classes'.[40] The government then promised the 'standardization' of wages to the NUR. The railwaymen, however, wanted 'standardization upwards' to ensure an advance that maintained their differential from skilled

railway workers and more than maintained their pre-war level of real
wages. The issue was sufficiently serious for Jimmy Thomas to fly to
Paris to consult the Prime Minister during the peace conference. A
national strike was avoided in March when the government gave a
verbal agreement to promote 'standardization upwards' and the war
bonuses were continued until the end of December. However, after a
favourable pay settlement for ASLEF in August and the breakdown
of talks between the maladroit Auckland Geddes and the NUR delegates on 16 September, a national conflict between the government
and the railwaymen suddenly loomed. Geddes's later offer of a 20 per
cent standard below current wages for remaining grades was not
acceptable. A clumsy intervention by Eric Geddes, whom Thomas
'hated', made matters worse.[41] On 26 September the strike
began—'quite unexpectedly—as a thief in the night', wrote Lloyd
George to his wife.[42] It was regarded by both sides as an industrial
disruption of unprecedented magnitude and seriousness.

The national railway strike lasted nine days. Its atmosphere seemed
a prelude to open class war. The unions achieved total solidarity
throughout the country. Despite the optimistic forecasts of ministers,
the rail services were paralysed. The Triple Alliance made several
soundings about calling for a general strike. In addition, the NUR
showed much sophistication and skill in appealing to public opinion
on behalf of railwaymen's wage and other claims. It used the Labour
Party's publicity services to support its cause; prominent advertise-
ments in the press and even in the cinema answered the government's
propaganda cogently, point by point. On the government's side, the
strike emergency apparatus went into full operation. Divisional Food
Controllers operated, with road transport freely used in ferrying food,
coal, and petrol around the country. Some of the effect of the strike
was frustrated: Covent Garden market functioned as normal. Tens of
thousands of troops went on full alert. There were inflammatory
statements from members of the government. Sir Eric Geddes spoke
of denying strike pay to the railwaymen, and sought to prevent even
the payment of wages in the week prior to the strike, a wholly illegal
suggestion. Lloyd George himself made some irresponsible contributions towards inflaming the passions of the hour. He denounced the
strike as 'an anarchist conspiracy' and accused Thomas, Cramp, and
the NUR executive of 'Prussianism'.[43]

Yet here was a national strike where the bridges between the government and a major union remained intact. It was much assisted by the moderation and good sense of the railwaymen's leaders and by Thomas's determination to avoid the intervention of the Triple Alliance at all costs. It was helped, too, by the good offices of the transport workers, for whom Harry Gosling acted as a go-between. The government also was anxious for a quick settlement, not only to prevent the paralysis of a rail stoppage, but also to set the tone for negotiations in other major industries. Auckland Geddes was brushed aside, and the Prime Minister himself effectively took over the negotiations. He was anxious to try to save face for Thomas 'who exercises a moderating influence at times and certainly did good work in the war'.[44] He agreed to grant Thomas some last-minute concessions, notably the 50s. minimum for a small category of railwaymen. The final stages of the negotiations on 4 October saw the Prime Minister engaged in frivolous banter with Thomas and Cramp—'Henderson, don't keep them standing on the door mat.'[45] In practice, the railwaymen won some solid points. Their wages were to be stabilized at their existing level until 30 September 1921, while negotiation for new standard rates would begin at once. A new sliding scale was proposed for railway workers under which each man would receive not less than 51s. a week as long as the cost of living stood at not less than 110 per cent above pre-war. After a brief period of anxiety at the start of 1920, these terms stuck, and the railways enjoyed comparative peace for the rest of the government's term of office. Lloyd George himself was privately exultant. 'The railwaymen have been thoroughly beaten & they know it. It will save much trouble in future. It has been very good business.' Auckland Geddes's comment was 'Nothing given away'; Churchill thought Thomas 'knew he was beaten' and that Lloyd George had deliberately offered some concessions 'to secure the Labour vote'. Curzon felt stirred to congratulate the Prime Minister for the patience and courage with which he had conducted 'the battle of the nation against an organized attack'.[46]

Bridgeman, writing after the event, was more measured. The strike had ended too soon. 'In order to save Thomas' face, the government invented a form of words which had the semblance of representing some kind of gains to the Railwaymen—& enabled them to present they had scored something by the strike.' Sir George Younger was worried that this tactic had gone too far, and that the NUR had been able to claim that 'the government was defeated and the strike achieved its object'.[47] But there was method in the government's moderation. Not only was a reasonable compromise worked out on wages, under which the men's wages suffered less than those of other workers when the slump came in late 1920. The whole argument was deflected on to the ground of partnership and conciliation which the war had made familiar. Instead of nationalization (which was excised from Geddes's bill), Lloyd George offered the NUR a genuine form of joint consultation with the management. In May 1921, National Wages Boards were set up, representing both sides of the industry (though not the consumer, as urged by Guild Socialists). The national rail strike, then, had genuinely constructive results, and gave the union a more creative and positive role. The *New Statesman* acknowledged the friendly atmosphere that survived in the industry and that the strike left no bitterness on either side.[48] On the railways, then, the crisis passed by with the unions and the government both set on a path of consensus and moderation.

The long-running saga over the miners' claims was very different. Like the railwaymen, the miners inherited an industry where production and working conditions had vastly improved under state control during the war.[49] National wage agreements, including a 'war wage' of 3s. a day, had been concluded for the first time. The miners ended the war in buoyant mood, with coal exports from South Wales and other coalfields once again booming. No other industry showed comparable increases in wages. On the other hand, the MFGB executive continued to move sharply to the left during the war years. Their President, the near-veteran Bob Smillie, an old Scottish associate of Keir Hardie's, their Vice-President, the Yorkshireman, Herbert Smith, and the General Secretary, the dynamic young Welshman, Frank Hodges, were all committed socialists.[50] The nationalization of the coal mines, together with forms of workers' participation in management, was firmly on the miners' programme for the first time. In February 1919, the miners submitted to the government claims for an advance of 30 per cent on basic wage rates, together with a six-hour day and nationalization. A nationwide stoppage was threatened. In much haste and alarm, the government offered a Royal Commission under the neutral chairmanship of Mr. Justice Sankey, with six representatives each nominated by the coal-owners and the miners. The terms of reference of this commission later caused much anger and confusion. It is clear that a two-tier inquiry was proposed, the first solely to consider working conditions and wages in the mines, the second to look in an unprejudiced fashion at the possibility of national-ization. Horne made it clear that these two exercises were quite distinct, and that any view of wage advances was unrelated to the broader issue of nationalization. The miners, however, interpreted the government's pledges in a very different sense, and much of the tragedy that enveloped industrial relations in the mines flowed from this misunderstanding.[51]

The outcome of the Sankey commission is a very familiar story. The miners, represented by Smillie, Hodges, and Smith, introduced the issue of public ownership in the discussions at an early stage. The coal-owners made a universally appalling impression as witnesses, through their intransigence on wages and their complacency towards social conditions in the mining communities. Finlay Gibson and Wallace Thorneycroft, representing the South Wales and Scottish coal-masters respectively, were particularly egregious examples, Gib-son for his evasiveness on daily wage rates, Thorneycroft for his ignorance on matters of health, safety, and housing. The latter at one point surmised (question 6,972) that 'coal dust in the lungs has a beneficial effect' on a miner's health. Smillie's and Hodges's probing interrogation tore their case to shreds. Sir Richard Redmayne, the Chief Inspector of Mines, who gave extensive evidence, described the present system of coal ownership as 'extravagant and wasteful'. Meanwhile royalty owners such as the Duke of Northumberland and the Marquess of Londonderry served only to indict the system they represented. The impact on Sankey's own mind was dramatic. Within a few days of the inquiry starting, he was writing in his diary: 'The owners' representatives proving no good. The men are getting it all their own way.' The owners he repeatedly dismissed as 'Hopeless'.[52] On the labour side, such intellectually formidable figures as Webb, Tawney, and Chiozza Money had a relatively easy task when con-fronted with detailed evidence of perhaps the worst-run segment of British capitalism. Sankey's first chairman's report in March was a compromise over wages, which gained the signatures of Balfour, Royden, and Duckham, the three relatively uncommitted members of the commission. A wage increase of 2s. a shift for adult miners—the 'Sankey wage'—was immediately implemented. Sankey's second report in July called for a system of public ownership under a Minister of Mines, with workers' participation in the administration of the coal

industry, notably through district councils. This won the support of
the six Labour representatives, and thus claimed a majority of seven
members of the thirteen-man commission. Five employers, in a
minority report, offered in effect a blanket defence of an unreconstructed privately-owned system. Sir Arthur Duckham offered a
compromise based on the amalgamation of collieries. But his scheme
differed significantly from Sankey's. Sankey's district councils would
be guided by public-interest considerations, whereas Duckham's
would still be governed by the wishes of private share-holders.[53] The
divisions on the Sankey commission brought much distress to its
chairman. But the public impact was dramatic. The Sankey report
became a litmus test of the government's willingness to accept public
ownership and socialization under pressure from a powerful,
nationally-organized union with the capacity to destroy the nation's
economy.

In fact, the prospects of harmony were as remote in the mining
industry as they were favourable on the railways. Unlike the railways,
both sides in the mining industry were utterly removed in their
interpretation of the major issues. The Coalowners' Association,
especially its President and Secretary, Evan Williams and Adam
Nimmo, were by-words for rigidity and insensitivity and for seeking
massive wage reductions as the panacea for their industry's ills. The
Association, which contained some diversity of opinion, was being
propelled by the wishes of the spokesmen of the cost-conscious
exporting coalfields of South Wales and eastern Scotland. For the
MFGB, Smillie, Hodges, and their colleagues were anxious to bring
nationalization to the fore so as to swamp all other issues. In these
circumstances, the government was largely helpless. It could not put
pressure on the coal-owners as it had done on the railway managers
since the latter had benefited directly from a government subsidy,
whereas the mine-owners had profits distributed for them by the
government. Few really expected the government to accept the public
ownership of the mines. Ministers like Churchill were careful to spell
out the difference in principle, as they saw it, between nationalizing a
service like the railways and nationalizing a manufacturing or extract-
ive industry.[54] The most the government could offer was an acceptance of Duckham's proposals for amalgamation, since these retained
the essence of the private system, together with the nationalization of
mining royalties. In the meantime, the government's decision on 9

July to raise the price of coal to the consumer by 6*s*. a ton (which the miners believed to be politically motivated) helped turn public opinion against the miners' claims. Lloyd George's announcement in the House on 19 August that the government had turned down the major proposal made by Sankey was anti-climactic. In debate in the Cabinet, only five ministers had favoured public ownership of the mines—the two Labour men, Barnes and Roberts; the old Bismarckian, Milner, and the two most radical Liberals, Addison and Montagu. Fisher had proposed a five-point reorganization of the mines as a compromise. The major figures in the government, headed by the Prime Minister and Bonar Law, were all hostile.[55] Nor could the miners really have expected otherwise, since they had framed their terms in such a way that the government would have had to offer total surrender. Since the miners were not yet financially prepared for a national strike, and the men's passions had been cooled by the 'Sankey wage', an uneasy truce prevailed until the following year, with government control of the mines renewed, and then renewed again until the following year.

The breakdown of agreement between the government and the Miners' Federation at a time when the coal industry was still vigorous and exports running at a high level had, of course, serious consequences for British industrial relations for the period down to the General Strike of 1926. In the immediate context of the Coalition's industrial strategy after 1918, however, it is less revealing than was the agreement arrived at with the railwaymen. Then, and later, the miners were truly a special case in more ways than one. Class bitterness and class solidarity in mining villages was without parallel in the rest of British industry. Under pressure from their militant areas in South Wales, Yorkshire, and Scotland, the MFGB was forced into a series of intransigent positions. They were confronted by coal-owners of monumental ineptitude as communicators and inhumanity as employers, who brushed aside proposals that they use the massive profits garnered by the industry since 1914 to promote improved living conditions for miners and their families. Even the most modest proposals for re-grouping uneconomic pits were rejected by them. With nationalization ruled out by the government, there was scarcely any common ground to detect between the parties to the dispute. The miners were unyielding. They would not divert the argument on to the less contentious ground of conciliation procedures or joint

management proposals. They held firm to the high ground of nationalization, or later of a national pool for wages and profits, with all its
practical difficulties. They were doggedly committed to what was
known in advance to be unacceptable. The miners captured much
public sympathy with their exposure of the privately-owned coal
industry. Some of it was lost with the 6s. rise in coal prices in July
1919. In a labour world where avenues of conciliation were successfully sought in several industries after the settlement of the rail strike,
the coal-mines remained a melancholy monument to class conflict and
disunity, as bleak as the slag heaps that brooded over the depressed
mining communities. They remained the supreme indictment of an
unreconstructed capitalism. The mining families of Yorkshire,
Durham, Northumberland, Nottinghamshire, South Wales, Fife-
shire, and elsewhere, with their inalienable legacy of poverty and
social deprivation throughout the inter-war period, were the inevitable casualties.

In fact, for much of 1920 the climate of labour relations generally
greatly improved. The government's handling of industrial relations
gained in sensitivity when Horne replaced Auckland Geddes at the
Board of Trade. Macnamara, a Liberal, was a tolerable replacement at
the department of Labour. More important, Lloyd George was now
bringing his full attention to bear on the domestic scene and resuming
his pre-war role as conciliator-in-chief of the trade unions. On the
other hand, it might be noted that the government's claim to represent
labour opinion directly more or less disappeared for ever in February
1920 when in rapid succession George Barnes and G. H. Roberts, two
'National Labour' remnants, left the administration; but they had
carried little weight and their departure had no effect on policy. *The
Times* noted that the new year began with a lull on the labour front.[56]
The railwaymen were occupied in working out the details of the new
proposals for joint management, while the miners for the moment had
set ideas of 'direct action' aside. Only the transport workers' campaign
for a 16s. daily minimum wage seemed likely to disturb the industrial
peace. Meanwhile, Labour, fortified by electoral success at Spen
Valley, was concentrating on political and constitutional pressure
rather than industrial.

The lull continued for some considerable time. It was greatly
assisted by the deceptively favourable economic climate that continued until the early summer. The sudden fall in share prices from

111.7 in March to 86.4 in April was not immediately recognized as the index of a massive trade depression that it really was. Wages increased for engineering and shipbuilding workers, railway shopmen, tinplate and steel workers, and cotton operatives, with the continuing competition between the NUR and ASLEF helping to force wages upwards on the railways. Money wage-rates, in fact, went on rising even after wholesale prices had fallen. In January 1921, wages were to stand at 18 per cent above the level for April 1920.[57]

The government itself contributed to this mood of optimism and growth. It was deeply committed to sustaining the trade unions and working with them in trying to achieve autonomy in industry. The fact that this inevitably entailed a policy of 'decontrol' in industry after the collectivist arrangements of wartime aroused scant alarm amongst many unions in the TUC since a resumption of free collective bargaining clearly entailed a more flexible system than the rigid statism of wartime. The mood of this period was set by the celebrated Shaw committee inquiring into dockers' pay, which produced a famous exchange between Ernest Bevin of the transport workers and Professor A. L. Bowley on the comparative number of calories required to sustain a docker and a Cambridge professor. The outcome was the Shaw committee's report which conceded every major point demanded by the dockers—a national daily minimum wage of 16s., a forty-four hour week, registration of dock labourers, and, especially significant to the government, a national joint council for the industry.[58] To the chagrin of port employers, the government accepted all of them. Repeatedly the refrain was heard in official circles that if reasonable concessions were not made to orthodox trade union leaders, then industrial anarchy and trade dislocation would follow.

The government's ca'canny policy had positive results. Strikes receded markedly compared with 1919. The Labour Party had less success to claim as a voice for discontented workers. The *New Statesman* noted how the impetus of earlier by-elections had been temporarily lost, and how at Horncastle, the Wrekin, Ashton-under-Lyne, and Paisley, Labour's vote had sagged, while fringe movements such as Horatio Bottomley's Independent group or the Anti-Waste movement drew the benefit of such protest as there was. Characteristically for a largely Fabian journal, it drew the conclusion that Labour should put forward more middle-class intellectuals as candidates, and fewer trade unionists.[59] At the municipal elections in November 1920, Labour suffered major setbacks compared with the previous years, especially in London. Labour's platform of expanding social expenditure was not alluring to the voters at a time of rising rates and growing municipal indebtedness. The government, then, approached labour against a background of some confidence. It could believe that it held the centre (or even left-centre) ground and that it was the die-hard extremists on the right, anxious to slash public spending, that formed the major threat to consensus now. The one major confrontation between labour and the government was the exception that proved the rule. The Councils of Action that sprang up in August 1920, as a result of union revulsion against the possible dispatch of arms to Poland to be used against the Red Armies, ended in anti-climax and reconciliation. Lloyd George, whatever the shifts and turns of his policy in eastern Europe, had no wish to send arms to Poland either. Quite apart from international considerations, this was no time either to stir up increasingly pacific trade unions or to add massively to government expenditure upon overseas adventures. The Councils of Action, then, whatever the legends that later shrouded their brief existence, as a symbol of effective 'direct action' for political ends, were pushing on a door that was already open.[60]

The government could, then, reasonably claim that its labour policies were not out of line with its commitment to preserve the wartime unity on a progressive basis and not merely as an anti-labour crusade. As always, though, the great exception was the mines. Here the gulf became wider than ever. Here also the government's attempts to play the honest broker between the two sides of the industry were clearly partisan. The proposed settlement for the mining industry, worked on in January 1920, were those agreed between Lord Gainford, Sir Adam Nimmo, and Sir Evan Williams of the Coalowners' Association, and the government.[61] It was laid down that the government would be granted powers to equalize profits in the different coalfields, and to control prices for the home consumer. There would be incentives for more efficient forms of production. It was agreed that decontrol of the mines was the ultimate objective: as a preliminary, the gap between the price of inland and exported coal would disappear. Profits in the coal industry would be used to reduce the cost of living for consumers (for instance, by maintaining the subsidies on wheat and bread) rather than to increase miners' wages which would merely generate another cycle of wage increases. One sole legacy of the Sankey reports survived. A Minister of Mines would be set up, but with few of the positive powers that Sankey had regarded as essential.

In May, Horne carried a proposal to increase the price of house coal by 14s. 2d. a ton, an essential prerequisite to making the collieries profit-making and to restoring uncontrolled competition.[62] The MFGB, totally rebuffed, retaliated with an immediate demand for a 2s.-per-shift wage increase, with a national pool to equalize profits and wages. They were, complained Wigram, the King's private secretary, 'in a truculent mood'.[63] At the end of August, a miners' ballot voted by 602,000 to 238,000 in favour of strike action to take effect by 27 September. 'An exceptionally bitter struggle was anticipated', the Cabinet grimly concluded.[64] Horne's proposals for relating wage increases to output, and then for offering arbitration, were rejected by the miners. On 23 September Lloyd George had a critical meeting with the entire MFGB executive, afforced by Thomas and Cramp of the NUR and Gosling and Robert Williams of the transport workers, at which he managed to gain a week's postponement for the strike. He played with some skill on the known divisions amongst the miners, the subtle shades of opinion that divided Smillie and Hodges from the more moderate counsels of Brace and Hartshorn. Meanwhile the *New Statesman* urged the miners to compromise and to accept arbitration on wages.[65] Smillie was also prepared to accept arbitration and offered to resign when his executive overruled him. But a later meeting failed totally. Now Lloyd George's negotiating flair deserted him. 'This time he was not so good,' Bridgeman recorded, 'getting into figures which he did not fully understand & aggressive in tone—and so was B. L. . . . He gave me the impression that he would rather like a strike & certainly gave the miners that view which made them all the more anxious to avoid it.'[66] The so-called 'datum line' strike called nationally by the miners began on 16 October, the first national stoppage by the miners since the minimum-wage strike of 1912. Addressing his colleagues, the Prime Minister radiated confidence.[67] The government was now physically better armed than it had been during the war. The fuel supplies of the gas, electricity, and railway services would last for six weeks. The Emergency Powers Act would ensure that the government could dig in and outface any pressures imposed on it by the Triple Alliance.

Yet, as so often in the past, it was Lloyd George who provided a way out. In less than a fortnight, the miners' strike was over. By a narrow margin on 2 November, the miners voted to return to work. There would be an immediate increase of 2s. a shift until 3 January. Thereafter would follow a sliding scale which took account both of output in terms of the annual production norm (or datum line) and also of the export price of coal. Lloyd George persuaded the coal-owners to abate 10 per cent of their profits if the necessary production was not secured—a 'brainwave' of Bridgeman's[68]—whereas the 2s. wage advance would not necessarily be withdrawn at the same time. The owners were also forced to take a more charitable view of the datum line of production against which the wage advance would operate. No one believed that it was more than a temporary truce: Fisher thought it could 'easily be represented as a miners' victory'.[69] But at least it gave a breathing space for the mines to work out the kind of wider-ranging agreements that prevailed in many other industries.

That winter, however, the situation in the mining industry became far more serious. The unions were now operating against a back-ground of production plunging downwards, and unemployment rising to over a million and a half. The post-war boom had decisively spent itself; wages were contracting or falling almost everywhere. The government's finance was no longer dictated by the need to placate labour at all costs. The commitment to return to gold (announced in November 1919), and the 'dear money' policy heralded by a 7 per cent bank rate from April 1920 to April 1921, illustrated the triumph of Treasury orthodoxy. Mass unemployment inevitably followed, with the miners foremost among the victims. At first, miners' wages and coal production held up well in the first six months of the slump that began in May. But by the start of 1921, no industry was to suffer more acutely than did coal mining. Exports of coal fell from 2,139,261 tons in May 1920 to virtually nothing. Export prices fell from 80s. to 40s. a ton. Markets in central and eastern Europe were lost to German and Polish competition, while the general stagnation of industry severely depressed the demand for coal at home.[70] The result was that any prospect of the government finding a viable solution for labour rela-tions in the mines disappeared. With huge losses mounting up through trying to guarantee the profits of the coal industry, losses that soared to £5m a month between January and March 1921, the government had no financial alternative but to end the subsidy to the mines and end all controls with effect from 31 March, five months earlier than planned. Wartime wage payments would come to an end. In reaction, the owners uninhibitedly published scales of proposed wage reductions, which amounted to 50 per cent in some districts. The MFGB campaign for renewed wage advances linked to a National Wages Board and a national pool had no hope of making headway, and a national miners' strike began on 1 April. The Cabinet was fully prepared for battle. It had the reassurance of knowing in advance that 28 battalions of troops were available at once, with others on call in Ireland, Malta, and even Upper Silesia. In addition, there were privateering groups of *condottieri* such as Page Croft's battalions of ex-servicemen.[71]

The miners' strike, with the even more alarming attendant threat of a general strike called by the Triple Alliance, was the *Götterdammerung* of the government's labour policies. Aristide Briand told the British Ambassador in Paris that it was the inevitable result of Lloyd George's adventurous policies at home and abroad, his 'dealings with Bolsheviks and playing with Revolution'. For day after day, the Prime Minister ground on with abortive attempts to begin talks with the miners' leaders, while keeping the government out of the strike directly so that it could be characterized as a normal trade dispute. He accepted a National Wages Board in principle. On the other hand, Laski, who saw him twice at this period, noted that he refused to announce publicly his private view that the coal industry was inefficiently run and the wage reductions demanded absurd.[72] The miners' reaction, symbolized in the immortal stolidity of Herbert Smith, was predictably stubborn and immobile. Even the radical Christopher Addison, commented on the 'extremism' of Frank Hodges, the Secretary of the MFGB; Bridgeman preferred to notice his 'priggishness'.[73] The damage to trade and investment mounted relentlessly. By 8 April unemployment had risen to 1,615,000, with a further 897,000 on short time. The total volume of exports shrank from £139m in May 1920 to only £50m in May 1921. Coal exports virtually disappeared and there was a huge fall in the tonnage of cargoes that entered British ports and were cleared there.[74] Undeterred, the miners pressed on with a demand for a national wages and profits pool which even the *New Statesman* thought an impractical alternative to public ownership. Lloyd George argued that it had the merits neither of private competition nor of national control.[75] As tempers rose, safety men were brought out in Fifeshire and elsewhere, leaving some mines flooded and lost for productive use for ever. This caused a great outcry, though Arnold Bennett did point out, fairly enough, that the newspapers had failed to mention that enginemen and pump staff had also received notice to quit just as had face-workers.[76] In response, the government set up a committee under Lord Birkenhead to consider national defence during the emergency. The Admiralty kept 2,500 men on protection service, while 56 infantry battalions were on duty, backed up by 194 under-strength battalions and an improvised defence force of over 60,000.[77]

In the end, the miners' strike dragged on until 1 July when sheer starvation forced the men back to work on the owners' vindictive terms, with wage cuts of extreme severity. A temporary government subsidy of £10m was a palliative to keep the mines afloat until 30 September. This, however, had been overshadowed by the momentous events of 14–15 April.[78] At the House of Commons on the evening of the 14th, Frank Hodges told a meeting of back-bench MPs, in answer to a question by Captain Colin Coote, the Coalition Liberal member for the Isle of Ely who had direct knowledge of the coal industry, that he was prepared to recommend a reconsideration of the wages question only by his executive, with the idea of a national pool set aside for the present. In other words, economic issues would take precedence over political. Who Hodges's companions were on that dramatic evening is not certain, but J. H. Thomas was certainly one, and Herbert Smith and Arthur Cook, the ex-Communist South Wales miners' representative, perhaps others. The MFGB executive later confirmed the substance of Hodges's statement (it had not been contradicted by his companions at the meeting who, according to Thomas, had not realized its significance);[79] but by a majority of one they voted to disavow it. Hodges was thus forced to tell the Prime Minister that a temporary settlement of wages could only follow the establishment of a national pool and that no purpose would be served by meeting the owners again. With divided counsels on the miners' executive, Lloyd George was able to step up the pressure on the faltering unions. That same Friday afternoon, the 15th, the railwaymen and transport workers in effect demolished the Triple Alliance by refusing to assist the miners with sympathetic strike action. The Triple Alliance was dead; the threat of a general strike had evaporated. First nationalization, then a nationally-based wages settlement, had had to be abandoned by the MFGB. The government could bide its time and pick off the miners as an individual and vulnerable target. The miners had obviously suffered a complete defeat. Membership of the union fell, there was mounting unemployment in the industry, wages fell to 47 per cent of their pre-war level for those miners still at work. The subsidy to the coal industry disappeared; decontrol ensured that the mines would revert to the full rigours of the private system, with all the social cost involved. Widespread victimization of militant miners by owners and managers became commonplace.

It was a tragic ending, a crushing defeat for the men. There were cries of betrayal by Frank Hodges himself, a Judas figure in labour circles for the rest of his days who was to finish up as an employer and even a coal-owner. It was also a humiliation for the TUC. Ramsay MacDonald, curiously for the future member for Aberavon, blamed the fact that the government, the miners, and the NUR were all under the volatile leadership of Welshmen.[80] The 'unrest' of the post-war era now abruptly came to an end, as depression and starvation removed the basic weapon of industrial power from the hands of organized workers. For the remainder of the term of the Coalition government, fifteen months in all from July 1921 to October 1922, a sullen truce prevailed, the legacy of the attempted appeasement of the unions by Lloyd George and his colleagues. The British revolution was off. Perhaps it had never been 'on' in the first place. Laski noted that a trade union leader who had denounced Lloyd George's trickery at Downing Street meetings had cursed the government with equal fervour for not providing a cup of tea at these conferences.[81] As Lenin had proclaimed, the creed of 'opportunism' had fatally gripped the British working-class mind.

The surrender of labour on Black Friday provided a disastrous comment on the national search for consensus in the years after 1918. The impact of the miners' strikes in older industrial communities in Wales, Scotland, the North, and North-East of England was catastrophic. The gulf between classes and regions in Britain seemed even wider than before. Class war seemed to have been sanctified by the Coalition government, with its legislative symbol in the Emergency Powers' Act. Meanwhile, the government's allies amongst the

coal-owning fraternity assuredly forgot nothing and learnt nothing in
the course of these tragic years. They only made Sankey's call for
public ownership, both on grounds of economies of scale and for social
reasons, more overwhelming than ever.

And yet, the prolonged series of crises in the mining industry can
still be regarded as not totally undermining the principles that the
Coalition government proclaimed and what, in part, it achieved. It
would be absurd to characterize the government's labour policy as a
huge success. To have presided over the permanent alienation of the
largest section of the industrial working class, to have allowed the
massive series of strikes in 1919–22, with forty million working days
lost on a yearly average for that period, is hardly a chronicle of
triumphant achievement. In the event, the benevolent inclinations of
the Ministry of Labour were dominated by the need to balance the
nation's books, and to implement decontrol which was believed to be
its corollary. It is not surprising that the events in the mines in 1920–1
led many contemporaries to believe that the Coalition's vision of unity
stemmed basically from hostility towards labour: Lloyd George's call
for the 'fusion' of the Liberal and Unionist parties in March 1920
relied heavily on this theme. Lord Robert Cecil, in a no-man's land on
the opposition benches, chided Austen Chamberlain a year later for
the government's 'perpetually considering plans for putting the miners in the wrong' and seeking 'a settlement which would discredit
labour'. The back-bench MPs, by being friendly and courteous to
Frank Hodges on 14 April, had averted a general strike, in contrast to
the government's abrasive attitude. Chamberlain's reply conceded
that he regarded the Labour Party as 'a serious menace to the nation',
partly because of its inexperience, but 'more seriously because of its
difference from every other party in the House of Commons in being
directed and controlled from outside Parliament'.[82] If Chamberlain, a
relatively moderate member of the administration, could display such
incomprehension towards his fellow MPs and towards labour in
general, the prospects of a meeting with the miners' executive then or
later were remote indeed.

On the other hand, these attitudes remained largely on the level of
rhetoric. There was no ultimate collision. By October 1922, for whatever reason (and mass unemployment must have been one major,
inglorious cause), the climate of industrial relations was more tranquil
than it had been in January 1919. This owed much to the moderation

and statesmanship of trade union leaders. Even amongst the miners, men such as Bob Smillie and Herbert Smith fought courageously to persuade the rank and file to accept a series of disappointing wage awards, in the face of the class-war postures of Cook or Ablett. The government can claim its meed of credit also. Its strategy was to sustain the authority of the unions, to ward off the syndicalists and the shop stewards, and to preserve meaningful and continuing relations with the authorized union leaders by offering them constant access to government. The weekly reports of the Ministry of Labour were a constant hymn to this theme. In addition, by associating the unions, much on the lines of the war years and the plans of the Ministry of Reconstruction, with positive schemes for joint consultation and management, by trying to give the unions a creative and not merely an introverted role coloured by a siege mentality, the government attempted to expand the range of labour relations. In this context, the settlement with the railwaymen and the national procedure for wage negotiations and manning agreements then set up was a useful model. Even in dealing with the miners in October 1920, at a time of tense and often fruitless negotiations, there emerged the germ of a more hopeful outlook, with proposals for raising productivity in a notoriously labour-intensive, high-cost industry, and associating the miners with more efficient methods of production, via the datum line, rather than simply with fairer methods of distribution.[83]

To back up its suggestions, the government could claim that its labour policies were among its more progressive during the Coalition's heyday of 1919–20. Quite apart from the imaginative range of social reforms introduced, government propaganda legitimately drew attention to the establishment of the legal forty-eight hour week, to the temporary spread of Trade Boards, to the greater voice for labour in consultation procedures and the extension of the Whitley Councils, to the levy on the purchase price of coal to improve social conditions in mining areas, and to the earlier increases in wages for skilled and unskilled workers, including a 2s. per shift increase for miners after the Sankey commission's various reports.[84] The government had steered well clear of more provocative policies. Schemes advocated by the *Daily Express* or Unionists such as Walter Guinness to form a cadre of anti-Bolshevik working-class speakers were not taken up. Nor did the government respond to demands to found a 'sound school of economics' to rebut 'Pigou . . . . and other wild men at

Cambridge [who] turn out a succession of wild young theorists who
join forces with the Ruskin College men and those turned out at the
rate of about 100 a month by the Socialist schools in London'.[85]
Liberal-minded men like Professor Pigou who endorsed a capital levy
and criticized the extreme speed of the policy of decontrol were left to
proclaim their theories without public rebuttal. Nor was the academic
freedom of the universities undermined by the need to ward off the
socialist challenge in ideas. The whole drift of government policy for
most of this period was to keep the class war at bay, or at least turn it
into a phoney war. Viewed by comparison with the industrial history
of Germany, France, Italy, Hungary, Canada, or the United States at
this identical period, the government succeeded. No blood was shed
anywhere, violence was minimal, social cohesion and a sense of
national identity remained firm.

Throughout these difficult years, then, the government sought to
appeal to, and to reinterpret, the consensus of the war period. A
constant theme is the need to govern through consent and to enlist the
support of the 'moral supremacy of the community' in dealing with
the trade unions. When settling with the railway clerks in February
1919, the Cabinet acknowledged that the press and public supported
the clerks' demand for the recognition of unionization amongst supervisory grades. Equally, it was felt that 'public opinion' supported a
renewal of the wartime wage bonuses for the railwaymen, even at the
cost of higher fares for middle-class railway users. Thomas Jones
assured the Prime Minister that 'public opinion' was sympathetic also
to the miners, and that there would be a general acceptance of the
principle of public ownership and a temporary advance in wages based
on the rising cost of living.[86] Up to Black Friday and beyond, the need
to proceed in harmony with public opinion was endlessly rehearsed.
Of whom this 'public' was precisely made up was the subject of wide
varieties of definition. Too often, it seemed to be a synonym for the
propertied classes in the home counties, or the forces of order as
opposed to those of social change. During the railway strike in
October 1919, the government was accused of making a specific bid to
enlist the political backing of the middle class.[87] On the other hand,
the Minister of Labour reminded his colleagues that public opinion
was predominantly labour opinion, and that the goodwill of the
majority of trade unionists and their families must be constantly
sought in labour disputes.[88] This view underlay, as has been seen, the

relatively quiet and unprovocative form of civil service strike organization directed by the Cabinet's Supply and Transport Committee. Ministers like Horne played some part here in cooling the passions of the governors; so, too, did some of the Coalitionist Liberals, notably Addison, Montagu, Fisher, and, frequently and with much effect, Churchill. The hard-liners in the administration (Birkenhead often being one) usually found the going difficult and unproductive.

Most important of all, despite some irresponsible oratorical excesses during major disputes with the NUR and the MFGB—'anarchist conspiracy' and the like—Lloyd George himself usually remained in the camp of the conciliators. From September 1919, after his return from Paris, he took personal charge of every major labour dispute. As an auxiliary minister of labour, his views were crucial. The doors of Downing Street to a wide variety of trade union deputations and delegations were ever open. In part, no doubt, his attitudes towards labour were the product of genuine compassion, as he had explained to Charles Masterman and others in the past. 'I know which side I am on.'[89] The social radicalism of pre-1914 had in some ways been reinforced for him by the experience of wartime, especially his time at the Ministry of Munitions. He could still draw on a reserve of credit of a unique relationship with the union leaders stretching back to his period at the Board of Trade in 1905–8, even if the new rank-and-file pressures and 'unofficial' movements amongst the engineers and others baffled him. He was at his best in close-quarter finessing with union delegations; this was recognized by his Cabinet colleagues even if they expressed concern at a Prime Minister's immersing himself so totally in detailed labour negotiations.[90] But Lloyd George's attitude was fired by something equally profound—a passion for social order. The menace to civilized society posed by Bolshevism and similar extreme leftist movements preoccupied him throughout this period. It lent an air of near desperation to his search for consensus. Lenin, in *Left-Wing Communism, an Infantile Disorder*, saw in Lloyd George a most formidable adversary, 'a very clever man [who] . . . has learned a great deal from the Marxists', so much so that he was moved to dedicate the book to him. The Paris peace conference confirmed for the Prime Minister the social and economic fragility of so many of the new regimes of central and eastern Europe. 'In a short time,' he declared to his colleagues, 'we might have three-quarters of Europe converted to

Bolshevism.' Britain might find herself standing alone 'for social order and common sense against anarchy'.[91] To preserve this order, social reconstruction must be pressed forward; Bourbon reaction was no answer. The trade unions must be maintained, and new and productive forms of collaboration with them unearthed. Only thus could the British workers be used to combat the steady decline in the nation's economic and trading position in the Coalition's later period.

On balance, then, the claim of the government to have sought a 'middle way' in labour relations is not a derisory one. There was no concerted attack on trade unionism as in 1927; private members' bills for amending the 1913 Trade Union Act on 'contracting out' got nowhere. Conversely, there was no general strike; 'direct action' slowly receded from memory. Class passions never ran to extremes. During the crisis of the miners' strike in April 1921, Laski commented on 'the stolidity of the Englishman. Pass Hyde Park where there are thirty thousand troops and he comments on the beauty of the horses.'[92] At the same time, leading trade unionists, Frank Hodges of the MFGB foremost among them, persistently denounced the affiliation of Labour with the newly-formed cadres of the Communist Party or with the Comintern. They were, declared Hodges, 'slaves of Moscow ... taking orders from the Asiatic mind'.[93] Above all, these years confirmed for Labour the prime necessity of pursuing the constitutional path, as Keir Hardie and the founding fathers had laid down twenty years earlier. In 1921–2, in the aftermath of the Triple Alliance, the successes of the Labour Party in by-elections and municipal elections were spectacular. Cabinet ministers noted how, in Kirkcaldy district, a successful Labour by-election candidate could inspire a fervour and a willingness to make financial sacrifice unknown to other parties.[94] The Labour Party, the symbol of the political capture of the commanding heights of the economy, became the focus for working-class discontent. It was an ambiguous, bitter-sweet achievement for the government. The politicizing of Labour was the major justification for the Coalition's approach to industrial relations in the post-war years. It was to prove a crucial factor in the Coalition's later collapse. Ramsay MacDonald was to be the heir to Lloyd George's peaceful revolution.

Ironically enough, it was during MacDonald's first Labour government in 1924, that supreme symbol of the workers' political

advance, that the unions found new barriers erected between themselves and Downing Street. They had lost at the hands of their own
'movement' that easy access to government, that constant open-ended
dialogue which had so freely characterized the bad old days of the
Lloyd George Coalition.

4

Priorities and Policies:
Social Reform

'The War has torn the scales from our eyes and forced us to see things as they really are. . . . We have to make a fresh start in a fresh world.'[1] Seebohm Rowntree's passionate declaration in 1918 may be taken as the manifesto of social reformers in the aftermath of the traumatic experiences of total war. It was taken as axiomatic and automatic that the basic inequalities and inhumanities within British society, on which the war had so dramatically focused attention, would provide the essential agenda for the legislative action of the post-war period. The New Liberalism of the Edwardian era, the piecemeal and haphazard social measures since the days of Disraeli would be subsumed in a massive and irresistible new programme of social reconstruction to which all parties and classes would lend their support. It was the inescapable social legacy of the unity of wartime. Before and after the armistice, Rowntree spelled out this programme in more detail.[2] There should be minimum wages for workers (44s. for men, 25s. for women), enforced by Trade Boards in unskilled trades; an investigation of the prospects for public ownership along the lines of that in the drink trade; a vast new programme of house building through the local authorities; a new framework for social security including universal and compulsory unemployment insurance and higher pensions; and a reduction of the working week to forty-eight hours.

Other reformers, taking their cue from the draft papers pouring from the Ministry of Reconstruction, added to this formidable programme for action—improved primary and secondary education, an overhaul of the Poor Law, restructured medical and hospital services, a new Ministry of Health. Social reform loomed large in the Coalition manifesto at the 1918 general election. Once returned to office, Lloyd George himself repeatedly emphasized in Cabinet, in parliament, through the press, and from the public platform the inescapable pledges he had repeatedly given to create a more socially just order. This, far more than the theme of 'making Germany pay', dominated his election speeches in November–December 1918. 'History' would condemn the government if it now failed to respond to 'the steadfast spirit of the workers' which 'had left an imperishable mark on the heart and conscience of the nation'. The Coalition government was judged at the time, and rightly judged, by the test of its pledges to create a 'fit country for heroes to live in'.[3] By that test, it has usually been subsequently condemned, with the Geddes Axe taken as the symbol of financial orthodoxy and of economy-minded businessmen crushing the experiments and the ideals kindled by the war. American historians, notably Bentley Gilbert and Paul Johnson, have dealt severely with what has been termed 'the failure of social reform'.[4] No area of policy has been more crucial in building up the dismal reputation of the post-war Coalition.

Lloyd George himself has been frequently attacked for jettisoning the reformers' hopes and for betraying his own radical past. The repeal of the land duties of 1909 carried out in Chamberlain's budget of 1920 has been seen as the burial of the reformism of the era of the 'People's Budget'. The explanations for this reversal, if such it was, have been varied. Some have seen the Prime Minister as full of good intentions that were simply swamped by the recession in trade and industry from mid-1920, which made the demands for 'economy' and the attack on 'waste' irresistible. Others have seen in Lloyd George after 1918 a changed animal, a man who now found his natural habitat amongst businessmen, captains of industry, and other guardians of the capitalist order, enemies of labour who regarded social reform as expensive and self-defeating. Professor Gilbert sees in him after 1918 simply 'the prisoner of the Tories',[5] a view based apparently on the debatable proposition that Conservatives and social reform were incompatible. There has, in addition, been a more convenient scapegoat, the hapless Dr. Addison, the optimistic medical practitioner of reconstruction remedies in 1918, and the government's major political sacrifice thereafter. His departure from the Lloyd George government in July 1921 has served as the supreme example of that government's betrayal of its pledges in 1918. He was variously attacked at the time and later for financial incompetence, for lack of tact in handling officials and deputations, for political ineptitude in not continuing the bureaucratic controls of wartime. The fact that his private papers were not available to Professors Gilbert and Johnson seems to have made their onslaught on Addison all the more uninhibited (and inaccurate). Addison, however, could not altogether complain. During his later distinguished career in the Labour Party from 1923 until his death in 1951 just after the downfall of the Attlee government, he used the experiences of 1919–21 as a supreme instance of the failure to grasp the new opportunities offered by 'war socialism'. From *The Betrayal of the Slums* (1922) onwards, he encouraged this picture of the social programmes of 1919–21 as a tale of folly and failure. He urged his colleagues in the 1945 Attlee government, in which his was a respected senior voice, to regard the period of Coalition government after 1918 as a model of what to avoid in undertaking post-war social reconstruction.[6] Addison's reputation, in part self-abused, never wholly recovered from the years of the Lloyd George government, especially for the failures of its housing programme. The credit of the administration has evaporated with it.

If, however, one casts back to the assumptions and circumstances that governed the course of events in January 1919, and ignores the convenient advantages offered the dialectician by hindsight, there can be no doubt that the government saw a sweeping social programme as a vital component of its drive for social unity. It was the positive aspect of its labour policy of conciliation. Lloyd George's commitment was strengthened by early negotiations with the Allied leaders on the need for the restoration of markets and purchasing power in a ravaged European continent, and thereby bringing stable employment to British workers. His government included a fair balance of social engineers and 'economists'. Amongst the Unionists, the Bismarckian paternalists, Milner and Eric Geddes, were countered by the fiscal orthodoxies of Austen Chamberlain—'not the man for new finance' commented Astor.[7] Horne veered somewhat between the two camps. Much of the impetus of the Coalition's reform programme, in fact, came from its less regarded Liberal wing. Addison, as has been seen, had drafted much of the proposed social policy for post-war at the Ministry of Reconstruction. A dull speaker, his was never a dominating voice in Cabinet. But he commanded much respect for his energy and enthusiasm, for his long connection with welfare policies dating back to his major role in passing the 1911 National Insurance Act, and for his close political association with the Prime Minister. Churchill was another Liberal minister anxious to expand social expenditure and to 'budget for hope, not for despair'.[8] Throughout the period 1919–21 he combined the view that the war had revealed appalling deficiencies in society which required urgent action, with the view that the particular spokesmen for working-class demands were unrepresentative or just destructive, and that the Labour Party was 'unfit to govern'. He generally gave Addison loyal support and defended him after he had been dismissed from office: their friendship survived to allow them to have private and amicable contacts about aircraft construction in 1937.[9] Edwin Montagu, another Liberal, the Secretary of State for India and formerly involved with reconstruction, was another consistent advocate of progressive social policies. And there was H. A. L. Fisher, Lloyd George's great intellectual discovery in 1916—'another Morley',[10] a term apparently intended as a compliment. He pioneered the 1918 Education Act and was generally regarded as a powerful academic voice on behalf of unreconstructed Liberalism, both in terms of domestic reform and an enlightened foreign and Irish policy. There were other reformist Liberals in the government also—Sir Alfred Mond (in his pre-1921 incarnation), Macnamara, Munro in the Cabinet, McCallum Scott and Tudor Walters in the junior ranks, even 'Bronco Bill' Sutherland in the premier's own entourage pleading for social experiment to give Coalition Liberalism a purpose and a soul.[11] The Garden Suburb, notably through Philip Kerr and Waldor Astor, also filtered proposals for social policies in the spring of 1919, usually linking them with plans for imperial development. The 'social imperialist' followers of Milner pressed hard for social and agricultural reform. In so far as its Liberal and Milnerite wings were alive and well, the Coalition's dedication to social reform was genuine enough.

Much remained to be done in restructuring the machinery of government to push on with effective social reform. Most of the initiative had come from the Ministry of Reconstruction which virtually disappeared after the armistice. The Local Government Board had provided a steady, depressing resistance to change, especially to the proposed formation of a new Ministry of Health. However, the removal of Hayes Fisher in November 1918, dismissed for mishandling the electoral register if not quite drowned in a butt of Malmsey as Lloyd George suggested,[12] had a stimulating effect, especially since he was shortly to be followed at the LGB by Addison. In addition, some of the most creative civil servants of the age—Morant, Newman, Heseltine, Carmichael, Anderson—were building on proposals emanating from the Ministry of Reconstruction and from the multitude of reports on social questions that poured forth in 1918. The Cabinet itself reconstituted the Home Affairs Committee in February 1919, after demands by Bonar Law and Addison, in the anticipation that the new session would prove one of vigorous action in domestic legislation.[13] If the other major Cabinet committee, the Finance Committee, tended to be dominated by Unionists, especially Chamberlain and Horne, the successive Chancellors of the Exchequer, the Home Affairs Committee was a platform for Liberalism. Fisher was its chairman throughout and it was to be entrusted with the technical details of processing the entire reconstruction programme. Later it was to be complained, by Churchill of all people, that the HAC was 'turning into a bill factory'.[14] Beyond the government, the convening of the National Industrial Conference was based on the premiss that labour and business would work in partnership in a broad programme to improve working conditions, though the precise relation of this to the 'controls' of the war period was left vague. With the machinery of government, the pattern of labour relations, the reformist ideology of such influential men as Rowntree all pointing in the same direction, there seems little room for doubt that the government intended a comprehensive social offensive to sustain the momentum built up between 1914 and 1918.

In the event, the 1919 and 1920 sessions were marked by a spate of social legislation without parallel since the heady days of the 1911 National Insurance Act. The Coalition became the vehicle for the New Liberalism *redivivus*. A range of new policies were put forward on a wide front, with the general acclaim of the political left, and reformers and welfare workers generally. The industrial troubles of this period, in the railways, the mines, and elsewhere, as has been seen, encouraged the view, as proclaimed by Horne and other ministers, that the answer to industrial discontent and to 'Bolshevist' propaganda lay in grappling vigorously with social distress. 'The unrest caused by the lack of houses cannot be exaggerated', commented the Ministry of Labour's 'directorate of intelligence'. It went on to report on the grave impact of the eviction of working-class tenants and of high food prices.[15] The return of Lloyd George to the domestic scene in August 1919, after the conclusion of the peace conference, encouraged this pressure for social change, both for humanitarian reasons and as the constructive antidote to red revolution.

Among the reforms of a preventative character, there was the early acceptance of universal unemployment insurance. William Beveridge's proposals to this effect had been rebuffed in 1918, much to their author's disgust.[16] However, it was known that the wartime extension of insurance would come to an end in the summer of 1919. It was agreed to be socially and politically unacceptable if the wartime 'donations' were not replaced with a more long-term system, especially in view of rising unemployment in textile and other trades. Ministers were doubtful whether unemployment insurance should be extended to all employments—agricultural labourers and domestic servants were the categories usually referred to as difficult cases. Addison, however, urged with the support of Churchill that unemployment and health insurance should be inseparably linked together.[17] In the end, the 'donation' was extended until March 1920 by which time the government had passed, through the agency of Horne, a permanent Unemployment Insurance Bill. It extended the principle to all trades covered by the health insurance scheme (save for farm labourers and domestic servants), on a contributory basis with benefits of 15s. a week and 12s. for women, for a maximum of fifteen weeks duration. This was opposed by the Labour Party which objected to another contributory 'poll-tax' (which the majority of the party had in fact accepted in 1911); but the bill swept through the House with scant criticism or even discussion. Twelve million workers came under this scheme for the first time. In the atmosphere of early 1920, this was a relatively uncontroversial measure, however dramatic its implications. It served as the basis henceforth for assisting the unemployed, whose numbers mounted alarmingly in the latter months of 1920. After pressure from Arthur Henderson, a committee of five employers and five labour representatives was set up, under the chairmanship of Horne.[18] The outcome was a considerable extension of the scheme in 1921 with the introduction of so-called 'uncovenanted' benefits, and a rise in the scale of benefits, inevitably since the unemployed could hardly have any savings to supplement. Later amendments to the Unemployment Insurance Act were introduced in a mood of panic in the light of the frightening collapse of trade in the winter of 1920–1, when unemployment soared to well over a million. The 'dole' became a by-word for public charity; the 'genuinely seeking work' test was to be especially notorious and socially divisive. In the light of the government's intentions in 1919, however, it may be taken as a fair indication of the commitment to renew the wartime consensus on the social front. Certainly, discussions in Cabinet suggest that the universal application of unemployment insurance was relatively uncontroversial and accepted as an imperative of domestic policy.

Other aspects of the government's social programme also showed signs of progress. Laming Worthington-Evans, an enlightened Unionist active in the Tory Social Reform group before the war, carried an extension of the scale of Old Age Pensions from £26. 5s. a year to £47. 5s. a year. Expenditure on education rose sharply, encouraged by the percentage grant system to local authorities. Fisher and Lewis, at the Board of Education, built on the foundations of the act of 1918 by encouraging a new school-building programme, and by supporting the day continuation schools. Evening classes of up to 320 hours a year were made possible. Teachers' salaries were a constant source of discontent, and the growing National Union of Teachers was vocal about them. But in 1921 the Burnham Scale was introduced and led to a considerable improvement in teachers' salaries and pension arrangements phased out over four years to satisfy 'economists'; a salary of £353 a year for men and £238 for women was approved. A standing committee of teachers' representatives and the local authorities was to keep salaries under constant review in the light of inflation. In 1922 it was reported that teachers' salaries had improved by 170 per cent over pre-war.[19]

Finally, despite the disagreement of Ernle, the Minister of Agriculture (who finally resigned and was replaced by Lord Lee of Fareham in August 1919), a new programme for the settlement of ex-servicemen on the land was begun. This was in deference to pledges given by Lloyd George at the time of the demobilization arrangements, pledges strongly renewed in an address by him to agriculturists at the Caxton Hall in October 1919. This policy was successfully sold to landowners and to Unionist MPs as a means of stabilizing rural society against the pressures of land speculators and of industrial trade unionists. A leading agricultural Unionist MP like Sir Ernest Pretyman (Chelmsford) warmly endorsed the Land Acquisition Bill. Walter Long abandoned his earlier belief that the purchase of holdings with state assistance would be tantamount to nationalization. More generally, under the aegis of Lee, a vigorous social reformer, and with the backing of Milner, Astor, and the social imperialist group of Unionists, the wartime assistance to farmers was continued. The 1920 Agriculture Act, negotiated between the government and the National Farmers Union (representing tenant farmers), continued the provisions of the 1917 Corn Production Act, with its framework of guaranteed prices to wheat and oats farmers, and of minimum wages, fixed by Wage Boards, for agricultural labourers. In February 1921, the government and the National Farmers Union agreed that millers would pay farmers up to a maximum price of 95s. a quarter for wheat of sound milling quality. Even in the conservative world of the land-owner and the tenant farmer, controls, bureaucracy, and collectivism appeared to be firmly entrenched.

One major new department came into being—the Ministry of Health. As agreed, Addison moved from the Local Government Board to take it over, in June 1919. In some ways, the new Ministry (which subsumed the LGB) was less well equipped with powers than the Ministry of Reconstruction's memorandums had envisaged during the war. In particular, there was the crucial point that nothing was done to overhaul the Poor Law or allot medical aid to local public health committees as the Maclean committee had recommended at the end of 1917. Addison's confidence was shaken at the outset by the loss of his major civil service assistant, John Anderson, who left to chair the Board of Inland Revenue.[20] In addition, the death of Sir Robert Morant was a cruel blow; it left the Ministry of Health, wrote Violet Markham, 'in a most critical situation'.[21] The ministry never posses-sed the executive force envisaged in Lord Rhondda's proposals back in early 1917. Even so, the unanimity within the government about the new ministry, and the response of political groups and health lobbies to it, is impressive. The new ministry, even if somewhat weakened, seemed another portent of the Coalition's determination to fulfil its pledges and impose new centralized control on the sprawling medical, hospital, and Poor Law services. Addison spoke optimisti-cally of going on to reform radically a system of Poor Law relief which had survived largely unchanged from the work of Chadwick and the Benthamite utilitarians almost a century earlier.

These various initiatives made up a considerable agenda for reform. Along with the forty-eight hour week and other possible measures

flowing from the National Industrial Conference, it seemed to show
that the government's course was firmly set in progressive directions.
So far, pressure by the Treasury for economy had been frustrated.
While military and naval expenditure was scaled down, and expensive
overseas commitments such as the intervention in Russia were terminated, social expenditure continued to mount, despite the agitation
against 'waste' stimulated in the Rothermere press. The momentum
for reform seemed to derive almost wholly from the Coalition
government, Edwin Montagu claimed exultantly.[22] In response to
fears, mainly coming from Unionist quarters but also loudly endorsed
by Asquith's wing of the Liberal Party (notably from Runciman) that
the country could not possible afford such colossal and open-ended
expenditure on social reform, government supporters responded that
there were sources yet untapped, notably wartime profits. Churchill
proclaimed the value of a capital levy, as did officials in the Inland
Revenue and also professional economists such as Professors A. C.
Pigou and A. H. Gibson.[23] In February 1920, Austen Chamberlain
was persuaded, perhaps largely for cosmetic reasons with difficult
by-elections coming up, to set up a fifteen-strong Select Committee on
War Wealth under the chairmanship of the Liberal, Sir William
Pearce. It included two Labour members (Hartshorn and Walsh).
The prospect of its adopting some kind of capital levy, as Webb and
the Labour Party demanded, was not ruled out. Until the summer of
1920, the 'socialists' clearly outstripped the 'economists' in the
government, with the Prime Minister's clear if erratic encouragement. Even such a cautious Scottish Unionist as Robert Horne had
emerged as a social engineer of considerable achievement. 'The
session has been wonderfully successful', wrote one Unionist to the
King.[24]

   However, all these aspects of social reform soon dwindled in
significance. By one ultimate test would the worth of the Coalition's
social intentions be judged, and its reputation made or lost. This was
the vital sphere of housing, truly 'an untrodden field of politics' save
for the incidental attention paid to it in Joseph Chamberlain's Unauthorized Programme in 1885 and Lloyd George's land campaign in
1913. No other social question had been illuminated with such appalling clarity during the war. No other failure of policy was subsequently more fiercely attacked than the programme of putting up
'homes for heroes'. Addison was throughout the key figure and it is

through a study of the vicissitudes of this housing drive in 1919–21 that the seriousness of the Coalition's reform programme can be measured.

Housing had been highlighted during the war as a supreme social need. The Commissions on Industrial Unrest in 1917 had stressed the effect of inadequate or slum housing and of high rents in generating discontent in mining and other communities. The Housing Advisory Panel under Lord Salisbury the same year had made some surprisingly radical proposals, including a national campaign for building 300,000 houses, with the state assisting local authorities with the finance by making up the difference between the valuation and the actual cost of houses. The Tudor Walters committee in 1918 urged direct state assistance to private builders. Addison at the Ministry of Reconstruction built up a powerful cadre to plan a house building and slum clearance programme, with Sir James Carmichael, formerly his assistant in the Ministry of Munitions, at its head. New links were forged with the private building industry, and steps taken to secure the early release of building workers from the armed forces. After a tantalizing lull while Auckland Geddes served at the Local Government Board until 10 January 1919, Addison at once got to work. Early in the following month, he circulated proposals in the Cabinet for local authorities to acquire houses and lend money to owners of working-class housing for improvements. For the next two years, housing was his obsession. Housing became the litmus test of the government's seriousness in pressing on with social reconstruction. 'Addison' (along with 'Fisher' and 'Mond') became the cry of those increasingly vocal right-wingers who saw in the government only a dangerous extension of war socialism and a new plunge into subsidized egalitarianism. 'Addison' represented much more than a personality (rather a self-effacing one as it happens, which has not helped his cause with later transatlantic critics). It expressed a mood, a mystique, a fusion of Seebohm Rowntree and Sidney Webb which had temporarily captured the public mind. In so far as Lloyd George insisted on grappling with labour difficulties in a 'fearlessly radical' fashion and had his own strong personal commitment to a housing programme, the menace of 'Addison' loomed in 10 Downing Street itself. Waldorf Astor saw Addison as sympathetic on health, maternity, and housing, a redeeming feature of what appeared to him otherwise as an 'Old Gang Ministry'.[25]

The basis of Addison's housing programme was revealed in his new bill introduced in March 1919 and which was to become law that July.[26] It was his main preoccupation as soon as he moved to the new Ministry of Health thereafter. The bill enshrined two basic principles. First, local authorities were compelled to fulfil the duty of providing houses and submitting schemes to the Ministry of Health. Secondly, there would be a state subsidy, covering the difference between the capital cost of a house and the amount it earned on rents that working-class tenants could afford, over and above the proceeds of a penny rate levied by the local authority. In addition, the procedure for demolishing slum property and acquiring land was stream-lined, and the compensation paid to slum owners much reduced. Addison bluntly criticized the inadequacies of local authorities in coping with the problem in the past. They had been timid, dilatory, and cost-conscious; as a result, there were 400,000 houses occupied that were unfit for human habitation. It was not a total measure. Much more needed to be done to relate the provision of houses to transport services, and to harmonize them with environmental requirements. The town planning aspects of the bill were justly criticized as inadequate. Nevertheless, the bill was a momentous, even revolutionary, one, and received a generally warm welcome, even from *The Times* (1 April). It set up house construction as a national priority for the first time, with eleven regional housing commissioners to goad the local authorities into action, and the state to pick up the bill. Fired by Addison's call for half a million new houses, the new housing commissariat went to work.

Addison began with a whirl of energy and optimism. Yet within six months, it was clear that his housing programmes were running into severe difficulties. Progress was disappointingly slow. By the end of October, while site applications were sufficient for 450,000 houses, in fact plans had been submitted to date for a mere 41,000. Worse, only 10,000 houses of the national programme were actually under construction, and a pathetic 180 of these were actually occupied.[27] Clearly at an early stage, the housing drive had lost momentum. A popular excuse for this later on was the restrictive financial policy of the government, intensified by the high interest rates and measures taken to maintain the pound at an artificially high value, which were regarded as essential remedies to the slump in 1920–1. But, in fact, there were structural problems inherent in the building industry and the structure of local government which extended far beyond Cabinet policy. In any case, the problems of the housing drive antedated the adoption of a deflationary policy by the Treasury by many months.

The first of these problems was the reluctance, or inability, of the local authorities to undertake the tasks allotted to them. Shackled by financial indebtedness since the war and by the cheese-paring caution of Ratepayer-dominated councils, the local councils were slow in submitting schemes to the ministry. Many of those that were submitted were peremptorily swept aside as mere token gestures. Secondly, building contractors were loath to take part in state housing schemes, and preferred to undertake enterprises that would bring quicker profits than building low-cost, high-density working-class houses. Warehouses, departmental stores, offices, theatres, cinemas, football stadia, and the like occupied the energies of fully thirty per cent of the building trade. Another sixty per cent (especially smaller builders) were engaged in the repair of existing property, and only ten per cent were engaged in actually building new houses.[28] Third, there was an alarming inflation in the cost of building materials and in the cost of transport required. A startling attack on this was launched by Tudor Walters, the Coalition Liberal member for Brightside and an expert on housing finance, who had chaired an important committee on housing at the end of 1918. He alleged that the public were paying at least £5m more than was economically justified for new houses. There was much talk of 'rings' in supplies for the house construction industry. For his pains, Walters was brought into the government in November 1919 as Paymaster-General with the special brief of dealing with housing finance. According to one view, he had become *de facto* Minister of Housing. Walters's interventions seem to have had some effect. By the end of 1920, according to Rothbarth's calculations, the rise in the prices of housing materials was lower than that for materials generally.[29] In any case, this could not now be held to be a prime reason for the delays in erecting new houses.

In addition to all these grave problems, the building trade was a prey to labour difficulties current throughout the economy at this period. Compared with pre-war, the building industry was 200,000 men short in 1919. Skilled workmen of all kinds had left the industry; in particular, bricklayers fell in number from 73,671 in 1914 to 53,063 in 1920. For the small total of houses under construction under the

Addison programme, a pitiful tally of 5,920 bricklayers was being employed.[30] Masons, joiners, slaters, and other skilled workmen were in equally short supply, and building was one trade, at least, where unemployment was virtually unknown and the demand for labour insatiable. Faced with this shortage of labour, the government's efforts to persuade the building trade unions to increase the supply of workmen were quite unavailing. There were proposals by the ministry to increase apprenticeships, to increase the flow of labour by upgrading unskilled men ('dilution' again), to provide a 'guaranteed working week' in return for a pledge by the unions to foreswear strikes or stoppages, and to prevent the competition for labour by contractors. All these efforts led nowhere. The building unions, well aware of the seasonal nature of their trade and the danger of mass lay-offs in the winter months, resisted dilution to the end. Indeed, by the spring of 1920, Lloyd George, in markedly anti-labour mood at this time as the 'fusion' moves got under way, was using the obstructiveness of the building trade unions in limiting entry into the industry and providing apprenticeships as a basic excuse for the failure of the government's housing drive.

These problems were inherent in the nature of the industry. It is naïve to assume that any easy solution lay in sight. Had there been, the ambitious Addison would have seized it with enthusiasm. Some historians have followed Tawney's attack on decontrol, contained in his famous article in the *Economic History Review* in 1943.[31] This was published at the height of sympathy for wartime controls (which later ministers such as Harold Wilson at the Board of Trade were subsequently to destroy in a massive 'bonfire'). These historians have seen in the failure to continue this kind of siege economy the roots of the government's ultimate failures in social reform. Philip Abrams's generalized onslaught on Addison, a curious blend of applied sociology and anti-feminism, is based—so it would appear—on the government's failure to retain the apparatus of wartime controls.[32] Addison is also attacked for failing to discern 'a substructure of economic imperatives' (presumably jargon for more socialism) and for failing to involve labour as directly in his programmes as the government involved 'middle-aged, propertied women'. The government should have 'imposed economic sanctions on the building industry', apparently through expropriation. He offers no clues as to how this might have been achieved in practical terms in peacetime—partly because his article, despite its title, really only covers the wartime years and is innocent of any analysis of 1919–20. Abrams does admit that labour had no wish to become involved in governmental planning. However, he ignores the role of the building trade unions whose influence shows how completely his line of attack misses the point. The licences of wartime had not been conducive to efficiency. They had already contributed to 'the high cost which has practically killed off private house building'.[33] The licence system for building that operated during the war was complex and costly. It had arisen haphazardly and was known to be short-term. Above all, it was unacceptable to the unions who regarded it as a form of wage control and of industrial conscription. Abrams's argument seems to assume that labour must favour collectivism, whereas it is clear that the building unions were as committed as were the building employers to the economics of the free market. Abrams's diagnosis is based on a premiss that no contemporary working in the building industry at any level could have accepted. It could have been imposed only by draconian methods of coercion without parallel in British society before or since; even then, there is no guarantee that such methods would have been efficient. Abrams—like other historians who have followed his argument implicitly[34]—also sets out his views while virtually ignoring the economic background to the housing programme, that severe slump in the economy which trade indices began to register from May 1920, and which made cuts in public spending as inevitable in 1920 as they did in 1975–7.

As for the comparison with the 'middle-aged women', brought in to advise the government (and whom Abrams treated in remarkably unliberated fashion, given the tone of much of his argument), it is notable that they included Beatrice Webb, presumably not held to be a partisan of decontrol. In general, Abrams's appeal to some theoretical form of 'military participation ratio' slides over all the practical difficulties of how houses actually were to be built, which the historian at least cannot fail to examine.[35] One solution canvassed at the time was the guild socialist idea of local building guilds which the Coles helped to sponsor in Manchester and some other cities. But these were obviously piecemeal local efforts; by the mid-1920s, guild socialism was an idea of the past. The only constructive alternative was the one that Addison and (until 1921) Mond tried to pursue, namely to accept society as it was and to try to persuade the unions to relent on their restrictive practices, offering a national settlement of wage rates, with a guaranteed working week, in return for some relaxation of trade union rules. Lloyd George offered assistance to persuade the unions to co-operate in a national building scheme, but in vain.[36]

For the employers, the only real possibility was to approach them directly by undertaking a limited state subsidy to private builders. It is testimony to the seriousness with which the commitment to housing reform was taken that the opposition of Chamberlain and the Treasury was overridden. The decision was made by the Cabinet on 20 November 1919 to subsidize private enterprise directly, the subsidy to run to a limit of £150 per house up to a limit of 100,000 houses to be completed over the next twelve months.[37] Never had the state intervened so directly in controlling housing as a nationally-run public service. No doubt, the fact that so many local authorities had returned Labour majorities in the recent municipal elections reinforced the government's resolve. But the dominant theme throughout was the essential need to fulfil the wartime pledges on houses and on those homes for heroes.

These decisions marked the second phase of Addison's housing campaign. Criticized in the press and on Unionist constituency platforms, Addison plodded on despite mounting cost. In view of the structural difficulties inherent in the building industry, it seems curious to imply, as does Professor Gilbert, that Addison's own alleged personal and other defects were largely responsible for the failure to build more houses. On the contrary, as Lord Birkenhead acknowledged at the time of Addison's resignation, he injected energy and dynamism into a situation in which any minister was bound to admit defeat, even if his political standing were more prestigious than that of Addison.[38] The local authorities, the building employers, the contractors, and the unions were the essential reasons for the failure to build more houses.

In addition, Addison encountered mounting difficulties with the Treasury which finally conspired with these other forces to break him politically. The power of the Treasury over all other departments was now greater than ever; as has been seen, in 1919 the head of the Treasury, Warren Fisher, had been recognized formally as head of the civil service. He had a veto over appointments in other departments: new ministries like Health or Labour were in no position to resist. In November 1919 the Treasury showed its power in the government's formal acceptance of the decision to move towards the return to the gold-exchange standard at the pre-war parity and to orthodox currency policies as recommended by the Cunliffe committee. Quite apart from the question of gold, the speculative boom from April 1919 onwards convinced the Cabinet (and even an economic radical like Keynes) that high interest rates and a curb on the money supply were essential to deal with rampant inflation. One corollary was the raising of bank rate to 6 per cent, a move which provoked Addison to angry but unavailing protest as it would obviously make it more and more difficult for local authorities to borrow money. In Chamberlain's view, they were already borrowing far too much, with severe disruption being caused in the capital market. It was estimated that the Treasury would be paying out £160m to the local authorities for housing over the next two years.[39] Reluctantly, Chamberlain did accept Addison's proposals for local housing bonds as a source of finance, but at 5½ per cent not at the favourable market rate of 6 per cent that Addison himself proposed.[40] The housing bond programme never really got off the ground, though Thomas Jones took the opportunity to convince Chamberlain that Labour-run local authorities in South Wales were genuinely trying to make the bond issue a success. 'In Merthyr, which is a hotbed of extreme Labour views, close upon £100,000 has been subscribed.'[41] Addison deserves some credit for making the best of a quite impossible situation. Gilbert's very one-sided account (which includes such curious references as to criticism from 'hitherto staunchly Liberal journals like the *Nation*') takes no account of the obstacles repeatedly placed in Addison's way by Treasury finance. Chamberlain repeatedly argued for changes in the rules of the building trade unions that he must have known perfectly well were impossible.[42] In the light of this, his department's policy made matters much worse. Bank rate went up again to 7 per cent in April 1920, and the charges required to finance the servicing of the National Debt became more and more impossible. Some local authorities seemed likely to go into virtual liquidation. The finance of Addison's schemes had been laid in ruins.

Even in these desperate circumstances, however, the housing programme went on. Subsidized houses were built in greater numbers now—about 100,000 in all by July 1921. Lloyd George defended Addison staunchly against every attack. He and Bonar Law tried to

persuade the Treasury to return to cheaper money to help the housing
bonds. There seems little cause to doubt that if economic circumstances had remained stable then social expenditure would have been
sustained. The cuts imposed on the army estimates and on capital-
ship construction passed housing and education by. A proposal for a
Geddes-type economies committee was rejected in July 1920. 'It
would probably proceed with representatives of Capital trying to cut
down every form of social expenditure while Labour tried to effect
reductions in the fighting services.'[43] In 1921–2, the net estimates on
Fisher's education programmes would reach a record £51m.[44] This
was partly, of course, the result of inflation which affected Fisher's
school-building programmes as much as they did Addison's council
houses. The Burnham agreements on teachers' salaries were another
major factor. Above all, in education as in housing, the central
government was trying to stir conservative local authorities to re-
double their efforts and expand their social provision. The free-
spending of which 'Addison, Fisher and co.'[45] were the culprits went
on almost unabated in 1920. Even the much-abused Addison schemes
were bearing fruit. In all, over 170,000 houses were to be completed
under them. As an experiment in public housing, the Addison act was
now showing results. The commitments to social reform, then,
remained a leading priority for a government still headed on a left-
ward, collectivist tack. On this the government presented a united
public face. In the Commons, Austen Chamberlain loyally rebuffed
the Anti-Waste lobby as reactionary. His businessman half-brother,
Neville, a stern critic of Excess Profits Duty, an old foe of Addison's
since the débâcle over national service in 1917, nevertheless warmly
backed the Ministry of Health's housing programme—which,
indeed, he himself was to develop in modified form when he went to
that department in 1923.[46]

In the grim winter of 1920–1, the programme of social reform
suddenly slowed down. Then it went into sharp reverse. The reasons
for this are not in doubt. It may well be that the Coalition Liberal
element in the government was increasingly lacking in influence. Its
most vigorous spokesman, Churchill, was fast moving to the right as a
result of his views on foreign and imperial policy, whatever his generous humanitarian impulses on social questions. The destitution he
witnessed in his Dundee constituency genuinely moved him. But his
political intimates now were essentially men who were most out of

sympathy with Addison and what he represented. For the rest, the 'Coaly Libs' were lost souls, rejected by their own Liberal brethren after the public brawl at Leamington in May 1920. They formed the leading targets for right-wing opportunists at by-elections. The Anti-Waste League's sensational victory at Dover in January 1921 made Addison and his socialist impulses a major scapegoat. But the overwhelming reason for the turn-about in social policy was one to which any government would have to subscribe, even if its views were more imaginative than that of 1921. The cost of social legislation after twelve months of rampant inflation followed by a shattering slump was becoming quite unacceptable. Chamberlain told the Cabinet Finance Committee in November 1920 that each house built under the Addison scheme was costing the exchequer £50–75 a year, and would do so for the next sixty years.[47] There was no incentive for the local authorities to economize. Addison did not attend these early meetings of the Finance Committee; in any case, his position was untenable. As it happened, his prestige suffered another chance blow on 15 December when the House of Lords rejected his Ministry of Health (Miscellaneous Provisions) Bill, designed to strengthen the powers of the local authorities in acquiring vacant housing and contributing to voluntary hospitals. For some reason, Professor Gilbert focuses blame on Addison's zeal for change rather than on the Lords' resistance to reform.[48] It is not clear whether he is blaming Addison for doing too much or too little. In the prevailing political and economic climate, the government had to admit defeat. Another commitment to reform had to be abandoned.

After some difficulty, Addison agreed finally in February 1921 to accept drastic new limits on expenditure on housing. A limit of £15m in expenditure would be imposed, and a total figure of 300,000 houses accepted as the upper limit. His circular to the local authorities, stating that the government would help them if prices should begin to fall, was withdrawn after criticism from Chamberlain. A departmental committee was appointed to inquire into the high cost of working-class dwellings. Soon after, the target of houses to be aimed at was withdrawn and amended to only 250,000.[49] The climax came suddenly with the resignation of Bonar Law from the government through ill-health. Austen Chamberlain succeeded him as leader of the Unionist Party and leader of the House. The balance of the government now tilted decisively against the social reformers.

Addison had anticipated this: 'Unless he [Chamberlain] becomes less reactionary than at present, it must mean a separation before too long.'[50] Horne replaced Chamberlain at the Treasury, full of his recent implementation of decontrol in the mines. He accepted in full the rigours of deflationist Treasury doctrine, with the priority of curbing public expenditure severely. A few days later, on 31 March, Addison was moved—apparently to his own surprise but to no one else's—to become Minister without Portfolio. Sir Alfred Mond replaced him at the Ministry of Health, the very epitome of the capitalist in politics. Addison's anger towards Lloyd George, whom he had served with such loyalty, knew no bounds. The Prime Minister, he noted, was too embarrassed to see him personally. 'These things are difficult to forget but they sadly illumine the defect in a great man's character.' Even the Carlton Club considered his move 'the base letting down of a friend'.[51] The Ministry without Portfolio was obviously a blind alley. Addison had lost all his effective influence. The cause of social reform perished with him.

The last episodes in the story of the Coalition's policy towards social questions were exceptionally dismal and generated much rancour. They drove a wedge between Lloyd George and Addison that lasted many years—in fact, until 1930 when Addison was now in a Labour Cabinet and Lloyd George, as the head of a fragmented third party, in the role of suppliant. The house-building programme slowed down remorselessly under Mond. No further tenders from local authorities were to be approved by the ministry. The government would go no further than honour its commitment to houses already approved and to encourage 'well-considered' schemes for slum clearances. Meanwhile the political pressure against 'waste' stepped up alarmingly. There was the formation of Lord Rothermere's Anti-Waste League in January 1921, with the vocal support of such newspapers as the *Sunday Pictorial* and the *Daily Mirror*. The victory of Polson in the Dover by-election in January was followed by striking successes in by-elections in the home counties, at the expense of Coalition Unionist candidates. In early June, there were two more Anti-Waste victories, at the Abbey division of Westminster, where Rothermere's nominee, Erskine, defeated the Conservative, Sir Herbert Jessel, himself no radical, and again at Hertford. The pressure against the phenomenon of 'Addison' became overwhelming. Lloyd George, harassed by a bewildering series of problems at home, in Europe, the Middle East, and above all in Ireland, could not afford to retain such a political liability. Addison himself was still usefully employed, notably as chairman of a Cabinet committee on rating and valuation, a prelude, as he still hoped, to the reform of the Poor Law.[52] However, he deeply resented the virtual suspension of his housing programmes under the aegis of Mond, and had no intention of submitting meekly to his demotion and the demolition of his policies. As the ferment developed, 'stirred up by the Anti-Wasters and the Northcliffe press', assisted by 'Lord Winterton and his small band of Tories', Addison turned on his attackers.[53] In the aftermath of the Anti-Waste by-election victories, he gave a most belligerent interview to the *Evening Standard* on 16 June. In this, he accused the Unionists of trying to drive him out of the government on account of his radicalism, and the right wing of the Coalition of using him as a scapegoat for the government's programme of social reform.

This brought his relationship to the government to crisis point. A motion had been put down in the name of a large number of Unionist back-benchers which criticized the £5,000 salary he drew as Minister without Portfolio. Austen Chamberlain told Lloyd George that the majority of Unionist members would go into the lobby in support of it, fortified by the Anti-Waste euphoria of the Abbey by-election. He was most reluctant to name a date for debating the motion for this reason.[54] Lloyd George's response strongly suggested that he was already committed to sacrificing Addison. The latter was trying to use the press to turn himself into a martyr over public health. 'Winston can afford these little exhibitions but in Addison they are quite intolerable.'[55] Chamberlain pursued the issue in further correspondence, while Younger added the helpful idea that Addison's salary might be paid from the Lloyd George fund![56] McCurdy, the Coalition Liberal chief whip in succession to Guest, reported that defeat in the Commons on the motion of Addison's salary seemed inescapable, especially since Addison had publicly accused the Coalition Unionists of disloyalty to their Liberal colleagues. No more than fifty Coalition Liberal votes could be relied on. Lloyd George's reply to his whip may serve as the *nunc dimittis* on social reform as far.as the government was concerned:

What I am especially concerned about is this agitation about Addison. I felt it coming for a very long time, long before Addison could be persuaded to leave the Ministry of Health. I did my best to get him to take the

Ministry of Portfolio a year or two ago. Whether he was succeeding or not, he was creating the impression of failure. However, he refused to take my advice on that occasion and I am very much afraid that it is now too late to save him.[57]

Addison himself was far from passive in this emergency. He elicited the support of powerful Unionists, Carson and Bonar Law, and from Birkenhead in the Cabinet. He wrote to Chamberlain to deny that he had impugned the Unionist Party. He also consulted closely with Liberal colleagues in the government, notably Shortt, Fisher, Montagu, and Hewart who could no doubt see the bell tolling for them also. Churchill was also 'keen on my not giving way' though he added that 'no official friend of yours is yet keen on playing the game to a colleague'. A senior Liberal back-bencher, Sir Thomas Robinson, told him that a couple of hundred members of parliament, headed by Carson, were organizing a dinner as a public tribute and gesture of support for Addison.[58] Above all, there still appeared to be a real prospect of help from Lloyd George. Addison saw him on 21 June to urge that he should defend the record of the Ministry of Health, and that he should place it on record that Addison never sought the post of Minister without Portfolio in the first place. Lloyd George was 'all amiability' and insisted on his friendship and loyalty to Addison, though characteristically he refused to pledge himself directly on the line he would take in the debate.[59] Two days later, the situation seemed much brighter for Addison. He breakfasted with the Prime Minister 'who seemed to have made up his mind to champion me properly'. He had now decided to rebut the Anti-Waste campaigners by proving from press cuttings the savings that Addison had effected while Minister of Munitions. Addison urged him 'not to give way or to give his minister away to the clamour. . . . It is now clear that there has been a Tory cabal against him lately and it has now come to light which makes it more important not to alienate his Liberal supporters.'[60] Addison, then, faced the vote with equanimity and misplaced confidence.

When the vote came, it was the pressure of Chamberlain and the Unionist majority which was decisive. Addison and his supporters simply lacked the firepower to stave off defeat. Lloyd George defended his minister in debate in very lukewarm fashion and made it clear that Addison's departure from the government at the end of the session was inevitable. This tactic made certain that the vote against the government was a token one, but it also confirmed that the most active reforming and radical influence in the government was on his way into the wilderness.

Addison, however, was still determined to fight to ensure that his housing programme retained some vestige of substance. Mond, his successor, had been one of his supporters in the drive for social reform in the Coalition's heyday in 1919–20. When Mond succeeded to the Ministry of Health, he himself did not assume that this meant a reversal of the social programme, however unbusinesslike the housing drive had been. Mond urged Lloyd George not to be swayed by Treasury officials into scrapping social reform or reversing his own programme of slum clearance:

The Liberal Coalitionists are very restless and the Safeguarding of Industries Bill has driven many of them into the lobbies against us. If we surrender entirely to the reactionary anti-waste crowd and give our own people no progressive or social reform scheme to talk about I am afraid the consequences will be to alienate our Liberals both in the House and in the country.[61]

In fact, though, Mond showed himself the most determined of 'economists' as far as the housing programme was concerned. Indeed, he was becoming increasingly doctrinaire as anti-socialism gripped the mind of the chief of the Mond–Brunner combine. In the famous debate on 'the failure of capitalism' on 20 March 1923 Mond was to rebuff Philip Snowden's attack by referring to the fact that building workers worked far more cheaply for private builders than for local authorities as he had discovered at the Ministry of Health;[62] apparently this was considered an impressive argument on behalf of private enterprise. Addison realized at once that Mond's policy amounted to the winding up of the expensive housing drive. On 4 July 1921 he reflected on the recommendations of the Cabinet Finance Committee, presided over by Horne. 'They were, if anything, a little worse than Mond's account. He told me he was not going to accept them but I'll bet he will. I am now sending round a remonstrance asking the whole Cabinet to consider it. Even if they do, I don't expect they will reverse it.'[63] This achieved, Addison relaxed in English fashion by watching a day's cricket in the Parks at Oxford. On 7 July his memorandum was duly circulated to the Cabinet. 'I am packing up papers today & no doubt shall be out on Monday when, at latest, it seems that the issue will have to be decided. . . . It is quite on the cards that L.G. may rule

that the Finance Comm[ittee] has authority to decide it. It hasn't but if
he says so it is the same so far as I am concerned.'[64] He looked forward
to the freedom (and the penury) of losing office after nearly seven
years as a minister.

Between 11 and 14 July the last rites were concluded. Addison's
memorandum (CP 3108), which protested about the conclusions on
housing reached at the Cabinet Finance Committee of 30 June, was
considered formally. After the housing programme had been scaled
down from 800,000 to 500,000 and then to 250,000, the government
now proposed a limit of only 176,000 houses to be completed, quite
without regard to tenders already accepted by the local authorities.
Addison, backed by Montagu and Churchill, strongly urged the
disappointment and dismay that would be felt amongst working-class
people. In fact, Bowley and Hodge were later to show (citing Northampton) that high rents meant that these new subsidized houses were
often beyond the means of working-class tenants anyhow even though
housing waiting lists were lengthening. Other ministers preferred to
emphasize the fact of trade depression and the strain of high taxation
upon the middle class.[65] The next day, at a conference of ministers,
Addison renewed his attack. It would be the dishonouring of a fundamental obligation on the part of the government, he claimed. He
urged that the suspension of the building programme be phased out
over three to four years, since otherwise there would be a complete
stoppage in new house-building, as contractors could not build to let
at an economic rent. Addison was overborne. The limit of 176,000
houses was confirmed as a Cabinet decision. 'No further assistance
[would] be given by the state for any houses for which contracts have
now been made.' As a further hammer blow, the Treasury's view was
accepted that a maximum annual contribution of only £200,000 would
be granted for slum clearance to assist local authorities over the
deficiency of capital charges in slum areas.[66] Earlier that day, Addison
had still been optimistic:

I went all out for them at the Cabinet & I think made a deep impression & gave
them a shock. I got vigorous support from Winston, Macnamara and to my
surprise Birkenhead and Worthington-Evans. L. G. backed up Mond who
made rather a hash of his case, but he clearly did so with a good deal of
uncertainty. . . . I don't intend to yield at all & on the whole inwardly long that
they will stick to the Cab. F. Cttee's findings & give me a chance of getting
on a good issue as you say. . . . My only misgiving is that they will all climb
down.[67]

Of this, there was scant prospect. Addison received some backing from his fellow Liberals, Macnamara and Fisher, at a Cabinet Committee, but his protests both against the limit of 176,000 houses and the sum of £200,000 allocated for the slums went unheeded. Mond's proposed housing programme (CP 3133) was endorsed. Addison's protests that this was profoundly uneconomic in view of the expenditure already incurred by the local authorities under housing schemes approved found insufficient support. In fact, the departmental committee he had appointed in February to investigate the high cost of working-class dwellings had attacked the ministry for flooding the housing market with contracts in excess of the resources available. It urged that, in future grants, the Exchequer Contribution should form only a percentage of the total deficit.[68] This was the final act. That night, Addison wrote out the last sentences of an angry letter of resignation he had already drafted in outline some days earlier. In this, he accused the Prime Minister and his colleagues of a 'breach of faith' and a 'betrayal of our solemn pledges to the people'. He wrote at fuller length to his wife later that day:

I have done it! I feel a great weight off my mind. . . . All but Horne wanted my suggestions but L.G. sent a message that they were to stick to the limit of 176,000. They all meekly gave way except myself who said I would never agree. Macnamara and Fisher were most anxious to find a bridge but L.G.'s veto stood in the way. . . . L.G. had got his head down and nothing availed.[69]

Addison, denounced for so long, suddenly became a popular hero. 'I had a great reception in the House—hearty and prolonged—apart from its merits I think everybody was delighted that anyhow a man would stand up for conviction and challenge L.G. Winston and co. think that L.G. is up against the biggest proposition of his life this time.'[70] The Nation, which had deemed Addison not to be a minister of 'constructive gifts or businesslike mind', nevertheless rejoiced that at last a member of the government had resigned on an issue of principle. The New Statesman, which stressed the 'hoax' now perpetrated on those who had purchased the housing bonds in 1920, found Addison's resignation to be 'creditable'. Even from Horatio Bottomley there came, for his own reasons, warm congratulations and an offer to Addison to join his Independent group in the Commons.[71] Certainly nothing became Addison in his career as a minister in the government more than the manner of his leaving it.

The departure of Addison, however, soon lost its immediacy of impact. After an angry exchange or two with Lloyd George and Mond in Commons debate, the new hero retired to the shadows as an independent Liberal to commune with such Wee Free friends as Wedgwood Benn. He alternated between thoughts of retirement from politics to resume his medical career after eleven years,[72] and picking up the threads of his old association with Labour leaders such as MacDonald and Henderson. As he had himself foreseen, the excitements of the Irish negotiations and of the Washington naval treaty soon overshadowed Lloyd George's little local difficulty. The pressure for emasculating social reform was remorseless now, and the austere and less combative Fisher found himself next in line of fire. The other 'spenders' were treated more leniently. Macnamara had considerable scope for enlarging the provision for unemployment in view of the massive increase in the jobless that continued that summer and autumn. Churchill, another of Addison's supporters and now a major force in the government, escaped with a rebuke when he criticized the government's programme for the unemployed. Lloyd George reminded him of the costliness of Addison's housing schemes. 'You supported him in this very fatuous policy with considerable vehemence and passion.' He entreated Churchill to 'judge more charitably the efforts put forth by your colleagues during the last two years. Abroad this policy has won a good deal of admiration and respect for this country.' Churchill replied by pointing out the difficulties experienced by the Dundee Town Council, among others, with the curtailment of the Addison housing programme: 'I had a bad time with them.'[73] But he accepted the Prime Minister's rebuke with good grace.

With Chamberlain and Horne rampant in the Cabinet, and the pressure for curbing state expenditure becoming still more overwhelming, the days of the social programme were numbered. On 2 August 1921, Horne's proposals for 'a strong independent committee' to make recommendations for the cutting down of national expenditure were accepted. There was some opposition on constitutional grounds as this committee was thought to be usurping the function of the Cabinet and would be quasi-executive in form. Churchill's dissent from the decision was formally recorded, and he threatened not to take part in the government's autumn propaganda campaign in the country. Fisher also opposed it strongly. But it went through, Lloyd

George writing a note to Mond commanding him to support it. Fisher sadly commented: 'The point is the PM is dead tired and wants to throw a sop to Anti-Waste before the recess.' The Prime Minister was indeed recuperating at this time after a temporary breakdown.[74] The idea of a non-partisan committee to review economies in expenditure had been considered in Cabinet before: Lloyd George had reached the conclusion that departmental action by itself was not enough. There had been suggestions that labour members might be included on such a committee—Frank Hodges's name had been mentioned.[75] But the composition of the committee revealed all too plainly the government's intentions. The five members (four of whom were Scots) were all leading figures in the business world—Lord Inchcape and Sir Joseph Maclay for shipping, Lord Faringdon and Sir Guy Granet from the railways, with as their chairman, Sir Eric Geddes. This was an intriguing choice. Geddes had been a minister until very recently. He had himself been accused of untrammelled expenditure in the course of his transport policies in 1919–21, while the size of his own pension had recently caused comment. In this atmosphere, there was no path for Geddes to pursue but to re-emerge as the champion of business efficiency of the most ruthless kind. As the Geddes committee speedily got to work in August and September, fortified by heavy hints from Inchcape to the shareholders of the P. and O. Shipping Line as to the kind of retrenchment that national survival required, it was clear that expenditure over the widest front, naval, military, and social, would be subjected to the harshest of financial tests. Inchcape denounced worthless spending on schools and houses, and on 'functionaries who are feeding on the people'.[76] Waldorf Astor and Fisher wrote of their alarm at the harm that could be done 'by soulless, irresponsible merchant princes'.[77] The commitment to social reform had been publicly cast to the fires long since. Geddes and his colleagues merely set light to the faggots.

The sacrifice of the social programmes of the Coalition government has rightly attracted much critical attention. The fiasco of the housing programmes in particular became a ready target for Labour and Liberal spokesmen, while the right used them as the paradigm of uncontrolled extravagance fuelled by the central government. Addison himself stoked the fires. His *Betrayal of the Slums* was a formidable indictment of the government's failure to carry out its pledges. Sutherland complained to his leader that the Geddes committee was a

vote-loser in urban by-elections, which enabled Labour to brand the
government as reactionary.[78] All this is beyond dispute, but it should
not be got out of perspective. The reversal of the government's social
programme in 1921–2 should be measured against the leading priority
it received in 1919–20. Until forced off course by overwhelming
economic and political pressures, the government made a genuine
effort to build on the wartime consensus with vigorous social policies.
This should not be measured simply by an abstract ideological criterion without reference to the economic context, nor by Mr. Abrams's
dedication to physical controls. Rather should it be assessed histori-
cally against the whole range of the government's policies, including
its anxiety to conciliate labour. To insist that the 'controls' of the war
years should have been retained is not germane to the central problem.
Particularly in the sphere of housing, these controls had little bearing
on making house building cheaper or more efficient, and, decisively,
they were unacceptable to the building trade unions. The issues of
social reform and of 'controls', other perhaps than in the maintenance
of full employment, are really quite distinct and there is no automatic
connection between them.

Social reform in 1919–22 rested on two main factors—political
drive and economic stability. Immediately after the 'coupon election'
both were clearly present, and a reasonably impartial assessment must
conclude that the social legislation of the government in this period
was far from negligible. In many ways it far outstripped the earlier
surge for reform in 1909–13. At the time, the Coalition was strongly
attacked by orthodox Conservatives, not necessarily die-hards, for
being too socialistic in its welfare policies:

Lloyd George as a prophet of anti-socialism does not compel conviction. The
government has been busy for two years 'extending the sphere of state action'
... Lloyd George classes all the grievances of which the people complain as
'attributable to conditions over which neither Government nor Parliament
have any control'. That is a big name to give the Fishers, Munros and
Addisons.'[79]

The implementation of universal state unemployment insurance, the
new expenditure on pensions and social security, the creation of the
Ministry of Health, the assistance to agricultural labourers, the educational programme launched by the Fisher act were in themselves a
formidable list of achievements. Addison's housing programme,
however many difficulties it faced in execution, introduced for the

first time the premiss that housing had become a social service and that the Exchequer should supplement the resources of the local authorities in meeting the cost. In all, 210,237 houses were completed in 1919–22 as against 30,000 only that were built without State assistance by private enterprise.[80] The Wheatley and Greenwood Acts of the first and second Labour governments built on Addison's foundations and made housing subsidies geared to the needs of working-class occupants their first priority. Addison had launched a revolution of its kind in 1919, a commentary on the imagination shown by the government at this period despite the erratic concern with social questions shown by its head.

The downfall of Addison, the downgrading of Fisher, the triumph of Anti-Waste with the appointment of the Geddes committee made all this seem later to be inadequate to the needs of the nation. In 1921 the government determined that financial considerations alone should be the yardstick for dictating the pace and scope of its social programme. Mond for Addison at the Ministry of Health was the symbol of this change. The fact remained that, despite the immense reversal in policy that followed, and the vast economies in most aspects of the domestic budget, save for education, in the wake of the Geddes report, enough survived of the reformist legislation of the immediate post-war years to make the unemployment and poverty of the rest of the 1920s bearable for the working class. The reforms of 1919–20 were the springboard for such later programmes as the Baldwin and MacDonald governments felt able to introduce. They played their modest part in warding off, so far as Britain was concerned, some of the worst effects of social division and political disintegration experienced by so many other European countries in the 1930s.

The social reform policies of the Coalition, then, were a serious contribution to reconstruction and to consensus. They were implemented by a government that often ran in advance of public opinion in trying to fulfil them. They ran aground for reasons that really would have defeated any government, even one as powerful as Lloyd George's in 1919–21. No doubt, many of the welfare benefits of that period went to sustain the living standards of the middle class. Much of the housing drive of post-1918 ended up by developing middle-class housing, quite apart from department stores and places of entertainment, designed for the residents of new suburbia and the fringes of great conurbations. Addison's act too often yielded the kind of comfortable semi-detached suburban properties in which E. D. Simon's housing committee took pride in Manchester. Bowley and Hodge showed later how overcrowding and housing shortages in old industrial towns such as Warrington had accelerated since 1919.[81] But no less true was this of the welfare reforms of 1945–51, passed by a Labour government to whom none of the political criticisms made by Professor Gilbert apply and which his closing remarks seem to take as a model.[82] Britain in 1919–22 was a nation with severe constraints on the scope for active government. Dr. Rodney Lowe has rightly emphasized the effects of civil service inertia on a domestic social programme, undermined from within by the new departments of Labour, Health, and Transport, and stifled from without by the Treasury, now more administratively powerful than ever before.[83] In addition, the war years had underlined the incapacity of even a powerfully equipped government to propel both sides of industry into harmonious action. The post-war housing policy confirmed this all the more clearly. All the government could do was to goad, stimulate, inspire, threaten—and keep its nerve politically. For much of the time, it worked. For many months, the government ignored pressure from the Treasury to retrench and to curb the inflationary excesses of its welfare programme. In the end, it succumbed to it as almost every British government from 1918 to the present day has had to do, given Britain's external financial predicament. 'Dear money' and a 7 per cent bank rate killed off the social programme. They were the product not of civil service defeatism but of key political decisions in the Cabinet, of that total reversal of domestic policy of which Addison was the victim and the Geddes report the testament. It is this betrayal of its social programme for which the Coalition was later condemned, and rightly so. But at least it could be said that for two years it made unemployment and structural poverty more bearable, strong and interventionist central government more acceptable, that it tried to create an image of social concern and communal involvement. In so far as the Addisons, Fishers, Hornes, Monds, and Churchills achieved part of these objectives for part of the time, in the face of pulverizing economic odds, they have a useful social testament. In the light of the choices available to the rulers of Britain in 1919, 'Addison' perhaps deserves its humble niche alongside 'Beveridge' in mapping out the road to 1945.

5

Priorities and Policies:
Overseas Affairs

Labour relations and social reform did not, however, comprise the supreme challenge to the stability or the credibility of the Coalition government in its effort to retain power on the basis of the wartime consensus. The centrality of overseas policy in the calculations of the government and especially of the Prime Minister, is crucial to the understanding of these years. Britain confronted a complex range of choices in world affairs after the armistice; indeed, it was its promise to achieve international reconstruction, no less than domestic, that lay at the heart of the Coalition's mandate in December 1918. With the war over, Britain enjoyed a unique influence in moulding the international fabric, through its victories in the field, its naval supremacy, the strength of its financial institutions, and the new vitality of the imperial relationship. Further, foreign affairs intersected with domestic problems in a variety of ways. There were direct interconnections such as the well-attested link between internal labour difficulties and the Allied attitude towards the new Bolshevik regime in Russia, or the widely accepted connection between a revival in trade and employment on the one hand and policies towards reparations and war debts on the other. More subtly, the peaks and troughs of the government's reputation in the handling of a bewildering array of foreign, imperial, Irish, and defence crises bore directly on its claim to reflect the national unity of a society embittered by the losses of wartime yet confident in its power and international influence in a way totally different from the introspective, defensive mood of Britain in 1945. Foreign affairs, then, are the key to many of the vital developments of these years, to those alternating phases of exultation and of fear that gripped the national psyche between 1919 and 1922 and which called for all the native guile of the Prime Minister in responding to them. They are also crucial to appreciating the standing of the government at any given moment in this period. Ultimately in 1922 Lloyd George's claim for a renewal of popular support lay in his being the bringer of peace, the hero of Washington and Genoa, not to mention the Irish settlement much nearer home. In the event, it was foreign affairs, and the warlike posture struck in the Near East which brought the government down, somewhat unexpectedly at a time when some of the domestic political and economic indicators were pointing favourably in its direction. If the years after 1919 may rightly be characterized as marking 'the impact of labour', in another sense it was the imprint of foreign policy which dominated these years and the minds of the governors. It made Millerand, Krassin, Rathenau, Poincaré, and Kemal more decisive in shoring up or undermining Lloyd George's position than all the onslaughts of machine politicians or press lords at home.

The main features of this period, according to popular tradition, are two-fold—an unprecedented interference by a quasi-presidential Prime Minister into the conduct of foreign and defence policy, and a consequently unstable international fabric, shot through with rational rivalries and resentments, which contained the seeds of a future world war. Lloyd George himself, by general consent, dominated British foreign policy in this era. This has often been taken to indicate a conduct of foreign affairs at once erratic and aggressive. Keynes's famous onslaught on the Versailles peace treaty set the tone. His *Economic Consequences* was an immense commercial success: it sold 100,000 hardback copies in all languages between 1919 and August 1920. It laid much of the blame on the British delegation for a Carthaginian, vindictive peace imposed on Germany which demanded impossible reparations terms and guaranteed future instability. It was a treaty, in Keynes's view, shaped by the jingo mood he saw as typical of the 'coupon election'. The fact that Keynes later modified his views in *A Revision of the Treaty* has received far less attention. Subsequently, Keynes argued, the victorious Anglo-French leaders pursued the unhappy task of trying to rivet insupportable terms upon the new Weimar Republic. It was saddled with 'war guilt' from the outset. When the peacemakers turned to eastern Europe, the outcome was the disastrous exercise in sabre-rattling that led to the fiasco of Chanak, with the threat of war with Turkey, in the face of hostility of virtually the entire world. Partisans of the League of Nations, such as Lord Robert Cecil, voiced the protests of those who saw in Lloyd Georgian foreign policy only cynicism and *realpolitik*. 'I have watched very closely Mr. Lloyd George's conduct of Foreign Affairs since I first accepted office in his Government, and I am profoundly convinced that there has never been a less satisfactory directory of our foreign policy in this country.' With regard to Russia, Asia Minor, central Europe, and the Genoa conference, 'he really is not a force for peace but for war'. Lloyd George's policy was volatile, at the mercy of short-term pressures from by-elections or newspaper headlines. 'Cannes and Genoa were in their way just as objectionable as Versailles and Paris.'[1] Both these judgements, the dominance of the Prime Minister over foreign policy and the implications of this in terms of an aggressive, provocative diplomacy need careful attention.

As to the first point, the interventions by the Prime Minister in the conduct of foreign affairs were, without doubt, unprecedented in recent years, although recollections of Disraeli and Salisbury in the past might have suggested that the balance between Downing Street and the Foreign Office was a shifting one at best. Lloyd George regarded international affairs as his leading priority now that the war had ended. As Professor Michael Fry has clearly shown, his concern with external affairs was already well-developed before 1914.[2] The Welsh radical heritage was overlain with a lively concern for Britain's imperial responsibilities and commitments, and her defence requirements. The war years, especially the period after December 1916 when Lloyd George himself largely shaped the main outlines of foreign policy, emphasize this concern to the point of obsession. It was the Prime Minister who dictated the main thrust of British foreign and defence policy in wartime conferences with Clemenceau, Orlando, and others. They reinforced his zeal for 'diplomacy by conference', a highly personal style of summit diplomacy which by-passed traditional Foreign Office channels and which called for the full deployment of the presidential mode. This tendency was much reinforced by the peace negotiations in Paris when the Supreme Council of Four (or Three), Lloyd George, Woodrow Wilson, and Clemenceau, with the occasional intervention of Orlando, determined the shaping of frontiers, the rise and fall of empires, and the structure of international relations from eastern Europe to the Pacific. Lloyd George certainly regarded the Foreign Office as hidebound and potentially reactionary. In policy towards the Soviet Union and negotiations with France, in particular, he relied on his own intuitions and his own entourage in the conduct of foreign affairs.

His main channels of advice were legacies of the war. The Cabinet Office, under the increasingly influential direction of Hankey, powerfully reinforced the Prime Minister's capacity for pulling together the threads of British foreign policy in a variety of theatres, and relating them to trade policy, labour relations, and many other matters. The famous Garden Suburb of private advisers, although much shrunken after the armistice, nevertheless boasted in Philip Kerr perhaps the Prime Minister's most intimate private confidant in the period 1919–20, a man who represented the Prime Minister's views to foreign heads of government or the domestic newspaper press, with the merest nod of acknowledgement to the Foreign Office. By July 1920 Churchill, himself at the War Office and always hankering after a wide range of responsibilities in foreign policy, could declare that 'At present the P.M. is conducting the business of the Foreign Office with Kerr's assistance. I don't think that any man who does not hold a leading position in the State should be permitted to exercise so much influence on important questions of policy as Kerr does.'[3] Kerr's extensive correspondence with the Prime Minister is testimony to the fruitful communion that the two enjoyed. It testifies also to the congruence with the Prime Minister's own ideas of Kerr's basic assumptions—his belief that Germany should be treated leniently over reparations and frontiers, that intervention in Russia should come to an end, that understanding with the United States should be encouraged especially on naval and Pacific questions.[4]

In May 1921 Kerr left to manage the *Daily Chronicle* as a pro-government newspaper, but his effective successor, Sir Edward Grigg, another old Milnerite imperialist, also exercised much influence. Grigg kept up the refrain of private advice in favour of appeasement, disarmament, and an emphasis on imperial development through the white dominions. He was a key figure at the time of Genoa. If these advisers were hard to locate against the background of the orthodox conduct of foreign policy, others were even more difficult to place. Lloyd George, as always, employed a multitude of contacts and advisers, many of them unexpected such as the 'Wee Free' Liberal member, Commander Kenworthy, military observers like Major Philip Gibbs, armaments tycoons such as Basil Zaharoff, and journalists in profusion. One striking figure, much used in trade and other negotiations with the Soviet Union in 1920–2 was E. F. Wise, formerly an official in the Ministry of Food, a man of decidedly left-wing views. He was later to be active in framing the ILP's 'Living Wage' schemes in 1926 and in forming the Socialist League in the 1930s. Wise's interventions on behalf of his master were wide-ranging. Curzon frequently protested about them. In August 1920 he complained that the Foreign Office was being circumvented in dealings with the Russian trade delegation by 'the ubiquitous Wise', aided by advice from Lloyd-Greame who was, after all, one of Curzon's under-secretaries. 'If [Wise] did not exist, we should have to invent him,' the Prime Minister playfully replied.[5]

The activities of Hankey, Kerr, Grigg, Wise, and others clearly show a period of the Foreign Office being by-passed by 10 Downing Street; it has been claimed that the office went into virtual eclipse after 1919.[6] Not only was Curzon frequently by-passed by the Prime Minister. The Treasury, through such officials as Bradbury, often circumvented the Foreign Office in dealings with the Reparations Commission. Lloyd George himself firmly believed in heads of governments dictating the major outlines of foreign relations, with the diplomatic advisers supplying the nuts and bolts on matters of detail. In his own case, he believed he had access to sources of commercial, financial, and industrial advice which the Foreign Office, weaned on the narrowly defined diplomacy of more stately days, could neither possess nor understand. He had also a profound distrust of professional diplomats, drawn from a social and educational background with which he had scant sympathy; he much preferred to work his own coterie of intimates. On the other hand, too much should not be made of the picture of Lloyd George railroading Foreign Office and colleagues along paths which they either did not comprehend or else positively detested. It is a picture that derives mainly from Curzon, with his well-known resentment of the Prime Minister's personal secretariat 'operating behind the back of the F.O., conducting intrigues, sending messages, holding interviews of which we were never informed until it was too late.' It was this 'backstairs business', he maintained, 'that sapped the strength of the Foreign Office'.[7] Certainly during the tenure of his predecessor, Balfour, Foreign Secretary until September 1919, Lloyd George dominated foreign relations consistently. Balfour did not mind; his policy was 'a free hand for the little man'. Curzon, an imperious autocrat, with a

profound belief in his own insight into foreign affairs particularly in
Asia, was a different matter. His succession to the Foreign Office in
place of Balfour was welcomed by the civil service which felt that one of
its own had returned. 'It was a great source of strength to us to have a
man in charge of the F.O. who actually directed foreign affairs instead
of allowing himself to be run by officials as Grey and A.J.B. had done,'
said Sir George Grahame of the Brussels embassy. But, he added, 'The
fear is that L.G.'s dislike of Curzon may prevent his appointment.'[8]
Difficulty between Curzon and the Prime Minister was predictable.
Earlier in the year, Curzon had vigorously attacked the conduct of the
Paris peace conference, 'arrived at in independence of any expert
authority and containing the seeds of certain failure'.[9] He instinctively
rebelled against the Lloyd Georgian method of personal diplomacy.
Lloyd George, for his part, disliked Curzon's adoption of the vice-regal
style. He took pride in announcing that Curzon was the one member of
his Cabinet that he consistently bullied.

And yet, it was protocol that Curzon largely objected to, rather than
the substance of Lloyd George's policies. There were clashes in abundance—often the product of irregularities by either side, let it be said.
For instance, in attempting to secure an Anglo-Russian trade agreement in 1920–1, it was the Foreign Office which frustrated the Prime
Minister's designs, rather than the other way around. Here and
elsewhere, permanent officials in the Foreign Office were often more
sympathetic to the Prime Minister's policies than Curzon himself
appeared to be. For instance, R. H. Hoare of the Northern department of the Foreign Office was a steadfast supporter of Lloyd
George's desire for an accommodation and a more stable commercial
and diplomatic relationship with Soviet Russia.[10] Beyond these
personal conflicts, on the content of policy Lloyd George and Curzon
were consistently in agreement. On scaling down French demands on
Germany, on the need for a plebiscite in Upper Silesia, on withdrawing British forces from Russia and Poland, on destroying the pan-
Islamic pretensions of the Turks and retaining control of the Straits,
on winding up the alliance with the Japanese, and in striving to forge a
closer *rapprochement* with an isolationist United States over naval
matters—even in their wary attitude towards the League of
Nations—Curzon and Lloyd George saw largely eye to eye.

So, too, did most of their colleagues. Here, at least, is an area where
Lloyd George had the vast bulk of his Unionist colleagues firmly

behind him—until the spring of 1922 when serious trouble loomed over first Russia, then Turkey. Bonar Law, Austen Chamberlain, Horne, and Worthington-Evans were among the Prime Minister's most loyal supporters in Cabinet, in upholding lines of policy that most of the Liberal ministers, Addison, Fisher, and Montagu for instance, thought were generally well in line with the Gladstonian tradition. Only Churchill, a brooding force for discontent particularly in relations with the Soviet Union, was a frequent critic. His promotion to Colonial Secretary in February 1921 was taken by Curzon as a portent of Churchill's growing encroachment on overseas policy as 'a sort of Asiatic Foreign Secretary'.[11] Until the spring of 1922, though, when the formal recognition of Russia suddenly became central to Lloyd George's designs, Churchill was relatively isolated. In any case, much of Lloyd George's policy, the quest for military and naval disarmament, the effort to preserve the *entente* with France despite all rebuffs, appealed to Churchill too. The view, therefore, that Lloyd George's foreign policy between 1919 and 1922 was the product of one wilful, autocratic personality, concealing an ignorance of external questions behind a cloud of 'brave new world' generalities, and foisting his whims on unwilling or deceived colleagues, is really a myth. All the evidence points the other way.

Another myth is the belief that Lloyd George's peculiar methods in handling foreign affairs led to an aggressive or chauvinist form of policy, as Keynes (in 1919 though not in 1922), Cecil, and most of the left professed to believe. As has been seen, the policy advisers closest to Lloyd George were apostles of appeasement and non-intervention, anxious to fight free of the jingo nationalism of the war years. Hankey and Kerr were the voices of a generous treatment of Germany at Fontainebleau in March 1919; so, too, was Thomas Jones, the later confidant of the Cliveden ménage; Grigg was the prophet of the re-casting of international relations at Genoa on the basis of disarmament and economic and financial stability; Frank Wise was the socialist advocate of friendship with Russia. Lloyd George himself shared these beliefs to the full. His distrust for the Foreign Office, apart from being part of a general mistrust of élitist 'experts' that dated back to his days at the Board of Trade, rested in some measure on the view that it reflected the Bourbon views of the reactionary, possessing classes anxious for a return to pre-1914. Lloyd George himself, even at the height of the 'coupon election', sensed that the national consensus, like his own viewpoint, was deeply hostile to a renewal of war. It was desperate for a permanent peace settlement built on effective guarantees and collective mechanisms, created by the Allied victors, for achieving international stability. Throughout the period 1919–22, as far as foreign affairs went, his critics came almost entirely from the right, from the hysterical anti-Germanism of the *National Review*, from the pro-French lobby symbolized by Wickham Steed, the new editor of *The Times*, from anti-Bolshevists with an unmuzzled Churchill at the head of the pack. In so far as Lloyd George's interpretation of the wartime consensus essentially linked conciliation and non-intervention abroad as the corollary of industrial peace and social reconstruction at home, his government took its tone from his direction of foreign affairs. Wars, vindictive reparations, the harbouring of ideological grudges against new regimes such as that in Russia, would dislocate trade and industrial stability, which made them unacceptable to most of the British right. They would set the international ethic in a mould of belligerence and nationalist rivalries, which made them anathema to the British left. The road to appeasement, based on an implicit revision of the Versailles treaty and the restoration of trade, markets, and stable currency exchange was also the way to a more stable Britain and a more prosperous Europe, and no doubt to a longer-lasting government of national unity as well.

One of the central factors shaping Lloyd George's anxiety to construct a peaceful mode of international relations lay in Britain's newly defined role as the centre of a world-wide imperial authority. The war had reinforced the call of empire. Since 1917, the Imperial Prime Ministers' meetings had become a regular forum for discussions upon common defence and commercial policies between the mother country and the dominions. The presence of Smuts in the War Cabinet was testimony to the new closeness of the relationship. The dominance of a man like Milner, with survivors of the 'kindergarten' like Sykes and Amery further down, was in itself a portent. The manifesto of the Coalition government in 1918 laid some emphasis on the imperial theme, including the need for preferential arrangements in tariffs, though not with sufficient emphasis to upset Liberal free traders. After the election, Milner went to the Colonial Office, with

Amery as his Under-Secretary. Austen Chamberlain's budget in 1919 made the first important concession to the principle of imperial preference, in a style reminiscent of his father as an unusually emotional Chamberlain recalled to the House. Selborne was but one of many who thrilled 'to the first Preference Budget'.[12] Britain ended the war with the imperial bond apparently as secure as ever, still the possessor of the greatest empire the world had seen. Imperial strategy, above all the defence of India, was still central to British overseas policy. The famous story of Lloyd George showing de Valera a map of the world with its multitudes of 'blotches of red' is evocative of British responses (though surely not of Irish) to the aftermath of war. The Paris peace conference was a powerful reminder of the collective influence of the British Empire delegation on a world-wide basis. Of course, much of this was illusory. The interventions of Billy Hughes of Australia showed with extreme clarity the basic nationalism that governed the outlook of the major dominions. The Imperial Prime Ministers' conferences tended to be centrifugal in emphasis. That of July 1921 was to be marked by vigorous protest, notably by Meighen of Canada, against the renewal of the British alliance with Japan, which conflicted with the essential Canadian interest of good relations with the United States.[13] Canada, Australia, and other dominion countries thought hemispherically or oceanically rather than imperially. The crisis at Chanak in September 1922, when only New Zealand and Newfoundland thought that Britain's zeal to preserve the security of the Dardanelles was of direct strategic or emotional concern to them, merely confirmed the pattern of previous years of imperial relations. Even so, relations between Britain and the white dominions remained at least a channel for communication, at best a force for inter-continental collaboration to serve as an element for stability in the post-war world.

Much more difficult for Lloyd George were those territories in Asia and Africa that Britain retained on a colonial or other basis. Indeed, after the peace treaties, Britain's commitments in these continents were even wider than before. The Geddes committee was starkly told by the War Office and the Admiralty in 1921 of the immense world-wide claims upon Britain's dwindling military, naval, and financial resources imposed by the territorial and mandate clauses of the peace treaty.[14]

Britain had emerged from the Paris conference with its imperial domain more extensive even than before. Former German colonies had been acquired by the Empire—Tanganyika and South-West Africa in Africa, New Guinea for Australia, and Samoa for New Zealand in the Pacific. Britain had also acquired extensive new mandated territories, in the Middle and Near East after the dissolution of the Turkish empire—Transjordan and (as confirmed at the San Remo conference in April 1920) Mesopotamia, with its supposed immense deposits of oil in the *vilayet* of Mosul in the far north. Lloyd George fought particularly hard for the latter which the Sykes-Picot treaty of wartime had 'mistakenly' given to France.[15] Regular British military garrisons were soon stationed in Mesopotamia (renamed Iraq) to support a proposed Arab kingdom, while the new additional mandate of Palestine demanded British forces on a long-term basis to preserve order and to protect Jewish minorities. Persia, with whom Curzon concluded treaty arrangements in the summer of 1919, also sucked in large numbers of British troops, ten battalions in all, while the uncertainty that resulted from the decay in the Turkish empire in Asia Minor resulted in Britain's being committed to stationing at least six battalions in Constantinople to defend the Straits. Egypt was yet another Middle Eastern military commitment for Britain. After the rise of a powerful nationalist movement in the spring of 1919, at least nine infantry battalions were stationed there, largely along the Suez Canal.[16] Most critical of all, there was India which absorbed the largest military detachment of all, partly to protect border areas from the Soviet Union, but mainly to ward off widespread internal insurrections by the Indians themselves. As for nearly a century, the size and disposition of Britain's army was being determined not by European considerations but by the need to keep down vast colonial or semi-colonial territories in an Empire which, in India, Egypt, and the Middle East, was gloomily held to be 'more unrestful' than ever. In addition, Britain had now for the first time for over a century a continental commitment as well. There was an obligation to the Supreme Allied Council to station troops in border regions of Germany, notably Upper Silesia in 1921. The need to police these vast and diverse territories conflicted with the government's declared priorities to run down its armed forces, cut defence costs, and minimize the possibilities of international conflict far from Britain's shores.

In practice, it became clear that the government, often with much reluctance, gradually was running down its imperial commitments.

By October 1922, there had been a steady if selective relinquishment of territorial control. This policy was begun during Milner's period at the Colonial Office; it was continued, more emphatically, under Churchill who succeeded Milner in February 1921. British policy, often erratic in conception and complicated by such factors as the confusion surrounding a peace settlement with Turkey, was a programme of phased withdrawal and a more indirect concept of empire in most theatres, from the eastern Mediterranean to the Indian subcontinent. The need for financial economy and for an end to inflationary government borrowing played a major part in all this. So, too, did the severe reductions in Britain's military and naval forces, heralded by the ending of conscription in early 1920, and continued in the progressive run-down of the British army to pre-1914 levels, despite the contrary pressures for using troops to quell labour unrest at home. Another factor was effective lobbying from local British representatives such as Sir Percy Cox, the High Commissioner at Baghdad, and his 'Oriental secretary', the scholar, Gertrude Bell, who urged that a more realistic approach be adopted to appease nationalist opinion in Asia. Importance was also attached to the effect of the government's interpretation of its imperial mandate upon domestic opinion in Britain, and on the fact that direct colonial rule on the traditional pattern would conflict with the mood of moderation and the quest for a middle way that the government sought at home.

These factors helped to dictate the steady withdrawal of British forces from Persia. This policy was strongly resisted by Curzon, who advocated the creation of 'a Moslem nexus of states' in the Middle East as buffer to protect India from possible Soviet incursion. Despite the Foreign Office, British troops were withdrawn from southern and eastern Persia by mid-1920. Curzon's vision of a Persia under direct British influence, somewhat on the lines of Egypt prior to 1914, came to nothing. The process of military withdrawal, enthusiastically supported by Churchill both at the War Office and the Colonial Office, was finally completed in its entirety by May 1921. British fears of driving Persia into the arms of the Bolsheviks by flouting Persian nationalist sentiment were often cited. Amicable relations with the new nationalist movement led by Reza Khan now became central to British calculations in the area. More hesitantly, British military commitments in Mesopotamia were also scaled down; Churchill could claim a saving there of £5.5m for the next financial year, 1921–2. The 'mandate' was replaced with a bilateral treaty with a newly elected Iraqi parliament. With the encouragement of Churchill, Feisal was installed as King of Iraq in August 1921. British dominance in the area was henceforth maintained in a more indirect fashion, through subsid-ized client relationships with Feisal in Iraq and Emir Abdullah in Transjordan, the latter a 'very agreeable and civilised Arab prince', according to Churchill.[17]

The urgent new problem of imperial control in the Middle East was Egypt, a vital meeting point of so many imperial lines of communica-tion. In the aftermath of the British advance through the old Turkish dominions, a major nationalist uprising broke out there in March 1919. The initial response by the Colonial Office was dismally charac-teristic of the traditional pattern of imperial rule in Ireland, India, and elsewhere. Leading nationalist figures, including Zaghloul Pasha their leader, were interned, and martial law riveted upon the Egyptian people. Tension between the Egyptian population and the British administration seemed to indicate that the government had another India on its hands. In fact, the response of the Lloyd George Coalition, even in a muddled fashion that won it little gratitude, was markedly different in tone from that of its predecessors, the Asquith govern-ment included. Under Allenby's paternalist rule, the temper of British control in Egypt was considerably moderated. Zaghloul was released from deportation in Malta. More significant, the British government mission sent off to Egypt under Milner in December 1919, and which reported in October 1920, adopted a very different attitude towards local nationalism. Cecil Hurst, its legal adviser, acknowledged that Britain stood at the parting of the ways in Egypt. Milner himself argued that a conciliatory attitude towards local nationalists such as Adly Pasha was vital for British Middle Eastern security. His mission, apart from three civil service advisers in Rodd, Maxwell, and Hurst, also included the Liberal journalist, J. A. Spen-der, and the Labour member, Brigadier-General Sir Owen Thomas. Milner's report recommended that the protectorate be abolished and Egypt granted self-government over its own internal affairs, with diplomatic recognition overseas. Reservations remained over the con-trol of the Suez Canal, over defence, the rights of European and other minorities, and the administration of the Sudan.[18] On 29 December 1920, the Cabinet engaged in full-scale debate over Milner's conclu-sions. The result left Milner 'very dissatisfied'. Chamberlain, Lee of

Fareham, the Liberals, Montagu, Addison, Munro, Fisher and, of course, Milner himself in effect endorsed them. Montagu, as usual, stressed the effect in inflaming Indian Moslem opinion. Eric Geddes, Worthington-Evans, and most crucially Curzon, Churchill, and Lloyd George himself came out against. Some emphasis was laid on the fact that Egyptian nationalist opinion was lukewarm about the Milner proposals in view of the limitations placed by them upon Egyptian sovereignty. Grigg recorded that 'the weight of Cabinet opinion, including that of the Prime Minister, has been against the Milner policy from the first'. He added that the dominions had endorsed the view that the withdrawal of British troops from Egypt would only add to the disorder and unrest there.[19] Curzon felt uneasy that Milner had treated secretly with Zaghloul, Adly Pasha, and other nationalist leaders in London before producing his report. There was much talk of a Milner–Zaghloul agreement. In addition, he disliked the fact that the role of the British High Commission in Cairo would in future be so shadowy.[20]

Despite all this, it was in the end a more liberal view that gained the day. In 1921, many pressures built up to encourage the adoption of something like Milner's proposals, even though their author had now left the government. In Egypt, new tension developed amongst the Wafd nationalists between Zaghloul and Adly; the British could now see the latter as a local aid to imperial strategic security. Within the British Cabinet, Curzon now advocated strongly that the protectorate in Egypt be replaced with a treaty; in part, this was to thwart Churchill's growing claims to direct British policy in the region, through the new Middle Eastern department under the Colonial Office. The fluctuating fortunes of British policy in Ireland, and the new contacts built up with the Sinn Fein leaders in the summer of 1921 also had implications for British attitudes towards the Wafd nationalists in Egypt. There were lengthy negotiations between Curzon and Adly Pasha in the autumn of that year. In December, there were fresh disturbances in Egypt itself, with Zaghloul once again arrested and deported. Finally in February 1922, with much reluctance, Lloyd George and his Cabinet accepted the view pressed strongly by Allenby, who threatened his resignation,[21] that sovereignty over its own internal affairs be accorded to Egypt. The so-called Allenby Declaration of 28 February 1922 formally brought the protectorate to an end. Curzon now could claim the credit for having forced the

Milner report upon the Cabinet's attention. The consequences for
Anglo-Egyptian relations were not happy ones. The Wafd movement,
and Zaghloul himself, refused to endorse the highly limited version of
independence imposed upon their country. As Dr. Darwin has clearly
shown, Britain's concessions to Egyptian nationalism were deliberately modest ones. They yielded only those aspects of internal
administration which it was not in Britain's interests to retain, and
maintained in full the broad outlines of imperial control as it had
survived since the 1880s.[22] There were important forces in the British
Cabinet which obstructed a more generous policy towards Egypt.
Churchill was as anxious to sustain the British presence in Egypt as he
was to withdraw it from Persia. Lloyd George himself seldom applied
his mind consistently to Egypt. Like advisers such as Kerr and Grigg,
he appears to have thought in terms of the framework of imperial
strategy and communications traditional prior to 1914, and to have
seen Egypt as a bargaining counter in coping with other nationalist
movements and in resisting political pressures at home. Philip Kerr
pressed on him the dangers of Zaghloul extending his contacts with
nationalist movements elsewhere and creating 'a Pan-Islamic Sinn
Fein machine'. British troops in the Suez Canal area remained a
source of tension down to 1954. The Anglo-French invasion of the
Canal zone in October 1956 was not an inappropriate commentary on
forty years of British imperial involvement in Egypt since 1914. And
yet the fact remains that, of all the options available to the Lloyd
George government in 1920–2, that of decentralization along the
liberal lines previously accorded to white territories within the
Empire, and of a substantial withdrawal in the face of local nationalist
opinion, was the course preferred.

In India also, a comparatively liberal course won the day. This owed
its success almost entirely to the relentless pressure from Edwin
Montagu, passionate advocate of extended self-government in India,
and an earnest suppliant for the Indian (especially the Indian Moslem)
viewpoint. He was particularly persistent in this line of argument
during the peace settlement with the Turks. He cited the growing
dominance of the Khilafat in Moslem politics, with their attachment
to the Sultan. The Montagu–Chelmsford reforms of 1919 were a
useful extension of the principle of 'dyarchy' in provincial self-
government in India, even though the coercive measures recommended by the Rowlatt commission were also implemented. The

immediate test of British rule in India, however, lay in the realm of law and order. The Congress movement, headed by Mahatma Gandhi, launched a massive campaign of passive civil disobedience or 'non-co-operation' in 1920, on behalf of *swaraj* or home rule. Passions were inflamed by the appalling horrors of the Jallianwalla Bagh in Amritsar when General Dyer's mismanagement of a local demonstration resulted in the shooting of at least three hundred Indians and the wounding of 2,000 others. The fate of Dyer at once became a touch-stone for die-hard sentiment about the tone of British rule in India. In practice, Montagu acted firmly if not always tactfully. Dyer was rightly dismissed, and a report accepted which severely criticized the authorities at Amritsar. When this affair came to be discussed in the Commons, the government ran into a flurry of right-wing protest.[23] Montagu's over-excited defence of Gladstonian principles of morality did not go down well on the Unionist benches. A Jew himself, Montagu was provoked by racialist insults from the opposition side. 'A strong anti-Jewish sentiment was shown by shouts and excitement among normally placid Tories of the backbench category,' reported Sutherland to the Prime Minister. Montagu, he noted, 'became more racial and more Yiddish in screaming tone and gesture'. The Liberal, J. L. Maffey, condemned Montagu's 'windy and unconvincing rhodomontades'. *The Times* blandly commented, 'Montagu is a Jew and in excitement has the mental idiom of the East.'[24] Churchill saved the day for the government in the debate, by making a tactful and restrained defence of the government's decision—and by using the 'moon-faced' Commander Kenworthy as the scapegoat for a digres-sion on anti-Bolshevism.[25]

Undeterred by the abuse and racialism he confronted in the political climate of 1919, still influenced by the 'aliens' agitation of wartime, Montagu pursued a resolutely and courageously liberal policy in India. He kept calm in the face of the growing strength of Gandhi's campaign of non-co-operation, and the massive involvement of Mos-lems from rural areas in the traditionally Hindu Congress movement. Usually, though not always, Montagu had the support of the new Viceroy who succeeded Chelmsford in 1921—Lord Reading, Lloyd George's old confrère from Marconi days and, as luck would have it, an Isaacs, another Jew. Reading's appointment followed a period of fevered uncertainty when Chamberlain, Fisher, and even Churchill were mooted as possible Viceroys.[26] By the end of 1921, tension in

India was markedly reduced. The scale of arrests and of civil disorder was clearly less pronounced than in 1919. Gandhi finally called off his non-co-operation campaign in February 1922. Reading took a placid view of Gandhi's activities; he even considered the calling of a round table conference to replace the dyarchy with something like full responsible government in the Indian provinces. Such a dramatic initiative, together with Reading's refusal to prosecute Gandhi, led to fierce attacks from the British Cabinet, though the Viceroy was backed up a liberal governor such as Lord Willingdon at Madras.

How far the relative liberalism of the Indian government's policies can be attributed to settled conviction by the government at Westminster may well be doubted. Montagu's allies in Cabinet were predictable—the Liberals, Addison, and Fisher. He faced much animosity from his colleagues, partly on racial grounds perhaps, partly because of his obsessional criticism of the government's 'bag and baggage' policy towards Turkey. Churchill frequently opposed a liberal policy in India and suggested at one critical moment that Gandhi be deported.[27] Curzon, the Foreign Secretary, deeply resented Montagu's stream of invective against British policy in the Near East, from the Sèvres treaty onwards. Curzon's own memories of Augustan rule at Delhi died hard. He flatly opposed 'granting democratic institutions to backward races which had no capacity for self-government'.[28] Lloyd George seldom applied his mind coherently to Indian problems. When he did, his instincts were paternalistic and illiberal. Down to 1935, Lloyd George was no ally of Indian nationalism. In a famous note, he once accused Montagu of 'behaving not so much as member of the British Cabinet, but a successor to the throne of Aurangzeb'.[29] Yet in practice, it was the views of the government of India, not those of Curzon or Lloyd George, which prevailed in British policy in Asia, from Iraq to Burmah. Disengagement was pursued, the threat of possible Bolshevik penetration successfully discounted. A policy of studious concession to the forces of nationalism in the Middle East and in India was the agreed concomitant of conciliation in Europe and peace at home.

The over-all tone of imperial policy in this period, then, was generally to reinforce the liberal temper of the government's outlook. None of the areas of major crisis—Egypt, Iraq, Persia, India—was left in a settled or stable condition as a result of the Lloyd George government's policies. The major questions had all been begged. The British mandate in Palestine, where wartime pledges to the Arabs and the Zionists were in hopeless contradiction with one another, was left in worse and bloodier disorder than ever. In India, the arrest of Gandhi presaged a period of further unrest. In general, though, it may be said that it was at least a more peaceful Empire when the government left office, one in which the economic and moral limitations upon the right of Britain to coerce its subject coloured populations into submission were more widely recognized. The government's interpretation of the realities of post-war imperial rule brought it into closer contact than before with the main drift of liberal–socialist critiques of empire. As elsewhere, it was the die-hard right which felt isolated and betrayed and which a new consensus was leaving far behind. If the government's domestic programme in some sense anticipated the road to 1945, its imperial policies at least left some pointers to the route to 1947.

There was, however, one vital area of imperial control which seemed dramatically at variance with the government's claim to be searching for a unity based on disengagement and peace. This, of course, was Ireland. This nation's political and social experiences had been for decades inextricably entwined with party politics and public policy in Britain. The condition of southern Ireland in the period after the 'coupon election' appeared as a mighty blemish upon the government's overseas policy, the one great indictment upon its record which all critics, from the ILP to Lord Northcliffe, could unite in condemning. The 'troubles' in Ireland did appalling damage to the government's reputation. Scott of the *Manchester Guardian*, happy to give the benefit of most doubts to Lloyd George's foreign and imperial policies, found that Ireland stuck in his gullet. When the Prime Minister publicly condoned the 'retaliation' policy employed by the Black and Tans and other auxiliary and para-military forces, Scott for a time broke off the close friendship he had enjoyed with Lloyd George for over twenty years.[30]

At the start of 1919, the British government had concluded that Ireland was not immediately susceptible to a political solution. Sinn Fein was irreconcilable, as its withdrawal from Westminster to form its own Dail in Dublin indicated. Its links with the more violent manifestations of the Irish republican movement through men like Michael Collins were beyond dispute. The British government in the latter months of 1918 had been imposing something very close to martial law under the aegis of the Lord Lieutenant, Sir John French. Districts such as western Cork were designated 'special military areas'.

The situation, already dangerous, rapidly became worse when the British government resumed its task after the 'coupon election'. The previous Chief Secretary for Ireland had been the mild, if unimaginative, Liberal, Edward Shortt, who had used his efforts to countermand French's operations. Just before the armistice, he had written to Lloyd George to insist that home rule for the whole of Ireland must on no account be postponed. North Country Liberals 'had heard it suggested in Tory quarters that Home Rule is for the present impossible owing to changed circumstances in Ireland. I am certain that if you even appear to lend countenance to such a policy the effect in the North will be deplorable.'[31] But in the ministerial changes after the election, Shortt moved to the Home Office, and was succeeded in Dublin Castle, by Ian MacPherson, another Liberal and a Scots Presbyterian with far less patience with Sinn Fein or with the general turmoil in southern Ireland. MacPherson took office amidst a barrage of hard-line advice. French told gloomily of industrial troubles in Belfast where 'hidden Bolshevik and Sinn Fein motives' were prompting the leaders, and of the murders in county Tipperary, where 'no one ever seems to speak about the Parliament now at all'. A Dubliner added that 'for ten weeks your government had abdicated as far as this country is concerned. The Sinn Fein gang have been permitted to posture as the only people who had anything to say on Irish affairs.'[32] Sir Horace Plunkett, of convention and creameries fame, told Addison that 'by declaring an Irish policy to which the majority of the Irish people will be violently opposed, Lloyd George has driven all the moderate men in the country, for the moment, out of politics'.[33]

MacPherson set to with a will, replacing the hiatus in policy with hard-line tactics on all fronts. By the end of May 1919 Sinn Fein had been declared a proscribed organization throughout the whole of Ireland. The Dail Eireann, of which de Valera was President and Arthur Griffith was Vice-President, was solemnly declared to be illegal. By the end of the year, British forces, together with an increasingly armed Royal Irish Constabulary, were in close-quarter combat with the IRA in most parts of southern and western Ireland.

It may well seem in retrospect surprising that a Cabinet, with a strong Liberal element and a self-professed Irish home ruler as its

Prime Minister, remained inactive for so long in the light of the increasingly tragic course of events in Ireland. It may be that Lloyd George's concentration on other issues, especially on the conduct of foreign affairs, until the summer of 1920 may have led to a policy of drift and of unthinking retaliation. Certainly the Prime Minister had never been a wholly committed enthusiast for home rule, ever since his near-decision to join Joseph Chamberlain and the Liberal Unionists back in 1886.[34] But it is also clear that the Cabinet throughout underestimated the seriousness of the task with which they were confronted, as the Salisbury Cabinet had done in South Africa in 1899–1902. Against all the evidence, the Cabinet's discussions repeatedly played down the numerical and military strength of the IRA and insisted on the moderate constitutionalism of the majority of the Irish population, whom they contrasted with the supposedly small majority of the 'murder gang'. The pattern of assuming that nationalist leaders formed a small and unrepresentative group and that 'men of violence' were but a hard-core minority of extremists was to recur in British attitudes towards the Irish problem over the next fifty years, but it reached its apotheosis in 1919–20. With totally unjustified complacency, the Cabinet agreed in November 1919 on setting up a Council of Ireland, with a home rule settlement for southern Ireland and for Ulster separately, much on the lines of the measure of 1912. Fisher and Kerr formally drafted a Home Rule Bill, which Ulster now accepted as a guarantee of sustaining the British connection through the granting of limited self-government to the six mainly Protestant north-east counties, but which the Dail Eireann inevitably and logically ignored.[35] This bill ground its way through parliament in 1920; it was an obvious irrelevance as far as the course of British imperial policy was concerned. Even this measure, which nearly all southern Irishmen now rejected, was too liberal in sentiment for Lord Salisbury. 'The P.M. makes me sick' was his considered verdict on the government's Irish policy.[36]

The approach of the Coalition in this period was highly ambiguous. In theory, Irish policy seemed to be based on the premiss of the election manifesto drafted by Lloyd George and Bonar Law in October 1918, that self-government for a united Ireland remained the objective, but that there should be no 'coercion' of Ulster and that the imperial connection in fiscal, defence, and other matters should be retained. In debates in the Cabinet, the tone remained moderate, with

Liberals like Fisher providing much of the initiative. MacPherson felt disgusted with the Prime Minister's inability to lend whole-hearted support to his own tough policy:

I never had a word of sympathy from the P.M. He preferred to have the views of a man who was notoriously a Jesuit, whose views on Irish affairs I shd. listen to but never accept. The same views were accepted by the Minister of Education, who had the P.M.'s ear. He was essentially a theorist, guided by the stupid egotist, Sir Horace Plunkett, who missed the Convention. The P.M. was guided also by Shortt who was admittedly the worst of all Chief Secretaries, who became Home Secretary. I have never heard one man of any shade of political opinion in Ireland say a kind word about him.[37]

On a theoretical level, then, a moderate, rational policy for Ireland seemed capable of being salvaged. In practice, the insistence that the 'criminal conspiracy' which Sinn Fein was felt to be meant that a law-and-order approach to Irish affairs rapidly became dominant. In the winter and spring of 1919–20, decisions were taken which had a profound impact on the handling of Irish policies. Although British troop detachments in Ireland were steadily run down (to a total of 25,000 bayonets in March 1920),[38] the military tactics against the IRA became more and more aggressive. On 29 March the appointment of General Sir Nevil Macready as commander of the British forces in Ireland meant that a much more vigorous policy of 'retaliation' would now be adopted, with scant regard for the cost to the civilian population. Even worse, the army was now backed by para-military auxiliaries who inflamed southern Irish Catholic opinion still further. A straw in the wind was the dismissal of Byrne, head of the Royal Irish Constabulary, in December 1919. French had long complained that his 'temperament and methods' made him quite unsuitable for his post.[39] In practice, this meant that a force for moderation was removed from the Irish administration. The Irish constabulary was now becoming increasingly militarized and afforced with non-Irish auxiliaries, many of them unemployed ex-servicemen. These were the so-called Black and Tans who more than any other factor turned the war against Sinn Fein into a national struggle between alien auxiliaries and mercenaries, and the native population, fought according to the methods of rural and urban guerrilla warfare. The Black and Tans were reinforced by the recruitment of 'Auxis' in July–August 1920, a special auxiliary detachment of the RIC, only loosely under either civilian or military control.

The new departure in British government policy was marked by the replacement of the discontented MacPherson as Chief Secretary by Sir Hamar Greenwood in April 1920. Greenwood was a Canadian whose imperial instincts made him deeply hostile to Sinn Fein and whose Liberal professions, based on a somewhat sanctimonious attachment to the temperance movement, were not much more than a veneer. Greenwood began with some sensible decisions. French was moved from the command of British troops in Ireland, while a new administrative structure was created to reinforce Dublin Castle. This was to bring new and positive influences to bear. Sir John Anderson, once Addison's white hope for the new Ministry of Health, and now transferred from the Inland Revenue to Dublin Castle, was to prove a consistent voice for sanity amidst the carnage of 'retaliation'.[40] His deputy, Alfred Cope, one of Lloyd George's key 'men of push and go' during the period at Munitions, and later on to be head of the Coalition Liberal party organization, was close in his relationship to the Prime Minister. His purpose was to keep channels of communication open to Sinn Fein. A series of undercover contacts were established with Arthur Griffith, Michael Collins, and others from the summer of 1920 onwards. These, however, were swamped by the policy of counter-violence which, astonishingly, became official British policy from this period. Greenwood's Restoration of Order in Ireland Act imposed something close to martial law.[41] It gave the authorities power to imprison without trial and to try prisoners by court-martial. The toll of violent incidents in Ireland mounted alarmingly. The Mayor of Cork, Terence McSwiney, began a lengthy hunger strike as a protest against the tenor of British policy. 'If you let him off you might as well give up Ireland altogether,' commented a harassed Prime Minister. Ireland, he gloomily concluded in Welsh, was a 'hell's broth'.[42] In due course, McSwiney died, with massive effect upon Irish-American opinion and on attitudes in Britain itself. The death of Kevin Barry at the hands of British troops was another famous inflammatory episode. The climax was reached on 'Bloody Sunday' (21 November 1920), when twelve innocent spectators were machine-gunned to death by the Auxis after a Gaelic football match at Croke Park, Dublin. On 11 December, martial law was formally proclaimed for the whole of Ireland, with a good deal of latitude in the manner in which local troops and police officials interpreted its operation. Despite the stepping up of military and police strength in

Ireland, however, especially in Munster where RIC strength built up
to 13,000 with Black and Tan assistance, the IRA seemed as vigorous
and implacable as ever, with Michael Collins's 'flying columns' inflict-
ing fear and havoc on the British authorities.

Set against the background of its general external and domestic
policy of conciliation and appeasement, the government's policy of
counter-violence and retaliation seems barely credible. Against all the
evidence, Lloyd George and Churchill, the War Minister, let the
police and the Auxis have their heads, and sanctioned a policy of
'counter-terrorism' throughout southern Ireland. Lloyd George himself was in truculent and intransigent mood towards the Irish that
winter. In a fateful pronouncement in his Caernarvon constituency in
October and again at the London Guildhall a few weeks later, he
addressed himself to the Irish question in the most inflexible terms.
The IRA was dismissed as 'the murder gang'; in any case, he proclaimed, 'we have murder by the throat'.[43] It was these speeches that
finally drove a permanent wedge between the Prime Minister and his
old ally, C. P. Scott, editor of the *Manchester Guardian* and custodian
of the Liberal conscience. Throughout that winter and spring, Lloyd
George lent his authority to backing up the hard-line approach in the
Cabinet, and in endorsing Greenwood's proclaimed policy of
reprisals. Even as late as 12 May 1921, when a group of largely Liberal
ministers suggested a military truce now that all-Ireland elections
were approaching, Lloyd George set his face against it. Montagu,
Addison, Fisher, Munro, and, interestingly enough, Churchill,
pleaded for the truce; Balfour, Horne, Chamberlain, and
Worthington-Evans were against it. So was Lloyd George. 'We lose
the day' if such a policy were adopted on the eve of possible negotiations.[44] As always, in questions external and domestic, Lloyd George
believed in bargaining for peace from a position of the maximum
possible strength. That decided it. The fighting went on.

After months of bloodshed, the Cabinet quite suddenly reversed
policy. In June it ended the policy of retaliation. This owed nothing at
all to Greenwood who considered that 'the Black and Tans had really
behaved extraordinarily well'.[45] Macready's request for a more rigorous application of martial law was turned down and on 24 June de
Valera and Sir James Craig, the Ulster Prime Minister, were invited
for negotiations. A truce came into effect on 11 July. A dialogue began
with de Valera in August and the scene was set for the prolonged

negotiations with the Sinn Fein leaders that lasted from early October until the dramatic signing of the Irish peace treaty on 6 December.

Many factors played their part in this reversal of a disastrous and quite unproductive policy of repression. The effect on overseas opinion was harmful to the government's foreign policy. With crucial discussions coming up with the United States government over naval disarmament and policy in the Pacific, this was no time needlessly to inflame an important section of American–Irish opinion, especially in the Democratic Party. The cost of maintaining so large a military establishment in Ireland also played its part, not least with the pressures for detailing some of a diminishing military presence in Ireland for use during labour disputes in Britain. The disorganization and inefficiency of the Irish military command in the face of determined guerrilla warfare was another factor. There was scant coordination between the police and army authorities, not least because of the underestimate consistently made of the military capacity of the IRA. General Tudor, commander-in-chief of the British troops, had been removed in February.

But the ultimate reason for the reversal of British policy was that its strategy of counter-violence was wholly at a variance with the mood of conciliation and unity that it sought to convey in its other domestic and external policies. In particular, the impact on British opinion was disastrous. Labour and Liberal spokesmen vied in condemnation of the 'troubles'. So did important sections of Conservative opinion: Lord Hugh Cecil deplored the policy of 'lawless reprisals'.[46] Wickham Steed and J. L. Garvin, editors of *The Times* and the *Observer* respectively, the former a strong partisan of Balkan nationalism, the latter an Irishman, were two Unionist editors whose indictments of the government's Irish policies had powerful effect. Their proprietors, Northcliffe and Waldorf Astor, warmly supported them. Just in time, Lloyd George radically changed course. He took seriously the leads and contacts that Cope had assembled for him in Ireland. He listened seriously to the moderate counsels of civil servants like Sir John Anderson who advocated dominion home rule for a united Ireland. He asked his private secretary, Edward Grigg, to draft the King's speech for the opening of the parliament at Belfast on 22 June in liberal and conciliatory terms. Thomas Jones, who sealed his lips on so many areas of policy, put pressure on Lloyd George to appear 'as the one man who could bring a peace that would be

accepted by this country and be at all satisfactory to Sinn Fein'.[47] In
the end, it was Lloyd George who emerged as the great peacemaker in
Ireland, too. He was to grant the twenty-six counties of Catholic
southern Ireland a greater measure of self-government than Parnell
had ever advocated, with the prospect of absorbing Ulster in the near
future also. Ultimately, Ireland was to join Egypt, India, and Iraq in
the government's imperial programme of the conciliation of nationalism and military withdrawal. The change in course in Ireland was
achieved only at appalling cost. Young members of parliament like
Oswald Mosley regarded the government's Irish policy as morally
repugnant; in later years, Mosley compared it to the revulsion of
young Americans in the 1960s to the bloody holocaust of Vietnam.
Segments of Liberal and nonconformist opinion from that moment on
regarded Lloyd George as having forfeited his claim to speak on behalf
of the Liberal ethic. Ireland was the blackest chapter of the
government's policy in any theatre, a monument to ignorance, racial
and religious prejudice, and ineptitude. For all that, the pendulum
swung, just in time perhaps, to direct the Coalition here also on the
road of sanity, decency, and peace.

   This record in imperial and Irish policy, as has been seen, presents a
mixed picture, although the basic pressures everywhere, economic,
political, and military, were to force the government towards disengagement and pacification. This record provided the essential background to the government's essential task in foreign policy, to restore
peace and economic stability to a shattered European continent. Here
there can be little dispute that the government interpreted both its
duty and (*pace* Keynes) its electoral mandate in terms of pursuing a
policy of reconciliation. As has been seen, this was the basic aspiration
of the Prime Minister who imposed his stamp on the conduct of
foreign affairs throughout, and of his immediate policy advisers,
Hankey, Kerr, Grigg, and Wise. Throughout the Paris peace conference, Lloyd George had been the leading advocate of moderation. He
had played, with more flair and some success, the role arrogated for
himself by President Woodrow Wilson. In Paris, as in the party
system of the United States, Wilson showed that his moralism was set
in a mould of pragmatic politics—not for nothing were his intimates
working politicians like Tumulty or McAdoo rather than the detached
academic intellectuals whose views Wilson was believed to reflect.[48]
Lloyd George did not see in Wilson at Paris the embattled champion

of principle. He complained to Donald Maclean that the President 'ran away from the battle of Liberalism when the pinch came'.[49] The Fontainebleau Memorandum of 25 March 1919, drafted it would appear largely by Kerr and Hankey with the assistance of Smuts and some advice from Montagu, became the basis of Lloyd George's perception of a post-war settlement. While it recognized French fears for national security and proposed an inter-Allied guarantee against any future German aggression, the memorandum took an approach towards German problems radically different from that of Clemenceau and the French delegation. Reparations, it urged, should be wound up as soon as practicable, and in any case radically scaled down from the outset. German frontiers should not be drawn in such a way that a large number of German nationals were placed under alien (especially Polish) rule. It argued against the transfer of Danzig, the Polish Corridor territories, or Upper Silesia to alien governments. Nor did it support the separation of the Rhineland from Germany, even though territories there should be demilitarized. As regards the Soviet Union, a serious effort should be made to initiate talks with the new Bolshevik regime, perhaps along the lines of the recent abortive effort made at Prinkipo on the Sea of Marmora.[50] The Fontainebleau Memorandum did not greatly influence the Paris negotiations at the time, though Lloyd George won some partial victories, notably over the status of Danzig. The French noted bitterly that the British produced the memorandum only when their own security was resolved. Its significance was rather that it provided a manifesto for future appeasement and re-negotiation of the Versailles settlement, which provided the framework for the British government's post-war approach towards Europe. It set Britain upon a path of using its newly-won continental authority as the inspiration for political conciliation and economic recovery, and of carrying domestic British opinion with it.

Lloyd George's concern with Europe centred on two great powers above all, the great pariah nations of Russia and Germany (with the latter bringing in the attendant problems of guarantees for French frontier security). They formed the twin poles of Lloyd Georgian ventures in foreign policy over the next three years. Up to Genoa and beyond, the appeasement of Russia and the appeasement of Germany formed his overwhelming external preoccupation. Linked with both was the hope that British industrial recovery and a stable pattern of

domestic labour relations could be placed on a firm footing. As time
went on, even the horrors in Ireland receded in importance. The need
for bringing Russia and Germany fully into the comity of nations
seemed to be the key to the success or failure of the Lloyd George
Coalition, and its quest for unity.

In Russia, the government inherited a dangerous and ambiguous
situation. At the armistice, there were many detachments of British
troops in various regions of Russia, from Murmansk to Vladivostok,
from the Caucasus to the Indian–Afghan border. With the outbreak of
civil war in Russia, these troops, originally sent to the east to protect
war supplies or possibly to resurrect the Russian front, came to be
used in assisting the White Russian forces under the various com-
mands of Denikin, Yudenich, and Kolchak. Almost unwittingly,
Britain seemed to have become involved in an open-ended anti-
Bolshevik crusade. Winston Churchill urged the Supreme Allied
Council in March 1919 to undertake full-scale armed intervention,
now that the Prinkipo negotiations had clearly failed.[51] Churchill,
indeed, was a persistent and unyielding advocate of assistance to the
White Russians throughout 1919, and of minimizing any commercial
or diplomatic ties with the Soviet Union thereafter. As late as March
1922 he was to lead a successful movement within the Cabinet against
the formal diplomatic recognition of the Soviet Union. Churchill's
rhetoric throughout this period was strident and extreme. He decried
the 'baboonery' of Bolshevism. He insisted, in writing to the Prime
Minister, that 'nothing can preserve either the Bolshevik system or
the Bolshevik regime. By mistakes on our part the agony of the
Russian people may be prolonged. But their relief is sure.' The
Bolsheviks were 'the enemies of the human race and must be put down
at any cost'. Over a year later, he argued passionately against concluding a trade agreement with the Russians. 'It seems to me you are on the
high road to embracing Bolshevism. I am going to keep off that and
denounce them on all possible occasions.' When John Baird, a junior
minister in the War Office, was told that Churchill had been an early
advocate of withdrawal from Russia, he greeted the news with understandable incredulity.[52]

However, Churchill's resistance was no more than a forceful and
noisy obstacle towards a rational approach towards the new Bolshevik
rulers. Lloyd George himself symbolized this approach and went a
fair way towards carrying it through. He confronted boldly the fervent

opposition of the right-wing press and of the die-hards who found in Churchill a fortuitous but lonely spokesman. Lloyd George was convinced at an early stage that British military and naval intervention in Russia must be wound up. Even in February 1919, he had made diplomatic overtures to Lenin and Trotsky during the abortive negotiations at Prinkipo. Fisher, the President of the Board of Education, was one of Lloyd George's major policy advisers at this period and probably drafted the Prinkipo note himself. He concluded that the White Russians were not worth lavish military or financial assistance. Yudenich was 'a reactionary' and the White Russians as a whole represented the propertied classes whose attitude had been the spur to revolution in 1917.[53] The Prime Minister dealt firmly with Churchill's protests. 'I have found your mind so obsessed by Russia,' he wrote. Churchill should now recognize the hopelessness of the campaigns of Denikin and Kolchak, the dangers involved in according diplomatic recognition to the Baltic states, and the unacceptable cost involved in sending British troops to Estonia and Latvia as Churchill wildly demanded.[54] Churchill should apply his feverish efforts to curtailing military expenditure instead. He launched a fierce attack on Churchill in full Cabinet, which Milner noted that the victim bore with remarkably good humour.[55] After various shifts and turns of policy, by the end of 1919 all British forces had been withdrawn from Russian soil, while the possibility of clashes in border incidents in Persia or Afghanistan was also being diminished. By February 1920, the Russian civil war was effectively over, Kolchak meeting his death before a Red firing squad.

The way was now open for Lloyd George to impose his policy of pursuing something approaching normal relations with the Bolshevik rulers. Like the Russian desk in the Foreign Office, and like his personal adviser, Frank Wise, Lloyd George felt convinced that the answer lay through trade—through building up the widest range of commercial and business contacts with the Russians on a non-ideological basis, and leaving to one side such delicate issues as the question of Russian debts to Britain and France and claims of British bond-holders. Lloyd George since his Board of Trade days 'believed in businessmen'. He regarded the commercial representatives of the Red regime, men like Krassin, as the eastern version of Sir Eric Geddes—hard-faced, hard-headed collectivists who had done very well out of the revolution.[56] In the spring of 1920, it was diplomatic factors which largely drove Lloyd George on, despite the open hostility of the French from Millerand downwards. As industrial recession struck Britain from May onwards, it was more defensive aspects that had most impact now, the belief that Russia would prove a vital and almost limitless new market for British manufactured goods, currently stagnating and deprived of their traditional outlets in central Europe and other manufacturing countries elsewhere. The Treasury's policy of persisting with an artificially high exchange rate of $4.87 for the pound until March 1919 had made the problem worse, though Lloyd George ignored the fact. It was Anglo–Russian trading prospects which formed the basis of Lloyd George's increasingly confident overtures to the Russians. The search for new markets in eastern Europe was viewed now as a crucial supplement to the government's measures at home to try to combat the slump in overseas trade—Board of Trade credit and insurance schemes to assist exporters, selective tariffs imposed on 'key' articles such as dye-stuffs and scientific glassware, and protection against 'dumping' and 'collapsed exchanges' such as the mark (or the rouble). These overtures by the British government culminated in May 1920 with the half-comedy of Krassin's visit to Britain at the head of a Soviet trade delegation, the first official contact between British and Soviet representatives. Even Curzon was forced to swallow his distaste and physically grasp what Churchill helpfully called 'the hairy paw of the baboon'. Lloyd George violently denounced the Foreign Secretary in full Cabinet for his obstructiveness.[57] The Prime Minister laid emphasis on the fact that Krassin was 'a good businessman' as opposed to the Foreign Minister, Maxim Litvinov, whom he dismissed as 'a dangerous revolutionary' intent on propaganda and subversion. With a growing agreement amongst British manufacturers and businessmen that the decline in Britain's trading position, with the loss of half the export trade since 1914, was the fundamental problem confronting the nation, Lloyd George's peaceable overtures to the Russians made considerable headway.

The one episode at apparent variance with this policy of appeasement was the exception that proved the rule. In August 1920, after the drive of the Red Army deep into Poland, a possible intervention by Britain on behalf of the Poles seemed to be looming. In a famous episode, hallowed in legend, the TUC and the Labour Party formed a Council of Action which threatened co-ordinated measures of a 'direct' kind nationwide, to ensure that British troops and military equipment would not be sent to Poland.[58] The *Jolly George* incident when London dockers refused to load a ship bound for Poland seemed the prototype for a far more direct application of industrial power to foreign policy. There was a tense meeting of Lloyd George and the Council of Action on 10 August. In fact, it is perfectly clear that the TUC were pushing at an open door. 'No arms to Poland' was Lloyd George's policy also, however, he might insist for the benefit of Unionists in the House of Commons on the need to protect Polish independence. To dispatch British troops to Poland would have been senseless in view of the crucial stage of the trade talks with Krassin and the Russian delegation. It would have been totally at variance with the British policy of withdrawing its forces from eastern Europe generally, and would have been a simple target for Anti-Waste zealots of whatever political persuasion. He told the Cabinet on 9 August 1920, and repeated the French President, Millerand, at a meeting at Hythe, that British public opinion was hostile to intervention in Poland, that the working class would be particularly antagonized, and that the Conservative press would be also. The House of Commons, from Sir Frederick Banbury to Josiah Wedgwood was 'absolutely unanimous' on not sending arms to Poland.[59] Earlier, on 20 July, Lloyd George had taken as his fundamental premiss the horror prevalent in Britain about the prospect of entering upon a new war. However much he might fulminate in the Commons about the unconstitutional nature of the Council of Action, in practice he had talked to its leaders, distinctly non-revolutionary political and industrial figures like Clynes, Thomas, and Bevin, and had urged them to persuade Kamenev and Krassin of the peaceful character of British intentions. His policy and that of the Council of Action, like Litvinov's view of peace, were one and indivisible.

That autumn, the policy of peace through trade made erratic headway. It culminated in the Cabinet's formally recording its agreement in principle that November. Lloyd George emphasized the fears of a slump that would continue for another eighteen months. Why should they not trade with the Bolsheviks? 'After all, we trade with cannibals in the Solomon Islands.'[60] Labour spokesmen, with their Russian sympathies, acted as unofficial sponsors of the government's policy. Conversely, businessmen, desperately concerned at the slump widespread throughout industry, saw in sales of farm equipment and other

capital goods, in a vast and undeveloped market, a new source of
stimulus and hope. Sir Robert Horne was himself the most forceful
advocate of the new demand for an Anglo–Russian trade agreement on
strictly pragmatic Board-of-Trade grounds, while he remained somewhat more realistic than did many in the Labour Party about what the
limits of this trading relationship might be. There were many
moments of deadlock. Philip Kerr could report in late December that
negotiations were still 'hanging in the balance' owing to difficulties
about Bolshevik propaganda in Britain and on gold deposits in Russia.[61] After many diplomatic adventures, Horne and Krassin signed a
trading agreement on 16 March 1921, a few hours as it happened
before the Soviet government launched a crushing attack on the
rebellious sailors in Kronstadt. The first steps had been taken by a
western government to regularize relations with the Soviet regime.

In many ways, the trade treaty with Russia was disappointing. A
more general peace treaty remained elusive, due in large measure to
the paranoid suspicion of Lenin and his colleagues about British
assistance for internal subversive groups within Russia. The trade
agreement did not in fact produce much trade. A total of £108m in the
first five years to 1926 was far below the more optimistic proclama-
tions of Lloyd George and the expectations of British exporters.[62] The
outcome remained that Lloyd George, alone among western leaders
and in the teeth of violent hostility from Churchill, Curzon, and other
ministers, imposed for the first time some degree of realism on the
non-Communist world's attitude to Soviet Bolshevism. Lloyd George
himself discounted the ideological and propagandist objectives of the
Russian leaders—no doubt, in large measure a reflection of his own
agnostic approach to political ideas. He would have echoed Franklin
Roosevelt's description of his own outlook—'A Christian and Democrat, that's all,'[63] with even the first in some doubt in Lloyd George's
case. He believed that ultimately the realities that would dictate
Russia's foreign policy would be its urgent need for capital goods and
for the restoration of commerce and normal financial relations with
other major nations. He was convinced that only commercial recognition, followed by diplomatic, was the route to stability and to international security. The appeasement of Russia was a major pivot of his
policy, and the first great landmark on the west's path to realism in
dealing with revolutionary Russia.

The appeasement of Russia went side by side with the appeasement of Germany in Lloyd George's grand design. More than any other of the peacemakers, he was profoundly disturbed by the outcome of the Versailles treaty, and was anxious for its revision. He regarded its handling of Germany's frontiers as pregnant of future unrest in Memel, Danzig, and Silesia in the east, and the Saarland and the Rhineland in the west. He thought the proposed scale of reparations now suggested as punitive and totally absurd. He would have agreed with Smuts, Montagu, and Fisher that the treaty that emerged was 'a French document' which potentially divided Europe into two armed camps.[64] He devoted his major diplomatic efforts over the next three years to an heroic effort to try to undo the damage caused by it to the fabric of European commerce, credit, and political stability.

The problem of Germany dominated much of Lloyd George's mind for this period. As Smuts commented, 'the immediate future of Europe depends on Germany and not on Russia'.[65] Lloyd George's method was clear—summit diplomacy on the model of wartime. Eyre Crowe's blunder in presenting what turned out to be something very similar to an ultimatum for Germany illustrated for Lloyd George the inadequacy of the Foreign Office in supplying the flexibility and sensitivity required. 'I very much prefer that great questions should be discussed between principals, meeting alternately in London, Paris and Italy & that details should be settled by communication between the Foreign Offices.'[66] The greatest of these 'great questions' was without doubt German reparations—on which Curzon and the Prime Minister were basically agreed. The Cunliffe report on reparations had proposed that they were to be assessed at £24,000m, representing the entire cost of the war to the Allies, payable at a rate of £1,200m a year. Lloyd George in his memoirs confirms that he and Bonar Law thought this a 'wild and fantastic chimera. It was incredible that men of such experience and responsibility should have appended their names to it.'[67]

Still, it was he who had appointed these men in the first instance, and had been responsible for the more moderate proposals of Sir John Bradbury and the British Treasury being set aside. Keynes, quite reasonably, pointed out that Cunliffe and Lord Sumner, the main authors of the reparations proposals, were ill-equipped for the task, and unqualified to form an expert view about German capacity to pay. Cunliffe was 'a banker, brought in for electioneering and parliamentary purposes', wrote Keynes.[68] According to Bradbury, Cunliffe, when asked why Germany was first being asked to pay £200m in gold, replied 'Because it's twice as much as they've got.' Sumner was a judge, quite at sea in the technicalities of quantifying national assets and liabilities. Austen Chamberlain argued in return that both Sumner and Keynes were prophesying about something:

which is not yet capable of exact determination. . . . But the treaty gives the Germans the opportunity of making definite proposals if they wish, and leave the Commission at liberty to make such arrangements for getting Germany on its legs in advance of reparation as to them may seem necessary or expedient. The real difficulty is getting things started.

Keynes's view, he claimed, would leave Germany with a lesser burden in relation to her population than that of France or Britain.[69]

Lloyd George set to with a will to counteract this damaging start for the post-war German settlement. By the start of 1920, relations with France had deteriorated sharply as a result. In particular, the failure of the American Senate to ratify the peace treaty meant that the promise of a formal Anglo–American military guarantee to France against possible future German aggression simply lapsed. Over German indemnities, over German disarmament, over the opening up of commercial and perhaps diplomatic relations with Russia, over Syria, Iraq, and Palestine, and the question of mandates in the Middle East, Britain and France, personified by Lloyd George and Millerand, were hopelessly at odds. In every case save for the significant exception of policy towards Turkey, Lloyd George's was the voice of moderation and conciliation.

At San Remo (19–26 April 1920), Lloyd George began the long haul of making sense of French claims for reparations from Germany. In the view of the normally hostile *New Statesman* and also the *Nation*, he achieved a considerable measure of success. The heads of the German government were invited to meet the Supreme Council at Spa to discuss the execution of the treaty in relation to reparations. The fantastic sum of £24,000m proposed by the Cunliffe committee in 1918 was already being whittled down. In practice, the process of the revision of the treaty had already begun. 'San Remo has cheered me up greatly.'[70] There were other features of the San Remo conference less acceptable to Liberal opinion, and to many Unionists also. The Middle East was carved up to mutual Anglo-French satisfaction, the Syrian mandate being accorded to France, that for Mesopotamia

(including the alleged oil deposits in Mosul) for Britain. The Cad-
man–Berthelot oil agreement was concluded, guaranteeing France a
quarter share of any oil discovered at Mosul. In the Near East, Lloyd
George's anti-Turk views carried the day. Venizelos, the Greek Prime
Minister, was rewarded with enormous new domains—Macedonia,
western and eastern Thrace on the European mainland, the majority
of islands in the Aegean sea, and even Smyrna in Asia Minor.
Albanians, Yugoslavs, Bulgarians, and Turks would be placed under
Greek rule to satisfy Lloyd George's Gladstonian obsession about the
Turks, and his Disraelian obsession about the straits. The Treaty of
Sèvres in August was to carve up the remnants of the Turkish
dominions. Still, the main issue at San Remo concerned reparations,
and here Lloyd George secured Anglo-French accord on the moderate
line of agreeing on a lump sum instead of the Germans paying instal-
ments on account. He also forced the French into withdrawing their
troops from five Ruhr towns (Frankfort, Darmstadt, Hannau,
Dieburg, and Homburg), dispatched there unilaterally on 6 April
when the Germans sent more troops into the Ruhr than the French
considered was justified to quell a Communist uprising. Britain
announced that she would refuse to participate in the conference of
Allied ambassadors until French troops were removed; they withdrew
from the Ruhr on 17 May. At a further conference at Boulogne on
21–2 June, Lloyd George and Millerand appeared to have agreed on
fixing a lump sum for Germany's indemnity, perhaps £4,500m spread
over the next thirty-five years. At Spa on 9 July, there were some
rough passages with the German delegates and especially with the
Chancellor, Hugo Stinnes, 'an entirely new kind of capitalist, dark
and fanatical', about coal deliveries as reparations. The prospect of
military sanctions on Germany loomed near. Again, however, the
range of reparations was scaled down. Despite resistance from Lloyd
George and Curzon, inter-Allied percentages were adopted as a basis
for calculation. The French proportion was assessed at 52 per cent,
the British at 22 per cent. Coal deliveries were fixed at £2m tons a
month for the next six months.[71] In accepting the general principle of
reparations, Lloyd George was voicing the broad consensus of opinion
in Britain, not only on the right wing. Keynes's proposed 'revision' of
the Versailles treaty would leave Germany still paying 36 milliard gold
marks. The *New Statesman* commented that 'it is obvious that Germany will have to pay an indemnity, and nobody denies that it is just

that she should'.[72] Where Lloyd George differed even from this
journal, radical as it was, and may be thought to have been more
enlightened, was in trying to make reparations payments as long-
drawn-out and harmless as possible.

At a further conference at Brussels in December, the next in the
long saga of Anglo–French meetings, the discussions between the
experts broke down. However, in practice a much more moderate
scale than that demanded by France was agreed. Lloyd George's
pressure on the French was paradoxically much assisted by the resistant, almost truculent, attitude adopted by successive German foreign
ministers towards the two series of forty-two annuities that the
Supreme Allied Council now proposed. This enabled the British
government to encourage the French by adopting a more belligerent
posture. At London in March 1921, Simons, the German Foreign
Minister, undiplomatically suggested a radical scaling down of the
Allied demands from £11,300m to only £1,500m. Lloyd George
issued an ultimatum, sanctions were applied, and British and French
troops occupied Dusseldorf, Duisburg, and Ruhrtort. A customs
cordon was created between these territories and the rest of Germany.
Lloyd George and Briand, now the French Foreign Secretary—a
Breton and a 'responsive personality' very much after the Prime
Minister's heart—even discussed the possible occupation of the Ruhr
as a whole. After the resignation of his Cabinet, the German Chancellor, Josef Wirth, had to accept the Allied schedule of payments,
reform his government, and accede to the Allied ultimatum on 11
May. In return, France had accepted a total sum of 132,000m gold
marks (or £6,600m) in place of the sums originally bandied about at
Paris in 1919.[73] Interest on the C Bonds, well over half the total, was
deferred: in effect the bulk of Germany's alleged obligations would
never be paid. By the summer of 1921 Lloyd George could claim that
his policy on reparations had steered a successful course between
passivity and vengeance. He had achieved this on the basis of a broad
range of agreement within the Cabinet and amongst the electorate.
Churchill had been a fierce critic of the government's policies in
relation to Russia and Turkey. On 2 June 1921 he told Lloyd George:
'we are drifting steadily and rapidly towards what will be in fact the
defeat of England by Turkey'. But he now solemnly recorded his
agreement with the decision to phase down, if not phase out, German
reparations payments. While he felt that the French occupation of the

Ruhr 'will happen anyhow', the extent of the reparations demanded by the French press and public would be an economic disaster for Europe and fuel an insatiable German desire for revenge.[74] On balance, Lloyd George could argue that he had both kept the *entente* with France in being, albeit on a somewhat shaky basis, and yet had imposed terms on Germany sufficiently moderate and even nebulous so that a dialogue remained possible with the leaders of the Weimar republic. Another pariah was slowly being ushered into the comity of nations after a period of isolation.

In addition, Lloyd George was turning his attention to the modification of the arrangements for Germany's frontiers as laid down at Versailles. By 1921, the key area was Upper Silesia, a region vital in both political and economic terms. In 1913, Upper Silesia had contributed almost 25 per cent of the entire coal production of Germany (43.4m tons). By comparison with Silesia, territories such as Lorraine and the Saar were of minor importance. While there was French pressure to have the bulk of this area transferred to Poland, Britain pointed out that Upper Silesia contained 275,000 Germans as against 233,000 Poles, with the bulk of the German population clearly contained in the industrial communes.[75] Lloyd George successfully insisted on a plebiscite but the commissioners, as not infrequently, interpreted its results in somewhat ambiguous terms. The French Commissioner, Le Rond, sought to award the bulk of the industrial communes to Poland; this would lead to a boycott by the Germans since they had little coking coal and were dependent on the Polish sphere for fuel for their foundries. In Upper Silesia, there was great racial tension. A Berlin socialist asked Arthur Ponsonby despairingly, 'Is there any prospect that in the Upper Silesia crisis Lloyd George will *remain* sensible?'[76] Unlike Ponsonby, he had scant faith in Briand; like others on the left in Europe he regarded Lloyd George as an erratic standard-bearer for his hopes. As events turned out, Lloyd George managed to salvage something out of the confusion. A plebiscite on 30 November 1921 showed a large majority (717,000–483,000) in favour of inclusion with Germany. Still the commissioners were hesitant; Chancellor Wirth thought their decision in April 1922 'a terrible blow'.[77] Despite an organized uprising by the Poles which harassed the Allied occupying powers, in August 1922 the League of Nations eventually managed to gain agreement with a partition of Upper Silesia on balance in Germany's favour. Here again Lloyd George had striven, with some success, to remove a source of national grievance and to assist in the restoration of German self-respect.

However, what is vital about Lloyd George's appeasement of Germany, as compared with that of Neville Chamberlain twenty years later, is that he recognized that concessions should be reciprocal, and not offered unilaterally and indiscriminately in response to German pressure. He recognized that there was a legitimate French problem, too, after devastating invasions in 1870 and again in 1914, with such immense loss of life and property. There was a prospect of Germany re-emerging as powerful as before: some kind of military guarantee of French security was therefore essential. He sought a balanced appeasement, based on strength not surrender. The treaty provisions of Versailles had not really met the French demand for territorial guarantees at all. Under Article 428 it was laid down that the west bank of the Rhine would be occupied by Allied forces for fifteen years. However, as has been seen, the more fundamental assurance that Britain and the United States would assist France in the case of German aggression had fallen through when the US Senate failed to ratify the treaty. Indeed, no-one with any appreciation of the long record of American isolationism in foreign policy towards Europe could have ever supposed that the Senate would look with favour on so sweeping a commitment to a continent three thousand miles away from the American eastern seaboard. Lloyd George, then, as part of his wider design of European reconciliation, with Russia and Germany brought in, sought to alleviate French anxiety. As the winter of 1921 drew in, amidst the catharsis of the Irish treaty negotiations which seemed to remove the one major domestic threat to the Coalition, Lloyd George looked with new favour on proposals for some kind of military guarantee of France's eastern frontier. Quarrels with France abounded by this time, over Silesia, over Turkey as usual, and over the rather curious issue as to whether French submarines should be included in the naval disarmament proposals agreed at the Washington conference. Still, Lloyd George had told d'Abernon, the British Ambassador to Berlin, on 21 June that he favoured some kind of long-term military guarantee to the French; so did Churchill although critical of some aspects of the conduct of Anglo–French relations.[78] On the other hand, Britain wanted 'no military adventures' and could have no truck with assisting France's new allies, the Poles, in territorial expansion in eastern Europe. When Lloyd George and Briand met in London on 18–21 December to discuss the latest round of discussions with the Germans over reparations payments, the issue of a British guarantee of France against German invasion came up centrally during the talks. In this more active and daring fashion, Lloyd George sought to provide the kind of security framework that alone could permanently guarantee the wider, more commercially stable Europe that he felt he could yet create.

In relation both to Russia and to German–French relations, then, Lloyd George was in general the voice of moderation and of 'no adventures'. He had significantly reduced the international temperature, save only in Asia Minor, and had minimized the areas where a wider conflagration could break out. Even Keynes by 1922 was seeing in him the major force for European peace. Lord Robert Cecil persistently attacked British foreign policy in these years as 'destitute of principle', from Germany to Mesopotamia. Even when Lloyd George was right, as over Upper Silesia, his methods were objectionable. 'Limehouse oratory is not a good vehicle for diplomacy.' But it is clear that the main thrust of Cecil's attack concerned the government's attitude to the League. Some years later, he wrote to Churchill that 'L.G. missed the greatest chances ever given to a man' after 1918. 'Clemenceau frankly regarded the League as an Anglo-Saxon fantasy. L.G. approved of it but never attempted to understand it, and indeed thought it of little importance except as a bargaining counter to the Americans.'[79]

Not everyone thought Lloyd George was so hostile to the League. One warm partisan of the Coalition, O. F. Maclagan, a confectionery manufacturer, linked his defence of the government and ideas of 'fusion' with his public campaigns for the League of Nations.[80] Lloyd George himself argued that he was pursuing the only realistic strategy by basing his policy on the dominant powers that had emerged victorious in the war rather than on an untried world organization without executive or coercive powers. The League had yet to 'prove its capacity to preserve the peace and liberty of the world'. His objectives were much those Cecil would have had in mind—indeed, Lloyd George's foreign policy, until the débâcle of Chanak, attracted steady if reluctant applause from those on the left during this period. However much its adherents, still bearing the bruises of the 'coupon election', would have disputed it, Lloyd George was the advocate of the effective objectives of the UDC. He sought peace and disarmament, however, through summit conclave rather than through the mirage of open diplomacy. By the end of 1921, he could point to an empire and a continent largely at peace. One observer could see at the start of 1922 the dawn of a more hopeful and prosperous era than the world had known since pre-war days.[81]

Along with peace, the government had pursued a policy of disarmament also, partly of course because of sheer financial necessity. Churchill agreed at a Cabinet meeting on 5 August 1919 to bring conscription to an early end. Expenditure on the armed forces was reduced from £604m in 1919 to £111m by 1922. Military battalions had been pulled back home from Mesopotamia to Ireland. Churchill at the War Office until March 1921, his successor, Worthington-Evans more emphatically so, had accepted the ten-year rule, that there would be no general war for at least ten years, as governing British military deployment and estimates. Even the British navy was being scaled down. In the five years after Jutland, Britain laid down not a single capital ship. After some diplomatic finessing between Britain and the United States about combining an international conference to deal with both Pacific affairs and also naval disarmament, the Washington conference got under way in November. Lloyd George himself, occupied with the Irish negotiations, chose not to attend. In any case, he feared that Washington might prove 'something of a fiasco'.[82] His own dealings with the USA had been somewhat remote since Versailles. As will be seen later, the outcome was a treaty for naval disarmament between Britain, the United States, Italy, France, and Japan, the only effective agreement on naval disarmament to be reached between 1918 and 1939. Lloyd George had argued at Paris in 1919 that it was idle to impose permanent limitations on German armaments unless the Allies imposed similar limitations on themselves. There was the further effect of leaving the Anglo–American relationship in somewhat better repair after tensions over Ireland, war debts, and the Japanese alliance, and lending an inter-continental dimension to Lloyd George's handling of the international scene.

Throughout this period, the conduct of British foreign and imperial policy had over all a rough consistency. This stemmed essentially from its highly personal direction by the Prime Minister. He and his advisers now took it for granted that the premier should take over from the Foreign Office and the Colonial Office the basic lines of external policy. Grigg spelled this out for the benefit of King George V.

Communications from the dominions prime ministers came via the British premier. The great departments of state interacted over foreign policy; only the Prime Minister could co-ordinate their operations. Most important of all:

Foreign affairs are now so closely connected with the main questions affecting political opinion in this country, e.g. trade depression, unemployment, limitation of armaments and the maintenance of peace as a basis for economic revival. . . . The fact that the Prime Minister is *par excellence* the man to whom both Parliament and the country look for an exposition of all Ministerial policy reinforces all other causes which are leading to the centralization of foreign policy in his hands.[83]

To critics of the presidential style, naturally, Lloyd George's method was dangerous. It led to the dangers of Caesarism, to intuitive, erratic diplomacy, and confused, ill-prepared encounters between heads of government in which a jumble of different political, economic, and strategic issues were muddled up and used as counters operating against one another.[84] 'Diplomacy by conference' was the very antithesis of the stately progressions of foreign office staffs and embassies: Genoa in April 1922 was its apotheosis. But the period from 1919 was in a unique sense a time when the international structure was in flux, and foreign politics at the mercy of new gusts of economic or ideological change. Lloyd George saw, or convinced himself that he saw, the interrelated aspects which led him to link withdrawal from the periphery of empire with the appeasement of the outcast nations excluded from the peace settlement. They could be fused together with the instinctive expertise which was the Prime Minister's special hallmark in diplomacy whether he were meeting foreign heads of state or trade union delegations at home.

Above all—and this was Lloyd George's supreme justification—he believed that foreign policy was the product less of timeless abstractions based on traditional concepts of power and special interest, than of the new pressures for change from the electors at home. This conviction drove him on throughout his talks with Wilson and Clemenceau. It was a new model diplomacy that he sought to conduct after 1919, to try to interpret afresh the mandate he had received at the polls. Contrary to Keynes's later picture, this was not a mandate for *revanche* or the pursuit of military adventures abroad. It was, or seemed to be, a mandate for the 'normalcy' of trade and peaceful relations applied to a world agitated anew by movements such as international communism and colonial nationalism. At every stage in his foreign policy, the touchstone for Lloyd George was the need to carry with him the consensus of opinion at home, and to relate demands for conciliation in the domestic industrial scene with a wider pacification, based not on the abstract generalities of the League of Nations, but on the realities of great power involvement in preserving international security. Even more emphatically than at home, Lloyd George's policy often moved in advance of public opinion. When political crisis came in October 1922, it was in part the most traditional elements in British life which turned against his European grand design. To fuse the 'normalcy' of the pre-war world, including the fabric of the Empire, with the dynamism of the popular movements released after the war, that 'deep sense of anger and revolt' noted in the Fontainebleau Memorandum, was Lloyd George's achievement. On the base of a truer national unity he sought to create a more united and tranquil world. Professor Ullman remarks, in summing up Lloyd George's Russian policy, that of all the peacemakers, he had the broadest vision. 'He was the best of his time.'[85] This wise judgement is capable of wider application. If Lloyd George's grand design ultimately collapsed through the sheer immensity of the problems that weighed it down, those who followed on after 1922 were scarcely more distinguished in bringing peace to their nation or stability to their world.

6

The Appeal to Opinion

Throughout this myriad of domestic and external policy preoccu-
pations, the government and its various opponents were agreed on
seeing one supreme yardstick for measuring the rightness of their
approach—the touchstone of opinion. In crisis after crisis, the same
test was applied, namely whether 'public opinion' endorsed or
opposed a given line of action. Naturally the various opposition
groups, the Independent Liberals, the Labour Party, and the Tory
die-hards, felt themselves to be unique custodians of the general will,
and to have a special access to the people denied to an autocratic and
semi-presidential government. But the Cabinet itself, far more than
Cabinets in pre-war days, constantly appealed to public opinion as the
final arbiter of policy. It was felt that public opinion had to be carried
along during labour disputes. This meant a relatively moderate
response to the railway clerks or even the miners.[1] It was felt that the
government should not flout public opinion by taking too aggressive a
stand in industrial troubles or by making its anti-strike contingency
planning too open and provocative. On the other hand, it was argued
that public opinion was impressed by the firm measures adopted in
standing up to the railwaymen in September 1919. 'A great impression had been made on the public last time by the perfection of the
Government's organization, and it would be very serious if the
Government did not live up to that high standard.'[2]

Public opinion, it was also urged, insisted on the fulfilment of the
government's pledges on housing and other aspects of social reform;
there lay the true antidote to Bolshevism, so Lloyd George claimed. On
the other hand, the public were also felt to be increasingly anxious at
the escalating cost of the government's social and other programmes,
and to be vehement for stringent economy.[3] Abroad, opinion, in
the view of Fisher, was enthusiastic for self-government for the Egyp-
tians; whereas Curzon felt certain that the public was turning against

the granting of democracy to backward races such as the Indians. The public was felt to be strongly against sending arms to Poland, but equally strongly in favour of dispatching arms to Chanak.[4] It wanted adequate reparations from Germany to pay for the costs of the war, but decidedly wanted no more war to enforce payment.[5] Cabinet positions for or against tariff protection for 'key industries', reprisals in Ireland, subsidies for wheat and other foodstuffs, were equally confidently based on this fundamental, but elusive, test.

Of course, of what elements this opinion was composed, where it was to be located, and what seriousness should be attached to its various forms of expression—by-elections, newspaper headlines, pressure-group activity, public demonstrations, and so forth —occasioned innumerable variations on the theme. Then, as now, politicians felt that if public opinion did not clearly exist, therefore it ought most conveniently to be manufactured. But, in general, politicians, as figures operating in a democratic order of politics, felt certain that public opinion existed, and that the only real problem was of communicating the truth to it without ambiguity, and then reaping the reward in public support and a lease of power. Politicians in 1919–22 did not, of course, possess public opinion polls or the aids to the gauging of opinion that exist in the later twentieth century. Dr. Gallup did not begin his operations until the 1930s in America. One of a rival poll's triumphs was to predict that Alf Landon, the Republican hope, would defeat Franklin Roosevelt in the 1936 presidential election: in the event, he carried two states to Roosevelt's forty-six. However, politicians in more recent years have not necessarily found that opinion polls enable them to attain either consistency of policy or accuracy in the timing of an election. Harold Wilson in June 1970 and Edward Heath in February 1974 may well have wished that they had relied on the more impressionistic kind of evidence favoured by their predecessors after the First World War. In assessing public opinion ministers after 1918 depended on the same kind of flow of miscellaneous information as they had done for decades—messages from party organizers in the constituencies and in central office, the tone of debate as reflected in meetings or in the correspondence columns of the newspapers, hints from journalists and political hangers-on, random guesses and wishful thinking. Most politicians took seriously, at least, the information that reached them via orthodox party channels. This could lead to shattering mistakes, such as Austen Chamberlain's certainty in October 1922 that the Newport by-election would sustain the Coalition in office by returning a Labour candidate. In fact, the Conservatives won the seat comfortably, as they were to do until 1929, and the government fell. Lloyd George, however, gloried in his isolation as a leader without a party machine of any substance to back him up. In a pre-television age, he preferred to rely on a kind of direct communion with 'the people', vaulting over parliament, press, and political parties, to achieve a kind of intimate symbiosis with his public. This had governed his political style since he entered politics as a Welsh outsider who flouted the orthodox party organizations even in his native land. It hardened into faith during the popular crusades over the People's Budget in 1909–10 and during his experiences as war leader after 1916. He did occasionally listen to one or two Liberal advisers on tactics, notably McCurdy and Macnamara whom he believed, on the basis of very little evidence, to be experts on the changing moods of the electorate. After 1918, though, fresh from an overwhelming endorsement at the polls, equipped with personal and political antennae that could penetrate the mass of 'interests' and 'responsive personalities' that he believed made up the political culture of Britain, Lloyd George strove anew to build on his unique reputation as a populist leader. Like Eric Hoffer's 'true believer' he had the gift of touching the hearts, minds, and souls of the people he led, of 'harnessing men's hungers and fears in a holy [or unholy] cause'.[6]

The principle of claiming that policies derived essentially from popular support and inspiration was, of course, commonplace. It had been current in British public life at least since the 1867 Reform Act. Constitutional authorities like Dicey, in examining the relationship between law and public opinion, had made much of the theory of the 'mandate'. It was part of the private fantasy world which politicians constructed for themselves, a world of rhetoric, self-delusion, and ambition against which outside stimuli from the wider public were projected. It had scant basis in history, logic, or sociological observation. None the less, politicians, believed it to enshrine a profound truth. In 1919–22, as before and after, they felt, in the words of Field Marshal Sir Henry Wilson, that 'if you get England on your side, there is nothing you can't do. If you don't, then there is nothing that you can do.'[7]

Nevertheless, there were serious grounds for supposing in 1919 that

British politics were to an unprecedented extent swayed by popular pressures of a new and unfamiliar kind, and that the character of post-war politics was totally different in character from the more slow-moving world of pre-1914. The Representation of the People Act passed early in 1918 had radically transformed the electorate.[8] In 1910, it has been calculated that about $7\frac{1}{2}$ million males were on the registers—about 60 per cent of the adult male population—and, of course, no females. At the 'coupon election' in December 1918, the electorate had been expanded to 21 million, of whom 8 million were women. This revolutionized the basis of political activity—though not necessarily, as will be seen, the politician's perception of it. Virtually all adult males were now enfranchised; the vote was clearly geared to residence and not to property, though such features as the plural vote attached to business premises and the like survived. Women over the age of thirty also had the vote, although on a more restricted property basis. As a result, the level of enfranchisement seems to have been much higher than in pre-war years, rising to a level of 94.9 per cent of the English male population in the autumn of 1921. Clearly this was a strange new world in which old landmarks had disappeared. At the same time, the constituencies were radically re-drawn, with many two-member seats abolished and more numerically equal constituencies than before.

But the politicians' conclusions, however, were erratic. One factor certainly did impinge on the consciousness of all political camps, as indicating a quite new atmosphere in public life. This was the existence of the women's vote to whom all parties laid claim. There were moves, indeed, to extend it further: Labour sought to enlarge it and grant it to all women over twenty-one on the same basis as men. Much attention was paid to the female vote in the 'coupon election'. Lloyd George ordered that special efforts be made to enlist it. He directed that Christabel Pankhurst and other well-known women's leaders of attested patriotism be employed as speakers.[9] Alone of the leading politicians of the day, he addressed a special meeting of women voters in December 1918, with Mrs. Fawcett in the chair; this took place in London's Queen's Hall on 9 December. Lloyd George later claimed that it was the women's vote which was the basis of the Coalition's success. He told Neville Chamberlain, in perhaps their first meeting since the war, in June 1921, 'Women had voted for us . . . in 1918 and we mustn't lose their vote. . . . Once having gone, they would not

come back, for women in politics were more constant than men.'
Chamberlain commented in his diary, 'I thought the little beast
showed his usual astuteness in all this.'[10] Women were thought to be
natural recruits for the Coalition cause. Women voters, wrote a
defeated Liberal of the York election, voted 'to make Germany pay'.[11]
Robertson, chairman of the Scottish Liberals, thought Asquith had
been defeated at East Fife 'by the soldiers and the women'.[12] Women
electors, 'bloodthirsty, cursing their hate', threatened ILP or pacifist
candidates such as MacDonald at Leicester or the Revd. Thomas
Nicholas at Aberdare with their lives.[13] Women, Coalitionists argued,
were 'moderate', anxious to avoid the extremes of socialism and
reaction, dedicated to the values of home and family, King and
country. They were particularly hostile to industrial militancy, as
shown by the miners.

On the other hand, the existence of women voters in such massive
numbers aroused some Coalition alarm also. They had 'no political
education' and were thus a prey to hucksters and purveyors of flashy
doctrines.[14] This made them potentially volatile and cannon fodder
for the appeal of the Wee Frees in by-elections. At the same time,
women were concerned with 'economic realities', with the cost of
living and the purchasing power of their husbands' wages. More than
other electors, they 'care most about social reform', added one
observer.[15] This, it was thought, made them susceptible to Labour.
Many recruits to Labour and even to the ILP were detected amongst
women voters by the political observers of the time: the prominence of
women such as Margaret Bondfield and Mary Macarthur in the
Labour movement was an obvious encouragement. Women, some
added, were inclined to rivet their gaze on the breakfast table and the
kitchen sink. They were 'parochial' and had a 'narrowing' effect on
politics.[16] The high abstractions of foreign policy or international
commerce, which underpinned the strategy of the Coalition were
simply above their heads. In this sense, then, the women's vote
captured in 1918 might easily be lost to the Coalition. The *Lloyd
George Liberal Magazine* urged Coalitionists in the constituencies to
form women's sections and to stress the qualities of the Prime
Minister who was agreed to have a unique appeal to women, whether
as individuals or in the mass. Addison, another Liberal, took a
different view of the character of the woman voter. 'Men were inclined
to practical compromise, whereas women were more inclined to insist

on the ideal': his zeal for reform, however, stopped a little short of the liberation of women.[17] The rise of Anti-Waste as a serious challenge to the government was linked closely with the women's vote. It was claimed that the Anti-Waste successes gained in Dover in January 1921 and at Hertford in June were the result of a revolt of women voters against high government spending and dearer food. The phenomenon of women in politics, then, aroused much attention and sophistical ingenuity. The election of Lady Astor for the Sutton division of Plymouth—the first woman MP save for a Sinn Feiner in 1918 who never left Ireland—was a portent here. At the time, though, it seemed interesting largely as the successful defence of a Coalition seat, even with a 13 per cent swing against the government. Sir George Younger strongly opposed the nomination of Lady Astor—'and the worst of it is the woman is sure to get in'.[18] Much more importance was attached to the victory of Mrs. Wintringham as an Independent Liberal in the Louth by-election in 1921 in succession to her late husband. She had fought a silent and inactive campaign, unlike the noisy Lady Astor.[19] Her triumph at a time when the Liberals' fortunes in by-elections were distinctly in decline was held to be a striking symbol of the power of women voters in dictating the priorities and securing the advancement of their sex.

The advent of women electors, therefore, had a marked impact on the rhetoric, the assumptions, and the apprehensions of politicians of all parties. They influenced the projection of party propaganda. They encouraged somewhat ineffectual attempts to enlist women candidates of the type of Mrs. Coombe Tennant, an ardent Lloyd George Liberal from Neath with valuable eisteddfodic credentials (she was a bard under the cryptic soubriquet of 'Mam o Nedd', 'the mother from Neath'). Otherwise, it is remarkable how slight the impact was of the massive enlargement of the electorate in 1918 upon the outlook of party organizers and workers.

Politicians at the local level did, of course, pay some heed to the effects of redistribution in 1918. Salvidge of Liverpool gave some characteristically knowledgeable advice to F. E. Smith, as he then was, about transferring from Walton to the new West Derby division in Liverpool.[20] But otherwise, the discussion of the responses of the electorate was astonishingly similar to those governing pre-war politics. The same regional and local variations were thought to govern politics after 1918. The allocation of 'coupons' in different

constituencies between the Liberal and Unionist whips followed
largely the traditional pattern. The Wrekin had always been a Liberal
area, and thus the new constituency bearing its name was allocated a
Coalition Liberal candidate. East End constituencies in London had
always had their recognized pockets of Liberal and Conservative
strength since 1885—Limehouse was Liberal, Mile End, Conservative, and so on—and so, it was assumed, things would remain.

The most that the party organizers, whips like Guest and Talbot,
managers like Younger and Salvidge, would acknowledge was that in
a generalized way the electorate was much larger. Addison thought
this a reassuring factor as a larger electorate would be less open to
'particularist influences' which he did not itemize.[21] But there were
many new, untried, and unknown individuals on the voting register,
perhaps more volatile, certainly harder to predict. This uncertainty
was especially paramount in the character of party politics after 1918
when traditional party labels were in abeyance with a Liberal–Conservative coalition confronted by shifting patterns of Labour, Liberal,
and independent Conservative opposition, with the Irish Nationalist
Party almost wiped out, and men like Lord Robert Cecil who almost
defied classification since their contacts ranged from Unity House
to Hatfield House. Professor Gilbert Murray found Oxford University
student politics 'very lively and interesting. The name Conservative
will very likely disappear, and the thing is evidently taking new
forms—Tory Democrat in general character. Religions and mysticism seem to be booming; also of course Labour.'[22] Sir Charles Petrie's
romantic Toryism, fostered in the new Oxford Carlton Club, was
countered by the austerity of G. D. H. Cole's 'scientific socialism' as
espoused by Oxford's many Fabians.

In this strange atmosphere, the Coalition's party organizers, Liberal and Conservative alike, showed scant appreciation of the structural changes in the electorate that had taken place, the newly
enrolled mass vote detached from the relatively fixed voting patterns
of pre-1914. The Labour Party, although in the judgement of three
later scholars the obvious beneficiaries of these franchise changes,[23]
also appeared to think within the same categories. 'Labour', comments Dr. McKibbin elsewhere, 'thought it was competing for the
same electorate as the Liberal Party.'[24] Hence, no doubt, the reason
for Labour's surprising and pointless emphasis on rural constituencies after 1918. Ramsay MacDonald in particular felt that Labour's

progress depended crucially on winning over the more radical layers
of the existing Liberal vote.[25] His experience with the essentially
Lib–Lab Union of Democratic Control, in which differences over
economic policy at home were papered over following the Union's
insistence on the prime importance of a 'democratic' foreign policy,
confirmed this basic assumption. Henderson returned to parliament
at the Widnes by-election in September 1919 on the open understanding that he was running as the 'progressive' candidate of anti-
government Liberals and Labour alike. After 1920, though, this kind
of renewed 'progressive alliance' faded away. Time after time, tacticians such as Sir William Sutherland insisted that the issues of pre-war
days, especially those dear to Liberals in the past such as temperance,
free trade, disestablishment, and education, were played out and had
run their course. The voters were 'grim realists', mainly preoccupied
with the cost of living and unemployment, 'casting about for lifelines
in their sea of troubles'. The things that mattered were:

the earnings that can keep a home together, and it is also the question which
touches the woman voter—and her enormous importance must be kept in
mind in every appeal. It is not suggested that these traditional questions
should be ignored but too much must not be expected of them. They are old
horses who have run a lot of races in their time but have hardly got the pace
needed today. They mean much to the elderly pundits in Liberal politics, but
less to the legions of new voters who take these things on their merits.[26]

The issues, then, were different. The party system was in flux. The
public psyche had been wrenched out of traditional patterns by the
impact of total war. Yet, the party managers concluded, politics and
public opinion should still be viewed in terms of the encasing mould of
familiar party politics that dated from the Gladstone–Disraeli era.
Whether party men called for 'fearlessly radical' initiatives or for 'no
adventures' at home or abroad,[27] they still related to the traditional
norms of political behaviour. Despite the war, they thought that little
fundamentally had changed in the structure of British politics or
society, though few perhaps would go so far as 'Eddy' Hartington in
claiming that the war had generated a new enthusiasm for the landed
aristocracy as a reaction to Labour Bolsheviks and philistine
businessmen politicians. (He cited an approach for him to stand as
candidate from the miners of Clay Cross as evidence for this view.)[28]
Otherwise, public opinion was something that party organizers could
confidently measure as information filtered through from the grass

roots. More schematic aids such as Addison's suggestion that Lloyd George create a 'policy section' in his private secretariat to assess the moods of the public were not followed up. Like everyone else, the party managers wanted 'normalcy' and 'business as usual' now that peace had returned. The existence of a Coalition government that claimed to reflect a united nation in a fundamentally novel fashion did not disturb the comfortable, prescriptive world of the known.

And yet, if men inquired at all into the character of British society after the war, and its implications for political life, it was recognized as axiomatic that profound changes had taken place. Social and cultural standards had been transformed. Sexual and generational barriers had fallen: with a surplus of bachelors in the age structure, it was 'a gay world' reported a correspondent of *The Times*.[29] Traditional social divisions, those between town and country, church and chapel, Anglo-Saxon and Celt, paled in significance when measured against the economic upheavals of wartime. As a result, Britain, it was universally agreed, was a less deferential society with the focuses of authority harder to locate, even in the more static rural areas of the nation.

The dominance of 'land' or a 'landed interest' in shaping the fabric of society was clearly receding into a distant past. Ownership of land was less of a social or an economic asset. Partly as a result of high taxation of wartime, partly of short-term factors such as the incentives offered by the changes in land valuation included in the 1919 budget, great estates broke up all over England and Wales. Landowners took advantage of favourable short-term conditions in a booming land market to sell up their holdings in what Professor F. M. L. Thompson has called the greatest upheaval in land ownership since the Norman conquest. About a quarter of England was believed to have changed ownership in the period 1918–22: 'England is changing hands', exclaimed *The Times*.[30] By 1925, the 'green revolution' had created a large new class of occupying freeholders, farmers who often found that with mortgages and growing indebtedness through a collapse in prices, they were more helpless under the sway of the banks than they had ever been during the relatively benevolent ascendancy of the private landlords. The authority of great landowners was much less imposing than it had been before the war. It was noticeable that landowners were excluded from the Royal Commission appointed in July 1919 to investigate agricultural prices, whereas tenant farmers and agricultural labourers' representatives such as George Dallas were prominent among its members. The relationship of land to politics had changed markedly, too. After 1918, the importance of landed wealth as a force to bind together the Conservative vote and to provoke agrarian radicals was clearly diminishing. Lloyd George's rural rhetoric, charged with class hostility towards the landlords before 1914, was now increasingly economic rather than social in emphasis. He now dwelt on the need to assist farmers with long-term credit and incentives to aid productivity—and to create new tenants through land acquisition and settlement. The repeal of the land duties of 1909 in Austen Chamberlain's budget of 1920—an uncontroversial measure since these duties had yielded no revenue in ten years—was a portent of a new era. It was the unity of agricultural society, as a productive economic concern, not its class divisions, that was now emphasized. This change affected urban land as well as rural. By the mid-1920s, the major threat to the healthy development of inner-city districts seemed to lie, not in the old absentee landlord whom radicals had denounced for generations past, but rather in speculative property-development companies. The enemy now was faceless, and all the more frightening for that.

The Unionist Party was profoundly affected by these changes. No longer was it sensitively attuned to the 'feudal' Toryism of the land-owner, of which squires like Walter Long or Henry Chaplin (both active in politics after 1918) had been the prototype. Larger landowners now looked askance at the growing influence of the National Farmers' Union, which represented occupying tenant farmers and favoured such proposals as security for capital and substantial compensation for disturbance or eviction. This led to divided counsels in the face of the government's varied agricultural policies after 1918. Unionist spokesmen for agricultural interests, men such as Pretyman, Lane-Fox, or Terrell, were not happy with the continuation of the 1917 Corn Production Act after the war. It had brought government control in the fixing of farm prices and the pushing up of labourers' wages through county Wages Boards. The 1920 Agricultural Amendment Act, which continued the wartime guarantee for wheat and oats prices, was suspect as being an arrangement between the government and the NFU, and was amended in the Lords after pressure by landowners. There was also a widespread outcry about the operations of the Wages Boards with all the red tape involved. On the other hand, when the government, quite without warning, reversed its policies completely in June–July 1921 and repealed Part I of the Agriculture Acts, which guaranteed wheat and oats prices, and fixed labourers' wages, the landed interest generally felt bereft, if not betrayed. A famous pamphlet referred to *The Great Betrayal*. Whatever landowners and farmers felt about bureaucratic controls on agriculture, the unilateral nature of the government's change of policy came as a great shock. At the time, very few Unionists MPs 'from farming backgrounds protested—only a handful like Cavendish-Bentinck and Thomas Davies, from Nottinghamshire and Gloucestershire respectively, together with Milnerites like Waldorf Astor who tried to rescue the Wages Boards on social grounds. The Commons Agricultural Committee, chaired by Captain Fitzroy (Daventry), remained mutely compliant. But by the end of 1921, it was obvious that the repeal of the Agriculture Acts had vastly increased the problems of farmers who had bought new land, entered into new contracts, and introduced new courses of cropping in the expectation of guaranteed high prices, and now saw the price of land and of farm produce collapse. Coalitionists who argued that decontrol must apply as much to wheat farmers as to the coal mines were denounced. By mid-1922, talk of 'betrayal' and of a farmers' revolt against the Unionist leadership comparable with 1846 was widespread. The hapless Griffith-Boscawen, an accident-prone Minister of Agriculture from February 1921, had to defend a policy which he himself admitted to be a 'terrible reversal', even if justifiable on financial grounds. It was not surprising that he was one of the Cabinet ministers to lead the push for Tory independence in October 1922.

Quite apart from the wide social implications of the loss of authority and the economic decline of the landed interest, the political impact of the 'betrayal' was considerable, especially for the Unionists. It was noted how few leading figures in the party stood up to defend the interests either of the landowner or the tenant farmer. Milner, that long-time imperialist advocate of 'efficiency' in food production, was a rare exception—and he left the government early in 1921. Bonar Law had no interest in agricultural problems, and Austen Chamberlain was little improvement. Nationally, the Unionist Party now derived its mass support and finance, not from the broad acres of England, certainly not from wheat-growing districts such as East Anglia, but from middle-class suburbia, and from business, manufacturing, and commercial interests whose political passions were fired by the menace of socialism in industrial areas. The landed interest felt isolated. To some degree, the rise of 'independent Conservatism' in opposition to the Coalition government in 1921–2 was an aristocratic reaction, the response of the Salisburys, the Selbornes, and the Devonshires to the passing of ancient patterns of deference, control, and stability. Even the 'landed interest' now seemed to be represented less by traditional landowners than by the quasi-collectivist National Farmers' Union, with its enthusiasm for wartime controls. Older landed proprietors, symbols of an organic society, infused with a High Anglican sense of Christian obligation, abused the Coalition and *arriviste*, vulgar leaders such as Lloyd George, Horne, or Birkenhead for the sake of the deferential world they felt they had lost.[31]

Religious deference also counted for much less after the war. The pre-1914 world when the pronouncements of Anglican bishops and nonconformist ministers could sway political multitudes, when the Commons could be paralysed into crisis over such issues as the 'right of entry' into provided schools in the early morning or the status of churchyards and chapels-of-ease, seemed now extraordinarily remote. The passage of the disestablishment of the church in Wales in August 1919 was typical of this change. Until the war, some Conservatives had thought this proposal even more disastrous and certainly more sacrilegious than even Irish home rule. Lord Robert Cecil, ever the individualist, resigned from the government on this very issue just before the 'coupon election'. In practice, Lloyd George returned from Versailles, and fudged up a settlement of disendowment in a fortnight, with the generous allocation of £1m to the Welsh church to cover the loss of vested interests during the war. Shortt, the Home Secretary, had little knowledge of the disendowment measure he was to introduce hours before he rose to address the House.[32] There were a few partisan zealots—nonconformists in Wales who felt that the church was being offered compensation for its previous possession of 'national' property such as tithe; churchmen like Samuel Hoare who still talked of plunder.[33] Nobody much cared: Lloyd George soon whisked it through. A year later he attended the enthronement of his old antagonist and comrade in intrigue, the Bishop of St. Asaph, as the first Archbishop of Wales. Religious education and tithe were largely dead issues, too. On the other hand, it was noticeable that the removal of purely sectarian questions did not make the Church of England any more outspoken or courageous in giving a moral lead on wider public issues. Indeed, Randall Davidson, the Archbishop of Canterbury, seemed more subject to dictation by the Erastian, secular authorities than ever. He was noticeably coy in giving a lead in denouncing the outrages and atrocities committed in Ireland under the aegis of the British government. Haldane thought him 'a Georgite by necessity'.[34] Only a few mavericks, led by Charles Gore, the Anglo-Catholic Bishop of Oxford, inspired protests in the newspapers and put pressure on MPs in protesting against British policy in Ireland. Nor did the labour troubles of these embattled years extract more than token comments from church leaders. In general, the impact of the Church of England upon politics was testimony to a narrowing constituency and a muffled message. Most Englishmen perhaps regarded it, as Churchill described the function of a flying buttress. They supported the church, but from the outside.

Nor was nonconformity any more influential or outspoken. Indeed, the period 1919–22 may be taken as that when the nonconformist impact on politics was finally seen to be sporadic and ineffectual. The free churches had been greatly disturbed by the impact of war. In general, the majority, taking their cue from Robertson Nicoll in the *British Weekly*, supported the war as a Christian cause. Rebels and pacifists such as the Fellowship of Reconciliation were ostracized by congregations and expelled by golf clubs. In 1919 the government was headed by the greatest champion of nonconformity that the age had produced, a man on intimate terms with Horton, Shakespeare, Scott Lidgett, Elvet Lewis, a man who paraded his devotion and his secure family life in Sunday morning attendances at Castle Street Welsh Baptist church near to Oxford Circus. The fact that its minister was a known socialist did not appear to mar the harmony of these occasions.[35] Not for nothing did the *Baptist Times* join with the *British Weekly* in endorsing the Coalition at the election in 1918. In many ways it was a government of nonconformists, with Unionists such as Law, Chamberlain, and Birkenhead of free church background and many nonconformists among the Liberal ministers. But this hardly mattered now as the government did little to satisfy nonconformist opinion on either of the key issues, temperance or education. Fisher caused much offence in Wales by refusing to endorse the Welsh Licensing Bill, a private members' measure, in March 1920. 'It was the only tactless speech I ever heard him make,' reflected his loyal

lieutenant, Herbert Lewis. The government did provide some help
when the bill was reintroduced in the 1921 session. With the assistance of Lloyd George in the Commons, and (ironically enough) Lord
Birkenhead in the Lords who frustrated Lord Plymouth's attempts to
obtain a referendum, the Welsh Licensing Bill received the royal
assent in August 1921. Its main provision was that Sunday Closing
was extended to Monmouthshire—which almost certainly helped lose
the Newport by-election for the Coalition in October 1922.[36] It did
little to assuage feelings of political inadequacy amongst nonconformist Liberals. On the critical question of Ireland, the nonconformist
conscience was hardly more outspoken than was the Anglican. When
the National Free Church Council did pronounce in March 1921, it
was mainly to denounce the 'terrorism' of the IRA and to express the
hope that the government would achieve a settlement 'consistent with
the spirit of Christ'. It was noticeable that the protests against the
'retaliation' policy in Ireland was largely secular in origin. Nonconformity after 1918 was clearly suffering from a crisis in morale, and
perhaps in identity, unable to focus on specific issues or to decide
unequivocally whether it remained loyal to the Baptist Prime Minister
or threw in its lot with the Wee Frees or Labour.

There were some signs that, even in Wales, free churchmen,
especially the Independents, 'the most political and republican of the
sects,' were in revolt against the government. In the by-election in
Cardiganshire in February 1921, in the Prime Minister's own pat-
rimony, Llewelyn Williams, a sworn enemy of the Prime Minister
since the introduction of conscription, polled over 11,000 votes in this
Welsh-speaking, Methodist-dominated county. It was urban voters,
seaside landladies and the like, who denied him victory. Chapels, even
families, were rent with savage quarrels for a generation to come.[37]
But here again nonconformists were being swept along by political
opinion, rather than leading it. In industrial areas it was reported that
Anglicans and free churchmen felt it their duty to incline publicly to
Labour so as to exert their spiritual authority in keeping working men
and women in the church. 'No nonconformist minister in these industrial constituencies dares nowadays to take the chair at a Liberal
meeting.' Many ministers openly supported D. R. Grenfell in the
Gower by-election in 1922 even though he admitted he adhered to no
Christian church.[38] Above all, nonconformists were paralysed by the
schism in the Liberal Party which made their impact on opinion in the

press or in by-elections all the more ineffective. There was the rare courageous protest from the veteran Dr. John Clifford—but he had joined the ILP many years before. It was noticeable that nonconformist conventions to promote temperance or some other worthy cause would often have Arthur Henderson or Philip Snowden as their leading speaker.

Religion, then, no more than land, dictated the course or the priorities of political debate. Another declining force by 1919 was the emphasis on non-English nationalism as a factor to shore up the Liberal vote and evoke the fury of Unionists and English patriots. Irish nationalism after 1918 was clearly an external, Irish problem. Memories of Parnell, the immediate impact of the 'troubles' in Ireland, and the rise of Sinn Fein continued to sway voters in Lancashire constituencies. In Liverpool, T. P. O'Connor still held on to the Scotland seat he had held virtually without challenge since 1885. In 1929 he was succeeded by another Irishman, David Logan, though one who took the Labour whip and who remained the MP for Scotland until 1962. In the Stockport by-election of March 1920, William O'Brien of the Irish TUC, temporarily resident in Wormwood Scrubs, ran as a Nationalist candidate and polled over 2,300 votes. Joe Devlin ran for another Liverpool seat, Exchange, in the 1922 election. Otherwise, Irish nationalism became effectively detached from British party political experience by the progress of Sinn Fein and its zeal to exclude itself as decisively as possible from the other parties. Everywhere, Irish working-class voters moved in large numbers to support the Labour Party. This was the more pronounced after the Labour Party's report, written by Arthur Greenwood early in 1921, which was scathingly critical of British policy in Ireland and which strongly endorsed Irish self-government. In many industrial constituencies in England, Wales, and Scotland a new Labour–Irish alliance was constructed. T. P. O'Connor urged Irish voters in Spen Valley to vote Labour; as a reward, he was to receive a Privy Councillorship from the first Labour government in 1924. In Glasgow, Irish Catholic strength was fundamental to the growth of the Labour Party and the return of the militant ILP 'Clydesiders' in the election of 1922. Forty years later, Catholic Labour voters in Glasgow and the Clyde region were the surest bulwark against a basically Protestant Scottish National Party. Irish particularism had become a prop for the Union and an ally in the British class struggle.

As for Scotland and Wales, their sub-nationalisms were extin-
guished by the centralizing imperatives of war and the assimilation of
their institutions in the London-based system. Scottish nationalism
had not been much of a factor in Edwardian politics. The Secretary-
ship of State had been gained, back in 1885, while it was clear that
Scottish Liberals were as divided by the issue of church disestablishment as Welsh Liberals were united by it. Scotland had retained its
own distinctive legal, religious, and educational institutions since the
Act of Union. There seemed little reason to press for governmental
separation, nor was Labour's theoretical commitment to 'home rule
all round' in its manifesto in 1918 taken very seriously. The Speaker's
conference in 1919 effectively killed off devolution as a major issue for
the next fifty years. In practice, the more nationally-minded Scots
often followed Maxton into the sectarianism of the ILP, while Labour
Head Office exerted its powerful influence against local separatism.
Alternatively they supported the cultural nationalism of poets like
Hugh MacDiarmid and his 'Scottish Renaissance'. The Scottish
National Party, founded in 1928, three years after Plaid Cymru in
Wales, was a feeble alternative to pre-1914 Scottish national politics,
and remained so for almost forty more years.[30]

Welsh nationalism had been far more buoyant than Scottish in
1914, and closely linked with the progress of the Liberal Party and of
Lloyd George in particular. The emergence of Lloyd George as Prime
Minister showed how limited this type of nationalism really was. In
1918 Wales was content with its place in the sun, national and imperial. Its sense of inferiority was finally erased by the presence of a kind
of Welsh Mafia in the Prime Minister's private entourage and Cabinet
secretariat—Welsh and in a good many cases Welsh-speaking as well.
The old Welsh national issues, disestablishment, land reform, temperance, church schools, were dead or dying. They perished with the
society, dominated by the rector and the squire, that gave them birth.
Welsh home rule attracted little attention. Endless conferences at
baroque hotels in Llandrindod Wells produced nothing more than
pious resolutions. Idealistic journals such as *Welsh Outlook*, founded
by Thomas Jones amongst others, disseminated their mildly
nationalistic gospel in an apathetic environment. After 1919, Wales
like Scotland rapidly moved to become a stronghold of the Labour
Party, which proclaimed the solidarity of the trade union movement
and of the working class in all nations. Keir Hardie's early nationalism

was forgotten by the Welsh Labour Party (and not resurrected until the 1960s). Lloyd George encouraged his fellow Welsh members to turn their attention to a Welsh Secretary of State—'go for the big thing'[40]—knowing full well that this was a dead cause, and had been since 1892. One of the last of the pre-war home rulers, E. T. John, erstwhile anti-conscriptionist and former Liberal member for east Denbighshire, spent his energy in campaigning in various hopeless rural seats as a Labour–Welsh home rule candidate. Along with Lloyd George's old journalistic colleague at Caernarvon, Beriah Gwynfe Evans, he sought to become the 'de Valera of Wales'[41] just as Tom Ellis had allegedly been its Parnell in the past. John, with all his earnestness, was a survivor from a past age. The 'little Bethel' world of 'Wales for the Welsh', which Hardie's *Merthyr Pioneer* had derided before 1914 was passing away.[42] Apart from a few university intellectuals and literati (who were to found Plaid Cymru in 1925) the fate of Welsh culture or of a Welsh language admittedly under severe pressure failed to stimulate the kind of concern that the older sectarian and class politics had done. The conclusion must be that, for Ireland, Scotland, and Wales, Celtic nationalism, along with the land and religion, had lost its capacity to dominate or significantly affect political alignments. If there was one unifying issue now, it was that transformation in the capitalist structure, well under way since the 1890s, completed by the war, which had divided people and communities in terms of class rather than of traditionalist sectionalists. It was class with which the Coalition had to come to terms; outside Ireland, they were all Unionists now. Whether class-based politics would prove to be less deferential or tolerant of authority than the older style of politics had been was an open question then and later.

The focusing of class affiliations upon specific issues after 1918 was difficult to assess. Public opinion in the new post-war world was subject to shifting crystallization and dissolution, as the colourful story of by-elections in the period shows. The degree of political commitment, however, as opposed to the commitment to economic interest embodied in trade unions or employers' organizations, was hard to ascertain. All observers agreed that the electors after 1918 were anything but politically apathetic. Polls in by-elections were frequently high, often over 70 per cent in industrial constituencies in the North of England or Wales where Labour posed a strong challenge, or where there were well-publicized independents such as the

Bottomley candidates in the two by-elections at the Wrekin in 1920. There was a poll of 82.3 per cent at Ashton-under-Lyne in January 1920, perhaps in part because the victorious Unionist, Sir Walter de Frece, received the active support of his wife, the music-hall celebrity, Vesta Tilley. Polls of over 80 per cent were recorded at key by-elections at Wolverhampton West and Cambridge in March 1922. Newspapers, whether 'quality' or popular, contained a much greater quantity of political material after 1918 than they were to do after 1945. But the direction and import of this intense political interest was far harder to determine.

One phenomenon of the post-war period that contemporaries often noted was the relative feebleness of local party organization, even some considerable time after the political vacuum created by the electoral truce of wartime. This was, of course, most marked in the Liberal Party as a result of the schism of 1918. Local Liberal associations became enfeebled, as did the organization of the party for fighting local elections; indeed between 1919 and 1922 a consistent feature of county and municipal elections is the collapse of the Liberal performance. In London, which the Progressives had controlled from 1889 to 1907, only a small rump of Progressives kept the old flag flying.[43] The great majority of local Liberal associations outside Wales remained faithful to Asquith, but they were felt to be middle-class and elderly, and lacking in life. In seats held by the Coalition Liberals, local organization was even more sketchy. Younger was told of how in Spen Valley, Dartford, and South Norfolk in 1919–20, the local associations had selected Independent Liberals as candidates, leaving the Coaly Libs with no organization of their own.[44] Coalition agents were especially hard to retain, since many of them feared for their pension rights after the split in their party.[45] Instead of relying on local grass-roots involvement, the Coalition Liberals tended to rely on the stimulus of their high command, ministers being dispatched from Whitehall into the constituencies, or alternatively the organization being supplied by Evan R. Davies or other members of the Downing Street secretariat. 'They arrive, spend money lavishly, but cut little ice.'[46]

The Unionist Party ought to have been in much more flourishing condition. After all, the 1918 Redistribution Act had created at least seventy safe Conservative seats in middle-class areas of the home counties and elsewhere. But Unionist organization, on which Coali-

tion Liberal candidates in by-elections had frequently to depend, had
necessarily run down in seats where a Liberal was given the 'coupon'
in 1918. Even in January 1922, concern that local party organization
was patchy and had largely disappeared in some areas underlay the
fears of Unionist party managers that an early general election would
be harmful to their cause. There was acute difficulty for Sir George
Younger in raising local party funds. Dr. Ramsden has written that
'the post-war Coalition did far more damage to the [Unionist] Party
than the war itself'.[47] The successive rebellions among constituency
Unionists in 1921–2 against the attachment of their party leaders to
Lloyd George's Coalition often took place quite outside the formal
organization of the local party, through Anti-Waste organizations or
ad hoc independent groups. In any case, local Unionists, like the
Liberals, were suffering from withdrawal symptoms, after the suppression of time-honoured causes like tariff reform, Irish home rule,
or (a theme particularly favoured amongst Unionists in the country)
revision of the powers of the House of Lords. Party organizers loudly
complained of 'middle class apathy'.

The Labour Party showed by far the greatest signs of vitality and
grass-roots enthusiasm in politics after 1918. Fisher noted how a
Labour by-election candidate could inspire a passion and a zeal for
self-sacrifice that the older parties could not begin to emulate.[48] But in
most of Labour's new strongholds, it was the trade unions rather than
the embryonic constituency or divisional Labour parties which provided the organizational core. For Labour at the grass roots, organization was largely a function of class. In rural constituencies, Labour
was inevitably weak. It was not much nearer to penetrating this
unfamiliar terrain four years after the end of the war, despite the
encouragement of winning agricultural labourers' votes in abundance
in the South Norfolk by-election in July 1920. In urban areas,
Labour was often ill-equipped for combat. In London, especially,
local Labour parties were hard to organize, and Herbert Morrison as
London organizer had an uphill task.[49] Labour's disappointing results
in London in the 1922 election showed how arduous was the road that
still lay ahead. In Birmingham, Liverpool, and Edinburgh, things
were not better. More than the other parties, Labour was able to
embody widespread, if often inarticulate, popular concern for a wide
range of social and economic issues in the political world of 1919–22.
But it had yet to take the form of mass participation in local or national

party politics, or in unambiguous commitment to the political or constitutional method.

Political protest tended to express itself in this period more freely in independent pressure groups, which flourished as never before. There were one-cause bodies of a cross-party type such as the Peace with Ireland Council which drew wide support from a range of critics of the government's Irish policy. There were interest-based bodies such as the Middle Class Union, founded in 1920 under the somewhat unexpected leadership of Lord Askwith, to resist egalitarian pressures being imposed on the salaried professions, small traders, and the like. Lord Robert Cecil complained that it reflected narrow commercial and propertied concerns and took inadequate account of such wider moral themes as (inevitably) the League of Nations.[50] The Anti-Waste League, founded by Lord Rothermere in January 1921, through the medium of his *Sunday Pictorial*, was a classic pressure-group of the period, enlisting businessmen and right-wing groups of diverse kinds, particularly in south-east England and the home counties.[51] It was here, in Dover, Hertford, and the Abbey division of Westminster, that the three Anti-Waste gains in by-elections were registered in 1921. As dissatisfaction with the Coalition amongst the Unionist right wing gained momentum, formal party organization tended to retreat, and protest groups of this type proliferated. Instead of political parties forming the basis for such bodies as the Budget League and its opposing organization before the war, the formal party machines in mid-1921 seemed, at least on the Coalition side, to be almost a reflection of Anti-Waste and freelance irregulars of this type. It was here that effective protest against the government was initially marshalled and subsequently translated into back-bench parliamentary protest through such men as Gretton, Gwynne, and McNeill. On the anti-government side, Labour was in large measure an economic pressure group in political guise. The initiative was retained largely by the TUC, a nexus of separatist groups which claimed to represent the vast majority of the nation's working force and its families. The power of the TUC, both formally in labour disputes and through such spontaneous creations as the Council of Action formed to resist the dispatch of 'arms to Poland', was in itself the most powerful testimony to how fluid and rudderless politics had become, and how peculiarly irrelevant was much of the party-inspired rhetoric of the Guests, Youngers, and Hendersons.

Another symptom of the uncertainty of the times and the unpredictability of locating and interpreting 'public opinion' was the role of the newspaper press in politics at this period. Increasingly the press was viewed as a cohesive entity—the Press with a capital P, rather than a range of individual journals. During the war years, to some extent the press had supplied the missing ingredients of party debate and political conflict. It was in the press that the great crises of wartime politics—the 'shell scandal', the sacking of Robertson, the Maurice debate, and so forth—took place. Military journalists like Colonel Repington suddenly acquired the power to make or unmake governments, or so it seemed. Lloyd George came to power in December 1916 amidst an apparently concerted press campaign, with Northcliffe, proprietor of *The Times* and the then editor, Geoffrey Robinson, as orchestrators-in-chief. Much attention was paid to the political role of press lords such as Northcliffe, Beaverbrook, and Rothermere in the 1917–18 period. The presence of Lloyd George in Downing Street after 1918 ensured in itself that the press would remain a powerful factor in politics. Asquith could claim that the Coalition was a government in which power was shared almost 'equally between Parliament and the Press'. As is well known, the Prime Minister went to great lengths to maintain a favourable coverage in the press. He went to some lengths to conciliate proprietors like Beaverbrook and Rothermere; he still maintained close contact with Riddell of the *News of the World*. He was anxious to have the Coalition reported in the press in an extensive and favourable way, as an essential means of sustaining his personal communion with the people. In a sense, Lloyd George's four years in office between 1918–22 were one long press conference, anticipating Roosevelt's style during the New Deal. Public policy and public relations went hand in hand as never before. The Prime Minister's close confidant, Philip Kerr, went to manage the *Daily Chronicle* in May 1921, the one clearly pro-government daily Liberal newspaper which had been acquired in a *coup* in October 1918 after the intervention of Dalziel, Weir, and other pro-Lloyd George capitalists. As events turned out, the Independent Liberal *Daily News*, bitterly hostile to the government at the time of the 'coupon election', became more sympathetic to the administration after Stuart Hodgson succeeded A. G. Gardiner as editor in 1919.[52] The Prime Minister sought other outlets also, and told Sutherland to cultivate them. In September 1919 he secured a special number of the *Future*, the staid journal of the English-Speaking Union, as a pro-government tract. It provided a means of publicizing the government's domestic and international achievements during its first eight months in office. He remonstrated with his wife: 'Why should you object to the "Future"? Is it your notion that Ministers should stand to be shot at and spat upon by every rapscallion who has a grievance against them and that they should never reply? I have just had enough of that and I mean to put up a fight.' The *Future* featured articles by the Prime Minister and all his leading ministerial colleagues, depicted in glamorized terms as they explained the progress of reconstruction. It sold well, copies printed being increased from 1½ million to three million to meet demand.[53] The weekly, *Outlook*, was also purchased as a pro-government organ by Lord Lee of Fareham, the new Minister of Agriculture, in the spring of 1919. The climax of the government's publicity drive, from Lloyd George's point of view, came with the production of the *Lloyd George Liberal Magazine* in October 1920 to rival the *Liberal Magazine* and boost the premier and his party. But its very appearance was a sign of weakness. It followed the failure of 'fusion', the expulsion of the Coalition Liberals from their party at Leamington, and the consequently indeterminate position of the Coaly Libs in the political firmament. Its very existence, however, at least showed the centrality attached by the head of the government, an old press man himself since the days of the Welsh National Publishing Company at Caernarvon in 1887, to the power of the printed word.

In the post-war years, great proprietors seemed to sway multitudes. Indeed, people thought increasingly after 1918 in terms of great proprietors rather than of great editors as before 1914. The age of the powerful editor was passing away, as was the culture of the Victorian Liberal man of letters that sustained it for so long. Robert Donald, A. G. Gardiner, J. A. Spender, all left editorial posts during this period. Finally in 1923 H. W. Massingham left the *Nation* amidst fierce controversy over his pro-Labour sympathies.[54] The claims made by the press lords were ample ones at this time. Rothermere clearly felt that his newspapers, the *Daily Mail* and the *Sunday Pictorial*, could magnify his Anti-Waste League into a national force, especially as his son, young Esmond Harmsworth, sat in the House as Independent Unionist and Anti-Waste member for the Isle of Thanet from

November 1919. Rothermere declared that the Anti-Waste victories
in by-elections in 1921 were triumphs for his newspapers. Beaverbrook's claims for the *Daily Express* were scarcely less inflated. The
campaign by the *Express* to end the embargo on Canadian cattle was
blamed for the defeat of Griffith-Boscawen, the new Minister of
Agriculture, in a by-election in Dudley in March 1921 (on an 80 per
cent poll), even though Dudley was largely industrial and cared little
for Canadian or imperial interests. Elsewhere, there were still
powerful editors with influence to dispense. On the right-wing opposition side, the *Morning Post*, edited by the aberrant Welshman, H. A.
Gwynne, served as the focus for right-wing dissidence, in the absence
of any effective die-hard organization within the Unionist Party. J. L.
Garvin's *Observer*, owned by Waldorf Astor, a government minister in
1918–21, was a powerful voice for centrist Unionist opinion, usually
sympathetic to the Prime Minister save over Ireland. On the Liberal
side, Scott in the *Manchester Guardian* alternated between moral
disapproval of Lloyd George in the strictest Gladstonian terms and
sympathetic handling of a Liberal premier in whose radicalism Scott
still desperately believed. Lloyd George spent much time and effort in
conciliating each in turn. He had some success, and probably enjoyed
a better press than, for example, Austen Chamberlain who tended to
treat press communications with impatience or disdain. If the Prime
Minister's response was anything to go by, then 'public opinion' in
this period meant essentially press opinion. The climax was reached in
August 1922 when he made a serious effort via Rothermere to purchase *The Times* after Northcliffe's death. The idea was to have
Printing House Square in safe Coalition hands, perhaps with the
Prime Minister himself doubling his role as editor-in-chief.[55]

Yet it is the record of *The Times* that shows up the hollowness of the
claim of the press to represent the public mind. After the war, *The
Times*, under Northcliffe's command, became a more popular and
aggressive newspaper than before; Northcliffe's pretensions were far
removed from the stately world of Delane. To this end, under the
editorship of Wickham Steed, from early 1919 to November 1922,
The Times pursued a prolonged and virulent campaign against the
Prime Minister. While it had much to say about politics at home, it
concentrated on his foreign policy, Steed adopting a revanchist pro-
French standpoint, and a highly sensationalist style of presentation.
The climax was reached at the Genoa conference when Steed ran

clearly fallacious stories to suggest that the *entente* with France was being dismantled, and that Lloyd George had informed Barthou to this effect. A few months earlier, in January 1922, *The Times* had tried to maximize Anglo-French animosity at the time of the Washington talks on naval disarmament by suggesting that Lord Lee, the First Lord of the Admiralty, was improperly quoting from French government sources on the issue of French submarines. On Ireland, Steed, a zealot for small nations in the Balkans, strongly attacked the policy of reprisals, and called for a liberal settlement. In domestic matters, *The Times* was sternly 'anti-waste', featuring regular dirges about the mounting tale of public indebtedness and of rising government expenditure. At the time of the publication of the Geddes report in January 1922, it tried to suggest, quite inaccurately, that the government were trying to bury its findings in a miasma of Cabinet committees designed to avoid the recommended economies. On the whole, Steed's attacks misfired. At times, they reinforced a powerful mood of popular criticism of one or other of the Coalition's programmes. More often, by their very unfairness and unreliability, they drew attention to the instability of Northcliffe rather than the inadequacy of Lloyd George. When Northcliffe died in August 1922, he was clearly a beaten man, his dreams of public influence unfulfilled. He had found that national newspapers were increasingly valued for their news or their entertainment, rather than as purveyors of the vagrant opinions of their proprietors. The influence of the weeklies, fortnightlies, and monthlies which formed the domain of the Edwardian man of letters was equally in decline; many began to go out of circulation from 1920 onwards.[56] Editors felt that they were baying in the wilderness, with scant contact with or effect on the views of the population in general. H. W. Massingham of the *Nation* is a key exhibit here, with the relative failure of his concerted efforts to create a Liberal–Labour progressive front against the Coalition. His journal attracted some of the most facile and brilliant writers of the day. Masterman, Tomlinson, and Woolf among others graced his columns. But the effect was to bury the *Nation* along with many of the causes it espoused, and to hasten the day when it would be swallowed up by the socialist *New Statesman*. Massingham left amid general rancour in April 1923 after discovering that Hubert Henderson, a Cambridge economics don, had been appointed editor without his being informed. In general, the press and public opinion were clearly to be demarcated as different entities in 1919–22; attempts to merge them together inevitably failed because of the futility of the enterprise.

In this shifting, fluid world, then, men and women tried to interpret the essence of the popular mood and to harness it to buttress or assail the government. What, in its fundamentals, was this public to whose opinion politicians paid such religious deference? Was it simply middle-class opinion, to be rallied against the railway strikes or the threat from the Triple Alliance? Was it the opinion of the newly enfranchised working men and women? Was it the opinion of the possessing and propertied classes rallying to the call of constitutionalism, capitalism, and order? Was it still the Athenaeum, Oxbridge world of 'high politics' where Liberal intellectuals such as Gilbert Murray presided? Wherever public opinion originated, however whimsical its manifestations, most politicians felt certain where it should finally be secured in safe anchorage. Public opinion should above all be harnessed to the 'centre', to shore up that grand national consensus born out of the unity of wartime. Britain, it was agreed, had emerged still a profoundly united nation, its commitment to its institutions and its past reinforced by the 'patriotism' of war. It was still relatively free from those sectional, regional, or religious cleavages that tended to make less fortunate European states more ungovernable: the decline of Victorian anticlericalism and of Celtic nationalism emphasized the oneness of Britain. The genius of politics, it was felt, lay in trying to interpret this deep sense of unity in political terms, to purge excesses and extremism whether of the left or the right. 'Our appeal must always be to the moderate men and women in the nation—that great mass of citizens who lie between the two extremes. .... We shall decline to listen to the voice of either the reactionary or the revolutionary.'[57] From that quest for the centre, that attempt to attract the great mass of untutored opinion towards a newly conceived national mean, much of the dynamism and uniqueness of British politics between 1919 and 1922 derived.

7

The Quest for the Centre

In June 1920 the Cabinet broke off from a technical discussion to reflect in more abstract terms on its political and moral role. The conclusion was self-fulfilling and reassuring:

The only justification for the existence of the present form of Government was that it attempted to hold the balance evenly and fairly between all classes of the community. The Government must show that they were not in the hands of the working class, nor tied to the protection of the capitalists. Just as in its Russian policy the Government had fearlessly, and on an independent review of its merits, adopted a policy which was generally acceptable to the working classes, so in the question now under discussion, they should not hesitate to adopt the policy favoured by the commercial interests.[1]

Herein lay the core of the justification for the Coalition government. It epitomized the 'national' interest as opposed to the sectionalism of labour or business. This concept, though, took many and often confused forms. Sometimes, an organic view was taken, with the Coalition representing all the different interests and classes in the community fused into one, a secular perpetuation of the historic symbiosis of wartime, including Liberal, Unionist, and Socialist, or the essence of all three. Alternatively, society was viewed in more stratified terms, with the Coalition representing the 'centre' or the 'middle ground', a moderate, rational approach, progressive though not revolutionary, finding the mean on each question on its merits, despite the sectional harassment of the self-styled 'left' and 'right'. In the latter interpretation, the Coalition stood conventionally on the central ground, detached from extremist assaults on either side like Wellington at Quatre Bras, fighting off the onslaughts of both in the pursuit of national objectives without the arrival of any political Blucher to help it out. In the former view, by contrast—one much favoured by Lloyd George—the Coalition, instead of standing firm in resistance to 'the left' and 'right', somehow comprehended them both. It stood for a different order of politics from that hitherto known in Britain, a higher synthesis which transcended the mundane world of petty partisanship, a world which had disappeared or lost its moral validity with the advent of total war. Either way, the significance of Coalition was clear. It embodied the quest both for unity and for the centre. Its purpose was symbolized by the electoral partnership of Coalition Unionists and Coalition Liberals, with some fringe Labour/NDP backing, in the Cabinet and the Commons. It embodied unity of command as surely as did the partnership of Foch and Haig in the crisis of wartime. Unity of command now implied a higher, moral almost sacred, unity throughout the nation itself.

But the contradictions inherent in this vision of the 'centre' were brought out in this Cabinet discussion of June 1920 referred to above. The occasion for this self-congratulatory outburst was a Cabinet decision to reject any form of special taxation on the immense profits made during the war. The rejection of Labour's proposals for a capital levy was, of course, no surprise. But even the modified version offered by the Board of Inland Revenue, headed by the distinctly non-socialist, John Anderson, was turned down. This scheme advocated a graduated scale which would apply to incomes of upwards of £25,000 and would include valuations of wealth for June 1914 and for June 1918, with appropriate abatements. It was expected to raise £500m over twelve years. In mitigation, the scale of Excess Profits Duty would be reduced. But it was reported to the Cabinet by Horne that the financial and business community were totally opposed to any kind of levy on wartime profits which, it was felt, would severely damage business confidence and the willingness to invest. Austen Chamberlain, who had with great reluctance acceded to the appointment of the Select Committee on Wartime Wealth, under the chairmanship of Sir William Pearce, earlier in the year, vehemently supported this view.[2] Already, then, unity was becoming synonymous with capitalism. The demands of ex-servicemen and of millions of trade unionists, who were confronted with wage cuts while the massive war profits remained untouched, were set aside in the interests of the 'centre' as identified with anti-socialism and anti-egalitarianism. Whatever the willingness of the Coalition to seek a middle ground in collective bargaining, in its colonial policy, and in foreign policy crises such as the Polish question, as far as any challenge to the basic economic fabric and the distribution of wealth went, the Coalition's 'moderation' was other men's conservatism. Even at the top, this change of emphasis was noted. Lloyd George, Riddell observed, now sang the praises of self-made businessmen and captains of industry: 'One Leverhulme or Ellerman is worth more to the world than say . . . 20,000 engine drivers and should be remunerated accordingly.' Socialism to him was the supreme and ever-present danger. 'His point of view has entirely changed.'[3]

Nevertheless, the initial impulse for discovering where 'the centre' lay and yoking it inextricably to the fortunes of the Lloyd George Coalition was a basic fact of life in the politics of the post-armistice period, one taken exceptionally seriously. It is difficult now, in a period when party conflict appears uniquely to mould political behaviour, to penetrate the mind of those after 1918 who supported the Coalition in the genuine belief that they were renewing that higher unity embodied by those who had fought in the trenches, and who felt therefore that a return to party warfare would be a betrayal of those who had made the supreme sacrifice during the war. For them, the 'coupon' enshrined an ultimate morality. Of course, in so many later accounts, the political arrangements which accompanied the transition from war to peace in 1918–19 have been denounced as a kind of corrupt bargain, in which the 'hard-faced' realists outgunned the moralists and idealists, from Lord Robert Cecil to George Lansbury. Here as elsewhere, the discussion has taken an Asquithian turn. The Wee Frees have triumphed in the pages of authors from J. A. Spender to Trevor Wilson in inverse ratio to their collapse as a major force in practical politics. The Asquithians have played the Greeks to the Coalitionists' Romans—or perhaps Turks would be a better analogy. It is worth spelling out, though, that there were many different kinds of pressure, perfectly reputable and with a broad measure of support, which in 1919–20 sought not only to sustain the Coalition but to make it the permanent foundation of a new kind of political order.

Naturally, it is in the ranks of the victors that these impulses were most apparent. The Cabinet that Lloyd George formed in January 1919 was genuinely fired by a conviction that party controversy was out-moded and that the government's programmes, seeking for a middle way between socialists and die-hards, represented a viable and valid consensus acceptable to men and women of goodwill. Lloyd George's Cabinet, in fact, was an exceptionally united one. Including, as it did, proud, autocratic, strong-willed figures like Churchill, Cur-

zon, Milner, and Montagu, side by side with more pliable men like
Shortt, Macnamara, Greenwood, or Lee of Fareham ('Lloyd George's
family', Curzon called them[4]), it conducted its operations in a remarkably harmonious fashion in which the party bickerings of the past
were subsumed. There were continuing sources of inter-party
difficulty, notably over the exact nature and scale of the inroads to be
made into free trade. Everyone agreed there should be some, and that
McKenna and Runciman, Gladstonians both, had made substantial
modifications of the tariff system during the war. But the precise
content of legislation on anti-dumping and the protection of 'key'
industries caused much difficulty in the government from the autumn
of 1919 onwards. However, too much can be made of issues of this
kind. Lloyd George was probably justified in discounting the
significance of anti-dumping as a major political issue. 'I think you
will hear very little more of that,' he told Scott. 'It has to be postponed
because it was part of the bargain.'[5] On the main lines of policy, even
in the face of unprecedented problems about labour, finance, Ireland,
and foreign affairs, the Cabinet's inner coherence compares favourably with that of most British governments during the course of the
present century. Sir Robert Horne was justified in claiming in
November 1921 that the Cabinet was a truly united force, and that
party labels carried little significance in the treatment of policies.[5] It
was, wrote Griffith-Boscawen later, 'really a happy family'.[6] What the
Coalition might lead to was unclear in 1919, but even Bonar Law had
looked forward with some equanimity to Lloyd George's possibly
becoming leader of the Unionist party as the natural consequence of
the alliance of wartime. The general assumption seemed to be that the
Coalition would continue in being, that the partnership of the Liberals
and Unionists within it (Labour was discounted at an early stage)
would become more and more intimate, and that this might lead to
some kind of fusion at the constituency level and perhaps all the way
up to the summit of politics.

This enthusiasm for the idea of unity, embodied in what was
thought to be a moderate, centrist-minded government, was certainly
shared in the House of Commons. In April 1919, a New Members'
Coalition Group was formed, and remained in being until the
government fell in October 1922.[7] Although it consisted mainly of
Unionists, a Coalition Liberal, Oscar Guest, the brother of the Liberal
chief whip, was elected chairman. Two young back-benchers, both

fresh from the trenches and fired with the ideals of wartime unity, were chosen as secretaries—Oswald Mosley, an aristocratic young Conservative, and Colin Coote, a Coalition Liberal. Their idealism was genuine; they were no mere time-servers. Later generations, Sir Colin Coote has recalled, 'may not now recall how few we survivors from the infantry of the Great War were and how absolute was our determination to see that our generation had not died in vain. What is now a cliché was then a faith, intensely held and swiftly frustrated.'[8] These Coalitionist back-benchers formed a powerful pressure-group urging 'fusion' upon the party whips in 1919–20. Colonel Walter Elliott, an able young Clydeside Unionist, was one powerful advocate of 'a permanent Coalition Party'. As a student at Glasgow, he had been a member of the Fabian Society. Trained as a medical doctor, he was a warm supporter of the Ministry of Health and Addison's housing programme. Not only had the Coalition, he believed, achieved much progressive legislation at home in the 1919 session. More generally he felt that Coalition must become a permanent feature of the British way of life, as of the Australian, with economic forces replacing political as the dominant features in contemporary society, and all the instability that this brought with it.[9] Another Unionist, Kingsley Wood, a Methodist solicitor, with experience of wartime housing and land schemes, felt that the Coalition symbolized the mass urge for social improvement. This was in the interest not only of the community as a whole. It was also in the interests of Conservatives, since the suppression of Liberal Unionism by 'Salisburyism' in the party after 1902 had led directly to the electoral débâcle of 1906.[10] Sir Ernest Wild, a celebrated lawyer (later notorious as counsel for Horatio Bottomley) and Unionist member for an East End constituency, went further. The Coalition, he maintained, was a lasting combination of idealistic men and women, not a temporary expedient. It had its moral imperatives, and even its 'soul', embodied by Lloyd George, a 'prodigy among statesmen'.[11]

On the Liberal side, too, there were forceful advocates for a permanent coalition. O. F. Maclagan, 'uncouponed' Liberal candidate for Rugby in the 1918 election and now an ardent Lloyd Georgian, equated the Coalition government with 'the broadest and truest Christianity'. It was the domestic equivalent of the League of Nations, of which Maclagan himself was a fervent partisan.[12] At a more powerful level in Coalition Liberal circles, Charles McCurdy, the chief whip from March 1921, produced an historical exegesis, designed to prove that, at least since 1886, the old forms of party conflict had eroded and that coalition had increasingly become the norm for British political life. The true enemy lay not in Coalition but in Caucus, which divided the national energies and shackled the national genius. Sir Herbert Lewis, Fisher's Under-Secretary at the Board of Education, a political ally of Lloyd George's in Wales since 1892 and a public figure of total integrity, saw in the Coalition the embodiment of 'the spirit of accommodation'. 'Party', in Lewis's words, 'would rather have no bread than half a loaf.'[13] Sir Gordon Hewart, the Attorney-General, favoured a more philosophical approach which relied, in its defence of the Coalition, partly on quotations from that classic Liberal text, John Morley's *Compromise*.[14]

These voices had their supporters in the press and elsewhere. Editors like Garvin, political ideologues like Philip Kerr, regarded a more permanent and more perfect union as the spiritual as well as the practical answer to the divisive pressures of post-war Britain. The problem, of course, was that these voices had no mass organization. All they could supply in grass-roots terms were the traditional mechanisms of Unionist and Liberal organization. These were necessarily conceived in pre-war terms to fight a pre-war party battle: Unionist Central Office clearly reflected this ethos, while Coalition Liberal headquarters was a small splinter-group from Abingdon Street. Without a national machinery to underpin the Coalition, all the way from Downing Street to ward level, the Coalition would remain on the level of rhetoric and abstraction. Its various challengers, Liberals, Labour, independent Unionists above all, would appear increasingly credible and gain in public standing accordingly.

In the period after the conclusion of the Versailles peace treaty in July 1919, a series of moves took place to try to form a centrist-type Coalition in more durable form. The major impulse had to come from the Prime Minister. His impact on the home front had been minimal during the months of the peace talks in Paris. 'He had practically disappeared from domestic politics,' wrote a pro-government journal.[15] Even after the Versailles treaty had been concluded, his quasi-presidential detachment remained very marked. He attended parliament twice a week for Prime Minister's question time. He would make the occasional weighty pronouncement in the Commons or in some other London venue on labour or foreign policy issues. But *The Times* commented, not altogether unfairly, 'If Mr. Lloyd George sat in the House of Lords as Lord Criccieth or Deauville, Parliament would hear him oftener than it does.'[16] Lloyd George's Olympian isolation from the day-to-day skirmishings of politics, which he left to the whips and to Bonar Law, only fired his zeal anew for extending the life of the Coalition and transforming its character. His dedication, present even during the 'coupon election', now became more and more evident, to turn the Coalition government into a coalition party. This, symbolized in the idea of 'fusion', was his essential political objective over the next few months.

In a discussion with Lord Riddell, Lloyd George discussed three possible courses of action in the light of the losses the Coalition had sustained in by-elections from West Leyton to Spen Valley.[17] Only one can have been seriously considered. The first was retirement after fourteen exhausting years in high office. This was unthinkable for one of Lloyd George's confidence in his own unique capacity to master the problems confronting Britain and Europe. He constantly insisted on his sound health and robust physique. The second was resignation in order to re-emerge as leader of the Coalition Liberals. This was equally unappealing. To cast oneself gratuitously as the head of the minority group in the Coalition, which had little local organization and was losing seats in by-elections, was also unthinkable. Liberalism of any variety, Lloyd George now professed, was outmoded, a dying creed. 'Liberal labels lead nowhere.' The third possible course was a genuine fusion between the two wings of the Coalition to give the government a more positive identity. 'No-one will take the Coalition brew.' That winter, he devoted much energy towards persuading his fellow Liberals in the government and in the country to break with their historic traditions and 'fuse' with the Unionists. 'National unity alone can save Britain, can save Europe, can save the world,' he declared to the Manchester Reform Club.[18] He described fusion as embodying the best of the old Liberalism. 'He had a good programme—Home Rule, Temperance, Purchase of Minerals, Security to Agricultural Tenant.' Even a name was proposed—'the United Reform Party'. H. A. L. Fisher was approached to draft the Liberal section of its programme, with Horne and Birkenhead to draft the Unionist part. But after this spate of bills was passed, 'there will have to be a period of administration'.[19] His emphasis now was on Liberalism as fossilized, a relic of the past, and on the need to transcend the Coalition since any reunion of the two Liberal sections was out of the question. At a meeting at Cobham on 4 February, Lloyd George presented these views to some leading Liberal ministers—Macnamara, Kellaway, Shortt, Munro, Addison, Fisher, Sutherland, Herbert Lewis, and Hewart. There was some resistance, especially from Fisher and Hewart, but this seemed of little consequence.[20] The logic of 'fusion' as the inevitable consequence of the train of events that had been launched in December 1916 seemed irresistible.

There was indigenous Coalition Liberal pressure for 'fusion' also, despite their divided counsels. In part, this was defensive, a response by the organizers to the fact that their political future without 'fusion' was a gloomy one. Increasingly, they were losing by-elections; increasingly, local Liberal associations were adopting Wee Frees as their prospective candidates, even in constituencies which had returned Coalitionists in the 'coupon election'. Spen Valley, where Colonel Fairfax came a poor third, well behind not only Labour but also Sir John Simon, the Asquithian, was the gravest warning yet. Without 'fusion', it seemed, the Coaly Libs would have no future any more than they had a past. Nor would they have any clearly guiding principles or priorities save in an arrangement which guaranteed both their client connection with Lloyd George and the aura of national unity that had presumably brought them into being. As an idea, 'Coalition Liberalism was in the air'.[21]

There were, however, more positive Liberal pressures also making for 'fusion'. The remarkable spate of legislation passed in the 1919 session bore a clear Liberal hallmark, especially with its emphasis on social reform. Many of the New Members' Group were Liberals as has been seen. To men such as Colin Coote or Oscar Guest or Leng Sturrock, or the Reverend Josiah Towyn Jones, the Coalition merely expressed in more durable form the traditional Liberal ethic of free enterprise and class harmony, an ethic under more severe challenge than ever before from an assertive socialism. The *Daily Chronicle*, a rather dull newspaper admittedly, was the vehicle for those holding such views, as were some local provincial Liberal newspapers such as the *South Wales News*. It was a Coalition Liberal, 'Politicus', who wrote the classic defence of the government's position under Sutherland's aegis, under the rather misleading title *Party not Faction*.[22] In the Cabinet, while most Liberal ministers were sceptical about the merits of 'fusion', and inclined to reflect on the sad fate of Joseph Chamberlain, there were two powerful voices calling insistently for 'fusion'.

Christopher Addison saw in 'fusion' the essential instrument for following up the collectivism of the war years and pushing on with a bold programme of social reconstruction such as he had himself initiated in health and housing. He pressed on Lloyd George the need for a central Coalition Whips' organization and a joint propaganda section to further communication between the Cabinet and the country. Then 'at the first opportune moment, the Party fusion that we have often discussed should be pressed on with a proper declaration of policy'.[23] Addison's motives for wanting 'fusion' were wholly positive. He believed that, with goading from himself and a few allies such as Fisher and Montagu, the Coalition was an agency for creative improvement. He believed further that Lloyd George was still essentially the man of 1911, the visionary populistic radical who had first brought Addison himself into front-line politics during the Insurance Bill crisis. The best of Labour and of Liberalism could be merged and taken several stages further. Nor, in the light of the early surge of social reform that the Coalition promoted, can Addison's views be said to be wholly unrealistic.

The other Liberal pressing for 'fusion' was Winston Churchill, the Secretary of State for War. His motives were largely negative. Significantly, where Addison proposed 'Reform' in the name of the new party, Churchill introduced the element of 'Constitution'.[24] For Churchill, the critical event in recent years had been not the end of war with Germany but the outbreak of Bolshevik revolution in Russia. It had gripped his mind obsessionally during the past twelve months, both in relation to aiding the Whites in the Russian civil war, and in using vigorous methods in warding off 'Bolshevik anarchy' during industrial unrest at home. For Churchill, 'fusion' signified order, constitutionalism, the class system, free enterprise with a human face. Its opponents, ranging from Philip Snowden to Lenin, were one and indivisible. His aggressive onslaughts on Labour, especially in a speech at Dundee in February where he first unveiled his oft-repeated opinion that Labour was 'unfit to govern',[25] demonstrated that to Churchill a constitutionalist centre party was a weapon to wage war on Labour. The rival approaches of Addison and Churchill, the social engineer and the class warrior, illustrated the conflicting elements in the Liberal mind. But at least they suggest that Coalition Liberal support for 'fusion' existed in some depth and variety.

The viewpoint of the Unionists, the dominant element in the Coalition, is less clear. The role of the leadership was obscure: Davidson told Baird that a stumbling block to the creation of a 'Central Party' which had recently been under discussion was to find a suitable position for Bonar Law.[26] At the level of the party managers and the Unionist whips, there is little doubt that 'fusion' was regarded as the enemy of that independent Conservative spirit which they existed to foster. Talbot, the Unionist chief whip, Younger, the party chairman, Fraser, the national agent, were adamant that Coalition and 'fusion' were clean different things. Coalition to them was a partnership, probably temporary, that left the party machinery in being and left the Tory ethic free to emerge again, open and independent. Talbot viewed with much suspicion any hint that the various supporters of the Coalition should even sit together as a block in the House, let alone that they should receive a joint whip.[27] Younger felt that 'the unreliability of L.G.' and 'the appalling entourage which infests Downing St.' were insuperable obstacles.[28] Even in 1919 pressures for a more assertive form of Unionism were building up. The extreme die-hard right, with its links with Page Croft's two-man National Party, could be safely disregarded. More dangerous was the emergence of a group of younger Unionists, Edward Wood, Samuel Hoare, William Ormsby-Gore, Hills, Lloyd-Greame, mainly from the party centre, critical of government policies both on industrial questions and on Ireland.[29]

Even so, a clear consensus was growing in the winter of 1919–20 amongst leading Unionists that 'fusion' was a political necessity even if not a particularly attractive one. Even Younger made some approving remarks in the London evening press. Baird felt that it was certain that 'L.G. will end with us'.[30] Senior ministers like Balfour regarded it as the creation of that organic unity for which the philosophy of Conservatism had always stood. Business-orientated ministers like Horne saw it as the mechanism for implementing the updated pragmatic social Toryism that dated from Disraeli and had been reinforced by the statism of the war years. Horne feared lest Tory right-wingers 'made it impossible for L.G. to stay with us'.[31] Lord Birkenhead, now emerging as a front-line political influence in the governmental firmament, enthusiastically proclaimed in a series of articles in the *Weekly Dispatch* the need for a 'national Party' to fight an anti-Bolshevik crusade. The Coalition as it existed at present was 'invertebrate and undefined'.[32] Above all, without much enthusiasm at first, 'fusion' was becoming more appealing to Bonar Law and Austen Chamberlain. At the very least, it would fill in organizational gaps in the constituencies. Logic and efficiency demanded electoral 'fusion': Bonar Law rallied party workers on 14 October 1919 to the vision of 'a permanently fused party'.[33] Indeed, 'fusion' was already being practised in the constituencies. In the by-election at Stockport in March 1920, Evan Davies, one of the Prime Minister's key private secretaries, acted as joint agent for both the Coalition candidates, Unionist and Liberal.[34] At the maximum, 'fusion' would rally constitutionalists everywhere to fight the trade unions and the 'so-called Labour Party'. In any case, without Lloyd George as a charismatic leader, the Unionist high command still felt apprehensive about facing the challenges of post-war politics after years of electoral truce. By March, Bonar Law and Lloyd George, now closer together than ever before, had agreed on a common strategy. This was preceded by strident declarations on behalf of 'fusion' by Churchill and Birkenhead. It was agreed that Lloyd George would address Coalition Liberal members on 18 March, and that Law would address Unionist members immediately afterwards. Neither would irrevocably commit himself to 'fusion', but each would indicate 'that we cannot go on as we are, that is with the United Party [*sic*] in the House of Commons, but with no such union in the constituencies.'[35]

'Fusion', as the political translation of national unity, could, then, be defended on higher and lower planes. It could plausibly be upheld as the logical outcome both of the war and of the progressive measures of the 1919 session, presented side by side with stern measures to deal with the railwaymen and miners, 'Supply and Transport Committees' and all. The essential problem, however, was that a strategy, defensible and respectable as a concept, had to be conducted in terms of traditional procedures. It had to be sold to suspicious party loyalists from Cabinet ministers down to constituency branch chairmen. Further, it depended for its success on the unique salesmanship of the Prime Minister. He alone in public life flaunted that coat of many colours with which the Coalitionism was kaleidoscopically identified. Here the Prime Minister's curiously unobserved weakness showed itself. He had a rare gift in handling deputations and dignitaries. He could charm businessmen and trade unionists down from the bough in flocks. But handling political party regulars was a less familiar exercise, remote from the presidential mode. On 16 and 18 March 1920, Lloyd George simply botched any opportunity he had. His career was never to look quite the same again.

On the 16th, resistance amongst Liberal ministers showed itself. Fisher, Montagu, Hewart, Munro, even Mond, all insisted on their commitment to historic Liberalism. The loss of their traditional party name caused especial heart-searching. Some ministers pointed out the problems that would arise in the constituencies. Herbert Lewis, usually docile, urged 'that in Wales it would be practically impossible to get anything in the shape of fusion between the local Associations.'[36] Lloyd George and Churchill tried to browbeat them, but this compounded the offence. Even a Coaly Lib was not to be bullied, let alone bought. At the vital meeting with the Coalition Liberal MPs at the Commons on 18 March, Lloyd George misread the signs of the times with even more fatal results. The draft of his speech had been scrutinized beforehand by Sutherland and others of his private staff. Sutherland bluntly wrote that, as drafted, the speech 'represents almost pure conservatism'. It contained nothing to fire the imagination of younger Liberals. There should be much more on the liberal aspects of the proposed programme of the new party in relation to foreign and imperial policy, India, Egypt, Ireland, 'democratic taxation', and licensing reform. 'Your speech now is *not* that of an enthusiastic progressive.'[37] But, as his talks with Fisher and other Liberals during the winter had shown, Lloyd George was not now in progressive mood. He appeared to be soured by the industrial conflicts after a relatively strike-free summer. His speech to the Liberal members had been prepared by him with unusual care over the previous two days. 'I have rarely seen him more highly strung,' commented Frances Stevenson.[38]

In fact, like many of Lloyd George's more carefully prepared utterances, it was a total failure. Almost incredibly, he chose to adopt a strongly conservative stance when addressing the hyper-sensitive Coalition Liberals, many of whom were openly yearning for reunion with their lost Asquithian comrades. The Prime Minister simply banged the anti-socialist drum as crudely as Churchill and with as little effect. He took the line once again that the British Labour Party and Lenin's Central Party Committee in Moscow were but different points on the same continuum. Labour's successses in by-elections opened the door, by implication, to Bolshevism. It was vital, therefore, for Coalitionists, Liberal and Unionist alike, to agree on a common programme and organization to fight Labour in industrial constituencies. This was the line of argument least likely to appeal to dissentient Liberals who concentrated instead on what the Prime Minister left out. Taking their cue from the dissentient ministers who had registered their clear protest two days earlier, they produced a stream of awkward questions about the future of Irish home rule, about licensing reform, above all about free trade which had already provoked Coalition Liberal back-bench protests about the Anti-Dumping Bill. Then there was the vital question of their historic identity and their party's sacred name. No voice at all was raised in enthusiastic support of 'fusion'. Each speaker, Wallace, France, Trevelyan Thompson, Kiley, and others, emphasized his Liberalism not his Coalitionism. The Prime Minister had seen the meeting in advance as providing a Liberal mandate for 'fusion'. In fact, the dread word could not even be uttered. As he had visualized might happen, he had to settle for the tame alternative of urging 'closer co-operation' with the Unionists in the constituencies. Even the mechanics of this were not explained with any precision. In reply to Colonel Murray and Tudor Rees, Lloyd George could reply only that the form of this 'closer co-operation' was 'not for me to dictate'.[39] The meeting was a miserable failure, compounded by the fact that someone present (Lloyd George himself suspected the disgruntled Ian MacPherson[40]) gave a full account of the proceedings to the press. With the Liberals so hesitant and reluctant, the great airship of a centre party never took off the ground. It stayed on its moorings, gently deflating.

It followed that the Unionists necessarily let 'fusion' drop as well. In fact, Bonar Law had been having last-minute reservations which led to an ill-tempered scene between him and Lloyd George on the 16th. 'Bonar is funking it now.'[41] A few days later, without emotion, Bonar Law wrote to Balfour explaining that Lloyd George's schemes had run into difficulties:

What we are thinking of now is getting Resolutions passed by both sections approving of closer co-operation and suggesting that a Committee representative of both sides should be appointed to make proposals for this purpose. The result of this will probably be not to attempt any real fusion of the Parties but to get co-operation something on the lines of the Liberal Unionists and Conservatives in the early days.

Bonar Law added revealingly that:

personally I am not sorry at the turn events have taken. I do not like the idea of complete fusion if it can be avoided but I had come to think, as I think you had also, that it was really inevitable if the Coalition were to continue, but it had always seemed to me more important from L.G.'s point of view than from ours. As a Party we were losing nothing and since the necessity of going slowly in the matter has come from L.G.'s own friends and not from ours I do not regret it.

Balfour himself had shown alarm at the more adventurous items on Fisher's draft programme for the new centre party: proportional representation, home rule for Wales and Scotland, labour legislation represented anything but moderation. The government therefore turned to the more immediate crisis of the French unilateral occupation of German towns in the Ruhr. There were still Unionists in the constituencies who favoured 'fusion': inevitably, this was in regions where Unionism was relatively weak, northern Scotland above all.[42] Some leading Unionists, notably Birkenhead and Horne, and, with increasing fervour, Austen Chamberlain, saw 'fusion' as the only effective means of fighting the Labour Party. Birkenhead, the leading Tory advocate of coalition in 1910, was now the most aggressive 'fusionist'. The fact remained that the vast majority of Unionists retained visions of independence for their party, and saw 'fusion' as essentially the badge of respectability for the stateless persons of Coalition Liberalism. The most that Unionists would offer was 'closer co-operation' in the constituencies in terms of propaganda and joint canvassing.

In this respect, there was one notable triumph to chalk up soon after the 'fusion' crisis. This was in Stockport in Lancashire where polling took place on 27 March and where there was a double vacancy in this two-member constituency. Contrary to Professor Bentley Gilbert's version, Greenwood, the Coalition Unionist, and Fildes, the Coalition Liberal, won comfortably over Labour, in a constituency which had been partly Labour since 1906. Their victory was achieved despite the siphoning off of some votes by right-wing Independents. Labour, it should be observed, was handicapped by some tension between its own candidate and the Co-operative representative, and by the loss of

some votes to an Irish Nationalist/trade unionist. Stockport, fought
with the Coalition candidates sharing a common platform and a
common agent, was the 'fusion' movement's one and only triumph.[43]
By the summer, the difficulties of 'closer co-operation' by the Unionists with Coaly Libs, who either had no constituency organization of
their own at all or else defiantly selected Wee Free candidates if they
had, were starker than ever. Coalition Liberal seats lost at Dartford,
the Wrekin, and South Norfolk were the result, whereas Unionist
seats were defended by Coalition candidates with much more success.
By the end of the year, Unionist managers were demanding that the
Coalition Liberals should either create their own machinery in each
constituency they held, or else openly or secretly finance the Unionist
organization. Younger concluded: 'Fusion is impossible or
inadvisable.'[44]

In retrospect, the failure of 'fusion' may be seen as an historic divide
in the story of the post-war Coalition. It was a severe rebuff for the
Prime Minister who had invested his own credit in the attempt. He
had failed to carry with him even his own band of indentured retainers. The 'fusionists' were exposed as an army of generals with no rank
and file. From that moment on, the Coalition always had an air of
impermanence. It had been unable to evolve from its earlier stage of
party composition; it was all trees and no wood. It seemed inevitable
that at some future stage its basic components, the party machines,
would reassert themselves and show up the basic fragmentation
within the Coalition. Henceforth, the strategy of 'fusion', repeatedly
proclaimed by Chamberlain on the Unionist side and by men such as
Guest and McCurdy on the Liberal, was repeatedly postponed to an
indefinite future. Long before 1922, it was clear that, at the earliest,
'fusion' would have to await the outcome of the next general election,
which would be fought on the binocular coalition basis of 1918. It was
small wonder that the main cries for 'fusion' came from desperate
Coaly Libs in the constituencies, especially in industrial areas like
Scotland, Wales, and the north of England where they had polled well
in 1918 and where the challenge of Labour was now so menacing.
Bereft of a distinct past, a viable present, or a definable future,
Coalition Liberals could foresee catastrophe at the polls. Reports from
the regions suggested a mood amongst many of them that was moving
closer to that of Unionists. In Scotland, they wanted 'a rest from
legislation'. In the North, they criticized 'grandiose schemes of

Secondary and Extension education', and 'fruitless expenditure' on housing. In the West Midlands, there was 'a very real desire for governmental economy'. Everywhere there was gloom with the spectre of Labour's 'extreme Bolshevik programme'.[45]

The one ray of hope was the stature of the Prime Minister as he moved decisively from international conferencing to the domestic scene. 'No alternative Premier can be suggested and with the possible exception of unemployment we can see nothing that can unseat him.'[46] At the local level, there was 'fusion' in abundance as businessmen and manufacturers amongst the Coalition Liberals—men like the Holts in Liverpool—joined with Unionists in sponsoring anti-Labour 'ratepapers' candidates in borough or municipal elections. Salvidge organized anti-Labour 'fusion' tickets in Liverpool, with a strongly Protestant slant.[47] But where it really mattered, in the parliamentary constituencies, Unionists were 'playing the party game' and treating their Liberal allies with disdain or contempt. Few Unionists at the constituency level, south of the Scottish border, upheld the banner of 'fusion' after April 1920; few had done so before. Years later, Sir Colin Coote could regard Edmund Talbot, the Unionist chief whip, as the true author of the collapse of 'fusion'.[48] But Talbot was responding to pressure from below. 'Fusion' had become the politics of weakness. It languished through its own irrelevance to the march of events.

In party terms, then, the attempt to respond to the cry for centrist government with the movement for 'fusion' never made much sense. There was minimal enthusiasm on the Unionist side. Coalition Liberals still retained enough faith in the old shibboleths to resist even their own leader. From central office to local associations in constituencies throughout the land, resistance to change was inevitable and overpowering.

But the whole point of the Coalition's appeal was that that party world should be transcended. From the standpoint of the main agents for change within the Coalition, especially policy-makers in the Cabinet, 'fusion' made more sense. The idea had been floated in a world where older patterns of politics were in disarray, when the level of party commitment appeared to be low in response to the unifying pressure of wartime. It could well be claimed that by the spring of 1920 the Coalition was in fact offering an alternative strategy in foreign and domestic affairs, both to the die-hards and to the

proponents of the capital levy. It had been far from a do-nothing
government to date. The 1920 session of parliament was faced with a
huge programme of legislation, covering the coal industry, the
government of Ireland, the forty-eight hour week, national unemployment insurance, a minimum wage, corn prices, liquor control,
and the 'safeguarding' of industry. It was going to be an exciting, even
exhausting, session. The Cabinet was still united. The indices of trade
and of production were still comparatively favourable. The pound was
stronger against the dollar, and stronger still against other currencies.
The class warfare of the autumn was becoming a distant memory by
the summer of 1920, save for the incurable rancour of the coal-mining
industry. The upsurge of militant Labour seemed to have made the
case for a Coalition all the more overwhelming. The wide range of
views to be found within the Coalition camp need not cause dismay.
After all, the Liberal government of 1906 had been supported by an
extraordinary array of opinion, from J. A. Hobson to Harold Cox,
from Chiozza Money to Hilaire Belloc. All the successful party
governments in the past had been coalitions of sections, interest
groups, and opinions. In contrast to coalition governments, say, in the
French Third Republic or in an Italy tottering into chaos, the British
version was providing coherent policies and powerful leadership.

There was, then, a yearning for unity in 1919–20 in Britain and the
Coalition came near to expressing it. It failed, of course, because of the
impossibly wide gulf between united leaders and disparate constituency parties, and because each element within the Coalition had its
own private concept of what unity was composed of and where the
centre was to be located. The positive content of Coalition centrism
was harder and harder to determine. The government now tended to
reflect more clearly its component parts. Fisher described the
Agriculture Bill in May as 'a very bad example of Coalition legislation,
the first part Tory, the second Radical'.[49] Lloyd George's own political role as its figure-head and totem was harder to predict also. The
failure of 'fusion' in March 1920 did not mean that the Coalition was
on the point of imminent collapse or that its search for a middle way in
policy was invalid. It did mean that increasingly the justification for
the Coalition had to be a negative one. The emphasis was now placed
on the dangers or the immaturity of its various challengers. Ministers
had to stress the inability of their variegated opponents, Liberal,
Labour, or die-hard, to form a credible government. By implication,

the idea of Coalition centrism, of a 'national' government, had become the lowest common factor in politics, rather than the highest. The abnormality of Coalition had to be represented as 'normalcy' in contrast to the even more bizarre alternatives to be found on the left and the right. As time passed, it was the inadequacy of its various challengers rather than its own merits that kept 'Lloyd George's Stage Army' in being. It is to this that we must now turn.

8

Minor Challengers:
Asquithians and Cecils

After the 'deluge' of the First World War, the Asquithian Liberals
were left beleaguered, the orphans of the storm. The triumph of
Lloyd George in 1918 seemed to have shattered the Liberal Party and
to have destroyed the Liberal ethic. Individual liberties, free enterprise, class conciliation, and world harmony seemed to disappear
beneath the waves of rhetoric of the 'coupon election'—rhetoric to
which, admittedly, Asquith and his supporters made their contribution. Over two million voters had supported 'uncouponed' Liberals at
the polls, but everywhere there were reports of shattered morale. In
the end, Asquith, Runciman, Simon, McKenna, Samuel, the white
knights of undefiled Liberalism, were among the fallen. The party
machine still remained firmly in Asquithian hands in all parts of
Britain save in Wales. The central office in Abingdon Street under the
direction of Lord Gladstone and Sir Robert Hudson, themselves two
survivors from the 1880s, remained poised for battle. There were still
major newspapers and periodicals that defended the Free Liberal
cause, the *Manchester Guardian* and the *Nation* prominent among
them. Names like Spender, Massingham, Gardiner, Hirst, illustrated
the Liberal talent to be found in editorial ranks. But it was hard to
claim that this was much more than a shell. The Liberal crisis was not
merely one of electoral assault from without but of self-immolation
from within.[1] At the rarefied levels of the Liberal intelligentsia, men
like Gilbert Murray or Charles Masterman testified to the cataclysmic
effect of the chauvinism and collectivism of the war and Lloyd George
combined, in shattering the repose and refinement of the Liberal
mind. The noblest Romans were in full retreat. Lloyd George and his
'couponed' Goths and Vandals had captured the very temple of their
civilization. Well might classically-educated Asquithians, in the
aftermath of their stunning experiences at the polls, meditate in
Gibbonian fashion on the crimes and follies of mankind.

The extent of the plight of the Independent Liberals soon became apparent when parliament reassembled. Twenty-eight Liberals had been returned to the House in different parts of the country without the assistance of the 'coupon'. Conversely at least two 'couponed' Liberals, Josiah Wedgwood (Newcastle-under-Lyme) and Evan Hayward (Seaham Harbour, Co. Durham), professed themselves to be 'impenitent Independent Radicals'. A gathering of just twenty-three 'Liberals without prefix or suffix' met in the House of Commons on 3 February under the chairmanship of Francis Acland.[2] They included three 'couponed' members, Hayward, P. W. Raffan, and Penry Williams. On the other hand, one or two Independents wisely stayed away. It was decided after an amiable discussion (with some dissent from Hilton Young who had refused the 'coupon' but who was soon to enter the Coalitionist ranks and serve in the government) to form themselves into a special party. To reserve the position of Asquith as head of the party, the new post of sessional chairman was created, and, with so few figures of substance left, Donald Maclean (Peebles), who had held only minor office before the war, was elected. J. M. Hogge and G. R. Thorne, two implacable anti-Coalitionists, became secretaries. These Independent Liberals were necessarily not a strong group. Apart from Maclean, only Wedgwood Benn, Acland, and George Lambert were their only figures of any substance or debating ability. Barely two dozen in number, they could not even claim to provide a token opposition since the 57-strong parliamentary Labour Party, under the chairmanship of William Adamson, a Fife-shire miner, now formed the official opposition.

The status of the new Independent Liberal group was obscure for some time. On 6 February, a gathering of over one hundred Liberal members met at the House. They were under the chairmanship of George Lambert, himself in an ambiguous position towards the government and whose very presence suggested some hopes of Liberal reunion. Four known Coalitionists, Sir Archibald Williamson, Sir Ivor Philipps, Albion Richardson, and Sir Thomas Whittaker, were appointed to join a committee to promote a union of all Liberal members. But after some debate, the non-Coalition Liberal members rejected a motion to merge with the Coalitionists. In their turn, they appointed four representatives, Wedgwood Benn, Penry Williams, Frank Briant, and Hogge, to confer with the four Coalition Liberals. This was clearly, a meaningless exercise. Although 'couponed' and un-couponed Liberals might claim to be advancing towards the same objectives, in practical terms a vast gulf existed between them. By the end of March, the committee had dissolved, negotiations having irretrievably broken down.[3] The ostensible cause of the breach was a Coalition Liberal suggestion that the Liberal Party in parliament should consist of members clearly nominated by local Liberal associations, a proposal which the Independents rejected. Basically, of course, there was an immense divide between those who chose to collaborate with the old Tory enemy on behalf of agreed objectives, and those who felt that a coalition of this type was unprincipled and immoral. The Independent Liberal group, cheerfully christened the 'Wee Frees', thus emerged as a distinct party, by its very presence challenging the claims of Lloyd George's much larger retinue of 136 to uphold the true Liberal faith.

The Independent Liberals were not a significant or influential group in the sessions of 1919 and 1920. On the major issues of international and industrial relations, the *Nation* complained, they were failing to make much impact. The Wee Frees failed to speak out clearly on behalf of democratic self-government in Ireland, India, or Egypt, of withdrawal from Russia, of modification of the Versailles treaty, of more harmonious industrial relations, of economy in governmental expenditure, or even of free trade. Liberals, non-Coalition and Coalition alike, had sat by while leaders of the government (including Liberal ministers like Churchill and Mond) swallowed doses of protection and imperial preference, had abandoned home rule for Ireland, had retained conscription, and had abandoned Lloyd George's pre-war land taxes. Austen Chamberlain's excessively rosy account of the national finances in October was allowed by Maclean to pass by with relatively little criticism—an index, it was thought, of the feebleness of the Liberal opposition.[4] Why Professor Wilson considers that the Wee Frees 'far outshone the Labour opposition' in the House is not clear.[5] All the evidence seems to suggest rather that the Independent Liberals were a relatively unimportant minority group, generally regarded with tolerant sympathy, who made little impression on any aspect of public debate. They had little that was distinctive or new to say. If radical Liberalism was required, the government's own social programme at this early stage more than fulfilled the need.

It is a curious commentary on the Asquithian viewpoint that the

Liberals continued to believe that they represented the real voice of opposition to the government, that their influence was out of all proportion to their numbers, and that the pronouncements of Maclean, Acland, or Hogge carried immense weight in Whitehall and the stock exchange. Never has the self-delusion inherent in the élitism and patrician superiority of the Liberal mode been shown up more starkly. The Liberal universe after 1918 is an inner-directed, narcissistic world in which abstract contemplation of the Liberal ethic in some isolation from the unhappy facts of life took command. It makes a good deal of sense—though it is not the complete picture—to consider Liberalism in these years in terms of the 'high politics' and high philosophy of the chosen few rather than in terms of grass-roots organization and the tides of opinion in the constituencies. The Liberals after 1918, although in opposition, were clearly a Court rather than a Country party—or at least they convinced themselves that that was how they appeared.

In fact, there were genuine signs in the country also for at least a year that Independent Liberalism was on the move, its artificially low strength in the House being supplemented by a period of growth much more in line with residual Liberal support in different parts of Britain. In the early months of the government, the Liberals registered three striking by-election victories, all at the expense of Coalition candidates. The first, on St. David's Day as it happened, was at West Leyton in north-east London. On a huge swing of 24.7 per cent, an Independent Liberal, A. E. Newbould, defeated a Coalition Unionist. This shook government Liberals. Mond wrote to Lloyd George that the Wee Frees were 'elated'. It was rumoured that Asquith, McKenna, Runciman, Samuel, and Simon 'will all be back in Parliament this year'. Mond attributed the defeat at West Leyton to the inadequacy of Mason, the Unionist candidate, 'unknown locally, a typical reactionary Tory and Director of Railways who, I believe, stated in answer to a question that he thought thirty shillings a week enough for any railway man'. The answer was for the government to press on with a vigorous social policy attractive to radical constituencies such as West Leyton. More important, Coalition Liberals should lay decisive claim to seats unfairly mortgaged by the Tories in 1918 but which were really Liberal to the core.[6] Perhaps West Leyton, taken with the swing to Labour in the Liverpool, West Derby, by-election a week earlier, may be taken as a protest vote, picked up by the Liberals in a contest where no Labour man was standing.

The same tendency was even more emphatic in the by-election at Hull Central on 29 March. On a low poll (as at West Leyton), Commander Kenworthy, the radical Independent Liberal, defeated a Coalition Unionist in a straight fight on a larger swing (32.9 per cent) than the Coalition was to suffer in any by-election until Labour won South-East Southwark in December 1921. Here the Unionist candidate, Lord Eustace Percy, was, unlike Mason, undoubtedly a strong and honourable one, even if ambivalent about Lloyd George. Nevertheless, Kenworthy's extraordinary victory, turning a Unionist majority of over 10,000 into a Liberal one of 917, reflected the deep forces of protest. Percy wrote after the poll that he had been 'fighting a kind of Bottomley irresponsibility compounded with Bolshevism'. Years later, he described his embarrassment at the 'puerilities' of his own campaign. Kenworthy's strongly left-wing attack made much of the issues of 'non-conscription' and free trade. He attacked the government for its delay in settling satisfactory peace terms and for the slow progress achieved in settling ex-servicemen on the land and in building houses as promised. Troubles in Palestine may have had some effect on the Jewish vote. Kenworthy's appeal, very attractive to Labour voters, resembled that of successful Commonwealth Party candidates in the period 1943–5.[7] It was emphatically radical, far to the left of Asquith and his immediate lieutenants. In fact, Kenworthy (who held Hull Central for the Liberals in the elections of 1922, 1923, and 1924) was later on to join the Labour Party, always his natural destination, and, disguised as Lord Strabolgi, to become a leading Labour peer. These two victories were followed by a third Liberal gain from the Unionists, in Central Aberdeenshire on 16 April. It was on a smaller swing but in some ways was more impressive since there was on this occasion a Labour candidate in the field as well.

These impressive victories were taken as indicating a sweeping resurgence of Liberalism as the true voice of anti-Coalition sentiment. In fact, they were a false dawn. Neither in the House nor in the country did Liberalism show much advance over the next eighteen months. The Liberal performance in by-elections was less striking thereafter. At Widnes in August, no Liberal candidate was put up, and Wee Frees in the area registered their support for Arthur Henderson. At Rusholme in Manchester on 7 October, the local Liberals did

experience a three-cornered contest when, to their dismay, the local
ILP put up Dr. Dunthorne as its candidate somewhat at the last
minute, and with the disapproval of Ramsay MacDonald amongst
others.[8] The Wee Free, Pringle, came a poor third with a mere 19.1
per cent of the votes, even though amateur psephologists had forecast
his return. Liberals also finished up third at Devonport (Sutton) and
St. Albans. Thereafter, they became more circumspect. When a
contest became due at the Wrekin, an area with a strong Liberal
tradition, early in 1920, no Wee Free came forward and the constituency was captured by a Bottomley candidate, C. F. Palmer, the
assistant editor of *John Bull*. Liberals next fought the seat in 1929.

The major success that Liberals could claim was less in making
inroads into Labour or Unionist territory than in waging civil war
against the Coaly Libs with some success. Here they had some
achievement. At Spen Valley, the local Liberal Association adopted
Sir John Simon, even though the deceased Liberal had been
'couponed' in 1918. In a famous contest, Labour headed the poll, but
Simon polled impressively and left the Coalition Liberal, Colonel
Fairfax, well down in third place. This was an embarrassing contest
for the Coalition Liberals. Their election machinery in Spen Valley
depended on the Unionists. Only one Liberal minister spoke on
behalf of Fairfax. He was Macnamara who was pilloried for it in the
press and was promptly disowned by his own Liberal Association in
North-West Camberwell (though this did not prevent his winning a
by-election there fairly comfortably in March 1920).[9] Unionist
ministers maintained their practice of not participating in by-
elections, a tradition observed until 1927. Even Field Marshal Haig
managed to damage the Coalition cause by making observations on
Simon's meritorious services in the RAF during the war.[10] Another
triumph of selection for the Independents came at Paisley, when the
death of Sir John McCallum, an 'uncouponed' Liberal, resulted in the
local Association unanimously adopting Asquith as their candidate.
To Freddie Guest's alarm, there was a possibility that the Unionists
might not even put up a candidate and would give Asquith a free run
against the Labour/Co-operative candidate, Biggar. On the other
hand, another Coaly Lib organizer, Dudley Ward, suggested that
Asquith might be left unopposed as the 'coupon' had been allocated in
somewhat fortuitous circumstances to a National Democratic Party
candidate at Paisley in 1918. In the event, the Coalition got the worst

of all worlds. The Unionists put up a dull candidate, J. A. D. McKean, who ran a half-hearted campaign and lost his deposit. Asquith, amidst immense enthusiasm at the National Liberal Club, defeated Biggar by 2,834 to become by far the most distinguished of the by-election victors over the government. Guest surmised that Asquith's victory was partly personal, partly the result of his gaining Tory votes to keep Labour out. The real significance of the election, Guest argued hopefully, was the defeat of Labour, the government's only effective challenger.[11]

Asquith's victory was an isolated one for the Independents at this time. There were other cases of local Liberal associations nominating a Wee Free, at Dartford, for example. But there was only one other Independent Liberal victory to record in 1920, and none at all in 1921. Tom Wintringham's victory at Louth in June in a straight fight with Christopher Turnor, a Coalition NDP candidate of highly eccentric views was a most unusual contest. Turnor, who campaigned for a better deal for farm labourers, was distrusted by Lincolnshire agriculturists. The 11.8 per cent swing to the Liberals was not paralleled elsewhere. Guest, typically, attributed it to the Unionists having stolen the 'coupon' in a *'traditional* Liberal seat'.[12] By 1921, the Independent Liberals were doing distinctly badly at the polls; they were suffering above all at the hands of Labour. A Wee Free seat was lost at Penistone, in Yorkshire, in March 1921, the hapless Pringle again being defeated. Even in Wales, that traditional Liberal territory since 1868, there was failure. 'Ireland is being run for all it is worth against you,' Lloyd George was told by the woman organizer for the North Wales Coalition Liberals.[13] On the other hand, the Independent Welsh Liberal Council, set up in rivalry to Lloyd George's official organization of which Lord St. David's was the president, was a feeble and backward-looking movement. Few Welsh hearts would be set on fire by its call to amend the 1919 disendowment arrangements for the Welsh church, to pass further licensing reform, or to set up an elected council for Wales. Lloyd Georgian Liberalism here, even under severe pressure, could still beat off the Asquithian challenge. In a famous by-election at Cardiganshire in February 1921, the veteran Independent Liberal, Llewelyn Williams, once a close associate of Lloyd George's who had broken with him over conscription in early 1916, was chosen by the Cardiganshire Liberal Association. Williams at this time was paranoid about the Prime Minister, a 'dictator' and 'a little Devil who plagues us so'.[14] Williams captured the popular imagination in the villages of Cardiganshire, but his opponent, Captain Evans, one of Lloyd George's private secretaries and a prudently selected local Methodist, triumphed by the margin of over 3,000 votes.[15] Watkin Davies, still in a private no-man's-land between Coalition Liberalism and Labour, felt now 'we must look to England and Scotland to deliver us from autocracy. Poor Wales!'[16] Liberalism in the county remained bitterly divided, symbolized by two rival Liberal clubs being set up at opposite ends of the main street in Aberystwyth. (The Asquithian club is still the Liberal club in the 1970s; the Lloyd Georgian premises, perhaps appropriately, are now an auction room.) A leading pro-Lloyd George minister, the Revd. R. D. Rees, was driven out after conflict with Asquithians within the Methodist congregation of Tabernacle chapel.[17] The fact remained that the electoral weakness of Asquithian Liberalism had again been underlined. Not until Isaac Foot defeated a Unionist in Bodmin in February 1922 would a Liberal gain once again be registered.

As an electoral force, then, Asquithian Liberalism soon lost its capacity to alarm as a major challenger to the government. The victories of West Leyton and Hull Central were transitory and unrepresentative of the popular mood. To Liberals of the faith, the real challenge offered by Liberalism resided outside the Commons, far beyond the hustings, at a plane of intellect and rationality far removed from petty party considerations. To a marked extent, the English intellectual world (and, in special national senses, those of Wales and Scotland as well) was a Liberal world. Great journals, great institutions, great universities still took their tone from Liberal intellectuals. It was ironic that the historian, H. A. L. Fisher, perhaps the most representative, highest Liberal of them all was firmly anchored within the Cabinet and proud of it.

In fact at the level of intellectual and literary debate, the Liberal challenge to the government petered out. The Liberal journals reverberated with protests against illiberal aspects of the government's policy. But in no case could the protests be said to be distinctly Liberal in emphasis or leadership. On the anti-dumping issue, with its menace to free trade, it was Coalition Liberals who were to the fore in protest, led by Wallace from Scotland and Gerald France from Yorkshire. They forced the government to drop the bill in 1919 and again in 1920 because its provisions relating to 'key industries'

and 'collapsed exchanges' were unacceptable to Coalition Liberals.[18]
On Ireland, opinion of all shades, from the Communists to Northcliffe, was vehement in criticism. The presence of George Lambert as
chairman of the Coalition Liberal group and of Hilton Young as
Financial Secretary of the Treasury showed how the forces of
Independent Liberalism could be weakened by pressure from the
big battalions. Churchill even thought that Wedgwood Benn could
be won over by the Coalition, which would leave only 'master Kenworthy', his *bête noire* (or perhaps *rouge*), as a significant Liberal
opponent.[19] The voice of protest in the Liberal press was muted or
uncertain. The *Daily News* became less hostile to the government
after Gardiner's departure. Scott in the *Guardian* preserved his links
with Lloyd George; his breach with the premier over the reprisals in the
winter of 1920–1 had been healed by the treaty twelve months later.
On the very eve of the 'fusion' manœuvres in February 1920, Scott
seriously believed that Lloyd George was 'feeling his way back to his
old position in the Liberal ranks' and perhaps to reconciliation with
Asquith.[20] In the *Nation*, Massingham's long campaign for a progressive alliance of Independent Liberals with Labour in an anti-
government coalition of the moderate left led nowhere. There was no
reason why it should, in view of the Liberals' commitment to free
enterprise and the presence of such men as Runciman and Simon as
leading spokesmen on industrial questions. Llewelyn Williams considered himself 'an old-fashioned Gladstonian Liberal' who had
rejected overtures from Labour.[21] Elsewhere, Liberals refused to soil
their hands. They compensated for electoral failure by an hauteur of
attitude which claimed to transcend politics itself. It was all a little too
much for most electors in a democracy to bear.

At various levels, the weakness of Liberalism in 1918–22 unfolded
to reveal itself. Asquith himself illustrated it by the feebleness of his
leadership of his party in the House. Apart from one stinging pronouncement on Ireland, he was remarkably passive after being
returned to the Commons for Paisley. Scott now agreed with Lloyd
George in seeing him as 'a great boulder blocking the way' of progress.
Scott himself found him 'immobile', a 'somewhat querulous and very
old, old man'. Llewelyn Williams, after seeing him at a Bar dinner,
complained about Asquith's long silence on political questions, apart
from one '"hellish" outburst'. Viscount Gladstone, president of the
party, used a sporting metaphor. 'Our stroke oar neither sets the time

nor rows his weight. . . . Beyond a weak ripple his speeches have no effect.' Brandy, depression, or old age had taken their toll of the once invincible Liberal 'sledgehammer'.[22] Without Asquith as a vigorous spokesman in the House, Independent Liberalism had not much to offer. More than once, Lloyd George had to remain silent in debate, to his disappointment, as the anticipated Asquithian attack never materialized. The performances of senior Liberals such as Grey, Runciman, and Simon in this period were hardly more decisive; McKenna had now become a major financial figure at the Midland Bank; Samuel had departed to administer Palestine; others such as Harcourt, McKinnon Wood, or Hobhouse had prudently left national politics altogether.

The activity of the Liberal Party machine was also unproductive. In early 1919, Sir Robert Hudson spent much effort in seeking to reorganize it on more efficient lines. This largely took the form of trying to strengthen the hand of the Liberal Central Association, which had not met since 1914, and of streamlining the machinery at Abingdon Street, with Maclean as its head, Wedgwood Benn as his parliamentary lieutenant, and Geoffrey Howard as link with the candidates in the constituencies. The position of the National Liberal Federation, however, should be modified. 'The old theory that the NLF must be independent of officialdom and the Parliamentary element may be pushed too far.'[23] The underlying idea was clearly to reinforce the old central caucus which had provided the skeletal links for the disparate elements of Liberalism since Hudson began work under Schnadhorst after the split over Irish home rule back in 1886. Later Viscount Gladstone took over as party organizer, a kind of Liberal version of Sir George Younger, to complement what was thought to be the new authority of the party after Asquith's return to parliament. It is clear, though, that this apparently impressive national machine was a frail one, short of agents and party professionals, short of funds also despite the ready cheque books of such rich sympathizers as Lord Cowdray. The revived party organization of the Liberals was no real basis for a sustained national challenge. Compared with the electoral machines being built up by Labour and being re-established by the Unionists, it looked ramshackle, a penny-farthing in the automobile age, to adapt Harold Wilson's later phrase.

The one successful tactic the party could pursue, as has been seen, was to add to the insecurity and confusion of the Coalitionists. After

Spen Valley and Paisley, the Independent Liberals declared war on
the Coaly Libs and rapidly severed any remaining ties with them.
However, the Coalitionists themselves took their part in creating a
mood of internecine combat. After the failure of the 'fusion' moves in
March 1920, Coalitionists from Guest downwards were convinced
that they had burnt their boats as far as the Asquithians were concerned, and that a more firmly based Coalition was their one hope of
survival. Several ministers, Churchill and MacPherson among them,
provocatively attended the annual meeting of the Scottish Liberal
Federation on 30 April and were severely heckled.[24] The famous
brawl at the National Liberal Federation meeting at Leamington on 7
May (which one historian describes as 'an organizational meeting'
of the Lloyd George Liberals), was the result of prepared belligerency
on both sides. A batch of Coalition Liberal ministers, Addison, Macnamara, Kellaway, Hewart, Herbert Lewis, and others, decided to
attend, along with fifty-odd Coalition Liberal MPs. There was predictable uproar, particularly when Addison, never one to shirk a fight,
made a fierce speech which denounced the sectarianism of the
Asquithians. It proclaimed the liberal policies of the government from
the abolition of conscription to the encouragement of home rule in
India. Addison, Hewart, and Kellaway led a mass walk-out by the
Coalitionists. It was obviously the 'great split' which Churchill had
long foreseen; but both sides accepted it as the recognition of the
political facts of life. Not until June 1921 did any Liberal back-
benchers on either side make any real attempt at a *rapprochement*.[25] In
any case, the Coalition Liberals were in confident mood after
Leamington. 'We had a lovely—and indeed an enjoyable—time at
Leamington. They gave us the very opportunity we wanted and I am
sure our meeting on Tuesday gave us a good start,' wrote Addison.
Hewart unashamedly harangued his Leicester Liberal Association on
the progressive character of the government.[26] The Coaly Libs were
also heartened by two comfortable by-election victories by Liberal
ministers, McCurdy at Northampton and Greenwood at Sunderland.
They felt assured that the revival of Independent Liberalism was a
mirage. Guest commented complacently on the annual meeting of
Independent Liberal agents—'No speakers, No candidates, No
money.' Lloyd George himself thought that 'Wee Freeism is almost an
extinct force'. In the light of the failures of the Asquithians in by-
elections and in providing the sinews of war, there seemed every

justification for this complacency. There seemed justification also for
the claims that Liberal objectives would be best furthered by remaining in the Coalition. Lloyd George boldly assured his colleagues that
the government included no genuine Conservatives at all. They were
all either Liberals or else 'Liberal-minded men'.[27]

Worst of all, the Independent Liberals were ineffective challengers
in the realm of ideas and policies. So many of their programmes were
theoretical in character. The specifics usually tended to concentrate
on issues like site-value rating and licensing reform which were
peripheral at best, or else consisted of saying ditto to the Coaly Libs on
free trade and Ireland. In the vital new areas of industrial and social
policy, the Independent Liberals cut a feeble figure. They were
notably silent on the root themes of social deprivation, economic
recession, and unemployment. Led by such as Runciman and Simon,
they tended to repeat the standard incantations on the need for
'retrenchment' and 'economy'. Even a radical like Masterman could
only echo the call for 'more treasury control' over spending.[28] After
much protest from Liberal candidates, the policy-making section of
the party did produce an industrial policy in January 1921, much on
the lines of Asquith's 'Paisley policy'.[29] Its dominant characteristic
was its generality. It was an uneasy compromise between collectivism
and *laissez-faire*, typical of the party at this period. While paying
half-hearted tribute to the government's policies of social reform, it
also called loudly for 'retrenchment'. While decrying the centralization introduced by Eric Geddes and other ministers, it also called for
the possible public ownership of certain unnamed industries where
there was no longer free competition. An ill-defined capital levy was
called for, to help reduce the National Debt. It was couched throughout in the kind of Christian abstractions favoured by Masterman, its
main author.

However, sections of the party pressed for more radical and more
concrete policies. At the annual conference of the NLF at Nottingham
in 1921, resolutions were carried which called for joint industrial
committees of employers and workers to fix minimum wages and
standard hours of work. The existing Trade Boards and Whitley
Councils would be adapted for this purpose, and consumers also
brought in. The abortive National Industrial Conference of 1919
would be recalled. In addition, other resolutions called for an attack
on trusts and monopolies, and for new initiatives to deal with

unemployment insurance on an industry-wide basis. The 'Manchester group', an impressive body intellectually, headed by Professor Ramsay Muir (a professor of history at Manchester University), Ernest Simon (head of the Manchester Housing Committee), and Philip Guedalla, a young Oxford graduate, urged a much more sympathetic attitude towards labour. They were on close personal terms with socialists like Tawney. Ramsay Muir himself advocated industrial co-partnership, profit-sharing schemes, and labour participation in the control of industry.[30] Muir even gave up his chair of Modern History to inaugurate the Liberal summer school movement at Grasmere in the Lake District in September 1921. From 1922 onwards, these schools were held annually at Oxford or Cambridge. They attracted some outstanding intellects from the start—J. M. Keynes, A. F. Pollard, Josiah Stamp, Leonard Hobhouse, Hubert Henderson, Comyns Carr, Walter Layton (co-director of the summer schools with Muir himself). Muir began a full-time career as Liberal organizer, candidate (for Rochdale), and propagandist, to try to concoct a new social and economic philosophy appropriate for Liberals in the postwar period. These eventually bore fruit in the imaginative schemes drawn up by the Liberals for land, industry, and employment in 1925–9—but by then Lloyd George was back at their head to offer drive and inspiration. The impact made by these initiatives on the Liberal leadership in 1921–2 was slight indeed. From Asquith downwards, no major figure in the party offered much encouragement to Muir and his friends. Traditional Cobdenites denounced this attempt to divert or beguile Liberals away from the fundamentals for which an earlier generation of Manchester Liberals had fought.[31] The party's manifesto in the general election of November 1922 was utterly traditional apart from some woolly references to 'co-operation between capital and labour'. As against Muir's appeal for Liberals to face up to such evils as the maldistribution of wealth, a more representative view was that of J. M. Robertson, that stern, free-thinking free trader, editor of Bradlaugh's old secularist journal, the *National Reformer*. He drew an indelible line between pure Liberals and the 'class-hating, class fanatics' of the Labour Party.[32] Here was a Rubicon that no Liberal Caesar could decently consider crossing.

Increasingly, then, it was apparent that the Independent Liberal Party, cut off from its main earlier inspiration, Lloyd George, was a passive, unexciting alternative to the Coalition. Professor Wilson has rightly called the Coalition Liberals in 1922 'coalitionists in a post-coalition world'.[33] By the same token, the Free Liberals were in 1919–22 Edwardian survivors, compromised between caucus politics and traditional shibboleths, Chamberlain and Gladstone fused into one. Their influence in the world of journalism, on which they much depended, was in manifest decline; as has been seen, Donald, Gardiner, Spender, and Massingham all left their editorial posts between 1919 and 1923. Francis Hirst's fanatically free-trade *Common Sense* folded up in early 1921. Neither in electoral muscle nor in intellectual vitality were the Asquithian Liberals, least of all their fading leader, effective or credible challengers to the much-abused but still competent Coalition government.

In a somewhat similar category may be placed another minority group of challengers, those miscellaneous high-minded Centrists identified with Lord Robert Cecil.[34] Their effectiveness rose and fell with the fortunes of their eccentric leader. Cecil was a man of unpredictable passions. He entered the post-war world in appropriate fashion by resigning from the government over the terms of Welsh disendowment. He sacrificed a positive role in the making of post-war Britain for the sake of glebes and churchyards. As a result of this quixotic gesture, he lost his place as a British Foreign Office minister at the Paris peace conference. He continued to take a close interest in Lloyd Georgian diplomacy thereafter. In May he complained to the Prime Minister that the terms of the treaty had departed sharply from the statement of war aims included in Lloyd George's speech to the trade unions in January 1918. He instanced the burden of reparations to be imposed on Germany, the indefensible nature of the territorial provisions relating to Upper Silesia, the Polish Corridor, and the Saar, and the resultant strain on relations with the United States.[35] He continued to smite Lloyd Georgian foreign policy hip and thigh over the next three years. Years later, he told Churchill that Lloyd George had missed an historic opportunity in Paris: he had allowed himself to be hectored by the newspapers into 'standing for a *vae victis* peace which I really believe he did not himself want'.[36]

But the roots of Cecil's attack on the government's foreign policy, indeed on the Coalition generally, really lay in his passionate, dogmatic adherence to the League of Nations. Along with such Liberal luminaries as Gilbert Murray and G. P. Gooch, Cecil became a root-and-branch evangelist for the League of extraordinary fervour. He was convinced that Lloyd George regarded the League with cynicism, as a bargaining counter with Woodrow Wilson. From the outset, Cecil was disturbed over such aspects as Britain's insistence on 'freedom of the seas' as interpreted in London, on Lloyd George's insistence on being consulted about the appointment of a secretary to the League, and on the alleged demand that the Americans should retain a smaller fleet than the British as a pre-condition of Britain's signing the draft treaty.[37] As the style of Lloyd George's foreign policy unfolded, with summit diplomacy between Britain and France by-passing the League, from San Remo to Genoa, Cecil's distaste became more vocal. There were, he conceded, some ministers who took the League seriously—H. A. L. Fisher notable amongst them—but Lloyd George's *realpolitik* swamped them all. The British government's circumvention of his beloved League seemed to Cecil to provide a classic instance of old-style nationalism rejecting the glowing opportunities present for creating a new international law and international morality.

Cecil's vision of the League was based on a kind of benevolent paternalism and an organic approach towards international questions. So, too, was his panacea for domestic troubles, namely industrial co-partnership. His ideas on this theme were invariably somewhat vague, and coloured by high Anglican euphoria. Addressing the 'Centre Group' of MPs at the Criterion restaurant in July 1919, he upheld a profit-sharing, co-partnership system which would produce the 'humanizing of industry'.[38] The conflicts between labour and capital were, he believed, psychological in origin. Change the mood, restore mutual confidence and Christian fellowship within industry, and disputes between masters and men over wage rates, differentials, and the like would wither away.

Cecil's apparent detachment from the party scene did not prevent him from joining some highly conventional bandwagons. Significantly, Younger rated him in October 1919 as 'Bonar Law's only possible successor' as Unionist leader.[39] He presided over the People's Union for Economy, and urged that a definite limit be placed upon public expenditure.[40] His appeal was hardly to be distinguished from the Anti-Waste League of Rothermere. He addressed the Middle Class Union, though he felt its base was too narrow and too reminiscent of 'the smaller trading, propertied and professional classes'. 'The L. of N. + Anti-Waste' was the programme he wanted to be pushed in by-elections.[41] What he sought above all was a union of landowners and labour against 'the intervening classes and the extremists'.[42] It was Bentinck's Young England come again in an even more inappropriate setting. He also flirted with such fellow aristocrats as 'Eddy' Hartington, Lord Bledisloe, and his cousin, Lord Salisbury, to enlist gentry of conscience and high sensibility against the money-grubbing Coalitionists. 'It is really a desperate business having a Welsh wizard to control the affairs of the country,' he lamented. 'I am beginning to believe that there is nothing so dangerous as cleverness in an administrator. Give me a stupid old country gentleman.'[43] As with a later Cecil intervention in high politics, a Celtic minister was being attacked for seeming too clever by half.

Cecil's moralistic laments, founded on the twin poles of the League overseas and co-partnership at home, gradually took him far from his original Unionist moorings. In the industrial troubles of 1919–20, his head tended to concur with the government, but his heart (perhaps his soul) to throb with sympathy for labour. He told Austen Chamberlain that he felt that the government's handling of the miners in April 1921 was biased and unduly based on a desire to put the workers in the wrong. On the other hand, he agreed with some of Chamberlain's attacks on 'the so-called Labour Party'. 'If any means offered them-selves which would produce another possible alternative, I should be much tempted to take them.'[44] By the summer of 1920 he had estab-lished himself as a leading critic of the government on foreign policy and industrial questions, and on Ireland as well. Salisbury felt with alarm that he was drifting towards the Labour Party. Finally, in February 1921 Balfour accepted, with much good humour, Cecil's private announcement that he was to sit amongst the opposition MPs.[45]

Cecil now was an imposing and potentially dangerous opponent for the government. He combined aristocratic lineage of an impeccable kind with experience of high office and expertise in foreign affairs. Oswald Mosley was one young new MP sufficiently impressed to cross the floor with him. Cecil acted as a vital catalyst in Mosley's rapid progression from Coalition Unionism to the Independent Labour Party between 1918 and 1924.[46] But Cecil had ambitious aspirations. He thought of forming a new party, a true 'centre' instead of the bogus centrism associated with the Coalition. He had discussed such a movement with the Asquithian leader, Donald Maclean, at the height

of the Polish crisis in August 1920. While Maclean expressed doubts
about the practicality of a new kind of anti-government coalition,
Cecil focused his gaze on its ultimate objectives—sound finance,
industrial partnership, and, inevitably, the League of Nations.[47] He
urged the Oxford Hellenist, Gilbert Murray, that they should appeal
to 'the non-political mass—the people who did not vote at the last
election & those conservatives who are not reactionary & passionately
desire clean and honest Govt.' What they should aim at was a 'ministry
of plain, blunt men who will advocate conciliation & union of Classes
at home, peace in Ireland, L. of N. foreign policy and above all
economic sanity & retrenchment'.[48]

Naturally, Independent Liberals believed that in their moderate
ranks a would-be centrist like Cecil could find his natural habitat.
Even the socialist Harold Laski was involved in persuading Cecil to
join the Liberals as 'the one way to beat L.-G. at the next election'.[49]
But Cecil believed that, on the contrary, official Liberalism was
generally thought to be dead, and Asquith himself discredited. He
made overtures to a progressive Tory like Arthur Steel-Maitland who
provided a link with friendly journalists in the Northcliffe press;
contacts were visualized with the *Manchester Guardian*, the Unionist
provincial press, St. Loe Strachey's *Spectator*, and even conceivably
with the Fabian *New Statesman*. Steel-Maitland agreed that any new
group must be much more than 'the old Liberal Party plus one or two
others who have crossed the floor'.[50] Cecil himself contemplated
support from a wide range of opinion in advocating the expulsion of
Lloyd George. He urged Lord Cowdray, the benevolent patron of
Independent Liberalism, that 'some middle party or combination'
must be formed to combat both Labour and Lloyd George at the next
election. Apart from some Asquithians, several Unionists 'more or
less in agreement with us' like Ormsby-Gore, Winterton, Hoare,
Hills, Cockerill, Birchall, and Elliot should be approached, plus a
Coaly Lib like Colin Coote.[51] The inclusion of a name such as Winterton's shows that it was far from a radical movement that Cecil had in
mind. On the other hand, Liberal journalists such as J. A. Spender of
the *Westminster Gazette* and Wilson Harris of the *Daily News* were
approached also, while Lord Gladstone pondered the merits of 'a
combination of the Cecil, Rothermere and general interest'.[52]

What Cecil wanted was a centrist movement that would overcome
the Lloyd George Coalition not by flashy or innovative programmes,

but by innate moral superiority. This dictated his idea of its leader. The former Foreign Secretary, Viscount Grey, had emerged into public life again after the disillusion of the war years, despite the handicap of his increasing blindness. He had had a brief and unproductive period as Ambassador to Washington under Lloyd George—with whom his relations had remained reasonably good, despite the impression left by Lloyd George in his *War Memoirs* years later. Grey was perhaps the one figure in public life unsullied by the war and the internecine political strife that followed it. He was a kind of progressive Pétain hovering in the wings. In the spring of 1921, Cecil inaugurated what has been termed 'a conspiracy', to project Grey as the head of a new centrist movement.[53] He enlisted some help from journalists, some from Liberal organization men like Gladstone, much from university-based idealists who shared Cecil's own passion for the League, notably Gilbert Murray, the very symbol of Greek polity. The objective of the campaign was to persuade Asquith to allow Grey to become the head of this movement. As Steel-Maitland none too tactfully wrote to Asquith, the intention was to persuade the public that it was truly a new party, not 'a domestic Liberal affair, with one former very eminent Liberal coming again out of retirement'. The purpose was to attract 'very many sober and sensible people who are disgusted with the Government, but are not for the most part members of the present Liberal Party'.[54] He urged Asquith not to write a public letter to Grey himself.

This high-minded intrigue never really got off the ground at all. It resembled more the discreet gavotte that precedes the election of the head of an Oxford or Cambridge college than a bid for power. There were three obvious difficulties. One was that the Independent Liberals were as reluctant to fuse with the Cecil group as they were with the Unionists. 'Liberals and Radicals must be left to fight under their own flag,' wrote Spender. 'It is a hard enough job in any case with L.G. twisting and turning and confusing all issues on one side, and Labour beating up all the discontents on the other.'[55] The second was that Asquith himself had manifestly no intention of giving up the party leadership or expressing any public desire to subordinate himself to Grey. When in October 1922 Cecil formally suggested that he step down as party leader in preparation for the coming election, he flatly declined. He believed, or so he claimed, that the Liberal Party would receive his resignation with alarm and 'he must keep his hands free'.[56]

As in 1910 and 1916, Asquith was ever the ambitious partisan, even in old age.

Thirdly, and most crucially, Grey himself was a most reluctant and elusive Messiah. The belief that he retained a yearning to head a new national crusade to throw out Lloyd George had scant empirical basis. Grey did not seem to respond to an early approach from Cecil some time in the spring of 1921. In October, he did make a major pronouncement at Berwick-on-Tweed, in his old constituency, a speech concocted in part with Runciman. Grey, so Runciman reported, was 'to urge the necessity for an independent or free opposition, indeed for a House of Commons untied from the present Government'.[57] Grey's speech, however, was couched in generalities apart from a sharp and effective attack on the government's policy in Ireland. This last might have done some good had it been delivered a few months earlier at the height of the 'reprisals' strategy. Now that full talks were in progress with Sinn Fein, it seemed somewhat self-indulgent, a form of retrospective radicalism. Soon Grey lapsed again into non-partisan disquisitions, then into more Delphic silence. Finally in February 1922 a stone was discovered in his kidney and he was removed from politics for many months. By the time of the fall of the government in October, he cut a negligible figure. The fact that Cecil was still touting him as a possible centrist leader showed how out of touch he was with political realities. All that remained now was further attempts by the Liberal machine to entice Cecil into the Independent Liberal camp. Here, it was claimed, was where real faith in the League truly resided. Gladstone, curiously enough, offered Cecil the Liberal nomination in Warrington which he ventured to claim was a sound Liberal seat: in fact, it had been solidly Conservative since 1885 apart from the freak result in 1906. Cecil dismissed the offer with some contempt. He still wanted an independent grouping, whereas Gladstone felt 'the whole trend of things is to go back to party formulations'.[58] The revolt of the high-minded had foundered on the low road of electoral calculations, with some ill-feeling all round. By the end of 1923, Cecil was back in his true harbour, that of progressive Conservatism, a sympathizer with Baldwin in the belief that he alone could render Lloyd George powerless.[59] He served in Baldwin's first two Cabinets. Years later, in his memoirs, he professed himself to be now a supporter of the Labour Party.

The misadventures of the Asquithians and the Cecil group are both really episodes in the sad tale of post-war Liberalism. They are both illustrations of the illusions entertained by intellectuals, the belief that they truly reflected the consensus of centrist opinion whereas Coalition centrism was the dishonest hucksterism of the wartime *arriviste*. Neither group was a credible challenger for power. In terms of ideological relevance, professional efficiency, mass support, and political style, both were anachronisms, albeit instructive ones. The Independent Liberals were clearly in decline, despite their illusory success in early by-elections in 1919. They were ill-suited for the democratic politics initiated by the franchise reform of 1918. That Liberals as a species were not necessarily ill-equipped for the rough and tumble of democratic politics is shown by the success of some of the Coalition Liberals. Lloyd George, Churchill, and Guest as executants, Addison and Montagu as reforming spirits, were able to adapt their style pragmatically without sacrificing the kind of priorities that had initially made them Liberals. Even Fisher, like Woodrow Wilson, was very much the academic with political antennae, while no-one could accuse 'Bronco Bill' Sutherland of being too much of a gentleman. The Independent Liberals were not able so to adapt. Like their leader, men such as Grey, Runciman, and Simon remained frozen in the mid-Victorian world of the later Gladstone.

If the Wee Frees conformed to their Gladstonian origins, the Cecil group harked back still further, to a middle grouping like the Peelites of the 1850s, or perhaps the Liberal Republicans of the Godkin school in America in 1872—cultivated, detached, a loose affiliation of idealistic paternalistic, public-spirited businessmen, afforced by the Cecil brand of *noblesse oblige*.[60] In the world of 1920 such a political approach was other-worldly. It was natural that Cecil himself, a kind of cross between Savonarola and Stafford Cripps, a High Church hot-gospeller for positive thinking and ethical purity, should regard the League of Nations as the foundation of his credo, a sort of Fortieth Article. The proven shortcomings of the League even by October 1922, the withdrawal of the United States, the evident fact that only by practical harmonizing of policies by the great powers, not through appeal to some vaguely conceived 'international opinion', could foreign affairs be conducted, Cecil left on one side. At the Imperial Conference in 1923, Cecil proclaimed that the League's 'executive instrument is not force but public opinion'. To him, the triumph of Lloyd George implied both the victory of *realpolitik* abroad and of

amorality at home. In each case, the government was the apotheosis of
the fixer. Cecil's crusade was doomed to fail. What E. H. Carr was to
call later 'the nemesis of utopianism' was to be confirmed on 10
September 1931 when Cecil told the League Assembly that there had
scarcely ever been 'a period in the world's history when war seems less
likely than it does at present';[61] eight days later, the Japanese invaded
Manchuria. It was hard enough for the Coalition to create a non-party
movement. At least it had the proven co-operation of the war years
and the aid of the whips on which to base itself. Cecil had nothing so
tangible—merely an aspiration and an ethic. Even the Anti-Waste
League, with three MPs, formed a larger group in the House. The
choice of the remote and failing Grey as the pied piper of the centrists
showed how rarefied Cecil's conceptions were. They tended to dis-
integrate as they ventured out from the senior common room. Confronted with the patrician Old Guard of the Asquith camp and these
high-minded conspirators, the Coalition and its supporters could feel
reassured. They were secure against the revivalists both of the dead
past and prophetic future. The real dangers lay elsewhere.

9

Major Challengers:
the Labour Party

Long before the war ended, Lloyd George and his associates had decided that the Labour Party would form the main opponent of whatever type of government they established when peacetime conditions returned. The Prime Minister had often expanded on this theme in 1917 and 1918. He told Riddell that after the war 'it may come to a fight between him and Henderson'.[1] During the 'coupon election' also, even if concealed by the euphoria of the hustings, Labour, not the Independent Liberals, was regarded as the real enemy of the Coalition. It was well known that Labour was far better organized, numerically much stronger with its mass trade-union affiliated membership, better financed and more professional in every sense, as a result of the new 1918 party constitution. Further, it was believed that the Russian revolution had stimulated in the Labour Party, as well as amongst industrial workers, a new passion for total social and economic change of the capitalist system. The impact of the 1917 revolution upon even such a staid and cautious figure as Arthur Henderson, at the time of the Stockholm conference, was remarkable. Lloyd George thought him unbalanced: 'he had more than a touch of the revolutionary malaria'.[2] Ramsay MacDonald, the acme of constitutional 'progressivism' when chairman of the Labour Party in 1911–14, now hailed the revolution as heralding a 'springtide of joy' all over Europe.[3] Revolutionary movements in Germany, Austria, France, Italy, and Hungary added to the fervour and excitement. Labour, then, provided for government strategists the real challenge to the consensus at the 'coupon election'. The Labour Party, wrote Philip Kerr, consisted of those 'who have always been for fraternization with the enemy and a compromise peace, and who are now really Bolsheviks and doing all they can to condemn this country to class hatred and social strife, ending in Bolshevist ruin'.[4] If Labour had

Henderson, Clynes, Thomas on the surface, there were Hodges, Smillie, Bob Williams, 'hot heads and feather-brains of the Noah Ablett type'[5] lurking below, the real nine-tenths of Labour's iceberg.

Lloyd George, as has been seen, continued to proclaim the need to ward off the threat of Labour. He urged the Cabinet to combine strong government and the preservation of order with far-sighted measures of social reform. Otherwise, Britain might join the three-quarters of Europe 'already converted to Bolshevism'.[6] It was the fear of Germany being swept away in a Red tide that underlay the lenient terms advocated during the peace negotiations in the Fontainebleau Memorandum. Side by side with his belief that the rulers of Soviet Russia could be approached on a regular commercial and even diplomatic basis and that trade with them was highly desirable was the conviction that Communism must be held short of the Vistula. The cessation of Comintern propaganda and internal subversion within the British trade union movement was a pre-condition of normalizing relations with Russia. Throughout 1920, the fear of Bolshevism, the belief that Labour was the demure front for much more dangerous assaults on the economic and political structure, was Lloyd George's fundamental theme and a major determinant of his strategy. If he reproved Churchill for his obsession with 'the baboonery of Bolshevism', Lloyd George himself made ample use of the Red bogey in pressing for some kind of 'fusion' or centrist combination of moderate constitutionalists. In May 1920, he told his Minister of Agriculture, Lee of Fareham, of his impatience with the pinpricks of the Asquithians. He wanted them out of the way to 'get to grips with the real enemy—Labour'.[7] His main advisers, Kerr, Sutherland, Guest, Grigg, were dedicated opponents of socialism. The rising tide of labour militancy in the winter of 1920–1, the crisis of Black Friday and the confrontation with the Triple Alliance, the further belief that Bolshevik subversives were lending succour and arms to Sinn Fein in Ireland, all intensified Lloyd George's zeal to crush Labour and his awareness of where the real opposition lay.

There was ample evidence to confirm the government's fears in 1919–21. Coalition party organizers testified to how Labour was ideally placed to exploit discontent amongst working-class voters. The initial unrest over the continuation of war-time shortages and the failure immediately to abolish conscription swelled Labour polls in

1919. By the latter part of 1920, the rising tide of unemployment, falling real wages, and a cost of living markedly higher than pre-war also told to Labour's advantage. By 1922, Labour was the main voice of protest at the unprecedented level of unemployment and the savage impact of the Geddes axe on the social services. The post-war period also saw a massive increase in Labour's industrial strength, confirming a period of steady growth that really dated from the 1911–14 period. The membership of the trade unions continued to increase after the armistice. By 1921 the TUC could record that its membership had reached 6,613,000. As a result, in the same period the affiliated membership of the Labour Party rose to over four and a half million. It numbered 2,350 local Labour Parties and Trades Councils in England and Wales, plus 62 in Scotland.[8] Apart from its traditional strongholds amongst miners, textile workers, railwaymen, iron and steel workers, engineers, shipbuilders, and pottery workers, Labour was now making inroads into lower middle-class groups such as railway clerks, post office workers, and elementary schoolteachers. The politically conscious working-class, wrote a new recruit, Charles Trevelyan, had gone over *en masse* to Labour.[9]

At the same time, the kind of middle-class professional or intellectual radical that the Fabians had sought to attract before the war now came over to Labour in vast numbers. The Union of Democratic Control brought in many who had opposed the war and who had crusaded for a democratic, negotiated peace. Pethick-Lawrence, Angell, Trevelyan, Ponsonby, Morel, and others all joined Labour and added enormously to its rhetorical striking power. So did J. A. Hobson who probably never became a party member. Tawney, the Webbs, Cole, for all their divergences in interpreting the message of socialism, added immense intellectual distinction. The demolition of the pretensions of the private coal-owners by Tawney and Webb during the Sankey commission in 1919 was a revelation. Partly in response to this socialist revival, the Independent Labour Party, although an eventual casualty of the structural changes in the Labour Party effected in 1918, grew rapidly in membership in 1919 and 1920. Party branches rose to 787 in 1920 and national membership was claimed to stand at 30,000.[10] Especially powerful in Glasgow, where Irish Catholics flocked to support the Clydesiders, Maxton, Maclean, Buchanan, Wheatley, and their colleagues, it had substantial support elsewhere. Sales of *Forward* and the *New Leader* leapt up.

MacDonald, something of an outcast after his electoral defeat at Leicester, refurbished his ILP credentials. As before the war, the ILP, even more than the constituency Labour Parties, seemed the essential channel for non-working-class radicals to work for democratic socialism.

The impact of this in political terms has already been partially discussed. Contemporaries realized that the return of only 57 Labour members, under the quiescent leadership first of Adamson, then of Clynes, in the 1918 election was an illusory reflection of Labour's real power.[11] The significant thing was the 2,375,202 votes that Labour had polled, and its marked appeal to the young, to ex-servicemen, and to women. Labour's electoral gains at Widnes and Bothwell and near-success in Swansea East in the summer of 1919 were a portent of its capacity to voice the protests of the discontented moderate left. The triumph of a little-known miner at Spen Valley in December showed how Labour could take on all comers in a three-cornered contest. Impressive victories in the municipal elections in November showed how Labour could make new inroads into urban communities more complex than unreconstructed mining or textile villages. The gains in the London boroughs were especially impressive. As it happened, Labour's advance in 1920 was less impressive, particularly in the first six months of the year before the post-war economic collapse and the sharp fall in wages and employment. Partly, of course, this was because vacancies occurred in seats relatively unpromising for Labour candidates. There were still two remarkable by-election victories. In Dartford in March, J. Mills won by a massive majority over a variety of opponents, but here the Coalition forces were in much disarray as the local Liberal Association put up an Asquithian. The eventual standard-bearer for the Coalition was an NDP man who came in a bad third. In South Norfolk in July, Labour gained a rare victory in an agricultural seat, with a popular candidate, George Edwards of the Agricultural Labourers' Union, winning at the expense of a Coalition Liberal who got little Unionist support. Otherwise, Labour's electoral performance was not over-impressive, even though it held on to its own seats, including three in South Wales, with some ease. The Stockport by-election in March, where there was tension between Labour and the Co-operative movement, was a particular disappointment. The municipal elections of November 1920 showed a series of Labour defeats. Herbert Morrison attributed them to increases in rates, with Labour candidates now bearing the brunt of the anger of ratepayers who sought cuts in municipal expenditure.[12] The London County Council elections in March 1922 were also to prove unproductive for Labour, as the defeat of Gosling by Benn at Kennington showed.

Nevertheless, the severe winter of 1920–1 and the inability of the government to make any effective impression on the toll of unemployment saw Labour's progress then continue dramatically. There were five parliamentary seats gained in 1921—Dudley in the West Midlands, Kirkcaldy District in Scotland, Penistone in the West Riding, Heywood and Radcliffe in Lancashire, South-West Southwark in London. Several more followed early in 1922, culminating in the smashing defeat of a government junior minister at Pontypridd in July by an ILP man, T. I. Mardy Jones, miners' agent for the Pontypridd district. In almost every type of constituency, Labour's poll increased, while Labour's spirits were sustained by the ever present tide of trade union militancy. The only exception, indeed, was the defeat of Ramsay MacDonald at Woolwich in March 1921. This was truly a special case.[13] A venomous government campaign was run against MacDonald, which stressed his wartime 'pacifism'. His opponent, Captain Gee, backed by Horatio Bottomley, was a V.C. who appealed to the patriotic arsenal workers on traditional wartime lines. Several of the local Labour Party refused to support their candidate; poor MacDonald was humiliated. The Coalition registered what was in fact their sole gain in a contested by-election in the entire period between 1919–22. Woolwich was a wholly exceptional result. Otherwise, the record of this period is of relentless Labour progress which appeared to justify the apprehensions of the government and the confidence of Labour leaders that a Henderson/Clynes/Thomas administration lay just around the corner.[14]

This is all familiar enough. What is much less often emphasized is the inadequacy of Labour's structure and programme in the immediate post-war period. For all its rapid growth as a movement of protest, Labour still lacked credibility as a party of power. While it posed a massive threat to the dominance of the Coalition government, it was a threat that the ministers felt with some confidence that they were able to contain. The most popular note was that struck by Winston Churchill. Addressing his constituents at Dundee on 13 February 1920, he repeatedly urged, in the face of much interruption, that

'Labour was unfit to govern the country'.[15] He gave three main reasons. First, Labour had 'made themselves into a class party, led by class leaders and fighting the battle of class interests in predominance over all other interests (Cheers)'. Secondly, Labour had no constructive programme for the regulation of the mines, for housing, for coping with unemployment, or for increasing the national wealth. Thirdly, Labour leaders had let themselves be deceived by the revolutionaries in Russia and had 'bowed down and chanted hymns and burned incense before the Russian idol'. Churchill's rhetoric was crude and intemperate. It was echoed by few other ministers in public, certainly by no other Liberal. It underlined the gulf that had existed between Churchill and the working-class mind since the unrest in the Welsh mining valleys in 1910. It provided an element of distrust, even of hatred, which coloured the outlook of rising young Labour leaders like Aneurin Bevan (a student at the Central Labour College at this period), and seriously damaged Churchill's standing as a spokesman for the national interest in the inter-war period. In the general election of 1945, and even those of 1950–1, Churchill's atavistic response to Labour was remembered and held against him, to the electoral detriment of his party in working-class areas. Only when the comparatively untainted figures of Eden and Macmillan assumed the Conservative leadership in the 1950s did the heritage of hatred that Churchill had left amongst miners and others finally evaporate. And yet, the fact remained that Churchill's public doubt that Labour was 'fit to govern' touched a responsive chord amongst the voters in the post-war period. Labour was relatively inexperienced. Its leaders came largely from one class of the community, one with no experience of running industrial or financial enterprises. It was, so it seemed, unpragmatic, notably over its attitude towards Russia, and a prey to an extremist fringe. With MacDonald, Snowden, and other experienced Labour leaders out of parliament, and Henderson tending to concentrate on building up the party central machine, Labour created an image of intemperate upheaval at variance with the mood of consensus which the Coalition sought to embody.

The first point to be noted is that, like its opponents, the Labour Party was a coalition as it had always been, a coalition of a somewhat inchoate kind. As before the war, it was a federation of mass trade unions, focused mainly upon social and economic advantages for their members, and of often middle-class socialists, drawn into the ILP and now into the new constituency Labour Parties. The division in the party was reflected in the sections which made up the new national executive, the majority of twelve trade unionists sitting somewhat uneasily with the five (later seven) representatives of the constituency parties, with the four women members drawn from either side. The constituency representatives invariably included members of the ILP whose impotence, after the structural reforms carried through by Henderson and Webb in 1918, has often tended to be exaggerated. A series of conflicts between the unions and the socialists after 1918 testified to the strains still inherent in the flexible protean 'Labour alliance' that Keir Hardie had created at the turn of the century. One after another, the ancillary institutions of the party, the Labour Research Department, under the direction of that austere intellectual, G. D. H. Cole, and the various policy advisory committees, were gradually stripped of their socialist components by the national executive, in response to trade union pressure. The Labour Research Department, indeed, was abolished in 1921, as a result of Henderson's anxiety to merge the research activities of the Labour Party and the TUC.[16] In exile after his defeat in 1918, MacDonald deplored the tension that existed between the unions and the ILP, the self-styled 'right' and 'left' which shackled Labour as an effective challenger to the government. He wrote to Oswald Garrison Villard of the New York *Nation*:

You will have seen what the ILP did at Southport as regards Moscow, and you will certainly have seen what Labour has done here as regards a General Strike. I have never felt so humiliated at being in a fiasco . . . and the blame is heavy upon the Left as upon the Right. . . . The poor miner is left in the lurch and the bonds of confidence in Labour are dangerously strained.[17]

Even allowing for MacDonald's peculiarly Celtic brand of brooding pessimism, especially marked in the period after his electoral defeat at Woolwich, the tension between the different wings of the party was undeniable. Constituency parties were the old assortment of trades councils, trade union branches, 'divisional' parties, and the like. As before, the Labour Party was a vast sprawling umbrella of intensely sectional trade unions, doctrinaire socialists, and recently arrived radicals whose philosophy was hardly distinguishable from the New Liberalism of pre-1914. In this last category came the single-taxers, men like Outhwaite, Hemmerde, Dundas White, and, above all, Josiah Wedgwood, who drifted into the Labour camp after 1918;[18]

Wedgwood, elected as a 'couponed' Liberal in 1918, became vice-chairman of the parliamentary Labour Party in 1921. Labour was 'a queer mixture', thought Laski, though perhaps 'the best of the lot'.[19]

Central figures like MacDonald and Snowden had to battle with each faction in turn. They had to try to divert the unions away from purely industrial action of a direct kind. They had to keep the ILP free from association with quasi-Communist bodies such as the Third International (the short-lived 'Two and a Half International' was the result here). They also had to keep the essential line of demarcation clear between Labour and the Independent Liberals. In this last connection, Henderson's open advocacy of a continuing alliance with the Liberals during the campaign in Widnes in August 1919 was a particular source of embarrassment. Henderson emphasized Labour's part in the wartime coalition; 'his colours were a combination of Liberal and Labour', wrote MacDonald.[20] Despite the growing power of centralization flowing from head office under Henderson's direction, there was still much to do to weld together these disparate units into a coherent party, fit to govern and to retain power.

Again, of the various components within this Labour alliance, the dominant element was clearly the trade unions. The overwhelming majority of the party membership and the bulk of its finance came from union sources, and the unions' control of the national executive and of the party conference, as enshrined in the 1918 constitution, confirmed that this was so. The trade union connection brought both strength and weakness to Labour's claim to be a national challenger for power. It brought financial security through the political levy. It provided, of course, a solid foundation for identification with the mass proletariat. It won much popular support through the campaign for nationalization of the mines. As Hardie had urged before 1914, it was crucial for Labour to be a preponderantly working-class movement, instead of a rootless middle-class group of Marxist intellectuals on the lines of the Italian socialists, or indeed the pre-war Social Democratic Federation in Britain. On the other hand, the trade unions were essentially sectional in their appeal with an abiding distrust of undue involvement with the state. They were hardly committed to the primacy of political or constitutional action, geared to the conquest of power within the state. The miners' leaders, men like Smillie, Smith, or Cook, scarcely thought in political terms at all. They pressed doggedly on with the demands for nationalization or 'a wages pool' without reference to the political context in which they were made. It is the political naïvety of the miners almost as much as the stupidity and inhumanity of the coal-owners which impresses one about the discussions before the Sankey commission. In the end, the miners pressed for everything, and gained almost nothing, not even the crumb of the nationalization of mining royalties, in an industry generally admitted to be hopelessly mismanaged.

While prominent union leaders, such as J. H Thomas of the NUR, remained anxious for parliamentary seats, increasingly leading figures in the union world placed their prime efforts and hopes on industrial activity. Ernest Bevin, briefly (and for the only time until 1931) a parliamentary candidate in 1918, is a case in point.[21] Like most of his colleagues, he believed that industrial action superseded political. The Labour Party was a parliamentary front for 'the movement', a public projection of the TUC. The pressures for 'direct action' or for varying forms of workers' control confirmed this tendency. It reached a climax with the Councils of Action created at the height of the 'Arms to Poland' crisis in August 1920. This generated the legend of the government having to surrender to spontaneous rank-and-file trade union pressure even though, as has been seen, Lloyd George had himself scant intention of sending either arms or troops to Poland. The Council of Action remained a symbol of industrial power, beguiling to trade union leaders of most shades of opinion, and an embarrassment to the parliamentary Labour Party. Even though the new general council of the TUC in 1921 was by no means dominated by the left wing, it retained its enthusiasm for the direct methods of the Council of Action. They provided the myth which sustained the unions just as the anti-strike committees run by Eric Geddes sustained the government. An unnecessary confrontation like that of 1926, in which the miners suffered cruelly, was the result. It was the product of a movement which prided itself on essentially having its focus outside parliament, on minimizing the authority of its leaders, and of being basically a defensive pressure-group designed simply to fight for the living standards of the working class, rather than as a dynamic party anxious to capture power and to reach out to all classes and sections of the community. Of course, in the situation prevailing after 1918, the Labour Party in parliament consisted largely of second-rate trade unionists, irregular in attendance, uninspiring in debate, amongst whom Clynes and Graham were the most impressive. Its chairman in 1919–20, Willie Adamson, was a dull performer, even on mining topics where he was outshone by Hartshorn and Brace. It was natural that Smillie, Hodges, Williams, Bevin, and other gifted union leaders could offer the glamour of active leadership. But it was not yet a recipe for a successful party or a successful government.

In these circumstances, the Labour Party presented a somewhat paralysed alternative to the policies of the government. They were criticized almost exclusively from a trade union standpoint; Labour's promise of united action on behalf of national objectives was inevitably suspect. By contrast with the alternatives offered by Lloyd George's ministers, the Labour response too often revealed its sectional, trade-based origin. One instance was the housing programme. It was universally agreed that there was an immense need for working-class housing at low rents, and that private builders had not come anywhere near to meeting this need. This was one of the main themes stressed by the Joint Industrial Conference in 1919 and by the trade union evidence before it. Yet the response of the building trade unions was throughout suspicious and negative. They refused to accept 'dilution' in any form. This was understandable, in view of the seasonal nature of building work. Less defensible was the refusal to make more apprenticeships available to ex-servicemen and others, and the rigid demarcations between different classes of building workers. There were many other reasons for the failure of the housing programme as has been seen—the inadequacies of the local authorities, the inefficiency of the private building industry, the anxiety of contractors for easy profits in speculative building for the wealthy, immense Treasury obstacles placed in the path of the Ministry of Health. But it must be said that the building trade unions played some part in the failure of a national house-building programme, in their unwillingness to meet the shortage of skilled labour which was agreed to be a major problem. This, in turn, handicapped the Labour Party in launching an effective attack on the government's housing policy under Addison and Mond. A similar approach governed the Labour Party's attitude towards the coal mines, where acceptance of the miners' demands on a national pool and other aspects of wages precluded co-operation with attempts to improve production or productivity in a notoriously labour-intensive industry, or assist in the rehabilitation of desperate mining communities. It all suggested that Labour was still an amalgam of sections rather than a cohesive party with national objectives.

It followed that Labour's support in the nation was partial also. The outstanding areas of Labour strength were in areas of concentrated heavy industry, preferably of a one-industry kind as in mining or textile towns. Many of Labour's strongholds were, in a sense, almost industrial villages, surviving from an earlier phase of industrialization, isolated mining communities such as Clay Cross, Chester-le-Street, or Ebbw Vale, with their fierce class loyalties and a warm sense of communal and cultural association. Labour was based essentially on Clydeside, Durham, Lancashire, the West Riding, and South Wales. In the major cities, as municipal elections showed in 1920–2, Labour had made less impact. In London, Birmingham, Liverpool, or Cardiff, with their conglomeration of trades and occupations and complex social structure, Labour found it hard to build up a viable form of party organization or to win mass support. In the 1922 general election, Labour captured ten seats out of sixty-two in the London boroughs, three in Manchester, two in Leeds, and none at all in Birmingham, Liverpool, Hull, Bristol, or Cardiff. Herbert Morrison's efforts to build up an autonomous form of organization for the London Labour Party were blunted by the stern centralism of Head Office. In all, Labour's tally of metropolitan borough seats in local elections fell from 572 in 1919 to 259 in 1922.[22] The triumph of Labour even in the poorer boroughs of the East End, heralded by the return of Lansbury for Poplar and C. R. Attlee for Limehouse in 1922, really lay some years off. All four Islington seats returned Conservatives in 1922, as did three Lambeth constituencies, Stoke Newington, and Mile End. Not until 1934, in a famous victory, did Morrison establish a permanent ascendancy for Labour in London, one which lasted until well after 1945. With Labour relatively weak in central city areas, as well as in areas of newer industries, chemicals, electrical industries, car manufacturing, consumer durables, and the like, its claim to be a contemporary, nationwide rival to the Coalition remained in doubt. In rural constituencies, Labour was handicapped by the depressed circumstances of agricultural labourers after 1921. Its successes between 1906 and 1922 were based on the legacy of the first industrial revolution rather than of the second.

Finally, even if Churchill's strictures were too extreme, Labour's programmes and its solutions for the manifold ills afflicting post-war Britain were still sketchy and often derivative. Labour had much to say on foreign affairs. Indeed, foreign and imperial policy—the peace treaties, Russia, India, Egypt, and so on—dominated the debates in the annual Labour Party conference between 1919 and 1923. Labour's views on foreign policy were an updated version of those of Morel and the Union of Democratic Control. Labour upheld the League of Nations, which it linked, none too persuasively, with the principle of open covenants openly arrived at. It urged peace with Russia and the economic rehabilitation of central Europe, assisted by loans and export credits, and including industrial co-operative societies established on an international basis. It attacked the punitive basis of the Versailles treaty on Keynesian lines and the 'system' of great power politics that resulted from it: Molly Hamilton thought this line of attack 'grossly exaggerated'. Contrary to later accounts, the Labour Party did support the principle that Germany should pay reparations to cover the damage to life and property for which she was said to be responsible. However, Labour wanted reparations scaled down, and the Reparations Commission to reach an early decision on the global amount that Germany should pay. The commission's operations should be placed under the aegis of the League of Nations, with a right of appeal.[23]

Labour increasingly projected itself as the truly international party, new-born, untrammelled by the national rivalries of pre-1914 which had led to the holocaust that followed. Ramsay MacDonald, his radical credentials glowingly refurbished by his opposition to the war, built up a unique reputation as the voice of internationalism and peace. Labour tended to argue that the route to economic recovery for Britain at home lay through the international sphere. The ending of reparations and war debts, the establishment of stable trading relations with Germany, Russia, and other European powers would restore markets and renew the buoyancy of the staple industries on which the economy (and Labour's electoral strength) were based. Much of this was admirable. It was also remarkably similar to the professions of the Liberals and the Cecil group—and to the practice of the Coalition government. While there were episodes in the foreign policy of the administration that Labour could attack—the partial intervention in Russia, the threat of arms to Poland, the aggressively anti-Turkish policy in Asia Minor—the general themes of Labour's

approach provided the basis of Lloyd Georgian diplomacy. In trying
to renegotiate major aspects of the Versailles settlement, appease
Germany, and bring the Soviet Union into the European system, in
trying above all to rebuild the shattered economies of central Europe
on the basis of international conciliation and guarantees in conference
after conference from San Remo in 1920 to The Hague in 1922, Lloyd
George was in practice the voice of British radicalism in foreign policy.
At the cost of repeated onslaughts from the Unionist right, and of
frequent sniping from Churchill within the Cabinet, Lloyd George's
foreign policy tended to negate the argument for a Labour government. He was pursuing most of Labour's objectives, but with greater
efficiency and greater realism.

Equally in much of its domestic programme, Labour found it hard
to strike a particularly distinct note. It was, of course, valiant for social
reform. It championed increased public expenditure on education,
pensions, minimum wages for industrial and agricultural workers,
unemployment insurance, housing, public transport. It had not produced any comprehensive scheme for linking its social programme
together as a coherent whole. Tawney and Cole were unable to construct the basic intellectual framework for Labour policy that
Beveridge and Keynes (both Liberals) were able to do in 1945. Nor
did Labour at any stage produce a financial policy which might make
practical sense of their idealistic and expensive social programmes.
Much of Labour's thinking (under which direct taxation was good and
indirect, bad) was a translation of old Liberal doctrines, symbolized
by the presence of Philip Snowden as Labour's all-purpose expert on
treasury affairs. This applied also to the speeches of Willie Graham
(Edinburgh Central), the parliamentary Labour Party's new discovery on financial and trade questions in 1918–22, famous for his
memory of statistics. The one novelty that Labour did offer was the
capital levy on individual property owners to redeem the National
Debt.[24] It was proposed that a rising scale of taxation would apply to
capital upwards of £5,000, until a 60 per cent rate applied to capital of
over £1m. Payment could be made in government securities such as
War Loan scrip, in industrial securities, or even in cash. Labour
claimed that this would raise at least £3,000m. and very rapidly too. It
would wipe out half the war debt of £7,500m. and make possible both
reductions in income tax and new funds for social expenditure.
Further, through the transfer of industrial shares and debentures, it

would give the nation part ownership of the railways, mines, land, the banks, insurance, and shipping—the 'equity share' approach to nationalization revived by Gaitskell in the 1950s. This scheme for a capital levy of which Pethick-Lawrence was the most effective and persistent advocate, received some authoritative backing. This came notably from the Liberal professor of economics at Cambridge (later unfairly attacked by Keynes), A. C. Pigou.[25] The idea of a levy originated from a well-founded concern about extortionate wartime profits, virtually tax-free. But the details of assessment and valuation—which aroused alarm from amongst the Co-operative societies who never liked the capital levy—were not worked out in detail. It was noticeable that when Labour came to office in 1924 that Snowden in his budget concentrated on such traditional items as 'a free breakfast table' and ignored his party's commitment to a capital levy. Two months earlier MacDonald had announced that a capital levy could not be enacted in that parliament. In any case, he went on, the levy was not 'a stage to socialism' but merely a technique for reducing the burden of debt charges upon industry.[26] In fact, from 1923 the party erased a capital levy from its programme. The idea had made sense during the post-war boom of 1919–20. It made less in the trade depression of 1921–3, with sagging investment and falling profits. Labour henceforth made scant effort to reduce inequalities in capital as opposed to inequalities in income, until the floating of the idea of a wealth tax by the party's national executive in the 1970s.

Even in its own special area of social reform, many of Labour's proposals were imprecise. On the Poor Law, which Beatrice Webb had effectively undermined in the minority report of the Poor Law Commission in 1909, Labour offered no clear diagnosis. It tended to expend its rhetoric in supporting the courageous but unconstructive efforts of Labour-controlled Boards of Guardians in areas such as Poplar to spend and spend on the poor beyond the precepts allowed by central government, in the hope that the whole shoddy system of 'less eligibility' would cave in from financial pressure, much as the Speenhamland system had caved in a century earlier. It was magnificent but it was not politics, even if George Lansbury acquired the mantle of martyrdom here, long before Bevin set fire to the faggots at Brighton in 1935. Nor was it electorally popular. 'Poplarism' cost Labour dear. The party won 143 seats on London Boards of Guar-

dians in 1919, only 112 in 1922.[27] Labour's ill-costed social programmes were much as put forward by Liberals of the Masterman-
Rowntree schools. They were designed to spend more in propping up
the casualties of the injustices of life, the old, the sick, the children,
the unemployed, not to provide a comprehensive system of social
security. In any case, some of what Labour demanded was being put
into practice by Addison, Fisher, Horne, and Macnamara. Wheatley's Housing Act of 1924 followed Addison's scheme of subsidies,
with more success. The Coalition government's programme on housing, education, labour, and employment in 1919–20, until trade
collapsed and 'economy' carried the day, combined much of the best
of Labour's policies, while being constrained by financial considerations to which Labour paid little heed.

   Labour's main thrust in domestic argument in 1919–22 was, in
fact, sociological, not economic or financial. It stood 'for the working
class', for protecting the wretched victim of capitalism in Jarrow,
Merthyr Tydfil, Clydeside, and Poplar. It had, to a degree remarkable
for a party which claimed to base its programme on a scientific
diagnosis of the economic structure and the seeds of its collapse, no
valid economic policy at all. There was no Labour policy for planning,
for revitalizing industry, for management of the economy. Apart from
a brief exposition of the capital levy by Snowden in 1919 (the motion
carried *nem. con.* without a debate),[28] there was not one discussion of
financial or economic policy at any of Labour's annual party conferences between 1919 and 1922. In financial debates, Labour's spokesmen cut a poor figure, when contrasted with Austen Chamberlain,
Horne, Mond, or Lloyd-Greame. Frankly, they were ignorant of
financial detail, and they gloried in that ignorance since their ultimate
claim was to prepare for a new society, not to try to administer or patch
up the present one. The acknowledged Labour expert on finance, was
Philip Snowden, and he had been defeated at the polls in 1918. His
Labour and National Finance (1920) was an orthodox enough document. When he returned in 1922, and even more when he appeared as
Labour's all-powerful Chancellor of the Exchequer in 1924 and 1929,
he proved to be an economist of quite extraordinary conservatism.
With remarkably little protest, he yoked Labour's programme not to
Webb, let alone to Marx, but to Cobden and Bright, if not Ricardo.
He was a fanatical free trader, an implacable opponent of social
expenditure that might unbalance the budget, suspicious of public

works, import boards, quotas, or other novelties. Labour followed his
head tamely enough. Henderson and Willie Graham, Labour's other
spokesmen in financial matters, took much the same line. On currency questions, wrote Sidney Webb, Labour was, 'as Lombard
Street would say, as sound as a bell'.[29] It followed that Labour in
1919–22 was ill-prepared if not unfit to govern, in that it had no new
analysis of the economic troubles of the nation. Its remedy for
economic stagnation was to prop up with subsidies the ailing staple
industries of coal, textiles, iron and steel, and shipbuilding. Its
remedy for trading deficits was stern deflation, 'living within your
means', and an unyielding commitment to free trade. The national
executive was particularly slow to produce new thinking on agriculture, apart from rehearsing the merits of the guaranteed minimum
wages for labourers achieved during the war and lost after 1921. More
original ideas came from E. F. Wise, Hobson, and the ILP who
stressed the need to increase capitalization and give farmers security of
tenure as a boost to more efficient methods of food production.
Throughout the 1920s, Labour's agricultural policies paled by comparison with those of Lloyd George and the Liberals, until at the end
of the decade Noel Buxton and the ex-Liberal, Christopher Addison,
began a new range of imaginative proposals including marketing
schemes and import boards.

On unemployment, which first emerged as a tragic menace during
the lifetime of the Coalition government from May–June 1920
onwards, Labour had really very little to offer. Its ideas had scarcely
advanced beyond the 'right to work' scheme proposed by Hardie and
MacDonald in 1907.[30] Like that former scheme, it was based on
traditional views of the trade cycle and of under-consumption, ideas
that J. A. Hobson had first made familiar to the British left in the
1890s. Symbolically, Hobson himself was allied to the ILP at this
time, and welded his economic theories to the pressure for increased
workers' purchasing power put forward by Maxton and the Clydesiders. The 'living wage' scheme of 1926 was the outcome, imaginative and forward-looking, but never accepted by the Labour leadership.
Meanwhile, Labour advanced a variety of proposals for grappling
with mass unemployment. It urged that the government provide
guarantees to exporters and traders to overseas countries where
markets had disappeared owing to the dislocation of war and the
collapse of credit in the importing country. This was much in line with

the practice of the Coalition government which introduced export credits from September 1919 onwards and found that they yielded remarkably little. From March 1921, the government announced that it was prepared to offer advances to cover 100 per cent of the cost of goods to British exporters, and to guarantee up to 85 per cent of the invoice price. But the advances made up to March 1921 had amounted to only £400,000.[31] The problem of markets being glutted with high-priced goods and the lowered purchasing power of the consumer remained. Only in fringe markets—Finland, the Baltic countries, the Balkans—did the export credit schemes have much impact. There was the alternative ter Meulen scheme (which Labour did not favour), a Dutch idea under which credit would be allocated internationally to different countries upon the security of specific assets, with gold bonds issued against the security of these assets. But this made no headway. Labour tended to overlook the practical financial difficulties in its call for export credits. These were most helpful in the smallest and least profitable markets. At home, Labour called, along the lines of 'living wage' and 'right to work' schemes, for adequate mainten-ance for the unemployed and their dependants, with wages not to fall below a reasonable subsistence level. Without a national policy for wages, this raised all manner of technical problems, and left the need for comprehensive unemployment insurance as urgent as ever. It has already been noted that the government had in 1920 made progress in this direction, through a national minimum wage, with agricultural labourers and domestic servants being excluded.

The nub of Labour's programme for the unemployed was more public works. This was really 'outdoor relief' in twentieth-century guise, a palliative not necessarily more effective or more appealing to the moral dignity of the unemployed than existing policies. In prac-tice, such government schemes as the building of arterial roads around London gave work to remarkably few unemployed people.[32] In any case, Labour's schemes for public works were largely nullified by financial orthodoxy. In 1929–31 it was to be seen how Treasury-minded the Labour Party was, with Snowden easily able to block extravagant-sounding public works proposals, even though the toll of unemployed was now almost three million. Public works plus 'adequate maintenance' was not much of a policy for grappling with unemployment. Again, it had little more to offer than did the government's efforts. Under the aegis of Macnamara, as Minister of

Labour, and Mond, as First Commissioner of· Works, modest counter-cyclical works programmes were initiated, and the principle of deficit financing at least considered. The St. David's committee was to make some useful suggestions about public schemes such as housing developments. In the end, the Coalition government failed to bring down the toll of unemployment. It may have been a problem to defeat any government at that time, confronted with the transitional character of the economy and the force of entrenched financial orthodoxy. The Coalition did not do well, and probably made matters worse by allowing an uncontrolled boom in 1919–20 to be followed by massive deflation of a self-defeating kind. All that may be added here is that there is no evidence, from the programmes that Labour put forward in 1919–22 or from its record in office in 1924 and 1929–31 that the Labour Party would have done any better. Indeed, in terms of administrative competence and the retention of public confidence, it might well have done a good deal worse.

The apex of Labour's programme was, of course, 'socialism'. In the famous debate in the Commons on 20 March 1923 on 'the failure of the capitalist system', Snowden and Tom Johnston spoke eloquently of the founding of a socialist commonwealth in the future, much as the prophet Hardie had foretold long ago.[33] But 'socialism' as an answer to the country's ills was so ill-defined and propagandist a concept in 1919–22 that it may be doubted how seriously it was ever entertained. Snowden's evangelical speech was a good deal less rigorous than the free-enterprise philippic offered in reply by Sir Alfred Mond. The content of this socialism was unclear. Presumably it went far beyond the advanced social reform plus a managed economy advocated by Liberals, Independent, and Coalitionist alike. It had something to do with workers' control, perhaps, and indeed Clause IV (or rather III b) in the 1918 constitution included a vague nod in this direction. But there was no serious effort to work out the mechanics of workers' control or public accountability, even in the mines, at this or any other stage. That was left to John Maclean and the tiny British Socialist Party;[34] the syndicalists in the Welsh mining valleys gradually turned either to Communist *étatisme* like Arthur Horner or right-wing Labourism like W. H. Mainwaring. In practice, advocates of industrial devolution or of decentralization like G. D. H. Cole and his Guild Socialists made scant impact. The Building Guilds set up to construct houses and flats in Manchester and other towns in 1920–1 petered out.[35] Cole joined the mainstream of the Labour movement once again.

Socialism in practical terms meant neither workers' control nor any form of syndicalism, but nationalization of the major industries of the country, perhaps of the institutions of distribution and exchange (the banks and insurance houses, for example) as well. The land might also be included. This was the acme of Labour's proposals throughout this period. In all the class-war rhetoric contained in the *Daily Herald* and expressed through a Marxist terminology, which makes the *Herald* an unrepresentative source for Labour thinking at this period, it was assumed that nationalization would end at a stroke the evils of capitalism. It would raise wages, improve industrial relations, establish public control, and generate new wealth. But public ownership was an aspiration not a programme. It was almost a substitute for thought since the advent of socialism was held to be so inevitable that its mechanics, financing, and institutional arrangements need not be worked out in detail. Labour in these years made much of nationalization in general, and little of nationalization in particular. The only industry where nationalization was pressed as an immediate objective was, of course, the coal mining industry. Here, there were workable schemes produced by Sankey and other members of the commission, including a good deal of democratic industrial self-government through district councils with real powers. The Miners' Federation put forward a bill to nationalize mines and minerals in 1919.[36] Tawney produced a fairly detailed sketch of public ownership for the mines with a national mining council to control production, distribution, exports, and finance. Frank Hodges also wrote an effective, but brief book on the subject.[37] But the Labour Party left these on one side and did not follow them up. The motion for the nationalization of the mines at the 1922 annual party conference at Edinburgh, moved by Frank Hodges, seconded by Emanuel Shinwell, was carried without opposition, indeed virtually without debate. There was never advanced at any stage between 1919 and 1922 a precise blueprint of how nationalization would be carried out in practice. Its financing, its mode of operation, its relation to parliament and to other publicly or privately owned industries was seldom discussed. MacDonald himself had little to say about these points in *Socialism: Critical and Constructive* (1922): it was heavily flavoured with the same quasi-Darwinian biological analogies that had featured his writings before the war. It included only the briefest comment on schemes for nationalization drawn up by the miners (notably Hodges) and the railwaymen; the only point made was that 'bureaucracy' would be eliminated'.[38] There was no Labour programme of nationalization, none that was presented to the nation in 1923, 1924, or 1929. When the ex-Liberal Christopher Addison appeared to flirt with the idea of the nationalization of land, on the lines of the 'cultivating tenure' in Lloyd George's 'Green Book', MacDonald carefully kept him out of the Ministry of Agriculture, or at least from Cabinet rank.[39] Labour's economic plans were still basically the 'advanced radicalism' of pre-war, with the class rhetoric and class solidarity of an entrenched industrial base. Beyond generalities Labour did not go. It did not criticize the strategy of the Coalition government in any fundamental sense because it did not regard itself so far as a credible challenger to it. It was the leadership of the opposition to which Labour aspired in 1919–22, ousting the Liberals as the left-wing alternative to Toryism, not the leadership of government. It was still the party of protest the founding fathers had created in Faringdon Street a generation ago.

The conclusion must be, then, that Labour, if hardly 'unfit to govern', was in this period some way short of presenting a valid alternative to the policies of the government, with all their shortcomings. Nor could it reasonably be claimed that Labour was a 'national' movement in the way that the National government was not. Labour was clearly a class party not a national one. It projected itself as a political façade for the TUC. Not until MacDonald became leader of the party in November 1922 and welded Labour's disparate *squadristi* into an effective parliamentary fighting force, operating on an orthodox party basis and openly seeking the votes of dissident Liberals and radicals, did Labour make an effective advance. In the period 1919–22, as has been seen, in many respects it was scarcely a political party at all. It was a vast pressure group, a labour 'interest' with the TUC calling the tune. Throughout this period, in the inter-party flux of these years, there was speculation that Labour might not transform itself into a clearly defined independent party at all. It might, as the *Nation* constantly hoped, provide the mass working-class support that the small band of Independent Liberals so desperately needed. It might make common cause with the Cecil centrists, or at least their more progressive elements. There were prospects, it was even rumoured, of Lloyd George himself recapturing his special relation with the Labour movement, built up at the Board of Trade in 1905–8 and renewed as recently as the early months of 1918 with the new overtures to the trade unions then. Sidney Webb once committed himself to the view that the Coalition could break up and Lloyd George again project himself as a leader of the left, including Labour—a view that brought a stern rebuke from H. N. Brailsford.[40] As late as February 1922, Arthur Henderson meditated on the possibility of Lloyd George trying to split the Labour Party as he had done the Liberals, with 'patriots' like Clynes, Hodge, Thomas, Brace, and Hartshorn aligned in opposition to the Bolshevist fringe.[41] Even a man like Frank Hodges, the miners' General Secretary, was thought to be eligible for such a combination.

Lloyd George, after all, was capable of moving as decisively to the left as to the right. In the autumn of 1921–2 there took place what the press called his 'swing to the left', including a new emphasis on palliatives to deal with unemployment, disarmament at Washington, and peace in Ireland. Thomas Jones, deputy-secretary to the Cabinet, had a curious conversation with Arthur Greenwood, formerly a civil servant at the Ministry of Reconstruction, and now in Labour's research department, on 18 January 1922.[42] Labour, so Greenwood insisted, would return a minimum of 150 successful candidates at the next election. It was currently well-disposed towards Lloyd George, because of Ireland, Genoa, and Reparations. 'If you are "sound" on Education and only in for reasonable economy that will help greatly.' Greenwood thought 'official co-operation impossible but limited unofficial understandings as to certain seats worth exploring especially as some of the seats of the leaders (e.g. Henderson) are insecure.' As events turned out, the full rigour of the axe of Geddes alienated a good deal of possible Labour sympathy with the government. Still, the prospects for some kind of *rapprochement* between Labour and a Prime Minister sorely harassed by a rampant die-hard Toryism in his domestic and foreign policy remained a possibility to the end. Lloyd George kept on good personal terms with men like Snowden and George Lansbury. There were limits to Labour's confidence and independence even now. Even the Geddes axe was not necessarily a fatal blow to co-operation, as Labour had campaigned as hard for 'economy' as anyone else, though naturally the main emphasis here tended to be on British military commitments in India, Mesopotamia, Persia, and Egypt.

All this is not to deny that Labour posed a formidable challenge to the government in 1919–22. It was already immensely more powerful than it had ever looked like being before August 1914. By 1922, it could claim over 2,400 divisional or local Labour Parties, while over 400 candidates had been adopted. Rather it is to emphasize that this Labour challenge had its limits in terms of Labour's organizational structure, its class base, its electoral support, and its ideology. Some of these problems were inevitably the temporary result of Labour's rapid rise in a few years from being a minor third force to becoming the effective opposition. It would have been unrealistic to expect that in only four or five years Labour could develop the style and coherence of better-endowed capitalist parties which had been in existence for generations. Some of the weaknesses of this period perhaps endured much longer. It took the period after the crisis of 1931 for Labour to evolve an effective amalgam of social democracy and Keynesianism as the basis for a realistic economic policy. It took the experience of the Second World War for Labour to provide (again with the assistance of Keynes) a credible antidote to mass unemployment.[43] It took the Butskellite years after 1951 for Labour to move away from the 'cloth cap' era of social protest to elaborate up-to-date forms of fiscal management (put into practice somewhat unhappily between 1964 and 1970, perhaps more successfully so after 1974). It took the years from 1974 for Labour to start renewing its links with the social democratic movements of continental Europe and to modify its isolationism. Labour, on the eve of the general election of 1922, had the capacity for almost unlimited growth. Its organizational structure was crystallizing, its ideas were beginning to mature. There was new inspiration from the Labour Party research and information bureau, founded in January 1922. Its permanent secretary was Arthur Greenwood, formerly an assistant of Addison's at the Ministry of Reconstruction, while its research workers included gifted socialists like Barbara Wootton and Hugh Dalton. MacDonald was managing to erode the almost paralysing sense of deference or inferiority innate in a party composed largely of poorly-educated working men, operating within a highly rigid class framework. Labour would, without doubt, soon be fit to govern. But that moment had not arrived in 1919–22. Apart from marginally affecting the climate of industrial relations, it is difficult to visualize any area of policy that a Labour government would have handled with more competence in the years after the armistice. It was still basically the voice of protest, geared to the long haul in the wilderness.

What can be said is that Labour in this period, despite all entice-ments and the dreams of men like Greenwood, clung on fiercely to its independence. The old magic of the 'party of progress', uniting Labour and radicals in a popular front, had evaporated. Labour still preserved its attachment to the parliamentary mode. Attempts to affiliate the Labour Party to the Communist International or to merge it with the nascent British Communist Party got nowhere. At the annual party conference at Edinburgh in June 1922, the motion for the affiliation of the Communists was defeated yet again, by 3,086,000 to 261,000. The most powerful onslaught, as has been seen, came from Frank Hodges of the miners whose well-cut blue suit and silk handkerchief aroused disgust among ILP delegates.[44] The Commun-ists stood for collectivist dictatorship, the Labour Party for democra-tic socialism. Labour and the Communists remained at arms' length, while efforts to merge the TUC into a kind of 'United Front,' pressed by Stalin as against Trotsky, Kamenev, and Zinoviev after 1925, also were fruitless.[45] With all its limitations, the Labour Party retained its commitment to the democratic process and its sensitivity to the British political tradition—and, through its powerful nonconformist heritage, the British religious tradition as well. Labour was not ready to govern in 1919–22 and it was fortunate that it did not do so. Under new leadership, and in more congenial circumstances after 1922, it was to advance with new purpose in the quest for socialism in our time.[46]

10

Major Challengers:
the Die-Hards

Labour's challenge to the Coalition government was long-term and predictable. After all, the Labour Party had broken with the government since before the 'coupon election'. The Labour component of the government was negligible—indeed, non-existent when Barnes and Roberts retired in February 1920. The challenge from the extreme right was more immediate and more insidiously dangerous since, of course, the government would survive or fall on the basis of the Unionists' staying faithful to it. Bonar Law was the key figure in the administration in party terms; his relationship with Lloyd George was the fulcrum on which it turned. The danger from the right, then, preoccupied ministers and defenders of the Coalition at a very early stage, even before the Paris peace negotiations were concluded. It took a very different form from the challenge from Labour. Where Labour was imprecise in many aspects of its doctrines, the extreme right was all too specific. Where Labour could count on an almost limitless mass following amongst working men and women, the right was short of numbers. Its strength lay in its connections in parliament and Fleet Street, and its ability to provide a megaphone for fundamental Tory instincts which the policies of the Coalition appeared to override.

For a long while, however, the Tory challenge was a muffled and indistinct one. A series of disparate issues arose which led to protest by sections within the Unionist Party, especially by back-benchers in the House of Commons. Lloyd George himself felt certain throughout of the existence of a powerful chorus of die-hard opponents, nationalist in outlook in foreign affairs, anti-socialist and inegalitarian at home. Indeed, a favourite tactic of the Prime Minister, particularly in the lead-up to the 'fusion' moves in the spring of 1920, was to parallel die-hard opposition with Labour 'bolshevism'. Who exactly these die-hards were, with their echoes of the 'ditchers' who had resisted the Parliament Bill in 1911, was not often made clear. There were very few orthodox Unionists, even 'uncouponed' ones, who opposed the government in the months after the 1918 general election. There was Brigadier Page Croft's two-man National Party, with its links with 'patriotic labour' via Havelock Wilson of the Seamen's Union; but this was a tiny and eccentric minority. Horatio Bottomley's Independent Party claimed to be radical in its attitude towards social change. Nevertheless, Lloyd George felt that if the die-hards did not exist, then, like Glendower, he must conjure their spirits up out of the vasty deep. Their very presence would confirm that the Coalition truly stood for the middle way, and was opposed with equal fervour by extremes of left and right. In March 1920, not many took him seriously. But by the end of the year, the spectre of die-hardism was haunting the adherents of the Coalition. There was a relentless stream of criticism and denigration of aspects of the government's policy. Each episode of die-hard criticism, relatively trivial at the time, proved to be a milestone in the road that led to October 1922.

In the early period of the government, it was foreign policy that generated most die-hard sniping. There were many Unionists in the House who took seriously those declarations in the course of the election about making Germany pay and hanging the Kaiser. Their passion was fanned by Leo Maxse's *National Review*, a monthly which served as a bell-wether for anti-Semitic, anti-German xenophobia on the far right, and also by the *Morning Post*, H. A. Gwynne's classic pillar of high Tory orthodoxy. They were often joined by St. Loe Strachey's *Spectator*, once Liberal and still free trade, but second to none in its strident anti-Semitism and hostility towards 'aliens'. *The Times* also took every opportunity to instil doubt about Lloyd George's seriousness over a peace settlement with Germany. This was partly the result of Northcliffe's private quarrel with Lloyd George during the war after the fiasco of his visit to the United States. Even more, it reflected the change in editorship when Geoffrey Dawson (né Robinson), the successor to Buckle since 1912, was followed by Wickham Steed. The latter was a crusader for many causes including Balkan nationalism and Irish freedom, but also a virulent opponent of Lloyd Georgian diplomacy. Steed arrogated for himself the mantle of defender of France and the preserver of the *entente cordiale.* He pursued Lloyd George's conduct of foreign policy with the passion of a vendetta; symbolically, his motor car collided with that of the Prime Minister during the Cannes conference in January 1922, though no-one was injured.[1]

Armed with these allies, an array of Unionist back-benchers, headed by the otherwise totally obscure Kennedy Jones, telegraphed the Prime Minister in Paris in early April 1919, expressing dismay at what was thought to be the over-lenient attitude shown by him and Wilson towards German reparations, frontier settlements, and the issue of war guilt. Lloyd George returned in full majesty to crush the rebels. His speech included a memorable assault on Northcliffe and *The Times* which Printing House Square never forgave nor forgot. But it was indicative of the importance that he attached to these critics of the right that he regarded it as a major crisis for the Coalition, despite its huge majority in the Commons.

The next episode in die-hard protest came on 23 October 1919, again over Britain's external relations. This arose from the restlessness occasioned by the government's Aliens Restriction Bill, handled by Auckland Geddes and Shortt. This measure failed to satisfy the xenophobic nationalism of the Unionist benches, which still flourished even though there were perhaps no more than 20,000 aliens in the country who had any connection with Austria or Germany. Sir Ernest Wild now accused aliens of introducing 'the white slave traffic, unnatural vice, the brothel keepers, ... the gambling hells' and of being the cause of at least 'one half of the vice' in the country. Pemberton Billing deplored the migration of 'Asiatic' aliens across London 'from the slums of Whitechapel to the sacred precincts of Park Lane'. 'And Westminster' another honourable member called out encouragingly.[2] Sir Edward Carson led the main attack—which evoked comparison with the famous revolt against Bonar Law during the Nigerian assets debate in November 1916. The result was the rare phenomenon of a government defeat by 72 votes over the holding of pilotage certificates by aliens (a somewhat sensitive issue between the British and French Foreign Offices). The opposition vote of 185 included 120 Coalition Unionists, as well as Liberals and Labour trade unionists. A delegation of those who had carried the amendment against the government was hastily invited to 10 Downing Street to confer with Lloyd George and some of his senior colleagues.[3] They included a broad spectrum of opinion: Carson, right-wing figures such as Joynson-Hicks and Kennedy Jones, centrist supporters of the Coalition such as Wild and Sir John Butcher, even Coalition Liberals like Sir Thomas Whittaker and John Hinds, together with—Pelion upon so many Ossas—Horatio Bottomley. The result was that the government had to agree to some significant concessions to put teeth into the Aliens Bill, to strengthen the powers of deportation, and to prevent 'aliens', loosely defined, from entering the civil service. These measures were in the 1930s to offer grave obstacles to Jewish victims of Hitler's purges who sought asylum in Britain. It was an interesting demonstration of back-bench power. Lord Hugh Cecil and other observers felt that the government's defeat was due partly to bad parliamentary management, partly to the absence of Bonar Law, partly to a reaction 'to the hectoring methods adopted by Auckland Geddes in particular'. It might also have been in part reaction to the uncompromising handling of the Electricity Supply Bill, by Eric Geddes, another tactless and maladroit parliamentary performer. The House, it was thought, 'resents the sudden leap into fame and power of the Geddes brothers and is impatient of Auckland Geddes' . . . rather dogmatic style'.[4] Even so, this episode can hardly be regarded as a major triumph for the die-hard right wing. Dislike of foreigners was a theme which united Unionists of many shades in 1919: it was to harden into racialism in the 1930s. The rebels over the Aliens Bill included many hard-core loyalists. The government, therefore, was able to brush this revolt aside.

In the course of the spring and summer of 1920, however, die-hard sentiment built up. Again it was in part external policy that led to rebellion. The disciplining of General Dyer after the massacre at Amritsar in the Punjab led to a massive protest on the right amongst those who felt that the shooting of a few hundred Indians was a fair price to pay for the security of the Raj. As has been seen, the climax came in the debate in July 1920 when Montagu was the victim of a fierce Unionist demonstration. This was fanned by his tactless approach and also by his Jewish antecedents which excited right-wingers of most shades. The large total of 129 Unionists, again headed by Carson, voted against the government, who scraped home by 230 votes to 129 on a censure motion with the aid of 40 Labour and 26 Wee Free members. Without Churchill's skilful defensive action, the government might well have been defeated. This time, the Amritsar protest could not be shuffled off by an isolated crisis. Die-hardism by this period was becoming well-defined and its supporters in the Commons and the press more effective.

There was a distinct group of right-wingers who pursued the government at every turn. There were Major Gretton, the brewer, Sir William Joynson-Hicks, an evangelical solicitor, Sir Frederick Banbury, Rupert Gwynne, Pretyman Newman, and a few others. They barely numbered two dozen in all, but their capacity for inflaming the passions of the Unionist rank and file was considerable. There were now cogent domestic causes of right-wing discontent. There were the shamelessly radical programmes of 'Addison, Fisher and co.' not to mention Eric Geddes's essays in centralization, with their contribution to the rising toll of government expenditure and national indebtedness. There were the government's attempts to humour their Coalition Liberal minority by watering down anti-dumping legislation. The government's financial policy also seemed unduly oppressive despite the apparently reassuring presence of Austen Chamberlain back at the Treasury, where he had first been appointed in 1903. His budget of 1919 was welcomed by most right-wingers for its elements of imperial preference on imported goods. On the other hand, it also imposed an Excess Profits Tax of 40 per cent on businessmen: Chamberlain's brother, Neville, reported that Birmingham jewellers were particularly incensed.[5] Despite the protests of chambers of commerce and of the FBI at this brake on trade and investment, the injury was actually compounded in the budget of 1920. Excess Profits Duty, far from being abolished, was actually raised to 60 per cent, while a further Corporation Tax of 1s. in the £ was imposed on the total profit of companies. These measures, taken along with higher duties on beer and spirits, enraged Unionist opinion. It was noted that the Labour benches were enthusiastic for the budget, despite the *New Statesman*'s hostility towards the operation of the EPD.[6] Further blows appeared to be looming from the hands of Chamberlain who seemed to be moving left as decisively as Balfour or Horne. A Royal Commission on the Income Tax was sitting and might bring further horrors. Further, it was known that the Select Committee on Wartime Wealth was soon to report; the government might outbid Labour by introducing its own capital levy. Some ministers, including Churchill and Addison, strongly favoured such a levy.[7] In retaliation, Sir Frederick Banbury organized a memorial from over a hundred Unionist back-benchers which totally rejected any idea of a levy on wartime profits. In the event, a Labour motion advocating a capital levy was defeated on 8 June by 244 to 81. Chamberlain justified his raising of the rate of EPD as the only fair and feasible alternative to a levy on wealth. He insisted to an FBI delegation that the 60 per cent rate must stay, and that it was not payable in the form of war loan.[8]

By now, the momentum of right-wing protest was gathering pace. The record of government setbacks in by-elections was one factor, for instance the victory by a Bottomley candidate at the Wrekin in February 1920. Criticism from within Unionist ranks was another. Lord Rothermere had concerted a newspaper agitation against government 'waste'. His son, Esmond Harmsworth, recently the Prime Minister's ADC at Paris, had stood for the Isle of Thanet in Kent on an Anti-Waste ticket in November 1919. But in curious circumstances he had been adopted by the local Unionist Association instead, and was elected as a one-man band for Anti-Waste. The movement for 'fusion' in March 1920 also agitated the far right. Their loss of a party identity might prove beyond repair, at the hands of a volatile, unprincipled Prime Minister. At a different level, Lord Salisbury expressed aristocratic resentment at the *arrivistes* who were now taking over the party under the leadership of Bonar Law and such acolytes as Salvidge. In May 1920, Salisbury joined with Lord Selborne in setting out the main principles of 'Independent Unionism'. These included a vigorous foreign policy; imperial solidarity; a reformed House of Lords; 'co-operation with the forces of religion'; 'a really national policy' including some social reform; the preservation of private enterprise and resistance to 'Nationalisation and Bolshevism'; rigid economy in public spending; the supremacy of the law over militant labour and Irish rebels; an Irish settlement which would protect the Ulster loyalists; 'clean and straightforward politics'; and the repudiation of 'unavowable methods of securing support'.[9] To back these principles, the machinery of the Unionist Party should be fully maintained while anything that resembled 'fusion' should be resisted. The crisis over General Dyer and Montagu's handling of the Amritsar affair was regarded as a test case for traditional conservatism of this type.

Some apprehension was voiced at Birmingham in June 1920 when the National Union of Conservative Associations met—for the first time since 1913. Here there was a hint of wider trouble. Sir Harry Foster on behalf of the executive was due to be put up to urge 'closer co-operation' within the Coalition to defend the·national interest against 'the Socialist Party'. But a delegate from the Shrewsbury Unionist Association was to move a resolution which viewed with dismay 'the ruinous and socialistic legislation passed since the armistice' and called for a more vigorous assertion of Unionist principles within the Coalition.[10] How widespread this mood of criticism was is unclear. The impression is that the number of dissident local associations was at this time very small, easily swamped by the loyalist battalions from Lancashire and Birmingham, marshalled by Lord Derby and Neville Chamberlain respectively. In any case, opinion was never tested; the motion was deflected without a vote being taken. Younger wrote with glee to Bonar Law that the conference, called at a potentially dangerous time when criticism of the government was widespread, had done a great deal of good. A neutral motion was adopted which asked all parties to combat 'the evils of Socialism', coupled with a demand that the Unionist organization remain at a peak of fighting efficiency.[11] This had the best of both worlds. It preserved the attachment to the Coalition, while offering a nod in the direction of party independence. Die-hards continue to find grass-roots support in their campaigns against extravagant government spending and the appeasement of socialism, but it was easily contained by party leaders. When Joynson-Hicks wrote to *The Times* on 16 December 1920 to demand either a closer liaison between Lloyd George and the Conservatives, or else a break with the Coalition, several Unionist members wrote in to denounce his complaints as reactionary and unrepresentative.

Until 1921, therefore, the die-hard revolt was sporadic and comfortably suppressed. The rebels were, in the main, figures of minor stature, with only the occasional presence and rasping oratory of Carson to lend them authority. Nor had the die-hard movement discovered a theme to arouse continuous concern. By the end of 1920, for example, the dismissal of Dyer was no longer a live issue, and Montagu was maintaining a more relaxed style of government throughout India with relatively little difficulty. Some of the die-hard causes were manifestly dead ones. For instance, much importance was attached by Salisbury and others to the government's pledge in the 1918 election manifesto to reform the House of Lords. In effect, this meant a substantial modification of the 1911 Parliament Act, giving the upper house powers of revising legislation, which would amount to suspending or even rejecting government measures until 'the nation could pronounce'. The rise of Labour roused fears of socialistic legislation being passed through the Commons. Of all issues, this was perhaps the one most in conflict with the mood of unity and of reconstruction which the government wanted to perpetuate. Milner, a sympathizer within the Cabinet with House of Lords reform, pointed out to Selborne that not only all Labour and Liberals, including the Coalition Liberals, would reject such a policy, but that even many liberal-minded Unionists would be hostile. There was scant public concern. 'No-one in the government has ever manifested any keen interest in the question.' Milner was damning the consequences no longer. He also argued that even a Labour government was likely to be non-socialist in character.[12] Such interest as was shown concerned not the powers of the upper house, but rather its composition, which their lordships felt to be sacrosanct, and believed to be menaced by Lloyd George's quotas of politically-promoted barons and viscounts. Clearly, diehardism had no popular leverage behind an anachronistic cause such as this.

In the new year, it all changed dramatically. Protest within Unionist constituency parties, sporadic and localized, was much fortified by a successful independent pressure-group. This was Lord Rothermere's new Anti-Waste movement, inaugurated in the sensationalist pages of the *Sunday Pictorial* in January 1921 and dedicated to fighting extravagance in government spending and the rising toll of the interest charges on the National Debt. The trade depression which now gripped the nation, the expenditure associated with Addison and Fisher, all lent fuel to this movement. It met with most support in Tory middle-class strongholds in the home counties and in London. In January, Sir Thomas Polson, Rothermere's nominee, scored a sensational victory at Dover over the official Unionist, J. J. Astor, by the margin of 3,130 votes. Polson concentrated exclusively on the theme of 'waste', on high taxes and rates, with Austen Chamberlain his particular target. His victory was attributed by the press to a revolt by the middle-class voter and by women generally; it gave new heart to die-hard sentiment. The Addison housing schemes gave further momentum to the Anti-Waste pressure behind the die-hard revolt. There was plenty of other ammunition now. The rising toll of the unemployed meant that liabilities in the unemployment insurance fund rose astronomically, reaching almost £20m by the middle of the year;[13] the losses on the railways continued to mount, fanned, it was claimed, by Geddes's over-ambitious schemes for national reorganization; while the outcome of the miners' strike from April to July proved no less costly with a state subsidy for the mines to last until the end of September, to cushion the fall in wages in less profitable coalfields. The heavy expenditure incurred in Mesopotamia and Persia was also as unpopular with the extreme right as it was with the left. This die-hard pressure for economy gained one early victory in 1921 when Austen Chamberlain was forced to re-establish the House of Commons Estimates Committee which had been suspended in 1914 and whose reintroduction the Chancellor had always resisted.

In addition, there was a major change in the balance of the government in March 1921. Bonar Law resigned and Austen Chamberlain succeeded him as leader both of the House and of the Unionist Party. This had two main effects. Chamberlain's rise to the leadership meant that the rebels were now confronted by a less tactful and good-humoured party leader, whose nonconformist, Liberal Unionist background was still remembered and resented. Again, the presence of Bonar Law was now an ambiguous one, since his health improved and he was able to return to political life and to attend debates in the House from mid-autumn. Although he remained loyal to the Coalition in his public pronouncements, notably over the Irish treaty, Law was careful to measure his distance from the government. His very presence in the House meant that the die-hards, hitherto insignificant figures who by no stretch of the imagination could be regarded as being of ministerial timber, now had the possible support of a statesman of major stature. Despite his professions of loyalty to his late colleagues—Salisbury felt that 'there was a good deal of the Lancelot Gobbo' in Bonar Law, 'a courageous and a shrinking Bonar Law wrestling with one another all the time'[14]—Law, simply by not being Chamberlain, was conceivable as a kind of leader of the opposition. He was the first such phenomenon the government had encountered since the election.

The new heart put into the die-hards over government spending was stimulated by two more remarkable victories for Anti-Waste in June. On 7 June, J. M. M. Erskine defeated the official Unionist, Sir Herbert Jessel, in the St. George's division of Westminster, on a low poll, by nearly 2,000 votes. Chamberlain now expressed alarm at the new inroads Anti-Waste was making into Unionist support for the government in south-east England. Lloyd George replied: 'We must take counsel lest we find ourselves caught between Labour in the North and anti-waste in the South.' Younger attributed this result to anti-Semitism directed at Jessel personally. 'Far too many Jews have been placed in prominent positions by the present Government.'[15] The threat was underlined a few days later when Murray F. Sueter scored a third Anti-Waste victory at Hertford, winning by 6,776 over a popular local Unionist, Sir Hildred Carlile. The Anti-Waste movement was becoming a stampede. Its immediate victim, as has been seen, was Addison. He was, in effect, jettisoned by Lloyd George for electoral reasons on 23 June when it was announced that his salary would shortly be terminated; Addison himself left the government three weeks later, his resignation over the housing programme anticipating his own sacrifice to Anti-Waste. On all fronts in constituencies throughout southern England, Unionist loyalty was being eroded by the Anti-Waste crusade.

A further crisis came with a by-election in the Abbey division of Westminster in August. All three candidates here claimed to be representing Anti-Waste and to be unconnected with the Coalition. Brigadier-General Nicholson, theoretically the official Unionist nominee, described himself as 'Constitutional and Independent Conservative Anti-Waste', as opposed to Lieutenant R. V. K. Applin, the Anti-Waste League's official candidate, and Arnold Lupton, a former Liberal MP for Sleaford who stood as 'Independent Liberal and Anti-Waste'.[16] Nicholson's victory by just over 1,000 on a low poll was indeed a dubious triumph for the government. It was followed by another desperate contest in London, in West Lewisham where Sir Philip Dawson, 'Conservative and Anti-Waste', defeated Lieutenant-Commander Windham, the Anti-Waste candidate, by just 747 votes. Mr. Punch depicted Lloyd George wryly contemplating the various Anti-Waste and anti-Coalition posters on a wall in Westminster. If he wished to win the next election, the premier concluded, 'I mustn't be identified with myself'.[17]

In fact, West Lewisham was the last serious contest by Lord Rothermere's private army. Anti-Waste gradually ceased to be a threat to the Coalition at the polls. On the other hand, its inroads into government strength were massive ones. It forced the government into a major surrender in August when the Geddes committee of businessmen was appointed to examine radical economies in public expenditure. This was a complete reversal of policy, one that appeared, to Churchill at least, to mark a constitutional abdication by the elected government in favour of an unelected body of businessmen. Also Anti-Waste had given a backbone to the die-hard movement which it could never achieve on its own. As recently as 13 June, Lord Selborne had told Salisbury that he exaggerated the degree of the Coalition's unpopularity amongst Unionists. Indeed, the government's handling of the coal strike had strengthened its hold amongst Conservatives in the west country and elsewhere. The die-hards, Selborne felt, had no leadership. Cecil had 'left us' while 'Austen and Horne are not going to throw over Lloyd George at this moment'.[18] By the end of the summer, matters were far more uncertain. A minister had been sacrificed, a major line of policy had been reversed, the government had shown signs of panic. One sign of the times was Gretton's writing to Chamberlain in July formally to announce his withdrawal of support from the government.[19] Unionism was being sacrificed on 'the slippery slope of coalition'. He explained later that while he had felt that the Coalition was necessary to deal with the difficult transition at the time of the armistice, since then 'it had shown no settled policy and no definite principles'.[20] Taxation remained a crushing burden, business stagnated, expenditure was rising almost without check. Sir Herbert Nield of the Council of the National Union was alarmed at Lloyd George's continuing profession of support for Liberal principles: this was sapping the foundations of Unionist support in south-east England.[21] Younger, the key figure of all as party manager, began to meditate on how long the Coalition could be kept in being. He, too, was being swept on by the swelling die-hard tide.

Anti-Waste agitation was reinforced by alarm over Ireland. This brought some new elements into the die-hard camp. The trend of the negotiations with Sinn Fein in October was very disturbing for many Unionists. There were the threats of surrender to the violent fanatics of Sinn Fein, of undermining the fabric of the Empire and the supremacy of the Crown, of sacrificing the Protestant loyalists of Ulster. Even Bonar Law was said to have expressed 'fury' with the government for 'throwing over Ulster'.[22] Events reached a climax with the National Union annual conference scheduled for 17 November, where die-hard protests over Ireland were certain to reach a crescendo. As ill-luck would have it, the conference would be held in

Liverpool. This had been a citadel of Tory Democracy since Disraelian times, founded on working-class Orange sentiment directed against the Irish Catholic immigrants who flocked into the constituencies of Scotland, Exchange, Abercromby, and Toxteth from across the water.

This was rightly felt to be a supreme test of the strength of die-hard opinion. Grigg commented on the persistence of die-hard protest over Ireland. 'Party labels have lost all their force and rank and file veer to winds of every description.'[23] The machinery of the National Constitutional Association, headed by Page Croft, had been used by Gretton and his friends to build up pressure and hold meetings. The Liverpool conference came immediately after a vote of censure in the Commons. During the debate, widespread Unionist anxiety had been expressed about the kind of settlement likely to be imposed in Ireland, especially with regard to the imperial connection, the financial and defence arrangements, and the possible union of the whole of Ireland. Certainly, the Unionist leadership took the die-hard protests much more seriously than it had done sixteen months earlier at Birmingham. Austen Chamberlain urged his half-brother, Neville, himself no friend of the Coalition or of Lloyd George, to ensure that Birmingham Unionists were well represented, as 'the malcontents' were undertaking 'a great whip up' for the Liverpool conference. Privately he assured his half-brother that he was more hopeful of a satisfactory settlement for Ireland than he had ever been before.[24] Meanwhile, Lord Derby, also in a somewhat ambiguous position towards the government by now and very critical of its foreign policy, lent his formidable influence, and the organizational skill of Archibald Salvidge of Liverpool, to keep the Lancashire delegates in line. 'The more I think of it the more difficult I think our meeting is going to be.' Salvidge, he reported, was prepared to move a motion which supported the Coalition on general grounds, and placed faith in Lloyd George's promise not to curtail the rights of Ulster. Derby added:

It is a good thing that he should bring in the maintenance of the Coalition government because he fought the Municipal Election here in the closest partnership with the Liberal Coalitionists, and everybody knows that it was owing to this alliance that we won the seats we did. He therefore will carry the whole of the Merseyside Delegates with him in that.

He himself would approach Younger beforehand about tactics, 'but I think it may be best to let the Die-Hards have a run, then for Salvidge to speak, also Worthington-Evans, and for me to come in only at the end'.[25] On the other side, Salisbury believed that Derby was worried by the Ulster sympathies of the Liverpool Unionists. 'I suspect he will occupy a strong position on the fence but the Liverpool contingent will be growingly [sic] anti-Government.'[26]

The main item on the agenda at Liverpool on 17 November was the die-hard motion moved by Gretton which amounted to a condemnation of the government for its policy on Ireland. There was an even more vehement amendment in the name of the Duke of Northumberland, another ennobled die-hard who was involved with the financing of the *Morning Post*. Salisbury actually believed that Gretton's motion would be carried 'easily, even unanimously',[27] and that that would take the wind out of the sails of Northumberland's amendment. In fact, the course of the debate showed that the die-hard protest movement still had some way to go if it was to pose a serious challenge to the Unionist leadership, let alone the government itself. Gretton's motion was supported by no major figure in the party. Bonar Law, who, in Astor's view, could have 'stampeded' many delegates, carefully stayed away from Liverpool altogether. Gretton's ineffective speech was supported only by extremists like Archer-Shee ('too violent', said Astor) and Ronald MacNeill, an Ulsterman and perhaps the most convincing of the die-hards. On the other hand, elder statesmen like Lord Midleton, on behalf of southern Irish Unionists, and Henry Chaplin spoke against the motion. The official line was upheld by Salvidge, applauded by a 'well-drilled clique' he had assembled in the audience.[28] Salvidge had beforehand denounced the 'ulterior motives' of these 'disgruntled critics'. Now he warmly defended a continuation of the negotiations with the southern Irish leaders. He claimed to be speaking on behalf of 'a united Liverpool'.[29] Worthington-Evans and (with more circumspection) Derby reaffirmed the government's pledges on the coercion of Ulster, the supremacy of the Crown, and retaining Ireland within the Empire. Out of 1,800 delegates, Gretton captured fewer than 70 for his motion. Northumberland's motion was not moved at all, 'it being explained that his lordship had a train to catch'. Later that evening, at a mass rally at the Sun Hall, Kensington, in Liverpool, Austen Chamberlain delivered a speech of remarkable fervour and eloquence. He placed clearly and honestly before the delegates the stark alternatives facing them if the Irish negotiations broke down. Remarkably enough, he even publicly recanted his own vote against self-government for the Transvaal and the Orange Free State back in 1906. This courageous speech brought warm congratulations from such varied Unionists as Sir Philip Magnus, Sir William Lane Mitchell, Waldorf Astor, and Edward Goulding.[30] The National Union after Liverpool seemed as much a docile 'handmaid to the party' under the leadership of Austen Chamberlain as it had been under that of Disraeli. But this was deceptive. Astor knew how much was owed to Derby who 'has thrown the whole of his influence to keep the Party straight and to get local Liverpool opinion loyal to Austen and the Govt.'. Derby had probably done as much as anyone 'to keep things straight'. Astor added, 'I am confident there wd. have been no overwhelming vote for the Govt. if Bonar had made his bid and had a good seconder.'[31]

The mood of the Unionist rank and file was known to be fragile after the Liverpool conference. It remained so after the signing of the agreement with the Sinn Feiners by the government on 6 December. This confirmed many of the fears, overt or implied, felt at the Liverpool meeting. 'Our people in the country are getting very jumpy,' reported Younger.[32] There was undoubtedly a good deal of unease, shortly to surface again when a Unionist reaction, of which Younger now became the voice, was to frustrate Lloyd George in his desire for a January general election. When Austen Chamberlain tested opinion amongst Unionist party organizers throughout the country, in late December, one after the other, from John Gilmour in Scotland to Herbert Jessel in London, reported that 'fusion' was unpopular, that there was rank-and-file pressure for reform of the House of Lords, and for other die-hard proposals to be implemented before a general election was held. 'A fused party will not gain Tory votes.'[33] There was growing sentiment voiced in such journals as the *Morning Post* and the *Yorkshire Post* for the winding up of the Coalition, with the restoration of free Toryism and the familiar party system. J. C. C. Davidson urged Bonar Law, still Delphic and remote, that they needed 'the re-establishment of a great Conservative Party with Honest Government, Drastic Economy, National Security and *No adventures* abroad or at home as its watchwords'. Lloyd George could produce only 'the same faces at every show, a façade of gilded or gold bricks with no real fabric behind it. . . . The Tory Party seems to be drifting away from him.'[34] Davidson's solution was for Derby to lead the party in the Lords and for Bonar Law himself to re-emerge as leader in the Commons. Encouraged by Anti-Waste and the Ulster loyalists, die-hardism was clearly permeating the fabric of the party over a wide area, instilling a mood of uncertainty and apprehension, as the Coalition lurched along free from open challenge.

On the other hand, the Liverpool conference also showed that concern for the future of the Coalition was not the same as anxiety to end it forthwith. On the contrary, die-hardism, for two or three more months, remained a challenge which the Coalition was able to neutralize. Indeed, its vigour enabled Austen Chamberlain, previously a somewhat grey and negative member of the government, to acquire a new stature as a pugnacious and eloquent defender of government policies, in speeches expressed with more courage than discretion and remembered all too well in October 1922. For all the publicity they attracted, the die-hards were still a shifting, relatively uninfluential opposition until the end of 1921. It is certainly a mistake to antedate the revolt which triumphed at the Carlton Club on 19 October 1922. To Salisbury, the 'Diehard movement is one of honest men who have risked their political reputation'.[35] Implicit in his tone was a sense of isolation, a feeling that he and his friends were swimming against the tide. In the early months of 1922, the party was still in the control of Austen Chamberlain, Horne, Birkenhead, and their colleagues. Chamberlain, though consistently underestimating the right-wing threat, was probably justified in dismissing the 'small die-hard section' which even critics like Hannon and Goulding declined to join,[36] Even *The Times* in early March 1922 assessed the number of those Unionist members actively working for the independence of their party from the Coalition at no greater than fifty.[37] None of them was a major figure in the party. With the conspicuous exception of the Geddes 'economies' committee, the die-hards had seen every phase of government policy, India, Egypt, Ireland, and foreign relations, turn against them. As the Coalition entered its fourth year in power the die-hards still lacked a leader and a compelling cause.

To assess the significance of the die-hard challenge to the Coalition in this period is peculiarly difficult. It was a more insidious, if more short-term, challenge than the overt attack from Labour; it was a process of infiltration from within. But at every stage, from the first murmurings over the peace treaty in March 1919 to the Irish peace settlement in January 1922 the die-hards threatened more than they could achieve. They might win indirect triumphs in by-elections, partly through the passion engendered by the Anti-Waste League. But it was striking how many rebellious 'independents', from Esmond Harmsworth onwards, entered the House full of ominous threats to the Coalition, and were promptly lost to view in the face of governmental power (and perhaps governmental competence) thereafter.

Certainly, if the die-hards did pose a challenge, it was not because their proposals were in any respect more realistic or promising than those of the ministers. On the contrary, in almost every instance, their policies would have been totally disastrous if actually carried out, and totally destructive of the mood of unity induced by the war. They would have dealt with mass unemployment through policies of financial deflation that would have depressed the economy still further. They would have responded to working-class discontent with a total suspension of social reform. They would have answered the demands of the miners with a blanket vindication of the Coalowners' Association with their obsession with huge wage reductions and a refusal to reform the structure of their obsolete industry. They would have dealt with Sinn Fein through military reprisals almost indefinitely which would have turned Ireland into a bloodbath. They would have reinstated General Dyer, the hero of the Amritsar massacre, and would have applied mindless coercion to the national demands of the Indian Congress. In foreign affairs, they would have revoked the naval disarmament agreed to at Washington, they would have continued assistance to the White Russians almost indefinitely, they would have imposed the full rigour of 'war guilt' upon Germany, together with huge indemnities condemned as impractical by almost every economist of repute. Their programmes would have been laced with the flavour of class war, xenophobic nationalism, and anti-Semitism. Nor did their policies make sense. It was absurd to preach 'anti-waste' and also massively increase Britain's military commitment in Ireland, Russia, and Egypt. It was absurd to decry the stagnation of trade and then reply with a dampening down of domestic demand and credit policies that cut back industrial investment. It was absurd to appeal for 'national unity' and interpret this in terms that could only alienate Jews, Irishmen, blacks, and perhaps even Welsh and Scots as well. Not one of the die-hards emerged in later years as a politician of major stature, save perhaps for Joynson-Hicks who served under Baldwin in

1924–9 as a predictably conservative, puritanical, unimaginative
Home Secretary. He was best remembered for his speech criticizing
the New Prayer Book. The rest, from the brewer, Gretton, downwards, languished in obscurity. The Coalition may well have pursued
contradictory and even unprincipled policies in relation to labour,
social reform, imperial and foreign policy. But there was a realism and
a moderation about its approach, even in the critical months of 1922,
which contrasted with the atavistic passions of the die-hard mind. Far
more than the Labour Party in this period, the Unionist/National
right wingers sought and deserved the role of permanent opposition.
They staked a permanent claim to the wilderness.

But, of course, many unworthy causes triumph in this sad world.
There can be no doubt that die-hardism, however ideologically primitive and organizationally weak, made substantial inroads into the
Unionist rank and file throughout 1921. It was increasingly powerful
in the National Union's executive committee. By the spring of the
following year, the whole party seemed to be seething with unrest, so
much so that the Prime Minister had to threaten to resign unless he
received a pledge of Unionist loyalty. Some of this was the inevitable
protest from local party workers against the unnatural political vacuum created by a Coalition in which the Unionist party served with its
independence clipped and its future indeterminate. Some of it
responded to a genuine nationwide concern for the abnormal
economic and external conditions in a Britain suffering from industrial decline and imperial disintegration on a scale unknown in its
recent history. Some was the natural reaction of party managers
against a dictatorial and unduly remote leadership which, under
Austen Chamberlain, seemed to be losing touch with constituency
opinion. Particular campaigns such as the drive to expel Addison, the
'anti-waste' movement, and the saga of the Irish negotiations gave a
kind of spurious unity to a series of disparate revolts. But to dislodge
the government, the die-hards needed to achieve much more than
they seemed to have done by the start of 1922. They needed the
unambiguous endorsement of party organizers from Younger downwards, in a way at variance with the traditions of British Toryism.
They needed credible leadership, to cut a better figure in debate. They
needed far stronger links with the centre and centre-left of the party,
such as in time they found in Baldwin and Griffith-Boscawen in
October 1922. They also needed a less negative style. Loyal Unionists

warmed to Salvidge's charge that Gretton and his friends were really mounting a 'Chamberlain Must Go' campaign.[38]

The die-hards' strongest card was an appeal to the decencies of normal party politics, in place of the presidential manœuvres of Lloyd George, the corruption of his fund, the intrigues of his Garden Suburb, his clandestine links with the press, and his contempt for the constitution. The die-hards could appeal to orthodoxy. But since their leaders and followers were unorthodox, supporters of General Dyer, Ulster Covenanters, White Russians, and the anti-strike battalions of 'civil guards', in opposition to their elected leadership, they could hardly link orthodoxy with moderation. The attitudes of men like J. C. C. Davidson, Neville Chamberlain, and Samuel Hoare in the latter months of 1921 suggest that a more mainstream version of Toryism was moving towards the direction of the die-hards. But it was still unformed, and relatively feeble, compared with the Coalition's stand on behalf of ordered progress and the middle way. For the average Unionist in 1919–22, the Coalition could offer the practice of Peel combined with the rhetoric of Disraeli; the die-hards were thus frustrated at every turn. In any case, the grass roots was no place for a Tory revolt to flourish. It needed support in parliament and in the government in substantial numbers, unless it were not to join fringe movements such as the Anti-Waste League and the Middle Class Union on the dust-heap of the Coalition's version of history.

On 1 February 1922 Lord Birkenhead addressed the New Members' Coalition Group which had remained in existence since the disappointments over 'fusion' two years earlier.[39] Buoyed up by the cuisine and the splendours of the Savoy Hotel, Birkenhead swept away, in his well-known contemptuous style, each of the challenges that was supposed to be threatening the existence of the government. Labour he dismissed for its 'consistent and abject poltroonery', during three difficult years. The Grey/Cecil group he brushed aside; they were no people to criticize failures in British diplomacy in view of Grey's record in July–August 1914. As for Unionists, he declared that they were happy to continue their partnership with the Prime Minister. At a period of mass unemployment, unrest in Egypt, India, and Ireland, it was no time to resume party politics. *The Times*, in reporting Birkenhead's speech, noted that a new campaign against independent Unionists such as Gretton was about to be launched. Erskine of the Anti-Waste League would be opposed by a Unionist whip at the next election in his constituency. Birkenhead's confidence was already becoming suspect by 1 February. He was never an accurate reader of the political entrails at any stage of his career. Nevertheless, the record from 1919 to 1922 gives some substance to his claims. Confronted with the declining Wee Frees and the almost apolitical Cecil centrists, with the class appeal of Labour and the fringe sectionalism of the die-hard right, the Coalition could claim to offer unity and stability. Its enemies to some degree cancelled one another out. A. J. Cook and Colonel Gretton acted in a mutually destructive partnership. Most tacticians agreed on one conclusion, that the nation required what President Warren G. Harding was to call 'normalcy'. Neither the *Marxisant* left nor a reactionary right conformed to the norms that the nation set for itself. With Scylla and Charybdis bent on destruction of each other, with the 'cabin boys' still firmly in their place, Lloyd George's ship of state, confidently if not serenely, steamed on regardless.

11

Lloyd George's Last Stand

In June 1920, at the time of the annual conference of the National Union of Unionist Associations, the Lloyd George government appeared to be in a strong, if not impregnable, position. The failure to achieve 'fusion' three months earlier had been forgotten; a confident government could face such pin-pricks as the Wee Free by-election victory at Louth (3 June) with complete equanimity. It appeared to be presiding over a nation and an Empire as powerful and prosperous as ever before in its history, fuelled by a massive injection of credit to the tune of over £500m from the banks and finance houses in the year April 1919–April 1920 'for industrial and other purposes'. The stock exchange was buoyant, the pound climbing upwards against the dollar, there was abnormally high demand in textiles and shipbuilding, unemployment seemed to have diminished almost to zero. Despite a series of progressive wage increases in major industries and an increase in money income of 25–35 per cent in the period April 1919–April 1920, the cost of living was beginning to fall: Selfridge's, the department store, decided to cut prices by ten per cent.[1] Austen Chamberlain's budget in April 1920 contemplated the economic scene with confidence. As has been seen, it did, indeed, increase taxes. Income tax was raised, with the supertax limit reduced to £2,000, while other rates were increased. Excess Profits Duty and Corporations Tax were imposed, despite business protests. There were also increases in the duty on beer and spirits; conversely, Lloyd George's land taxes of 1909 were abolished. However, Chamberlain's explanation that he had to raise new taxes to make some reduction in the floating debt was generally accepted, as was his defence of EPD as an alternative to Labour's capital levy. Chamberlain budgeted confidently for a large surplus on the Treasury account. Indeed, it was to rise even beyond his expectations, to £278m after the high earnings of the previous financial year. Chamberlain's financial survey was projected against an apparent background of strong confidence. The labour unrest of the winter had markedly subsided; employment was returning to normal. Politically, this was reflected in Lloyd George's presiding over the nation almost without challenge. Lee of Fareham thought his domination of the Cabinet was 'complete and wonderful' with Churchill the only minister who even tried to measure swords with him. Lloyd George's insight was 'almost uncanny—and of course his experience is by now far greater than that of anyone else—perhaps anywhere in the world'.[2] As the socialist, Harold Laski, was to write gloomily, 'Lloyd George will be in for the next ten years, so that one might as well cultivate one's private garden and be screened from public view.'[3]

When the Unionists met again, at Liverpool in November 1921, the prospects were very different. Lloyd George was now at bay, having withstood tirades of criticism and policy failures without parallel in recent history. The government seemed to be on the run. This was in part because problems present in the summer of 1920 were still very much alive. The crises of empire in India and Egypt were no nearer a solution. Ireland was enjoying a truce, after years of bloodshed, but no one could guess what the outcome of the negotiations with Sinn Fein might be. Relations with Russia, naval talks with the United States, the scale and exaction of German reparations added to the mood of unease and despondency, and to the government's lowered reputation.

But the real change, without doubt, was the collapse of the economy. In the late spring of 1920, the boom broke and gave way to industrial stagnation and mass unemployment without parallel.[4] They were to paralyse the economy almost until the onset of another world war. The speculative boom of 1919–20, fuelled by Chamberlain's grossly mistaken policy of budgeting for large surpluses, far outstripped purchasing power at home and abroad. The feverish buying of commodities, flotation of new companies, and issue of new shares were quite unreal. Domestic prices suddenly broke in the summer of 1920; the export trade collapsed similarly a few months later. As early as 29 July 1920, the Cabinet was anticipating a 'serious slump' in the autumn.[5] By December, the total of unemployed had risen to 540,000 and it increased steadily thereafter. The impact of the two national miners' strikes of October–November 1920 and April–July 1921 made this all the more severe. 'We may have the worst period of unemployment any of us have known,' Lloyd George declared during the winter. He reported that the FBI foresaw it lasting for at least another eighteen months.[6] The most frightening of the economic indices published month by month was the slump in the export trades: by the end of 1920, this was reflected in coal exports as in everything else. Over-all exports, which had totalled £137m in value in July 1920 had shrunk to £96m by December, and to a mere £43m by May 1921. In every major industry, orders fell off, markets disappeared, and men were laid off in hundreds of thousands. By the mid-summer of 1921, after the coal strike, the total of unemployed amounted to over 2,171,000 (17.8 per cent of the insured working population) with a further 832,000 on systematic short time. At the end of 1921, non-strike unemployment ran to 18 per cent of the labour force. It was a phenomenon with which local government services and the embryonic national insurance fund were quite unable to cope.

The basic cause lay in the collapse, first of domestic, then of foreign, demand, after the immediate post-war re-stocking and replacement of capital equipment. The slump did not originate from extremes of deflation at all. But the Treasury, which had aggravated the boom in 1919 with a credit bonanza, now aggravated the slump with a restrictive policy which contracted economic activity still further. In the winter of 1919–20, the 'dear money' party of the Treasury—Chamberlain, backed up by key Treasury officials such as Blackett, Niemeyer, and Hawtrey—won a crucial victory. They had the vigorous support of Montague Norman, the Governor of the Bank of England. From November 1919, notes in circulation had been contracted, and bank notes set aside to the currency note reserve; the money supply began to grow at a slower rate. Treasury bills were sold in vast quantities. Finally on 15 April 1920, the bank rate was raised sharply to 7 per cent. It remained at this high level for a further twelve months, which saw stagnant trade and rapidly falling wholesale prices. *The Economist* Index on commodity prices fell to its lowest point since September 1916. Gilt-edged and other securities languished. Consols stood at 45 at the start of 1921 and only 50 at the end. The outcome was a collapse of confidence in the British economy and of its productive base. Businessmen, frenetic in their optimism in 1919–20, became, equally irrationally, sunk in deepest gloom. Industrial investment in physical assets and stocks fell right away. Private sector domestic fixed-capital formation, according to C. H.

Feinstein's calculations, fell from £379m in 1920 to £299m in 1921 and to £261m in 1922.[7] It was not to touch £300m again until 1929. Herein lay the roots of a long-term economic decline from which, sixty years later, the nation had not recovered.

Some blamed government finance for this relentless slump in the economy. Excessive expenditure and over-high taxation were popular explanations much canvassed in the press at the time. More plausibly, economists after 1945 were almost unanimous in pointing to the government's extreme 'dear money' policy after 1918 as a crucial factor in causing the depression to be infinitely more severe in its effects, and far harder to reverse. However, it should be pointed out that expert opinion at the time was agreed that deflationary finance was inescapable as a corrective to the heady speculative boom of 1919. There lay in the background the government's commitment, finally announced by Austen Chamberlain to the Commons on 15 December 1919, to accept the recommendations of the Cunliffe committee to aim to return to gold at the pre-war parity. The corollaries to this crucial decision, as urged by Basil Blackett (Permanent Secretary to the Treasury until 1922) and his successor Otto Niemeyer, were the cessation of government borrowing, the limitation of note issue, and much higher interest rates. Keynes later attacked their approach on his *Treatise on Money* in 1930. However, even the supposedly unorthodox and radical Keynes had also insisted in February 1920 that the Treasury adopt a 'swift and severe dose of dear money', not as a commitment to return to gold, but in order to check extreme inflation and to bring some realism to the conduct of business. The announcement of the 7 per cent bank rate on 15 April (Keynes had recommended 8 or conceivably 10 per cent) met with general acceptance from economists, whatever dismay it inspired amongst social reformers who saw programmes for housing and welfare severely curtailed as a result. In any case, high bank rate, and similarly severe interest charges elsewhere, did not in themselves cause the slump, even if they made it worse. Well before April 1920, there had been signs of a decline of home consumer demand, and of a falling off of bank lending. Overseas, percipient observers could point to the problems of over-production, of fluctuating exchange rates, and, most crucially, of a world-wide slump in demand which saw the markets for manufactured and agricultural products falling away almost everywhere. Britain suffered from this massive international trade depression in common with every other leading industrial nation. Not until June 1921 was it to be reported that for the first time for over a year there were hints of new orders coming in and the curve of wholesale prices rising. An increase in exports of 7.6 per cent was recorded in September. But whether the slump be assigned to short- or long-term, domestic or external causes, whatever the technical arguments for or against a return to gold and a consequent pegging of the pound–dollar exchange rate, a government which claimed the credit for the post-war boom was equally clearly saddled with the responsibility for structural depression.

It was against this background of economic collapse and consequent social discontent that the Coalition government was struggling throughout 1921. The policy consequences have already been sur- veyed. The Government's social reform programme lay in ruins, its major architect ejected from the Cabinet. The policy for the reconcili- ation of labour almost fell to pieces after Black Friday, with a rash of Labour gains in by-elections thereafter. The government's foreign and defence policy had to be re-shaped because of the commitment to sharp economy in overseas commitments and the need to base a successful diplomacy on financial and economic recovery. At all points, Lloyd George suddenly seemed a desperate man: perhaps this underlay his temporary physical breakdown in June 1921. He was now in an increasingly isolated position. In the Cabinet, his own Coalition Liberals were an enfeebled influence, with Churchill, their major representative, following his own course on issues ranging from unemployment insurance to the settlement of the Near East. The Unionists were less in harmony with the Prime Minister, too. Austen Chamberlain, for all that he was 'loyal, straight and sensible',[8] was unable to strike up the warm rapport with the mercurial premier that Bonar Law had built up during the four years up to his resignation in March 1921. With the stamp of personal authority so emphatic on the government's programme on all fronts, the press naturally used the Prime Minister as its essential target. He could not complain at the publicity now as he had attracted it deliberately for so long. His highly personal style of governing added to his problems, notably his private methods of political finance through the disbursement of honours, and his presidential style of rule through 'conferences of ministers' and *ad hoc* committees rather than through formal Cabinets. The summoning of the Cabinet to Inverness town hall in September 1921 to accommodate the Prime Minister's convalescence in the highlands symbolized his autocratic methods. The *Lloyd George Liberal Magazine*, first issued in October 1920 and with 30,000 copies printed monthly, boosted Coalition Liberal morale. But it also drew attention to the nature of the Coaly Libs as a one-man band, goaded into unnatural harmony by a frenetic conductor of aberrant genius. Lloyd George's personal control of the central machine of government was not what it had been previously. In the Cabinet secretariat, Hankey continued to play a somewhat grey role, while Thomas Jones was busy mending his fences with Bonar Law. The Garden Suburb of private advisers was disappearing, its major figure, Philip Kerr, having departed in May 1921 to manage the pro-government *Daily Chronicle*. His successor, Edward Grigg, a liberal-minded imperialist of humane sympathies, free from Kerr's brand of exotic mysticism, enjoyed less scope than had his predecessor. The rest of Lloyd George's private entourage, men like Geoffrey Shakespeare, Evan Davies, and the free-wheeling, free-loading manager of publicity and patronage, 'Bronco Bill' Sutherland, were functionaries on a lower level from the body of advisers such as Adams, Kerr, and Astor who surrounded the leader in 1917–18. Lloyd George, then, seemed something of a beleaguered figure, one close to fighting out his last stand.

But the Prime Minister still had the capacity to dominate and to inspire. In the autumn of 1921, while the Irish negotiations were still at their most delicate, Lloyd George strove once again to grasp the initiative, to re-shape his strategy, and to rehabilitate the authority of his government. As before, the theme was unity and consensus, as alternatives to the sectionalism of Labour and the die-hards, and the fragmentation offered by Asquith or Cecil. With its policies hanging in the balance almost everywhere, the Coalition, under the militant leadership of its chief, reached out for a new mandate, re-defined to take account of the political setbacks and economic calamities endured in the past twelve months.

This counter-attack took the form of what *The Times* chose to term 'the swing to the left'.[9] It was certainly long overdue, in view of the government's surrender of its most innovative domestic programmes with the appointment of the Geddes committee and the certainty of massive economies to follow. At home, the main preoccupation now was a desperate attempt to refurbish the unemployment insurance scheme for a task for which it was wholly unprepared to deal—the existence of a permanent pool of well over one million unemployed workers. Here the record was one of makeshifts in policy. Two problems of vital consequence arose. The first was to extend the duration of insurance benefits. The original act of 1920 had limited benefits to one week for six weeks' contribution, while no claimant could draw benefit for more than twenty-six weeks in any year. Obviously by the spring of 1921, these cautious calculations were meaningless. Almost a million workers were about to run out of benefit, a few months after the scheme had come into operation. The 'one-in-six' rule was abandoned and 'uncovenanted' benefits, over and above what the individual was entitled to, were authorized by the Cabinet in February 1921.[10] Two further periods of eligibility were laid down, of sixteen weeks' duration each, to cover the period up to July 1922. In addition, the Cabinet abandoned its resistance to paying unemployment benefit to the half million workers who were on short time though not technically unemployed. Clearly the insurance aspects of the unemployment scheme, with all its actuarial calculations, had been abandoned in favour of a large charitable welfare donation of almost unlimited length of time.

Secondly, the scale of benefits was sharply increased. In February 1921, Macnamara introduced a bill, which Labour severely criticized but dared not resist, to increase benefits to 18s. for civilian unemployment workers, later raised to 20s. under Labour pressure.[11] It had been agreed that the deficit of £15m would be met either with a direct grant from the Treasury or from the Insurance Fund. This met with strong opposition from Horne, now at the Exchequer, but the fact remained that even 20s. was hardly enough for a married worker with a family to support. A major change was, therefore, added in November when the principle of dependants' allowances was introduced, with 5s. payable weekly for a dependent wife or husband, and 1s. a week per child up to a total of four children.[12] Despite fierce criticism by the Labour spokesman, Tom Shaw, it passed through all of its stages in the Commons in just a week. Clearly, the entire financing of the insurance scheme had been transformed, partly as the result of economic necessity of keeping the unemployed in subsistence, partly of simple fear as violence accompanied demonstrations by organizations of unemployed men that autumn. The suddenness and scale of mass unemployment had demolished the assumptions on which Horne's scheme of 1920 had been based.

But these panic measures, accompanied as they were by the 'genuinely seeking work' provision who so incensed the working-class unemployed, hardly added up to a change in direction in domestic policy. There was no real 'swing to the left' here at all, merely a panic recourse to charity. In all other respects, the government's domestic programme was becalmed. Decontrol had taken its toll of the rationalization schemes intended for transport: their sponsor, Sir Eric Geddes, had left the government. Even though bank rate was steadily reduced in 1922 from 7 to 5 per cent, social reform was in suspense. Only education maintained its former share of the budget, mainly through the new salaries for school-teachers agreed through the Burnham committee. Otherwise, the Geddes committee overshadowed the government's entire domestic policy and threatened to emasculate it entirely. It was possible that Lloyd George might salvage some credit, as Arthur Greenwood suggested, by trying to resist the full impact of whatever Geddes recommended; but this was highly unlikely in view of the intense pressure for 'anti-waste' from Fleet Street to the Treasury. At home, the government had run out of steam and had nothing new to offer. A rally in share prices in January and February from 78.6 to 81.4 dimly heralded an economic 'upturn' which must be the administration's only hope.[13]

Beyond the shores of England, it was very different. It was its external policy which offered a lifeline to the government now, with a prospect of re-establishing its credentials among progressive opinion. In particular, Ireland, for long the black exception to a generally peaceable external policy, suddenly became the government's great claim to liberal virtue. It had been probable, at least from February 1921, that Lloyd George, as he applied his mind with more purpose to Irish affairs and turned increasingly to domestic political management, would strive for peace in Ireland. The 'reprisals' policy under Greenwood's direction was costly and unsuccessful. Macready and Anderson reported that coercion had failed. It was repugnant to the conscience of many of the government's Liberal and some Unionist supporters. Since the cause of the southern Irish Unionists had been conceded in principle during the latter stages of the war, some kind of imaginative gesture of self-government for the twenty-six counties of southern Ireland was always on the cards.

Lloyd George had had his antennae directed towards talks with Sinn Fein, under the mediation of Alfred Cope, long before the

King's conciliatory remarks to the all-Ireland parliament in June (of which too much has been made by historians as an example of royal influence and which, in any case, were drafted by Sir Edward Grigg for the King to read out).[14] The tragicomedy of Lloyd George's overtures to de Valera at least produced several meetings in August. In early October, talks began in earnest between a British Cabinet deputation, headed by the Prime Minister, and the Sinn Fein delegation, headed, mercifully, by Griffith and Collins since de Valera chose to remain in Dublin. At the same time, the truce between the British forces and the IRA was continued almost indefinitely. With the expectations raised by the talks with Sinn Fein, it was scarcely conceivable that Lloyd George could allow them to end in failure. Austen Chamberlain's bold remarks to the Unionists gathered in Liverpool on 17 November implied some kind of dominion status, on the same lines as that enjoyed by Canada or Australia. The series of issues that came up during the talks—the Oath of Allegiance, the preservation of the framework of the Empire, the maintenance of British defence rights in Ireland, a just settlement of the related issues of land purchase and the national debt—could none of them prove decisive. The major stumbling block, of course, could be Ulster. Even Alderman Salvidge, with all his ingrained loyalty towards the government, was adamant that no pressure could be put on Ulster to enter an all-Ireland parliament, especially now that it had its own legislature in Belfast. No such coercion of Ulster was politically possible for Lloyd George. He could not have begun to carry it through his Cabinet, let alone the Commons. In any event, neither the Sinn Fein delegates nor the Prime Minister intended to have a break on Ulster. This is precisely what would have occurred had the creation of a unified Irish state under a Dublin parliament been carried through. The crisis atmosphere of 5 December 1921, culminating in Griffith's acceptance of Lloyd George's peace terms on behalf of his delegation, has lacked nothing in drama in Churchill's and other accounts. But this is somewhat unreal. Days earlier, Griffith and Collins, after successful persuasion by Thomas Jones, had separately conceded the principle of a partition of Ireland in the first instance, with a boundary commission left to determine the future status of the six Protestant counties of the north-east.[15] Lloyd George could, politically, deliver nothing less. The Sinn Feiners could reasonably ask for nothing more, especially when Griffith honourably confessed that on 13 November he had

privately agreed to a boundary commission in principle. In return for
a free-trade agreement, the Irish delegates accepted an Oath of
Allegiance invented by the unlikely combination of Winston Churchill and Harold Laski. The *Daily Chronicle*, Lloyd George's own
organ, stated that if talks broke down with the Sinn Fein delegation,
they would be followed, not by resumed fighting, but by further
negotiation.[16] Peace was logical and inevitable.

The debate on the Irish treaty in the House of Commons on 15
December was a triumph for the government, its first for many
months. A settlement which ended years of bloodshed and coercion in
Ireland had the inevitable support of Labour and Liberal members of
all shades. The vast majority of Unionists also gave their blessing to a
settlement which preserved the separation of Ulster and preserved
(indeed, extended) the supremacy of the Empire. Bonar Law, who
had discreetly kept his silence while the negotiations were progress-
ing, and had declined various offers from Salvidge and Salisbury to
state his views openly, now declared his approval of the government's
settlement. Only the usual die-hards, men like Gretton, a few Irish
hard-liners like McNeill and Carson, came out in opposition. In the
Lords, Birkenhead delivered a memorable rebuke at Carson's
expense. Ireland quite suddenly became the government's badge of
honour and respectability, its major asset. When, after a desperately
anxious debate, the Sinn Fein dail in Dublin voted in January by 64
votes to 57 to uphold the treaty even though for a time it implied the
partition of Ireland, the government's cup was filled. For the first time
in a year, it could point to an achievement of outstanding magnitude, a
genuinely creative compromise between the IRA and the die-hards
which, with the goodwill of most Irishmen, brought a dark age of
crisis and violence to its close.

Quite fortuitously, the Irish settlement coincided almost exactly in
time with another diplomatic triumph, another peaceful settlement in
line with the promises of 1918. On 13 December, a four-power treaty
was signed in Washington between the United States, France, Japan,
and Great Britain, covering future plans for 'insular possessions and
insular dominions' in the Pacific. Substantial progress had also been
made at Washington in the sphere of naval disarmament. On 6 February 1922 a major international pact was signed between the British
Empire, the United States, France, Italy, and Japan, of which the
most significant feature was the declaration of a ten-year naval holiday

in the construction of capital ships. This was a somewhat accidental achievement for Anglo-American diplomacy. British foreign policy under Lloyd George had largely concentrated on the pacification of Europe, and on Germany and Russia in particular. However, the wider dimensions of imperial policy were also of much importance, especially in the Pacific. Britain ended the war with over forty Dreadnought battleships, many of them almost obsolete, and a desperate anxiety to economize on her naval commitments. In 1918, the ten-year rule had been adopted by the British Cabinet: it accepted that there would be no major war over the next ten years. This was followed by the acceptance by the Admiralty of the one-power standard which adopted the premiss of naval equality with the United States. Good relations with the USA were vital in the Far East, even though they were soured by America's refusal to participate either in the League of Nations or in the pacification of Europe after the peace treaties. Partly because of this, proposals by Jellicoe in early 1920 that a large new Pacific fleet of twenty capital ships, including four carriers, should be built, were set aside. There were also powerful considerations of economy. Lloyd George warned against an increase in naval expenditure. 'The campaign of economy was not merely a newspaper agitation; there was a genuine alarm throughout the constituencies and the popular cries were "No Government Control" and "Rigorous Economy".'[17]

The issue most crucial to Britain's naval commitments and to Anglo-American relations in 1921 was the status of the Anglo-Japanese alliance which had been successively renewed from 1902 onwards, and was due for further renewal in the summer of 1921. The alliance with Japan was thought by the government to have been beneficial during the war, and to have saved Britain expense in patrolling the Pacific. On the other hand, it was clearly provocative to the United States; while the suggestion of building a naval base at Singapore, mooted during these years, was potentially aimed at the Japanese. Indeed, during the Washington conference, American and Dutch representatives privately urged the British to persist with the base at Singapore.[18] Britain faced the anomalous position that Japan was both her ally and also the greatest putative threat to her imperial possessions in Asia and Oceania. On 30 May 1921 the Cabinet discussed at length its attitude to the renewal of the alliance with Japan.[19] Curzon and Lloyd George both summed up in favour of a renewal of the alliance on a four- to five-year basis. It was argued that the existence of the alliance absolved Britain from greater military and naval expenditure in the Far East. Churchill was one of those in favour of temporary renewal; however, he pointed out the problems in maintaining the one-power standard for the British navy if Japan and the United States continued to compete in naval armaments. As Colonial Secretary he had to emphasize Canadian dislike of the alliance. The conference of Imperial Prime Ministers which met in London in June and July revealed a wide division of opinion. Meighen of Canada violently attacked the alliance with Japan because it would upset the United States, on which Canada so much depended. Hughes of Australia, on the other hand, argued strongly for its renewal. The conference ended somewhat unsatisfactorily with a dubious legal judgement by Birkenhead, which Lloyd George gleefully brandished, to the effect that no formal decision either for or against renewal of the alliance was necessary since it could only be terminated by either side with twelve months' notice. The affair dragged on, with Empire and Cabinet much divided.

The British government intended to call an international conference to discuss Pacific and Far Eastern questions, to precede one on naval disarmament. But it was out-manœuvred when the American Secretary of State, Charles Evans Hughes, unexpectedly issued invitations to an omnibus conference to be held in Washington in November, at which the Far East and naval disarmament would be discussed side by side. Britain's response was not immediately one of immense enthusiasm. Lloyd George himself, much preoccupied at this time with the Irish negotiations, refused to make it clear whether he would attend the Washington conference himself. He feared it might prove 'something of a fiasco'.[20] In the end, the veteran, Balfour, headed the British delegation (which claimed to speak for the Empire), with Lee of Fareham, the First Lord of the Admiralty (who had an American wife), Hankey, and Sir Auckland Geddes (now Ambassador in Washington), as his colleagues. The conference began on 12 November with sweeping proposals from Hughes for a ten-year naval holiday, with Britain to retain just twenty-two capital ships of 600,000 tonnage, and a 5:5:3 ratio between the British, American, and Japanese navies. Beatty and the Admiralty were unenthusiastic; but on 10 December, a few days after the Irish treaty, there came a telegram from Lloyd George insisting that the British delegation accept the main lines of the American proposals, including the ten-year naval holiday. The four-power treaty on the Pacific was signed just three days later, in effect marking the end of the Anglo-Japanese alliance, a quiet burial after years of argument. Subsequently, with Lee as its main spokesman, the British delegation took the lead in making sweeping proposals for naval disarmament, including the offer on 22 December to scrap the whole of the British submarine fleet. The conference as a whole went well. It was marked by a vigorous, open mood which contemporaries contrasted with the atmosphere of enervating intrigue in Paris three years earlier. Balfour, in particular, responded to it with surprising energy. With the new cordiality between London and Washington that resulted from the ending of the Anglo-Japanese alliance, the concluding of the naval treaty on 6 February was relatively straightforward. There was also signed a nine-power treaty on China which codified and expanded the American doctrine of the Open Door.

Here, then, was another area where the government had taken the lead in promoting peace. There was acclaim from all sides. Even H. A. Gwynne of the die-hard *Morning Post* praised the 'splendid results' of Washington.[21] With all its limitations, the Washington treaty did make impossible the building up of a large Far Eastern battleship fleet by Britain. It marked the only serious achievement in naval disarmament in the entire inter-war period. Britain had, in fact, given up thoughts of naval dominance before the Washington treaties were signed. The Geddes committee reasonably commented that ever since the Great War 'We have abandoned all ideas of naval supremacy.'[22] Perhaps, in a longer perspective, it might be added that such ideas of supremacy were effectively abandoned with the alliance with Japan in 1902, when Japan's naval monopoly in the western Pacific was implicitly recognized. Britain's position during the conference emerged as moderate and conciliatory. It was in marked contrast to that adopted by the French who shackled the negotiations at every stage. Despite fierce pressure from Lee and Curzon, the French refused to countenance any diminution in their submarine fleet, even though they were hardly menaced from the sea, least of all by Britain. The French also demanded that they retain ten capital ships, as well as 90,000 tonnage of submarines, despite their own serious financial difficulties at this time. The Washington conference came to a satisfactory conclusion despite the obstructiveness of the French. Lloyd

George's sudden surge of interest in it, including the decision to change policy and accept the ten-year naval holiday reveals its political uses at this time. For a nation with a zeal for economy at home and tranquillity abroad, the three treaties signed at Washington represented a genuine achievement which most closely conformed to the national needs.

Ireland and Washington coincided with further drives for international peace. By the winter of 1921, the crisis in Anglo-Russian relations appeared to be ending. The trade treaty, signed the previous March, had the benevolent endorsement of the British FBI; it had lost its capacity to enrage the die-hards. Even Churchill had had little to say about Russia for many months. In any case, his departmental commitments at the Colonial Office (where he had succeeded Milner in February 1921), first in Egypt and the Middle East, later in Ireland, later still in Kenya, more than taxed even his formidable energies. The new thaw in Anglo-Russian relations encouraged Lloyd George to move towards a still more ambitious phase in international conciliation.

In the latter part of 1921, many British and French businessmen, alarmed at the contraction of world markets and of trade, pondered a broader approach to the Bolshevik regime in which a consortium of western bankers and businessmen would propose the more formal entry of the Soviet Union into commercial relations with the rest of Europe. The Russians made their counter-proposals for a different kind of conference at which the rival claims of Russia and the western powers could each be weighed. Lloyd George, during a series of meetings with the French premier, Briand, in London on 18–22 December 1922, proposed combining both, and having a general European conference to consider ways of remedying the paralysis of the European financial and commercial system.[23] The refusal of the Americans to widen the Washington conference into a wider affair made a European alternative inevitable. On 20 December, Horne, Worthington-Evans, Loucheur for France, and also Walter Rathenau, the German industrialist and former Minister for Reconstruction, had agreed at a secret meeting on measures to promote European economic recovery; these would include a syndicate of industrialists with a working capital of £10m in the first instance.[24]

Lloyd George characteristically seized on linking the idea of an economic conference with political considerations. At the conference with Briand at Cannes in early January, he was to propose not only a European economic conference, but also a harmonization of differences between Britain and France elsewhere, including a resolution of German reparations and a pact to guarantee French territorial security. The downfall of Briand's ministry during the Cannes conference on 12 January, and the advent of Poincaré as Prime Minister instead, cast a pall over the prospects for a European conference, about which Poincaré was plainly sceptical. Nevertheless, the movement for a conference—to be convened, it now transpired, at Genoa in March or April—had a momentum of its own. It was welcomed by the Germans: they had already declared that they could not meet the demands for reparations payment scheduled for 15 January or 15 February. The Russians also were enthusiastic; on 27 January the Central Committee of the Soviet Union announced that it accepted the invitation to attend the Genoa conference, and announced an unusually large delegation to attend, with the Foreign Minister, Chicherin, as its head, and Lenin himself as its titular president. Genoa had its obvious difficulties. The French were obstructive. The Americans, inevitably, would not be there. The League of Nations was being by-passed, as the Cecil group protested. There were obvious dangers of mixing up political and economic objectives in one grand summit conference, of turning Genoa into another Versailles. Nevertheless, the general reception (outside Printing House Square) was encouraging.

With Ireland and then Washington largely behind him, with growing hopes for peace in Egypt as well, Lloyd George during the Christmas period could point to Genoa as perhaps the crowning achievement of his administration, making immediate peace with ultimate prosperity truly possible. Churchill could claim that 'the word of Britain has counted as it has never counted before, leading the quest for general appeasement and world recovery'.[25] The political potentialities of Genoa were immense. It could appeal both to the isolationism of the right and the internationalism of the left. It would, of course, deflect attention from mass unemployment and a stagnant economy at home. It could make the anticipated economies to be demanded by the Geddes committee part and parcel of a logical scheme of disarmament and the revival of Britain's export trade. Above all, it provided Lloyd George with a clear opportunity of regaining the political initiative. He had suffered a dismal series of rebuffs, culminating in a sensational

Labour victory at a by-election in South-East Southwark on 14 December. The victorious candidate here, T. E. Naylor, of the London Society of Compositors, gained a clear majority of the votes cast: in any case, his union had a powerful appeal in Southwark, a constituency close to Fleet Street, where many printing workers lived. The swing against the government, 39.7 per cent compared with the general election, was the largest of any in the course of that parliament, greater even than those at West Leyton and Hull Central back in the spring of 1919. Now truly was the time for the Coalition to pull itself together and exploit the peace issue to see a new and wider mandate.

In the euphoric aftermath of these achievements in external policy, Lloyd George decided, some time before Christmas, that he wanted an early general election. This would confirm the alliance with the Unionists, and leave the delicate question of future relations between the two wings of the Coalition for peaceful discussion at leisure after the polls. This was not a bad time to select, politically. The Wee Frees had made little headway for eighteen months. The die-hards had been flattened by Salvidge and Chamberlain at Liverpool. There was the continuing menace from Labour, but here was one opponent that Lloyd George welcomed, since its very existence gave point to the government's claim to stand as the custodians of tradition and ordered progress. Precisely who Lloyd George's confidants were in these critical days is not wholly clear, but Birkenhead, one of the quadrumvirate popularly thought to make up an 'inner Cabinet' or 'directorate' (Chamberlain, Churchill, and Horne being the others), was certainly prominent. Negotiations about a possible election seem to have begun at a dinner at his home on 19 December.[26] Churchill's reaction was very guarded. Horne's view is not known directly, but he was unlikely to have been hostile in view of his success in promoting Treasury ideas of economy and imposing them on the government's programme. Only Austen Chamberlain was from the first distinctly hostile, and anxious to consult more widely among party organizers. But that did not necessarily present a decisive obstacle to what was, after all, one of the Prime Minister's traditional constitutional powers, the right to call a general election at a moment of his own choosing.

Austen Chamberlain, in sounding out Unionist opinion about the prospects for an early election, gave two slightly different versions of the situation. Writing to Younger, the party chairman, he phrased it that Lloyd George was 'greatly attracted to the idea of an election early in the New Year', and Birkenhead 'equally strongly in favour of it'. But Lloyd George, he added, had not made a final decision 'though there is no doubt where his inclinations lie'.[27] Writing with more freedom to his brother, Neville, the same day, Austen reported that Lloyd George 'strongly favoured' a dissolution and that he was supported in this view by Birkenhead, McCurdy, and by Macnamara 'whom the Prime Minister considers a shrewd electioneer'.[28] Austen Chamberlain himself was opposed and Churchill hesitant. In writing to Younger, Chamberlain gave policy considerations to justify his opposition to having an early election—the delicate state of Ireland and the effect in undermining what remained of financial and commercial confidence. To Neville, however, the Unionist leader emphasized party aspects—the impossibility of consolidating the Coalition into a united party before an election held so early, and the general impact on Unionist morale. An election now might result not only in the return of an undue proportion of die-hards but also of many 'independent Conservatives, unpledged to the support of a Coalition government'. Chamberlain also wrote around to Unionist party organizers in different parts of England, Wales, and Scotland, seeking their views on the choice between an immediate election, an election in about eighteen months' time taking the form of a renewed appeal by the Coalition on the present basis, or a still later election to support a 'new party formed within the Coalition'. Clearly, he was making possible a rebellion by the party organizers to frustrate Lloyd George's intentions.

If there was uncertainty and doubt in the Coalition Unionist camp, some Coalition Liberals, like the Prime Minister, saw the prospect of an early election as a sudden dawn after a wild and stormy night. Latterly, they had been sorely shaken over the Safeguarding of Industries Bill and its threat to free trade over the 'key industries' provisions. Their chief whip, Charles McCurdy, now proclaimed that Coalition Liberal organizers all over the country were confident about an early election and the return of Lloyd George with a large majority, apart from the concern expressed in some areas about the effect of unemployment on the government's chances. He was convinced, despite all the recent evidence from by-elections up to South-East Southwark, that the Liberal wing of the Coalition was steadily gaining in strength. The settlement of the Irish question created a new climate in which the government could appeal to the country. 'It is a mistake to suppose that Coalition has grown more unpopular among the electors.'[29] To balance McCurdy's absurd over-optimism, Sutherland, another Liberal adviser on tactics, was more cautious. There was still no sign of a general revival of trade, despite some hopeful symptoms in the South Wales coal trade. The Geddes report could enable Labour to brand the government as reactionaries. Labour's recent success at Southwark confirmed its ability to serve as the residuary legatees of popular discontent, while there were signs that the Independent Liberals might support Labour candidates in key seats, as had occurred at Southwark. The Irish vote was no longer reliable, with its links with Labour, and the Irish treaty was not necessarily a vote-winner in any case. On the other hand, Sutherland left it open as to whether the government could successfully go to the country on a 'peace and prosperity' ticket. He took comfort from the collapse of the 'extremists' in Labour's ranks in mining and other industrial areas. He urged Lloyd George to adopt a bold progressive stance, to break free from the 'bourgeoisie crust' with which a largely middle-class Coalition Liberalism was associated in the public mind, especially in the North. Events, he thought, were working in the government's favour, especially in Washington and Ireland. The government should now stress that it was not just a rich man's administration and emphasize its policies over unemployment relief, pensions, and progressive taxation.[30]

But it was the Unionists alone who could determine or demolish the Prime Minister's plan for an election. By the end of the year, Austen Chamberlain had received shattering proof from all over the country that Unionists almost everywhere were totally opposed to an early election and doubtful about further overtures in the direction of 'fusion'' in future months. Only Williams in the West of England would even consider an early appeal to the country.[31] Neville Chamberlain, writing both publicly and privately to his brother, expressed the views of Midlands Unionists with extreme clarity. There was, he reported, wide discontent with the Coalition in Birmingham; even Austen's own seat in West Birmingham was no longer secure, so Central Office agents declared. Unionists in the Midlands opposed any early 'fusion'; many would secede rather than accept Lloyd George as the head of a new party. His private view was that the Coalition ought to be dissolved, but he recognized its impracticability 'until somebody has the happy idea of "p'isoning Lloyd George's rum and water"'. He listed six specific arguments. Many Unionists were uncertain about the virtues of the Irish settlement. House of Lords reform remained to be undertaken. 'The Coalition has no friends to speak of: businessmen loathe it. They are sore about E.P.D. and C.P.T.' The Geddes economies proposed for education were much disliked by teachers. Labour's activities at the time of the Council of Action and the miners' strike had now been forgotten. Finally, unemployment and the depressed state of business were paramount issues, and obviously told to the disadvantage of the government.[32] A variety of sources of advice were brought to bear by other correspondents. Lloyd-Greame, a government trade minister, reported that Scottish chambers of commerce were against an early election. Amery, an expert on foreign affairs, pronounced that Washington, Cannes, and Ireland would not arouse much enthusiasm amongst Unionist voters. The editor of the *Scotsman* condemned Sutherland's and McCurdy's 'stunt' tactics in trying to whip up a press campaign in favour of an early election.[33]

Most damaging of all, Tory Central Office was adamant against an appeal to the country. Malcolm Fraser, the chief party agent, wrote that 'it would split the Unionist party from top to toe'. A host of Independent Conservatives would spring up, whereas there was no clear attraction offered by the Coalition 'with its numerous facets of sects and creeds'. He contrasted the massive growth of the Labour Party since 1918 with the fact that the Coalition had won only 47 per cent of the votes cast in contested by-elections in that period, as opposed to 61 per cent in 1918. Among government supporters, Fraser claimed, 'neither wing is really proud of the achievements of the Coalition'. There was strong feeling about the burden of taxation and the scale of government expenditure, as shown in the St. George's by-election, while he, also, asserted that neither Ireland nor Washington would be electoral assets.[34] Where Fraser was despondent, Younger was belligerent. It was futile to imagine that any alternative administration could cope with unemployment and industrial difficulties any better than the present government. 'Our people in the country are getting very jumpy.'[35] Chamberlain duly reported these virtually unanimous views to Lloyd George on 4 January, just after the Prime Minister's departure for the conference with Briand at Cannes. Unionists everywhere were hostile to a Coalition; many would break

away from the Coalition and provoke three-cornered fights if an early
election were held. Agricultural districts were strongly against an
election, while in industrial areas 'unemployment will play havoc with
us'.[36]

Still, it was by no means certain that Lloyd George would bow
before these Unionist pressures. On 3 January *The Times* reported that
'a February general election was regarded as almost a certainty'. The
government's campaign would emphasize the Geddes economies, the
revival of trade, proposals for a European economic conference to be
presented to the delegates at Cannes, peace in Ireland, disarmament in
Washington. Lloyd George's projected speech to a mass Coalition
Liberal rally at Westminster Hall on 20 January would be the
starting-point for a new campaign, based on partnership and unity of
action with the Unionists, rather than on direct fusion.

But the Unionist party organizers turned to more direct pressures
than merely communicating their views to Chamberlain. Conservative Central Office now organized a press campaign against a snap
election. From 30 December onwards, remarkably full accounts had
appeared in *The Times* and the *Morning Post* setting forth the arguments within the government for and against a general election. In
particular, Chamberlain's letters to party workers were paraphrased
in great detail. Chamberlain himself denied that he had authorized
these press leakages; curiously enough, he attributed them to Birkenhead. Churchill, who complained about them on Lloyd George's
behalf, believed, more plausibly, that Malcolm Fraser was the
source.[37] They were followed by an even more unorthodox challenge.
On 5 January, an interview with Younger appeared in the press in
which he revealed, in effect, the private debate amongst ministers on
the possibility of an early election. He argued strongly that the Coalition ought not to go to the country until it had finished its task. In
particular, he mentioned the need for fulfilling the government's
pledges on the reform of the House of Lords. This led to immediate
Coalition Liberal protests; but Younger promptly compounded the
offence with a further interview, this time with the Press Association,
published on 6 January. In even more forthright tones, Younger
referred to the 'unfulfilled pledges' of the government. Apart from
reform of the Lords, he mentioned the need for a permanent settlement in Ireland, for reviving trade and industry, and for carrying out
the economies recommended by Geddes. The arguments for an early

election were based on 'pure opportunism and a narrow party spirit'. He also circularized local party chairmen, giving his views against an election.[38] The following day, *The Times* carried a remarkably full survey of the views of local Unionists, as conveyed confidentially to Austen Chamberlain, including those of Neville Chamberlain, Sir Herbert Jessel in London, and Unionist spokesmen in Manchester, Nottingham, and Plymouth. The views of leading Unionist politicians were also cited, Birkenhead, Horne, and Worthington-Evans being in favour of an early election, Austen Chamberlain against, with Bonar Law and Derby undecided. The views of Manchester Coalition Liberals, as given to Hewart, with their unexpectedly strong opposition to an early election were also given. In all, Younger gave four interviews, two to the *Evening News*, one to the *Evening Standard*, and one to the Press Association, all equally devastating.

It was a marked sign of the government's political difficulties that, in the face of these stark challenges from Younger, it could neither discipline him nor dismiss him. Churchill felt that Younger's tactics had seriously prejudiced Conservative opinion, and that he himself must now resist holding an election in January or February. He, Birkenhead, and Derby proposed that no action be taken until Lloyd George returned from Cannes.[39] Lloyd George himself, in a cable, fumed that 'Younger had behaved disgracefully', especially in revealing to the press a private document from McCurdy, and in suggesting that the idea of a general election was a Coalition Liberal stunt. In the meantime, he looked forward to a successful outcome for the Cannes conference: 'I think we are on the way to a solution of the reparation problem.'[40] Even in the face of the Prime Minister's anger, however, and of the withering scorn of Birkenhead who dismissed him as a 'cabin boy' who sought to take over the bridge, Younger was quite impenitent. A veteran organizer himself and a septuagenarian, he was in no mood to apologize to Lloyd George or anyone else. He denounced Sutherland's press 'stunts'. He threatened to teach 'Sutherland & co' that they could treat neither the great Unionist Party nor himself as 'a negligible quantity'. He told Horne bluntly that Unionists in the country expected immediate action to implement the Geddes report: it should not be mere 'window dressing'.[41] It was clear, too, that Chamberlain in general backed up Younger's unorthodox methods. He told McCurdy on 10 January, in a long discussion, that he himself had reservations about an election, whichever date were selected. Any closer form of union would be fatal to the prospects of the party. After the press disclosures, he felt that it would be impossible to agree to an early election and remain Unionist leader. McCurdy told Lloyd George by telegram, 'I think you should consider the situation that split is certain of entire Conservative Party and revolt possible whenever this parliament ends.' He commented, resignedly, that Chamberlain was 'perhaps obsessed with the idea of his duty to the Conservative Party'. He and Leslie Wilson, the Unionist whip, were being misled by the stream of letters against an election that they were receiving from party workers, since these were being orchestrated by Younger.[42]

McCurdy continued to insist for some days that Younger had overplayed his hand, and that the great majority of Unionists were not opposed to an early election. He went so far as to claim that Chamberlain was misinformed as to the real opinion of the Tory rank and file in the country, 'the great majority of whom see no real alternative to Coalition as form of Government and desire no alternative to yourself as Leader. He also fails to realize the strength of the non-party vote which goes to swell Liberal, Labour and Tory returns.'[43] This was obviously wishful thinking. McCurdy cited no firm evidence at all for his assessment of Tory opinion, nor did any exist. By the time Lloyd George returned home from Cannes on 13 January, McCurdy was virtually alone in advocating an early election.

The only thing that could conceivably have salvaged an immediate election for Lloyd George now would have been some highly dramatic diplomatic breakthrough at Cannes. In fact, the downfall of Briand as French Prime Minister and his replacement by Poincaré, who promptly disavowed virtually every agreement that Briand and Lloyd George had reached, meant that the British premier came home empty-handed. All over the country, chairmen of Unionist constituencies were telling Younger, and he was telling the world at the top of his voice, of their opposition to an election, and of the certainty of a mass Unionist secession if one were held. Derby at the Manchester Constitutional Club on the 14th took a similar line and urged instead a continuation of the Coalition on present lines, with retrenchment as its main theme. He underlined the disenchantment with government policy that he had felt privately for some months by adding some sharp criticisms of the conduct of the negotiations at Cannes. They ought not, he thought, to have been conducted in the first instance by heads of government.[44] At a private dinner with Chamberlain, Horne, Birkenhead, and Churchill on the evening of the 13th, Lloyd George found that the option of an early election was ruled out. In any case, the Irish treaty, the budget, and above all Genoa were all looming up, and in need of government attention without any distraction. The Prime Minister had to admit defeat. On the 17th, *The Times*'s correspondent reported 'there will be no February election—that is settled'.[45] Lloyd George himself still affected an air of indifference, or alternatively of keeping his opponents guessing. He told Scott that Younger was 'playing his game' by relieving the Prime Minister of the risk of an early election before he had had time to put together a new political combination. Grigg wrote to Cromer that the 'P.M. is really somewhat indifferent' about the prospect of an election. However, he did add that there was a major weakness, namely that while the Unionists were a party without (he claimed) a leader, the Prime Minister was a leader without a party.[46] Lloyd George's pretence that the decision when and how to call a general election was his alone was being exploded. He had no alternatives left, whereas Younger's prestige was growing all the time. The grand rally of Coalition Liberals at Central Hall, Westminster on 22 January was anticlimactic. Lloyd George himself, in the opinion of one in the audience who had not heard him speak since 1913, 'spoke with more restraint and less eloquence'.[47] He dismissed the idea of a general election. He himself, he claimed, had never started the rumour in the first place. His emphasis now was on the long haul, on continuity in policy with Genoa and Geddes coming up. Now, above all times, was a time for international and national confidence to be sustained. Nationalism not sectionalism was the need of the hour. The great election scare was over three weeks after it had begun. Relieved speculators on the stock exchange, so Arthur Kiddy reported in the *Spectator*, could now cash in, another crisis in the market over.[48]

Without doubt, this episode marked a serious decline in the Prime Minister's authority. The fact that he had the bad luck that it coincided with a political crisis in Paris that led to the fall of the French government added to the impression of weakness. A Prime Minister who could not call an election when he chose, who could not control the majority component of his government, and who could not take action against a party official when he revealed private government communications, was clearly on the run. Austen Chamberlain was also thought to be 'discredited for lack of leadership'.[49] Lloyd George himself was badly advised throughout. The main voices on behalf of an election were two. On the Unionist side, Birkenhead was almost the worst adviser that could have been chosen, with his record of erratic party behaviour since the coalition manœuvres of 1910 and his contemptuous dismissal of Unionist machine politicians. On the Liberal side, McCurdy, even less inhibited than Freddie Guest, provided Lloyd George with a stream of over-confident misinformation. He had even told Lloyd George that Churchill had become committed to an early dissolution: 'he is indignant with Younger and expresses desire for immediate election'.[50] This was clearly incorrect. Sutherland was more guarded, and few other leading Coalition Liberals—in fact, probably none save Guest and Macnamara—agreed with McCurdy. It is clear that, if an election had been held, Lloyd George would have been faced with a Unionist revolt that would have destroyed the Coalition at a stroke. As it was, widespread unease resulted. Small wonder that Austen Chamberlain complained to Derby that the threat of a dissolution of parliament seemed 'for the moment to have shattered my work'.[51]

By most orthodox calculations, Lloyd George's belief that he could capitalize on the 'swing to the left' by gaining a new mandate from the electors early in 1922 seems to be a total illusion. By the same token, his view that he could soldier on and renew the unity of the government and of the nation, rallying the middle ground against Labour and the die-hards, seems at best an act of faith. But the whole essence of his role, isolated as it was, was that he could appeal over the heads of the party managers. He hoped to restore his private communion with the political nation whose symbol he had become and whose essential unity he claimed to represent. It was not, perhaps, a wholly ridiculous claim. The party managers, the Youngers and Frasers, based their assessments on what the rank-and-file activists in the constituencies could be persuaded to swallow. The fact that they gave such prominence to so irrelevant an issue as the reform of the House of Lords, in which even Unionist voters manifested scant interest, showed the limits of their perspective. The party managers based their judgements on sectional, party-based considerations, on the mobilization of men, the buying off of protest groups, and the manipulation of pressures and interests. Lloyd George based his appeal to the nation not on 'high politics' but on high policy. In 1922, more than at any time earlier in his career, his view of the political future was shaped by trying to enlarge his appeal by a dynamic and constructive programme at home and abroad. This was the end to which Cabinet and parliamentary manœuvrings were devoted. More than at any time during his premiership, Lloyd George now trod the high road. His emphasis on foreign policy, in particular the preparations for the international conference to be convened at Genoa, illustrates very clearly the rarefied view of public affairs that he now took. The political and tactical niceties urged, accurately or inaccurately, by McCurdy and Sutherland, were subordinated to the great aim of shoring up a new political base which would bring his policies to fruition and would restore peace to a shattered Continent. This would benefit Britain itself also, both directly in stimulating trade and employment, and indirectly since 'Britain was the one stable country of the world.'[52]

Now above all times Lloyd George's appeal for unity must be made to work. Now he must try to vault over parties, pressure-groups, and parliament to communicate with the mass electorate, a communication founded not on the manipulation of the media but on firmly based and successful policies. His failure to achieve an early election revealed more clearly than ever the need for sustaining this mystical unity which his government claimed to embody. Unity in the conflict between capital and labour, unity within the Empire, unity in pushing on with the appeasement and reconciliation of Europe, unity at a more parochial level between the different wings of the government, were more than ever paramount. Lloyd George does not seem to have been downcast by his defeat at the hands of Sir George Younger in January 1922. Rather it confirmed his commitment to a vision in which he symbolized the spirit of a nation at one with itself and at peace with a wider world.

12

The Downfall of the Coalition: Class Consciousness

The Coalition was based on the premiss of social unity. At its inception in 1918, it took its cue from its leader in claiming that it would perpetuate the class collaboration of the war years in a new and productive partnership. Lloyd George believed that the war had been a solvent of traditional social barriers: conflict between social classes was now as outmoded as conflict between political parties. He claimed that it was a social, as well as political, coalition. The claim that labour was comprehended within the umbrella of the Coalition, as clearly as were business interests, was genuinely held. The trade unions were negotiable groups just as were the FBI and the Chambers of Commerce; they were bound in industrial partnership with the employers as they had been in some sense since the conclusion of the Treasury agreement in March 1915, when strikes and wartime profits had—at least, in theory—been traded off, against each other. The state, through the mediation of the Ministry of Labour, was present as broker to help create a framework in which pragmatic partnership and free collective bargaining could proceed side by side. The Coalition did not begin its life as an anti-labour front. From 1919 onwards, the unions enjoyed easy and frequent access to government, a relationship that by 1926 they had clearly lost. Even so, by the time of Black Friday in April 1921, an anti-labour front was what the government closely resembled. The private rhetoric of Cabinet ministers had viewed the unions as a sectional enemy whose more extreme claims should be resisted by all available means. The brief honeymoon period of the National Industrial Conference was long forgotten. The whole tide of governmental policy in the period of 'decontrol' was running against the demands of organized labour. Well before 1914, British workers had evolved a degree of institutionalized collective consciousness without parallel in any industrial nation in the world, save perhaps for

Germany. The course of government after 1918 was probably to intensify that class consciousness still further. The pre-war pattern of workers being concentrated in labour-intensive industries, and being employed in larger units of production was confirmed by the war years. An atmosphere of isolation and withdrawal was created in the world of labour. This meant that the reality of social division and conflict made a mockery of a governmental system which paid obeisance to national unity. Here, no less fundamentally than in the 'high politics' of the Tory back-bench revolt in October 1922, lay the roots of the downfall of Lloyd George and his Coalition government.

This basic division within society had been sufficiently pronounced in the eighteen months of boom that followed the armistice as mass unions, more powerful and prosperous than ever before, tried to build on the gains in wages achieved during the war. It was difficult for the government, even in this period, to sustain an amicable working relationship with the articulate working class, although, as has been seen, some success was achieved in settling accounts with the railwaymen's union after the national rail strike in the autumn of 1919. Meaningful contact between the government and labour almost disappeared when the massive slump, and the huge unemployment that followed, began in the summer of 1920. By the Christmas of 1921, the very time when Lloyd George was meditating that his achievements in the fields of overseas peace and disarmament might justify an appeal to the electors, unemployment stood at over two million, 18 per cent of the insured working population. In every major staple industry, in engineering, shipbuilding, iron and steel, textiles, and—finally and most disastrously—in coal-mining, the active labour force fell to an unprecedented low level. It cannot be said that the government was caught wholly unawares, or that it anticipated that an early upturn in the trade cycle would bring renewed prosperity. On the contrary, the Cabinet recognized from the summer of 1920 onwards that a massive trade slump was coming and that it would be on a prolonged, worldwide scale hitherto unknown.

Nevertheless, the government's efforts to cope with mass unemployment were totally unsuccessful. They even emphasized the sectional nature of their objectives. As has been seen, the attempt to extend the range of unemployment insurance was a belated, unhappy affair, with Macnamara, the Minister of Labour, introducing a series of half measures that remained inadequate for the problem.[1] Although the dole was now provided for an almost unlimited extension of time and a fund set up to maintain wives and dependent children, at the fall of the Coalition government in October 1922 the benefits offered were still only 15s. for an unemployed man and 12s. for an unemployed woman. The fiction was maintained that these were to supplement the savings thriftily accumulated by the unemployed workers, even though in the financial conditions of 1919–22 such an idea was absurd. Further, more objectionable features of the system were introduced. Macnamara's scheme of March 1921 included the notorious 'genuinely seeking work' test which placed the onus on the applicant for unemployment benefit, and left him open to rigorous scrutiny of his skills, his savings, and even his personal character. More, the benefits were enforced in an atmosphere which, especially after the Geddes report, implied rigid economy. The dissent of Horne, the Chancellor, was recorded when the Cabinet agreed in March 1922 to preserve benefits at the existing financial levels.[2] Certain categories of workers were excluded altogether, including wives whose husbands were in full-time employment, and single men and women who lived with relatives. While the Coalition government prided itself on the intro-duction of universal insurance against unemployment, working-class men and women saw it rather as the author of the 'means test' and system of inquisitorial relief which imposed indignities upon the working class unknown in any other aspect of state policy, central or local. In addition, the meagre benefits provided were an incentive to underfeeding and malnutrition. How, after all, could a child be maintained in full health on 1s. a week?

More positively, the Coalition did try from an early stage to initiate measures that would moderate the impact of the slump in trade. A Cabinet Committee on Unemployment was set up in August 1920, under the chairmanship of Worthington-Evans, a committee over which the Prime Minister himself was later frequently to preside.[3] Here were considered a series of disparate proposals for reducing unemployment. Efforts were to be made to enlist another 25,000 apprentices in the building trade unions, to assist in Addison's hous-ing drive, with a guaranteed working week. New schemes for arterial road building were to be started, such as the North Circular Road in London. However, Sir Henry Maybury, the Director-General of the Ministry of Transport, pointed out that unskilled labour would be used on a large scale only in the early stages of road construction. The repair of existing roads would need more skilled men and this would probably lead to difficulties with the trade unions concerned.[4] Sir Alfred Mond, the Commissioner of Works until March 1921, was simultaneously exhorted to exercise economy and to provide work for unemployed workers on government building projects. The Overseas Trade Department, under Lloyd-Greame, was empowered to assist manufacturers and traders by authorizing export credits for trade with countries with depreciated currencies. But all these were palliatives of an unsystematic and limited kind. The housing drive, as has been seen, ground to a halt in 1921. The road-building programme absorbed only a few thousand unemployed workers. A government report (CP 2517) indicated that by February 1921 only 774 workers were being employed on London's arterial roads, instead of the 11,700 who should have been engaged.[5] The Ministry of Works's efforts were equally modest. The export-credits scheme was widely criticized by economists. It applied in the first instance only to countries where the market risks were high and where the governments concerned had not the resources to trade widely with Britain in any case. In general, the Cabinet Unemployment Committee was an ineffective body, hemmed in by pressure first from Chamberlain, then from Horne at the Exchequer. Amidst general agreement, Chamberlain pointed out that the state had never previously devoted expenditure above £300,000 to cope with unemployment.[6] The government was in any case committed to returning to gold as recommended by the Cunliffe committee. With the new zeal for economy in 1921, and some signs of achievement for this hard policy as the pound rose steadily against the dollar from a low point of $3.20, there was little prospect of these earlier precedents being superseded.

In December 1920, a new phase of government policy was begun. This was the appointment of a special Cabinet committee under Viscount St. David's, a former colleague of the Prime Minister's in the Welsh Parliamentary Party prior to 1910 and president of the Welsh National Liberal Council. Its object was specifically to initiate public works projects to alleviate unemployment. It was authorized to spend a sum of up to £3m to assist the local authorities in carrying out 'useful works', other than the housing and road schemes for which provision had already been made.[7] To underline the gravity with which he regarded the problem of the unemployed, Lloyd George actually held a conference at Downing Street on the afternoon of Christmas Day, with those present including Macnamara, the Minister of Labour, Sir Allen Smith of the Engineering Employers' Federation, and Arthur Henderson. Smith and Henderson jointly proposed that a compulsory levy of one penny in the pound be imposed on employers and employed alike, and that the state set up 'a great national fund' for the relief of industrial distress.[8] A committee of five heads of industry, including Smith and Adam Nimmo, the coal-owner, and five labour representatives was set up to assess the practicality of such a scheme. In fact, this committee soon disappeared from view, as a result of the breakdown of communication between the two sides of industry; the optimism of the National Industrial Conference in 1919 had indeed disappeared. On the other hand, the St. David's committee did produce some useful activity. Its funds were increased to £10m as unemployment deteriorated still further in October 1921. By the end of the year, it was reported that the committee had approved 660 separate local public-works schemes, public utilities, and other ventures. A further 600 schemes were under consideration which would exceed the total of £10m by £4.5m. This raised once again the fundamental problem of finance. The Treasury was being committed to spending £600,000 a year, whereas Horne reported that it could not exceed a limit of £200,000. After much debate, with Churchill a vigorous supporter of more active policies, the Cabinet agreed to raise the limit to £13m but only on condition that a more stringent test of what unemployment consisted was applied.[9]

In fact, the Treasury's control hamstrung the St. David's committee throughout. Nor could it hope to make more than a marginal impact on the problem of mass unemployment. By September 1921, the situation was even more desperate. The total of unemployed stood at over 1.5m even though the immediate effects of the coal strike had passed away. The Directorate of Intelligence sent highly alarmist reports to the Cabinet about the threat to law and order contained in mass demonstrations of the unemployed, especially in London, and how they were being exploited by Communists and other 'agitators'.[10] Poor Law Boards of Guardians were facing bankruptcy, with high charges on interest repayment and sinking fund payments. Macnamara reported that the unemployment insurance benefit of 15s. could no longer be supplemented from relief from Guardians or from trade union funds as had been possible the previous winter. By 1 April, a further half a million men would have exhausted their eight-week benefit.[11] At the same time, the Treasury maintained an inflexible attitude towards social relief. Horne's budget of April 1921 was quite inappropriate for the tasks with which it was confronted. Its only major change was to abolish Excess Profits Duty which was agreed to have become a liability in view of the provision for repayment when profits fell below standard.[12] Over all, the budget still anticipated a large surplus for the year. Clearly, some new departure in policy was essential, lest the social cleavage induced by unemployment on such a scale become unbridgeable.

In the summer of 1921, immediately after the appointment of the Geddes economies committee, the Lloyd George government took steps to acknowledge that unemployment had become by far its major domestic priority. At the same time as the arrangements being agreed for the negotiations with the Irish Sinn Fein leaders, during Lloyd George's recuperative holiday at Gairloch in the Scottish highlands, the Cabinet strove to provide a new initiative and a new strategy in grappling with unemployment. The Cabinet Committee on Unemployment met on 12 September under the chairmanship of Mond, with Horne, Baldwin (President of the Board of Trade), and Macnamara also present. It was agreed to extend state assistance to necessitous Poor Law authorities, to provide more capital to stimulate public works through the St. David's committee, and to widen the scope of unemployment insurance. Hopeful signs of new prospects of employment were said to be discerned in road construction and shipbuilding.[13] Conferences with bankers, manufacturers, and traders on the part of the Prime Minister seemed to herald more ambitious programmes, perhaps inducements to the banks to give more generous credit and financial support to industrialists. There was the prospect of granting more assistance to the needier Poor Law authorities, as a result of the savings from the closing of over 150 labour exchanges and cutting costs on insurance and housing. Generally, there was widespread agreement that the government must play a more vigorous part in stimulating public works and industrial enterprise, lest a wholly unacceptable sum of tens of millions be spent to maintain a permanent army of over a million unemployed workers.

This new urgency by the government failed to impress eight Labour mayors in London, where the impact of unemployment was more severe. On 16 September, they had a meeting with Mond, where they urged state loans to subsidize public utility schemes run by the local authorities. Then, in a well-publicized journey, the mayors headed by Herbert Morrison, the Mayor of Hackney, travelled by train to Inverness in the far north, and compelled a private discussion at Gairloch with Lloyd George himself.[14] Clearly, by this time, un-employment had transcended every issue save Ireland amongst the government's priorities. On 1–2 October, Lloyd George had dis-cussions with bankers and industrialists at Gairloch, together with professional economists such as Walter Layton. When parliament reassembled in mid-October, a dramatic new initiative from the government was generally expected.

In fact, the government's initiative fell flat. It was, perhaps, more imaginative than the proposals of the Labour mayors who concen-trated, understandably enough, on the human problems of relief and whose proposals for positive action largely amounted to a rehearsal of the public works experiments offered by Labour spokesmen since the days of Keir Hardie. The government was unenthusiastic about open-ended relief assistance, quite apart from the passion for 'economy'. Its main adviser on unemployment programmes now was Hilton Young, a former Wee Free Liberal who had crossed the floor and joined the government as Financial Secretary to the Treasury. Grigg was amongst those who much admired his intellectual capac-ity—'the best mind of his age in politics'.[15] Young's emphasis was on long-term projects of capital development in Britain and the Empire, and the stimulation of markets in Europe through favourable credit policies.[16] Faced with such diagnoses, it is not surprising that the government's original plans for assistance to the banks in the short term to provide credit to businesses by government guarantees were whittled away in the Cabinet. Lloyd George's announcement of the government's programme for unemployment on 19 October accepted that high unemployment was likely to be present for the foreseeable future. There would be money made available for relief works, £10m in all, plus a further £1m to extend unemployment benefit, and £300,000 granted to help ex-servicemen emigrate to the dominions—this a final gesture of despair. But the main emphasis was to be on much longer-term measures, £26m for export credits to assist traders in overseas markets, special facilities for developing trade with countries whose prospects offered adequate guarantees, £25m for loans concluded specifically to promote employment in the United Kingdom. In effect, the government's emphasis was on the long haul.

Hilton Young's declaration at Gairloch that inflation was preferable to mass starvation was forgotten. The overtures from the TUC and the Labour mayors ended with angry recriminations all round. And with this, the government's much-trumpeted initiative was spent.[17]

For the rest of its time in office, the government introduced no new measures of any consequence to try to relieve unemployment with positive action. Lloyd George's statement of October 1921 was to remain the last comprehensive statement by the government on the roots of unemployment and the possible range of remedies for it. Any further initiatives were to be frustrated by the pressure for 'economy' in social spending, and by the prevalent view, expressed forcibly by Lloyd George to the Labour mayors at Gairloch, that the only real remedy for unemployment was simply to wait for better times. This conclusion on the part of the government represented the conventional wisdom of those pre-Keynesian days, wisdom to which Keynes himself broadly subscribed at this period. On balance, the government's proposals were more positive than those of its opponents. The Labour Party, from the London mayors downwards, was as weak in advocating constructive remedies for stimulating industry as it was strong in advocating more charitable expenditure upon relief. Within the Treasury itself, in the circulars of ministers such as Mond and Hilton Young, more imaginative proposals were being suggested, outlining schemes of counter-cyclical government expenditure in place of deflation, and moving towards the concept of the 'multiplier' as far as generating employment was concerned.[18] Churchill was a forceful, though unsuccessful, critic of 'the austere bankers' policy which it has been since the banks got the traders in their power after the short post-war boom' and which had been directly responsible for creating well over a million unemployed, as the social cost of writing off immense quantities of industrial capital. He complained that there were no precise directives from the Treasury on major questions. For example, was it intended to pay off the internal National Debt at its present inflated value, in relation to pre-war standards, or at its full face value of £7m?[19] In the end, the fact that the government could offer no more than a compromise between aiding the local authorities and trying to stimulate trade in the long term—together with such novelties as the inquiries with bankers and manufacturers—may have offered the best that any government, so ill-equipped with

macro-economic advice compared with governments since 1940, may
have been able to achieve. In any case, no simple solutions existed for
deep-rooted structural problems in British industry and in the pattern
of trade which dated from the later nineteenth century. Where the
government could be attacked was in making its public works and
employment policies the slaves of its financial policy—and in a highly
erratic fashion. Churchill eloquently showed how politics had fluctu-
ated between paying off the public debt through a dampening down of
purchasing power, and inflating the currency to encourage enterprise
and investment. Neither policy had been consistently followed, while
such hopeful initiatives as Addison's housing campaign had been
totally reversed. Hamstrung by the Treasury, politically constrained
by the Anti-Waste movement, the government had to give up any
thoughts of reviving the economy at home, and had simply to concentrate on the optimistic view that Britain's traditional exporting staple
industries would pull her through in the end. Salvation was thought to
lie in increasing exports and restoring currency stability in Europe,
west and east. Hence the new authority given from April 1921 to
Lloyd-Greame at the Overseas Trade department, and the importance
attached to the conference at Genoa, not least in opening up the
Russian market. It was pointed out that European markets had taken
36.9 per cent of British exports at the end of 1920 but only 30.7 per
cent a year later.[20] In the foreseeable future—at least until the spring
of 1923 according to most forecasts—the government felt that it could
do little beyond bailing out the local authorities and practising
economy to make relief programmes more effective. In political
terms, this simply meant that the social division between the mass
unemployed in the older industrial regions and those with more secure
prospects in service employment, commerce, and newer industries
elsewhere, became one of the fundamental props of the government's
programme.

This was much reinforced by the impact of the Geddes reports on
government economies. These reports went through a somewhat
tortuous process in the government's hands. They were in the hands
of ministers by mid-December, but there was a suspicious delay in
publishing them, attributed in sections of the press to the political
crisis occasioned by Lloyd George's hope of calling a general election.
Not until 6 February was it decided to publish them after pressure by
the Unionist chief whip, Leslie Wilson.[21] In the first week of January,

two major Cabinet committees were appointed to consider how best to implement the economies for which the businessmen on Geddes's committee had called. One, under the chairmanship of Churchill, a fierce critic of the entire principle of appointing the Geddes committee, dealt with defence departments; the other, chaired by Austen Chamberlain, covered the domestic civil service estimates.[22] Not until the end of February did a government conclusion emerge, and the full extent of the cuts in expenditure become apparent. In fact, the main impact of Geddes fell on defence. The committee had been asked by the Chancellor to try to reduce the estimates by the huge total of £100m. In the event, Geddes proposed cuts of approximately £76m, of which £46.5m would fall on the armed services. Of this, about £21m each would be pared off the estimates of the military and naval departments, while economies in the air force would account for a further £5m. Naturally, there was stern resistance. The War Office fought hard against the economies proposed. There was, it pointed out, 'evidence of world-wide conspiracy fomented by all the elements most hostile to British interests—Sinn Feiners and Socialists at our own doors, Russian Bolsheviks, Turkish and Egyptian Nationalists, and Indian Seditionists'.[23] The Admiralty fought even harder: Beatty was backed up strongly by Churchill and by Lee of Fareham who stormed back from Washington to join in the resistance. In the end, the naval authorities won some concessions. While there would be a general economy in personnel, naval stores, and stocks, the two battleships proposed for 1922–3 would indeed go ahead, despite the opposition of the Geddes committee. In the end, the reduction of £19.3m in the naval estimates was markedly below what Geddes had recommended as the minimum acceptable requirement.[24] Of course, the cuts were still substantial. They encouraged a further contraction in Britain's role as a world power, and anticipated the further run-down promoted, ironically, by Churchill while at the Treasury under Baldwin after 1924.

On the other hand, the economies in military and naval expenditure merely recognized the inescapable fact, underlined by the disarmament measures agreed to in the Washington naval talks, that Britain's resources no longer made possible anything resembling the old two-power standard, or any formal recognition of naval supremacy. The cuts in social spending, however, amounting—if Geddes was followed—to a total of £24m, including £18m on education, although smaller, amounted to a more abrupt and serious reversal of policy. The argument about where, and how severely, the Geddes axe would fall on social expenditure was prolonged and fierce, a public as well as a private argument.

The economies in the housing programme, over £2m in all, went through without much debate. They marked the last rites for Addison's programme for subsidized housing, and the ending of all further contracts with the local authorities. The attempt to build working-class housing on a mass scale was buried, with Mond as the undertaker. Again, the economies in unemployment insurance were accepted, although such drastic measures as the closure of all labour exchanges or placing the financial burden on individual industries were not. Economies in public health ensured that nothing would be done to implement reforms such as the regionalizing of hospitals advocated by the Dawson committee in 1920. What caused the most prolonged and bitter controversy, in a way that cast doubt on the government's basic priorities, was the £18m cuts in the educational budget proposed by the Geddes committee. Certainly, expenditure in education had formed the largest part of the social spending by the local authorities. In particular, teachers' salaries had risen dramatically, with the introduction of the Burnham Scale, until they had reached a level 170 per cent above that of pre-war. On the other hand, the 1918 Education Act, introduced by H. A. L. Fisher, had been one of the most solid innovations of the Coalition government. It was backed by a powerful pressure-group, the increasingly vocal National Union of Teachers, under its General Secretary, the former Liberal MP, J. H. Yoxall. Geddes now made proposals that would have reduced the estimates for education for 1922–3 from £50m to £32m, which would have emasculated the entire programme of primary, secondary, and technical education in the maintained sector. Geddes made several proposals as to how this would be achieved. The lower age limit of entry would be raised from five years to six, while many small schools would be closed. The standard of staffing would be diminished from one teacher per 32 children to one per 50. Teachers, it was also suggested, might offer a voluntary poll-tax towards their superannuation fund. The costs for teacher-training would be increased, technical schools cut back, the University Tutorial Classes abolished. Finally, the percentage grant system of payment by the Treasury to local authorities would be changed to a block grant. The abandonment of the day-continuation schools, on which Fisher and Sir Herbert Lewis, his Under-Secretary, had set such store, was confirmed.

These proposals were resisted with unexpected fierceness by the Board of Education, particularly the suggested increase in the size of classes and the adjustment of teachers' salaries under the Burnham Scale. Fisher himself had been something of a declining force in the government since his early authority in Irish and foreign policy questions in 1919. Now, buffeted by educational pressure groups of all kinds, he produced some vigorous opposition. He wanted the raising of the school-entry age to be optional. The Burnham Scale should be upheld—'it would be most impolitic from the political point of view to alienate the [teachers] at the present moment'.[26] His economies would amount to only £3m instead of the £18m called for. Backed up by Munro, the Secretary of State for Scotland, he defended the percentage grant system: it guaranteed the proportion spent by the local councils upon education, and was 'an instrument of progress'. He had previously denied that his circulars had been an incitement to extravagance by the local authorities.[27] The growth of educational expenditure was the result of a system begun before his act in 1918.

Fisher had to face heavy salvos from Horne, the Chancellor, who had attacked the Geddes proposals himself for being too modest.[28] He reminded his colleagues that 'the people were overburdened with taxation' and that 'the commercial community' felt that levels of taxation were not only hindering the growth of new business but were hampering the operation of present enterprises. Businessmen, the only evidence that Horne felt worth citing, believed that heavy cuts must be made both in defence and in education. 'Even if the whole of the economies recommended by the Geddes Committee were effected, there would be a deficit on the Budget for the coming year.' He went on: 'If the Budget were not balanced, the Government would be exposed to a most formidable attack by the business community and he was doubtful if the Government would survive it.' Like Fisher, Horne had political considerations well in mind. The savings proposed by the Geddes committee ought, in all, to be increased to £100m. On the committee set up to consider the implementation of the Geddes proposals, chaired by Austen Chamberlain, Horne strongly attacked the attitude of the schoolteachers.[29] It was incredible that the only profession to retain the benefits of remuneration fixed when the cost of living was at its highest in 1919 should be the teachers. Lloyd George now joined in himself, as a champion of sweeping cuts in spending on state education. He had never himself been deeply involved in movements for developing public education, even in the Wales of the 1890s where higher education had been a kind of badge of nationality, with the national university as its symbol. He prided himself always on being a self-made product of self-education, who preferred the common sense of the common man to bookish learning. Haldane had found Lloyd George something of an obstacle to his scheme for a national system of education back in 1913, with the Welshman insisting that land took priority over education in the government's programme.[30] Lloyd George now suggested to Lord Burnham that teachers might either revise their pension arrangements, or else have their annual salary increments stopped for a term of years, a view which Burnham and Fisher both strongly resisted. Lloyd George was certain that there should be economies in the size of classes. 'He was sure that the brighter children would learn as readily and as quickly in a class of seventy as they would in a much smaller class.'[31] Of course, no evidence was provided to back up this assertion. The Prime Minister hoped that the number of teachers would be reduced very rapidly and an average of classes of 60 to 70 aimed at through the country.

Even the Prime Minister, however, could not wholly undermine the public educational system. The issue of teachers' salaries was in fact beyond the Cabinet's control since they had been fixed by legal contract in 1919. Lord Burnham reported that new scales had been agreed upon as recently as June 1921. Much public support would rally behind the teachers in 'a conflict where the latter would use to the utmost their great and growing political influence'. Already, in fact, there were widespread revolts against the proposed economies in education from a wide range of groups. Not only Liberal and Labour voices were raised in protest. Education was a less emotive issue than, say, housing or unemployment insurance, now that the religious issue had been largely defused. Many Conservatives had taken a leading part in promoting elementary education and also local universities. Neville Chamberlain specifically cited public resentment over the education cuts as a major reason for not holding a general election in January or February.[32] A Unionist newspaper like the *Observer* was highly critical also. Meanwhile, in two huge swings against the government in successive by-elections in February, there were Labour gains at Manchester (Clayton) and North Camberwell. In both, the victorious candidates, J. E. Sutton and Charles Ammon, made great play with the attacks on the elementary education system, and working-class parents responded accordingly.[33] On 21 February, the day after the Camberwell by-election, the Cabinet acknowledged finally that the proposed cuts were losing them votes. The proposed exclusion of children under six from school 'was undoubtedly exercising a deleterious effect in the constituencies'.[34] In the end, the whole scale of the economies proposed by Geddes was much diminished in the face of political pressure. Horne had aimed at total economies of up to £100m. The Cabinet agreed on £64m. In place of the cuts in the education estimates of £18m as demanded by Geddes, £6.5m only were agreed on. It was acknowledged that nothing could be done about teachers' salaries in view of their contractual arrangements through the Burnham committee, while the exclusion of children under six from school was also turned down 'as it would involve a storm of opposition in the larger urban centres'. For these non-economic and non-educational reasons, the worst impact of Geddes was blunted. Lloyd George now characteristically reversed his views on educational economies. 'They do not appeal to the people' and would turn the teachers into 'Bolsheviks'.[35] He accepted Philip Snowden's view that 'all the schoolmasters and schoolmistresses have been working like blacks for the Labour man' in the Clayton by-election, and that this accounted for the Labour victory. On 1 March Horne had reluctantly to report to the Commons that neither the decision to exclude children under six from school, nor the cuts in teachers' salaries, would be implemented, though there would be a 5 per cent levy for superannuation. Nor would the percentage grant system be abolished, but rather reviewed by a committee which would consider its merits as opposed to the block grant method. In fact, this Meston committee never published its report: in 1925, the new Permanent Secretary, Symonds, was to call in vain for 'Meston's long-delayed report'.[36] Fisher and the Education Board had something to show for their rearguard action.

Nevertheless, the cuts in educational and other social services were a sorry spectacle, and did the government's education programme, and its claim to be striking an even balance between the different classes, immense harm. The *Nation* commented that, like Macnamara on unemployment, Fisher had entirely sold the pass on the basic issues of educational policy. 'Dr. Addison at least had the pluck to resign when his housing policy was thrown overboard.'[37] Fisher, once a commanding figure in the government, was now an unhappy, beleaguered professor at bay. Even with the modifications made by the Cabinet, the cuts both in primary and secondary education were severe enough. Classes of fifty or over were now authorized as the norm. Teachers took a cut in their living standards, while their numbers were likely to be reduced from anything up to 6,000 in three years, owing to the attack on the training colleges. School-building programmes were suspended and no increase made in the proportion of free places in secondary schools. It was no thanks to Fisher that the percentage grant system was maintained. The National Union of Teachers, with young radical figures like the Welshman, W. G. Cove rising within it, became a formidable and articulate pressure group inciting public condemnation of the government.[38] On 16 May the government was to suffer a humiliating defeat when the proposed 5 per cent levy on teachers for superannuation was turned down in the Commons. Fisher tentatively offered his resignation.[39]

More generally, the economies in education illustrated the general flow of government policy, a policy of accepting social imbalances and deferring when in doubt to the ill-informed views of the business community unless overwhelming public pressure, such as over the school entry age, forced a retreat. The effect of the government's policy was to reduce still further its claim to represent a broad national consensus. It was not only the TUC who pointed out that the opportunities for working-class children would be seriously affected at every stage in the educational ladder supposedly erected by Fisher in 1918. There would be larger classes in elementary schools, and less money to spend in renovating antiquated and insanitary Victorian school buildings. There would be a steady decline in the number of pupils attending state secondary schools, despite the rise in the child population. There would also be far fewer scholarships for universities and other institutions of higher education. As for education, so for housing, state insurance and the remaining pillars of the government's domestic programme. Under the economic pressures of the slump and the political pressures of Geddes, backed up by Anti-Waste, the business community, and the Rothermere and Northcliffe press, the government took a decision to make the two nations of the land that degree the more separate, and to ensure that measures of social expenditure designed to bridge the gulf between them would be that degree more ineffective. Lloyd George's national consensus, in short, heightened national inequality.

Despite the retreat conducted by the Coalition government in 1921–2 along the whole range of its social policies, most studies found that social conditions generally showed a marked improvement compared with pre-war days, simply on account of the war. Bowley and Hogg in 1924 found that only 6.5 per cent of the population might fall below the poverty line, compared with 11 per cent in 1913.[40] The wages of unskilled men had risen by double in the same period, whereas the cost of living had risen by only 70 per cent, and the average working week had fallen from 55 hours to 48. Medical indices were also reassuring, in relation to malnutrition among children or the health of the aged. The economic standards prevailing between different social classes were more uniform, the working class was less concentrated and homogeneous, the barriers between workers in different grades and social categories were more blurred. Nevertheless, the period of Lloyd George's Coalition, for all the intentions of ministers like Addison and Fisher, appeared to see social division and class consciousness become still more intense.

This was the result of three factors above all. First, by presiding over a period of mass unemployment which it found itself unable significantly to relieve, the Coalition government delayed substantially the further raising of economic standards that the war had begun. As has been seen, Bowley and Hogg found that the total of those living in primary poverty was 6.5 per cent. But for mass unemployment in mining areas, however, this figure should have been just over 3 per cent. Secondly, by placing the main emphasis on cutting down public expenditure and alleviating the burden of direct taxation, the government removed the major weapon at its disposal in grappling with social inequality. Throughout the slump of 1920–2, the government was obsessed with budgeting for a surplus by cutting back expenditure. It cited the rally in share prices from 81.4 in March 1922 to 93.0 in May as proof of its success.[41] The pound climbed back to $4.43 against the dollar, and bank rate was lowered to $4\frac{1}{2}$ per cent. Nor was the government's taxation policy in the least egalitarian. No measures were taken to tax wartime profits: the report of June 1920 from the Select Committee on War Wealth proved to be wholly barren. Horne's budget in May 1922 actually had as its centre-piece a substantial reduction of income tax from a standard rate of 6s. to 5s. This was accompanied by muddled calculations which left him with a surplus of £101m on the year, instead of a deficit, a surplus which was used to pay off creditors through debt redemption. Years later, Tawney ironically commented that 'it is improbable that when the history of the first decade of the peace comes to be written it will give a prominent place to the effects of high taxation'.[42] Partly as a result of this financial policy, the promising initiatives in social policy undertaken in 1919 were reversed. Surveys in the mid-1920s found that very few houses for rent by working-class families were built between 1913 and 1924, that overcrowding in houses in older industrial areas actually became worse during the period,[43] that school places for working-class children were reduced with the occupational opportunities that went with them, and that the more hopeful pattern in the statistics for malnutrition, child mortality, and provision for the old discerned just after the war did not continue. And thirdly, although this is almost impossible to measure with any degree of precision, the government's approach made class consciousness and hostility within each section an instrument of policy. By 1921–2 it seemed that policy, especially in the case of Horne, was being programmed by business and commercial organizations, whereas demands by working-class organizations and pressure groups were those of outsiders, isolated from the central decision-making process. A government pledged to social unity had made social division and injustice all the more glaring.

As far as the working class is concerned, the record of this period, with its massive labour unrest and tension between the unions and the government, suggests that class consciousness was heightened. Later sociologists concluded that the working-class sense of relative deprivation, in terms of power and status, was intensified after the war. After 1918, a smaller proportion of the population was employed in manual or other working occupations. The census of 1921 showed that the 'wage-earner' category had fallen to 15m. But for that 15m, the experiences of 1919–22 probably strengthened their solidarity and sense of class self-reliance as profoundly as did the war years themselves or the upsurge of the trade unions in the 1911–14 period. The gulf between skilled and unskilled workers narrowed, as both collaborated in militant workshop organizations. The great strikes of the period, the railwaymen's strike of 1919, the miners' strike of 1920–1, other stoppages by engineers, transport workers, iron founders, and even the police are marked by a degree of cohesion and solidarity more pronounced even than in 1911–14. Workers' demands had progressed also, from narrower wage questions to broader issues of industrial management and control. In mining communities, it is significant that the pockets of 'Lib–Labbery', which survived down to the war and cost the Labour party some by-elections in the Midlands in 1912–13, had been largely eliminated. The appeal of class had outstripped the call of community—or of nationality in Wales and Scotland. In coalfield after coalfield, there is a unanimity of response which is impressive, and which survived to resist the so-called 'Spencer' unions enlisted by the coal-owners as a strike-breaking weapon after 1927. Pro-government candidates in by-elections in mining areas, such as George Hay Morgan in Abertillery in 1920, spoke of their helplessness in communicating with, or penetrating the mind of, the miner and his family.[44] There is a remarkable solidarity, too, about working-class participation in pressure movements such as the TUC's campaign against the education cuts envisaged in the Geddes report. Politically, of course, the Labour Party was the beneficiary. Contemporaries noted the mass enthusiasm, energy, self-sacrifice that marked Labour's efforts in by-election campaigns.

In some ways, working-class life became more bourgeoisified—and, perhaps, therefore, more bearable—in the post-war period. It was less violent, less fraught, with less drunkenness and newer, cheaper forms of mass entertainment. The thousands of working men who flocked to see Aston Villa win the first post-war Cup Final in 1920 by 1–0 seemed a more affluent assembly than the cloth-cap multitudes who attended football matches before the war, and of whose politicization Keir Hardie and Ramsay MacDonald had once despaired.[45] The presence of King George V at such a working-class festival as the Cup Final was perhaps a symbol of changing times. In terms of focusing upon political and economic objectives, this greater strength and respectability made the working-class reaction all the more clear-cut and aggressive. How much this continued growth of working-class consciousness is due to the policies of the government is hard to determine. Some of it was a legacy of the incorporative impulse and economic gains of the war years. Much of it was a response to the hardening attitudes of leading employers such as Allen

Smith of the Engineers' Federation who referred to his workmen as 'the enemy'.[46] But it seems not unreasonable to conclude that the post-war Coalition's public stance of hostility towards the unions during every major industrial confrontation, and its failure to give priority in its programmes for policies to cope with unemployment, added to the embitterment of working-class people. It strengthened their fierce loyalty to their working comrades and to their industrial and political leaders. It added to the magnetic appeal of Ramsay MacDonald who emerged as an evangelist of genius for the labour cause in the post-1918 period.[47] If Lloyd George claimed that his supporters in the House represented the Chambers of Commerce and his opponents the TUC, this polarization was partly of his own making. Between 1919 and 1922 his special relationship with organized labour, cherished since 1906, was destroyed. Even in the 'coupon election', he had traded on his traditional appeal in the older industrial areas, South Wales, Yorkshire, and Lancashire, the North East, industrial Scotland. Coalition Liberalism drew much of its transient strength from these communities. By October 1922, Coalition Liberalism and Lloyd George were fugitives from these very regions, at the mercy of a working-class movement which felt itself to be the victim and the enemy of the regime.

If working-class consciousness may well have accentuated during this post-war period, middle-class consciousness certainly did so. The 1921 census showed that the sections of the population which might be categorized as 'middle class' had increased sharply during the war; it continued to do so thereafter. The professional class rose from 2.4m in 1911 to 3.1m in 1921, numbering by now almost one fifth of the workforce.[48] The numbers of professional men, doctors, lawyers, architects, and the like increased steadily. More dramatically did those in civil service, administrative, and clerical occupations. Suburbs and commuter districts mushroomed outwards into the countryside to accommodate the rising salariat of the 'white collar worker'. Many of them were distinctly impecunious since professional advancement bore no relation to the ownership of capital or the distribution of urban property which remained largely unaffected by the war; but rising expectations accompanied rising numbers. Again, the managerial classes required for industry built up relentlessly during these years. By 1921, Britain's professional/managerial middle class was increasingly dominant in social power, the more so as the landed aristocracy of pre-war years was hectically engaged in selling off its estates, rural and urban, to take advantage of buoyant market conditions for land.

On the other hand, this was a middle class which felt itself to be, in major respects, a casualty of the war, and suffering a real cut in its living standards. The journals of these years were full of lamentations at the crushing blows endured stoically by the middle class amidst the post-war inflation.[49] Indeed, professional and managerial groups, usually on fixed incomes, markedly failed to match the determined efforts made by organized workers in 1919–20 to keep abreast of the rising cost of living. Often, there was even talk of the death of the middle class in this period, and the vast political dangers that would ensue if it were not revived, artificially or otherwise. *The Times*'s medical correspondent associated the decline of the birth-rate since the war with the decline of the middle class, with the decline of middle-class families, and the reluctance of the middle-class male to marry as his salary would not support a family. The 'lower middle class', those with an income of perhaps between £300 and £800, were a source of particular anxiety, as they were 'the backbone of the nation', who had supplied officers during the war and recruits for the learned professions in peacetime.[50] Correspondents pressured for governmental action to make it profitable for the middle class to have children through new tax allowances. It was the alleged plight of the middle class that prompted the agitation, which seared into the mind of Horne at the Treasury, to alleviate the burden of taxation. Even the Labour Party, with its high proportion of middle-class recruits after 1918, especially through the ILP, was not loath to deplore the sad plight of the middle class. The burdens of 'this deserving class' were 'almost intolerable', Snowden wrote. 'The middle class has been squeezed nearly dry,' the (middle-class) Labour candidate for South Hereford in 1922 complained.[51] Philip Snowden and Ramsay Mac-Donald were anxious to stress that Labour's plans for a war-debt redemption levy on capital posed no threat to the commercial and professional classes, or to capitalist enterprises such as the co-operative societies. On the contrary, the middle class would benefit from a capital levy by receiving a cut in the tax on earned income.[52] There was also, of course, much familiar middle-class lament at the decline in domestic servants at this period, even though they still numbered well over a million in 1921.

How seriously this lament for the middle class was taken is a moot point, but there were some significant pointers in 1919–22. There was a rash of 'Middle Class Unions', appealing mainly to smaller businessmen, rentiers, and tradesmen on a fiercely anti-socialist basis. The most prominent, rather surprisingly, was headed by Lord Askwith, until recently conciliator at the Board of Trade, but now deeply despondent at the labour unrest of 1919–20.[53] There is some evidence of middle-class coherence emerging during strikes and periods of industrial tension. Just as the working class responded with growing solidarity and cohesion, so lower middle-class groups such as clerical workers and minor civil servants, even though increasingly organized in white-collar unions, clung all the more passionately to order and free enterprise. With the exception of schoolteachers, they were a useful support to governmental resistance to the General Strike in 1926. In 1919 some of them were enthusiastic drivers of milk lorries to frustrate the national rail strike. They remained discontented with the government to the end of its days, despite somewhat improved economic fortunes for those in employment in 1921–2 with sharply falling prices, a firmer pound, and bank rate falling from 5 per cent on 16 February to only 3 per cent on 13 July. The class awareness of the white-collar worker was no sure source of support for Lloyd George and his Coalition. On the contrary, it encouraged further cries for 'economy', and for an inexpensive, even isolationist, foreign policy; a government which appeared to be dragging its feet in either case stood condemned. In 1922 Lloyd George's administration was losing support as emphatically in the suburbs of the south east as it was in the industrial coalfields of Wales and the North. If these middle-class protesters had an ideal, it lay not in the outmoded die-hard Toryism of pre-war but rather in an up-to-date independent Conservatism, as the voice of the salaried, rate-paying, owner-occupier. Middle-class group awareness fuelled the Tory rebellion against the government in the latter months of 1922. It provided the natural, anxious clientele for the unifying bromides of Stanley Baldwin, just as the workers responded to the heady idealism of Maxton or MacDonald. 'Socialism in Our Time' and 'Peace in Our Time, O Lord!' emerged as the two rival visions, ideological alternatives to the Lloyd George era.

The result of its social and economic policies, therefore, was for the Coalition to produce a more divided, more sectional society, with classes at war with each other and with the government. A simpler class stratification replaced the mixture of class and status distinctions prior to 1914.[54] Peacetime conditions fostered class war, demolished the middle ground hacked away in 1919, and undermined the pretensions for a Coalition government which social upheaval was making irrelevant.

13

The Downfall of the Coalition: Foreign Policy

If the government's first premiss was social unity, the second was international peace. In the absence of the United States as a consistent participant in international affairs, this largely depended on British leadership. It was the urge to extend this leadership, through a flexible system of appeasement and external guarantee, that motivated Lloyd George at the start of 1922. He was now in heroic mood, the last of the Big Three at Versailles still at the head of his nation, his spirits rekindled by the successful outcome of the Irish treaty. He felt that developments in Russian and German internal politics made some kind of grand international *rapprochement* feasible for the first time since the Versailles treaty. He also felt that it would prove the surest method of restoring credibility to the Coalition and of imposing discipline within its ranks. Hence the crucial importance that he attached to the coming conference at Genoa. He told Riddell that he did not intend to 'resign or to ride for a fall. . . . He looks to the [Genoa] conference to restore his star to the zenith.'[1] Of course, there were serious constraints on the Prime Minister's ability to exert any initiative in foreign affairs. There was the growing pressure for economy, recently sanctified by Geddes, which worked against British intervention overseas, either militarily in a guarantee to France, or in naval terms in the Pacific. And, of course, there was the political constraint in the shape of growing Unionist disaffection in the country, with the possibility of its finding a focus some time in Bonar Law. Right-wing constraints on Lloyd George operated abroad as well as at home, especially after the rebuff of failing to call an election in January 1922. They were reinforced in the press, especially in *The Times*, where Wickham Steed used his avenues of contact with the Quai d'Orsay to pursue a lengthy campaign of vilification of Lloyd George's foreign policy. Still, the Prime Minister felt reasonably confident that he could transcend these financial and political difficulties, until he felt able to call a general election. No alternative foreign policy presented itself with any conviction—and no alternative Prime Minister.

One immediate obstacle continued to loom in the Prime Minister's path. Tension between Downing Street and the Foreign Office, symbolized in the suspicions of Curzon discussed above, was still as pronounced as ever. Lloyd George continued to irritate his Foreign Secretary with his unorthodox methods and his use of personal advisers such as Grigg and Wise. Even Benes, the Prime Minister of Czechoslovakia, on one famous occasion in February 1922, was used to circumvent the Foreign Office in putting pressure on France.[2] In 1921-2, Curzon's resentment was focused above all on Lloyd George's highly personal approaches to the Greek government in dealing with a settlement of Asia Minor. Curzon was later to instance the secret negotiations in March 1921 between Philip Kerr and an emissary of the Greek Foreign Minister, Calegeropoulos, which involved Britain in a military and financial commitment to the Greek army in Asia Minor in attacking Angora and trying to destroy the forces of the Turkish nationalist leader, Mustapha Kemal.[3] These negotiations were as unknown to the Foreign Office as were earlier and later approaches to the Reparations Commission, about which Curzon learnt from the Berlin embassy and the German newspapers. Curzon later complained, in self-pitying fashion, that there had been a concerted campaign against him, led by Lloyd George, supported by Churchill and Birkenhead, with the serpentine figure of Balfour in the background. This had the purpose of removing him from the Foreign Office when he fell ill in the early summer of 1922. He added that Derby had been approached to take his place, entirely at variance with pledges that the Prime Minister had given him.[4]

As before, however, too much can be made of these episodes. On major issues, the Foreign Office and 10 Downing Street still thought as one. Curzon certainly had no objection to being excluded from the Washington conference, nor from the discussions at Genoa. Indeed, contrary to the view given by F. S. Northedge, he would have been present at Genoa had he not had a recurrence of his back troubles.[5] Lloyd George continued to show some concern to protect the Foreign Office from the incursions of other departments, notably the War Office. Most important of all, Lloyd George and Curzon saw eye to eye on the broad outlines of policy agreed at Cannes and proposed at Genoa. On German reparations, relations with Russia, negotiations with the United States over war debts, even until September 1922 on major aspects of the handling of relations with Turkey and control of the straits, Curzon and Lloyd George did not seriously diverge. After the Irish treaty, Curzon startled the Cabinet with the warmth of his personal tribute to the Prime Minister.[6] Grey, amongst others, was to criticize the 'conference' method as opposed to the 'council' method of conducting international diplomacy. But even Curzon accepted the growing fact of personal liaison between heads of government who alone could harmonize the interconnected strands of strategy, finance, commerce, and political authority. In general, it may be said that Lloyd George's major initiatives in foreign policy in 1922 reflected the broad consensus of the Cabinet, including the Foreign Secretary. In so far as they were aimed at appeasement and disarmament, they reflected the national consensus as well.

Lloyd George's grand design began at Cannes on the French Riviera where Lloyd George met Aristide Briand, the French Prime Minister and Foreign Minister combined, from 6 January onwards. Through a meeting of heads of government, Lloyd George tried to resolve with interrelated policies German reparations, French insecurity, and European economic recovery. He was accompanied by Grigg and Thomas Jones, since Hankey was in Washington. It was this kind of summit diplomacy that gave the appearance of trying to substitute great power *realpolitik* and secret conclave for the open deliberations of the League of Nations. Gilbert Murray, though, was probably right in writing later that it was 'the hostility between L. G. and Lord Robert [that] has had the effect of making L. G. appear anti-League'. He added that this impression was reinforced by 'the attacks on the League by Grigg and other Imperialists'. On the other hand, over Upper Silesia it had been Lloyd George who had persuaded Briand the previous August to call the League in to adjudicate.[7]

At Cannes, Lloyd George repeated the proposed scheme for an international conference, to include Germany and the Soviet Union, to be held at Genoa in March and April. After some hesitancy, Briand accepted it. Discussion then centred on trying finally to resolve the impasse over German reparations payments. This was vital because the German government had declared itself unable to meet its

scheduled payments for either January or February. As a decisive
gambit, Lloyd George for the first time boldly met the French demand
for territorial security.[8] This focused on the left bank of the Rhine, the
region of France's major diplomatic defeat in 1919, since the Anglo-
American promise to protect France against German attack on her soil
had lapsed with the failure of the US Congress to ratify the treaty.
Lloyd George made it plain that any British commitment would relate
only to France's eastern boundary. He could not accept any definition
of French 'security', whether based on the notion of 'indirect aggression' or not, which left it open for Britain to become embroiled in the
internal affairs of Poland or other eastern European countries. He
emphasized that Britain's main concern was to guarantee French soil
against unprovoked direct attack, not an open-ended offensive and
defensive military alliance. Briand countered by urging that any
British guarantee must be supplemented by a technical military convention arranged by the two general staffs. Thus, in the elegant
surroundings of the Villa Valetta at Cannes, Lloyd George and Briand
moved closer together in trying to define a guarantee that would meet
both French demands and British reservations. Nearby, at Le Cercle
Nautique, Horne and other economics ministers turned away from
ploughing the sands yet again over German indemnities to a wider
discussion of international action to promote trade and economic
recovery in central Europe. The two exercises necessarily became
distinct, which led to Italian protests that they were being deliberately
excluded from the Anglo-French conclaves on a military guarantee. In
a conversation with Bonomi, the Italian Prime Minister, on 10 January, Lloyd George rebutted this firmly enough.[9]

By 11 January, the day of the fateful game of golf between the
British and French prime ministers on the neighbouring Cannes golf
links, negotiations seemed to be moving rapidly towards an historic
agreement. Britain offered a treaty with six articles. Of these, the first
was the most crucial—'that in the event of direct and unprovoked
aggression against the soil of France by Germany, Great Britain will
come to the immediate assistance of France with her naval, military
and air forces'. Article Five laid down that the treaty would last for ten
years and would be renewable. Many later commentators saw in this a
proposed degree of involvement in continental Europe quite out of
line with British traditions in foreign policy and one out of phase with
current policies of military disengagement. Hankey, far away in

Washington, wrote to his wife that he would have blocked this entang-
lement in continental affairs, and that the guarantee reflected the
particular views of Grigg and Churchill.[10] It is certainly the case that
Churchill, ever a patron of the *entente*, warmly backed the guarantee to
France. But so, too, did the British Cabinet as a whole. On 10 January
1922 there was universal agreement with the draft articles, as dispatched from Lloyd George at Cannes to his Cabinet colleagues.
Curzon was as confident as anyone:

While it did not throw heavy obligations upon us, they would be of great value
to France. . . . Under the proposed guarantee . . . we should not have to make
any special military preparations. Our military policy would remain unef-
fected [*sic*] and we should only provide the military force required for the
needs of the British Empire. If Germany attacked France the whole of the
resources of the British Empire would be available to support France. Such a
guarantee would give confidence in France, would help the thoughtful section
of French opinion to fight the Chauvinist party in France. Such a guarantee
would also give us a free hand with regard to Germany. . . . By helping
Germany we might under existing conditions expose to the charge of deserting
France, but if France was our ally no such charge could be made.[11]

Germany, it was optimistically recorded, would welcome such a
guarantee, and Germany was also the key to the situation in Russia. A
general easement in Europe would then result. Francophile ministers
like Austen Chamberlain warmly concurred. Lloyd George, then,
clearly carried his colleagues with him in what was felt to be a policy
not out of line with traditional British objectives. The state of public
opinion is more doubtful. Labour Party opinion, which failed to
accept Lloyd George's main point on the sensitive interrelationship of
German reparations to French security, was hostile to any Anglo-
French pact. The idea was compared (quite misleadingly) with the
military conversations of January 1906 and the consequent approach
of world war. It would encourage French nationalist ambitions; it was
also objectionable for by-passing the League of Nations. Some Conservative opinion, however, may well have been more sympathetic at
this reinterpretation of the *entente* with France.

But the obstacles in Lloyd George's path lay not in London but in
Paris. The prospect that Briand was sacrificing vital French strategic
interests, and that German reparations were being submerged by
schemes for a wider European reconstruction, led to a parliamentary
crisis. Briand was summoned back to Paris by President Millerand.
There was a vital debate in the National Assembly on the 12th; Briand

was defeated and promptly resigned. He fell from power, a French contemporary wrote, 'non parce qu'il avait tort, mais parce que ses compatriotes tardèrent trop à partager son point de vue'.[12] Briand was succeeded as Prime Minister and Foreign Minister by the Lorrainer, Raymond Poincaré, as truculently anti-German in 1922 as he had been in 1914. A meeting between him and Lloyd George in Paris on 14 January did not go well. Poincaré made it clear that Britain had not conceded nearly enough in her proposed articles at Cannes. He wanted the pact to be tied to a specific military convention, and the time-limit to be lengthened so that France would not be exposed when the fifteen-year occupation of the west bank of the Rhine came to an end in 1933. In reply, Lloyd George described the proposal for a military convention as 'the height of unreason'; there was no agreement on any issue.[13] The French Ambassador in London, St. Aulaire, presented six French demands to Curzon on 26 January. These contained several proposals to which Britain objected, including close co-operation between the two general staffs; making the breach of Articles 42 and 43 of the Covenant by Germany a special *casus foederis* which would justify British military assistance to France; and extending the treaty to eastern Europe.[14] Clearly on this basis, there was scant likelihood of Britain's going beyond what she had offered at Cannes. It would have implied a degree of continental involvement unprecedented in British history since the days of Marlborough. It was unacceptable to the left and the right alike in Britain, as Poincaré must have known. The Cannes initiative, then, led nowhere. The *entente* was left less cordial than at any time since 1918. When Lloyd George met Poincaré at Boulogne on 25 February, to discuss the preliminaries over Genoa and also differences over the Near East, the French Prime Minister courteously dined on his own, leaving Lloyd George to order his own lunch at the local railway station.[15] Clearly, in his grand design for European reconciliation, Lloyd George would get little help from the French. Poincaré, wrote Grigg, was out to 'wreck' Genoa.[16]

This was a grave blow, but not necessarily a fatal one. Lloyd George believed that there were other levers that could be used to set the machinery of international collaboration in motion; in particular there were Germany and Russia, both of whom were crucial to the conference at Genoa, now firmly timed for 10 April. Each presented special difficulties. The German Foreign Minister, Walter Rathenau (so appointed by Chancellor Josef Wirth soon after Cannes), although a businessman, was remarkably open-minded towards Russia, and anxious to promote a joint European venture to assist in the rehabilitation of the Russian market.[17] He was aware of the decline in the value of the German mark after the new gold payments fixed by the Reparations Commission. There were even hints that the Germans might even conclude their own agreement with Russia, although Rathenau was careful to make no commitment when Chicherin passed through Berlin on his way to Genoa. In the meantime, Rathenau, like most Germans, was alarmed at Poincaré's re-emergence in France, and concerned that his presence (or absence) at Genoa would doom the conference at birth. Rashly, he voiced fears that Poincaré had gained the better of Lloyd George during those frigid conversations at Boulogne. This did not foster good relations with the British Prime Minister.

Russia was a more serious problem. Lloyd George had long been convinced that the Anglo-Russian trade treaty of March 1921 was merely the first stage towards a full *de jure* recognition of the Soviet Union for diplomatic and commercial purposes. Lenin and the Politburo made it clear that, for Genoa to yield any fruit at all, Russia would be satisfied with nothing less. The intractable problems of how to placate anti-Bolshevik western powers anxious to have Russia redeem her debts and cease propagandist activity and internal subversion in the west, and how at the same time to restore Russia to full economic and diplomatic status in the comity of nations, exercised Lloyd George, above all other problems, from now on.

Anglo-Russian relations had been in a fluid state since the trade treaty a year earlier. In many ways, that treaty in itself was a substantive recognition of the *de facto* existence of the Soviet Union as a great power with whom Britain was able to conclude major commercial negotiations. At his meeting with Poincaré at Boulogne on 25 February, Lloyd George had proposed leaving the issue of Russian recognition to await how the Russian delegation actually conducted itself at Genoa. He pointed out that Allied financiers would not invest money to assist in the rehabilitation of Russian markets unless there was some kind of formal recognition. Poincaré flatly refused, and insisted that each nation ought to have a free hand in its attitude towards the recognition of the Soviet Union. The issue of the debts and financial obligations of previous pre-revolution Russian governments seemed to him an insuperable obstacle. Cecil Hurst, the British Foreign Office legal adviser, argued, in the pragmatic British way, that the London view was that 'if one negotiated a treaty with another Government upon a footing of equality and called upon that Government in the treaty to take action upon the footing that it is a state, the treaty itself amounts to a recognition *de jure*'. The issue was one that involved the government of Russia in general, quite apart from its particular rulers. In the future, 'the financiers want to lend their money to Russia and not to Lenin'. Fromageot, the French representative, replied that if the conclusion of a treaty with the Russian government was regarded as *de jure* recognition, then the French government would not sign it, and would not recognize agreements concluded at Genoa.[18]

These divisions between Britain and France were more than diplomatic niceties. They went straight to the heart of the Prime Minister's grand scheme for Genoa. More, they raised the basic commitment of his government and its supporters, and of public opinion generally, to the blend of appeasement and intervention that formed the basis of his foreign policy. The recognition of Russia soon became a question which threatened the survival of the Coalition. Of course, die-hard opinion in parliament, Gretton and his allies, naturally found in the recognition of Bolshevik Russia another prime target for attack. More generally, there was disquiet amongst the Prime Minister's Unionist colleagues about the Russia policy, with Horne, the architect of the trade treaty, one of the few advocates of recognition on strictly pragmatic grounds. Austen Chamberlain himself was extremely dubious. He felt that Britain could not simply recognize Russia on her own, without the concurrence of France and the United States. In any case, 'extreme communist elements' were gaining the upper hand in Moscow again.[19]

But the main problem now concerned Churchill. Since the conclusion of the Irish treaty, Churchill had been a key figure in maintaining the unity of the government, still a Liberal in name and to some extent in outlook. He had been critical of several major aspects of government policy over the past six months—unemployment policy and the Geddes axe at home, Germany and Turkey overseas. However, the general diplomatic approach to Genoa gained his general support. The recognition of Russia, inevitably, seemed to him a flirtation with evil. The issue had been specifically deferred for future decision, when the Cabinet had approved the resolutions to be submitted at Cannes back in December, largely at Churchill's insistence. Birkenhead and Chamberlain now tried to appease him, but in vain. Chamberlain warned Lloyd George of the dangers of Churchill's resigning 'because he was more Tory than the Tory ministers'.[20] In reply, Lloyd George fiercely declined to be dictated to either by the French or the Unionist Party over the recognition of Russia; he added, 'Winston is obsessed by the defeat inflicted upon his military projects by the Bolshevik Armies.'[21] However, he well appreciated that Churchill's resignation might lead to a disastrous early election. In practice, Lloyd George, now brooding in a prolonged isolation at Criccieth, realized that he had no alternative but to produce a carefully phrased compromise to patch his government together. Grigg explained that the Prime Minister's idea 'was to make peace and this is not assisted by highly technical discussion on what constitutes *de jure* recognition and what does not'.[22] But the Prime Minister had to go much further than these generalities to produce some kind of consensus in his Cabinet.

At the crucial Cabinet meeting on 28 March, Lloyd George carried a much modified form of recognition in the face of heavy fire from Churchill.[23] He argued that some degree of recognition was inevitable for the concluding of trade negotiations. 'Access to the Courts of law was essential for the carrying on of Trade.' However, full diplomatic recognition must await Russian agreement to the decisions carried out in Genoa, and embodied in the Cannes resolutions. Chargés d'affaires in London and Moscow were the limit to which he would go. Churchill bitterly attacked even this restricted proposal. 'He was bitterly sorry that at a time of strong Conservative majorities in a country deeply devoted to the monarchy, it was proposed to accord this supreme favour and patronage to the Bolsheviks.' After emollient interventions by Austen Chamberlain and Stanley Baldwin, the proposal for chargés d'affaires was accepted, with the proviso that Britain would not act in isolation from the general consensus of opinion at Genoa. It was agreed that a vote of confidence on the policy to be adopted at Genoa would be taken in the House on 3 April. Churchill blustered about 'taking sides against Russia as a whole in favour of a band of dastardly criminals'. However, the Prime Minister assured him that there would be no full diplomatic recognition and no decision without the full agreement of the Cabinet.

In this edgy crisis-ridden atmosphere, the scheme of European pacification to be undertaken at Genoa was launched. The press was full of well-informed accounts of the divisions in the Cabinet and rumours of an early election. Wickham Steed in *The Times* wrote passionately on the strains within the *entente* with France. The final hurdle was the Commons on 3 April. Here Lloyd George was restrained and cautious, 'lacking in fire and energy'.[24] He dwelt on Russia's potential as the greatest undeveloped country in the world, and the need, acknowledged even by Lenin, for new trading links with the west in the light of the failures of Russia's internal economic programmes. The aggression on the government side came, once again, from Austen Chamberlain who dealt fiercely with Joynson-Hicks and other die-hards. The only opposing voices came from a handful on the extreme right and the government won its usual easy victory on the division. But it was apparent that this only concealed the precarious nature of the mandate that the Prime Minister had been granted. The weeks of retreat in North Wales in March had given an alarming impression of a drifting, leaderless government. For all that, Lloyd George retained his mood of optimism as Genoa approached. At least the substance and the timing of the recognition of Russia, after 'a probationary period', had been left in his hands. In domestic terms, he had a relatively free hand with regard to reparations, French security, and European trade, even from Churchill. The constraints lay overseas, chiefly in Paris.

Above all, a generous mood of idealism remained about the possibilities for Genoa, as the starting-point for a new and truly Liberal policy of reconciliation. Many on the left warmly endorsed Lloyd George's stand in resisting Poincaré over reparations, as did a partly repentant Keynes. These hopes were finely expressed by Edward Grigg, perhaps closer to the Prime Minister at this time than at any phase in his career. He was depressed by many features of the forthcoming talks at Genoa—the failure to produce any long-term proposals for settling German reparations, France's handling of the juridical aspects of the recognition of Russia, Wickham Steed's links with the Quai d'Orsay in playing upon divisions within the British Cabinet. But there were inspiring alternatives. 'Here, then, the lists are set for a real issue—peace, appeasement, reconstruction on the one hand; on the other, the old doctrines of intervention, ascendancy and vengeance.' Such a policy would bring the Americans into European affairs in the light of the gun-flashes from the great artillery which you would bring to bear on the old reactionary camps. . . . I write like a Liberal, you will say. I am

one on this issue, and two thirds of the Unionist Party will prove so too when
they are brought up against it. . . . At present, the Die-Hards are watching you
as the old reactionaries in Europe watched Napoleon in 1814, fighting the
most brilliant campaign of his whole history from a soldier's standpoint, but
exhausting himself and his army when both needed breathing space for a fresh
start. How different would have been his history in 1815 if he had not
overfought the campaign of 1814, winning brilliant battles for an inadequate
result.[25]

With these perhaps unwise evocations of the preliminaries to
Waterloo, Grigg urged his leader on to one supreme final effort.

The conference at last got under way at Genoa on 10 April. There
was one notable absentee. The American Secretary of State, Charles
Evans Hughes, had announced that the USA would not attend the
Genoa conference as its purpose was essentially political, not
economic.[26] But this was wholly predictable. It was still clearly felt
that Genoa was a great international occasion. Lloyd George opened
its sessions with an eloquent and uplifting appeal for reconciliation
which made a deep impression on those present. Much of the work at
Genoa was technical, conducted through three of the four subcommissions, Financial, Economic, and Transportation. Here some
useful work was put in trying to prevent fluctuations in national
currencies and instability in exchanges, in removing obstacles to the
free flow of trade, and in creating an international framework for
transport and communications. But these were minor enterprises.
The main interest centred throughout in the plenary sessions of the
heads of the governments (in fact, the French representative,
Barthou, was Justice Minister) in the elegant Palazzo di San Giorgio—or Lloyd Giorgio as local wags had it. All such themes as a
settlement of reparations and a European non-aggression pact were
ventilated and referred to the Political Subcommission. Much attention focused also on the comings and goings at Lloyd George's private
residence, the Villa d'Albertis, six miles out of Genoa. Here, the
glowing prospects for agreement at Genoa rapidly disappeared,
amidst a dangerous swirl of accusations and intrigue. A secret bilateral
treaty between Russia and Germany was already well advanced before
the Genoa conference ever began. Radek and Seeckt had agreed in
Berlin on 15 March for German engineers and technicians to provide
assistance for Russia. However, these agreements remained in the
shadows at Genoa for a week, while Rathenau, the German Foreign

Minister, tried in vain to gain a private audience with Lloyd George. The latter, meanwhile, had secret conclaves at his villa with a series of Russian representatives, notably Chicherin, Litvinov, and Krassin. Then on Easter Sunday, 16 April, Rathenau and Chicherin signed the notorious 'treaty' of Rapallo at the Hotel St. Margharita in that resort. Much of it consisted of building up political and consular contacts. Stresemann was later to claim that Lloyd George had been kept fully informed throughout.[27] No reference was made to any military arrangements. But the effect was dramatic. It was a declaration of independence by the two pariah nations, to settle whose problems Genoa had largely been called. Lloyd George's claims were shattered. The French claimed that Rapallo was really aimed at the territorial integrity of Poland. Barthou spoke of withdrawing from the conference forthwith. Nationalism—in this case, the nationalism of the vanquished—had demolished the conference's claims of building a new international order. 'Only the Hun can do these things,' Grigg lamented.[28]

Lloyd George stayed on at Genoa until 18 May, trying to restore some kind of order out of the chaos. He resumed diplomatic contacts with the Russians, using Frank Wise as an intermediary once again. He revived the idea of a Prinkipo-type meeting with the Russian leaders. He alarmed Lloyd-Greame, the minister involved, by offering the Russians a massive credit without the authorization of the British Cabinet.[29] He entered into detailed discussions of Russian proposals on a war debt settlement. All this disturbed Austen Chamberlain who urged caution on the Prime Minister, via Worthington-Evans (who was amongst those at Genoa); he feared that the Prime Minister was losing touch with opinion at home. 'No-one here will be prepared for financial assistance on our part unless the Russian Government sincerely accepted the terms settled by the Cabinet before the Prime Minister's departure.' A satisfactory settlement of European economic problems was urgently required, but 'the worst thing that could happen would be that you should bring back an agreement from Genoa of such a character that we could not ratify it here'.[30] Horne wrote to convey the alarm felt by King George V at the negotiations with the Soviet regime. Definite stipulations should be made, so the King felt, 'that all propaganda by Bolsheviks—or propaganda on the borders of India or any other part of our Empire—should cease', as a precondition to any financial aid.[31]

These fears were unnecessary since Genoa was rapidly lapsing into stalemate. Ruined by Rapallo, Lloyd George's overtures to the Russians yielded nothing. By the end of April, Britain, France, Belgium, Italy, and Japan had agreed on a contingency package of aid to Russia; but this soon foundered on disagreement between the Allies on the draft terms of a reply to the Russian government. Equally fruitless were the talks on the other major theme of the conference—German indemnities. Repeated bullying by Lloyd George of Barthou, the French Justice Minister (whom Hankey thought 'a decent fellow'[32]), led nowhere. A fierce speech by Poincaré at Bar-le-Duc on 24 April, in which he appeared to threaten a unilateral invasion of Germany by France if the Germans defaulted on their next payment of indemnities, marked the failure of this policy also. Renewed disagreements over the Near East worsened Anglo-French relations still further. Lloyd George remained outwardly confident. Grigg admiringly told Austen Chamberlain that 'the PM must be a wonderful fellow. The poisonous attacks on him by the Northcliffe Press are a disgrace and Wickham Steed's articles are not those of an Englishman. As if the ousting of the P.M. would be the cure for all the evils from which the Nation is suffering! We should certainly be more up to our necks in the mess than we are now.'[33] The Prime Minister offered a last series of linked proposals, under which Germany's liability to pay would be greatly reduced, the French share of payments, proportionately, would be much increased, an international loan would be floated to assist Germany—but which would largely go to France in the form of advance reparations payments—and there would be a promise to France of a continued moratorium in respect of her war debt to Great Britain.[34]

But the conference was wrecked long before that. In the event, the Political Subcommission went into early eclipse, with Germany expelled after Rapallo, and France and Belgium withdrawing at a later stage. The nations which produced the final draft communiqué to the Russian government included only Britain, Italy, Japan, Poland, Rumania, Switzerland, and Sweden, a mere rump of the world's major powers. In any case, the Russians rejected this final document. In the end, it was lamely decided to postpone all the difficult issues to a further conference at The Hague in June, to which war debts and credits, and outstanding questions relating to private property in Russia, would be referred. After much wrangling, it was agreed that two separate conferences were to be held at The Hague, one which the Russians would attend, and one from which they would be excluded. Genoa had yielded no decision on any major question. Lloyd George's report on the conference to the Commons on 25 May was a muted affair, enlivened only by spirited replies to Asquith, Cecil, and Kenworthy. His replies concealed the fact that his last throw had failed.

Genoa was a watershed in international diplomacy and in the history of the Coalition. Never again would such a large, rambling assembly, on the lines of Paris in 1919, be convened, until San Francisco in 1945. It is easy to criticize the form and style of events at Genoa. There was too little detailed preparation, too much generalized optimism, too many disparate issues muddled up with one another. In many ways, it was a parody of summit diplomacy at its worst. 'Badly prepared', it ended in 'discreditable collapse', wrote Wickham Steed with satisfaction.[35] Surrounding the conference was the perennial air of personal intrigue and newspaper scare-mongering, from which Lloyd George suffered, but which he also did his best to mobilize, especially in putting pressure on the French. The longer it lasted, the more emphatically unproductive Genoa was. In its original terms of reference—world trade and economic collaboration—Genoa in some respects was revealing. The 'Genoa resolutions', largely drafted by R. G. Hawtrey and Basil Blackett of the Treasury, brilliantly encapsulated the best pre-Keynesian economic wisdom of the time, in calling for a universal return to gold, for stable exchanges and price levels. Worthington-Evans romantically described them as 'a financial code' worthy to rank with that of Justinian.[36] Lloyd George could point also to the effective work of the three subcommissions in dealing with finance, economics, and transport. Worthington-Evans, another of those who had ploughed the sands at Genoa, pointed out the safeguards that would surround foreign aid to Russia and others, as well as to political achievements such as the non-aggression pact with Russia and signed in all by thirty-four nations.[37] But it was all very intangible, and cruel reward for the high hopes that Lloyd George had encouraged the nation to build up.

In the short term, it may well be that the Prime Minister reaped some personal prestige, through the impressive figure he had cut in the plenary sessions, and in withstanding the vindictive and unfair attacks from Wickham Steed and 'Pertinax' in the Anglo-French press. But in broader perspective, Genoa helped undermine further not only the credibility of the government, but also the national aspirations which it claimed to keep afloat. The government's conciliatory foreign policy had won widespread support until the end of 1921.When it went into more active mood from January 1922 onwards, public unease grew. Cannes suggested, especially to the left, the dangers of providing military guarantees to sustain western European security; the very idea recalled the march to war between 1906 and 1914.[38] Genoa, by contrast, suggested how exposed Britain would become if it took the lead as a peacemaker. Right-wing critics, anxious not to have their country as policeman of the world, did not want her as the world's referee either. On the left and the right, the government's foreign policy from Cannes to Genoa fuelled the isolationist mood. The subtle interrelationships that Lloyd George adduced between external security and domestic prosperity, between European peace and military guarantees, made little impact. The country was not in heroic mood. It was happy to forget the revision of the peace treaties and let Europe amble on in its own chaotic fashion. Lloyd George was not the main agent of failure at Genoa. On the contrary, he strove throughout most valiantly for moderation in relation to German reparations, relations with Russia, and disarmament. It was the nationalist aspirations of Poincaré and, in their fashion, of Rathenau and Lenin, which thwarted him and his vision of international order. But because Lloyd George and Genoa had become so intertwined in public debate in the spring of 1922, the failure of Genoa hastened on the downfall of the Prime Minister. He was yoked with a view of world leadership which was rejected equally by a tired, timid public at home, and by inflexibly nationalist antagonists abroad. Genoa was perhaps the one hope of effective international action to clear up the legacies of the First World War in the twenty years between 1919 and 1939. Its main promise had lain in the political rather than in the economic sphere: Keynes shortly denounced the Genoa Resolutions on Currency, with their rigid adherence to the gold-exchange standard, as 'a barbarous relic'.[39] But politically, too, Genoa was fruitless. It was a noble failure, but failure nevertheless.

In the summer of 1922, everything seemed to be turning out for the worst in the government's foreign policy. The two conferences at The Hague at the end of June predictably yielded only more sterility. On 10 July, Lloyd George told the Commons that there was only deadlock and that the British delegates were being brought home. The main interest at The Hague lay in Maxim Litvinoff's demands, on behalf of the Soviet government, for £322,400,000 of credits over the next three years. The terms on which it was hoped they would be granted were inevitably unacceptable to the western powers. Krassin's proposals for compensation for the confiscation of private property were turned down as unacceptable by his own government.[40] Relations with the Soviet Union became as distant as at any stage since Prinkipo. Frank Wise continued to produce memorandums of much good sense, questioning on pre-Keynesian grounds the desirability of an insistence on gold in meeting international monetary obligations and urging the reasons for the *de jure* recognition of Russia. But Rapallo and Genoa had killed all that.[41] German reparations also led to more fruitless bickering. A conference of experts from Britain and France in early August in London broke down once again. On the one hand, the German government was asking for a moratorium on cash payments for the rest of 1922. On the other hand, Poincaré insisted that no such extension be granted save on the surrender of specified mines, lands, and forests by the German government. He publicly declared his distrust of the Reparations Commission. Lloyd George himself urged that reparations be linked to the value of German exports and suggested collecting a percentage (perhaps 25 per cent) before they left German ports.[42] The disturbed temper of the Weimar Republic in Germany was illustrated by the murder of Walter Rathenau by an anti-Semitic fanatic on 24 June. Lloyd George's longer-term hopes for admitting Germany to the League of Nations were more remote than ever.

In other spheres also, the government's alliances were in some confusion. The accord with the United States achieved in Washington soon began to founder. The British were irritated with the Americans' refusal to do anything to assist the political reconciliation or economic recovery of Europe: this was the price of the election of Harding and the Republicans in 1920, with their rejection of 'Wilsonianism'. On their side, the Americans were angry over the vexed issue of Allied war debts to America. Britain's debts amounted to $4,000m outstanding, but the Allied governments insisted that debts to America should be linked with the issue of German indemnities to Britain and France. There was much criticism in Britain over the allocation made in Horne's budget in 1922 to cover debt payments to the United States from October, as the three-year moratorium was ending. Lloyd

George asked in vain for a cancellation of all inter-Allied debts. He urged his colleagues not to 'cringe' before the Americans who were pushing up tariffs on British goods to quite exorbitant levels.[43] Britain's eventual response was the so-called Balfour Note of 1 August. It complained that the USA was demanding that Britain fund her debt to her immediately. But Britain's allies must first meet their obligations to her in turn. Britain would claim from Europe no more than the United States demanded from her. As Professor Fry has shown, it placed the responsibility for the non-settlement of debts squarely on the United States.[44] The 'Atlanticists' within the British administration, who included both Philip Kerr and Edward Grigg, were 'miserable' at the British attitude which they felt would deter the Americans from future assistance to Europe and lead Americans to believe that Britain was shamming bankrupt.[45] On a less starry-eyed level, Chamberlain and Horne both sought to placate the USA and asked that their dissent from the Balfour Note be formally recorded.[46] Keynes shortly afterwards denounced the Note as being based on the fallacious principle that 'the less Germany pays, the more France shall pay'.[47] At the time, Basil Blackett of the Treasury strongly criticized the Note as disingenuous, and urged that Britain straightforwardly fund the debt incurred during the war.[48] On the other hand, Harvey, the US Ambassador in London, admitted that 'business interests and newspaper comment' backed up the British government's stand.[49] In America, the effect of the Note was to strengthen the distaste of isolationists for providing aid to perfidious imperial powers in the Old World. Critics warmed to Coolidge's comment that Britain had 'hired' the money in the first place. Anglo-American relations entered a more glacial phase, difficulties over the debt being accentuated by further prospective naval competition in the Pacific and tension over a possible British naval base at Singapore. In the New World, too, Britain's role as a sincere and dependable international conciliator was made to look tawdry and unreal.

The prestige of the government in its conduct of foreign policy was diminished still further by the course of events in Asia Minor. At least at Cannes and Genoa, and in relations with Russia and Germany, the government's failures were largely those of the well-intentioned peacemaker. However, Lloyd George's image as a man of peace was seriously tarnished by his fatal involvement in Greek-Turkish rivalry in the Near East. Since the end of the war, he had lent every effort towards encouraging Greek attempts to retain not only eastern and western Thrace in continental Europe, but large segments of Asia Minor as well, especially around Smyrna with its large Greek population. He was a passionate enthusiast for the Greeks on traditional Liberal lines. He was an especial admirer of the Liberal Prime Minister, Venizelos. When the latter was defeated in the Greek elections in November 1920, Lloyd George wrote a personal letter full of shock and distress. 'This is the kind of thing that makes one despair of democracy.'[50] Lloyd George's outlook neatly blended the views of Gladstone and Disraeli. He adhered 'to the Gladstonian tradition which regards the Turk as a curse'.[51] The Turks, truly 'unspeakable', had 'forfeited their title to rule majorities of other peoples', Kerr added. d'Abernon, the Ambassador in Berlin, noted Lloyd George's 'little Bethel mentality' on this question.[52] Kemal, the Turkish nationalist leader, was 'no better than a carpet-seller in a bazaar'.

Apart from this moralistic heritage, weaned during the horrors of Bulgaria and Armenia during Lloyd George's political youth, there was the Disraelian mantle of imperial concern with the Straits and the routes to India. Sympathy for Greece, combined with a passion for preserving the 'freedom' of passage through the straits, led to the one great aberration in Lloyd George's foreign policy, the one area of belligerent commitment, totally at variance with his otherwise conciliatory policy. He was even to propose the expulsion of the Turks from Constantinople, Balfour and Curzon alone supporting him. There was always difficulty in getting the Cabinet to endorse so one-sided a policy. Churchill was usually a supporter of a more measured approach towards Greek-Turkish rivalry: only through an accommodation with Kemal, he argued, could the new Kingdom of Iraq be stabilized. Turkey could become a barrier to Russian ambitions in the Near East.[53] Montagu, with at first the support of Milner, loudly voiced the anxieties of Indian Moslems at so aggressively anti-Turkish an attitude. Liberals in the Cabinet generally resisted the 'bag and baggage' policy.[54] Still, Lloyd George got his way at every decisive stage. Curzon strongly supported him in his anxiety for control of the Straits and for destroying the Turks' imperial pretensions as the basis for a Middle East settlement. At San Remo in April 1920, he secured the reluctant support of Millerand and the French government to a vast expansion of the Greek domain. Later in the year, the Treaty of Sèvres massively carved up the Turkish

dominions and allocated huge areas of Asia Minor and of the Mediterranean islands as well to Greek rule. The pivot of Allied policy in this
area, the one region still awaiting a peace settlement after the armistice, was the maintenance of Greek hegemony as the surest guarantee
of British imperial interests.

It soon became clear that Lloyd George had backed the wrong
horse. Kemal was an astute diplomat; he conducted sorties with the
Russians and, more spectacularly, with the French government.
Poincaré was as pro-Turkish as any Tory die-hard; he eventually
withdrew French troops from the Asian mainland and threw diplomatic support behind Kemal. The Greeks, by contrast, simply lacked the
military capacity to impose their authority on Asia Minor. As early as
January 1921, the Greek army had been repulsed by the Turks at the
battle of Inonu. Undismayed, Lloyd George and Kerr had held secret
conclaves with Gounaris and Calegoropoulos, the Greek Prime
Minister and Foreign Minister respectively, in London between 21
February and 10 March. In effect, Britain agreed not to deter Greek
offensives into the heart of Asia Minor, even to Angora itself. A
so-called autonomous province of Smyrna was in time proposed to be
detached from Turkey. Churchill criticized this policy which would
make a general pacification in the Middle East impossible. Lloyd
George sharply rejoined that he could not accept Churchill's stark view
that 'surrender or war were the only possible alternatives'.[55] Curzon
had to resist Lloyd George's 'usual passionate haste' for a new and
even more severe treaty of Sèvres.[56] In fact, the incompetence of the
Greek army repeatedly frustrated Lloyd George's Philhellene
ambitions. A second Greek offensive, in March 1921 shortly after the
London conference, perished once again at Inonu, at the hands of
Ismet Pasha (who later adopted the name of the battlefield). A third
offensive led to a humiliating defeat in September for the much larger
Greek army at the twenty-two day battle at the Sakarya river with the
loss of 18,000 men. The Greek army languished in Anatolia during the
bitter winter of 1921–2, rapidly declining in morale, equipment, and
fighting capacity.[57] The Greeks had lost all hope of imposing an Ionian
settlement by force of arms, and relied on Britain to bail them out.

By the summer of 1922, despite prolonged and unresolved Anglo-
French differences over Asia Minor, the situation remained much as
before. Talks in Paris on the Near East in March yielded nothing. The
Greek army in Asia was isolated and evidently incapable of advancing

further towards Angora. Alternatively, 50,000 Greek forces massed in eastern Thrace might hope to occupy Constantinople to redress these humiliations in Asia Minor. Western Thrace, including the sacred city of Adrianople, the Greeks always insisted was theirs. The Cabinet's official position was as unrelentingly anti-Turk as ever; even Curzon's occasional resolution seemed to melt away. The one irreconcilable critic was Edwin Montagu, the Secretary for India. After lengthy quarrels, first with Curzon over Egypt and then with Churchill over Asian settlers in the Kenyan highlands, he finally left the Cabinet in spectacular circumstances in March. He had a violent public row with Curzon over Montagu's unauthorized publication of a telegram by the Viceroy of India, Lord Reading, which expressed the unease of many Indians about the government's attitude towards Turkey. Montagu seemed to stand convicted of releasing private documents in breach of confidences given in Cabinet.[56] Curzon loftily wrote that he could not be dictated to over Thrace by 'a subordinate branch of the British Government 6,000 miles away'. However, Montagu left the government with more panache than had Addison the previous July. Montagu made a rousing speech before his Cambridge constituents soon after his resignation. In this, he denounced the one-man band which the government had become, under which collective responsibility by the Cabinet had been supplanted by quasi-presidential dictatorship. Montagu, a courageous voice of liberal humanism on Indian matters, symbolized the growing disenchantment of its more radical wing with the Coalition's policies. It left men like Fisher and Macnamara the more isolated. On the other hand, while Addison's departure stimulated a national debate on the government's failures in social reform, the fact that Montagu's resignation was in protest against policy in the Near East somehow lost its impact. It was soon subsumed by popular interest in Genoa. Montagu passed into the shadows, a brilliant, bitter survivor, with the government's Turkish policy quite unchanged. It was Mustapha Kemal who did Montagu's work for him and dashed Lloyd George's foreign policy into fragments.

The preliminary was a disastrously unbalanced speech by Lloyd George in the Commons on 4 August. Here, he echoed the passionately Hellenic views he had affirmed in a secret meeting with Venizelos at the Commons on 30 May.[59] In this speech, he accused the Turks of committing wartime atrocities, and of refusing reasonable diplomatic overtures for peace thereafter. Indirectly, he seemed to pledge British support and financial aid for the Greeks in yet another offensive, including a blockade of Asia Minor. For the Independent Liberals, Donald Maclean warmly applauded these sentiments. But Derby, writing to Bonar Law, condemned Lloyd George's 'insane love of the Greeks'. He added, 'How could you expect the Turks to negotiate with a man who could make such a speech?' Curzon, abroad at the time, thought it simply 'deplorable'.[60] In retaliation, Kemal's forces smashed through the Greek army's defences on 26 August near Afium Karahissar. Within days, the Greeks were in full and headlong retreat. Kemal's armies poured into Smyrna which was put to fire and sword in biblical fashion, with huge loss of life (perhaps 120,000 in all) amongst its Greek inhabitants. The Turks then pushed on towards the Dardanelles, and threatened with 40,000 troops the position held by the British at Chanak. This was General 'Tim' Harington's scanty force of one squadron and two battalions.

The British government responded in highly belligerent fashion. Even Churchill, previously a fierce critic of the pro-Greek policy in the Near East, was now transformed into a fire-eating defender of British imperial interests. The Prime Minister and the service ministers, along with the chiefs of staff, Beatty, the First Sea Lord, Cavan, Chief of the Imperial General Staff, and Trenchard of the RAF, co-ordinated plans to bring in naval reinforcements assisted by two squadrons of aeroplanes, to protect the Dardanelles and the Bosporus and the British-held position at Chanak. Beatty was ordered to ensure that 'no Kemalist forces be allowed to cross the salt water' to the European mainland. Artillery would be brought up at Gallipoli to cover the narrow straits.[61] Finally, at an ominous meeting of the Cabinet on 27 September, the decision was taken to reinforce Harington with military forces, and to accept the probability of fighting between British and Turkish troops. Military reinforcements were to be sent from Britain, Egypt, Malta, Gibraltar, and Cyprus, together with the bulk of the Mediterranean Fleet and some of the Atlantic Fleet.[62] The one tranquillizing factor was Harington himself at Chanak, who, with the British High Commissioner at Constantinople, Sir Horace Rumbold, sought to hold off a confrontation with the Turks until negotiations could begin. 'I thought it was peace my country wanted,' Harington later declared.[63] Lloyd George, always the foe of political generals, rebuked him for his presumption.

'General Harington was so much concerned with the political situation—which was not rightly his—that he did not devote sufficient attention to the military situation.' He defended the presence of massed Greek troops in eastern Thrace, near the approaches to Constantinople. 'He would not be surprised if, in a few weeks, the Greeks were not as formidable a force as that under Mustafa Kemal.'[64] He took some heart from a bloodless revolution in Greece which led to the abdication of King Constantine on 27 September. 'I think it is just possible God may take a hand. It looks like it.'[65]

For two weeks more, war over Chanak hung in the balance. Then delicate negotiations with Ismet Pasha at Mudania bore fruit; a settlement was signed on 11 October. With effect from 15 October, it was agreed that Greek troops would retire from eastern Thrace, while Turkish forces would retire fifteen kilometres from Chanak. Both sides could save face, and Lloyd George even claim to have won a famous diplomatic victory. Robert Boothby was later to write that it was the only time that Britain stood up to a potential aggressor between 1918 and 1939.[66] That, however, was precisely the problem. The Chanak affair conflicted mightily with a national yearning for peaceful isolation. In fact, Lloyd George's pro-Greek pretensions had been shattered anyway. Venizelos's mirage of a vast new Greek empire in the eastern Mediterranean had vanished into thin air, while Turkey under Kemal was to consolidate itself as a developing modern state. The claims made for Britain's imperial authority during the Chanak affair proved equally unreal. One after the other, the dominions made it plain that Britain's preoccupation with the strategic and economic importance of the Dardanelles was no concern of theirs. Mackenzie King, who had become Liberal Prime Minister of Canada in succession to the Conservative, Meighen, was especially resistant. He was incensed that Britain, through an uncharacteristic error in detail by Churchill as Colonial Secretary, published her appeal to the dominions for help before he received it himself. Only New Zealand and Newfoundland, two minor brethren, pledged what help they could muster. Shorn of imperial support, Britain found allies in Europe alarmingly scarce also. It was well known that the Russians were establishing links with the Turks. The Balkan countries, Yugoslavia, Rumania, and Bulgaria, were scracely more enthusiastic about Greek hegemony in south-eastern Europe than Turkish. Italy, deep in the throes of political confusion on the eve of Mussolini's march on

Rome, could offer no assistance to anyone. Most important of all, Poincaré flatly refused either to assist in convening a Balkan confer- ence on the Near East or in lending any naval or military aid for the British force at Chanak.[67] In practice, Harington and Charpy, the British and French commanders on the straits, struck up a good relationship since neither wished to take action against the Turks. Despite a famous confrontation on 3 October between Poincaré and Curzon in Paris, in which Poincaré accused Britain of putting unfair pressure on Rumania and after which Curzon was left prostrated with exhaustion and shock,[68] the French refused to budge. Poincaré left Lloyd George's Philhellene quixotries to perish in their own good time.

All this bore directly on the pretensions of the Coalition at home. The government's anti-Turkish policies led to a surge of Tory opposi- tion. Since the days of Disraeli, the Conservatives had been the pro-Turk party. Derby finally announced his break with the Coalition at this point; he claimed that Kemal represented all right-thinking and patriotic Turkish opinion.[69] Younger, while publicly calling for a show of 'strength and determination' towards Turkey, made it plain that Lloyd George's obsessive hostility towards the Turks was in complete conflict with Tory traditions. 'To compare a Turk with a miserable Levantine Greek is to compare gold with dross.' He took some comfort from the thought that at least Venizelos was a Cretan, not a genuine Greek.[70] Salisbury denounced the anti-Mahommedan policy in Asia Minor which was inconsistent with the government's policy in India and ran the risk of estranging France. Only the 'road of humiliation lay ahead'. He tried to put pressure on Bonar Law who agreed with him, so he claimed, that Chanak made the fall of the Coalition all the more inevitable.[71]

This pressure built up within the Cabinet where a 'peace party' was soon discernible. Curzon, the architect of the Treaty of Sèvres, had lately been showing growing alarm at the government's Near Eastern policy. It was heightened by what he believed to be the Lloyd George/Birkenhead/Churchill/Balfour *putsch* to remove him from the Foreign Office. While he supported the Cabinet's decision to send reinforcements to assist Harington, he was concerned at the warlike turn that events in Asia Minor were taking. On 27 September he told the Cabinet 'that he did not hold quite such strong views on the retention of Chanak as some of his colleagues'. He strove to avoid any

appearance of a government censure of Harington. He claimed that
war with Turkey would gain little support from country or parliament. He ridiculed Lloyd George's scheme for a grand international
conference at Venice. The Prime Minister would not attend, Curzon
wrote to the British Ambassador in Paris, but 'would send me to fight
the battle and to bear the brunt of defeat'.[72] But Curzon was notorious
for waiting for others to take the lead in any revolt against Lloyd
George. An ally was now at hand. This was Griffith-Boscawen, who
had had a miserable time as Minister of Agriculture since February
1921. He had infuriated the farmers by having to repeal the Agriculture Act and had even lost his seat at Dudley in the by-election
consequent to his being promoted to the Cabinet. Boscawen was now
to emerge as the key figure of protest, certainly more so than Baldwin,
the President of the Board of Trade, whose Carlton Club speech was
later to lend him the aura of arch-critic of the Coalition but who in fact
had been remarkably timid when accepting the government's right to
remain in office. 'We were glad enough to join with Lloyd George in
1918,' Baldwin remarked.[73] Boscawen was already upset at the Prime
Minister's refusal to renew guaranteed prices to wheat farmers, which
caused grave risk to Tory strength in English rural constituencies.
Now he wrote to Chamberlain and to Curzon in agitated fashion on 2
October, when it seemed probable that an ultimatum to Kemal would
lead to British troops opening fire on the very eve of the conference at
Mudania:

I am certain the average Englishman is dead against war in general, but I
believe that he would fight for the freedom of the Dardanelles and to protect
the graves in the Gallipoli peninsula, but he would insist that every effort
should be made in the first instance and I am certain he would not fight for
anything else. I don't believe the country cares anything about Thrace and
Conservatives generally would prefer to see the Turks there rather than the
Greeks. *A good understanding with Turkey was our old policy* and it is essential
having regard to the enormous Mahommedan population of the British
Empire.[74]

Writing to Curzon, he declared that a good understanding with Turkey was the 'policy of Palmerston and Beaconsfield'. He added that
Lords Peel and Crawford of Balcarres were ministers who agreed with
his views.[75] They all feared a snap 'khaki' election called to rescue the
government from its domestic difficulties. Curzon replied firmly that
he had no intention of 'being pushed or cajoled (so far as the F.O. is

concerned) into war' in the face of 'some of our colleagues who have got the smell of gunpowder in their nostrils and are reckless of the consequences'. He warmly defended Harington's coolness of judgement at Chanak, especially in delaying the issue of the ultimatum to the Turks.[76] Gradually, the peace section of the Cabinet wore down the militants, Lloyd George, Birkenhead, Churchill, Worthington-Evans, and possibly Horne (with the acquiescence also of Chamberlain and Balfour). On 1 October, Boscawen, Peel, Crawford, and Lee of Fareham (First Lord of the Admiralty and a key minister in the Chanak crisis) met to deprecate hasty action over eastern Thrace. By 5 October, it became clear that they had a notable Liberal ally, Sir Alfred Mond. Despite his Gladstonian onslaughts on the 'unspeakable Turk' for the benefit of his Welsh nonconformist constituents in Swansea, Mond declared privately that Britain ought to stand aside from a war between the Greeks and the Turks, especially since they had been deserted by the French and other allies.[77] Other Liberal ministers, Fisher, Shortt, Munro, and Macnamara, were hardly enthusiasts for war-mongering. Finally on 7 October, Lloyd George agreed, to the evident disappointment of Churchill and Birkenhead, that a telegram ought to be sent to Curzon to endorse the agreement he had reached with Poincaré in Paris. Harington would further be given instructions to withdraw from Scutari and Constantinople, if necessary.[78] Lloyd George himself finally accepted Boscawen's view that Thrace was a faraway country of which they knew nothing, and for whose future, as for that of Czechoslovakia in 1938, Britain would never take up arms. The bringer of peace with honour at Versailles, the hero of Genoa, had been crushingly defeated by his own peace party; he was an unsuccessful as a maker of war as he had been an architect of reconciliation. His admirer, Lee of Fareham, conceded that Lloyd George had 'lost his ascendancy' in the Cabinet in the face of the 'moderation and commonsense of the Cabinet as a whole'.[79]

On each occasion, from Cannes to Chanak, Lloyd George's foreign policy had failed to produce results. It had done his reputation and that of his government great harm. Some of this was personal. 'L.G. has lost all authority at home and still more abroad. The change in his international reputation at Geneva this year was very marked,' Cecil wrote on 9 October, with typical exaggeration.[80] 'The extent of the distrust of him is really very remarkable.' The French, the Swiss, the Czechs, the Americans, and the Italians all took much the same view.

'I believe that it is really true that, so long as he is directing British affairs it will be very difficult to make any serious advance towards European peace. The Greek defeat is regarded as a great blow for him personally.'[81] Cecil's partisan view was not far from the truth by October 1922. What was at stake ultimately, though, was more than one man's highly personal methods of conducting international diplomacy, trying to find a way of circumventing the hopeless morass of world problems left by the war, which conventional statesmanship through foreign office channels had failed to diminish. The real casualty of Lloyd George's misadventures in foreign affairs was the view that the British government had a unique responsibility, in the vacuum left by American withdrawal and French intransigence, to lead the world forward toward a new era of reconciliation. This would be achieved by a combination of appeasement of the major powers, especially Germany and Russia, and active intervention in key areas of which France's eastern boundary and the Dardanelles were the most vital. The method would be inter-allied summit diplomacy rather than the more rarefied channels of the League of Nations, about which Cecil, Murray, and their LNU friends had such inflated hopes. The Coalition had come to be harnessed to a vigorous concept of dynamic diplomacy, both for wider political reasons and for direct economic assistance for a stagnant British trade and industry. 'Prosperity with honour' might have been inscribed on Lloyd George's scrap of paper had he returned from Genoa with anything to show for his labours.

As discussions in the Cabinet and leading articles in the newspapers showed, the public mood since Versailles was resistant towards such initiatives. The left in general had drunk deep of the cup of isolationism. Keynes's *Economic Consequences of the Peace*, with its dire warnings of the effects of reparations upon Germany's economic future (warnings which Keynes himself was beginning to modify by 1922) had been a triumphant best-seller, a talisman for the rejection of international negotiations on behalf of old-fashioned nationalist objectives. 'Extraordinarily brilliant', Cecil called it.[82] It greatly encouraged the post-war isolationist, almost pacifist, mood, the feeling that wars were punitive and pointless. So, too, did the Union of Democratic Control, led by such men as Morel, Ponsonby, and Trevelyan, with its insistence that open, democratic diplomacy would alone provide the basis for a stable and durable peace. By 1922 the Labour and Independent Liberal parties, headed by the newly charismatic figure of Ramsay MacDonald, were organs for the propaganda of the UDC. Anti-war tracts by Ponsonby, Hobson, Angell, and Morel sold as never before; the UDC's foreign policy, its onslaughts on 'the system of Versailles', was virtually the Labour Party's foreign policy. The UDC retained its belief in Britain's international influence. Like later dissenting groups, the Peace Ballot movement in the 1930s, the Campaign for Nuclear Disarmament in the 1960s, it believed that a bold moral gesture of disarmament by Britain would capture the imagination of a world that still looked to Britain for a lead. But this heady, generalized internationalism went with an instant suspicion of specific commitments. At the height of the Chanak crisis on 21 September, Arthur Henderson and a TUC delegation gave Lloyd George their views on the Turkish crisis; they were views that would have been warmly endorsed by Cobden and the advocates of 'no foreign policy' in the past. In vain did Lloyd George point out to them that Britain had to act, even if alone, since the USA would not take responsibility for Armenia, France for Cilicia, Italy for Southern Anatolia, nor Greece for the *vilayet* of Smyrna.[83] As with the trade unions, so with the radical intelligentsia. Foreign affairs, a revulsion against the war of 1914–18, had carried an entire generation of intellectuals into the Labour party via the UDC or the ILP or both. Foreign affairs were the touchstone of their rejection of the government's attempted consensus now.

On the right, isolationism was no less marked, though necessarily for less philosophic and more pragmatic reasons. There were also deep human sentiments, which General Harington himself, surprisingly, embodied: 'I had seen enough of war, through four years connected with the defence of the Ypres Salient, to convince me that our country wanted no more war.'[84] In the Cabinet, Boscawen and, belatedly, Baldwin, in arguing against war during the Chanak crisis, were taking a strictly neutralist line. On the grounds urged by Boscawen, despite his remarks about defending the graves at Gallipoli, it seems improbable that he would have accepted British military or naval intervention anywhere, other perhaps than keeping black and brown natives in the Empire in good order. Apart from a band of die-hards, unimportant by 1922, who still dreamed of an ideological crusade against the Soviet Union, the bulk of Conservatives, on grounds of the need for economy and of suspicion of an ideologically motivated foreign policy, were firm against foreign intervention. They were edging away from their identification with the peace treaty of Versailles, and the need to protect its settlement. Instead of revising the peace treaties, they would just let them gather dust. On 7 October 1922, a famous letter by Bonar Law appeared in *The Times*. He included some conventional support for the government. It had been right to resist a Turkish invasion into Europe. Otherwise, the same horrors would have occurred in Thrace as had taken place in Anatolia. But the nub of his argument—and one celebrated phrase—lingered in the mind. Britain could not alone act 'as policeman of the world'. Conservatives wanted to retain the *entente* with France, settle their debts with the United States, allow the League harmlessly to talk away, and settle for a quiet life. In foreign affairs, as to some degree at home, the Coalition government had lost friends for being too active, too innovative, too anxious to involve Britain in shoring up international security.

There was, perhaps, a conflict between two concepts of appeasement. The one, favoured by Lloyd George between 1919 and 1922 and still championed by him even in the later 1930s, sought to blend reconciliation with a positive build-up of military and naval guarantees to stabilize areas such as the Rhineland or the Near East. The Genoa idea and the Cannes resolutions went together. The other version of appeasement preferred a more passive role, played out in the traditional style of the Foreign Office as for decades past, in which a combination of poverty and timidity would dictate a policy of withdrawal from each theatre in turn. This was the policy inherited and developed by Baldwin and his fellow rebels against the confrontation at Chanak. By an erratic route, it led to the surrender at Munich, then, quite inconsistently, to the guarantee to Poland in March 1939 wholly at variance with post- (and indeed pre-) Lloyd Georgian foreign policy. In the later 1930s, Conservative ministers such as Halifax and Hoare chose to forget that they themselves had called for an even more punitive treatment of Germany during the Paris peace conference in April 1919.

Six months after he fell from power, Lloyd George reflected, with typical exaggeration, on the change in British external policy since the days of the Coalition. 'As long as we were in office we prevented the Turks from going to Constantinople, the French from going into the Ruhr, and the American hand from coming into our till. Now they have all got there.'[85] The contrast (like nostalgic recollection of Cromwell's strong foreign policy prevalent in England after the restoration of the Stuarts) is not perhaps a complete distortion. In preferring appeasement in the passive voice and the subjunctive mood to the erratic affirmatives of the Coalition government, the nation made its choice, a choice for a new internal unity founded on withdrawal from the instability and crises of a dangerous world.

14

The Downfall of the Coalition: Party Politics

The growth of class division at home and the tide of isolationism in foreign policy were underlying forces working to undermine the Coalition government. But the immediately decisive element would, of course, be the preservation of that political partnership forged in the 'coupon' arrangements of 1918 and still in being, despite the growing Unionist rebelliousness since the Irish treaty. That partnership had suffered a crisis of credibility in January 1922 with Lloyd George's failure to gain agreement over the calling of a general election. He had been humiliated by Younger, and a Unionist secession from the government seemed imminent. In fact, the crisis passed over fairly rapidly and a period of quiet followed. Austen Chamberlain was quick to point out that Unionist attachment to the Coalition remained powerful. The formation of the so-called 'National Liberal' party on 20 January gave new status to the demoralized Coalition Liberals after so many electoral and policy defeats. The discussions on the Geddes report took the steam out of the Anti-Waste movement and served to unify the administration. By February, the government seemed to have re-formed ranks and to have accepted the continuation of a loose alliance between its major wings with no thought of 'fusion'. As has been seen, Birkenhead, the Lord Chancellor, addressed the New Members' Coalition group on 1 February in a mood of some confidence.[1] The Coalition, he claimed, had no serious opponents; the nation shared his view that this was no time to plunge again into the perilous waters of party politics. Nor did the Prime Minister look like a man on the run. Thelma Cazalet Keir pointed out that, despised as he was in smart society in Belgravia and Mayfair, he attracted instant applause from the audiences in music halls, or in cinemas when his familiar face, long mane, and Inverness cloak appeared on the screen.[2]

Birkenhead's analysis contained his usual arrogant over-optimism.

Miss Keir, a friend of Megan Lloyd George, was in part giving way to
hero-worship. Yet the fact remained that, after the election crisis of
early January, the government entered upon calmer waters. Apart
from a very difficult period in mid-March when the Prime Minister's
seclusion in Criccieth gave rise to wild rumours and damaging uncertainty, the next few months were uneventful, even dull, in terms of
political manœuvre. The dominant part played by foreign affairs,
especially the convening of the conference at Genoa, dulled the
passions of domestic partisans. Even as late as mid-June 1922, the
government still seemed almost impregnable. After a disastrous
period in February, when three by-elections were lost in six days
—Manchester (Clayton) and North Camberwell to Labour, Bodmin
to Isaac Foot for the Liberals—the electors seemed somewhat less
hostile. There was a notable Coalition victory at West Wolverhampton in March. A non-political supporter of the government, Sir
Robert Bird, held the swing in this highly marginal seat down to less
than two per cent against a prominent trade unionist opponent.[3] Soon
afterwards, Cambridge was held by an official Conservative, despite
the threat of some difficulty caused by the resignation of Montagu (a
Cambridgeshire MP) from the government. The same month, Salvidge held the Coalitionists in line defending the Exchange division of
Liverpool without opposition. Inverness in the Scottish highlands and
Chertsey in the home counties were also retained. In Chertsey, the
Independent Liberals unsuccessfully put up General Sir Hubert
Gough, as a military critic of the government's supposedly warlike
foreign policy. Finally, a by-election in the City of London on 19 May
witnessed a clear defeat for Sir Thomas Vansittart Bowater, an advocate of 'anti-waste', by an official Conservative. Evidently, since
the Geddes report, this particular threat to the government had
been neutralized. Generally, the threat of a reviving party politics
had been staved off, and the fabric of unity, on the surface,
maintained.

At a more profound level, each wing of the Coalition was showing
signs of discontent that required only a new crisis to ignite them. The
less important of the two, though far from trivial, were the Coalition
Liberals. Their morale was not manifestly raised by the formation of
the National Liberal Party after meetings at Central Hall, Westminster, on 21–2 January. A Welsh observer found the proceedings rather
dull and an Independent Liberal demonstration at the same venue on

the 23rd 'far superior both in point of numbers and enthusiasm'.[4] The Liberal element in the government was now gravely weakened. Addison had gone. Montagu followed in March over policy towards Turkey, accompanying his departure with fierce blasts at the Prime Minister's style of leadership. Hewart, the Attorney-General, was removed from the government to become Lord Chief Justice. He was followed in office by a Unionist, Sir Ernest Pollock, while his seat at East Leicester was lost to Labour in the by-election on a swing of 33 per cent. Churchill, now insisting that 'Liberalism was the truest form of conservatism', was an ambiguous figure.[5] Shortt, Munro, Greenwood, and probably Macnamara did not count. Fisher, the Minister of Education, the last plausibly radical figure in the administration, was a declining force, presiding miserably over the economies partially forced on him by the Geddes committee. It was little wonder that he approached Lloyd George with the suggestion that he and the Coalition Liberals generally should withdraw from the government after Genoa. He clutched at the straw of the Prime Minister's wanting 'an early election and a fresh base of Coalition power'.[6] Hilton Young was also an advocate of an early election as the sole means of giving the Liberal element in the government credibility.[7] Meanwhile McCurdy continued to provide a stream of absurdly over-confident memorandums, urging Lloyd George to use an early election as a weapon with which to discipline the Unionist rebels. 'If an election is held on the lines I have suggested, the Coalition Liberals will be returned in the largest possible numbers.'[8]

Deprived of key personnel, the Coaly Libs were seeing their programmes stripped bare also. The Irish treaty brought them no credit, while the Geddes economies were no policy for a radical party. Behind them, the bemused Coalition Liberal MPs continued to voice extreme unease about the government's deviations from the strict orthodoxies of free trade. The Anti-Dumping Bill of 1921 was now on the statute book, despite resistance from the government's Liberal supporters. The heavy duties on imports dumped below the cost of production in British ports, and the protection afforded home industry against 'collapsed exchanges' such as the German mark, seemed to open the door to almost limitless interference in the free flow of imports and exports. Wedgwood Benn's motion of protest on 14 February found only 18 Coalition Liberal members voting in support of the government, while 19 voted against and 87 were either absent or abstained.

These last included several ministers, including Churchill, a prominent critic of the 'key industries' sections of the bill.[9] In the event,
there was nothing that the Liberals could do, though a group of
back-benchers led by John Wallace and Gerald France continued to
badger Stanley Baldwin about the Board of Trade's handling of the
operation of the bill. In June, another crisis blew up to trouble the free
trade conscience, namely the import of fabric gloves and the question
of whether this included glove fabrics as well. Lancashire Liberals
were up in arms, and Captain William Edge, member for Bolton and a
junior whip, wrote to announce his resignation from the
government.[10] He had paired in favour of Benn's motion on 14
February.

The Coalition Liberals were now helpless. The Wee Frees would
not have them; they had no option but to cling to the unpopular rock
of coalition. The Coalition Liberal Association in Bolton endorsed
Edge's resignation on fabric gloves yet proclaimed its 'unswerving
loyalty' to the government. Wedgwood Benn noted in May that
another motion on the restriction of imports found no support from
Coalitionists. 'The Coalition Liberal revolt against them has completely died away. . . . The House is not very much interested in these
Free Trade debates.' All in all, the Coalition Liberals cut a somewhat
pathetic figure. Mond, Macnamara, and Kellaway reported on their
party organization in May and suggested that Greenwood succeeded
McCurdy as chief whip; but they admitted that this would have no
impact 'as policy remains unsettled'.[11] They were not encouraged by
their leader's attitude. He remained cut off from his party and treated
his Liberal colleagues with scant regard. None of them, save for
Churchill, was a close associate. Lloyd George insisted that the
government as a whole was faithful to Liberal principles. 'Balfour and
Chamberlain were both now practically Liberals.' Balfour, for
instance, was 'in matters of foreign policy far more Liberal than
Grey'.[12] When approaches were made by J. M. Hogge on behalf of
some left-wing Wee Frees to sound out the Prime Minister over
possible Liberal reunion, he met with no encouragement. Fortnightly
lunches attended by about forty Coalition and Independent Liberal
MPs yielded nothing. A proposed dinner of reconciliation at the Ritz
was cancelled. Margot Asquith characteristically attributed the whole
movement to Scott of the *Manchester Guardian*—'a popinjay of vanity'.
'Reunion has always been rot' was her considered judgement.[13]

The Coalition Unionist disaffection with the government was very much more serious. The events of January 1922 had left their scars. Younger now openly called for a 'bill of divorcement' between the two wings of the Coalition,[14] though he seemed to be referring to some undefined period subsequent to the next general election. Chamberlain had more and more difficulty in keeping his troops in loyal formation; he had to concede that there would be no more 'coupons'. Bonar Law, on returning to London in February, found a 'greater difference in the opinion of the Unionist party towards the Coalition'.[15] Chamberlain had to meet thirty-five die-hard MPs on 13 February to receive a public recital of their complaints. The Coalition, he was told, had shown 'no settled policy'.[16] When he announced his renewed commitment to Coalition at the Oxford Carlton Club on 3 March, he was rebuked by Sir Alexander Leith of the National Unionist Council, which was obviously far more hostile to Coalition than were the party leaders.[17] In declaring that 'when we go to the country we go as a government', Chamberlain was said to have been going beyond previous positions adopted by the Coalition. It was noticeable that Worthington-Evans, speaking to his Colchester constituents on the same night as Chamberlain's speech, was more circumspect. He went so far as to admit that an independent Conservative administration was a perfectly practical proposition, though not one he would currently urge.[18] One indication of Unionist discontent came when Montagu's resignation on 10 March left the India Office vacant—'like Dr. Addison, thrown to the wolves of reaction', wrote the *Nation*.[19] In rapid succession, three leading Unionist peers, Derby, Devonshire, and Crawford declined the Prime Minister's invitation to succeed him. In the end, the appointment of the minor figure of Lord Peel, formerly the Minister of Transport, was both a testimony to the growing enfeeblement of the government at its highest levels, and the Prime Minister's inability to use his powers of patronage to any great effect. The die-hard minority, Gretton at the helm, found increasing sympathy, with unrest continuing in Ireland, India, and Egypt, and the furore that surrounded the possible recognition of Soviet Russia at Genoa.

Matters reached a crisis point between 10 and 27 March when Lloyd George, under doctor's orders with severe neuralgia and eye trouble, retired home to Criccieth to brood in seclusion about his political future. His enforced separation from Frances Stevenson, with telephone conversations constantly overheard by the Lloyd George family, added to his personal strain.[20] The background to it all lay in his exasperation with the mounting Unionist criticism of his leadership and his insistence on gaining a vote of confidence from his Cabinet colleagues prior to Genoa. He complained bitterly of 'Younger and Tory indiscipline'. In somewhat guarded terms, he wrote to Chamberlain on 27 February offering his resignation unless his Tory colleagues offered him unambiguous support.[21] This was, predictably, turned down. Throughout his period of absence, during which Lloyd George was observed pottering quietly around Criccieth and taking his due meed of interest in Welsh sermons at Capel Zion, Dame Margaret's own Methodist chapel, rumour and uncertainty reached a new pitch. Lloyd George's decision to retire from public life was widely anticipated. Certainly, there were those such as Grigg and Hilton Young who advised him to resign in the expectation that he would return on the rebound six months later fresher and more powerful than ever. During this period, Tory mutinies seemed to multiply. A meeting of 200 Unionist members in the House came close to repudiating Chamberlain's leadership and produced all kinds of discontented mutterings at the policy and conduct of the Coalition.[22] Walter Long told Chamberlain that Lloyd George was destroying their party by hanging on to office.[23] Chamberlain had to write to the Prime Minister in some agitation, urging him to make some clear statement of his intentions, and in particular to declare himself as firmly on behalf of the Coalition as Chamberlain himself and Balfour had done for the Unionists. Otherwise, attacks by the Wee Frees went unanswered. Chamberlain professed to be still sanguine about the ineffectiveness of the revolts by small bevies of die-hards. 'If we keep our heads and stand to our guns we shall win all along the line.'[24]

For most Unionists, the government seemed to be doing nothing right at this period. Dining at the Carlton Club, Waldorf Astor was 'much struck' by the feeling 'against L.G. personally. It seems to be stronger even than the feeling against the Govt. as a whole.'[25] Garvin thought that Lloyd George's government had long outlived its usefulness. Unionists felt that the government's foreign policies were reckless in the extreme, with their flirtations with Bolshevism. There was chaos in Ireland, with IRA assaults along the Ulster border. At home, there were the expensive hazards of Lloyd George's 'swing to the left'. Reform of the Lords was totally ignored. Salvidge was a lone supporter of the government on the National Union's executive committee. Loyalists in rural constituencies deplored also the repeal of the Agriculture Act in 1921, with its guaranteed prices to wheat and other farmers. Some farmers, no doubt, were glad to see the end of experiments in state control such as the Agricultural Wages Board, even at the cost of the guarantee, as Milner claimed. Many more were convinced that to scrap Treasury guarantees to keep prices up at the very time that the boom in business had collapsed was a gross betrayal. Griffith-Boscawen, the Minister of Agriculture, was the target for fierce protest in Tory rural strongholds. He had to display his embarrassment in the pages of the *Lloyd George Liberal Magazine* and to lament that he had had to repeal the successful policies of food production launched by Ernle and Lee of Fareham.[26] Nor could he extract any alternative form of assistance from Lloyd George and Horne, now that 'economy' and 'decontrol' were in such vogue, for agriculture as for industry. Poor Griffith-Boscawen, already humiliated in the by-election at Dudley in March 1921, was to suffer heavy defeat by a Liberal in his rural constituency in Somerset at the 1922 election. He never entered parliament again, the scapegoat for the new era of depression on the land. In March 1922, with Lloyd George incommunicado at Criccieth, grievances from farmers and others continued to fester, to the government's discredit.

However, as soon as Lloyd George returned from Criccieth, the climate at once improved. Unionist discontent, even though the serious wave to date, began again to ebb. The Cabinet hammered out a compromise over the recognition of Russia which appeared to satisfy the critics, save for a few die-hards like Joynson-Hicks who were routed in debate. Grigg reported that Lloyd George failed to see why he should resign and seem to yield 'to the howls of enemies like Northcliffe'.[27] Meanwhile, unrest in India, after an initial surge of disappointment at the departure of Edwin Montagu, almost disappeared. The later months of 1922 were the most tranquil period that the subcontinent had experienced since 1919. In these circumstances, Unionist rebellion again seemed remote and peripheral. During the month and a half that the Prime Minister was at Genoa, there were no signs of any domestic upheaval to upset the government. Indeed, the fact that Lloyd George could stay away for so lengthy a period was testimony to the confidence still widespread in government circles. Chamberlain, while he admitted that there was discontent in London and the home counties among Tory loyalists, thought that Coalition sentiment still flourished in the Midlands, the North, and Scotland.[28] Horne's budget, which included a cut in the basic rate of income tax from 6s. to 5s. in the pound, was popular amongst Unionists everywhere. There were also slightly firmer signs of improved trade, rising market prices, and a more buoyant industrial advance. The index of industrial equities rose from 78.6 in January to 96.7 in August.[29] No great strikes were on the horizon. Sterling was remarkably firm. Until the latter part of June, therefore, the government still remained firmly in the saddle, well able to cope with sporadic sniper fire from its right flank.

The truth was that, even after Genoa, Unionist criticism of the Coalition was relatively ineffective. The rebels were still virtually leaderless, with no serious encouragement from within the government—certainly not from Baldwin whose distaste for Coalition politics was kept very private indeed. Bonar Law seemed sunk in a slough of melancholy passivity. Unionist attacks were unfocused, lighting variously on a vast range of issues, foreign and domestic, great and small, and rebuffed with some ease by Chamberlain as the objectives of Coalition policy shifted. Conservatives (the term most generally used since December 1921) had to confine their attacks within very general terms. 'The combined results of the war and of the emergency alliance of political opponents have combined to divorce Ministers from the sentiments which stir the minds of the electorate,' complained J. S. Sandars. Chamberlain and his colleagues were 'talking a language the constituencies do not understand'.[30] The present parliamentary system deterred able young men from entering politics at all and reduced back-benchers to cynical lobby fodder. Stamfordham agreed and added that a government with a huge majority 'stifled the growth of Parliamentary capacity'. McCurdy was quoted as believing that 'the house was tired when it was elected'.[31] These reflections were a substitute for a more precise strategy for getting rid of the government. Salisbury was more and more incensed at the course of events. 'I am not prepared to support the Coalition on any terms', not even reform of the upper house.[32] But he, too, was at a loss to find a mechanism for translating widespread discontent amongst party workers, constituency chairmen, and back-benchers into something effective.

Then in June came a new phase of protest which was much more damaging. Almost by chance, the Unionist rebels alighted on an issue which was both emotive and struck at the heart of the methods of the government, and more especially of its leader. It was also a theme which, for the first time, roused murmurs of rebellion from within the administration itself. The uproar about the so-called 'honours scandal', in which Lloyd George's political fund was the central issue, fortuitously became the cause of a new upheaval which rocked the government to its foundations. In itself, the honours question was a trivial enough matter. Lloyd George's practice differed in scale but not in kind from the practice of Prime Ministers since the days of Palmerston: he offered peerages and other honours in return for contributions to party funds. Certainly, Lloyd George's creation of new peers on such a massive scale—in part, a product of a Welsh contempt for the upper house and its hereditary basis, in part a reflection of his own *arriviste* background—was unusual. The cash nexus was more explicit than it had been under Asquith or Balfour. Still, the practice was well-established, and generally felt to be a harmless safeguard against the widespread political corruption endemic in the politics of France or the United States. It was better to sell titles than to sell policies. The Unionists themselves benefited from the sale of honours: as Dr. Ramsden has observed, they adopted an obvious double standard. Their complaint, at the Central Office level, was not ethical at all, but concerned the practical issue of the allocation of the proceeds. 'Freddie [Guest] is nobbling our men,' complained Younger, when a Unionist benefactor appeared on the Liberals' list. The Coaly Libs were reaping the monetary rewards that ought to have come the way of Unionist coffers in return for ennobling obscure knights of the shire or other Tory supporters. In addition, he tried to draw a distinction between Lloyd George's filling his political coffers and the Unionists' 'placing subscriptions in trust'.[33] But the overriding necessity for Lloyd George, as Bonar Law and Austen Chamberlain were realists enough to understand, was that he was in a political limbo after the 'coupon election'. The Liberal Party funds were in the hands of his Asquithian opponents; save in Wales, Lloyd George had nothing. The sale of peerages and other honours, even if accompanied by Sutherland's unique style of personal persuasion in the convivial atmosphere of London's clubland, was simply a political tactic. The Lloyd George fund was a political fund, pure and simple, not a source of personal wealth for a Prime Minister still relatively poor. Despite the fund, Lloyd George was still apprehensive for his financial future after he should fall from power. His personal income was almost as precarious now as when, an impecunious Welsh back-bencher in the 1890s, he had involved himself in an unsuccessful syndicate to prospect the alleged gold reserves in Patagonia.[34] In August 1922, Lloyd George was overjoyed when he was able to sign an advance contract for his war memoirs which guaranteed him a minimum of £90,000 for the future.[35]

Much of the outcry about the sale of honours was humbug. But, for all that, it related directly and sensitively to the very essence of the government, namely the Prime Minister's methods of retaining his personal ascendancy. Lloyd George himself correctly surmised that the root of the agitation lay in 'the dislike of the Tories of his having a party fund of his own'.[36] Further, the quality of the recruits he added to the House of Lords was a sensitive issue to Tory fundamentalists, already dismayed at reform of the House of Lords being postponed, and at the dilution of the quality of the old pre-war landed aristocracy by the *nouveaux riches* who had profited from the war. A particularly controversial honours list at the end of June, raised a general outcry; included was the name of Sir Joseph Robinson, a South African capitalist whose dubious business methods were widely publicized. Two hundred Unionist members now signed a motion to demand an all-party inquiry into the method by which political honours were awarded. They also pressed for an early debate and the government had little option but to agree. This revolt was much broader in base than any of its predecessors. Outside the ranks of government, it saw Salisbury ally himself with the die-hard group which Gretton and his followers had kept going in such discouraging circumstances for so long. Within the government, five under-secretaries, Edward Wood, Winterton, and Bridgeman, followed later by Tryon and Peter Pease, approached the chief whip, Leslie Wilson.[37] They informed him that they would be unable to support the government in the debate in the House, unless a joint committee of the Lords and Commons were appointed, to remain in permanent session and to vet the Prime Minister's honours list before it was sent to the King. This evidence of latent erosion in the junior ranks of the government could not be ignored. In the debate in the House on 17 July, Lloyd George was forced to agree to a Royal Commission to inquire into the entire practice of granting honours. He admitted privately to Thomas Jones that he had given scant attention to such recipients as Robinson in the recent past. He told his private secretary, Geoffrey Shakespeare, that he knew little about the methods adopted by the whips in attracting political funds or rewarding the donors.[38]

The government survived the debate with its usual ease. A Royal Commission buried the question. But it had been an awkward crisis; the rumbles of Unionist discontent continued until the session came to a merciful end on 4 August. It was a difficult period for the government. The Coalition Liberals were upset about the duty on fabric gloves. A by-election at Pontypridd on 27 July saw Labour capture the seat with a large swing against the Coalition. Unionist alarm at the renewed disorder in Ireland had been heightened when Field Marshal Sir Henry Wilson (now an Ulster MP) was assassinated by an IRA gunman outside his home in Eaton Place in London. The Unionist under-secretaries remained unhappy and anxious for a greater show of independence by their party. Bridgeman recorded that 'somewhere about this time a strong feeling in the country against the continuance of the Coalition at a general election' encouraged some of the under-secretaries to seek an urgent interview with Austen Chamberlain.[39] Sir Robert 'Peter' Sanders, formerly a chief whip and closely in touch with constituency opinion, was the chief spokesman at a meeting of almost all Unionist junior ministers and non-Cabinet ministers at Austen Chamberlain's room in the Commons on 20 July. Apart from general murmurs of sympathy, this yielded nothing. A further meeting was then held of the junior ministers, headed by Sanders, Bridgeman, Gibbs, Amery, and the two law officers, Pollock and Scott, with all the Unionist members of the Cabinet. This went extremely badly. Chamberlain began with a mild rebuke about the irregularity of the proceedings. Balfour alleged that the junior ministers were calling for Lloyd George's resignation simply because of Coalition Liberal unease about fabric gloves. The temperature was markedly raised by Lord Birkenhead, in whose room the meeting took place. He accused the deputation of timidity in the face of 'a few old die-hard majors'. He went on to give them 'a sort of schoolboy lecture on loyalty'. He berated his old legal associate, the Attorney-General, Sir Ernest Pollock, for 'impropriety and folly'. The junior ministers went off in high anger, against Birkenhead in particular. Bridgeman reflected on how remarkable it was that, of all the Unionist Cabinet ministers, only Leslie Scott should show the least uncertainty about the firmness of his attachment to the Coalition.[40] Certainly Baldwin gave no such indication. This entire ferment, initially sparked off by the trivial issue of the summer honours list, had little organic relation to earlier movements for Tory independence down to the spring of 1922. Yet it left the Conservatives in extreme disarray, their loyalty to their elected leaders, for all their solidarity in defending the cause of Coalition, in quite unusual doubt.

Well before the House reassembled in early October, it was obvious that the partnership which underpinned the Coalition at Westminster was splitting asunder. Sutherland continued to send Lloyd George soothing memorandums about the security of his position.[41] Younger's main support, he claimed, came from those few seats where Central Office paid the expenses. The Industrial Tory group did not support him. Younger was said to be unpopular. At the Constitutional Club, 'he was denounced for every crime in the Calendar, including the making of bad beer and the selling of it in the most miserable tied houses in the trade'. Younger's problem was just 'swollen head'. Sutherland added, 'The Prime Minister's friends regard the Prime Minister as being in a strong position.'

How far Lloyd George gave credence to this emollient and somewhat absurd advice is uncertain. He had always tended to rely on intuition rather than hard information from party workers where elections were concerned; in the past it had invariably worked. It seems clear that electoral prospects were peculiarly remote from his mind now as the Greek–Turkish conflict reached a crisis point in early September and the threat of war with Turkey over Chanak came ever closer. As the Greek cause became militarily more hopeless, so Lloyd George's commitment became more resolute. The well-known Turcophile sympathies of the Conservative rank and file, from Younger downwards, were brushed aside. So was Derby's announcement on 1 September, to the shock of Chamberlain, that he was breaking with the Coalition because of its policy towards Turkey.[42] The evidence was there in abundance that insurrection against the Coalition amongst the Tory rank and file was widespread; Chanak gave them a cause as never before. The chief whip, Leslie Wilson, told Chamberlain that over 180 independent Conservatives would be run against Coalitionist candidates at the forthcoming election. He warned of the growing strength of Lord Salisbury's following. He added, perhaps more ominously, that it was most unlikely that Conservatives would agree to going before the electorate another time on the basis of coalition.[43]

These premonitions were brushed aside by Lloyd George, Chamberlain, Birkenhead, Horne, and Churchill, the dominant voices within the Cabinet. On 17 September it was decided by this inner group to hold an early election to deflect the autumn meeting of the National Union's annual conference and to exploit patriotic sentiment over the crisis with the Turks.[44] Even *The Times* thought that 'the political horizon so far as home affairs are concerned is clearer than it has been for many months'.[45] There was no particular reason why the Cabinet should defer to constituency opinion in the Unionist Party, or consider it to be decisive. The political unity of the Coalition flowed down from the summit. It was imposed at Cabinet level on the party machines, and imposed by the executive on the legislative as during the war years. It drew strength from the imperatives of strong, active government, and from the sectionalism of its various opponents, from Gretton to the ILP. There seemed little to suggest, especially after the happy outcome of the Turkish affair at the Treaty of Mudania, that the government's bellicosity and pro-Greek partisanship would lead to its downfall.

Two events loomed up as decisive in the timing and management of the forthcoming election. The more immediate was a by-election at Newport where an Independent Conservative, Reginald Clarry, was in the field. This was not necessarily a conclusive test for the Coalition, which had brushed aside so many by-election catastrophes over the past four years as the product of an uninformed and volatile public opinion. The Coalition's position in Newport was a weak one. Its supposed candidate was a Liberal, Lyndon Moore, who announced that he would stand 'without prefix or suffix' as an independent; his attachment to the Coalition was most indeterminate. There was a widespread belief that Labour would win the seat, as it had won others in South Wales of late. Later legends made the Newport result the acid test for the future of the Coalition; but it was not decisive at the time. Chamberlain himself magnified Newport into excessive prominence by openly anticipating a Labour victory that would, through the defeat of Clarry, cement the Coalition more firmly together.[46]

The second, and more decisive event, was the forthcoming meeting of the National Union scheduled for 15 November. It was recognized that this would be a difficult occasion for the party leadership, far more so than the meeting at Liverpool held during the talks with Sinn Fein twelve months earlier. Chamberlain evidently intended it to be a forum for calling the rebels to heel and imposing party discipline on his assorted critics. There was a general expectation that it would be the preliminary to an election in which the Coalition partners, while fighting the campaign on a separate but equal basis, would ask for a new lease of power—unless tactical necessity led the government to appeal to the country even before 15 November. With Lloyd George seemingly more firmly in the saddle than ever as a result of the military and naval preparations for the Chanak crisis, and his only conceivable rival, Bonar Law, still unwilling to declare any kind of separate position distinct from that of the Coalition, there seemed little room for doubt that the big battalions would triumph again, if less convincingly than before.

What turned the scales in October 1922 was that for the first time in four years, a sizeable faction within the Cabinet itself moved towards an independent position. This gave the sectaries and secretaries in the Conservative lower ranks a kind of authority and conviction they had never implied in in years of criticism and complaint. On the other hand, there can be little doubt that the government, while its position was becoming more precarious overall, could have withstood even this challenge had it not mishandled the political crisis at every stage. Lloyd George and Austen Chamberlain in a special sense brought about their own downfall, Lloyd George by pushing on with an extreme anti-Turkish policy, culminating in his Manchester speech on 14 October at a point of fanaticism that few Liberals and virtually no Tories could reasonably accept, Chamberlain by an insensitive and over-confident view of his own strength as party leader.

The early discontent in the Cabinet over the Chanak policy had been neutralized. Curzon had certainly been a voice of dissent throughout. He had told the Cabinet that he had doubts about the importance of retaining Chanak at all, and cited public opinion as a decisive force against committing the nation to war. In the event, Mudania was, in part, his diplomatic triumph. There were other members of the Cabinet clearly forming a peace faction, such as Lee of Fareham and Mond. By 7 October they had won their point. The threat of war with Turkey receded; even the Prime Minister acknowledged the permanent presence of the Turks on the European mainland, including most of eastern Thrace, as well as over the whole of

Asia Minor. The two Unionists most disturbed by the Chanak policy were Boscawen, the Minister of Agriculture, and Baldwin, the President of the Board of Trade, one pro-Turk, the other generally pacifist. Neither posed a crucial threat to the government. Boscawen was a somewhat haunted figure during this period, his policy for agriculture in ruins. His private rebellion against the government of which he was a key member was a recent conversion. As recently as 4 August 1922, after the clash between Birkenhead and the junior Unionist ministers, he had written to Pollock sympathetically, declaring his determination to fight for the Coalition. 'I feel myself so strongly', Boscawen wrote then, 'that the Prime Minister is a great national asset and he has been so loyal to us that I could never be a party to any movement against him so long as he desires to remain in his present position.' Chamberlain's position, he added, 'is very difficult but he has earned the sympathy and respect of all of us and we must support him and help him where we can'.[47]

Less than two months later, Boscawen's unwavering loyalty to the Coalition had somehow melted away: of course, the Chanak crisis had intervened and this impressed the mind of an old-fashioned pro-Turk Tory. Even in early October, however, he was more immediately worried about the collapse of farm prices than about the Near East, after the repeal of the subsidies granted to wheat and oats farmers under Part I of the old Corn Production Act. On 10 October, the Cabinet finally turned down his new agricultural proposals (CP 4629) to assist the farmers. Lloyd George, for long a staunch champion of the small farmers, now took a leading part in arguing against help to the farming community either by reduction of their rates or by providing state loans to farmers who had bought farms since the war. Horne and the Treasury were adamant against change, on financial grounds. Above all, the political point was urged that manufacturers, urban shopkeepers, and the Labour movement would see it as 'a dole to landlords' at a time when state assistance had already been refused to urban local authorities and to the miners. Ministers pointedly noted that four-fifths of members of parliament represented urban constituencies. Boscawen wrote to Austen Chamberlain later that day, to offer his resignation even though he stressed that he differed from his colleagues on no other issue.[48] On the 12th, after a private discussion, he abruptly withdrew his resignation. Again, though, Boscawen complained to Chamberlain solely about the needs of the farming community. The hundred and fifty or so agricultural members on the Unionist side had been notably loyal to the government. Fitzroy, Pretyman, Lane-Fox, Townley, Courthope, Spender Clay, Murrough Wilson 'are amongst our best friends'.[49] This was still short of a declaration of revolt, even if such a gesture from the hapless Boscawen would have had any decisive impact.

Nor was Baldwin at the Board of Trade any more bold. His reactions to the crisis were particularly secretive, his options more open than those of any member of the government. His private yearning for 'a cleaner atmosphere' was not publicly unveiled. Then on the morning of the 12th, he declared his difficulty in joining with the other Unionist ministers in following Lloyd George's leadership at another election. Baldwin was now entering upon a severe crisis of conscience. Hitherto he had been another second-ranking member of the administration whose genuine qualms of conscience could be contained with some ease. Pollock was greatly surprised on 16 October to receive a private note from Baldwin declaring that he could no longer accept Lloyd George's leadership.[50]

The collapse of the government occurred quite suddenly and spectacularly in the period 13–19 October. This had nothing directly to do with the sale of honours, nor even with the Turkish crisis. The latter was now over after the agreement at Mudania on the 12th, settled with honour and prudence in the judgement of most ministers, thanks mainly to Curzon. These two issues drew attention to the elements of personal autocracy that governed the Coalition's approach, but were not decisive in themselves. What was crucial now was Chamberlain's insistence that the government must proclaim an early general election, perhaps before the National Union meeting was held. At this, Curzon, Baldwin, and Boscawen came together from 14 October in common agreement that they would resign if the leadership tried to force an immediate election upon them. Against all the omens, Chamberlain pushed on in doctrinaire fashion, behaving with far less finesse than he had done in January when his leader had proposed an election. As Mr. Cowling has written, he and Birkenhead were determined to push their critics into a corner, and this proved fatal.[51] Lloyd George made an extraordinary speech at the Manchester Free Trade Hall on the 14th which combined the usual commitment to Coalition with a ringing declaration of his Liberal faith as instanced by his Gladstonian attitude towards Turkey. Despite this, Chamberlain maintained that the basic structure and policy of the Coalition were no different from before. He had told Birmingham Unionists on the 13th that he remained 'a convinced and unrepentant Coalitionist'.[52] At a meeting on the afternoon of the 16th at the Carlton Club, discontent was widely voiced about the need to hold an early election; complaint came even from previously loyal MPs such as Sir William Bull. Baldwin and Boscawen now made it plain that in that case they would leave the government. In the *Observer*, once regarded as 'Lloyd George's Sunday newspaper', Garvin now called openly for Lloyd George to resign.[53]

The famous 'revolt of the under-secretaries', dormant since July, was now given new life. Later that day, the 16th, at 5.0 p.m., the junior ministers met Chamberlain and were presented with the proposal for an early election. After some indecision, the two law ministers, Leslie Scott and Sir Ernest Pollock, 'capitulated'; but the remainder, led by Amery, insisted that the Unionist Party must go to the country at the next election with its own leaders and its own programme.[54] Baldwin indicated privately that he shared this view. On the other hand, it was agreed that there would be co-operation with like-minded elements in the Liberal Party, and what was put forward was still something less than a complete break with the Coalition. 'A reconstituted Coalition' was what Ormsby-Gore demanded.[55] He also criticized Bonar Law's letter to *The Times* for its threat towards the French. Chamberlain now reacted in even more intemperate fashion. He summoned a meeting for the Carlton Club on the morning of the 19th. At this, all Unionist MPs would attend, and the various dissidents presumably made to toe the line. In reaction, on the 17th the revolt became still more organized. The rebellious under-secretaries, including Bridgeman and Wood, met Baldwin and Boscawen, to draw up a statement to insist that Chamberlain run his party on an independent basis at the next election. A meeting of Pollock, Gilmour, and Wood (representing pro-government, undecided, and anti-government opinion respectively) with Chamberlain on the evening of the 17th failed to obtain any hint of concession from the Unionist leader. Wood then wrote separately to announce his resignation from the government.[56] A group of influential back-benchers, marshalled by Samuel Hoare, and mainly from the party centre, was also brought in. It was now agreed that Chamberlain and the other party leaders would have to be opposed at the Carlton Club. Hoare and thirty associates drafted a motion to the effect that the

Unionists should leave the Coalition forthwith. On the 18th, the National Union executive empowered Younger to call an emergency conference before any snap election were held. It was already clear that the Carlton Club meeting would see a division within Tory ranks on a scale unequalled since 1846.

Nevertheless, the combined forces of two Cabinet ministers (given moral support by Curzon, who, however, as a peer would be ineligible to vote at the Carlton Club), even if added to the majority of junior ministers and a substantial and growing tally of the Unionist Party, still seemed unlikely to prevail against almost every figure of major stature in the party. Loyalty in Tory ranks was a byword. The one imponderable element now was Bonar Law, who spent his time in isolation between 14 and 18 October, after persuading Boscawen earlier not to resign, and after trying to act as mediator between Chamberlain and the junior ministers. Even after his letter to *The Times* on 7 October, with its memorable reference to Britain's acting alone as 'policeman of the world', he refused to commit himself. He talked of resigning his seat and it seemed that he would probably not attend the Carlton Club meeting at all. 'No change—boneless' was Salisbury's verdict after telephoning Law on the 13th. On the other hand, at a private meeting with Lloyd George on 9 October, Law had urged him to bring the government to an end.[57] Much pressure was put on Bonar Law on the 18th as it was clear that his influence would be decisive. Whether the argument put by back-bench rebels, led by Hoare (with whom Law had played tennis), or the personal beguilement of Beaverbrook was the more crucial is not clear. Pollock attributed Law's attitude to his lack of an English public school education![58] More plausibly, it was the sense of the broad range of opponents of the government on the Unionist side, including now former loyalists as Pretyman and Lane-Fox, both discontented agriculturalists. By the evening of the 18th, though, Bonar Law had made up his mind to come to the Carlton Club meeting, though to what end remained uncertain.

On the morning of the 19th, the Carlton Club meeting was buoyed up before it began by the dramatic news of the decisive victory of Clarry, the Independent Conservative, in the Newport by-election, announced during the night. Clearly, this must have reinforced the tide of opinion running against Chamberlain, even though it could not technically be considered a defeat for the Coalition. Lyndon Moore, the Liberal, had disavowed any connection with the government. The election seems to have turned partly on such local issues as Sunday Closing in Monmouthshire which Clarry and Welsh licensed victuallers opposed; no doubt, it was partly a simple reaction against Labour.

At the same time, the actual pattern of the debate at the Carlton Club seems to have played a major part in making the decision of the members assembled there an overwhelming one. The meeting began with a brief statement by Curzon which explained his ineligibility to attend the debate. There followed a singularly ill-judged and inordinately lengthy speech by Austen Chamberlain, quite unbending in giving reasons for keeping the Coalition in being. He left it unclear whether a Coalition would be reconstructed after what he expected to be a victorious election campaign, but the general drift of his argument was that a Coalition, even though somewhat looser in form than in 1919–22, would continue into an indefinite future. Presumably Lloyd George would remain at its head. Once again, Chamberlain's argument relied heavily on the threat from Labour which made it imperative for Liberal and Conservative 'constitutionalists' to cling together to preserve British capitalism. It was a difficult speech to make, but it was badly made nevertheless. Bridgeman, a personal friend of Chamberlain, thought it 'unconvincing'.[59] But, apart from a later intervention by Balfour, it was the only speech made that morning actually in favour of the Coalition's remaining in being. Chamberlain was followed by Baldwin whose brief, but devastating, attack on Lloyd George, as a 'dynamic force' who threatened to split the Conservatives as he had done his own party, made a profound impression, not least as it was recognized that Baldwin had become a pivot in the various movements against the Coalition during the past few days. Significantly enough, there was then moved what was in effect Samuel Hoare's motion in favour of Tory independence. It was moved by Ernest Pretyman and George Lane-Fox, members for Essex and Yorkshire constituencies respectively, both until very recently devoted country supporters of their leaders and in no sense representative of die-hard sentiment. Pretyman had actually moved Chamberlain's election as party leader in March 1921. They were backed up by Mildmay, member for Totnes and again from the party centre, and then by Henry Craik, an extreme die-hard who flayed the government's Indian, Irish, and Egyptian policies in a wild tirade, which, according to Bridgeman, 'no one listened to'[60] and which was quite at variance with the generally restrained and sombre tone of the meeting.

The decisive intervention was that by Bonar Law. Until he spoke, no one present felt sure of the outcome. His speech was 'badly delivered but uncompromising' and 'betrayed the hand of his familiar spirit, Beaverbrook'. Astor was told that the general impression was that it was 'weak'.[61] But the verdict was now assured. Law's statement contained friendly enough comment upon both Chamberlain and Lloyd George. More than most Conservatives, he had sensed that the nature of political priorities had changed since the war. He was far removed from the Ulster extremist partisan of pre-1914. His essential plea, however, was that there was a limit to the price that must be paid for national unity. The break-up of the party was an unacceptable sacrifice, as was the right of the party to be consulted on such key issues as the holding of a general election. Bridgeman commented on the profound impact of his intervention: 'If he had spoken for Coalition I am pretty sure we would not have won.' Before the end, Leslie Wilson, the chief whip, also supported Law, surprising Chamberlain and Pollock by his 'apostasy'.[62] By the large margin of 187 votes to 87, the members of parliament there present voted down the Coalition. Soon afterwards, after a characteristically gay farewell to his private staff at Downing Street, Lloyd George went to Buckingham Palace to tender his resignation.

The fundamental issue now was not whether Lloyd George could retain the support of many Unionist members. It lay in whether Bonar Law would be able to construct a credible and effective government, in the absence of Chamberlain, Horne, Balfour, Birkenhead, Lee of Fareham, Worthington-Evans, Pollock, Scott, Gilmour, C. D. Murray, Mitchell Thomson, and other senior Unionists. Within two days all doubt was cast aside. Law could turn not only to senior ex-ministers such as Curzon and Baldwin, but also others with ministerial experience such as Steel-Maitland, Lloyd-Greame, Bridgeman, and Wood—and also Neville Chamberlain, abroad in Canada at the time of the Carlton Club meeting but for long a declared opponent of the Coalition and one with a loathing of Lloyd George and all his works. In addition, the commitment to independence amongst those who followed Chamberlain was not crystal clear in every case. George Gibbs, after much doubt, resumed his old post in the Household under Bonar Law. Worthington-Evans and Gilmour were two others who gave Bonar Law's new administration their blessing, even if they felt unable to join it. Gilmour actually appeared on a platform with Bonar Law in Scotland.[63] The new government, if unspectacular, was a perfectly respectable body in appearance, and clearly one that had Central Office and the overwhelming mass of party organizers, save for the special case of Liverpool, behind it. Bonar Law at once called the general election that Lloyd George had wanted since Christmas but had been frustrated by the Coalition from achieving. The Bonar Law government heralded in the clearest possible terms the return of political normality, founded on orthodox party machines and rivalries. The main obvious opposition, the Labour Party, was even more clearly a decisive testimony to party independence. While ambiguity continued to shroud both the Liberal and Unionist wings of the former Coalition, it was within a few days transparent that the era of Coalition was irreparably over.

At one level, the political explanation for the downfall of the Coalition on 19 October 1922 may be seen at the level of high political manœuvrings. This is clearly a most important dimension which deserves emphasis. In the vital period between the virtual ending of the Chanak crisis on 12 October and the Carlton Club meeting a week later, the leaders of the Coalition mishandled the issues and the personal relations involved at every stage. On the Unionist side, Chamberlain's insensitive and rash belief that he could crush his variegated critics at the Carlton Club after driving them to the wall was founded on a series of miscalculations. He had even delayed the Carlton Club meeting until the Newport election was known, since, against all reasonable expectation, he anticipated a Labour victory there. He underestimated Baldwin and Boscawen, he underestimated the junior ministers, he grossly underestimated and antagonized the broad-based range of back-bench critics that Hoare had assembled. Like Woodrow Wilson and the League of Nations covenant, when it was debated by the US Senate in 1919–20, Chamberlain would accept no 'reservations', no limitations on the government's right to choose its own election on its own issues in its own time, no limitations on its future strategy and composition. A sensitive party leader (a Baldwin or a Harold Wilson) would never have made such an error, compounded as it was by the offensive behaviour of Birkenhead. For some reason the Lord Chancellor considered himself and his brother Harold as experts on the mood of party workers; he made the rift

between Coalitionists and anti-Coalitionists in the party far more
bitter.

But if Chamberlain's tactical errors were serious ones, Lloyd
George's wayward and almost senseless strategy made Chamberlain's
plight, and his misconceived loyalty, far worse. At least Chamberlain's Birmingham speech on 13 October was addressed to his own
party supporters. Lloyd George's Manchester speech the next day
treated all parties alike as if they barely existed. In the crisis of
Coalition from 2 October onwards, Lloyd George, his judgement
apparently deranged by his aggressive stance over Turkey and the
Near East, followed an erratic and almost meaningless course of
action. At one remove, the Turkish crisis served to emphasize his
Liberal credentials, as shown in his ill-starred Manchester speech.
Grigg, whose sober judgement seems to have been equally upset
during this crisis, saw Lloyd George on the eve of his Manchester
speech, 'chanting war songs with the fire of the crusader burning in his
heart and blazing eyes . . . determined to make the conscience of the
country respond to the policy of peace and humanity'. Lloyd George
reminded Grigg of what he chose revealingly to term 'that delightful
nigger song, "singing with a sword in my hand"'.[64] But it was not
Liberal war chants but something more measured and more appealing
to Tory sentiment that the crisis demanded. On the other hand, Lloyd
George acknowledged that his own Coalition Liberal Party was almost
defunct. More generally, Liberalism itself was 'done for. All the
Liberal side will be represented by Labour,'[65] he told his Liberal
colleagues on 4 October. What comfort they took from these bleak
remarks is not recorded. Talking to C. P. Scott, however, Lloyd
George took the opposite tack, namely that the ministers of the
Coalition represented something beyond Liberalism and a new synthesis compounded of the best of the old party system. Chamberlain, he
told Scott on the 23rd, was 'a Liberal', Balfour 'a democrat', Balfour
'had become a Liberal in his old age like Gladstone'. Horne was the
'son of a Scottish Presbyterian minister—not much of Toryism in
that'. As an added endorsement, 'he was a Gladstonian in finance. He
has resisted all temptations to easy and popular finance.'[66] Scott
rightly concluded that Liberal renunion was impossible, and that he
was 'closely bound to the Conservatives who have stood by him'.
Lloyd George admitted that the great potentates of the old Coalition
had no machinery in the constituencies. The analogy to which he now

turned was that of the Peelites who had supplied the Liberal Party with intellectual reinforcement seventy years earlier.[67] It was a parallel hopelessly irrelevant to the world of organized mass parties in 1922, a comment on his lifelong carelessness about party considerations and intuitive liking for personal connections. He would have done well to recall his own observations on Theodore Roosevelt, an American progressive whose New Nationalism he greatly admired, but who broke fatally away from his own Republican Party in the 1912 presidential campaign. 'He ought never to have quarrelled with the machine.'[68] Lloyd George's updated New Nationalism, British style, left him equally stranded and alone.

His Coalition Liberals perforce had to follow his lead. Only Mond insisted that 'there was no future in clinging to the Tories'. During the subsequent general election campaign, he called for Lloyd George to revert to the radicalism of earlier years with a great campaign in Wales. He should even insist on his Gladstonian credentials and appeal to 'callow Liberal Nonconformists' for having stood up to the Turks at Chanak. This was the more curious as Mond was a well-known member of the 'peace party' in the Cabinet at the time of the Chanak crisis. It probably reflected his own precarious position in Swansea where he faced fierce Tory as well as Labour opposition, partly on anti-Semitic grounds once again.[69] All the other Liberal ministers—Macnamara, Shortt, even Fisher—agreed that they should stay detached but 'should adopt a programme to which our Conservative colleagues can subscribe'.[70] Churchill, still a Liberal in name, also agreed in re-erecting the platforms of the dead Coalition with his own distinctly anti-socialist bias, directed against the ILP challenge from E. D. Morel at Dundee. All this was really a hopeless policy, a blind faith in the non-existent middle ground of Coalitionism which the political earthquake of 13–19 October had destroyed. In following their tactically blind leader down the abyss, the Coalition Liberals chose the certain path of extinction. As the supreme instance of a party of generals with no rank and file, they were the supreme casualties of the out-of-date strategy of 'high politics'.

Clearly, then, miscalculations by the leaders of the Coalition, Chamberlain and above all Lloyd George, played a major part in leading to the rout at the Carlton Club. But a survey of the record of party manœuvrings from Genoa onwards can surely leave one in little doubt that a Unionist revolt against the Coalition would inevitably have arisen as soon as some issue emerged to unite the various factions of discontent. Each crisis—the recognition of Russia, the honours scandal, the confrontation with Turkey—uncovered new layers of disaffection and left the Tory leadership that degree more exposed. Even if Chamberlain had somehow bullied the majority of the party at the Carlton Club into accepting an early election, and into continuing the Coalition for the immediate future, any such government could have no guarantee of stability, especially against a background of over a million and a half unemployed and unresolved crises all over Europe from the Ruhr to Smyrna. There were still important pockets of Coalition support in the land, perfectly respectable and by no means pocket boroughs of the party leadership. Sheffield and Glasgow were major centres of Conservative Coalitionism. In Liverpool, Salvidge kept his cohorts largely in line, their enthusiasm for 'fusion' reinforced by the dramatic surge of Catholic Irish support in Liverpool for the Labour Party. The one Liverpool member in the late government, Leslie Scott, remained faithful to Lloyd George in 1922 and proved a noted apostle of class collaboration throughout the 1920s. The eighty-six Coalitionists who backed Chamberlain were by no means latter-day 'King's Friends', the elderly, or the corrupt. They included figures of intellectual distinction like Sir Philip Sassoon, Sir Philip Magnus, and Sir Halford Mackinder, and rising young men like Walter Elliot and Kingsley Wood. The Oxford University Junior Carlton Club wired Chamberlain its support, though Oxford Tories such as Sir Charles Petrie took the opposite view. But these were pockets only. In the strongest Tory areas of Britain, in London and the home counties still stirred by the cries of 'anti-waste', in the rural strongholds left helpless by Boscawen's failure to provide them with agricultural relief or rating reform, even in Chamberlain's own Birmingham where Steel-Maitland, Amery, Meysey-Thompson (and *in absentia* Neville Chamberlain) had all voted the Coalition down, the flight from the late form of government was irresistible. However tentative Bonar Law's intervention at the Carlton Club had been, his appeal for a patriotism based on party unity rather than on Coalition struck the essential note. So, too, did Baldwin's forthright attack on Lloyd George's personal methods of leadership. In the end, the revolt succeeded in October 1922 because it was so broadly-based, far more so than the various fringe die-hard protests from Amritsar days onwards. The vast majority of the under-secretaries, and of Hoare's back-bench rebels, were loyalists of the party centre. Their shift of allegiance left the former ministers—impressive *en bloc* but including men like Balfour, Birkenhead, and Lee of Fareham utterly detached from the constituencies or grass-roots sentiment—hopelessly isolated. In such circumstances, the belated vengeance of the Tory centrists on Lloyd George and his camp followers was peaceful, inevitable, a revolution as bloodless as its predecessors of 1916 and 1918.

What was the ultimate root cause of the Tory revolt against the Coalition? It was not really that the ethical standards of the late government, symbolized by the quasi-corruption of the Lloyd George fund, shocked decent-minded Broad Churchmen. Nor did the Coalition's policies really excite widespread dissent. The main lines of domestic and foreign policy were by 1922 well in line with Tory expectations; Bonar Law in October 1922 pledged himself largely to continue them. At home, the Geddes economies and the stern front against Labour were profoundly appealing. Abroad, the general policy of peace and disengagement was well in accord with a growing Tory isolationism, though admittedly the very different kind of policy pursued at Chanak was a sobering shock. In the last analysis, what Tories came to want in the spring and summer of 1922 was a reassertion of the autonomy of party, for its own sake. That key decisions over the calling of an election or the renewing of the framework of a bipartisan Coalition should be imposed on the rank and file by a distant and arrogant leadership, at the behest of the foremost opportunist in British politics, seemed disturbing, even immoral. Austen Chamberlain and other ministers, doughty partisans themselves in pre-war days and fiercely hostile to Lloyd George's own coalition scheme in 1910, had come to believe in the evolution of a corporate style of government in which the logic of policy would cause the organization of the traditional parties to transform themselves of their own accord. By October 1922, it seemed inevitable to men such as Chamberlain and Horne that a broad unity over policy decision-making should flow into electoral decision-making as well. For generations, to quote Raikes in the 1870s, Conservative Party machinery had been the 'handmaid' to the party leadership. Still more so would it be subservient when that leadership was invested with the special aura of unity inherited after the war and confirmed during the cumulative crises of the post-war years. But to orthodox party men, which

Bridgeman and Hoare, Ormsby-Gore and Pretyman basically were, their party had its own historic traditions, moral values, and personal loyalties. As Hoare's manifesto put it on 16 October, 'the vital need is not so much to form a government as to keep the party united'. Significantly, every major figure in the party organization present at the Carlton Club—Younger, Leslie Wilson, Sanders, Steel-Maitland, Shirley Benn—all voted against the Coalition.[71] Party embodied the essential virtues of a sectional world. It had only undergone suspended animation from December 1918. It was permanently in being, ready for instant resurrection. High policy and national unity were not what politics was basically about. The true Tory, like the committed socialist, flourished on the partisanship and sectionalism of a divided society. It might at worst lead to class hostility and renewed party warfare which might again drain away the national energies as in 1910–14. At best, perhaps it was the surest guarantee of democracy. By viewing party autonomy as the key both to social cohesion and to political liberty, as Burke had done a century and a half earlier, the Conservatives reasserted their independence. They tore down the remaining prop from a construct of consensus and unity which growing class consciousness and national isolationism had been long undermining. The New Tories appealed successfully to the Old. At the Carlton Club on 19 October 1922, British politicians once again happily adjusted their sights to a more parochial but more reassuring world.

15

Farewell to Unity

'The Coalition is Dead. Long Live the Coalition' was McCurdy's almost valedictory pronouncement on the fall of the Lloyd George government.[1] In fact, those who believed in life after death in this connection were few indeed. Those who desired such intimations of immortality were fewer still. The Coalition fell generally unlamented, amidst a sense that political loyalties had been normalized and the political atmosphere purified. It is a striking commentary on the mood of 1922 that, after the fall of Lloyd George, in sharp contrast to the mood after the fall of Churchill in 1945, the idea of coalition became markedly unpopular. Whereas after 1945 the vast majority of Conservative and Labour leaders looked back on their partnership during five years of wartime coalition as a time of creative, even noble, achievement in which they could take legitimate pride, the survivors of 1922 mostly viewed the previous four years with embarrassment. The difference was, of course, that the resumption of party and sectional conflict after 1918 had taken place largely within the framework of the Coalition, which served to discredit the very idea of unity, whereas after 1945 the resumption of party politics, from the moment victory was achieved in Europe, left the previous memories of coalition intact and undefiled. The very idea of national unity on the pattern of wartime collaboration was devalued after 1918, as was the political leader most personally associated with it.

It took just over a year for the legacy of the fall of the Coalition to be purged, and its survivors set free for party conflict once again. Bonar Law at once called a general election for November 1922, one in which the heirs of the Lloyd George government were inevitably in a vulnerable position. Resumed party strife between free Conservatives, Labour, and Independent Liberals left the pockets of centrists in control only of a middle ground that was steadily shrinking. At the election, there were two main categories of survivors. The more numerous were the old Coalition Liberals, National Liberals as they were now christened. Bonar Law tactfully managed to give them a free run in most constituencies, by removing the threat of any Conservative opponents. But they faced problems enough since the main Coaly Lib strongholds had been in industrial seats in South Wales, the North of England, and Scotland, where the challenge of Labour was most fierce. The National Liberals fought a half-hearted and irrelevant campaign in 1922. Their leader was disengaged in mind, his ideas still riveted on the analogies of the Peelites seventy years earlier, his speeches proclaiming the eternal values of a Coalition that had obviously ceased to exist. In the election campaign, the National Liberal machine was a disorganized affair, with disagreeable individuals who deterred a high-minded temporary recruit to National Unionist ranks like John Reith.[2] Lord Rothermere's expectation that Lloyd George could put up two hundred candidates soon collapsed. The National Liberals expected to suffer heavy casualties, and they did. Their parliamentary representation fell by over half, from about 130 to only 55. The fallen included Greenwood, Guest, Kellaway, and, most spectacularly of all, Churchill, defeated at Dundee by the twin assault of the ILP and a Prohibitionist, and in any case removed from the fray after an appendix operation. Throughout the campaign, the National Liberals cut a somewhat pathetic picture, with their leader adopting a variety of erratic positions from constituency to constituency. In general, the main line was to give independent support to the new Conservative government, though this was far from wholly reciprocated. Younger, unlike Bonar Law, resisted any blanket pact with the National Liberals, and over 35 of them in the end faced Conservative opponents at the polls. Over thirty of them in fact were defeated by Conservatives and only in Wales did they manage to hang on to seats in the face of Tory opposition. In the circumstances, to hold on to over fifty seats was a meritorious achievement. It was at least a useful bargaining counter for Lloyd George. But it did not erase the impression that the National Liberals were now a rootless personal connection in search of a viable political role.

The lot of former Coalition Unionists who remained true to their previous professions was even unhappier. Once Bonar Law had gained a clear majority at the polls, they faced a difficult and uncertain future. The fact that they included such figures as Austen Chamberlain, Worthington-Evans, and Horne, with backing from Birkenhead, Balfour, and Lee of Fareham in the Lords, did not make their impact any more substantial. They were not a homogeneous group in attitude. It was known that Worthington-Evans, for example, had given his blessing to the new Bonar Law government. He had pledged himself never again to serve under Lloyd George except under the inconceivable circumstances of the majority of the Conservative MPs declaring their support for him.[3] There was nothing remotely resembling a mass movement of Coalition Conservatives. Even in Liverpool, their strong citadel, Salvidge, whose attachment to Chamberlain did not waver throughout the 1922 campaign, had the mortification of noting that virtually all the local Conservatives elected declared their support for Bonar Law. The sole exception was Leslie Scott in the Exchange division who in any case was mainly pre-occupied with fighting off the challenge of Devlin, the Irish National-ist. Almost half of the 87 who voted for a continuation of the Coalition at the Carlton Club meeting went out of politics entirely or else were defeated at the polls. Nothing remotely like the mass schism that had torn the Liberals apart after 1918 seemed possible. The Unionist minority of MPs, numbering barely fifty after the polls, seemed doomed to the impotence of an isolation created for themselves out of past loyalties and present pride.

Throughout the session of 1923, during which first Bonar Law and then Baldwin grappled no more successfully with the external and domestic problems left by the Coalition, the two surviving groups, the National Liberals and the independent Conservatives, cut off from their historic roots and acting quite separately from one another, looked around for a credible and worthwhile role. Throughout the first half of 1923, there were a series of back-bench moves, prompted by Hogge among others, to try to unite the two Liberal parties in the House, but by the summer recess nothing had been achieved. The memories of recent party infighting were too fresh. In any case Lloyd George's followers gave general support to the Conservative administration while deploring its 'weakness' in foreign policy such as Baldwin's expensive settlement of the American debt, or Curzon's making peace with the Turks at Lausanne. The emergence of Baldwin as Conservative Prime Minister in May 1923 made Liberal reunion much more likely. His very presence, as a leading agent of the split in October 1922, made nonsense of any talk of a common front between the Conservatives and any group headed by Lloyd George.

Once Baldwin entered Downing Street, Lloyd George made a series of speeches which re-emphasized his Liberal credentials, including his lifelong devotion to free trade. They were a clear prelude to party reunion. Moves in various constituencies, notably in Wales, heralded a fusion of the Lloyd Georgian and Asquithian factions, who, between them, could claim over 120 MPs. The process was completed in October–November while Lloyd George was abroad on a highly lucrative lecture tour in the United States. There were rumours that he might return and offer a new alliance to dissident Conservatives on the basis of an imperial preference scheme, though no direct evidence for this widely held belief has ever been unearthed. In any case, Baldwin did Lloyd George's work for him. After consulting very few colleagues, he declared for protection of the home market in a speech at Plymouth on 26 October. This at once reunited the two Liberal armies in defence of free trade. Soon after Lloyd George's return from the United States on 9 November, a joint committee of Liberals, including Asquith and Simon, Lloyd George and Mond, hammered out a joint election manifesto, and agreed to fight as a united party all over the country. Only in Camborne and Cardiganshire in the distant Celtic fringe (where in each case rival Liberal candidates fought each other) was reunion not achieved. Such embarrassing legacies as the Lloyd George Fund were discreetly forgotten. So the Coalition Liberals once more became party regulars. Their help was worth having. They included considerable grass-roots strength in Scotland and Wales; they included some able young politicians like Archibald Sinclair and Leslie Hore-Belisha as well as major figures like Mond, Macnamara, Fisher, Grigg, and Hilton Young. Churchill was still officially recorded as a Liberal during his unsuccessful campaign to win Leicester in the December 1923 election. There was the Lloyd George fund as a potential crock of gold. And, of course, Lloyd George himself was recognized as still the dominant inspiration for Liberals everywhere, supplying a dynamism and originality that the tired ranks of the Asquithian leadership could not match.

Coalition Liberalism, then, died in December 1923. Its separate organization and publications such as the *Lloyd George Liberal Magazine* were wound up. But the Coalition Liberal ethos survived, and took the revealing form of a steady drift to the right by most of the more prominent Coalitionists who remained in Liberal ranks. The anti-socialist Constitutional Party, briefly flourished in 1923–4 and claimed such ex-ministers as Hamar Greenwood and, for a time, Churchill before he entered the Baldwin Cabinet in October 1924 as a formally enrolled Conservative. Freddie Guest and Hilton Young had pacts with Conservatives in their constituencies. By 1929, Mond and Hilton Young had joined the Conservatives, after fierce disputes with Lloyd George over his land reform programme. McCurdy was enlisted as a propagandist for Lord Beaverbrook's Empire Free Trade crusade. Even Edward Grigg, for long Lloyd George's devoted associate, 'heart and soul for Lloyd George' while member for Oldham in 1922–5,[4] also moved right and became a National Liberal in 1931 after a period as governor of Kenya. In the difficult passages for the parliamentary Liberal Party during the second minority Labour government of 1929–31, Lloyd George's commitment to support the Labour government led to further defections from old-time Liberals identified with the Coalition cause including Geoffrey Shakespeare, Sir Robert Hutchinson, and Leslie Hore-Belisha. Their dominant memory of the Coalition era was the anti-Labour rhetoric of 1920. Labour for them was still 'unfit to govern' even after two attempts with Liberal support. The decline of National Liberalism from a broad centrist movement into a small anti-socialist rump marked the final demise of the Liberal element contained within the fabric of national unity between 1918 and 1922. The one significant exception to the rule was Christopher Addison who, alone of this group, joined Labour. He held high office in 1930–1 under MacDonald and even higher office in 1945–51 under Attlee whose close confidant he became. Addison alone kept the 1918 flag of Reconstruction aloft as his old comrades-in-arms drifted into oblivion.

Coalition Conservatism had an even more brief duration. Austen Chamberlain regarded the new Bonar Law government in 1922–3 with immense scorn; it was a second-eleven team clearly out of its depth. He told Lee of Fareham in February 1923 that they should keep aloof from the government and let it wallow in its own mistakes.[5] On paper, he could count on up to fifty supporters in the Commons and the Lords, and was still a major element in a fluid party situation, with five groups coexisting after the November 1922 general election. Had Curzon become Prime Minister in May 1923 the Chamberlain group would have had more leverage and been able to declare terms to the new party leader as the price for unity. Baldwin's emergence ruined all that: it made the Conservative reunion as inevitable as the

Liberal. There had already been breaks in ranks. Early in 1923 Walter Elliot and F. C. Thompson had accepted office under Bonar Law. Then in May, Worthington-Evans was offered the Cabinet office of Postmaster-General by Baldwin. He wrote to Chamberlain saying that he felt he ought to accept: 'I stood out last time because I would not throw over Lloyd George or act contrary to the advice you gave the Party and because I was not satisfied with B.L.'s action towards you, but Lloyd George is now bent on reuniting the Liberal Party, and in the nature of things will soon be attacking this government.' He pointed out that he, Horne, Sassoon, Birkenhead, and Locker-Lampson had collectively agreed that Chamberlain should lead the party in the Commons if Curzon became premier; but this was now irrelevant.[6] Chamberlain did not demur, although complaining that he was himself 'under no illusions as to my unpopularity with the Die-Hards who are in the ascendant in the management and councils of the Party. . . . I think indeed that I am as much out of favour for having held my tongue as F.E. for having made speeches.'[7] As it happened, Baldwin came very close to offering Chamberlain cabinet rank as Lord Privy Seal, but was vetoed by Amery and some others. This move would certainly have brought back Horne and conceivably Birkenhead as well. In fact, Baldwin mishandled an interview with Chamberlain disastrously. Chamberlain, who had rushed back from holiday expecting to be offered high Cabinet office was presented with the prospect of going to the British embassy in Washington instead.[8] He left in high dudgeon, and for a moment the isolation of the independent Conservatives was more pronounced than ever.

It would not in the nature of things last long. Baldwin's Plymouth speech that October in favour of protection of the home market was obviously aimed at party unity. Chamberlain, who had kept closely in touch with Horne, Pollock, Scott, Bull, Chilcott, and Locker-Lampson as a hard core of ex-Coalitionists,[9] at once announced his enthusiastic desire to patch up old quarrels. The Conservative Party fought the December 1923 general election on a united basis, albeit unsuccessfully. When the election of October 1924 saw Baldwin returned to power with a large majority, Chamberlain went to the Foreign Office, Worthington-Evans to the War Office, Birkenhead (amidst general misgivings) to the India Office, and Gilmour to the Scottish Office. The major potentates had been rewarded, with the conspicuous exception of Horne who had expected the Treasury but found that mighty portfolio going to a newly acquired recruit, the ex-Coalition Liberal, Winston Churchill, instead. Lee of Fareham, now a figure of minor consequence, reflected, rather unfairly, that 'Austen never did have much punch or drive about getting things done for his colleagues or followers.'[10] Horne then faded away as a senior back-bench figure, consulted as a key adviser during the financial crisis of August 1931, but thereafter a figure in isolation during the years of National government. For Austen Chamberlain, as for almost all his followers of two years earlier, the world of party was now the only loyalty that counted.

In these circumstances, the politics of post-1924 were a reaction in stark form against the former Coalition. The presence of Baldwin and MacDonald at the head of the two major parties ensured that, quite apart from the logic of the separation that had taken place in 1922–4. The only conceivable stirrer of the embers of Coalition was the ever volatile Lloyd George.[11] At various times in the 1920s, he seemed to meditate an approach to Labour on the pattern of the Progressive alliance of pre-1914. He supposedly had negotiations with Mr. and Mrs. Snowden along these lines in 1926 following the defeat of the General Strike and the marked anti-trade union reaction that Baldwin's government then displayed.[12] But at times, too, the grand old memories of the post-1918 Coalition came flooding back. With the assistance of friendly press associated such as Garvin in the *Observer* and the Rothermere press, feelers were put out about some kind of centrist movement to present an alternative to an allegedly socialistic Labour Party and Baldwin's static and uninspiring regime. In 1928 and 1929 there were rumours that some such move was afoot, with Rothermere directly implicated.[13] In February 1929 Lloyd George had a 'very secret' talk with Churchill,[14] now somewhat discontented within the Baldwin government after the failure of his schemes for rating reform—and the likely prospect that Neville Chamberlain was overtaking him as second-ranking figure in the party to Baldwin. It was agreed that if the Conservatives were returned as the second largest party after the next election, they should approach the Liberals, whose leader Lloyd George again was. A compromise programme was sketched out, including tariff reform, no tariffs on basic commodities, and the reconstruction of the government to tackle unemployment somewhat on the lines of the Liberals' Yellow Book.

These murmurings were never conveyed to Baldwin. Had they

been they would assuredly have met with as short shrift from the Tory rank and file as the proposed Lib–Lab alignment would have done on the Labour side. Even after Labour's return at the 1929 general election, with the Liberals having again agreed to give it conditional support in the Commons, Lloyd George was again talking of a 'working understanding' between Liberals and Conservatives, lest 'the socialists be in for at least 7 years'.[15] But these combinations, which Lloyd George could invent by the score, were simply out of date. Conservative disaffection with Baldwin was already being siphoned off by Beaverbrook's Empire Free Trade movement. The prospect of a centrist alliance with the Liberals was once again an anachronism. Churchill became increasingly as obsessed with the highly un-Liberal cause of resistance to Indian nationalism as he had been with anti-Bolshevism ten years earlier. Lloyd George now moved closer to Labour; in June 1931 there was a real prospect of his entering Mac-Donald's Cabinet.[16] When a government of 'National' pretensions was put together in August 1931 it was the work of the critics of the old post-war Coalition, Baldwin and MacDonald. In addition, Hoare, Wood, Neville Chamberlain, all important figures in the revolt against the Coalition in October 1922, played key roles. No major ex-Coalitionist was included. Birkenhead was dead, Horne forgotten, Churchill isolated over India, Chamberlain deliberately kept out. The coalition of 1931 was largely a movement of party leaders designed to expunge memories of the Coalition of 1918. Lloyd George, just as much as the Labour Party, was by definition to be excluded. There were no supra-party figures now, no political businessmen or *manqué* academics. It was a ramp not of the bankers but of the party regulars. It was national unity deliberately conceived from a narrow perspective, with keeping Labour and Lloyd George out as the key to the restoration of national solvency. The contrast with the more broad-based 'unity' of 1918 was very apparent. In 1931, as in 1922, Lloyd George was relegated to the shadows. Even for one with his sanguine belief in political immortality, the prospect of resurrection now had surely departed for ever.

It is not surprising that the politicians of the 1922–40 period should have wanted to obliterate the post-war Coalition from their minds. Without necessarily endorsing the 'rule of the pigmies' interpretation of these years, it is possible to see the essential role of the politicians then as to keep the giants of 1918–22 at bay, Lloyd George and

Churchill above all, and to preserve at all costs the regime of the party regulars. Baldwin, Hoare, and Neville Chamberlain were still fighting the memories of the post-war Coalition in 1935 when they manœuvred to keep Lloyd George out of the National government and to have the civil servants undermine the arguments behind his public works and other 'New Deal' schemes to generate new employment and economic recovery. They were still fighting the legacy of Coalition in May 1940 when desperate attempts were made, after the Norway debate, first to retain Neville Chamberlain as Prime Minister, then to elevate Halifax whom, indeed, many Labour men at first preferred. Moves later that year to bring Lloyd George into Churchill's government, with the backing of such survivors of 1916 as Garvin and Grigg, foundered upon the same implacable memories.

Every major stream of opinion flowing through British political life from the early 1920s represented a reaction against the Coalition and all its works. The Labour Party was the heir both of the trade union solidarity of the era of Black Friday and of the critique of post-Versailles foreign policy launched by E. D. Morel and the Union of Democratic Control. The safe Conservatism which dominated British politics down to 1945, with its powerful suburban, middle-class base, stemmed from the tide of sentiment in favour of party autonomy in the 1920–2 period, with overtones of business efficiency that dated from 'anti-waste'.

In between, the Liberal Party, with much reason, regarded itself as the major victim of the 'coupon' and of Lloyd George's manœuvres in 1918–22. Naturally, its spokesmen in the intellectual and journalistic worlds spent much energy exorcizing the dead demon of Coalition. The fact that many of the former Liberal critics of that era—Keynes, Henderson, Layton, Robbins among them—flocked to join Lloyd George in devising new schemes to promote economic recovery in the later 1920s did not moderate the fervour with which Independent Liberals, far beyond the Asquith family entourage, denounced the phase of high politics which had reduced them to impotence. This went beyond hostility towards Lloyd George personally, though that was venomous enough. At least after August 1931 Labour could focus on a small handful of men, MacDonald, Snowden, and Thomas above all, who had betrayed them. The party machine, the unions, the vast mass of grass-roots Labour sentiment in the constituencies, were united in denouncing their traitorous leader. The divisions wrought partly by Lloyd George in Liberal ranks after 1918 were far more fundamental, not least the way in which the Coalition had confused the Liberal ethic and had enabled Lloyd George and his supporters to deny that their government had in any respect departed from Liberal principles of peace, retrenchment, and reform. Hence the destructive introspection which tortured the Liberal mind during the immediate post-war years, which found release only in turning on the spectre of Coalition as the *fons et origo* of the downfall of Liberalism.

It is not surprising that political partisans, and their successors after 1945, should have responded to the immediate post-1918 period in this fashion. It is not surprising either that cross-party movements such as the 'Next Five Years' movement headed by Harold Macmillan in the mid-1930s should have concentrated on being an intellectual and ideological pressure-group rather than a kind of centrist 'popular front' on Lloyd Georgian lines. Its named supporters did include old Coalitionists like Herbert Fisher and George Barnes, but its composition and purpose were really quite different.[17] What is more surprising is the failure of many historians and political commentators far removed from these partisan controversies to examine the post-war Coalition with any seriousness. Those few who have done so, for example Charles Mowat in his magisterial survey of inter-war Britain, tended to become excessively partisan the other way, in using the Coalition of 1918-22 as a starting-point for abuse of the 'pigmies and second-class brains' who allegedly governed Britain between 1922 and 1940.[18] As a consequence, they provoked an even more powerful reaction against the Lloyd George Coalition, with the result that men like Baldwin and Neville Chamberlain have lately emerged with even more titanic and unreal stature.

It would be indeed foolish to press the case for the Lloyd George peacetime Coalition too strongly. Its policies, especially in relation to unemployment and to Franco–German relations, were in extreme disarray when it left office. There were desperately dark passages such as the policy of reprisals adopted during the 'troubles' in Ireland. The later reversal of this policy with the unexpectedly generous Free State Treaty hardly removed the sense of disgust felt by wide sections of British opinion, from Lord Hugh Cecil to John Maclean and the British Socialist Party, at the atrocities committed in the name of the British government. Its Irish policy seriously diminished the quality of the Coalition government, even when due allowance is made for the counter-violence of the IRA and its over-romanticized leader, Michael Collins. The Coalition finally fell from office after a series of policies in the Near East, culminating in the Chanak crisis, which deprived Britain of every major ally in Europe and the Empire, policies which were full of duplicity and quite unrelated to Britain's commercial or strategic needs. The apparent belief of Lloyd George, Birkenhead, and Churchill that Chanak would create a 'jingo' mood favourable for a popular 'khaki' general election compounded their follies, and they deserved to suffer the supreme political penalty.

The Coalition years were not a halcyon period for British public life. It was not an encouraging time to be a radical, still less a socialist, in the face of the anti-Bolshevist rhetoric being pumped out from Cabinet ministers downwards. It was probably a distasteful time to be a conventional, decent-minded Conservative as well. But there is something to be put on the other side, and that has too seldom been considered, especially by those anxious to chastise Lloyd George's last phase in politics.

The post-war Coalition, of course, entered upon a peculiarly difficult inheritance. It came to power when Britain's financial position had been severely shaken with the loss of investment income through the sale of overseas assets and the accumulation of a National Debt of unprecedented scale. Britain's defence position had been transformed with the acknowledged ending of a century of naval supremacy. At the same time, there were imperial commitments acquired during the war and at Versailles, especially in the Middle East, which strained British military, naval, and financial resources still further. The changing energy pattern, with oil beginning to displace coal for industrial and naval purposes, added another tier of economic and strategic difficulties. Britain's naval mobility, based on coal, was disappearing: oil-fuelling bases at Singapore, Colombo, and Aden were now required. At home, there were the indisputable signs of economic run-down and mass unemployment in the staple industries of the economy, with the growth of infinitely more powerful and class-conscious trade unions in the older industrial regions, fiercely resistant to technological change and understandably hostile to governments or capitalist employers who proposed them. More generally, the war had brought about a profound social dissolution, bringing into prominence new groups such as organized labour, dissolving old loyalties to church, region, or community. This left the morale of the governors of the old society in disarray, poised between an apprehensive middle-class salariat whose status seemed to be in decline and an aggressive proletariat whose economic prospects had marginally improved.

The government of 1918—any government—would have had to adjust to a major crisis in the national psychology as the unknown, unquantifiable effects of total war worked to the surface. Any administration that tried to reassert the imperatives of national unity in this period of exceptional flux faced immense difficulties.

In the end, the Coalition failed to do so. Its vision of national unity became distorted and out-dated. It was undermined throughout the 1920–2 period by the growing sectionalism of class and of party by a nation which felt most secure in living on its conflicts and divisions. It was constrained by bureaucratic inertia and economic orthodoxy within the civil service. But in the interim, some steps were taken which played a valuable part in the hurricane that struck the European continent after 1929. The Coalition sought to effect a compromise between stability and change. It was genuinely felt that its purpose was to conserve the fabric of British government and of financial and commercial institutions, but through a strong, active government and in some key areas through radical change. Enough was achieved here to provide a platform on which Conservative and Labour governments after 1922 could take their stand. The policies of social reform begun by Addison and other apostles of reconstruction after 1918 were not wholly nullified by inertia in the Ministry of Labour or elsewhere in the civil service, nor by the economies imposed by the axe of Geddes. By providing a wider range of interventions by central government, especially in education and subsidized housing, it launched some vital new initiatives. Alone of the post-war governments in Europe or North America, that elected in Britain sought to make social reform foremost amongst its priorities. That it finally succumbed to the pressures of the Treasury and to deflationist finance is not surprising. The accepted wisdom of the day decreed such a course, while the broad international origins of the economic crisis, stemming from the collapse of domestic and overseas demand, defied immediate remedy by any government.

In any case, the Coalition government's handling of these intractable economic difficulties, which have plagued successive Chancellors in the six decades since the First World War, was not, perhaps, so deplorable. Governments prior to 1940 were relatively primitive in their economic and statistical equipment. There was no economic section of the Cabinet. There were no techniques for measuring aggregate demand, for providing reliable indices of taxation and expenditure, or enabling the budget to be used as the key regulator of the economy in the manner familiar in the post-Keynes era. Still, the Coalition weathered the financial tempests of 1920–2 reasonably well: indeed, in the 'pump-priming' schemes aired at Gairloch it was comparatively adventurous. Its monetary policy was not inflexible. The severe deflation and high interest rates of 1920–1, largely caused by concern for the reserves and the need to return to gold, were corrected. They had, in any event, been endorsed by Keynes himself at the time: in February 1920 he urged Chamberlain to administer 'a swift and severe dose of dear money' as a corrective to inflationary speculation.[19] In close collaboration with the New York Federal Reserve Bank, interest rates were brought down steadily from April 1921, with bank rate being lowered to 3 per cent in July 1922, the lowest point of the decade. Sterling was remarkably strong in the foreign exchange market throughout 1922, even when American prices stopped falling. At the time of the downfall of the Coalition, the dollar exchange rate had risen to $4.47. Bankers on both sides of the Atlantic assumed that sterling could safely return to gold at the rate of $4.86 as soon as reparations and inter-Allied debts were cleared up. In addition, the balance of payments was generally strong, despite capital outflows resulting from foreign loans. In 1922 there was a surplus of £201m on the current account, thanks to a large surplus of £264m from 'invisibles' such as freight and insurance.[20] Never again in the entire inter-war period would there be so cheerful a picture; indeed, there was to be more often than not a large deficit. The prevailing mood in late 1922 was one of restrained optimism. Stock exchange prices rallied sharply; industrial production showed a steady recovery that was maintained for some years to come. By the time the Coalition government fell from office, the financial and exchange system, if not the 'real economy' as measured by domestic capital formation, was distinctly on the mend.

The challenge of labour was met with a variety of responses by the Coalition. Many of them, especially on the part of Lloyd George, were undeniably belligerent. Even so, in view of the range of options available to the post-war government, its reaction to labour militancy was relatively subdued and civilized. Some effort was made to harness the wartime power of the trade unions to constructive purpose, and to deflect labour–employer confrontations away from dogmatic controversies over nationalization to areas where collaboration could take place: the railways are, of course, the leading example here. Certainly, one legacy of the era of Coalition was a confirmed distrust of central government on the part of the unions. This is a comment in part on the defensive psychology of the TUC, anxious to cling on to the economic gains of the war rather than to re-shape or modernize the economy. In part it reflects the peculiarly tragic circumstances of the coal-mining industry which infected other, more tranquil, industries with its poison of embittered folk memories and of capitalist inhumanity. On the other side, it might be noted that an explosive confrontation between labour and the government, widely foretold by observers from Joynson-Hicks to Lenin, did not take place. There was no general strike and, except for the brief period of mid-April 1921, no serious sign of one. The Triple Alliance crumbled away as the loose, ill-defined alignment it was. There was no punitive legislation against trade unions, as Tory back-benchers like Colonel Meysey-Thompson wanted in 1922, and as they were to achieve in 1927 under a weaker administration after the General Strike. There was no organized para-military or civil strike-breaking apparatus created by the government. What was set up, in the form of the OMS, was a kind of minimum framework for maintaining services and supplies in the case of a nationwide industrial dispute, under civil service direction, and as unprovocative as possible. It was not glorious but it played its part in dampening down the passions of class conflict for the rest of the decade (despite the General Strike) and in keeping some kind of dialogue in being between successive governments and the representatives of hundreds of thousands of embittered, exploited working men and women.

In foreign affairs, the Coalition was seen at its most adventurous. Alone of the post-war governments in Europe or North America, it sought an active, dynamic foreign policy. It tried to reconcile Franco–German rivalries, to assuage fears of the French for their national security, to reduce to credible proportions German reparations payments, and to bring the great pariah, the Soviet Union, into the international community. From Versailles to Genoa, Lloyd George sought to give Britain a creative role of leadership, appropriate for a major victorious power which was not, like France, paralysed by the impact of physical catastrophe and the Pétain mentality, and which had not, like the United States, defaulted on its international responsibilities. Lloyd George, with the assistance of Horne and most of the Unionists in the government, felt that these matters were organically linked to Britain's economic recovery, especially in the search for stable markets and for regularized exchanges, based ultimately on gold, between the major powers. Here again, the Coalition had no decisive achievement to show. Nationalist rivalries, chauvinist sentiments, the dead hand of American isolationism were too much for it. Lloyd George found at Genoa that he could not do it all on his own. Wickham Steed and Northcliffe, with their disloyal sniping and irresponsible reporting, he could cope with. Poincaré, Rathenau, Chicherin, Kemal, and Warren Gamaliel Harding, in their various fashions, were insuperable. For all that, the quest for world peace was not an ignoble one. At least, the Coalition did wind up the intervention in Russia, and the attendant threat of international war; it reduced tension between France and Germany at a critical period, foreshadowing the later 'spirit of Locarno'; it created some basis for that new, revised view of the peace treaties for which Keynes had so eloquently called, a revision which later British governments felt it impossible to attempt. Lloyd George was succeeded by appeasers of a more passive school, but that was hardly his fault. It was, indeed, a direct legacy of post-war neo-isolationism compounded of the writings of Keynes and the UDC, and of the Little Englandism of Turcophile Tories, which helped overthrow the government in October 1922. Elsewhere, by pursuing a relatively restrained and sympathetic policy towards nationalist movements in Egypt and India, by withdrawing military detachments from Persia and Mesopotamia, albeit very slowly, the Coalition made its contribution to a peaceful world—and, through the Washington conference, a disarmed world as well. Abroad as at home, it had helped towards a change of attitude which offered some prospects of a future free from war.

The strength and weakness of the Coalition was that it relied on policy and decision-making. Far from being consumed by high politics and manœuvrings in which policies were projected as so many ploys or bribes to beguile a range of floating political interests, the government intended to govern. The public records of this period do not make any sense unless it is accepted that broad policy objectives were constantly in view. Lloyd George, Churchill, Birkenhead, in the end even Austen Chamberlain, came to believe that, given firm government, conceived from a supra-party perspective, popular support would necessarily follow. Perhaps significantly, the word 'bipartisan' first entered the language in 1920. The Coalition certainly did not undermine democratic institutions in Britain. On the contrary, its leading figures went to great lengths to placate parliament, to preserve civil liberties, and to allow the clash of public debate to flow unheeded.

How sensible it is to compare the British experience with that of other major nations in the post-war period may be questioned. In Germany and Italy, the outcome of the war was a massive reaction against liberal parliamentary forms of government, with weak and ineffective legislatures and extra-constitutional authority exercised by the army or unofficial *squadristi*. The roots of the later totalitarian dictatorships of Hitler and Mussolini were already discernible in October 1922. On the other hand, Germany's experiment with liberalism dated only from 1919 while the Kingdom of Italy had for fifty years been a byword for political instability and social confusion. France, perhaps a more useful comparison with Britain, witnessed savage street fighting and industrial violence in 1919–20. It emerged from the post-war period politically and socially divided as never before, with the structure of the Third Republic even more frail, the *Cartel des Gauches* in full retreat, and the largest Communist Party in western Europe as testimony to the unbridgeable divisions within French society. Even the United States, scarred by the 'red scare' mentality of Attorney-General Mitchell Palmer and by the vigorous extension of espionage and sedition legislation, was no haven of liberal democracy in 1919–20. It entered the 1920s steeped in isolationism and in socio-political conservatism, the gains of Wilson's New Freedom thrown away, liberals and socialists in full flight with only La Follette's unavailing campaign as 'Progressive' candidate for the presidency in 1924 as a temporary refuge. Legacies of the war years included a resurgence of the Ku Klux Klan, prohibition, and nativist restrictions on immigration to America of non-'Teutonic' stock. By comparison with these other countries, Britain's democracy survived the post-war years in good fettle. Its government had genuinely attempted to maintain vigorous decision-making with a full range of institutions making for public accountability. The Coalition's vision of 'reconstruction' was always conceived within the accepted democratic framework, with non-political organizations such as the trade unions and the FBI brought in. The depoliticization of the British army, the low profile of the British police, the dissolution of paramilitary groups such as the Black and Tans were confirmed. The fact that British parliamentary democracy survived the economic holocaust of the 1930s in such good order, with no-one more dangerous than Oswald Mosley threatening to undermine it, owes much to the discretion and calm judgement of those who governed it in these difficult crisis years of 1918 to 1922.

The Coalition fell not because it had governed badly, certainly not because it had been immoral or unusually corrupt, but because major sections within British society rebelled against the constraints of unity. The apostles of unrestrained party warfare, Labour, Liberal, and independent Conservative, had behind them in 1922 a growing sense of sectional and class cleavage. They embodied also the belief that firm government interpreted in terms of an adventurous, internationalist foreign policy had its dangers; it threatened to supply new roles of leadership to a quiescent, insular nation where the pomp and circumstance of Empire exhibitions were a therapy and a substitute for a genuinely international role. From 1922 Britain deliberately chose the path of caution, of inward-looking nationalism, of internal manœuvrings between groups concerned with the distributive rather than with the productive aspects of wealth and power. After the Second World War, British people pursued this path with even more enthusiasm. They treated their prospects of leading a united western Europe, for instance, with disdain or even alarm. Even Churchill's pronouncements on this front added up to little more than rhetoric. In 1951–5 his second administration did nothing to further the European ideal. Meanwhile, Labour's socialist internationalism was seen to have died with Keir Hardie. For most British people of most political affiliations, domestic conflicts, the handling of inflation, the nationalization of major industries, the financing of the welfare state, comprehensive schools, policies to curb industrial strikes, political competition to appease racist fears about black immigration, were all far more absorbing. The effect of the Carlton Club meeting in October 1922, with its overtones of alarm at Britain's acting as 'policeman of the world', was to generate a deep instinct—subconscious at first, conscious long before the 1956 Suez crisis made it obvious—that

Britain was no longer a great power, and no longer wanted to be. Obviously, as in 1922 most British people preferred it that way.

With all its limitations, the Lloyd George Coalition did suggest some wider and more interesting horizons. Its vision was limited in all kinds of ways, not least by the influence of the Treasury which emasculated some of its more imaginative ventures. In any case, it would be absurd to argue that men like Chamberlain, Horne, Worthington-Evans, Addison, Mond, Fisher, Macnamara, or Barnes were men of dramatic or penetrating vision, respectable, honest, and efficient though they were. Some of the Coalition's personnel — Auckland Geddes and Hamar Greenwood, for instance — were manifestly inadequate for the offices they filled. Eric Geddes, too, was in some ways an anachronism, floundering in an unfamiliar political milieu and switching wildly from extravagant schemes for the reorganization of transport and electricity, to the extreme economy of the report on public expenditure. Birkenhead, an outstanding legal figure as Lord Chancellor, was politically erratic, choleric, and undermined by alcohol. Churchill had imagination and was more far-sighted on domestic matters than his biographers have always recognized. But his imagination was too often geared to a disappearing world. His attachment to late-Victorian legends of imperial greatness, founded on India, and his anti-Bolshevik obsession in foreign and labour policy made his influence erratic and often dangerous. Few of the Coalition's more creative passages owed much to Churchill; many of them were obstructed by him. He rose to full stature in March 1922 when he led the extreme right wing in resisting the formal diplomatic recognition of the Soviet Union.

But, however varied their capacity or vision, the government's ministers did give effective and generally loyal support to their head. Here there was much to generate enthusiasm, even inspiration. Many desperate mistakes were made at the level of tactics, notably an obsession with the newspaper press and with the manipulation of honours that is reminiscent of the pages of the Crossman diaries in the later 1960s. Yet Lloyd George salvaged enough of his earlier reforming zeal, combined with a fresh perception of foreign affairs, more realistic in tone than the Cecil centrists with their faith in the League, to make his government active and effective. For long, indeed until after the Irish treaty in December 1921, the contrast was immense between the strength of the Coalition and the sheer inadequacy of its various opponents—a Labour Party not yet capable of handling power and sectional in outlook; a Liberal/centrist movement increasingly apolitical and out-of-touch with the economic changes of post-1914; a die-hard Tory movement which offered little but negation and reaction on every front of policy. That these opponents were at least kept out of power for four vital years was cause for gratification. The only plausible heir, the Labour Party, was able to form a government later on when its structure of leadership, if not many of its policies, was more convincing. In 1945, Labour clearly upheld the standard of social reform which the Coalition had tried to appropriate in 1918. In the meantime, the Coalition could claim the ambiguous title of being a government that helped politicize Labour and make it fit to govern.

Until that time arrived, the Coalition, above all through Lloyd George himself, offered some kind of vision of social harmony and international conciliation which many young men and women entering politics in 1919 found neither ignoble nor undeserving of support. The Coalition tried to seize the opportunity, fleeting though it was, to take advantage of the war years and to create a middle way for a nation at peace with itself and in fruitful collaboration with its allies. Since 1922, no consistent route, middle way, or other version, has been charted. Churchill's highly successful coalition of 1940 was clearly intended for the duration of the war years only. Otherwise, as Herbert Croly had foretold years before 1914, Britain's 'national idea' was undermined by 'political privilege and social favouritism',[21] accompanied by a reaction against collective planning prevalent throughout industrial management and trade unions alike. It is not necessary to adopt Croly's organic corporate vision of the 'new nationalism' for Britain to see the impact of sectionalism and class conflict in sapping Britain's political initiative and economic strength since 1922. For all its failures, the Lloyd George Coalition of 1918–22, alone of peacetime British governments this century, tried to harness political consensus for positive ends. It rose above the political trivialities of the honours scandal or the 1922 Committee to offer its own, inadequate Grand Design. It is this effort, unavailing though it be, that truly represents a world we have lost.

Appendix I:
Members of the Cabinet
January 1919–October 1922

The five-man War Cabinet (Lloyd George, Curzon, Law, Barnes, Chamberlain) still operated until October 1919.

Prime Minister	David Lloyd George (Lib.)
Lord Chancellor	Lord Birkenhead (Un.)
Lord President	Lord Curzon (Un.) (from Oct. 1919) Arthur Balfour (Un.)
Lord Privy Seal	A. Bonar Law (Un.) (from Mar. 1921) Austen Chamberlain (Un.)
Chancellor of the Exchequer	Austen Chamberlain (Un.) (from Apr. 1921) Sir Robert Horne (Un.)
Home Secretary	Edward Shortt (Lib.)
Foreign Secretary	Arthur Balfour (Un.) (from Oct. 1919) Lord Curzon (Un.)
Colonial Secretary	Lord Milner (Un.) (from Feb. 1921) Winston Churchill (Lib.)
Secretary for War	Winston Churchill (Lib.) (from Feb. 1921) L. Worthington-Evans (Un.)
Secretary for India	Edwin Montagu (Lib.) (from Mar. 1922) Lord Peel (Un.)
Secretary for Scotland	R. Munro (Lib.)
Chief Secretary for Ireland	I. MacPherson (Lib.) (from Apr. 1920) Sir Hamar Greenwood (Lib.)
Viceroy of Ireland	Lord French (from Apr. 1921) Lord Fitzalan
First Lord of the Admiralty	Walter Long (Un.) (from Feb. 1921) Lord Lee of Fareham (Un.)

President of the Board of Trade	Sir Albert Stanley (Un.) (from May 1919) Sir Auckland Geddes (Un.) (from Mar. 1920) Sir Robert Horne (Un.) (from Apr. 1921) Stanley Baldwin (Un.)
President of the Local Government Board (Minister of Health from June 1919)	Dr. Christopher Addison (Lib.) (from Mar. 1921) Sir Alfred Mond (Lib.)
President of the Board of Agriculture (Minister of Agriculture from Aug. 1919)	R. E. Prothero (Lord Ernle) (Un.) (from Aug. 1919) Lord Lee of Fareham (Un.) (from Feb. 1921) Sir A. Griffith-Boscawen (Un.)
President of the Board of Education	H. A. L. Fisher (Lib.)
Minister of Munitions	Lord Inverforth (ministry abolished, Feb. 1921)
Ministry of Labour	Sir Robert Horne (Un.) (from Mar. 1920) T. J. Macnamara (Lib.)
Ministers without Portfolio	George Barnes (to Jan. 1920) (Lab.) Sir Eric Geddes (Minister of Transport with a seat in the Cabinet from Aug. 1919 to Nov. 1921) (Un.) Dr. Christopher Addison (Mar.–July 1921) (Lib.)
First Commissioner of Works	Earl of Crawford (Apr. 1921 to Oct. 1922: enters Cabinet, Apr. 1922) (Un.)

Appendix II:
Contested By-Elections 1919–1922

Date	Constituency	Result	*Percentage swing against Coalition*
1919			
26 Feb.	Liverpool, West Derby	Co. Un. hold	10.9
1 Mar.	West Leyton	Lib. *gain* from Co. Un.	24.7
19–24 Mar.	Oxford University	Co. Un. hold	
29 Mar.	Hull Central	Lib. *gain* from Co. Un.	32.9
16 Apr.	Aberdeen, Central	Lib. *gain* from Co. Un.	3.3
10 July	Swansea, East	Co. Lib. hold	10.5
16 July	Lanark, Bothwell	Lab. *gain* from Co. Un.	
30 Aug.	Widnes	Lab. *gain* from Co. Un.	11.9
6 Sept.	Pontefract	Co. Lib. hold	8.9
7 Oct.	Manchester, Rusholme	Co. Un. hold	17.5
11 Nov.	Croydon, South	Co. Un. hold	
13 Nov.	Durham, Chester-le-Street	Lab. hold	
15 Nov.	Plymouth, Sutton	Co. Un. hold	13.4
15 Nov.	Isle of Thanet	Ind. Cons. hold	
10 Dec.	St. Albans	Co. Un. hold	
17 Dec.	Bromley	Co. Un. hold	
20 Dec.	Spen Valley	Lab. *gain* from Co. Lib.	11.9
1920			
31 Jan.	Ashton-under-Lyne	Co. Un. hold	
7 Feb.	The Wrekin	Ind. *gain* from Co. Lib.	
12 Feb.	Paisley	Lib. hold	17.2
25 Feb.	Horncastle	Co. Un. hold	0.4
10 Mar.	Argyll	Co. Lib. hold	
27 Mar.	Dartford	Lab. *gain* from Co. Lib.	
27 Mar.	Stockport (2 seats)	Co. Un. and Co. Lib. hold*	

* Technically, Stockport was won by Co. Un. and Co. Lab. in the 1918 election.

Date	Constituency	Result	Percentage swing against Coalition
31 Mar.	Camberwell, North-West	Co. Lib. hold	
31 Mar.	Basingstoke	Co. Un. hold	
1 Apr.	Northampton	Co. Lib. hold	7.1
9 Apr.	Edinburgh, North	Co. Un. hold	9.7
9 Apr.	Edinburgh, South	Co. Un. hold	17.3
24 Apr.	Sunderland	Co. Lib. hold	
3 June	Louth	Lib. *gain* from Co. Un.	11.8
17 June	Nelson and Colne	Lab. hold	
27 July	Norfolk, South	Lab. *gain* from Co. Lib.	19.9
28 July	Suffolk, Woodbridge	Co. Un. hold	
25 Sept.	Ilford	Co. Un. hold	7.9
20 Nov.	The Wrekin	Ind. hold	
21 Dec.	Rhondda, West	Lab. hold	
21 Dec.	Abertillery	Lab. hold	
1921			
11 Jan.	Hereford	Co. Un. hold	
12 Jan.	Dover	Anti-Waste *gain* from Co. Un.	
18 Feb.	Cardiganshire	Co. Lib. hold	
2 Mar.	Woolwich, East	Co. Un. *gain* from Lab.	
3 Mar.	Dudley	Lab. *gain* from Co. Un.	10.9
4 Mar.	Kirkcaldy District	Lab. *gain* from Co. Lib.	
5 Mar.	Penistone	Lab. *gain* from Co. Lib.	
8 Apr.	Taunton	Co. Un. hold	11.3
19 Apr.	Worcestershire, Bewdley	Co. Un. hold	
23 Apr.	Bedford	Co. Lib. hold	
4 May	Hastings	Co. Un. hold	11.3
13 May	Penrith and Cockermouth	Co. Un. hold	
7 June	Westminster, St. George's	Anti-Waste *gain* from Co. Un.	
8 June	Lancashire, Heywood	Lab. *gain* from Co. Lib.	17.1
16 June	Hertford	Anti-Waste *gain* from Ind.	
24 Aug.	Caerphilly	Lab. hold	
25 Aug.	Westminster, Abbey	Co. Un. hold	
13 Sept.	Lewisham, West	Cons. hold	
22 Sept.	Louth	Lib. hold	
5 Oct.	Lancashire, Westhoughton	Lab. hold	
10 Nov.	Hornsey	Cons. hold	
14 Dec.	Southwark, South-East	Lab. *gain* from Co. Lib.	39.7

Date	Constituency	Result	Percentage swing against Coalition
1922			
17 Jan.	Tamworth	Co. Un. hold	
18 Feb.	Manchester, Clayton	Lab. *gain* from Co. Un.	18.7
20 Feb.	Camberwell, North	Lab. *gain* from Co. Un.	22.4
24 Feb.	Bodmin	Lib. *gain* from Co. Un.	14.8
7 Mar.	Wolverhampton, West	Co. Un. hold	1.9
16 Mar.	Cambridge	Cons. hold	16.5
16 Mar.	Inverness	Co. Lib. hold	
24 Mar.	Surrey, Chertsey	Cons. hold	
30 Mar.	Leicester, East	Lab. *gain* from Co. Lib.	33.0
19 May	City of London	Cons. hold	
29 June	Nottingham, East	Co. Un. hold	10.7
20 July	Gower	Lab. hold	
25 July	Pontypridd	Lab. *gain* from Co. Lib.	13.8
18 Aug.	Hackney, South	Co. Cons. *gain* from Ind.	
18 Oct.	Newport	Ind. Cons. *gain* from Co. Lib.	

Note: in the case of Unionist candidates, the terms 'Co. Un.', 'Co. Cons.', or 'Cons.' have been used variously, according to the self-designation of the candidates involved.

Appendix III:
Unemployment Percentage,
1914–1925

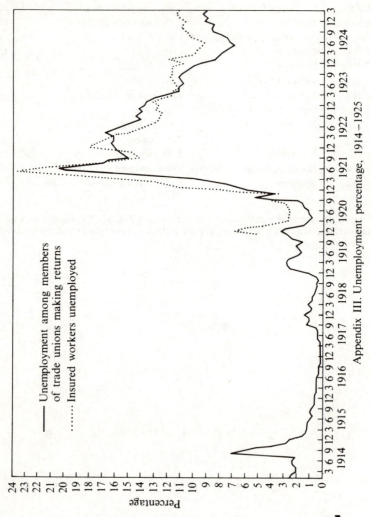

Appendix III. Unemployment percentage, 1914–1925

Source: E. V. Morgan, *Studies in British Financial Policy 1914–1925* (1961).

Appendix IV:
Indices of Wholesale Prices,
1919–1925

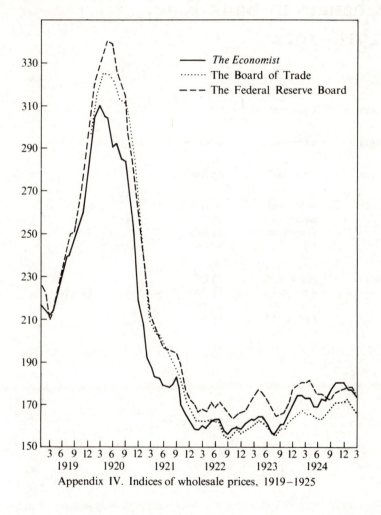

Appendix IV. Indices of wholesale prices, 1919–1925

Source: E. V. Morgan, *Studies in British Financial Policy 1914–1925* (1961).

Appendix V:
Changes in Bank Rate,
1918–1922

1918	5 per cent	
1919	6 per cent	6 Nov.
1920	7 per cent	15 Apr.
1921	6½ per cent	28 Apr.
	6 per cent	23 June
	5½ per cent	21 July
	5 per cent	3 Nov.
1922	4½ per cent	16 Feb.
	4 per cent	13 Apr.
	3½ per cent	15 June
	3 per cent	13 July

FOOTNOTES TO CHAPTER I

[1] Thomas Jones, *A Diary with Letters, 1931–50* (Oxford, 1950), p. xxxii.
[2] 'Cato' (Frank Owen and Michael Foot), *The Guilty Men* (1940), p. 19.
[3] Originally applied to Lloyd George: A. J. P. Taylor, *English History, 1914–1945* (Oxford, 1965), p. 74.
[4] Lord Robbins, *Autobiography of an Economist* (1971), pp. 112–13.
[5] Memorandum by Lord Asquith, 5 Oct. 1926 (British Library, Spender Papers, Add. MS. 46388, ff. 109–13).
[6] Josiah Wedgwood, *Memoirs of a Fighting Life* (1940), p. 146; J. M. Kenworthy, *Sailors, Statesmen—and Others* (1933), p. 158.
[7] C. P. Scott diary, 6 Dec. 1922 (BL, Scott Papers, Add. MS. 50906, ff. 207–8).
[8] e. g. Salisbury to Bonar Law, 4 Mar. 1922 (H. of Lords Record Office, Bonar Law Papers, 107/2/2).
[9] A. J. P. Taylor (ed.), *Lloyd George: a Diary by Frances Stevenson* (1972), p. 323.
[10] Carlton Club to Austen Chamberlain, Oct. 1922 (Univ. of Birmingham, Austen Chamberlain Papers, 33/1/29).
[11] J. Barnes and K. Middlemas, *Baldwin* (1969), p. 318.
[12] Austen Chamberlain to Lord Robert Cecil, 26 Apr. 1921 (A. Chamberlain Papers, AC/24/3/16).
[13] J. B. Priestley, *Postscripts* (1940), p. 42; cf. Harold Laski, 'Coalitions and the Constitution', *New Statesman and Nation*, 23 Oct. 1943
[14] Charles Mallet, *Mr. Lloyd George: a Study* (1930). Mallet attacked Lloyd George, among other things, for his penchant for 'programmes': elections were not won on the basis of mere programmes. He called for the Liberal Party 'to return to the moral force of Mr. Gladstone'.
[15] Watkin Davies, *Lloyd George, 1863–1914* (1939), pp. 279–81, 289.
[16] Davies's diary for 1921–2 (National Library of Wales, Watkin Davies Papers).
[17] H. C. G. Matthew, *The Liberal Imperialists* (Oxford, 1973), *passim*, for Rosebery; Kenneth O. Morgan, *Keir Hardie: Radical and Socialist* (1975), p. 131.
[18] On this, see Bernard Semmel, *Imperialism and Social Reform* (1960).
[19] This memorandum is printed in Kenneth O. Morgan, *The Age of Lloyd George* (1978, new ed.), pp. 150–5.
[20] D. Lloyd George, *War Memoirs* (1938), i, 20–3. Lloyd George, extraordinarily enough, blames the failure of the coalition scheme on Akers-Douglas, the then Unionist chief whip.
[21] Bodleian Library, Asquith Papers, vol. xxvi, ff. 12–38.
[22] The fullest account of this crisis is in Cameron Hazlehurst, *Politicians at War, July 1914–May 1915* (1971), pp. 227 ff.
[23] Addison to his wife, 2 Aug. 1916 (Bodleian, Addison Papers, Box 111); P. A.

Lockwood, 'Milner's Entry into the War Cabinet', *Historical Journal*, VII (1964). For the Ministry of Munitions generally, see R. J. Q. Adams, *Arms and the Wizard* (1978).

[24] This has been argued by some historians, notably A. J. P. Taylor, *Politics in the First World War* (1959), p. 76.

[25] See Cate Haste, *Keep the Home Fires Burning* (1977).

[26] Christopher Addison, *Politics from Within 1914–1918* (1924), i. 272–4 (9 Dec. 1916).

[27] *Parl.Deb.*, 5th Ser., Vol. 108, pp. 2347 ff.

[28] See Peter K. Cline, 'Eric Geddes and the "Experiment" with Businessmen in Government, 1915–22', in K. D. Brown (ed.), *Essays in Anti-Labour History* (1974), 74–104.

[29] Thomas Jones to his wife, 12 Dec. 1916 (National Library of Wales, Thomas Jones Papers, X/7). The full phrase was 'a fluid person moving amongst people who mattered'.

[30] See J. A. Turner, 'The Formation of Lloyd George's "Garden Suburb"', *Historical Journal*, XX, No. 1 (1977), 165–84.

[31] Lord Riddell, *War Diary* (1933), pp. 243, 324, for Lloyd George comparing Milner's creed with his own.

[32] W. B. Worsfold, *The War and Social Reform* (1919), p. 53, citing the Director-General of Food Production.

[33] R. H. Tawney, 'The Abolition of Economic Controls, 1918–21', *Economic History Review* XIII, No. 1 (1943), 1 ff.

[34] Cf. *History of the Ministry of Munitions*, VII (1922), part 1, 72–103.

[35] William Ashworth, *Economic History of England, 1870–1939* (1960), p. 284.

[36] *Final Report of Committee on Commercial and Industrial Policy* (Cd. 9035), P.P. (1918), XIII, especially paras. 114–19 (p. 26).

[37] e.g. *Report of the Commission of Inquiry on Industrial Unrest*, No. 7 division, 1917 (Cd. 8668).

[38] Political Diary, Feb. 1918 (Bridgeman Papers).

[39] W. W. Craik, *The Central Labour College* (1964); J. Hinton, *The First Shop Stewards Movement* (1973), a Marxist account.

[40] Cf. Raymond Moley, *After Seven Years* (New York, 1939), p. 13. The remark originally applied to Thomas Jefferson.

[41] J. M. Winter, *Socialism and the Challenge of War* (1974), p. 169. For public health, see *idem*, 'The Impact of the First World War on Civilian Health in Britain', *Economic History Review*, XXX, No. 3 (Aug. 1977), 487 ff.

[42] *Report of Housing Panel, Ministry of Reconstruction* (Cd. 9087).

[43] J. A. Hobson, *Democracy after the War* (1918), pp. 166, 174 ff.

[44] José Harris, *William Beveridge* (Oxford, 1977), pp. 250 ff.

[45] Cf. Royden Harrison, 'The War Emergency Workers National Committee, 1914–1920', in Asa Briggs and John Saville (eds.), *Essays in Labour History, 1886–1923*, II (1971), pp. 211–59; Norman Mackenzie (ed.), *The Letters of Sidney and Beatrice Webb*, Vol. III (1978), pp. 34 ff.

[46] Sidney Webb to Bernard Shaw, 18 Aug. 1915 (*Letters of Sidney and Beatrice Webb*, iii. p. 61). He also urged compulsory training of all youth from 14 to 21 'in *everything* needed for citizenship'.

[47] Memorandum printed in *Thomas Jones: Whitehall Diary*, Vol. I (Oxford, 1969); E. Montagu to Lloyd George, 25 June 1917 (Lloyd George Papers, F/59/3/19).

[48] This is the view taken in Paul Barton Johnson, *Land Fit for Heroes* (Chicago, 1968), which is, nevertheless, a very useful mine of information on the Ministry of Reconstruction.

[49] Bridgeman, Political Diary, Feb. 1918.

⁵⁰ 'List of government appointments held by Lord Addison, 1914–1951' (Addison Papers, Box 137). This document was an application to Winston Churchill for a state pension in November 1951.
⁵¹ Johnson, pp. 71–2.
⁵² Memorandums in Addison Papers, Box 72.
⁵³ Addison to his wife, 22 Aug. 1918 (Addison Papers, Box 111); *Four and a Half Years, 1914–1919*, Vol. II (1934), pp. 562–5.

FOOTNOTES TO CHAPTER II

¹ Addison, *Four and a Half Years*, ii. 458–9. This description of Astor comes from Walter Long to Bonar Law, 16 July 1918 (Lloyd George Papers, F/30/2/38).
² Guest to Lloyd George, 13 Dec. 1917, and memorandum of Dec. 1917 (Lloyd George Papers, F/21/2/10 and F/168/2/3). Lord Riddell, *War Diary*, p. 309 (27 Jan. 1918).
³ Stephen Roskill, *Hankey, Man of Secrets*, Vol. I (1970), pp. 544–5, citing Hankey's diary of 9 May 1918.
⁴ Guest to Lloyd George, 17 May 1918 (Lloyd George Papers, F/21/2/22).
⁵ Guest to Lloyd George, 7 Sept. 1918 (ibid., F/21/2/36); H. A. Taylor, *Robert Donald* (1934), pp. 175–93.
⁶ Memorandum on the 'Election question' (4 Sept. 1918) (Addison Papers, Box 72).
⁷ Materials on 'Policy for Government Committee' (ibid).
⁸ For these events, see Roy Douglas, 'The Background to the "Coupon" Election arrangements', *English Historical Review*, LXXXVI (Apr. 1971), 326 ff.
⁹ Guest to Lloyd George, 20 July 1918 (Lloyd George Papers, F/21/2/28).
¹⁰ Page diaries, Feb. 1917 (Houghton Library, Harvard, Page Papers, b MS. Am. 1090.5(2)).
¹¹ Bridgeman, Political Diary, Feb. 1918, p. 279.
¹² Bonar Law to Balfour, 5 Oct. 1919 (BL, Balfour Papers, Add. MS. 49693, ff. 272–80).
¹³ J. M. Keynes, *Economic Consequences of the Peace* (1919), pp. 133–6.
¹⁴ C. P. Scott diary, 6–8 Aug. 1918 (BL Scott Papers, Add. MS. 50905, f. 93).
¹⁵ See correspondence of Freddie Guest with Lloyd George (Lloyd George Papers, F/21/2, *passim*).
¹⁶ Trevor Wilson, *The Downfall of the Liberal Party, 1914–1935* (1966), chapter 6. Cf, Edward David, 'The Liberal Party Divided 1916–18', *Historical Journal*, XIII (1970), 509–33.
¹⁷ Guest to Lloyd George, 29 Oct. 1918 (Lloyd George Papers, F/21/2/46).
¹⁸ Younger to J. C. C. Davidson, 2 Dec. 1918 (Bonar Law Papers, 95/2).
¹⁹ 'Memorandum on Election Questions', 4 Sept. 1918 (Addison Papers, box 72).
²⁰ Guest to Lloyd George, 16 Aug. 1918 (Lloyd George Papers, F/21/2/31).
²¹ Salisbury to Selborne, 30 Aug. 1918 (Bodleian, Selborne Papers, 1/7).
²² Salvidge to Bonar Law, 22 Nov. 1918 (Bonar Law Papers, 95/3).
²³ Younger to Bonar Law, 28 Nov. 1918 (ibid).
²⁴ Maud P. Mead to Bonar Law, 20 Nov. 1918 (ibid.).
²⁵ Lloyd George to Bonar Law, 20 Nov. 1918 (Lloyd George Papers, F/30/2/55). He wrote that the Women's Party had been useful in fighting 'the Bolshevist and Pacifist element' in industrial areas such as South Wales and Glasgow.
²⁶ Note of 24 July 1918 (Addison Papers, Box 72).
²⁷ Barnes to J. T. Davies, 29 Aug. 1918 (Lloyd George Papers, F/4/2/32), and memorandum by Macnamara (ibid., F/6/2/49).

[28] Salisbury to Selborne, 12 June 1918 (Selborne Papers, 1/7).

[29] Lloyd George to Bonar Law, 29 Aug. 1918 (Lloyd George Papers, F/30/2/45).

[30] Law to Lloyd George, 22 Oct. 1918 (ibid., F/30/2/51). Cf. Kenneth O. Morgan, *Wales in British Politics, 1868–1922* (Cardiff, 1970 new ed.), pp. 286–7.

[31] Cf. Fisher to Lloyd George, 11 Oct. 1919 (Lloyd George Papers, F/16/7/29). On the aftermath of the convention, see R. B. McDowell, *The Irish Convention, 1917–18* (1970), chapter V.

[32] S. D. Waley, *Edwin Montagu* (Bombay, 1964), pp. 187–90; Churchill to Lloyd George, 7 Nov. 1918, Lloyd George to Churchill, 7 Nov. 1918 (Lloyd George Papers, F/8/2/37–8). The phrase, 'master and servant' (which Churchill used), appears in Robert Boothby, *I Fight to Live* (1947), p. 45.

[33] H. A. L. Fisher diary, 12 Nov. 1918 (Bodleian, Fisher Papers); *The Times*, 13 Nov. 1918.

[34] Guest to Lloyd George, 21 Oct. 1919 (Lloyd George Papers, F/21/2/43).

[35] Mary Stocks, *Ernest Simon of Manchester* (Manchester, 1963), pp. 57–9.

[36] See John Stubbs, 'Lord Milner and Patriotic Labour, 1914–18', *English Historical Review*, LXXXVII (Oct. 1972).

[37] See Marvin Swartz, *The Union of Democratic Control in British Politics* (Oxford, 1971), esp. pp. 85–104; Keith Robbins, *The Abolition of War* (Cardiff, 1976).

[38] Keynes, *Economic Consequences of the Peace*, pp. 127–33.

[39] Kerr to Lloyd George, 20 Nov. 1918 (Lloyd George Papers, F/89/1/13).

[40] *The Times*, 14 Dec. 1918. Cf. Trevor Wilson, p. 139, where this is wrongly attributed to the Bristol speech instead.

[41] *Contemporary Review*, Feb. 1919, p. 135.

[42] *Nation*, 4 Jan. 1919.

[43] *The Times*, 14 Dec. 1918.

[44] F. W. S. Craig, *British Parliamentary Election Statistics, 1918–1968* (Glasgow, 1968), p. 43.

[45] See *Labour Voice*, 30 Nov. 1918, for Brace's views, and ibid., 28 Dec. 1918, for Hartshorn's.

[46] Cf. David Marquand, *Ramsay MacDonald* (1977), pp. 207 ff., for Leicester; Trevelyan to Ponsonby, 'Election day, 1918' (Bodleian, Ponsonby Papers, Eng. Hist. c. 667, f. 100–1) for Elland; and Kenneth O. Morgan, 'The Merthyr of Keir Hardie', in G. Williams (ed.), *Merthyr Politics* (Cardiff, 1966), p. 78, for Aberdare.

[47] Notes on an Interview with Lloyd George, 27 June 1918 (Ponsonby Papers, Eng. Hist. c.667, ff. 60–8).

[48] See J. M. McEwen, 'The Coupon Election of 1918 and the Unionist Members of Parliament', *Journal of Modern History* (Sept. 1962), 294–306.

[49] *Spectator*, 4 Jan. 1919.

[50] *Outlook*, 4 Jan. 1919.

[51] Worthington-Evans Papers, file on 1918 election (Bodleian, Worthington-Evans Papers, MS. Eng. Hist. c. 892).

[52] *Nation*, 30 Nov. 1918.

[53] Lloyd George to Chamberlain, 9 Jan. 1919 (Lloyd George Papers, F/7/2/20).

[54] Churchill to Lloyd George, 26 Dec. 1919 (Lloyd George Papers, F/8/2/49). He referred specifically to Montagu, Isaacs, and Samuel, though not to Mond.

[55] Hankey's diary, 19 Dec. 1918, cited in Martin Gilbert (ed.), *Winston S. Churchill, Companion Volume IV*, part I, p. 443.

[56] Smith had been a member of the Tory Social Reform Committee before 1914.

[57] *The Economist*, 23 Nov. 1918.

[58] Cabinet minutes, 23 Jan. 1919 (Public Record Office, CAB 23/9).

[59] Ibid., 6 Dec. 1918, WC 510 (CAB 23/8).

[60] Montagu to Lloyd George, 16 Dec. 1918 (Lloyd George Papers, F/40/2/24).

FOOTNOTES TO CHAPTER III

[1] Ernest Hatch, 'The Uprising of Labour: an Alternative Government', *The Nineteenth Century and After* (Jan. 1920), 19–26.

[2] Maurice Cowling, *The Impact of Labour 1920–1924*(Cambridge, 1971), pp. 1–2.

[3] *New Statesman*, 20 Sept. 1919.

[4] Cabinet minutes, 31 Jan. 1919, WC 523 (CAB 23/9).

[5] Ibid.

[6] Bonar Law to Davidson, 20 Mar. 1919 (House of Lords Record Office, Davidson Papers).

[7] Cabinet minutes, 31 Jan. 1919 (CAB 23/9).

[8] Ibid., 4 Feb. 1919, WC 525 (CAB 23/9).

[9] Arno Mayer, *Politics and Diplomacy of Peacemaking* (1968), pp. 604–66.

[10] Lloyd George to Bonar Law, 19 and 20 Mar. 1919 (Lloyd George Papers, F/30/3/31–2).

[11] H. Laski to Oliver Wendell Holmes, 30 Apr. 1921, in M. Howe (ed.), *The Holmes–Laski Letters* (Oxford, 1953), i. 333.

[12] *Thomas Jones: Whitehall Diary*, i. 101 (Jones's notes on Cabinet conference of 2 Feb. 1920).

[13] Guest to Lloyd George, 20 July 1918 (Lloyd George Papers, F/21/2/28); Kenneth O. Morgan, '1900–1924', in David Butler (ed.), *Coalitions in British Politics* (1978), p. 34.

[14] Lloyd George to Bonar Law, 29 Jan. 1919 (Lloyd George Papers, F/30/3/10).

[15] Cabinet minutes, 4 Feb. 1919.

[16] Bridgeman, Political Diary, 17 Apr. 1920.

[17] Cf. 'A Student of Politics', *The Times*, 24 Dec. 1920.

[18] Lord Beaverbrook, *The Decline and Fall of Lloyd George* (1963), p. 103; Sir A. Griffith-Boscawen, *Memories* (1925), p. 223.

[19] For an excellent discussion of this, see Rodney Lowe, 'The Ministry of Labour, 1916–1924: a Graveyard of Social Reform?', *Public Administration* (Winter 1974), 415–38.

[20] 'Reports of a Revolutionary Organization', 11, 25 Sept. 1919, ST 8144, 8228 (CAB 24/88, 24/89); cf. *New Statesman*, 19 Nov. 1921, for a reference to the WEA.

[21] 'Report from Ministry of Labour for the week ending 8 October 1919', ST 8290 (CAB 24/89).

[22] John Baird diary, 9 Sept. 1919 (National Library of Australia).

[23] P. J. Grigg, *Prejudice and Judgement* (1948), pp. 72–3.

[24] Sir Harold Butler, *Confident Morning* (1950), p. 141.

[25] R. Smillie, *My Life for Labour* (1924), pp. 278–9; Addison to his wife, 6 Apr. 1921 (Addison Papers, Box 135).

[26] *Report of the Nineteenth Annual Conference of the Labour Party*, held at Southport, 25–7 June 1919, p. 128.

[27] Minutes of Conference of Ministers 16 Jan. 1920 (CAB 23/35).

[28] Memorandum by War Office to Geddes Committee on Public Expenditure, 1921 (CAB 27/164).

[29] Notes on Conference at Lympne, 23 Apr. 1921 (Worthington-Evans Papers).

[30] Cabinet minutes, 4 Feb. 1919, WC 525 (CAB 23/9).

[31] It was appointed on 4 Feb. 1919 (CAB 27/59).

[32] Major-General Sir Wyndham Childs, *Episodes and Reflections* (1930), p. 185; 'G. H'. to Shortt, 22 Oct. 1922: transcripts in Nuffield College Library (Shortt papers, 1/45).

[33] It existed, technically, from 14 Oct. 1919 to 29 Nov. 1921 (CAB 27/73–84).

[34] Shortt memorandum, CP 78 (CAB 24/92).

[35] Finance Committee, 15 Oct. 1919 (CAB 27/31).

[36] Cabinet minutes, 2 Feb., 20 June 1920 (CAB 23/20 and 23/21) for Geddes's interventions; memorandums in Thomas Jones Papers, C6.

[37] Cabinet minutes, 28 Mar. 1946 (CAB 128/7).

[38] *Report of Provisional Joint Committee presented to the meeting of the Industrial Conference, April 4 1919* (Cmd. 139); R. Charles, *The Development of Industrial Relations in Britain, 1911–1939* (1973), pp. 229–49: Butler, *Confident Morning*, pp. 142–3; R. Lowe, 'The Erosion of State Intervention in Britain, 1917–24', *Economic History Review*, XXXI, No. 2 (May 1978), 273–6; R. Lowe, 'The Failure of Consensus in Britain: the National Industrial Conference, 1919–1921', *Historical Journal*, XXI, No. 3 (1978), 649–75.

[39] Churchill to Bonar Law, 5 July 1919 (Bonar Law Papers, 97/5); Waldorf Astor to J. L. Garvin, 10 Jan. 1919 (University of Texas, Garvin MSS.).

[40] Cabinet minutes, 6 Dec. 1918, WC 510 (CAB 23/8).

[41] Baird diary, 4 Oct. 1919.

[42] Lloyd George to his wife, 26 Sept. 1919, in Kenneth O. Morgan (ed.), *Lloyd George: Family Letters, 1885–1936* (1975), p. 190.

[43] *The Times*, 29 Sept. 1919.

[44] Baird diary, 5 Oct. 1919.

[45] Fisher diary, 5 Oct. 1919.

[46] Lloyd George to his wife, 7 Oct. 1919, *Family Letters*, p. 191; Fisher diary, 5 Oct. 1919, for Auckland Geddes's view; Baird diary, 5 October 1919, for Churchill's; Curzon to Lloyd George, 6 Oct. 1919 (Lloyd George Papers, F/12/1/46), for Curzon's.

[47] Bridgeman, Political Diary, 17 Aug. 1920; Baird diary, 13 Oct. 1919, for Younger's comment.

[48] *New Statesman*, 11 Oct. 1919.

[49] For excellent discussions of the post-war situation in the mining industry, see M. W. Kirby, *The British Coalmining Industry, 1870–1946* (1977), pp. 24–65; G. A. Phillips, *The General Strike* (1976), pp. 23–42; S. M. H. Armitage, *The Politics of De-control in Industry* (1969), pp. 131–67.

[50] See R. Smillie, *My Life for Labour;* Joyce M. Bellamy and John Saville (eds.), *Dictionary of Labour Biography*, Vol. II (London 1974), sub 'Smith'; Frank Hodges, *My Adventures as a Labour Leader* (1925). Technically, Hodges came from Gloucestershire but moved to the Welsh mines at an early age.

[51] Cabinet minutes, 7 Feb. 1919 (CAB 23/9); Armitage, op. cit., pp. 121–2.

[52] Sankey's diary, 6, 10, 13 Mar. 1919 (Bodleian, Sankey Papers, MS. Eng. Hist. e 273); *Coal Industry Commission: Reports and Minutes of Evidence*, Vols I and II (Cmd. 359, 360), *passim.*

[53] H. D. Henderson, 'The Reports of the Coal Industry Commission', *Economic Journal* (Sept. 1919), 265–78.

[54] Churchill to Bonar Law, 5 July 1919 (Bonar Law Papers, 97/5).

[55] Cabinet minutes, 7 Aug. 1919 (CBA 23/15).

[56] *The Times*, 2 Jan. 1920.

[57] Ibid., 19 Apr. 1920; A. L. Bowley, *Prices and Wages in the United Kingdom, 1914–20* (New York, 1921), p. 106.

[58] *Report of a Court of Inquiry concerning Transport Workers* (Cmd. 936), pp. 6–7; *The Times*, 1 Apr. 1920; Alan Bullock, *The Life and Times of Ernest Bevin*, Vol. 1 (1960), pp. 116–33. Technically, the report was signed by seven committee members out of nine.

[59] *New Statesman*, 13 Mar. 1920.

[60] See L. J. Macfarlane, 'Hands off Russia: British Labour and the Russo-Polish War, 1920', *Past and Present* (Dec. 1967), 126–52; and below, pp. 136–7.

[61] Cabinet minutes, 27 Jan. 1920 (CAB 23/20).

[62] Ibid., 6 May 1920 (CAB 23/21).

[63] Wigram to Sir E. Grigg, 26 Aug. 1920 (Bodleian, Grigg Papers).

[64] Cabinet minutes, 17 Aug. 1920 (CAB 23/22).

[65] *New Statesman*, 16 Oct. 1920.

[66] Bridgeman, Political Diary, 24 Sept.–1 Oct 1920.

[67] Cabinet minutes, 25 Oct. 1920 (CAB 23/35).

[68] Bridgeman, Political Diary, 18–25 Oct. 1920.

[69] Fisher diary, 26 Oct. 1920.

[70] Kirby, p. 53.

[71] Minutes of Conference of Ministers, 4 Apr. 1921 (CAB 23/25); Lord Page Croft, *My Life of Strife* (1940), p. 151.

[72] Lord Hardinge to Curzon, 9 Apr. 1921 (P.R.O., FO/800/156, ff. 280–1); Laski to Holmes, 30 Apr. 1921 (*Holmes–Laski Letters*, i. 332).

[73] Addison to his wife, 12 Apr. 1921 (Addison Papers, Box 135); Bridgeman, Political Diary, Sept.–Oct. 1920—'Hodges is the prig of the party.'

[74] 'The After-Effects of the Coal Strike on Investors', *Financial Review of Reviews* (July–Aug. 1921), 151 ff.).

[75] Statement in Thomas Jones Papers, C/6; *New Statesman*, 16 Apr. 1921.

[76] Arnold Bennett to R. D. Blumenfeld, 1 Apr. 1921, James Hepburn (ed.), *Letters of Arnold Bennett*, Vol. III (Oxford, 1971), p. 143.

[77] Cabinet conclusions, 7, 9 Apr. 1921 (CAB 23/38); War Office memorandum sent to Geddes Committee on Public Expenditure (CAB 27/164).

[78] *Thomas Jones: Whitehall Diary*, i. 150–1; Cabinet conclusions, 15 Apr. 1921 (CAB 23/25); *The Times* 14–16 Apr. 1921; letter by Sir Colin Coote to the author, 19 Nov. 1976; F. Hodges, *My Adventures as a Labour Leader* (1925), pp. 132–5.

[79] Waldorf Astor to J. L. Garvin, 18 July 1921 (Reading University, Astor MSS., Box 62); *The Times*, 16 Apr. 1921.

[80] Ramsay MacDonald to Oswald Garrison Villard, 17 Apr. 1921 (Harvard University, Houghton Library, Villard Papers 6 MS Am. 1323).

[81] Laski to Holmes, 13 Apr. 1921 (*Holmes–Laski Letters*, i. 328).

[82] Cecil to Chamberlain, 20 Apr. 1921, Chamberlain to Cecil, 26 Apr. 1921 (Austen Chamberlain Papers, AC 24/3/15–16).

[83] Kirby, pp. 51–2.

[84] *Future*, Sept. 1919; *Nineteen Sixteen–Nineteen Twenty* (1920), chapter 7.

[85] Baird diary, 9 Sept. 1919, citing Walter Guinness.

[86] Thomas Jones to Lloyd George, 17 Mar. 1919 (Lloyd George Papers, F/23/4/36).

[87] *New Statesman*, 4 Oct. 1919.

[88] Report from the Minister of Labour for the week ending 1 Oct. 1919, GT 8256 (CAB 24/89).

[89] Lucy Masterman, *C. F. G. Masterman* (1939), p. 234. This cites a comment by Lloyd George in 1912 in which he contrasts the mining employers—'plump, well-fed men, well dressed'—with the union's representatives—'great, gaunt fellows, pale with working underground, their faces all torn with anxiety and hard work'.

[90] Cabinet minutes, 26 Oct. 1920 (CAB 23/23).

[91] Lenin, op. cit., Peking, 1965 (new ed.), pp. 82–3; ibid., 3 Mar. 1919 WC 539 (CAB 23/9).

[92] Laski to Holmes, 13 Apr. 1921 (*Holmes–Laski Letters*, i. 328).

[93] *Report of the Twenty-Second Annual Conference of the Labour Party*, held at Edinburgh, 27–30 June 1922, p. 128.

[94] Fisher diary, 24 Mar. 1921.

FOOTNOTES TO CHAPTER IV

[1] Seebohm Rowntree, *The Human Needs of Labour* (1918), pp. 9, 135.
[2] Ibid., and *idem*, 'Prospects and Tasks of Social Reconstruction', *Contemporary Review* (Jan. 1919), 1–9.
[3] Lloyd George's speech at Wolverhampton, 23 Nov. 1918.
[4] Johnson, *Land Fit for Heroes*, pp. 432–99, Bentley Gilbert, *British Social Policy, 1914–1939* (1970), *passim*.
[5] Gilbert, p. 306.
[6] Cabinet minutes, 20 Nov. 1945, Cab. 54(54) (CAB 128/2).
[7] Waldorf to J. L. Garvin, 10 Jan. 1919 (Garvin Papers).
[8] Churchill to Lloyd George, 12 Apr. 1922 (Lloyd George Papers, F/10/2/63).
[9] Martin Gilbert, *Winston S. Churchill*, Vol. V (1977), p. 874.
[10] C. P. Scott diary, 30 Nov.–1 Dec. 1919 Scott Papers, Add. MS. 50905, f. 211).
[11] Sutherland to Lloyd George, 2 Jan. 1922 (Lloyd George Papers, F/35/1/1).
[12] Lloyd George to Bonar Law, Dec. 1918 (ibid., F/30/2/5).
[13] Bonar Law to Lloyd George, 27 Jan. 1919 (Lloyd George Papers, F/30/3/7); Addison's memorandum on the Home Affairs Committee, 17 June 1918, (Addison Papers, Box 69).
[14] Churchill to Lloyd George, 6 July 1922 (Lloyd George Papers, F/10/3/15).
[15] Report on Revolutionary Organizations in the United Kingdom, 25 Sept. 1919 (GT 8228, CAB 24/89).
[16] Harris, *Beveridge*, pp. 256–8.
[17] Cabinet minutes, 14 Aug. 1919 (CAB 23/11).
[18] Ibid., 28 Dec. 1920 (CAB 23/23).
[19] See Herbert Lewis Papers, MSS. 1–54 (National Library of Wales); Memorandum by the Financial Secretary to the Treasury to the Geddes committee, 1921 (CAB 27/165).
[20] Sir A. Newsholme, *The Last Thirty Years in Public Health* (1936), pp. 105 ff; Addison to Bonar Law, 27 Aug. 1919 (Davidson Papers).
[21] Violet Markham to Thomas Jones, 18 Mar. 1920 (*Whitehall Diary*, i. 107).
[22] Edwin Montagu to Lloyd George, 10 July 1919 (Lloyd George Papers, F/40/2/57).
[23] A. C. Pigou, *A Capital Levy: A Levy on War Wealth* (1920); Gibson, in A. W. Kirkaldy (ed.), *British Finance during and after the War, 1914–21* (1921), p. 396.
[24] J. C. C. Davidson to Lord Stamfordham, 27 Dec. 1919 (Davidson Papers).
[25] Circular to Cabinet on Housing, 6 Feb. 1919 (CAB 24/5: G 235); Astor to Garvin, 10 Jan. 1919 (Garvin Papers); Guest to Lloyd George, 15 Nov. 1918 (Lloyd George Papers, F/21/2/47).
[26] *Parl.Deb.*, 5th ser., CXIV, pp. 1713 ff. (7 Apr. 1919).
[27] Ministry of Health memorandum, 27 Oct. 1919, CP3 (CAB 24/92).
[28] *The Times*, 18 Nov. 1919.
[29] *New Statesman*, 8 Nov. 1919; A. C. Pigou, *Aspects of British Economic History, 1918–1925* (1947), p. 91. The Tudor Walters committee (Cd. 9191) spoke of a shortage of 500,000 working-class houses.
[30] Report, Proceedings, and Memoranda of Cabinet Committee on Housing, 1920 (CAB 27/89).
[31] *Economic History Review*, XIII, 'The Abolition of Economic Controls, 1918–21', No. 1 (1943), 1–30.
[32] P. Abrams, 'The Failure of Social Reform, 1918–20', *Past and Present* (Apr. 1963), 43–64. Abrams does not explain in detail of what these controls consisted. See A. C. Pigou, 'Government Control in War and Peace', *Economic Journal* (Dec. 1918), 363 ff.,

for a critical discussion of administrative controls on production, rationing, and price controls.

    [33] 'The Present Position of House Building': Ministry of Health memorandum, 11 Nov. 1919, CP 93 (CAB 24/92).

    [34] e.g. Arthur Marwick, *Britain in the Century of Total War* (1968), p. 125; P. R. Wilding, 'Government and Housing: a Study in the Development of Social Policy, 1906–1939' (unpublished University of Manchester Ph.D. thesis, 1970), *passim*.

    [36] *Parl.Deb.*, 5th ser., Vol. 125, pp. 34–7 (10 Feb. 1920).

    [37] Cabinet minutes, 20 Nov. 1919 (CAB 23/18).

    [38] Gilbert, p. 145; Birkenhead to Addison, 23 June 1921 (Addison Papers, Box 126).

    [39] Cabinet minutes, 14 Nov. 1919 (CAB 23/18).

    [40] Addison memorandum on Housing Bonds, 28 Jan. 1920 (CAB 27/72): cf. Housing (Additional Powers) Act, 1919.

    [41] Thomas Jones to Chamberlain, 13 Aug. 1920 (Thomas Jones Papers, W/2).

    [42] Gilbert, p. 151. The *Nation* was Independent Liberal and had always been fiercely opposed to the government. For Chamberlain's views on housing finance, see memorandum of 20 May 1920 (CP 1330, CAB 24/106).

    [43] Cabinet Finance Committee, 22 July 1920 (CAB 27/71).

    [44] *Memorandum on Board of Education Estimates*, 1938 (Cmd. 5678). The precise figure was £51,014,665.

    [45] Joseph Nall to Sir G. Younger, 2 Dec. 1920 (Bonar Law Papers, 99/8/4).

    [46] K. Feiling, *Life of Neville Chamberlain* 1946), p. 89; *New Statesman*, 21 Mar. 1923; memorandum by Neville Chamberlain, 29 Dec. 1921 (Austen Chamberlain Papers AC 32/2/14). Chamberlain's bill of 1923 proposed smaller houses and a subsidy limited to £6 per house, for a period of twenty years.

    [47] Cabinet Finance Committee, 29 Nov. 1920 (CAB 27/71).

    [48] Gilbert, pp. 135–6.

    [49] Cabinet Finance Committee, 17 Feb. 1921 (CAB 27/71).

    [50] Addison to his wife, 17 Mar. 1921 (Addison Papers, Box 135).

    [51] Addison to his wife, 5 Apr. 1921 (ibid.).

    [52] Report (CAB 27/131).

    [53] Addison to his wife, 15 June 1921 (Addison Papers, Box 135).

    [54] Chamberlain to Lloyd George, 9 June 1921 (Lloyd George Papers, F/7/4/5).

    [55] Lloyd George to Chamberlain, 9 June 1921 (ibid., F/7/4/6).

    [56] Chamberlain to Lloyd George, 15 June 1929 (ibid., F/7/4/11).

    [57] Lloyd George to McCurdy, 14 June 1921 (ibid., F/34/4/12).

    [58] Addison to his wife, 21 June 1921 (Addison Papers, Box 135).

    [59] Ibid.

    [60] Ibid., 23 June 1921.

    [61] Ibid.

    [62] *Parl. Deb.*, 5th ser., Vol. 161, p. 2498.

    [63] Addison to his wife, 5 July 1921 (Addison Papers, Box 135).

    [64] Ibid., 7 July 1921.

    [65] A. L. Bowley and M. Hogg, *Has Poverty Diminished?* (1925), p. 60.

    [66] Conference of Ministers, 12 July 1921 (CAB 23/36).

    [67] Addison to his wife, 12 July 1921 (Addison Papers, Box 135).

    [68] Conclusion of Conference of Ministers, 13 July 1921 (CAB 23/36); *Report of Departmental Committee on High Cost of Building Working-Class Dwellings, 1921* (Cmd. 1447), reporting in early July 1921.

    [69] Addison to his wife, 14 July 1921 (Addison Papers, Box 135).

    [70] Ibid.

[71] *Nation*, 30 July 1921; *New Statesman*, 16 July 1921; Bottomley to Addison, 15 July 1921.

[72] Wedgwood Benn diary, 8 Mar. 1922 (House of Lords Record Office, Stansgate Papers, ST66).

[73] Lloyd George to Churchill, 1 Oct. 1921, Churchill to Lloyd George, 8 Oct. 1921 (Lloyd George Papers, F/10/1/1, 10).

[74] Lloyd George to Bonar Law, 7 June 1921 (ibid., F/31/1/58); *Lloyd George: a Diary by Frances Stevenson*, p. 220.

[75] Finance Committee, 22 July 1920 (CAB 27/71).

[76] *Spectator*, 24 Dec. 1921; Hector Bolitho, *James Lyle Mackay, First Earl of Inchcape* (1936), pp. 170–2.

[77] Astor to Garvin, 'Thursday' (Dec. 1921) (Garvin Papers); Fisher to Lloyd George, 8 Dec. 1921 (Lloyd George Papers, F/16/7/74).

[78] Sutherland memorandum, 19 Dec. 1921 (Austen Chamberlain Papers, AC/32/2/7).

[79] *Dundee Advertiser*, 26 Mar. 1921.

[80] Pigou, *Aspects of British Economic History*, p. 89, citing L. R. Connor in *Statistical Journal* (1936). Wilding (p. 431) gives a total of 198,181 to April 1923.

[81] Bowley and Hogg, p. 5.

[82] Gilbert, p. 308.

[83] Rodney Lowe, 'The Erosion of State Intervention in Britain, 1917–24', 270–86. This excellent article focuses on a national minimum wage and on the implementation of trade boards in 'sweated industries'. Although perhaps tilting the argument unduly away from political decision-making in favour of bureaucratic pressures, this discussion breaks vital new ground in trying to estimate civil service influence on government domestic policy in the post-war era. For some stimulating general comments on the problem as a whole, including the difficulties of finding evidence, see Max Beloff, 'The Whitehall Factor: the role of the Higher Civil Service, 1919–39', in G. Peele and C. Cook (eds.), *The Politics of Reappraisal, 1918–1939* (1975), pp. 209–31.

FOOTNOTES TO CHAPTER V

[1] Mary Agnes Hamilton, *Remembering my Good Friends* (1944), p. 105; Lord Robert Cecil to Mrs. Fawcett, 31 May 1922, Cecil to Smuts, 25 July 1922 (BL, Cecil Papers, Add. MS. 51163, ff. 97–9, 104–6).

[2] Michael Fry, *Lloyd George and Foreign Policy*, Vol. I (Montreal, 1977).

[3] Riddell, *Intimate Diary of the Peace Conference and After*, p. 223 (22 July 1920).

[4] Cf. Kerr to Lloyd George, 2 Sept. 1920 (Lloyd George Papers, F/90/1/18).

[5] Curzon to Lloyd George, 5 Aug. 1921 (ibid., F/13/2/38); Fisher diary, 17 Aug. 1920.

[6] See Alan Sharp, 'The Foreign Office in Eclipse, 1919–22', *History* (June 1976), 198–218. This admirable article concludes that much of the blame must rest on Curzon himself for inability to assert himself.

[7] Curzon memorandum (India Office Library, MS.Eur F/112/319); Curzon to Austen Chamberlain, 3 Oct. 1921 (Chamberlain Papers, AC/24/3/32); cf. memorandum by J. W. Headlam-Morley, 18 Oct. 1920 (FO/800/149, ff. 106–7).

[8] Blanche Dugdale, *Arthur James Balfour* (1936), II. 196; Baird diary, 9 Sept. 1919.

[9] Curzon to Austen Chamberlain, 7 May 1919 (Chamberlain Papers, AC/24/1/29).

[10] R. H. Ullman, *The Anglo-Soviet Accord* (Oxford, 1973), pp. 15–17.

[11] M. Gilbert, *Churchill*, IV, 528. Cf. Curzon to Milner, 13 Feb. 1921, where he talks of Churchill 'spreading his wings over the entire universe' (Bodleian, Milner Papers, 207).

[12] Selborne to Austen Chamberlain, 2 May 1919 (Chamberlain Papers, AC/24/1/47).

[13] I. H. Nish, *Alliance in Decline* (Oxford, 1972), pp. 335–7.

[14] Memorandums by War Office and Admiralty to the Geddes committee, 1921 (CAB 27/164).

[15] Memorandum by Balfour, in Kerr to Lloyd George, 9 Sept. 1919 (Lloyd George Papers, F/89/4/19).

[16] War Office memorandum, CP 3619 (CAB 27/164).

[17] Gilbert, *Churchill*, IV, p. 598.

[18] Report of the Milner Mission to Egypt (Cmd. 1131). It was circulated to the Cabinet on 12 Oct. 1920 (Trinity College, Cambridge, Montagu Papers, AS III–436). Also cf. memorandum by Sir Cecil Hurst, 'The proposed understanding with Egypt', 8 Oct. 1920 (Bodleian, Milner Papers, MS. Eng. Hist. c. 698, ff. 175–82).

[19] Fisher diary, 29 Dec. 1920; Grigg to Valentine Chirol, 28 Dec. 1920 (Grigg Papers); Milner's diary, 29 Dec. 1920 (Milner Papers, dep. 91).

[20] Montagu Papers, AS III–1/436. Milner's diary shows that he met Zaghloul and other Wafd leaders on 25 May, 10 June, and 13 August. For an admirable discussion of the British Cabinet's policy towards Egypt in this period, see G. J. Darwin, 'The Lloyd George Coalition Government and Britain's Imperial Policy in Egypt and the Middle East, 1918–1922' (unpublished Oxford University D.Phil. thesis, 1976), chapters IV and V, *passim*.

[21] Allenby telegram decypher, 20 Jan. 1922 (FO/800/153, f. 140).

[22] Curzon to Montagu, 1 Apr. 1921 (Montagu Papers, AS I–12); Darwin, pp. 193–203, 406–11.

[23] For an excellent description of the debate, see Gilbert, *Churchill*, iv. 401–11.

[24] Sutherland to Lloyd George, ? July 1920 (Lloyd George Papers, F/22/2/5); J. L. Maffey to Lord Chelmsford, 10 July 1920, cited in Judith M. Brown, *Gandhi's Rise to Power: Indian Politics, 1915–1922* (Cambridge, 1972), p. 243; *The Times*, 9 July 1920.

[25] Sutherland to Lloyd George, loc. cit.

[26] Montagu to Lloyd George, 26 Oct., 7 Dec. 1920 (Montagu Papers, AS IV–3/710, 724).

[27] Cabinet minutes, 6 Feb. 1922 (CAB 23/29); Churchill to Montagu, 8 Oct. 1921 (Montagu Papers, AS–3/68 (16).

[28] Cabinet minutes, 9 Feb. 1922 (CAB 23/29).

[29] Lloyd George to Montagu, 25 Apr. 1920 (Lloyd George Papers, F/40/3/5). See *Lloyd George: a Diary by Frances Stevenson*, p. 257 (21 Feb. 1934), where Lloyd George is quoted as saying: 'We should keep a strong hand in India. So long as the natives stick to rice, we shan't have much trouble. But when they take to eating wheat, that is when we shall have to look out.'

[30] J. L. Hammond, *C. P. Scott of the Manchester Guardian* (1934), pp. 271 ff.

[31] Shortt to Lloyd George, 10 Nov. 1918 (Lloyd George Papers, F/45/6/13).

[32] French to MacPherson, 31 Jan. 1919, A. M. Sullivan to MacPherson, 22 Feb. 1919 (Bodleian, MacPherson Papers, MS.Eng.Hist. c. 490).

[33] Plunkett to Addison, 2 Dec. 1918 (Addison Papers, Box 69).

[34] Kenneth O. Morgan, *Lloyd George* (1974), pp. 26–9.

[35] Cabinet Committee on Ireland, report, 4 Nov. 1919, CP 56 (CAB 27/68).

[36] Salisbury to Lord Selborne, 19 Sept. 1919 (Bodleian, Selborne Papers, I/7, f. 64).

[37] Memorandum by MacPherson, 20 Dec. 1919 (MacPherson Papers, loc. cit., ff. 180–3).

[38] Charles Townsend, *The British Campaign in Ireland, 1919–1921* (Oxford, 1975), pp. 43–4.

[39] French to MacPherson, 4 Nov., 10 Dec. 1919 (MacPherson Papers, loc. cit., ff. 139, 171).

[40] J. Wheeler-Bennett, *Sir John Anderson, Viscount Waverley* (1962), pp. 58–77.

[41] It became law on 9 August.

[42] Lloyd George to his wife, 2, 11 Sept. 1920, *Family Letters*, pp. 192–3.

[43] *The Times*, 11 Oct., 10 Nov. 1920.

[44] Fisher diary, 12 May 1920.

[45] Lord d'Abernon diary, 21 Aug. 1922 (BL, d'Abernon Papers, Add. MS. 48954B, f. 45).

[46] Cecil to Sandars, 30 Dec. 1920 (Bodleian, Sandars Papers).

[47] Thomas Jones to Bonar Law, 22 July 1921 (Thomas Jones Papers).

[48] Arthur Link, *Woodrow Wilson: the New Freedom* (Princeton, N.J., 1956), pp. 4–6.

[49] Interview with Donald Maclean, 7 Nov. 1919 (Bodleian, Maclean Papers, ff. 208–12).

[50] D. Lloyd George, *The Truth about the Peace Treaties*, Vol. I (1938), pp. 404–16.

[51] Cabinet minutes, 17 Mar. 1919 (CAB 23/9).

[52] Kerr to Lloyd George, 15 Feb. 1919 (Lloyd George Papers, F/89/2/16); Churchill to Lloyd George, 20 Sept. 1920 (ibid., F/9/1/15); Baird diary, 6 Sept. 1919; Cabinet minutes, 18 Nov. 1920 (CAB 23/23).

[53] Lloyd George's note on Churchill memorandum on the Russian situation, 30 Aug. 1919 (Lloyd George Papers, F/9/1/15).

[54] Lloyd George to Churchill, 22 Sept. 1919 (ibid., F/9/1/20).

[55] Milner diary, 8 Oct. 1919 (Milner Papers).

[56] Riddell, p. 198 (30 May 1920).

[57] Fisher diary, 7 June 1920.

[58] L. Macfarlane, 'Hands off Russia: British Labour and the Russo-Polish War, 1920', *Past and Present* (Dec. 1967), 126–52.

[59] Cabinet minutes, 9 Aug. 1920 (CAB 23/22); note to Lloyd George, 9 Aug. 1920 (Lloyd George Papers, F/99).

[60] Cabinet minutes, 17 Nov. 1920 (CAB 23/23).

[61] Kerr to Milner, 28 Dec. 1920 (Milner Papers, MS. Eng. Hist. c. 701).

[62] Ullmann, p. 454.

[63] Frances Perkins, *The Roosevelt I Knew* (New York, 1946), p. 330.

[64] Fisher diary, 31 May 1919; Smuts to Lord Robert Cecil, 5 July 1922 (Cecil Papers, Add. MS. 51163, ff. 99–103).

[65] Smuts to Cecil (loc. cit.).

[66] Lloyd George to Curzon, 10 Dec. 1919 (Lloyd George Papers, F/12/2/11).

[67] Lloyd George, *The Truth about the Peace Treaties*, i. 461.

[68] Keynes to Chamberlain, 28 Dec. 1919 (Chamberlain Papers, AC 35/1/10).

[69] Chamberlain to Selborne, 13 Feb. 1920 (Selborne Papers, II/87, f. 63). In the interval, Chamberlain had read the *Economic Consequences*, with much relish.

[70] *New Statesman*, 1 May 1920; *Nation*, May 1920; Violet Markham to Thomas Jones, 4 May 1920 (*Whitehall Diary*, i. 113).

[71] P. Kerr to Curzon, 25 June 1920 (FO/800/153, ff. 289–90); R. Butler and J. P. T. Bury (eds.), *Documents on British Foreign Policy, 1919–1939*, First Series, VIII, pp. 643–4.

[72] J. M. Keynes, *A Revision of the Treaty* (1922), pp. 169 ff. This was in place of the original claim of 138 milliard.

[73] 'Arrangement for the Discharge of Germany's Liability for Reparations under the Treaty of Versailles', *DBFP*, First Ser., XV, pp. 566–9 (3 May 1921).

[74] Churchill to Lloyd George, 2 June 1921 (Grigg Papers).

[75] Cabinet memorandum on 'Germany's Capacity to Pay', Sept. 1921 (Worthington-Evans Papers, M.S. Eng. Hist. c. 915).

[76] ? to Ponsonby, 6 June 1921 (Ponsonby Papers, ff. 54–5).

[77] Brand to Grigg, 20 Apr. 1921 (Grigg Papers).

[78] d'Abernon, *An Ambassador of Peace*, i. 185; Churchill to Lloyd George, 28 Nov. 1921 (Lloyd George Papers, F/10/1/48).

[79] Cecil to Grey, 12 Apr. 1921, Cecil to Churchill, 8 Jan. 1929 (Cecil Papers, Add. MS. 51073, ff. 79–81, 113–14); Cecil to Gilbert Murray, 18 May 1921 (Bodleian, Murray Papers, Box 16C).

[80] Information from Mr. Michael Maclagan, to whom the author expresses gratitude.

[81] Philip Gibbs, in *Review of Reviews* (Jan. 1922), 1 ff.

[82] Grigg to Curzon, 18 Sept. 1921 (Grigg Papers).

[83] Grigg to Stamfordham, 25 Jan. 1922 (ibid.).

[84] Valentine Chirol, 'Four Years of Lloyd Georgian Foreign Policy', *Edinburgh Review* (Jan. 1923), 1–20.

[85] Ullman, p. 473.

FOOTNOTES TO CHAPTER VI

[1] Cabinet minutes, 30 Jan. 1919 (CAB 23/9); Ministry of Labour report for the week ending 1 Oct. 1919 (CAB 24/89); Thomas Jones to Lloyd George, 17 Mar. 1919 (Lloyd George Papers, F/23/4/36).

[2] Conclusions of Conference of Ministers, 2 Feb. 1920 (CAB 23/37).

[3] Cabinet minutes, 3 Mar. 1919 (CAB 23/9); Finance Committee, 7 Dec. 1920 (CAB 27/71).

[4] Cabinet minutes, 2 Feb. 1922 (CAB 23/39); Lloyd George to Bonar Law, 4 Sept. 1920 (Lloyd George Papers, F/31/1/44); Lloyd George to Curzon, 15 Sept. 1922 (Lloyd George Papers, F/13/3/33); Riddell, *Intimate Diary of the Peace Conference and After*, p. 389 (24 Sept. 1922).

[5] Kerr to Lloyd George, 2 Sept. 1920 (Lloyd George Papers, F/90/1/18).

[6] Eric Hoffer, *The True Believer* (New York, 1951).

[7] D. G. Boyce, *Englishmen and Irish Troubles, 1918–1922* (1972), p. 83. Also see Dr. Boyce's 'Public Opinion and Historians', *History* (June 1978), for a thoughtful discussion of this theme.

[8] H. C. G. Matthew, R. I. McKibbin, J. A. Kay, 'The Franchise Factor in the Rise of the Labour Party', *English Historical Review*, XCIII (Oct. 1976), 723–52.

[9] Mond to Bonar Law, 11 Dec. 1918 (Bonar Law Papers, 96/4).

[10] Feiling, *Chamberlain*, pp. 90–1.

[11] Arnold Rowntree to Ponsonby, 3 Jan. 1919 (Ponsonby Papers).

[12] Fisher diary, 9 Jan. 1919.

[13] Marquand, *Ramsay MacDonald*, p. 235; private information from the late Rev. T. E. Nicholas. Women had made much of the 'white feather' offered to pacifists during the war.

[14] W. C. Jenkins to Mond, 10 Aug. 1922 (Lloyd George Papers, F/37/2/17).

[15] Worsfold, *The War and Social Reform*, p. 230.

[16] Malcolm Fraser to Austen Chamberlain, 31 Dec. 1921 (Chamberlain Papers, AC/32/2/7).

[17] *The Times*, 28 Feb. 1921. Addison was criticized by Lady Rhondda and others for failure to appoint women to the Welsh Board of Health and other bodies.

[18] Baird diary, 27 Oct. 1919.

[19] *The Times*, 24 Sept. 1921.

[20] Stanley Salvidge, *Salvidge of Liverpool* (1934), p. 163. Salvidge also warned Bonar Law about the change in the electoral character of Bootle.

[21] *The Times*, 28 Feb. 1921.

[22] Gilbert Murray to H. A. L. Fisher, 8 June 1919 (Murray Papers, Box 19).

[23] Matthew, McKibbin, and Kay, loc. cit.

[24] R. I. McKibbin, *The Evolution of the Labour Party 1910–1924* (Oxford, 1976), p. 118.

[25] Marquand, *Ramsay MacDonald*, p. 289.

[26] Sutherland to Lloyd George, 2 Jan. 1922 (Lloyd George Papers, F/35/1/1).

[27] Guest to Lloyd George, 15 Nov. 1918 (Lloyd George Papers, F/21/2/47); Davidson to Bonar Law, 13 Jan. 1922 (Bonar Law Papers, 107/2).

[28] Hartington to Lord R. Cecil, ? 1921 (Cecil Papers, Add. MS. 51163, f. 43).

[29] *The Times*, 11 Nov. 1919.

[30] F. M. L. Thompson, *English Landed Society in the Nineteenth Century* (1963), p. 333; *The Times*, 19 May 1920, cited in Thompson, p. 331; speech by Griffith-Boscawen in the Commons, 17 Nov. 1920.

[31] On agriculture, see E. H. Whetham, 'The Agriculture Act, 1920, and its Repeal—"the Great Betrayal"', *Agricultural History Review* (1972); *Annual Reports* and *Yearbooks* of the National Farmers' Union for 1920–2; Sir Arthur Griffith-Boscawen, 'The Decontrol of Agriculture', *Lloyd George Liberal Magazine* (July 1921), 578–9; *idem, Memories*, pp. 235–7; and Maurice Cowling, *The Impact of Labour*, pp. 87–90 for a brilliant analysis of the landed 'connection'.

[32] T. Huws Davies to Sir Henry Primrose, 3 Aug. 1919 (National Library of Wales, Huws Davies Papers, 16,354C).

[33] J. A. Cross, *Sir Samuel Hoare* (1977), pp. 30–5.

[34] Cited in Michael Bentley, *The Liberal Mind, 1914–1929* (Cambridge, 1977), p. 196.

[35] This was the Revd. James Nicholas, minister of Castle Street, 1916–35 (Walter P. John and Gwilym T. Hughes, *Hanes Castle Street a'r Bedyddwyr* (Llandyssul, 1959), pp. 68 ff.).

[36] Herbert Lewis to Lloyd George, Mar. 1920, 'not sent' (Herbert Lewis Papers, additional deposit); Lord Clwyd to Herbert Lewis, 12, 16, 17 Aug. 1921 (Plas Penucha MSS.); Lewis's diary, 26 Mar. 1920; John Ramsden, 'The Newport By-Election', in Chris Cook and J. Ramsden (eds.), *By-Elections in British Politics* (1973), p. 35.

[37] Kenneth O. Morgan, 'Cardiganshire Politics: the Liberal Ascendancy', *Ceredigion* (1967), pp. 332–5.

[38] W. C. Jenkins to Mond, 10 Aug. 1922 (Lloyd George Papers, F/37/2/17).

[39] Christopher Harvie, *Scotland and Nationalism* (1977), pp. 45–51.

[40] *Welsh Outlook* (Jan. 1921), p. 302.

[41] Beriah G. Evans to John, 5 May 1922, D. R. Grenfell to John, 18 Dec. 1923 (National Library of Wales, John Papers).

[42] *Merthyr Pioneer*, 14 Mar. 1914.

[43] Though Sir John Benn (Progressive) did defeat the transport workers' leader, Harry Gosling, in the LCC election for Kennington in March 1922.

[44] Sir R. Sanders to Younger, 2 Dec. 1920 (Bonar Law Papers, 99/8/4).

[45] *Annual Report* of the Coalition Liberal Organization, 1920, p. 32 (Lloyd George Papers, F/168/2/16).

[46] Younger to Bonar Law, 12 Aug. 1920 (Bonar Law Papers, 99/4/16).

[47] M. Fraser to Austen Chamberlain, 31 Dec. 1921 (Chamberlain Papers AC32/1/4a); J. A. Ramsden, 'The Organization of the Conservative and Unionist Party in Britain, 1910 to 1930' (unpublished Oxford University D.Phil., 1974), p. 46.

[48] Fisher diary, 24 Mar. 1921.

[49] McKibbin, *Evolution of the Labour Party*, pp. 170–4.

[50] Cecil to Lord Salisbury, 18 May 1921 (Cecil Papers, Add. MS. 51085, ff. 90–5).

[51] *Sunday Pictorial*, Jan.–Feb. 1921, *passim*.

⁵² S. Koss, *Fleet Street Radical* (1973), p. 289. This was on orders from the Cadburys.
⁵³ *The Times*, 18 Sept. 1919.
⁵⁴ A. Havighurst, *Radical Journalist* (Cambridge, 1974), pp. 293–302.
⁵⁵ *History of The Times, Part II*, pp. 694–9.
⁵⁶ See John Gross, *The Rise and Fall of the Man of Letters* (Penguin Books ed., 1973), chapter IV, for a stimulating discussion of Liberal littérateurs.
⁵⁷ *Lloyd George Liberal Magazine* (Oct. 1920), 12. From an interview with Harold Spender.

FOOTNOTES TO CHAPTER VII

¹ Cabinet conclusions, 4 June 1920 (CAB 23/21).
² *Report from the Select Committee on Increase of Wealth (War)*, P.P. (1920), VII, 55–389; Chamberlain to Garvin, 31 Oct. 1919 (Chamberlain Papers, AC/24/1/35).
³ Riddell, *Intimate Diary of the Peace Conference and After*, p. 179.
⁴ Curzon to Hardinge, 12 Jan. 1921, cited in Alan J. Sharp, 'The Foreign Office in Eclipse, 1919–22', 204, n. 47.
⁵ C. P. Scott diary, Dec. 1919 (Add. MS. 50905, f. 220).
⁶ *The Times*, 19 Nov. 1921; Griffith-Boscawen, *Memories*, p. 232.
⁷ Guest to Lloyd George, 8 July 1918 (Lloyd George Papers, F/21/4/1); Colin Coote, *Editorial* (1965), p. 103.
⁸ Sir Colin Coote to the author, 19 Nov. 1976 (quoted by permission).
⁹ Walter Elliot, 'For a Permanent Coalition Party', *Review of Reviews* (Jan. 1920), 31–4; Colin Coote, *A Companion of Honour* (1965), pp. 45 ff.
¹⁰ Letter in *The Times*, 16 Dec. 1920.
¹¹ E. Wild, 'The Coalition', *Nineteenth Century and After* (Mar. 1920), 397 ff.
¹² O. F. Maclagan, *Coalition Government* (1920).
¹³ C. McCurdy, 'Coalition, Caucus and Commonsense', *Fortnightly Review*, (Mar. 1921, 353 ff.; 'Notes on the Coalition Government, 1920' (Herbert Lewis Papers, 38).
¹⁴ Sir G. Hewart, *The Lloyd George Government: What it had done and Why it is still Needed* (1920), p. 15; idem., 'Coalition and Democracy', *Sunday Times*, 7 Aug. 1921.
¹⁵ *Outlook*, Apr. 1919.
¹⁶ *The Times*, 11 Nov. 1919.
¹⁷ Riddell, pp. 164–6.
¹⁸ Fisher diary, 4 Feb. 1920; *The Times*, 8 Dec. 1919.
¹⁹ Fisher diary, 28 Jan. 1920.
²⁰ Ibid., 4 Feb. 1920.
²¹ *Annual Report of Coalition Liberal Organization*, 1920.
²² Material in Addison Papers, Boxes 68 and 123.
²³ Addison to Lloyd George, 3 Mar. 1920 (Lloyd George Papers, F/1/6/4).
²⁴ Churchill to Lloyd George, 21 Feb. 1920 (ibid., F/9/2/9).
²⁵ *The Times*, 16 Feb. 1920.
²⁶ Baird diary, 8 Oct. 1919.
²⁷ Bonar Law to Lloyd George, 27 Jan. 1919 (Lloyd George Papers, F/30/3/7).
²⁸ Baird diary, 9 Oct. 1919.
²⁹ *The Times*, 20 Aug. 1919.
³⁰ *Evening Standard*, 13 Jan. 1920; Baird diary, 9 Oct. 1919.
³¹ Baird diary, 16 Nov. 1919.
³² *Weekly Dispatch*, 11 Jan.–21 Mar. 1920.
³³ *The Times*, 15 Oct. 1919.
³⁴ Ibid., 18 Mar. 1920.

[35] *Morning Post*, 13 Mar. 1920; *Observer*, 14 Mar. 1920; Bonar Law to Balfour, 12 Mar. 1920 (Bonar Law Papers 96/4).

[36] Fisher diary, 16 Mar. 1920; Herbert Lewis diary, 16 Mar. 1920 (Plas Penucha MSS.).

[37] Lloyd George Papers, F/242.

[38] *Lloyd George: a Diary by Frances Stevenson*, p. 206.

[39] *The Times*, 19 Mar. 1920; *Manchester Guardian*, 19 Mar. 1920.

[40] *Lloyd George: a Diary by Frances Stevenson*, p. 206.

[41] Ibid., p. 205.

[42] Bonar Law to Balfour, 24 Mar. 1920 (Bonar Law Papers, 96/4); Balfour to Lloyd George, 9 Feb. 1920 (Lloyd George Papers, F/3/5/1); Sir John Gilmour to Law, 16 Mar. 1920 (Bonar Law Papers, 96/4).

[43] For Stockport, see G. J. Wardle to Lloyd George, 9 Mar. 1920 (Lloyd George Papers, F/27/6/29), and the *Manchester Guardian*, Mar. 1920, *passim*. Bentley Gilbert incomprehensibly claims that Lord Salisbury 'obtained the defeat of the official Coalition candidate' [*sic*] at Stockport (*British Social Policy*, p. 42).

[44] Younger to Davidson, 4 Dec. 1920 (Bonar Law Papers, 99/8/4).

[45] *Annual Report of the Coalition Liberal Organization*, 1920.

[46] Ibid.

[47] I am grateful to Mr. Philip Waller for letting me see in advance the MS. of his valuable book on Liverpool.

[48] Sir Colin Coote to the author, loc. cit.

[49] Fisher diary, 18 May 1920.

FOOTNOTES TO CHAPTER VIII

[1] There is an interesting discussion of this theme in M. Bentley, *The Liberal Mind*.

[2] *The Times*, 4 Jan., 4 Feb. 1919.

[3] Ibid., 7 Feb. 1919; *Liberal Magazine* (Apr. 1919), 134–6.

[4] *The Economist*, 14 June 1919; *New Statesman*, 1 Nov. 1919.

[5] Trevor Wilson, *Downfall of the Liberal Party*, p. 191.

[6] Mond to Lloyd George, 15 Mar. 1919 (Lloyd George Papers, F/36/6/46).

[7] Lord E. Percy to Sir Alfred Zimmern, 14 Apr. 1919 (Bodleian, Zimmern Papers, Box 1); Lord Eustace Percy, *Some Memories* (1958), p. 74; Kenworthy, *Sailors, Statesmen—and Others*, pp. 151–4.

[8] *New Statesman*, 20 Sept. 1919.

[9] *Manchester Guardian*, 13 Dec. 1919.

[10] Cabinet minutes, 17 Dec. 1919 (CAB 23/20). It was agreed that Guest should arrange for a question to be put to Churchill about Col. Fairfax's war service.

[11] Guest to Lloyd George, 15 Jan., 25 Feb. 1920 (Lloyd George Papers, F/22/1/3, 13).

[12] Guest to Lloyd George, 18 June 1920 (ibid., F/22/1/45).

[13] Mrs. Price White to Mrs. Coombe Tennant, 24 Mar. 1921 (ibid., F/96/1/15).

[14] Llewelyn Williams to Ponsonby, 12 Oct. 1920 (Ponsonby Papers).

[15] See Kenneth O. Morgan, 'Cardiganshire Politics', *Ceredigion* (1967), loc. cit.

[16] Watkin Davies diary, 19 Feb. 1921 (Davies Papers).

[17] Goronwy Rees, *A Chapter of Accidents* (1972), pp. 13–18.

[18] *Manchester Guardian*, 3, 6 December 1919.

[19] Churchill to Lloyd George, 14 July 1921 (Lloyd George Papers, F/9/1/13).

[20] C. P. Scott diary, 15–17 Mar. 1920 (Scott Papers, Add. MS. 50906, ff. 13–14).

[21] Llewelyn Williams to Ponsonby, 12 Oct. 1920 (Ponsonby Papers).

[22] C. P. Scott diary, 9 Aug. 1921 (Scott Papers, Add. MS. 50906, ff. 78 ff.); Williams

to Ponsonby, loc. cit.; Gladstone to Cecil, 22 Apr. 1922 (Cecil Papers, Add. MS. 51163, ff. 85–7).

[23] Hudson to Maclean, 12 Jan. 1919 (Maclean Papers, Dep. 49–50, c. 465, ff. 121–32).

[24] *The Times*, 1 May 1920.

[25] *Manchester Guardian*, 8 May 1920; Fisher diary, 6 Nov. 1918; McCurdy memorandum, June 1921 (Lloyd George Papers, F/34/1/4); Bentley Gilbert, p. 44.

[26] Addison to Lloyd George, 13 May 1920 (Lloyd George Papers, F/1/6/8); cf. Sir Gordon Hewart, *The Lloyd George Government*.

[27] Guest to Lloyd George, 18 June 1920 (Lloyd George Papers, F/22/3/45); Lloyd George to Austen Chamberlain, 9 June 1920 (ibid., F/7/4/6); Fisher diary, 24 Mar. 1921.

[28] C. F. G. Masterman, 'The General Election—and After', *Contemporary Review* (Feb. 1919), 127.

[29] *Spectator*, 29 Jan. 1921; *Manchester Guardian*, Jan. 1921.

[30] *The Times*, 28 Sept. 1921; Mary Stocks, *Ernest Simon of Manchester*, pp. 61, 69; Ramsay Muir, *Liberalism and Industry* (1920), and *Politics and Progress* (1923); Philip Guedalla, *The Industrial Future: a Liberal Policy* (1922). For Muir more generally, see Stuart Hodgson (ed.), *Ramsay Muir: an Autobiography and some Essays* (1943).

[31] C. Sheridan Jones, *The Call to Liberalism* (1921).

[32] J. M. Robertson, *Liberalism and Labour* (1921) and *Mr. Lloyd George and Liberalism* (1923), pp. 122–3.

[33] Trevor Wilson, p. 237.

[34] Apart from the Cecil Papers in the British Library, his autobiography, *All the Way* (1949), is of much interest.

[35] Cecil to Lloyd George, 27 May 1919 (Cecil Papers, Add. MS. 51076, ff. 38–41).

[36] Cecil to Churchill, 8 Jan. 1929 (ibid., Add. MS. 51073, f. 113).

[37] Cecil to Lloyd George, 4 Apr. 1919 (ibid., Add. MS. 51076, ff. 35–6).

[38] *The Times*, 1 Aug. 1919.

[39] Baird diary, 9 Oct. 1919.

[40] *The Times*, 19 Mar. 1921.

[41] Cecil to Salisbury, 18 May 1921 (Cecil Papers, Add. MS. 51085, ff. 90–5); Cecil to Murray, 26 August 1921 (Murray Papers, Box 16C).

[42] Cecil to Salisbury, 6 May 1921 (Cecil Papers, Add. MS. 51085, ff. 83–4).

[43] Cecil to Gertrude Bell, 11 Apr. 1921 (ibid., Add. MS., 51163, ff. 1–3).

[44] Cecil to Chamberlain, 20, 27 Apr. 1921 (Chamberlain Papers, AC/24/3/15, 17).

[45] Balfour to Cecil, 6 Feb. 1921 (Cecil Papers, Add. MS. 51071, ff. 35–6).

[46] R. Skidelsky, *Mosley* (1975), pp. 93–5.

[47] Bodleian, Maclean Papers, c. 466.

[48] Cecil to Murray, 26 Aug. 1921 (Murray Papers, Box 16c).

[49] Laski to Holmes, 12 Jan. 1921 (*Holmes–Laski Letters*, i. 305).

[50] Steel-Maitland to Cecil, 5 Aug. 1921 (Cecil Papers, Add. MS. 51071, ff. 120–5).

[51] Cecil to Cowdray, 9 July 1921 (ibid., Add. MS. 51163, ff. 6–8).

[52] Wedgwood Benn diary, 1 Feb. 1922 Stansgate Papers, ST/66).

[53] See Michael Bentley, 'Liberal Politics and the Grey Conspiracy of 1921', *Historical Journal* (June 1977), 461–78.

[54] Steel-Maitland to Asquith, 29 July 1921 (Cecil Papers, Add. MS. 51071, ff. 109–11).

[55] Spender to Cecil, 2 Sept. 1921 (ibid., Add. MS. 51163, ff. 17–18).

[56] Asquith to Cecil, 19 Oct. 1922 (ibid., Add. MS. 51073, ff. 34–9); cf. Cecil to Murray, 9 Apr. 1921 (Murray Papers, Box 16c).

[57] Runciman to Cecil, 22 Aug. 1921 (Cecil Papers, Add. MS. 51163, ff. 10–11).

[58] Gladstone to Cecil, 21 Sept. 1922 (ibid., ff. 116–17); Gladstone to Murray, 20 Apr. 1922 (Murray Papers, Box 59). Warrington also went Liberal in January 1910.

[59] Cecil to Margot Asquith, 4 Dec. 1923 (Cecil Papers, Add. MS. 51073, f. 43).

[60] Cf. John Sproat, *The Best Men* (Oxford, 1968).

[61] E. H. Carr, *Twenty Years Crisis* (2nd ed., 1951), p. 38.

FOOTNOTES TO CHAPTER IX

[1] Riddell, *War Diary*, p. 309 (27 Jan. 1918).

[2] Lloyd George, *War Memoirs*, ii. 1127.

[3] *Report of Annual Conference of the Independent Labour Party*, 1917.

[4] Kerr to Lloyd George, 20 Nov. 1918 (Lloyd George Papers, F/89/1/13).

[5] Lloyd George to Bonar Law, 20 Mar. 1919 (ibid., F/30/3/32).

[6] Cabinet minutes, 3 Mar. 1919 (CAB 23/9).

[7] Alan Clark (ed.), *A Long Innings: the Private Papers of Lord Lee of Farham* (1974), p. 196.

[8] Malcolm Fraser to Austen Chamberlain, 31 Dec. 1921 (Chamberlain Papers, AC/32/4/1a).

[9] C. P. Trevelyan, *From Liberalism to Labour* (1921), p. 60. Cf. A. Siegfried, *Post-War Britain* (1924), pp. 279–80.

[19] R. E. Dowse, *Left in the Centre* 1966), pp. 70–2. In fact, ILP membership appears to have declined from 1921 onwards.

[11] E. Hatch, 'The Uprising of Labour', *Nineteenth Century and After* (Jan. 1920), 17–26; cf. J. B. Firth, 'The Return of Mr. Asquith', *Fortnightly Review* (1920), 357–8.

[12] *The Times*, 3 Nov. 1920.

[13] Marquand, *Ramsay MacDonald*, pp. 273–5.

[14] MacDonald to Ponsonby, 2 June 1922 (Ponsonby Papers).

[15] *The Times*, 14 Feb. 1920.

[16] See McKibbin, *Evolution of the Labour Party*, pp. 206–34.

[17] MacDonald to O. G. Villard, 17 Apr. 1921 (Villard Papers).

[18] See R. Douglas, *Land, People and Politics* (1976), pp. 174–5.

[19] Laski to Holmes, 15 Apr. 1922 (*Holmes—Laski Letters*, i. 415).

[20] MacDonald to Villard, 4 Sept. 1919 (Villard Papers).

[21] A. Bullock, *Life and Times of Ernest Bevin*, i. 321–2.

[22] B. Donoghue and G. W. Jones, *Herbert Morrison* (1973), appendix, p. 655.

[23] Henderson to Lloyd George, 7 Jan. 1920 (Lloyd George Papers F/27/3/39); M. A. Hamilton, *Remembering my Good Friends*, p. 106.

[24] On the capital levy, see F. W. Pethick-Lawrence, *A Levy on Capital* (1920); Sidney Webb, *National Finance and the Capital Levy* (1920); *Labour and the War Debt* (1922); Philip Snowden, *Labour and National Finance* (1920), pp. 68–81, and *If Labour Rules* (1923).

[25] A. C. Pigou, *A Levy on Capital* (1920). Keynes's attack on Pigou as an alleged exponent of traditional economics appears in his *General Theory* (1936), pp. 272–9.

[26] *Par. Deb.*, 5th ser., Vol. 169, pp. 1095–7 (14 Feb. 1924).

[27] Donoghue and Jones, p. 655.

[28] *Annual Conference of the Labour Party*, 1919, pp. 146 ff.

[29] Cited in P. Snowden, *Labour and National Finance*, p. 124.

[30] See R. Skidelsky, *Politicians and the Slump* (1968), pp. 27 ff.

[31] A. W. Kirkaldy (ed.), *British Finance during and after the War*, p. 376.

[32] See Cabinet Committee on Unemployment, 1920–2 (CAB 27/114).

[33] *Parl. Deb.*, 5th ser., Vol. 161, pp. 2472 ff.

[34] Cf. R. Challinor, *Origins of British Bolshevism* (1977).

³⁵ Margaret Cole, *G. D. H. Cole*, pp. 102, 121.

³⁶ H. D. Henderson, 'Reports of the Coal Industry Commission', *Economic Journal* (Sept. 1919), 265–78; Sir J. Sankey, *Chairman's Report on Coal Industry Commission*, 1919 (Cmd. 210). For a summary of the MFGB mines' nationalization bill, see R. Page Arnot, *The Miners: Years of Struggle* (1953), pp. 220–3.

³⁹ R. H. Tawney, 'The Nationalization of the Mines' (Labour Party pamphlet, 1919), reprinted in Rita Hinden (ed.), *The Radical Tradition* (Penguin Books, 1966), pp. 123–43; Frank Hodges, *Nationalisation of the Mines* (1920), pp. 84–132.

³⁸ R. MacDonald, *Socialism: Critical and Constructive*, pp. 145–7.

³⁹ Addison to MacDonald, 9 June 1929 (P.R.O., MacDonald Papers, 5/40).

⁴⁰ *Nation*, 21, 28 Feb. 1920.

⁴¹ C. P. Scott diary, 28 Feb. 1922, (Scott Papers, Add. MS. 50906, f. 147).

⁴² Lloyd George Papers, F/100.

⁴³ Paul Addison, *The Road to 1945* (1975), *passim*.

⁴⁴ See above, p. 78; cf. John Paton, *Left Turn!* (1936), p. 101, for a comment on Hodges's appearance.

⁴⁵ D. Calhoun, *The United Front* (Cambridge, 1975), *passim*.

⁴⁶ Since writing this chapter, I have had the benefit of reading (and, indeed, examining) C. J. Howard's admirable 'Henderson, MacDonald and Leadership in the Labour Party, 1914–1922' (Cambridge University Ph.D. thesis, 1978) which follows similar lines of argument to my own. He concludes that the Labour Party at this time was 'an organisers' party, not a fountain-head of ideas' (p. 313).

FOOTNOTES TO CHAPTER X

¹ H. Wickham Steed, *Through Thirty Years 1892–1922* (1924), pp. 368 ff; *History of The Times*, Vol. IV, part I, pp. 480 ff.

² Parl. Deb., 5th ser., Vol. 120, p. 86 (22 Oct. 1919). The next speaker, Ormsby-Gore, strongly attacked Billing's speech as anti-Semitic.

³ *The Times*. 25 Oct. 1919.

⁴ Bairy diary, 24 Oct. 1919.

⁵ Neville Chamberlain to Austen Chamberlain, 29 Dec. 1921 (Chamberlain Papers, AC/32/2/13).

⁶ *The Times*, 20 Apr. 1920; *New Statesman*, 24 Apr. 1920.

⁷ For Churchill, see his recorded dissent after a Cabinet decision not to go ahead with a levy on war wealth, 4 June 1920 (CAB 23/21). In the event, the Royal Commission on Income Tax (Cmd. 615) concentrated on technical adjustments such as differentiation in assessment, graduation, and the raising of personal allowances.

⁸ *The Times*, 2 July 1920.

⁹ Memorandum, May 1920 (Selborne Papers, I/7, ff. 96–7).

¹⁰ *The Times*, 2 June 1920.

¹¹ Younger to Bonar Law, 14 June 1920 (Lloyd George Papers, F/31/1/36).

¹² Milner to Selborne, 6 May 1921 (Selborne Papers, I/12, f. 315).

¹³ *The Times*, 11 June 1921.

¹⁴ Salisbury to Selborne, 15 Nov. 1921 (Selborne Papers, I/7, f. 113).

¹⁵ Chamberlain to Lloyd George, 9 June 1921, Lloyd George to Chamberlain, 9 June 1921 (Lloyd George Papers, F/7/4/5, 6); Younger to Chamberlain, 10 June 1921 (ibid., F/7/4/6).

¹⁶ *The Times*, 17–27 Aug. 1921; *Morning Post*, 17–27 Aug. 1921.

¹⁷ *Punch*, 31 Aug. 1921.

¹⁸ Selborne to Salisbury, 13 June 1921 (Selborne Papers, I/7, ff. 103–5).

¹⁹ Gretton to Chamberlain, 19 July 1921 (Chamberlain Papers, AC/24/3/46).

[20] Gretton memorandum, 19 Feb. 1922 (ibid., AC/33/1/10).

[21] Sir H. Nield to Chamberlain, 2, 15 Aug. 1921 (ibid., AC/24/3/78, 80).

[22] Salisbury to Selborne, 15 Nov. 1921 (Selborne Papers, loc. cit.).

[23] Grigg to Lord Cromer, 15 Nov. 1921 (Grigg Papers).

[24] Austen Chamberlain to Neville Chamberlain, 13 Nov. 1921 (Chamberlain Papers, AC/32/1/2).

[25] Derby to Austen Chamberlain, 14 Nov. 1921 (ibid., AC/32/1/3).

[26] Salisbury to Selborne, 15 Nov. 1921 (Selborne Papers, loc. cit.).

[27] Ibid.

[28] Waldorf Astor to Garvin, 'Thursday evening' 1921 (Garvin Papers).

[29] *The Times*, 18 Nov. 1921.

[30] Chamberlain Papers, AC/32/12 ff.

[31] Astor to Garvin, 'Thursday' and 'Thursday evening' 1921 (Garvin Papers).

[32] Younger to Austen Chamberlain, 4 Jan. 1922 (Chamberlain Papers, AC/32/2/21).

[33] R. Sanders to Chamberlain, 2 Jan. 1922 (ibid., AC/32/3/16).

[34] Davidson to Bonar Law, 13 Jan. 1922 (Bonar Law Papers, 107/2).

[35] Salisbury to Bonar Law, 4 Mar. 1922 (ibid., 107/2/21).

[36] Memorandum by Austen Chamberlain to Lloyd George, 18 Mar. 1922 (Lloyd George Papers, F/86/1/30).

[37] *The Times*, 3 Mar. 1922.

[38] Ibid., 17 Nov. 1921.

[39] Ibid., 2 Feb. 1922.

FOOTNOTES TO CHAPTER XI

[1] *Review of Reviews* (June 1920), p. 376.

[2] Clark (ed.), *A Long Innings*, p. 209 (13 May 1920).

[3] Laski to Holmes, 6 July 1921 (*Holmes–Laski Letters*, i. 348).

[4] On this see Pigou, *Aspects of British Economic History*; E. V. Morgan, *Studies in British Financial Policy, 1914–25* (1952); R. G. Hawtrey, *Currency and Credit* (4th edition, 1950); Susan Howson, 'The Origins of Dear Money, 1919–20', *Economic History Review*, XXVII, No. 1 (1974), 88–107; C. H. Feinstein, *Domestic Capital Formation in the United Kingdom, 1920–38* (1965); *Spectator*, 1 Jan., 31 Dec. 1921.

[5] Cabinet minutes, 29 July 1920 (CAB 23/22).

[6] Ibid., 17 Nov. 1920 (CAB 23/23).

[7] C. H. Feinstein, *National Income, Expenditure and Output of the United Kingdom, 1855–1965* (Cambridge, 1972), T85: Table 39: 'Gross Domestic Fixed Capital Formation at Current Prices'. The gross figure is somewhat more favourable owing to investment by the local authorities, mainly in housing (£141m in 1921).

[8] Lloyd George to Bonar Law, 7 June 1921 (Lloyd George Papers, F/31/1/58).

[9] *The Times*, 12 Jan. 1922.

[10] Cabinet minutes, 11 Feb. 1921 (CAB 23/24).

[11] *Parl. Deb.*, 5th ser., Vol. 138, pp. 993 ff. (Macnamara's speech, 23 Feb. 1921).

[12] Ibid., Vol. 147, pp. 471 ff. (Macnamara's speech on second reading, 24 Oct. 1921).

[13] Arthur Kiddy in the *Spectator* (25 Feb. 1922) attributed this largely to the glut of money arising from the unprecedented stagnation in trade.

[14] Thomas Jones to Lloyd George 15 June 1921 (Thomas Jones Papers, G2/4).

[15] D. G. Boyce, 'Public Opinion and Historians', 137; Viscount Pakenham, *Peace by Ordeal* (1972 edn.), pp. 177 ff; F. S. L. Lyons, *Ireland since the Famine* (London 1973 edn.), p. 435.

¹⁶ Laski to Holmes, 8 Dec. 1921 (*Holmes–Laski Letters*, i. 386–7); Lord Longford and T. P. O'Neill, *Eamon de Valera* (1970), p. 166.
¹⁷ For the Washington Treaty, see R. L. Buell, *The Washington Conference* (New York, 1922),*passim*; Nish,*Alliance in Decline*, pp. 354–83; S. W. Roskill,*Naval Policy between the Wars*, Vol. I (1968), pp. 300–30; minutes of Cabinet Finance Committee, 7 Dec. 1920 (CAB 27/71).
¹⁸ Clark (ed.), *A Good Innings*, p. 292 (17 July 1929).
¹⁹ Cabinet minutes, 30 May 1921 (CAB 23/35).
²⁰ Grigg to Cromer, 14 Sept. 1921 (Grigg Papers).
²¹ Gwynne to Balfour, 15 Mar. 1922 (Balfour Papers, Add. MS. 49797, ff. 162–3).
²² Report of Geddes Committee (CAB 27/164), p. 6.
²³ *DBFP*, 1st Ser., Vol. XV, pp. 760–804.
²⁴ Ibid., p. 776.
²⁵ *The Times*, 21 January 1922.
²⁶ Cowling, *Impact of Labour*, p. 133.
²⁷ Chamberlain to Younger, 21 Dec. 1921 (Chamberlain Papers, AC/32/2/2).
²⁸ Austen Chamberlain to Neville Chamberlain, 21 Dec. 1921 (ibid., AC/32/2/3).
²⁹ McCurdy memorandum, 20 Dec. 1921 (ibid., AC/32/2/8); McCurdy to Lloyd George, 5 Jan. 1922 (Lloyd George Papers, F/35/1/3).
³⁰ Sutherland memorandum on 'The Political Situation', 19 Dec. 1921 (Chamberlain Papers, AC/32/2/7); Sutherland memorandum, 2 Jan. 1922 (Lloyd George Papers, F/35/1/1).
³¹ J. Williams to Austen Chamberlain, 27 Dec. 1921 (Chamberlain Papers, AC/32/2/5).
³² Neville Chamberlain to Austen Chamberlain, 28 and 29 Dec. 1921 (ibid., AC/32/2/12–14).
³³ Lloyd-Greame to Chamberlain, 7 Jan. 1922, Amery to Chamberlain, 11 Jan. 1922, J. P. Croal to Chamberlain, 7 Jan. 1922 (ibid., 32/2/40).
³⁴ Fraser to Chamberlain, 31 Dec. 1922 (ibid., AC/32/4/1a).
³⁵ Younger to Chamberlain, 28 Dec. 1821, 4 Jan. 1922 (ibid., AC/32/2/15a, 21).
³⁶ Chamberlain to Lloyd George, 4 Jan. 1922 (Lloyd George Papers, F/7/5/1).
³⁷ Churchill to Lloyd George, cable, Jan. 1922 (ibid., F/10/2/1); cf. 'A Short Diary of a Press Campaign' (Austen Chamberlain Papers, AC/32/4/15).
³⁸ *The Times*, 11 Jan. 1922.
³⁹ Churchill to Lloyd George, cable, Jan. 1922 (loc. cit.).
⁴⁰ Lloyd George to Austen Chamberlain, 10 Jan. 1922 (Lloyd George Papers, F/7/5/3).
⁴¹ Younger to Chamberlain, 9, 12 Jan. 1922 (Chamberlain Papers, AC/32/3/23, 29).
⁴² McCurdy to Lloyd George, telegram, 11 Jan. 1922 (Lloyd George Papers, F/35/1/13).
⁴³ McCurdy to Lloyd George, Jan. 1922 (ibid., F/35/1/19).
⁴⁴ *The Times*, 16 Jan. 1922.
⁴⁵ Ibid., 17 Jan. 1922.
⁴⁶ C. P. Scott diary, 17–20 Jan. 1922 (Scott Papers, Add. MS. 50906, ff. 131–2); Grigg to Cromer, 19 Jan. 1922 (Grigg Papers).
⁴⁷ Watkin Davies diary, 22 Jan. 1922 (Davies Papers).
⁴⁸ *Spectator*, 21 Jan. 1922.
⁴⁹ Guest to Lloyd George, 16 Jan. 1922 (Lloyd George Papers, F/22/3/37).
⁵⁰ McCurdy to Lloyd George, telegram, 11 Jan. 1922 (loc. cit.).
⁵¹ Chamberlain to Derby, 12 Jan. 1922 (Chamberlain Papers, AC/32/2/34).
⁵² *The Times*, 23 Jan. 1922.

FOOTNOTES TO CHAPTER XII

[1] There is an interesting discussion in A. Deacon, 'Concession and Coercion: the Politics of Unemployment Insurance in the Twenties', in Briggs and Saville (eds.), *Essays in Labour History*, III (1977), pp. 9–35.

[2] Cabinet minutes, 22 Mar. 1922 (CAB 23/39).

[3] CAB 27/114.

[4] Cabinet Committee on Unemployment: minutes of meeting of 14 Sept. 1920. (CAB 27/114).

[5] Cabinet conclusions, 7 Feb. 1921 (CAB 23/24).

[6] Cabinet conclusions, 13 Dec. 1920 (CAB 23/23).

[7] Ministry of Labour Papers (CP 2315): Cabinet conclusions, 17 Dec. 1920 (CAB 23/23).

[8] Cabinet minutes, 31 Dec. 1920 (CAB 23/23).

[9] Cabinet conclusions, 6 Oct. 1921, 16 Dec., 22 Dec. 1921 (CAB 23/37).

[10] Special Weekly Report, CP 3361 (CB 24/128).

[11] Cabinet conclusions, 24 Jan. 1921 (CAB 23/38); Cabinet Committee on Unemployment: minutes of meeting of 7 Mar. 1921 (CAB 27/114).

[12] E. V. Morgan, *Studies in British Financial Policy, 1914–1925* (1961), p. 96.

[134] CAB 27/114.

[14] *The Times*, 17 Sept. 1921; Donoghue and Jones, *Herbert Morrison*, p. 49.

[15] Grigg to Lloyd George, 23 Mar. 1922 (Lloyd George Papers, F/86/1/35).

[16] Proposals of the Young committee, CP 3363 (CAB 23/37).

[17] *The Times*, 20 Oct. 1921; Lloyd George to C. W. Bowerman, 10 Oct. 1921 (Lloyd George Papers, F/27/3/48).

[18] See, for example, memorandums by Mond of 6 Sept. 1921 (CAB 24/127) and 7 Sept. 1922 (Lloyd George Papers, F/253).

[19] 'The Unemployment Situation', CP 3345, 28 Sept. 1921 (CAB 24/128).

[20] Note by Lloyd-Greame on 'Trade Prospects for 1922', 24 Dec. 1921 (Grigg Papers).

[21] Cabinet minutes, 6 Feb. 1922 (CAB 23/29).

[22] CAB 27/164.

[23] 'War Office Memorandum', CP 3619, p. 5 (ibid.).

[24] Report and Proceedings of Cabinet Committee to Examine the Report of the Geddes Committee, Part I (Defence Departments) (ibid.).

[25] Report of the Committee on Economies in Public Expenditure (Cmd. 1581); Sir Herbert Lewis to Lloyd George, 'Nadolig' [Christmas] 1920 (Lloyd George Papers, F/32/1/24).

[26] Minutes of Cabinet committee, 1922, p. 53 (CAB 27/165).

[27] Ibid.; Fisher to Hankey, 7 Dec. 1920 (CAB 27/72).

[28] Cabinet conclusions, 15 Feb. 1922 (CAB 23/29).

[29] Report, Proceedings, and Memoranda of the Cabinet Committee appointed to examine Parts I and II of the first interim report of the Committee on National Expenditure (GRC (CSD) series), proceedings of 26 Jan. 1922.

[30] Eric Ashby and Mary Anderson, *Portrait of Haldane at Work on Education* (1975), p. 115.

[31] Report, Proceedings, and Memoranda of the Cabinet Committee, proceedings of 26 Jan. 1922 (CAB 27/165).

[32] Neville Chamberlain to Austen Chamberlain, 29 Dec. 1921 (Chamberlain Papers, AC 32/2/14).

[33] Cf. *Nation*, 18, 25 February 1922; *The Times*, 20, 21 Feb. 1922.

[34] Cabinet conclusions, 21 Feb. 1922 (CAB 23/29).

[35] Lord Riddell, *Intimate Diary of the Peace Conference and After*, p. 357.
[36] B. Simon, *The Politics of Educational Reform, 1920–1940* (1974), p. 89.
[37] *Nation*, 4 Mar. 1922.
[38] Cove was elected Labour MP for Aberavon in 1929.
[39] *Parl. Deb.*, 5th ser., Vol. 154, pp. 263 ff.; Austen Chamberlain to Fisher, 17 May 1922 (Fisher Papers, Box 1).
[40] Bowley and Hogg, *Has Poverty Diminished?*, p. 7.
[41] E. V. Morgan, *op cit.* p. 78.
[42] R. H. Tawney, *Equality* (1929), p. 222.
[43] Bowley and Hogg, p. 60.
[44] Guest to Lloyd George, 6 Jan. 1921 (Lloyd George Papers, F/22/3/2).
[45] *Labour Leader*, 29 Apr. 1899.
[46] J. C. C. Davidson's memorandum in Robert Rhodes James (ed.), *Memoirs of a Conservative* (1969), p. 106, cf. the AEU lock-out of March–June 1922.
[47] See Marquand, *Ramsay MacDonald*, p. 296.
[48] See G. S. Bain, *The Growth of White Collar Unionism* (1970), pp. 12 ff.
[49] e.g. *Outlook*, 22 Feb. 1919.
[50] *The Times*, 11 Nov. 1919.
[51] Philip Snowden, *Labour and National Finance* (1920), p. 45; James J. Dodd, *If Labour Wins* (1923), p. 38.
[52] Snowden, *If Labour Rules*, pp. 30 ff.
[53] Lord Askwith, *Industrial Problems and Disputes* (1919), pp. 470 ff.
[54] Cf. B. A. Waites, 'The Effect of the First World War on Class and Status in England, 1910–1920', *Journal of Contemporary History* (Jan. 1976), 27–48. For a general discussion, see W. G. Runciman, *Relative Deprivation and Social Justice* (1966), pp. 55 ff.

FOOTNOTES TO CHAPTER XIII

[1] Riddell, *Intimate Diary of the Peace Conference and After*, p. 368 (23 Mar. 1922).
[2] Lord Hardinge, *Old Diplomacy* (1947), p. 270.
[3] M. Calogeropoulos to Curzon, 1 Mar. 1921 (India Office, MS. Eur. F112/319: Curzon F/1/7).
[4] Curzon Memorandum, 30 Nov. 1922 (ibid.).
[5] Curzon to Lloyd George, 6 Apr. 1922 (Lloyd George Papers, F/13/3/15); cf. F. S. Northedge, *The Troubled Giant* (1966), p. 210.
[6] Cabinet minutes, 6 Dec. 1921 (CAB 23/27).
[7] Murray to H. A. L. Fisher, 26 Aug. 1924 (Murray Papers, Box 19); Conversation between British and French Prime Ministers, 12 Aug. 1921 (*DBFP*, 1st ser., Vol. xv, p. 699).
[8] Conversation between Lloyd George and Briand, Jan. 1922 (FO 371: W/198/50/17).
[9] *DBFP*, 1st ser., Vol. XIX, p. 89.
[10] Hankey to his wife, 11 Jan. 1922, quoted in Roskill, *Hankey: Man of Secrets*, ii. 255.
[11] Cabinet conclusions, 10 Jan. 1922 (CAB 23/29).
[12] Alfred Aubert, *Briand* (Paris, 1928), p. 156.
[13] Papers respecting Negotiations for an Anglo-French Pact, 1924 (Cmd. 2169).
[14] J. P. Selsam, *The Attempts to Form an Anglo-French Alliance 1919–1924* (Philadelphia, 1936), p. 44.
[15] d'Abernon, *An Ambassador of Peace*, ii. 263.

[16] Grigg to Lloyd George, 14 Mar. 1922 (Grigg Papers).

[17] See James Joll, 'Rathenau', in *Intellectuals in Politics* (1960), pp. 120–1.

[18] Memorandum on 'De Jure Recognition of Russia' (Worthington-Evans Papers, MS. Eng. Hist., c. 929).

[19] Chamberlain to Lloyd George, 21 Mar. 1922 (Lloyd George Papers, F/7/5/20;.

[20] Ibid.

[21] Lloyd George to Chamberlain, 22 Mar. 1922 (ibid., F/7/5/31).

[22] Grigg to Brand, 30 Mar. 1922 (Grigg Papers).

[23] Cabinet conclusions, 28 Mar. 1922 (CAB 23/29).

[24] *Parl. Deb.*, 5th ser., Vol. 152, pp. 1885–904; *Review of Reviews* (Apr. 1922), 290–1.

[25] Grigg to Lloyd George, 17 Mar. 1922 (Lloyd George Papers F/86/1/29).

[26] Hughes to Ricci (Italian ambassador in Washington), 8 Mar. 1922 (*US Foreign Relations*, 1922, i. 392–3).

[27] See Gerald Freund, *Unholy Alliance* (1957), pp. 106 ff.; d'Abernon, ii. 235 (17 Aug. 1923).

[28] Grigg to Chamberlain, 18 Apr. 1922 (Grigg Papers).

[29] Earl of Swinton, *Sixty Years of Power* (1966), p. 50.

[30] Chamberlain to Worthington-Evans, 3 May 1922 (Worthington-Evans Papers, MS. Eng. Hist. c. 930).

[31] Horne to Worthington-Evans, 23 Apr. 1922 (ibid., ff. 53–4).

[32] Roskill, ii. 273.

[33] Grigg to Chamberlain, 4 May 1922 (Grigg Papers).

[34] Wilson Harris, *Contemporary Review* (June 1922).

[35] Wickham Steed, *Through Thirty Years*, p. 383.

[36] Memorandums in Worthington-Evans Papers, MS. Eng. Hist. c. 933.

[37] *Parl. Deb.*, 5th ser., Vol. 154, pp. 1449 ff. (19 May 1922).

[38] Cf. *New Statesman*, 28 Jan. 1922.

[38] J. M. Keynes, 'Alternative Aims in Monetary Policy', *Collected Writings of John Maynard Keynes*, IX (1972), pp. 179–80.

[40] Viscount Swinton, *I Remember* (1948), pp. 23–5.

[41] Memorandum by Wise, 16 Oct. 1922 (Grigg Papers).

[42] Cabinet Finance Committee, 31 July 1922 (CAB 27/71).

[43] Cabinet conclusions, 25 July 1922 (CAB 23/30).

[44] Fry, *Illusions of Security*, p. 195.

[45] Grigg to Lloyd George, 5 July 1922 (Grigg Papers).

[46] Cabinet 42 (22), 25 July 1922 (CAB 23/30).

[47] J. M. Keynes, 'The Balfour Note and Inter-Allied Debts', *Nation*, 24 Jan. 1925.

[48] Basil Blackett memorandum, 12 July 1922 (Lloyd George Papers, F/86/2/8).

[49] Harvey to Secretary of State Hughes, 4 Aug. 1922 (*US Foreign Relations*, 1922, i. 410).

[50] Lloyd George to E. Venizelos, 17 Nov. 1920 (Grigg Papers).

[51] C. P. Scott diary, 23 Oct. 1922 (Add. MS. 50906, f. 196).

[51] C. P. Scott diary, 23 Oct. 1922 (Scott Papers, Add. MS. 50906, f. 196).

[52] Kerr to Montagu, 3 May 1920 (Montagu Papers, AS IV–6/893); d'Abernon diary, 25 Sept. 1922 (d'Abernon Papers, Add. MS. 48954B, f. 95).

[53] Milner to Montagu, 2 Dec. 1919 (Montagu Papers, AS I–6/167(5)); Churchill memorandum on Near East, 23 Nov. 1920 (Lloyd George Papers, F/92/13/4).

[54] Fisher to Montagu, 18 Feb. 1920 (Montagu Papers, AS I–12/237(1)).

[55] Minutes of Conference of Ministers, 18 Feb. 1921 (CAB 23/38); M. Llewellyn Smith, *Ionian Vision* (1973), pp. 189 ff.

56 Curzon to Montagu, 12 Aug. 1921 (Montagu Papers, AS IV–6/919).
57 Llewellyn Smith, pp. 234 ff.; David Walder, *The Chanak Affair* (1969), pp. 150–4.
58 Curzon to Montagu, 6 Mar. 1922 (Montagu Papers, AS I–12/263(76)).
59 *Parl. Deb.*, 5th ser., Vol. 157, pp. 1997–2006; cf. MS. on meeting of Lloyd George and Venizelos (Lloyd George Papers, F/86/2/3).
60 Derby to Bonar Law, 22 Aug. 1922 (Bonar Law Papers, 107/2/57); Curzon MSS. (India Office, MS. Eur. F/112/319).
61 Conferences of Ministers, September 1922, *passim* (CAB 23/39); Curzon telegram to Sir H. Rumbold, 16 Sept. 1922 (FO/800/157, ff. 383–5).
62 Ibid., 27 Sept. 1922 (no. 148).
63 General Harington, *Tim Harington Looks Back* (1940), p. 127.
64 Conference of Ministers, 28, 30 Sept. 1922 (CAB 23/39).
65 Lloyd George to Mrs. Lloyd George, 28 Sept. 1922, *Family Letters*, p. 196.
66 Boothby, *I Fight to Live*, p. 28.
67 Conference of Ministers, 18 Sept. 1922 (CAB 23/39).
68 Cf. Viscount d'Abernon, ii. 111 (3 Oct. 1922).
69 Derby to Chamberlain, 1 Sept. 1922 (Chamberlain Papers, AC/33/2/12).
70 Younger to Chamberlain, 16 Sept. 1922 (ibid., AC/33/2/20). Cf. Younger's letter in *The Times*, 30 Sept. 1922.
71 Salisbury to Selborne, 16, 26 Sept. 1922 (Selborne Papers, I/7, ff. 126–33).
72 Cabinet minutes, 27 Sept. 1922 (CAB 23/39); Curzon to Lord Hardinge, 16 Sept. 1922 (FO/800/157, ff. 386–7); Curzon MSS. (India Office, MS. Eur. F/112/319).
73 See *The Times*, 18 Mar. 1922.
74 A. Griffith-Boscawen to Chamberlain, 2 Oct. 1922 (Griffith-Boscawen Papers, Eng. Hist. c. 396, ff. 89–90).
75 Griffith-Boscawen to Curzon, 2 Oct. 1922 (ibid.).
76 Curzon to Boscawen, 2 Oct. 1922 (ibid., f. 92;.
77 Mond to Lloyd George, 5 Nov. 1922 (Lloyd George Papers. G/14/5/2); 'Notes on the Eastern Crisis' by Griffith-Boscawen (Griffith-Boscawen Papers, Eng. Hist., c. 396, f. 104).
78 Notes on the Eastern Crisis' (ibid., f. 105).
79 Clark (ed.), *A Good Innings*, p. 230 (8 Oct. 1922).
80 Cecil to Asquith, 9 Oct. 1922 (Cecil Papers, Add. MS. 51073, ff. 30–3).
81 Cecil to Lady Gladstone, 16 Sept. 1922 (ibid. Add. MS. 51163, ff. 113–15).
82 Cecil to Gilbert Murray, 1 Jan. 1920 (Murray Papers, Box 16C).
83 Lloyd George: Statement on the Freedom of the Straits to TUC Parliamentary Committee (FO/371: E9701/27/44); *The Times*, 22 Sept. 1922.
84 Harington, p. 151.
85 Viscount d'Abernon, ii. p. 185 (28 Mar. 1923).

FOOTNOTES TO CHAPTER XIV

1 *The Times*, 2 Feb. 1922. See above, p. 253.
2 Clark (ed.), *A Good Innings*, p. 226.
3 *The Times*, 2–8 Mar. 1922.
4 Watkin Davies's diary, 23 Jan. 1922 (Davies Papers).
5 Speech at East Leicester, *The Times*, 27 Mar. 1922.
6 Fisher to Lloyd George, 30 Mar. 1922 (Lloyd George Papers, F/16/7/84); Fisher diary, 28 Mar. 1922.
7 Hilton Young to Grigg, 23 Mar. 1922 (Lloyd George Papers, F/86/1/35).
8 McCurdy memorandum, Mar. 1922 (ibid., F/35/1/37).

[9] Churchill to Lloyd George, 15 June 1922 (ibid., F/10/3/5).

[10] Edge to Lloyd George, 28 July 1922 (ibid., F/35/1/48); *Manchester Guardian*, 3 Aug. 1922.

[11] Wedgwood Benn diary, 8 May 1922 (Stansgate Papers); Mond to Lloyd George, May 1922 (Lloyd George Papers, F/37/2/15).

[12] C. P. Scott diary, 28 Feb.–2 Mar. 1922 (Scott Papers, Add. MS. 50906, f. 161).

[13] Margot Asquith to H. A. Gwynne, 18 Nov. (?) 1922 (Bodleian, Gwynne Papers, Box 14); *The Times*, 22 June 1921. The organizers were A. E. Newbould, Independent Liberal member for Leyton, and J. M. Wallace, Coalition Liberal member for Dunfermline.

[14] *The Times*, 23 Feb. 1922.

[15] Balfour memorandum of a conversation with Bonar Law (Balfour Papers, Add. MS. 49693, f. 300).

[16] Austen Chamberlain Papers, AC/33/1/9–10; *Morning Post*, 13 Feb. 1922.

[17] Chamberlain to Leith, 7 Mar. 1922 (Chamberlain Papers, AC/33/1/24).

[18] *The Times*, 4 Mar. 1922.

[19] *Nation*, 18 Mar. 1922.

[20] Lloyd George to Frances Stevenson, 15–24 Mar. 1922, in A. J. P. Taylor (ed.), *My Darling Pussy* (1975), pp. 35–41.

[21] Fisher diary, 29 Feb. 1922; Lloyd George to Chamberlain, 27 Feb. 1922 (Lloyd George Papers, F/7/5/6).

[22] *The Times*, 15 Mar. 1922.

[23] Long to Chamberlain, 27 Mar. 1922 (Chamberlain Papers, AC/33/1/53).

[24] Chamberlain to Lloyd George, 18 Mar. 1922 (Lloyd George Papers, F/86/1/30).

[25] Astor to Garvin, 'Tuesday' 1922 (Garvin Papers).

[26] Milner to Selborne, 13 June 1921 (Selborne Papers, I/12 f. 319); 'The Decontrol of Agriculture', *Lloyd George Liberal Magazine* (July 1921), pp. 518–19.

[27] Grigg to Brand, 30 Mar. 1922 (Grigg Papers).

[28] Chamberlain to Walter Long, 27 Apr. 1922 (Chamberlain Papers, AC/33/1/62).

[29] *Bankers' Magazine*, figures, cited in E. V. Morgan, *Studies in British Financial Policy*, p. 78 (Table 4).

[30] Sandars to Lord Stamfordham, ? Mar. 1922 (Sandars Papers, f. 47).

[31] Stamfordham to Sandars, 15 Mar. 1922 (ibid., ff. 52–3).

[32] Salisbury to Selborne, 4 May 1922 (Selborne Papers, f. 116).

[33] Younger to Bonar Law, 2 Jan. 1921, quoted in Lord Beaverbrook, *The Decline and Fall of Lloyd George* (1963), p. 243; J. A. Ramsden, 'The Organization of the Conservative and Unionist Party', pp. 342–4.

[34] John Grigg, *The Young Lloyd George* (1973), pp. 178–94.

[35] d'Abernon diary, 21 Aug. 1922 (d'Abernon Papers, Add. MS. 48954B, f. 45).

[36] *Thomas Jones: Whitehall Diary*, i. 203 (11 July 1922).

[37] Bridgeman, Political Diary, 1922.

[38] *Parl. Deb.*, 5th ser., Vol. 156, pp. 1759–70 (Lloyd George's speech); Geoffrey Shakespeare, *Let Candles be Brought in* 1949), p. 108; *Thomas Jones: Whitehall Diary*, i. 203 (11 July 1922).

[39] Bridgeman, loc. cit.; Austen Chamberlain Papers, AC/33/2/4.

[40] Bridgeman, loc. cit.; Pollock MS. on 'The Fall of the Coalition Government' (Bodleian, Hanworth Papers, MS. Eng. Hist. d. 432), ff. 68 ff.

[41] Sutherland to Lloyd George, 3 Sept. 1922 (Lloyd George Papers, F/35/1/55).

[42] Derby to Chamberlain, 1 Sept. 1922 (Chamberlain Papers, AC/33/2/12).

[43] Wilson to Chamberlain, 21 and ? Sept. 1922 (ibid., AC/33/2/25, 26).

[44] See Younger to Chamberlain, 22 Sept. 1922 (ibid., AC/33/2/21) for a strong pro-

test. The prospect of Lloyd George again heading them as a government 'appalled' him.

⁴⁵ *The Times*, 14 Sept. 1922.

⁴⁶ See John Ramsden, 'The Newport By-Election', in C. Cook and J. Ramsden (eds.), *By-Elections in British Politics* (1973), pp. 14 ff.

⁴⁷ Griffith-Boscawen to Pollock, 4 Aug. 1922 (Hanworth Papers loc cit., f. 75b).

⁴⁸ Cabinet conclusions, 5, 10 Oct. 1922 (CAB 23/31); Boscawen to Chamberlain, 10 Oct. 1922 (Chamberlain Papers, AC/33/2/47).

⁴⁹ Griffith-Boscawen Papers, f. 119; Griffith-Boscawen to Chamberlain, 12 Oct. 1922 (Chamberlain Papers, AC/33/2/29).

⁵⁰ Robert Rhodes James (ed.), *Memoirs of a Conservative*, p. 112; Barnes and Middlemas, *Baldwin* pp. 115–16; Pollock MS., 'Fall of the Coalition Government', f. 154.

⁵¹ Cowling, *Impact of Labour*, p. 194.

⁵² *The Times*, 14 Oct. 1922.

⁵³ *Observer*, 8 Oct. 1922; Norman Lester to Garvin, 10 Oct. 1922 (Garvin Papers).

⁵⁴ Bridgeman, Political Diary, 1922, p. 77; Pollock MS., 'Fall of the Coalition Government', f. 151.

⁵⁵ Ormsby-Gore, letter to *The Times*, 9 Oct. 1922.

⁵⁶ Pollock MS., 'Fall of the Coalition Government', ff. 155–6; Wood to Chamberlain, 17 Oct. 1922 (Chamberlain Papers, AC/32/2/84).

⁵⁷ Salisbury to Selborne, 13 Oct. 1922 (Selborne Papers I/7, f. 137); Beaverbrook, *The Decline and Fall of Lloyd George*, p. 177.

⁵⁸ Pollock MS., 'Fall of the Coalition Government', ff. 161–2; Cross, *Sir Samuel Hoare*, pp. 72–8.

⁵⁹ Bridgeman, Political Diary, 1922, p. 79.

⁶⁰ Ibid.

⁶¹ Ibid.; Astor to Garvin, 19 Oct. 1922 (Garvin Papers).

⁶² Bridgeman, loc. cit., p. 79; Pollock MS., 'Fall of the Coalition Government', f. 163.

⁶³ *The Times*, 26 Oct. 1922; G. Gibbs to Pollock, 3 Nov. 1922 (Hanworth Papers, ff. 192–9).

⁶⁴ Grigg to Lady Astor, 11 Oct. 1922 (Grigg Papers).

⁶⁵ Fisher diary, 4 Oct. 1922.

⁶⁶ C. P. Scott diary, 23 Oct. 1922 (Scott Papers, Add. MS. 50906, f. 196).

⁶⁷ Ibid (f. 202).

⁶⁸ Harold Spender, *The Prime Minister* (1920), p. 359.

⁶⁹ Mond to Lloyd George, 5 Nov. 1922 (Lloyd George Papers, F/14/5/2). Mond was to hang on to his Swansea seat by 802 votes in 1922 but lost it to Labour in 1923. He reappeared as Liberal member for Carmarthen in 1924.

⁷⁰ Fisher diary, 19 Oct. 1922.

⁷¹ Manifesto in *The Times*, 16 Oct. 1922; Ramsden, 'The Newport By-Election', p. 48.

FOOTNOTES TO CHAPTER XV

¹ McCurdy notes, 9 Sept. 1922 (Lloyd George Papers, F/35/1/50).

² Charles Stuart (ed.), *The Reith Diaries* (1976), p. 86.

³ Worthington-Evans to W. Coats Hutton, 9 Nov. 1922 (Worthington-Evans Papers, MS. Eng. Hist., c. 892).

⁴ Grigg to Lady Astor, 3 Nov. 1922 (Grigg Papers).

⁵ Clark (ed.), *A Good Innings*, p. 236.

[6] Worthington-Evans to Chamberlain, 22 May 1923, Worthington-Evans memorandum (Worthington-Evans Papers, MS. Eng. Hist., c. 922).

[7] Chamberlain to Worthington-Evans, 24 May 1923 (ibid.).

[8] Worthington-Evans memorandum (ibid.); Cowling, *Impact of Labour*, p. 270.

[9] Worthington-Evans memorandum.

[10] Clark (ed.), *A Good Innings*, p. 257 (6 Nov. 1924).

[11] For an excellent treatment of Lloyd George in the 1922–31 period, see John Campbell, *Lloyd George: The Goat in the Wilderness* (1977).

[12] Ibid. 147–8.

[13] Lord Rothermere to Lloyd George, 14 Sept., 18 Oct. 1928 (Lloyd George Papers G/17/1/32).

[14] Notes of conversation of Lloyd George and Churchill, 18 Feb. 1929 (ibid., G/4/4/23).

[15] Lloyd George to Churchill, 16 Oct. 1929 (ibid., G/4/4/24).

[16] Marquand, *Ramsay MacDonald*, pp. 599–603.

[17] *The Next Five Years: an Essay in Political Agreement* (1935), pp. vi–vii.

[18] C. L. Mowat, *Britain Between the Wars, 1918–1940* (1955), p. 142.

[19] See Susan Howson, '"A Dear Money Man"? Keynes on Monetary Policy, 1919–20', *Economic Journal*, LXXXIII (1973), 456–64.

[20] C. H. Feinstein, *National Income, Expenditure and Output of the United Kingdom*, T82: Table 37, Balance of Payments, Current Account, 1900–65; R. S. Sayers, *The Bank of England 1892–1944* (Cambridge, 1976), Vol. III, Appendix 32, pp. 307–17. Sayers's figures are based on *Board of Trade Journal* figures.

[21] Herbert Croly, *The Promise of American Life* (paperback ed., 1963), pp. 230–9.

Select Bibliography

A. Manuscript Collections

1. Private Papers

Addison Papers (Bodleian Library, Oxford, and in private hands)
Asquith Papers (Bodleian Library, Oxford)
Astor Papers (University of Reading: transcripts by courtesy of Professor J. Stubbs)
Baird Papers (National Library of Australia: transcripts by courtesy of Mr. P. A. Williamson)
Earl Balfour Papers (British Library)
Bridgeman Papers (courtesy of Viscount Bridgeman)
Burns Papers (British Library)
Viscount Cecil Papers (British Library)
Austen Chamberlain Papers (University of Birmingham Library)
Curzon Papers (India Office Library)
d'Abernon Papers (British Library)
Davidson Papers (House of Lords Record Library)
T. Huws Davies Papers (National Library of Wales, Aberystwyth)
Watkin Davies Papers (National Library of Wales, Aberystwyth)
Fisher Papers (Bodleian Library, Oxford)
Garvin Papers (University of Texas: transcripts by courtesy of Professor J. Stubbs)
Viscount Gladstone Papers (British Library)
Griffith-Boscawen Papers (Bodleian Library, Oxford)
Grigg Papers (microfilm in Bodleian Library, Oxford)
Gwynne Papers (Bodleian Library, Oxford)
Hanworth (Pollock) Papers (Bodleian Library, Oxford)
E. T. John Papers (National Library of Wales, Aberystwyth)
Thomas Jones Papers (National Library of Wales, Aberystwyth; courtesy of Mr. Tristan Jones)
Bonar Law Papers (House of Lords Record Office)

Sir Herbert Lewis Papers (National Library of Wales, Aberystwyth)
Sir Herbert Lewis Papers (Plas Penucha: courtesy of Mrs. K. Idwal Jones)
Lloyd George Papers (House of Lords Record Office)
Lloyd George Papers (National Library of Wales, Aberystwyth)
MacDonald Papers (Public Record Office)
Maclean Papers (Bodleian Library, Oxford)
MacPherson Papers (Bodleian Library, Oxford)
Milner Papers (Bodleian Library, Oxford)
Montagu Papers (Trinity College, Cambridge)
Gilbert Murray Papers (Bodleian Library, Oxford)
W. H. Page Papers (Houghton Library, Harvard University)
Ponsonby Papers (Bodleian Library, Oxford)
J. Bryn Roberts Papers (National Library of Wales, Aberystwyth)
Samuel Papers (House of Lords Record Office)
Sandars Papers (Bodleian Library, Oxford)
Sankey Papers (Bodleian Library, Oxford)
C. P. Scott Papers (British Library)
Selborne Papers (Bodleian Library, Oxford)
Shortt Papers (handlist in Nuffield College, Oxford)
J. A. Spender Papers (British Library)
Stansgate (Wedgwood Benn) Papers (House of Lords Record Office)
Villard Papers (Houghton Library, Harvard University)
Worthington-Evans Papers (Bodleian Library, Oxford)
Zimmern Papers (Bodleian Library, Oxford)

2. Public Records

Cabinet: CAB 23 (Cabinet Minutes, 1917–22)
         CAB 24 (Cabinet Papers)
         CAB 26 (Home Affairs Committee)
         CAB 27 (Cabinet Committees)
         CAB 128 (Cabinet Minutes, 1945–6)
Foreign Office: FO 371
         FO 800 (Curzon correspondence)
Health and Housing: HLG 48

B. Official Papers

Hansard, *Parliamentary Debates*, Fifth Series
Census of England and Wales, 1921: General Report with Appendices
Final Report of the Committee on Commercial and Industrial Policy (Cd. 9035),
   P.P. (1918), XIII, 239.

Report of Advisory Housing Panel, Ministry of Reconstruction (Cd. 9087), P.P. (1918), XXVI, 437.

Committee on Currency and Foreign Exchanges after the War: First Interim Report (Cd. 9182), P.P. (1918), VII, 853.

ibid., *Second Interim Report* (Cmd. 464), P.P. (1919), XIII, 593.

Report of the Provisional Joint Committee presented at a meeting of Industrial Conference, Central Hall, Westminster, April 4, 1919 (Cmd. 139), P.P. (1919), XXIV, 1.

Coal Industry Commission: Report and Minutes of Evidence, Vols. I and II (Cmd. 359, 360), P.P. (1919), XI, 373 and XII, 1

Report from the Select Committee on Increase of Wealth (War) (Cmd. 594 for memoranda), P.P. (1920), VII, 55

First Annual Report of the Ministry of Health, 1919–29 (Cmd. 923), P.P. (1920), XVII, 1

Transport Workers Court of Inquiry: Vol. I, Report and Minutes of Evidence (Cmd. 936), P.P. (1920), XXIV, 279

Second Annual Report of the Ministry of Health, 1920–1 (Cmd. 1446), P.P. (1921), XIII, 1

Report of the Departmental Committee on the High Cost of Building Working-Class Dwellings (Cmnd. 1447), P.P. (1921), XIII, 919

Third Annual Report of the Ministry of Health (Cmd. 1713), P.P. (1922), VIII, 1

First Interim Report of the Committee on National Expenditure (Cmnd. 1581), P.P. (1922), IX, 1

Second Interim Report of the Committee on National Expenditure (Cmd. 1582), P.P. (1922), IX, 173

Third Interim Report of the Committee on National Expenditure (Cmd. 1589), P.P. (1922), IX, 287

C. Newspapers, Periodicals, and Reports

1. Newspapers

Daily Chronicle
Daily News
Evening Standard
Labour Voice
Manchester Guardian
Morning Post
Observer
South Wales Daily News
Sunday Pictorial
The Times
Western Mail
Westminster Gazette

2. Periodicals

Contemporary Review
Economic Journal
The Economist
Financial Review of Reviews
Fortnightly Review
Future
Lancet
Liberal Magazine
Lloyd George Liberal Magazine
Nation
National Review
New Statesman
Nineteenth Century and After
Outlook
Review of Reviews
Socialist Review
Spectator

3. Reports

Annual Reports of the following organizations:
   Federation of British Industry
   Independent Labour Party
   Labour Party
   National Farmers' Union
   National Liberal Federation
   Trades Union Congress

D. Biographies *and* Memoirs *(arranged in order of subject; place of publication London unless otherwise stated)*

Addison, Dr. Christopher, *Politics from Within, 1914–1918*, 2 Vols. (1924)
—— *Four and a Half Years, 1914–1919*, 2 Vols. (1934)
Anderson, Sir John, *John Anderson, Viscount Waverley*, J. Wheeler-Bennett (1962)
Asquith, Herbert Henry, *Asquith*, Stephen Koss (1976)
Balfour, Arthur James, *Arthur James Balfour*, Blanche Dugdale, 2 Vols. (1936)
Beaverbrook, Lord, *Beaverbrook*, A. J. P. Taylor (1972)
Bennett, Arnold, *The Letters of Arnold Bennett*, ed. J. Hepburn, 3 Vols. (Oxford, 1970)

Bibliography

417

Beveridge, William, *William Beveridge*, José Harris (Oxford, 1977)
Bevin, Ernest, *The Life and Times of Ernest Bevin*, Alan Bullock, Vol. I (1960)
Birkenhead, Lord, *'F.E.'*, The Earl of Birkenhead (1959)
—— 'Lord Birkenhead', in *Lives of the Lord Chancellors*, R. F. V. Heuston (Oxford, 1964)
Boothby, Robert, *I Fight to Live* (1947)
Butler, Sir Harold, *Confident Morning* (1950)
Cecil of Chelwood, Viscount, *All the Way* (1949)
Chamberlain, Austen, *The Life and Letters of the Rt. Hon. Sir Austen Chamberlain*, Sir Charles Petrie, 2 Vols. (1940)
Chamberlain, Neville, *The Life of Neville Chamberlain*, Keith Feiling (1946)
Childs, Sir Wyndham, *Episodes and Reflections* (1930)
Churchill, Winston, *Winston Churchill*, Henry Pelling (1974)
—— *Winston S. Churchill*, Vol. IV, Martin Gilbert (1975)
Cole, G. D. H., *The Life of G. D. H. Cole*, Margaret Cole (1971)
Coote, Colin, *Editorial* (1965)
Croft, Sir Henry Page, *My Life of Strife* (1949)
Curzon, Marquess, *The Life of Lord Curzon*, by the Earl of Ronaldshay, Vol. III (1928)
d'Abernon, Viscount, *An Ambassador of Peace*, 3 Vols. (1929)
Derby, Earl of, *Lord Derby, King of Lancashire*, Randolph Churchill (1959)
Donald, Robert, *Robert Donald*, H. A. Taylor (1934)
Elliot, Walter, *A Companion of Honour*, Colin Coote (1962)
Ernle, Viscount, *Whippingham to Westminster* (1938)
Fisher, H. A. L., *An Unfinished Autobiography* (1940)
Gardiner, A. G., *Fleet Street Radical*, by Stephen Koss (1973)
Grey, Viscount, *Sir Edward Grey*, Keith Robbins (1971)
Griffith-Boscawen, Sir Arthur, *Memories* (1925)
Grigg, Sir James, *Prejudice and Judgement* (1948)
Hamilton, Mary Agnes, *Remembering my Good Friends* (1944)
Hankey, Sir Maurice, *Hankey: Man of Secrets*, S. W. Roskill, 2 Vols. (1970, 1972)
Harington, General Timothy, *Tim Harington Looks Back* (1940)
Harris, Sir Percy, *Forty Years in and out of Parliament* (1947)
Hewins, W. A. S., *The Apologia of an Imperialist*, 2 Vols. (1929)
Hoare, Sir Samuel, *Sir Samuel Hoare*, J. A. Cross (1977)
Inchcape, Lord, *James Lyle Mackay, First Earl of Inchcape*, Hector Bolitho (1936)
Jones, Thomas, *Thomas Jones: Whitehall Diary*, ed. Keith Middlemas, 3 Vols. (Oxford, 1969–71)
Kenworthy, J. M., *Sailors, Statesmen—and Others* (1933)
Laski, Harold, *The Holmes–Laski Letters*, ed. Mark Howe, 2 Vols. (Oxford, 1953)
Law, Andrew Bonar, *The Unknown Prime Minister* Robert Blake (1955)
Lee of Fareham, Lord, *A Good Innings: the Private Papers of Lord Lee of Fareham*, ed. Alan Clark (1974)
Lloyd George, David, *War Memoirs*, 2 Vols. (1938 ed.)

—— *Lloyd George: a diary by Frances Stevenson*, ed. A. J. P. Taylor (1971)
—— *Lloyd George: Family Letters, 1885–1936*, ed. Kenneth O. Morgan (Oxford and Cardiff, 1973)
—— *My Darling Pussy*, ed. A. J. P. Taylor (1975)
—— *Lloyd George*, by Peter Rowland (1976)
—— *Lloyd George: The Goat in the Wilderness*, John Campbell (1977)
MacDonald, Ramsay, *Ramsay MacDonald*, David Marquand (1977)
Midleton, Earl of, *Records and Reactions, 1856–1939* (1939)
Milner, Alfred, *Proconsul in Politics*, Alfred Gollin (1964)
Montagu, Edwin, *Edwin Montagu*, S. D. Waley (Bombay, 1964)
Morrison, Herbert, *Herbert Morrison*, B. Donoughue and G. W. Jones (1973)
Muir, Ramsay, *Ramsay Muir: an Autobiography and some Essays*, ed. Stuart Hodgson (1943)
Mosley, Sir Oswald, *Mosley*, Robert Skidelsky (1975)
Paton, John, *Left Turn!* (1936)
Percy, Lord Eustace, *Some Memories* (1958)
Pethick-Lawrence, Frederick W., *Pethick-Lawrence*, Vera Brittain (1963)
Rees, Sir J. Tudor, *Reserved Judgement* (1956)
Rees, Goronwy, *A Chapter of Accidents* (1972)
Riddell, Lord, *War Diary* (1933)
—— *An Intimate Diary of the Peace Conference and After, 1918–23* (1933)
Rowntree, Seebohm, *Seebohm Rowntree*, Asa Briggs (1963)
Scott, C. P., *C. P. Scott of the Manchester Guardian*, J. L. Hammond (1934)
—— *The Diaries of C. P. Scott*, ed. Trevor Wilson (1970)
Shakespeare, Sir Geoffrey, *Let Candles be Brought in* (1949)
Simon, E. D., *Ernest Simon of Manchester*, Mary Stocks (Manchester, 1963)
Steed, H. Wickham, *Through Thirty Years, 1892–1922* (1924)
Swinton, Earl of, *I Remember* (1948)
—— *Sixty Years of Power* (1966)
de Valera, Eamon, *Eamon de Valera*, Lord Longford and T. P. O'Neill (1970)
Webb, Sidney and Beatrice, *Our Partnership*, Beatrice Webb, eds. B. Drake and Margaret Cole (1948)
—— *The Letters of Sidney and Beatrice Webb*, Vol. III, ed. Norman Mackenzie (Cambridge and London, 1978)
Wedgwood, Josiah, *Memoirs of a Fighting Life* (1940)
Winterton, Earl, *Orders of the day* (1953)

E. Other Published Works
(place of publication London unless otherwise stated)

Armitage, Susan, *The Politics of Decontrol in Industry* (1969)
Arnot, R. Page, *The Miners: Years of Struggle* (1953)
Askwith, Lord, *Industrial Problems and Disputes* (1920)

Bagwell, Philip S., *The Railwaymen* (1963)
Beaverbrook, Lord, *Men and Power, 1917–1918* (1956)
—— *The Decline and Fall of Lloyd George* (1963)
Bentley, Michael, *The Liberal Mind, 1914–1929* (Cambridge, 1977)
Blake, Robert, *The Conservative Party from Peel to Churchill* (Oxford, 1970)
Bowley, A. L. and Hogg, M., *Has Poverty Diminished?* (1925)
Bowley, M., *Housing and the State* (1944)
Boyce, D. G., *Englishmen and Irish Troubles, 1918–1922* (1972)
Briggs, Asa and Saville, John (eds.), *Essays in Labour History*, Vols. II and III
    (1971, 1977)
Brockway, A. Fenner, *Lloyd George and the Traffic in Honours* (1922)
Brown, Judith M., *Gandhi's Rise to Power: Indian Politics, 1915–1922* (Cam-
    bridge, 1972)
Brown, Kenneth D. (ed.), *Essays in Anti-Labour History* (1972)
Buell, R. L., *The Washington Conference* (New York, 1922)
Butler, David (ed.), *Coalitions in British Politics* (1978)
Calhoun, Daniel F., *The United Front* (Cambridge, 1975)
Chamberlain, Austen, *The Unionist Party and Future Policy* (1922)
Charles, Roger, *The Development of Industrial Relations in Britain, 1911–1939*
    (1973)
Cook, C. and Ramsden, J. (eds.), *By-Elections in British Politics* (1973)
Cowling, Maurice, *The Impact of Labour, 1920–1924* (Cambridge, 1971)
Craig, Gordon, and Gilbert, F. (eds.), *The Diplomats, 1919–1939* (1961)
Documents on British Foreign Policy, 1919–1939, First Series, I–XX
Dodd, J. J., *If Labour Wins* (1923)
Dodds, Elliott, *Is Liberalism Dead?* (1920)
—— *Liberalism in Action* (1922)
Douglas, Roy, *Land, People and Politics* (1976)
Essays in Liberalism (1922)
Feinstein, C. H., *National Income, Expenditure and Output of the United
    Kingdom, 1855–1965* (Cambridge, 1972)
Fraser, J. A. Lovat, *Why a Tory Joined the Labour Party* (1921)
Freund, Gerald, *Unholy Alliance* (1957)
Fry, Michael, *Illusions of Security* (Toronto, 1977)
—— *Lloyd George and Foreign Policy*, Vol. I (Montreal, 1976)
Garratt, G. T., *The Mugwumps and the Labour Party* (1932)
Gilbert, Bentley, *British Social Policy, 1914–1939* (1970)
Gilbert, Martin, *The Roots of Appeasement* (1966)
Guedalla, Philip, *The Industrial Future: a Liberal Policy* (1922)
Hankey, Lord, *The Supreme Command at the Paris Peace Conference* (1963)
Hewart, Sir Gordon, *The Lloyd George Government: What it has done and why it
    is still needed* (1920)
Hinton, J., *The First Shop Stewards Movement* (1973)
History of The Times, The, Vol. IV (1952)
Hobson, J. A., *Democracy after the War* (1918)
—— *Taxation in the New State* (1919)
—— *Problems of a New World* (1921)

Hodges, Frank, *The Nationalisation of the Mines* (1920)
Johnson, Paul Barton, *Land Fit for Heroes* (Chicago, 1968)
Joll, James, *Intellectuals in Politics* (1960)
Jones, C. Sheridan, *The Call to Liberalism* (1921)
Keynes, J. M., *The Economic Consequences of the Peace* (1919)
—— *A Revision of the Treaty* (1922)
—— *Essays in Persuasion* (1931)
Kinnear, M., *The Fall of Lloyd George: the Political Crisis of 1922* (1973)
Kirby, M., *The British Coalmining Industry, 1870–1946* (1977)
Kirkaldy, A. W. (ed.), *British Finance during and after the War, 1914–1921* (1921)
Labour and the War Debt (1922)
Llewellyn Smith, M., *Ionian Vision* (1973)
Lloyd George, David, *The Truth about Reparations and War-Debts* (1932)
—— *The Truth about the Peace Treaties*, 2 Vols. (1938)
Lyons, F. S. L., *Ireland since the Famine* (1973)
MacLagan, O. F., *Coalition Government: a League of Parties as an Efficient Method of Government* (1922)
Marwick, Arthur, *The Deluge* (1965)
Mayer, Arno J., *The Politics of Diplomacy and Peacemaking* (1968)
McKibbin, R. I., *The Evolution of the Labour Party, 1910–1924* (Oxford, 1976)
Monroe, Elizabeth, *Britain's Moment in the Middle East, 1914–1956* (1964)
Moore, R. J., *The Crisis of Indian Unity, 1917–1940* (Oxford, 1974)
Morgan, E. V., *Studies in British Financial Policy, 1914–1925* (1961)
Morgan, Kenneth O., *Wales in British Politics, 1868–1922* (Cardiff, 2nd ed., 1970)
Mowat, C. L., *Britain between the Wars, 1918–1940* (1955)
Muir, Ramsay, *Liberalism and Industry* (1920)
—— *Politics and Progress* (1923)
Newsholme, Sir Arthur, *The Last Thirty Years in Public Health* (1936)
Nicolson, Harold, *Peacemaking* (1919)
Nish, I. H., *Alliance in Decline* (Oxford, 1972)
Northedge, F. S., *The Troubled Giant* (1966)
Pakenham, Viscount, *Peace by Ordeal* (1972 edn.)
Parker, R. A. C., *Europe, 1919–1939* (1969)
Pelling, Henry, *Popular Politics and Society in Late Victorian and Edwardian Britain* (1968)
Pethick-Lawrence, Frederick, *A Levy on Capital* (1920)
—— *The Capital Levy: How Labour would settle the War Debt* (1922)
Pigou, A. C., *A Capital Levy: A Levy on War Wealth* (1920)
—— *Aspects of British Economic History, 1918–1925* (1947)
'Politicus', *Party not Faction: the Necessity for Coalition Government* (1921)
Pugh, M., *Electoral Reform in War and Peace, 1906–18* (1978)
Roberts, Harry, *England: a National Policy for Labour* (1923)
Robertson, J. M., *Liberalism and Labour* (1921)

—— *Mr. Lloyd George and Liberalism* (1923)
Roskill, S. W., *British Naval Policy between the Wars*, Vol. I (1968)
Rowntree, B. Seebohm, *The Human Needs of Labour* (1918)
Runciman, W. G., *Relative Deprivation and Social Justice* (1966)
Sabine, B. E. V., *A History of Income Tax* (1966)
Selsam, J. Paul, *The Attempt to Form an Anglo-French Alliance, 1919–1924* (Philadelphia, 1936)
Siegfried, André, *Post-War Britain* (1924)
Snowden, Philip, *Labour and National Finance* (1920)
—— *If Labour Rules* (1923)
Snyder, R. K., *The Tariff Problem in Great Britain, 1918–1923* (Palo Alto, 1944)
Storey, H., *The Case Against the Lloyd George Coalition* (1920)
—— *The Liberal Handbook* (1923)
Sutherland, Sir William, *Nineteen Sixteen—Nineteen Twenty: the Lloyd George Coalition in War and Peace* (1920)
Swartz, Marvin, *The Union of Democratic Control in British Politics* (Oxford, 1971)
Taylor, A. J. P., *English History, 1914–1945* (Oxford, 1965)
—— (ed.), *Lloyd George: Twelve Essays* (1971)
Townshend, Charles, *The British Campaign in Ireland, 1919–1921* (Oxford, 1975)
Trevelyan, Charles P., *From Liberalism to Labour* (1921)
Ullman, R. H., *Britain and the Russian Civil War* (Oxford, 1968)
—— *The Anglo-Soviet Accord* (Oxford, 1973)
Walder, David, *The Chanak Affair* (1969)
Webb, Sidney, *National Finance and the Capital Levy* (1920)
What Coalition Government has done: a Catechism (Labour Party, 1922)
Whetham, Edith H., *The Agrarian History of England and Wales*, Vol. VIII *1914–1939* (Cambridge, 1978)
Wilson, Trevor, *The Downfall of the Liberal Party, 1914–1935* (1966)
Winter, J. M., *Socialism and the Challenge of War* (1973)
Wolfers, Arnold, *Britain and France between two World Wars* (Hamden, Connecticut, 1963)
Worsfold, W. B., *The War and Social Reform* (1919)
Wrigley, C., *Lloyd George and the Labour Movement* (Hassocks, Sussex, 1976)

F. ARTICLES

P. Abrams, 'The Failure of Social Reform, 1918–1920', *Past and Present* (Apr. 1963)
M. Bentley, 'Liberal Politics and the Grey Conspiracy of 1921', *Historical Journal* (June 1977)

D. G. Boyce, 'Public Opinion and Historians', *History* (June 1978)
P. K. Cline, 'Reopening the case of the Lloyd George Coalition and the Post-War Economic Transition, 1918–19', *Journal of British Studies* (Nov. 1970)
D. H. Close, 'The Collapse of Resistance to Democracy: Conservatives, Adult Suffrage and Second Chamber Reform, 1911–1928', *Historical Journal* (Dec. 1977)
E. David, 'The Liberal Party Divided, 1916–18', ibid. (Sept. 1970)
R. Douglas, 'The Background to the "Coupon" Election Arrangements', *English Historical Review* (Apr. 1971)
J. A. Dowie, '1919–20 is in need of attention', *Economic History Review* (1975)
Susan Howson, '"A Dear Money Man?" Keynes on Monetary Policy, 1919–20', *Economic Journal*, (1973)
—— 'The Origins of Dear Money, 1920', *Economic History Review* (1974)
G. Gareth Jones, 'The British Government and the Oil Companies, 1912–1924: the search for an Oil Policy', *Historical Journal* (Sept. 1977)
R. Lowe, 'The Ministry of Labour, 1916–1924: a Graveyard of Social Reform?', *Public Administration* (Autumn 1974)
—— 'The Erosion of State Intervention in Britain, 1917–24', *Economic History Review* (May 1978)
——, 'The Failure of Consensus in Britain: the National Industrial Conference, 1919–1921', *Historical Journal* (Sept. 1978)
J. M. McEwen, 'The Coupon Election of 1918 and the Unionist Members of Parliament', *Journal of Modern History* (Sept. 1962)
L. J. MacFarlane, 'Hands off Russia: British Labour and the Russo-Polish War, 1920', *Past and Present* (Dec. 1967)
Kenneth O. Morgan, 'Lloyd George's Premiership: a study in "Prime Ministerial Government"', *Historical Journal* (Jan. 1970)
A. C. Pigou, '1946 and 1919', *Lloyd's Bank Review* (July 1946)
W. D. Rubinstein, 'Henry Page Croft and the National Party, 1917–22', *Journal of Contemporary History* (Jan. 1974)
A. J. Sharp, 'The Foreign Office in Eclipse, 1919–22', *History* (June 1976)
R. H. Tawney, 'The British Coal Industry and the Question of Nationalization', *Quarterly Journal of Economics* (Nov. 1920)
—— 'The Abolition of Economic Controls, 1918–21', *Economic History Review* (1943)
B. A. Waites, 'The Effect of the First World War on Class and Status in England, 1910–1920', *Journal of Contemporary History* (Jan. 1976)
E. H. Whetham, 'The Agriculture Act, 1920, and its Repeal–"the Great Betrayal"', *Agricultural History Review* (1972)
J. M. Winter, 'The Impact of the First World War on Civilian Health in Britain', *Economic History Review* (Aug. 1977)

G. Unpublished Theses

G. M. Bayliss, 'The Outsider: Aspects of the Political Career of Sir Alfred Mond First Lord Melchett' (University of Wales Ph.D., 1969)

G. J. Darwin, 'The Lloyd George Coalition Government and Britain's Imperial Policy in Egypt and the Middle East, 1918–1922' (Oxford University D.Phil., 1976)

C. J. Howard, 'Henderson, MacDonald and Leadership in the Labour Party, 1914–1922' (Cambridge University Ph.D., 1978)

J. A. Ramsden, 'The Organization of the Conservative and Unionist Party in Britain, 1910 to 1930' (Oxford University D.Phil., 1974)

J. A. Turner, 'Lloyd George's Private Secretariat, 1917–1918' (Oxford University D.Phil., 1976)

P. R. Wilding, 'Government and Housing: a study in the Development of Social Policy, 1906–1939' (University of Manchester Ph.D., 1970)

Note: Two important works that appeared while this book was in the press are Peter Clarke, *Liberals and Social Democrats* (Cambridge, 1978) and John Ramsden, *The Age of Balfour and Baldwin, 1902–1940* (London, 1978).

Index

Abdullah, 120

Aberdeen Central (by-election), 196

Abertillery (by-election), 297

Ablett, Noah, 75, 214

Acland, Sir Francis Dyke, 43, 193, 195

Adams, Professor W. G. S., 17, 260

Adamson, William, 43, 193, 216, 222

Addison, Dr. Christopher, at Ministry of Munitions, 13, 19; and Lloyd George becoming premier, 14; as Minister of Reconstruction, 23–5, 81, 82; and formation of post-war coalition, 27–9, 34, 36; and social expenditure, 5, 84, 85, 243, 252; as Minister of Health, 87–8; and housing programme, 89–98, 105–8, 222, 282, 288, 290; departure from the government, 99–104; and labour unrest, 55, 65, 71, 77; and Egypt, 121; and India, 124; and Ireland, 126, 130; and women, 153–4; and 'fusion', 181, 182; and Liberal schism, 202; backs capital levy, 240; in MacDonald government, 1, 228, 232, 361; in Attlee government, 361; also mentioned, 3, 157, 211, 227, 374

Adly Pasha, 120–1

Agriculture, 17–18, 39, 86–7, 157–9, 228, 325, 337, 345–6

Agriculture Act (1920), 158–9, 190, 325, 337

Aitken, Max: see Beaverbrook

Aliens Bill, 238–9

Allenby, Field Marshal Lord, 120–1

America: see United States

Amery, Leopold C. S., 11, 25, 116, 117, 341, 354

Ammon, Charles G., 293

Amritsar massacre, 123, 239–41, 251, 354

Anderson, Sir John, 56, 84, 129, 131, 175, 262

Angell, Norman, 38, 215, 328

Anglo-Japanese alliance, 265–7

Anti-Dumping Bill, 177, 186, 199–200, 333

Anti-Waste League, 67, 97–8, 107, 154, 168, 206, 244–6, 254, 288, 294, 331

Applin, R. V. K., 245

Archer-Shee, Sir Martin, 248

Army, 146, 289

Ashton-under-Lyne (by-election), 67, 166

Askwith, Lord, 52, 168

Asquith, Herbert Henry, 3, 10, 11–14, 23, 36, 37, 43, 88, 153, 192, 196–8, 200–1, 204, 209, 315, 360

Asquith, Margot, 334

Assheton, Ralph, 5

Associated Society of Locomotive Engineers and Firemen (ASLEF), 59, 60, 67

Astor, Hon. J. J., 243

Astor, Lady Nancy, 154

Astor, Waldorf, 17, 27, 82, 83, 87, 89, 131, 159, 171, 248, 249, 260, 336

Attlee, Clement R., 57, 82, 223, 361

Australia, 117, 118, 266

Baird, John, 134, 183

Baldwin, Stanley, 1, 2, 5, 6, 107, 210, 252, 285, 300, 310, 325, 328, 334, 342, 345, 346, 349–50, 359–62, 364–6

Balfour, Arthur, Earl, 30, 44, 49, 113, 130, 186–7, 240, 266–7, 303, 318, 319, 324, 326, 334, 341, 349, 350, 352

Balfour, Sir Arthur, 63

Banbury, Sir Frederick, 137, 240

Bank Rate, 70, 108, 257, 262, 294, 300, 369

Barnes, George, 15, 37, 39, 48, 65, 236, 366, 374

Barry, Kevin, 129

Barthou, Joseph, 312–14

Beatty, Earl, 266, 289, 322

Beaverbrook, Lord, 3, 14, 34, 50, 169, 171, 348, 361, 364

Beck, A. C. T., 29

de Valera, Eamon, 35, 117, 126, 130, 363
Venice, 325
Venizelos, Eleutherios, 141, 319, 321, 323, 325
Versailles, Treaty of, 31, 110, 139, 141, 144, 179, 224, 302, 367
Villard, Oswald Garrison, 219

Wafd party, 121–2
Wales, 162, 164–5, 198–9, 292, 360. Also see South Wales
Wallace, J. M., 186, 199, 334, 410n.
Walsh, Stephen, 88
Walters, Tudor, 83, 89, 91
War Wealth, Committee on, 88, 175, 240, 295–6
Ward, Dudley, 25, 29, 197
Warrington, 210
Washington, Treaty of, 104, 146, 251, 264–8, 289
Webb, Beatrice, 23, 93
Webb, Sidney, 21–2, 63, 89, 215, 219, 228, 233
Wedgwood, Josiah, 4, 43, 137, 193, 219
Weekly Dispatch, 184
Weir, A.: see Inverforth
Welsh Church, 34, 159
Welsh Licensing Bill, 161–2
Welsh Outlook, 164
West Leyton (by-election), 195, 199
West Wolverhampton (by-election), 166, 332
Westminster (Abbey) (by-election), 98, 168, 245
Westminster (St. George's) (by-election), 244
Wheatley, John, 215, 227
White Russians, 134–5
Whitley Councils, 24, 29, 38, 57, 75, 203
Whittaker, Sir Thomas, 193, 239
Widnes (by-election), 47, 156, 196, 216, 220
Wigram, Lord, 69
Wild, Sir Ernest, 178, 239
Wilhelm II, Kaiser, 38–9
Williams, Sir Evan, 64, 68
Williams, Penry, 193
Williams, Robert, 69, 214, 222
Williams, W. Llewelyn, 162, 198–9, 200

Williamson, Sir A., 193
Willingdon, Lord, 124
Wilson, Harold, 150, 351
Wilson, Field Marshal Sir Henry, 151, 341
Wilson, Sir Horace, 52
Wilson, J. Havelock, 237
Wilson, Leslie, 276, 288, 342, 356
Wilson, Sir Murrough, 346
Wilson, Woodrow, 111, 132–3, 147, 206, 351, 372
Windham, Lieutenant-Commander, 245
Winterton, Earl, 208, 340
Wintringham, Mrs. M., 154, 198
Wintringham, T., 198
Wirth, Josef, 142, 307
Wise, E. F., 113, 115, 135, 228, 303, 313, 317
Wolverhampton, 39
Women, 13, 39–40, 152–4
Wood, Hon. Edward, 183, 329, 340, 347, 350, 364, 365
Wood, Kingsley, 178, 352
Woolwich (by-election), 217, 219
Wootton, Barbara, 234
Working class, 296–8
World War, First, 11–15, 21–3, 25–30, 40–1
World War, Second, 234
Worthington-Evans, Sir Laming, 42, 86, 115, 121, 130, 146, 248, 268, 275, 282, 313, 315, 326, 350, 359, 362, 374
Wrekin, The (by-elections), 67, 155, 166, 188, 197, 241

'X Committee', 17

Yorkshire, 65, 199
Young, Sir E. Hilton, 3, 43, 193, 200, 286–7, 333, 336, 360, 361
Younger, Sir George, 5, 32, 33, 61–2, 155, 183, 188, 206, 245, 246, 249, 273–9, 324, 331, 335, 336, 339, 342, 356
Yoxall, J. H., 290
Yudenich, General Nikolai N., 134, 135

Zaghloul Pasha, 120–2
Zaharoff, Basil, 112
Zinoviev, Grigorii, 235